Public Sector Housing Law

Other works on housing law by David Hughes

Public Sector Housing Law (1st edn, 1981; 2nd edn, 1987; 3rd edn, 1999, Butterworths).

Housing and Relationship Breakdown (2nd (revised) edn, 1993, The National Housing and Town Planning Council), jointly with T G Buck and C A Stacey.

Neighbour Disputes (1993, Institute of Housing), jointly with V A Karn, R Lickiss, J Crawley.

A New Century of Social Housing (1991, Leicester University Press), edited jointly with S G Lowe.

Social Housing Law and Policy (1995, Butterworths), jointly with S G Lowe.

Tenants Complaints and the Reform of Housing Management (1997, Dartmouth), jointly with V A Karn and R Lickiss.

Cases and Material on Housing Law (1999, Blackstone Press Ltd), jointly with M Davis, V Matthew and N Smith.

Other works by Stuart Lowe

Urban Social Movements: The City After Castells (1986, Macmillan).

A New Century of Social Housing (1991, Leicester University Press), edited jointly with D Hughes.

Social Housing Law and Policy (1995, Butterworths), jointly with D J Hughes.

'Homelessness and the Law', in R Burrows, N Pleace and D Quilgars (eds) *Homelessness and Social Policy* (1997, Routledge).

'Homes and Castles: was it inevitable that Britain became a "nation of home owners"' in J Goodwin (ed) *Built to Last – Reflections on British Housing Policy* (2nd edn, 1998, Shelter).

Housing Abandonment in Britain: Studies in the Causes and Consequences of Low Demand Housing (1998, Centre for Housing Policy, University of York), edited jointly with P Keenan and S Spencer.

Forthcoming

Housing Policy Analysis: Britain in Comparative Perspective, to be published by Macmillan

Public Sector Housing Law

Third edition

David Hughes

LLB (Liverpool), LLM (Cantab), FRSA.
Professor of Law in the Environmental Law Institute at De Montfort
 University, Leicester.
Hon Legal Consultant to the National Housing and Town Planning Council.
 Occasional Adviser to the House Builders' Federation.
Co-editor of 'Environmental Law and Management'.

Stuart Lowe

BA (Hons) in Political Theory and Institutions (Sheffield), Dip. Applied
 Social Studies [Community Development and Organisation] (Wales),
 PhD (Sheffield).
Senior Lecturer in Social Policy in the Department of Social Policy and Social
 Work, University of York.

Butterworths
London Edinburgh Dublin
2000

United Kingdom	Butterworths, a Division of Reed Elsevier (UK) Ltd, Halsbury House, 35 Chancery Lane, LONDON WC2A 1EL and 4 Hill Street, EDINBURGH EH2 3JZ
Australia	Butterworths, a Division of Reed International Books Australia Pty Ltd, CHATSWOOD, New South Wales
Canada	Butterworths Canada Ltd, MARKHAM, Ontario
Hong Kong	Butterworths Asia (Hong Kong), HONG KONG
India	Butterworths India, NEW DELHI
Ireland	Butterworth (Ireland) Ltd, DUBLIN
Malaysia	Malayan Law Journal Sdn Bhd, KUALA LUMPUR
New Zealand	Butterworths of New Zealand Ltd, WELLINGTON
Singapore	Butterworths Asia, SINGAPORE
South Africa	Butterworths Publishers (Pty) Ltd, DURBAN
USA	Lexis Law Publishing, CHARLOTTESVILLE, Virginia

A CIP Catalogue record for this book is available from the British Library.

ISBN 0 406 98301 1

Printed and bound by Hobbs the Printer Ltd, Totton, Hampshire

Visit us at our website: http://www.butterworths.co.uk

Preface

The first edition of this title appeared in 1981, with a second edition in 1987, both under the sole authorship of David Hughes. The book was intended then, as now, to be a scholarly legal text, containing both exposition and analysis of the Law of Housing. But there was always another aim, and that was to set the law in a wider social, political and economic context. When in the early 1990s an opportunity arose for a further edition of the title, coupled with the opportunity of bringing into the 'authoring team' someone skilled in the policy of housing and the analysis of society, it seemed entirely appropriate to recognise that with a change of title, and hence 'Social Housing Law and Policy' was born. The basic aim of the book, however, always remained the same, namely to provide a clear statement of the law coupled with analysis and critical comment, primarily of a traditional doctrinally analytical variety, all set in the wider framework of the law's social, economic, and political setting. If a new aim was added to those it was to make the work even more useful to the large number of local government officers in legal and housing departments who had come to rely on the earlier editions in their work. The aim here was to show how law and policy interact, and often conflict, so that what may be a declared object of housing policy may be dramatically altered in the outcome as a result of having to be expressed in a legal form. In the light of hindsight, with which, of course, we are all wise, the title we chose suggested to some a far more radical reappraisal of both law and policy, while to those seeking a 'traditional' text it smacked of critical legal theory. We were also disadvantaged by the passing into law of the Housing Act 1996 shortly after publication, which, though we had tried as hard as possible to accommodate it in the text by referring to the white papers which preceded it, inevitably gave the text a dated atmosphere early on in the 'shelf life' of the book.

For the current edition we have therefore made considerable changes. First of these is a return to the original title, so that there can be no doubt what the prime focus of the book is – namely it is a law book, but a law book about an area of law that cannot be understood without an appreciation of wider issues. We have accordingly somewhat restructured the book. Chapter 1 outlines the history and development of our national scheme of social housing provision, by which we mean what has come to be the system for providing non-profit making housing for those unable to purchase a home for themselves, coupled with provision for the homeless, and the law relating to housing conditions and standards across the sectors. The subsequent chapters examine that body of law in greater detail, but do not omit to set the legal material in its wider setting. It can of course be objected that this is only a partial treatment of the law of housing, which could be defined to include the law of house transfer – conveyancing – and house creation and siting – building standards and planning. Indeed there is room for a debate on what the proper sphere of housing law is, and perhaps there is room for a further debate as to whether there is even a proper sphere, on the basis that housing law as the child of policy is really now better thought of as a series of sub areas of issues as diverse as land policy, sustainable development, urban regeneration, social exclusion, and crime and disorder. It is arguable that the current law of housing is rapidly becoming entirely consequential on those issues, rather than being a recognisable body of coherent principles concerned with the provision and management of decent housing at affordable prices for all.

Even so, for the moment we believe there is on a pragmatically recognisable basis something that is still worthy of the name 'Public Sector Housing Law'. Local authorities are still great landlords, even if their functions are increasingly being taken over by other forms of registered social landlords; though surely the very invention and use of that classification under the 1996 legislation indicates that the public sector still has a major role in housing. Authorities also have to ensure that housing standards are maintained, and there may come a time, perhaps not far off in relation to houses in multiple occupation, when a major role for authorities will be the examination and certification of all landlords as 'fit and proper' to be letting out property. That would indeed give authorities a major strategic role in relation to housing provision in their areas. Those authorities also have to provide safety net accommodation for the homeless.

Thus, while the subject matter of this book is eclectic, it nevertheless revolves around certain core issues which are concerned with the provision and oversight of accommodation for those in our society who are less well able to fend for themselves in comparison to others. It was not ever thus with this body of law. There was a time when it might have been thought that municipally provided housing could become a, perhaps the, mainstay of housing accommodation in this country. In some parts of it, that did eventuate. In those days it was not unknown for there to be a grand, perhaps unrealistic, vision of what could be achieved by the creation of healthy, socially balanced communities based on municipal provision. At the very least, for many people such housing provided a way out of squalor and urban deprivation which it is hard for anyone to imagine today. As a tribute to the planners, builders and providers of that housing, our cover picture is of the most famous council house in England, 42, Forthlin Road, Liverpool, where we are told, Jim and Mary McCartney were glad to take their young sons Paul and Michael, and where the world heard some of the first Beatles' songs – even if Jim did think it should be 'She loves you, yes, yes, yes!'

David Hughes

Stuart Lowe

(Unless otherwise stated the law is given as at 28 September 1999, though the kindness of our publishers has enabled us to make a few later additions)

Contents

Preface   v
Table of statutes   xv
Table of cases   xxvii

CHAPTER ONE

A brief history of social housing   1

Introduction   1
Why 'council housing'?   5
The public health origins   6
'... the sty that made the pig'   10
Subsidies and the private landlords   13
The 1914–18 war and 'Homes Fit for Heroes'   15
The first Labour Government, 1924   20
Housing for the poor?   22
Slum clearance   23
The situation in 1939   25
After World War Two   26
The 1945 Labour Government   26
The high-rise era   29
The 1957 Rent Act   30
The new housing crisis   31
'The party of council housing'?   32
From redevelopment to rehabilitation   34
Labour and owner occupation   36

Housing subsidies under the Conservatives 38
The rise of housing associations 40
The Thatcher years 41
The 'enabling role' and beyond 45
The new world for housing associations 48
The Major Government 48
New Labour 51
Conclusion 54
Further reading 54

CHAPTER TWO

The provision and disposal of social housing 56

What is social housing and who provides it? 56
The housing authorities 57
Provision of housing by housing associations, and other 'registered
    social landlords' 59
THE DISPOSAL OF SOCIAL HOUSING 67
Introduction 67
The sale of council houses 67
The 'right to buy' under the Housing Act 1985 (as amended) 70
Rent into mortgage 81
The powers of the Secretary of State 89
GENERAL POWERS OF DISPOSAL 90
Voluntary stock transfers 91
The effect of transfer on RTB 95
Part III of the 1988 Act (HATs) 96
Further reading 100

CHAPTER THREE

**Social housing: its allocation, the rights and status of
its tenants 101**

THE STATUS OF HOUSING OCCUPATION 101
ALLOCATION POLICIES (COUNCIL HOUSING) 106
Reform 108
Discrimination in housing allocation on racial and sexual grounds 109
Discrimination and disability 112
The statutory rules on allocation 113
The Allocation Scheme 121
ALLOCATION POLICIES (REGISTERED SOCIAL LANDLORDS) 125
THE REQUIREMENTS FOR THE COMMENCEMENT OF A TENANCY 126

INTRODUCTORY TENANCIES 127
Security of tenure 135
GROUNDS FOR POSSESSION (INITIAL ISSUES) 137
Suitable alternative accommodation 137
General considerations affecting discretionary grounds
     of possession 147
Use of possession proceedings in cases of arrears 149
OTHER INDIVIDUAL RIGHTS OF SECURE TENANTS 158
Subletting and assignment 158
Improvements 159
THE COLLECTIVE RIGHTS OF SECURE TENANTS 161
Variation of terms and publicity 161
Tenant participation in housing management 162
The rise and fall of compulsory competitive tendering 164
Inspection powers 165
Transfer arrangements 167
Proactive tenant management 167
One cautionary note 170
Further developments – moving towards 'best value', consultation on
     central guidance 170
What are these tenant participation compacts? 170
Further key points about the policy 171
TENURE OF HOUSING ASSOCIATION DWELLINGS AND DWELLINGS OF
     OTHER REGISTERED SOCIAL LANDLORDS 173
Assured tenancies: the basic position 174
Security of tenure 176
Periodic tenancies 176
Fixed term tenancies 176
Procedure for obtaining possession 177
Security of tenure: ASTs 184
Modification of the assured tenancy regime for association,
     etc, tenants 185
THE ACCOUNTABILITY OF SOCIAL LANDLORDS 187
The Housing Corporation's regulatory powers in practice 187
Adjudicatory systems 190
Ombudsmen 190
Procedure 191
The effectiveness of the LO in providing a remedy 192
An Ombudsman for tenants of registered social landlords 194
Particular powers and obligations relating to the determination
     of investigations 196
Registered social landlords – further guidance on accountability 198
Complaints mechanisms 199
Informatory systems: reports to tenants 200

CONCLUSION 201
Further reading 202

CHAPTER FOUR

The legalities of housing finance, rents and subsidies 204

Local authority capital spending 204
Housing Revenue Accounts (HRAs) 207
Current expenditure 209
Financial arrangements of registered social landlords 219
Rents under registered social landlords 225
The new law of renting under the Housing Act 1988 228
Further reading 233

CHAPTER FIVE

Housing and relationships 234

General housing rights within relationships 234
Housing rights while a relationship subsists 235
Housing rights on disintegration of a relationship 243
The long term rights of the parties on the break-up
    of a relationship 248
Succession rights 266
Further reading 274

CHAPTER SIX

Homelessness 276

Historical context 276
The legal nature of homelessness 279
The official statistics 279
The law 281
The homeless in law 283
Initial contact with the local authority 286
Eligibility for assistance 290
The interim duty to accommodate 294
Priority need 295
The duties owed to the homeless 298
Intentional homelessness 298
Referral 309
The duties owed to the homeless 312
Duties of notification 322

Offences   323
Protecting the property of the homeless   323
Challenging decisions made under the Act and enforcing
    the duties   324
Duties under the Children Act 1989   332
The law and homelessness: an assessment   334
Further reading   336

CHAPTER SEVEN

Housing standards   338

Historical context   338
Landlords' obligations in tort   340
Liability under the Occupiers' Liability Act 1957   346
LANDLORDS' OBLIGATIONS IN CONTRACT   346
At common law   346
Under statute   348
Remedies for breaches of covenant   355
PUBLIC LAW REMEDIES FOR DEALING WITH
    SUB-STANDARD HOUSING   361
The 1989 fitness requirements   362
General guidance on the fitness standard   364
The Code   366
The courses of action available   368
Individual houses (including flats)   368
The legal procedures   370
HOUSING RENEWAL AND IMPROVEMENT   390
Renewal areas   390
Grant aid   393
The types of grant available   394
General restrictions on grant aid   398
Means testing   398
Decisions, notification and payment   399
Grant payment conditions   400
General grant conditions   401
Supplementary provision   403
Group repair schemes (GRS)   403
Home repair assistance (HRA)   405
REMEDIES UNDER THE ENVIRONMENTAL PROTECTION
    ACT 1990   405
The procedure for taking action in respect of a statutory nuisance   409
Rehousing displaced residents   419
Further reading   421

CHAPTER EIGHT

Multi-occupancy and overcrowding 422

Introduction 422
The current problem and the policy response to
    multiple occupation 423
The supervision of multi-occupation under the Housing Acts 429
Local authority housing and fire precaution powers 435
Overcrowding 460
Further reading 464

Index 465

Table of statutes

References in this Table to *Statutes*, are to Halsbury's Statutes of England, fourth edition, showing the volume and page at which the annotated text may be found.

References printed in **bold** type indicate where the Act is set out in part or in full.

PAGE

Access to Justice Act 1999
  s 27 419
Addison Act 1919 .... 6, 16, 17,
                   18, 19, 22
Acquisition of Land Act 1981 (9
    Statutes 366) 60, 392
  Pt II (ss 10-15) 382
Acquisition of Land (Assessment of
  Compensation)
  Act 1919 361
Adoption Act 1976 (6 *Statutes*
  220) 239
Arbitration Act 1950 (2 *Statutes*
  571) 190
Arbitration Act 1979 (2 *Statutes*
  650) 190
Artizans and Labourers Dwelling Act
  1868 (Torrens Act) 7, 8,
                 338, 361
Artizans and Labourers Dwellings
  Improvement Act 1875 (Cross
  Act) 7, 8, 338, 361
Asylum and Immigration Act
  1996 .... 115, 290
Audit Commission Act 1998 165
Charities Act 1960 (5 *Statutes* 805): 62
Children Act 1989 (6 *Statutes*
  387): 239, 241, 243, 249, 257
  s 20(1) 278, 332, 333

PAGE

Children Act 1989—*contd*
  s 20(3) 332, 333
  24(2) 333
  27 .... 278, 333, 334
  (1) 332
  29(9) 334
  105(1) 332
  Sch 1
    para 1 ...... 76, 84, 88, 158,
           267, 269, 272, 402
Companies Act 1985 (8 *Statutes*
  104) 63
  s 736 96
County Courts Act 1984
  s 188 157
Courts and Legal Services Act 1990
  (11 *Statutes* 1211)
  s 58 419
  58A 419
Crime and Disorder Act 1998 ... 248
  s 1 247
  5 157
  17 157
Defective Premises Act 1972 (31
  Statutes 245)
  s 1 .... **342**
  3(1) **343**
  (2) (a) **343**
  4 349

PAGE

Defective Premises Act 1972—*contd*
s 4(1) **343**
    (2) **345**
    (4) 345
    (6) 345
6 345
    (3) 343
7(2) 343
Disability Discrimination Act 1995
s 1 112
22,24 112
Domestic Proceedings and Magistrates'
    Courts Act 1978 (27 *Statutes*
    816)
s 16 .... 245, 246
Domestic Violence and Matrimonial
    Proceedings Act 1976 (27
    Statutes 812) 245, 246
Environmental Protection Act 1990
    (35 *Statutes* 791) .. 405, 407,
                                                415
s 79(4) 411
    (7) 406
80 .... 389, 409
81(3), (4) 409, 410
81A 410
81B 410
82 .... 416, 418, 419
    (1) 411
    (2) 412
    (3) 411, 420
    (6) 411, 414
    (7) 410, 411
    (9) 410
    (11) 414
    (12) 413, 414
Sch 3 410
Family Law Act 1996: 243, 245, 246,
                                    248, 260, 262,
                                    274, 306
s 30 236
33 .... 237, 240, 241, 242
    (2) 238
    (5) 236, 238
    (7) 239
34 237
35 .... 237, 240, 242
    (5) 240
    (8) 241
36 .... 237, 242
    (8) 241
37 .... 237, 242
38 .... 237, 242

PAGE

Family Law Act 1996—*contd*
s 40 242
42 246
53 249
62 237
    (3) 238
        (c) 239
63(1) 238
Sch 7 .... 251, 252, 268, 272
Fire Precautions Act 1971 (35
    Statutes 280) 430, 448
s 1 448
10(1) 458
10A 459
10B 459
House Purchase and Housing Act
    1959 393
Housing Act 1885 .... 11, 12
Housing Act 1923 . 18, 19, 22, 31, 41
Housing Act 1924 21
Housing Act 1930 .. 23, 24, 339, 361
Housing Act 1935 ..... 24, 214, 361
Housing Act 1949 361
Housing Act 1961 31
Housing Act 1964 .... 31, 32, 361
Housing Act 1969 (23 *Statutes*
    293) 35, 361, 390
Housing Act 1974 (23 *Statutes*
    297) 35, 40, 41, 205,
                    220, 361, 390, 393
Housing Act 1980 (23 *Statutes*
    321) 2, 4, 42, 43, 53,
                    68, 201, 209
s 89 .... 149, 185
Housing Act 1985 (21 *Statutes*
    35) 50, 56, 67, 70,
                    174, 235, 236, 249,
                    278, 281, 294, 321,
                    347, 349, 390, 415,
                    416,448
s 1 57
Pt II (ss 8-57) 57, 212
s 8 57
9(3) 58
    (5) 58
10,11 58
11A 58, 213
12 .... 58, 213
13 58
15(1) 58
17 .... 59, 454
21 106
22 .... 108, 113, 122

PAGE

Housing Act 1985—*contd*
s 23 .... 5 8
24 .... 2 1 5
(2)-(4) 2 1 6
25 .... 2 1 7
27 ..... 163, 164, 167, 169, 170
27AA 1 6 7
27AB 1 6 7
29 .... 5 7
32,33 .... 9 0
34 .... 9 1
(4) 9 0
35 .... 9 0
37 .... 9 1
44(1) 1 0 5
57 .... 9 1
Pt III (ss 58-78) 49, 278
s 75 .... 2 8 6
Pt IV (ss 79-117) 131, 162
s 79 .... 1 3 1
(3) 1 0 6
80 .... 1 3 1
81 .... 131, 259
82 .... 1 3 5
83 .... 135, 136
83A 1 3 6
(3) 2 6 0
84 .... 1 3 7
(2) (b), (c) 1 7 3
(3), (4) 1 3 6
85 .... 1 4 7
87 .... 72, 269, 270, 271
88(1)-(4) 2 7 1
89 .... 2 6 8
(3), (4) 2 6 9
90 .... 2 6 9
91 .... 134, 158, 267
(3) (b) 2 4 8
92 .... 80, 114, 144, 159,
160, 267, 271
(2A) 159, 160
93 .... 1 3 4
(1) (a), (b) 1 5 8
(2) 1 5 8
94 .... 1 5 8
96 .... 3 5 9
97 .... 1 5 9
99 .... 1 6 0
99A 160, 161
(8) 1 6 0
99B 160, 161
100,101 .... 1 6 1
102,103 .... 161, 216

PAGE

Housing Act 1985—*contd*
s 104 .... 162, 360
(3) 1 6 2
105 .... 130, 162, 163, 168, 201
106(5) 1 2 4
106A 9 1
110 .... 116, 135
111A 2 1 7
113 .... 260, 269, 270, 271, 402
Pt V (ss 118-188) 74, 162
s 118 .... 7 0
(2) 7 1
119 .... 7 0
120 .... 7 2
121 .... 7 3
122(1) 7 6
(2) 74, 75
123 .... 71, 72
124 .... 7 6
125 .... 74, 76, 78, 79, 80
125A 76, 77
(2) 7 7
125B 76, 77, 78
125D 77, 79
125E 77, 79
(4) 7 9
126(1) (a), (b) 7 4
127 .... 74, 76
128(3) 7 9
(5) 7 9
129 .... 74, 76
(2A) 7 4
(2B) 7 4
130,131 .... 7 5
136 .... 8 0
(2) 7 9
137(1), (2) 8 0
138(1)-(3) 8 1
139(1) 8 4
(2) 81, 134
140 .... 79, 80, 84
141 .... 79, 80, 84
143 .... 8 2
143A 8 2
143B 79, 82
(6) 8 2
144 ..... 79, 136, 137, 155, 156
146 .... 80, 82
147 .... 8 3
149 .... 8 3
150 .... 8 3
151 .... 8 4
151A 8 4

PAGE

Housing Act 1985—*contd*
s 151B 84
152,153 84
153A 81
153B 81
155 .... 76, 90
156 76
157 87
    (2)(b) 88
158 89
159 .... 76, 88
160 .... 76, 88
164 .... 89, 90
165-170 .... 89, 90
171A,B 95
171C 95, 96
171D-K 95
181 76
183 70
184(1), (2) 70
186 71
187 .... 74, 78
189 .... 370, 371, 372, 373,
           379, 395, 398, 442
    (1) 368
    (1A) 368
190 .... 371, 373, 379, 395,
           398, 389, 442
190A 370
    (1A) 371
    (1B) 371, 372
    (1C) 371
    (2), (3) 371
    (5) 371
191A 372
192 194
193 373
    (2) 373
    (2A) 373
194 373
195 373
197 373
198 373
198A 371, 373
203(3) 373
207 .... 370, 371, 377
Pt IX (ss 264-323) 448
s 264 .... 369, 373, 375, 379, 402
    (1), (2) 368
265 .... 369, 375, 358, 379
    (1) 368, 374
    (2) 368, 374
267(1) 374

PAGE

Housing Act 1985—*contd*
s 267(2) 373
268(1A) 374
    (2) 374
269 .... 374, 448
    (2A) 374
270(5) 375
271-278 375
279 374
280(1) 318
283 375
    (2) 376
284 375
286 376
287 (1)-(3) 376
288 376
289 .... 369, 380
    (2)(a), (b) 380
    (2B)-(2E) 380
    (2F)(a)-(c) 381
    (4) 381
    (5B) 381
290 .... 382, 384
291 384
293(1) 381
300 376
301 384
302(c) 350
Pt X (ss 324-344) 460, 462
s 324, 325 460
326(2)(b) 460
327 461
329 .... 461, 462
330 461
331 .... 461, 462
332, 333 462
334, 335 463
338, 339 462
342 462
343 460
Pt XI (ss 345-400) 429, 457
s 345 .... 429, 433, 434
346 435
346A 435
347, 348 435
348A 436
    (2) 437
348B-F 437
348C 438
348D 438
348E 438
348G 435, 451
349 438

PAGE

Housing Act 1985—contd
s 350 438
352 .... 385, 389, 396, 398,
423, 441, 443, 444,
445, 446, 447, 449,
452, 455, 458
(1A) 398, 441
(2) 442
(2A) 442
(3), (4) 442
(5A) 442
(7), (8) 442
352A 444
353 445
353A 455
(2) 455
354 .... 441, 445, 446, 451, 452
(2) 445
(8) 445
355 450
(2) 445
356 451
357 446
358 451
(2) 450
359 450
361-363 450
364 451
365 .... 441, 446, 448
(2) 446
(2A) 446
(3) 447
368 .... 442, 448, 451
369 .... 430, 451
(5) 439
372 .... 439, 440, 445, 449, 452
373 441
375 449
376 451
(1), (2) 449
377 449
377A 444, 445
(7) 444
379(2) 452
381(2) 452
382 452
384 .... 452, 453
385 452
387 (3) 452
389 453
392, 393 453
395 (1), (2) 450
395A 424, 455

PAGE

Housing Act 1985—contd
s 398 .... 377, 435, 436
(6) 440
428 208
429A 168
450A 77, 78
450B 78
450C 78
Pt XV (ss 460-526) 161
s 578 382
578A 382
583 384
584A 375
584B 375
Pt XVIII (ss 604-625) 392
s 604 .... 362, 385, 386, 423, 442
(3) 447
604A 365, 366, 372
(2) 369
605 .... 362, 391, 424, 447
606 362
607 59
621A 78, 86
622 317
Sch 1 322
para 1A 132
Sch 2 .... 135, 136, 137, 138,
139, 141, 143, 144,
145, 146, 147, 149,
159, 259
Pt IV 137, 257
para 10A 93
Sch 3 159
Sch 3A 91
para 5 92
6 92
Sch 4 .... 70, 75
Sch 5 72
para 1-3 95
Sch 6 .... 84, 89
para 2(1) 87
12 74
16A 79, 85
16B 77, 85
16C 78, 79, 85
16D 78
Sch 6A
para 2 84
Sch 9A
para 6 95
Sch 10 .... 373, 449
Sch 13
para 4 453

PAGE

Housing Act 1988 (23 *Statutes*
  735) 3, 45, 46, 47, 48,
      50, 67, 68, 151, 219,
      220, 224, 228, 235, 236,
      249, 294, 375, 376
Pt I (ss 1-45) 173
s 1 174
3 174
5(1), (2) 176, 177
7 177
  (1), (7) 176
8 177
8A 260
9(3) 176
11(1) 180
13 .... 229, 231
  (1)(b) 230
  (5) 230
14 .... 229, 231
  (7), (8) 231
15 248
  (1), (3) 273
17(2) 273
  (4), (5) 273
19A 106, 175, 176, 184
20 175
  (4) 184
21(1)-(3) 184
  (5)-(7) 185
22 232
27(8)(a) 258
40 177
41-43 231
46 61
49 185
60 96
62-65 97
67 97
72 97
74 97
75 98
79(2) 98
81(8)(a) 98
83, 84 98
84A 99
Pt IV (ss 93-114) 100
s 133 90
137 111
Sch 1 174
  Pt I 174
Sch 2 .... 137, 177, 178, 179, 180,
      181, 182, 183, 260
  Pt I 178

PAGE

Housing Act 1988—*contd*
  Pt III 181
  Sch 2A 175, 232
    para 2 186
  Sch 7 97
  Sch 8 97
Housing Act 1996 ...... 3, 100, 107,
      108, 135, 273, 175,
      197, 281, 290, 436,
      437
Pt I Ch I (ss 1-7) 62
s 1 63
  (2) 223
2 .... 63, 223
3 .... 63, 223
4(4) 64
5 64
8-15 69
16 .... 68, 69
17 69
18 .... 64, 68, 223
19 224
19A 232
20 224
21 224
22 65
23 .... 65, 224
25 68
27 .... 65, 224
30 .... 65, 187
31-35 65
36 .... 65, 66, 125, 175, 185
37, 38 66
40-43 66
44 .... 66, 67
45 .... 66, 67
46 67
49 66
50 66
51(2) 195
53 223
56 223
63 (2) 223
73 454
86 356
Pt V Ch 1 (ss 124-143) 127
s 124 127
125 128
127 .... 128, 129
128(3) 128
  (4) 129
129 129
130 128

PAGE

Housing Act 1996—*contd*
s 131 .... 129, 272
132,133 .... 130, 272
134 272
136,137 130
140 130
144 138
145 259
149 260
152 .... 154, 155, 156
  (1)(a) 155
153 156
  (7) 156
Pt VI (ss 159-174) 271
s 159 113
  (1) 114
161 (1) 114
162 118
  (1), (4) 114
163 119
164 .... 119, 120
  (5) 114
165(5) 114
166 120
167 121
  (1) 114
  (2) 125
  (3) 122
  (5) 114, 123
  (7) 114, 124
168 .... 114, 121
169 113
  (1) 114
170 126
Pt VII (ss 175-218) 49, 52,
                    133, 271, 318
s 175 (1)-(4) 283
176 .... 283, 305
177 283
  (1) 285
178 .... 283, 285
179-181 282
182 281
183 286
184 .... 286, 289, 322
  (3), (4) 324
  (6) 323
185 .... 290, 292
186 .... 292, 294
188 .... 294, 295, 312,
                    316, 318, 323,
                    328
189 295

PAGE

Housing Act 1996—*contd*
s 190 .... 308, 316, 318,
                323, 324, 328, 329
  (1) 298
  (2), (3) 312
191 .... 315, 324, 329
  (1) **298**
  (2), (3) 299
  (4) 300
192 .... 324, 329
  (1) 298
  (2) 116
193 .... 123, 311, 312, 314,
                316, 323, 324, 329
  (1) 298
  (5) 313, 321, 329
  (6)(a)-(d) 313
  (7)-(9) 313
194(3) 116
  (5) 314
195 .... 314, 323, 324, 329
  (1) 298
  (2) 123, 316
  (5) 315
196 .... 315, 324, 329
197 .... 316, 324, 329
  (2) 116, 311
  (4), (5) 315
198(1) 324
  (4) 309
  (5) 310, 324
199 .... 309, 310, 316
200 .... 309, 311, 318, 323, 328
  (3), (4) 325
201 157
202 .... 326, 329, 330, 331
  (1) 324
    (b) 329
  (2)-(4) 325
203(5) 325
204 .... 327, 329, 331
  (4) 318, 328
205 .... 295, 316
206 .... 295, 316
  (2) 317
207 316
  (2) 317
208 .... 316, 317
209 .... 176, 316
  (2), (3) 318
210 .... 315, 316
211 (1)-(4) 323
212 323

PAGE

Housing Act 1996—*contd*
s 213 .... 176, 322
  214 323
Sch 1 .... 61, 64, 170
       para 22 188
     24 188
Sch 2 195
Sch 17 322
     para 3 318
Housing and Building Control Act
    1984 (35 *Statutes* 618) ... 43
Housing and Planning Act 1986 . 278
Housing and Town Planning etc Act
    1919 .... 16, 17
Housing Associations Act 1985 (21
    Statutes 710) 67
s 1 61
  (1)(b) 63
  28 188
  36A 125, 175, 185, 273
  75(5) 109
  76 59
  78,79 59
  88,89 60
  90(3)-(6) 60
  92-94 60
  95-98 60
  106(1) 60
Sch 1 Pt III 64
Pt IV 64
Sch 6 59
Housing Finance Act
    1972 .... 39, 40, 215
Housing Grants, Construction
    and Regeneration Act
    1996 .... 377, 393
s 1 394
  2 394
  3 398
  4 394
  5 394
  7 394
  8 394
  11 395
  12 395
  13 395
   (4) 396
  17 396
  19 396
  20 396
  21 396
  22 396
  24 .... 397, 398

PAGE

Housing Grants, Construction
    and Regeneration Act
    1996—*contd*
s 25 398
  27-29 398
  30(5) 398
  31 399
  33 399
  34 399
   (5), (6) 400
  35 400
  36 400
  37-40 400
  41 401
  42 401
  44(3)(a), (b) 401
  45 401
  47 401
  48-51 402
  52 403
  53 402
  54 402
  57 .... 396, 403
  60 403
  62 403
   (6) 404
  63-66 404
  69-71 405
Pt III (ss 74-102) 59
s 76 405
  77 405
  81-85 377
  86 .... 378, 389
  87 379
  88 379
  92 405
  93 405
  96 404
  100 405
  101 404
  131-134 381
  135 .... 381, 382
  136 .... 381, 382
  137 381
  138 .... 381, 382
  139, 140 381
Housing (Homeless Persons) Act
    1977 .... 38, 276
Housing of the Working Classes Act
    1885
s 12 348
Housing of the Working Classes Act
    1890 .... 2, 12, 15, 42

PAGE

Housing Repairs and Rents Act 1954
   (23 *Statutes* 463) 29
Housing (Rural Workers) Act
   1926 338
Housing (Scotland) Act 1987
   s 20(2)(a) 249
Housing Subsidies Act 1956 29
Housing Subsidies Act 1967 37
Immigration Act 1971 (31 *Statutes*
   52) 115
Industrial and Provident Societies
   Act 1965 (21 *Statutes*
   1090) 61, 62, 63
Inheritance (Provision for Family and
   Dependants) Act 1975 (17
   Statutes 388)
   s 2 .... 76, 84, 88, 402
Land Compensation Act 1961 (9
   Statutes 163) 375, 382
Land Compensation Act 1973 (9
   Statutes 258)
   s 29(2) 382
      (3) 383
      (6) 382
    30 383
    32 383
    38 383
    39 .... 384, **419**, 420
Landlord and Tenant Act 1954
   Pt II 134, 174
Landlord and Tenant Act 1985 (23
   Statutes 333) 104
   s 8 .... 348, 350, 351
      (3) 349
    11 .... 162, 344, 349,
                  350, 361
      (1)(a) 351
      (1A) 350
      (1B) 351
      (3) 354
    12 .... 162, 350
    13 .... 162, 350
    14-16 162
    17 355
    18-30 86
    21(4) 87
    31 227
Landlord and Tenant Act 1987 (23
   Statutes 382)
   s 21 356
    22 356
    24 356
    48 136

PAGE

Land Registration Act 1925 (37
   Statutes 516) 73, 95
   s 123 81
Law of Property Act 1925 (37 *Statutes*
   72) 126, 255, 380
   s 36(2) 259
    53(1)(a) 268
    54(1) 268
     (2) 346
Law of Property (Miscellaneous
   Provisions) Act 1989
   s 1 268
Leasehold Reform, Housing and Urban
   Development Act 1993: 79, 82
   s 121 360
    135 93
Local Government Act 1858 9
Local Government Act 1888 (25
   Statutes 39) 11, 49
Local Government Act 1972 (25
   Statutes 166) 57
   s 195 277
    222 154
   Sch 23 277
Local Government Act 1974 (25
   Statutes 495) 195
   s 25(1)(a) 190
    26 191
     (1) 190
     (6) 192
    34(3) 190
Local Government Act 1978 (25
   Statutes 566)
   s 1 194
Local Government Act 1988 (25
   Statutes 870) 164
   s 2(3) 164
Local Government Act 1992 (25
   Statutes 1248) 49, 57, 164
Local Government Act 1999 189, 202
   s 3 164
    4 165
    5 165
    9 165
    10 166
    (2)-(4) 166
    11 166
    15 166
    21 164
Local Government and Housing
   Act 1989 (25 *Statutes*
   987) 45, 204, 207, 361
   s 26 193

PAGE

Local Government and Housing
    Act 1989—*contd*
Pt IV (ss 39-66) 208
s 39 208
  40 208
  43(8) 208
  44 208
  45 208
  53 208
  54 .... 208, 209
  55 209
  56 209
  58 209
  59(2) 209
  62 208
Pt VI (ss 74-88) 45
s 74(4) 212
  75 212
  76 211
  77 212
  79 .... 211, 212
  80 213
  80A 213
  86 214
  87 212
Pt VII (ss 89-100) 371
s 90 391
  91 392
  92 392
  93(2) 392
  95 393
  96 393
  98 390
Pt VIII (ss 101-138) 393
s 112,113 392
  115 392
  161 90
  167(1) 200
Sch 4 212
Sch 9 439
Local Government, Planning and
    Land Act 1980 . 49, 164, 206
Local Government (Wales) Act 1994
    (25 *Statutes* 1292) 57
s 1 57
  17 57
Sch 1 57
Sch 8 57
Matrimonial and Family Proceedings
    Act 1984 (27 *Statutes* 857)
s 17 .... 76, 84, 88, 402
  (1) 158, 267, 269, 272
  22 248

PAGE

Matrimonial Causes Act 1973 (27
    Statutes 734) 241, 251
s 23 .... 76, 88
  23A 84, 158
  24 .... 76, 84, 88, 158,
          256, 267, 269, 271,
               272, 402
  24A 76, 84, 88, 402
  37(2)(a), (b) 256
Matrimonial Homes Act 1983 (27
    Statutes 614)
s 1 .... 245, 246
  7 248
Sch 1 248
National Assistance Act 1948 (40
    Statutes 18)
s 2(1) 277
  17 277
  21 .... 293, 294
  (1) 292
    (a) 278
    (b) 277
National Health Service and
    Community Care Act 1990
    (30 *Statutes* 1001, 40 *Statutes*
    242)
s 47 293
  67(2) 278
National Parks and Access to the
    Countryside Act 1949 (32
    Statutes 63)
s 87 87
Occupiers' Liablility Act 1957 (31
    Statutes 238)
s 2 346
  3(1) **346**
Police and Criminal Evidence Act
    1984 (12 *Statutes* 801)
s 24 139
Powers of Criminal Courts Act 1973
    (12 *Statutes* 558)
s 35 414
Prosecution of Offences Act 1985
    (12 *Statutes* 895)
s 16-19 414
Protection from Eviction Act 1977
    (23 *Statutes* 302) 294
s 3 175
  5 .... 135, 253, 254
  (1)(b) 258
Protection from Harassment Act
    1997 248
s 1-3 247

PAGE

Public Health Act 1875 (35 *Statutes*
29) 8, 9, 405
Public Health Act 1936 (35 *Statutes*
117) 405, 416
Race Relations Act 1976 (6 *Statutes*
828)
s 1(1)(a) 110
(b) 111
3(1) 110
21 .... **109-110**
47 111
58 110
Registered Homes Act 1984 (35
Statutes 577) 446
Rent Act 1957 .... 30, 31
Rent Act 1965 .... 38, 39
Rent Act 1977 (23 *Statutes*
514) 220, 231, 232, 231,
279, 271, 375,
376, 382
Pt IV (ss 62-75) 225
s 67 225
67A 225
70 225
(2) 227
70A 225
71 .... 225, 227
72 .... 225, 228
Pt VI (ss 86-97) 173, 225
s 87 225
88 225
93 225
94 225
101 462

PAGE

Rent Act 1977—*contd*
Sch 11 225
Sex Discrimination Act 1975 (6
Statutes 753)
s 1 112
30 112
Sexual Offences Act 1956 (12
Statutes 229)
s 22, 23 139
Social Security Act 1980 (40 *Statutes*
116) 278
Supplementary Benefits Act 1976
(40 *Statutes* 97)
Sch 5 278
Supreme Court Act 1981 (11 *Statutes*
966)
s 31(4)(a) 331
Town and Country Planning Act
1947 27
Town and Country Planning Act
1953 28
Town and Country Planning Act 1990
(46 *Statutes* 514)
s 55(1) **426**, 427
(2)(a) **426**
(3)(a) **426**, 427
171B 428
Tribunals and Inquiries Act 1971
s 13 .... 226, 231
Trusts of Land and Appointment of
Trustees Act 1996
s 11 255
Working Classes Act 1890 ... 10, 338

Table of cases

A

Abbeyfield (Harpenden) Society Ltd v Woods [1968] 1 All ER 352n, [1968] 1
    WLR 374, 19 P & CR 36, 204 Estates Gazette 799, 111 Sol Jo 968, CA: 102
Abingdon RDC v O'Gorman [1968] 2 QB 811, [1968] 3 All ER 79, [1968]
    3 WLR 240, 19 P & CR 725, 207 Estates Gazette 245, 112 Sol Jo
    584, CA 151
Adami v Lincoln Grange Management Ltd (1997) 30 HLR 982, [1998] 1
    EGLR 58, [1998] 17 EG 148, [1998] 03 LS Gaz R 25, 142 Sol Jo LB 37,
    CA 348
Adeoso (otherwise Ametepe) v Adeoso [1981] 1 All ER 107, [1980] 1 WLR
    1535, 124 Sol Jo 847, CA 245
Ainsbury v Millington [1987] 1 All ER 929, [1987] 1 WLR 379n, 131 Sol Jo
    361, [1987] LS Gaz R 1241, HL 245
Al Hassani v Merrigan (1987) 20 HLR 238, [1988] 1 EGLR 93, [1988] 03
    EG 88, CA 349
Ali v Tower Hamlets London Borough Council [1993] QB 407, [1992] 3 All
    ER 512, [1992] 3 WLR 208, [1993] 2 FCR 406, [1993] Fam Law 123,
    90 LGR 501, 24 HLR 474, [1992] 20 LS Gaz R 35, 136 Sol Jo LB 113,
    CA 331
Ali v Westminster City Council [1999] 1 All ER 450, [1999] 1 WLR 384,
    31 HLR 349, CA 328
Ali v Wolkind. See Wolkind v Ali
Anderson v Dundee City Council [1999] 11 ELM 24 407
Andrews v Schooling [1991] 3 All ER 723, [1991] 1 WLR 783, 23 HLR 316,
    26 Con LR 31, 53 BLR 68, 135 Sol Jo 446, CA 342
Anstruther-Gough-Calthorpe v McOscar [1924] 1 KB 716, [1923] All ER Rep
    198, 130 LT 691, sub nom Calthorpe v McOscar 93 LJKB 273, 68 Sol Jo
    367, 40 TLR 223, CA 347

PAGE

Asco Developments Ltd v Lowes (1978) 248 Estates Gazette 683 357
Ashbridge Investments Ltd v Minister of Housing and Local Government
    [1965] 3 All ER 371, 129 JP 580, 63 LGR 400, 109 Sol Jo 595, sub nom
    Re Stalybridge (Castle Hall No 7) and (Acres Lane and Lawton Street)
    Compulsory Purchase Order 1963, Ashbridge Investments Ltd v Minister
    of Housing and Local Government [1965] 1 WLR 1320, CA 362
Attley v Cherwell District Council (1989) 21 HLR 613, CA 133
Auckland Harbour Board v R [1924] AC 318, 93 LJPC 126, 130 LT 621, PC: 224
Awua v Brent London Borough Council. See R v Brent London Borough
    Council, ex p Awua

B

B, ex p (1994) Times, 3 May 297
B v B [1994] 2 FCR 228, sub nom Brown v Brown [1994] 1 FLR 233, [1993]
    Fam Law 661, CA 239
B v B (occupation order) [1999] 2 FCR 251, [1999] 1 FLR 715, [1999] Fam
    Law 208, CA 240
Backhouse v Lambeth London Borough Council (1972) 116 Sol Jo 802 215
Bainbridge, Re, South Shields (D'Arcy Street) Compulsory Purchase Order 1937
    [1939] 1 KB 500, 103 JP 107, 108 LJKB 386, 83 Sol Jo 259, sub nom Re
    South Shields (D'Arcy Street) Compulsory Purchase Order 1937,
    Bainbridge's Application [1939] 1 All ER 419, 55 TLR 409, sub nom
    Bainbridge v Minister of Health 37 LGR 275, 160 LT 392 380
Ball v LCC [1949] 2 KB 159, [1949] 1 All ER 1056113 JP 315,, 47 LGR 591,
    93 Sol Jo 404, 65 TLR 533, CA 340
Barnes v Gorsuch (1981) 43 P & CR 294, 2 HLR 134, 263 Estates Gazette 253,
    CA 175
Barnes v Sheffield City Council (1995) 27 HLR 719, CA 432
Basingstoke and Deane Borough Council v Paice (1995) 27 HLR 433, [1995]
    2 EGLR 9, [1995] 44 EG 139, 159 LG Rev 909, [1995] NPC 46, CA ... 132
Bass Charrington (North) Ltd v Minister of Housing and Local Government
    (1970) 22 P & CR 31, [1970] RVR 416 382
Bassetlaw District Council v Renshaw [1992] 1 All ER 925, [1993] Fam Law
    16, 90 LGR 145, 23 HLR 603, [1991] 2 EGLR 254, CA 272
Bater v Bater [1999] 4 All ER 944, [1999] EGCS 111, sub nom Bater v
    Greenwich London Borough Council [1999] 3 FCR 254, [1999] Fam Law
    694, [1999] 33 LS Gaz R 30, CA 256
Baxter v Camden London Borough Council [1999] 4 All ER 449, [1999] 45
    EG 179, [1999] 42 LS Gaz R 41, [1999] NLJR 1618, 143 Sol Jo LB 249,
    sub nom Baxter v Camden London Borough Council (No 2) [1999] 3
    WLR 939, HL 340
Begum (Nipa) v Tower Hamlets London Borough Council (1999) Times,
    9 November, CA 284, 327, 329
Belcher v Reading Corpn [1950] Ch 380, [1949] 2 All ER 969, 114 JP 21,
    48 LGR 71, 93 Sol Jo 742, 65 TLR 773 215
Bell v Secretary of State for the Environment [1989] 1 EGLR 27, [1989] 13
    EG 70 454
Bennett v Preston District Council (1983) Environmental Health (April) 407
Berryman v Hounslow London Borough Council (1996) 30 HLR 567, [1997]
    PIQR P 83, CA 354
Billings (AC) & Sons Ltd v Riden [1958] AC 240, [1957] 3 All ER 1, [1957]
    3 WLR 496, 101 Sol Jo 645, HL 340

PAGE

Bird v Hildage [1948] 1 KB 91, [1947] 2 All ER 7, [1948] LJR 196, 91 Sol Jo
559, 177 LT 97, 63 TLR 405, CA 150
Birmingham Corpn v Minister of Housing and Local Government and
Habib Ullah [1964] 1 QB 178, [1963] 3 All ER 668, [1963] 3 WLR
937, 128 JP 33, 61 LGR 623, 15 P & CR 404, [1963] RVR 712, 107
Sol Jo 812 427
Birmingham District Council v Kelly (1985) 17 HLR 572, [1986] 2 EGLR
239 .... 407, 417
Birmingham District Council v McMahon (1987) 151 JP 709, 86 LGR 63,
19 HLR 452 412
Bishop Auckland Local Board v Bishop Auckland Iron and Steel Co (1882) 10
QBD 138, 52 LJMC 38, 47 JP 389, 31 WR 288, 48 LT 223, DC 408
Blake v Barking and Dagenham London Borough Council (1996) 30 HLR 963,
[1996] EGCS 145 77
Boldack v East Lindsey District Council (1998) 31 HLR 41, CA 341, 346
Botross v London Borough of Hammersmith and Fulham (1994) 27 HLR 179,
16 Cr App Rep (S) 622 408
Boyle v Verrall (1996) 29 HLR 436, [1997] 1 EGLR 25, [1997] 04 EG 145,
CA 178
Bradford Metropolitan City Council v McMahon [1993] 4 All ER 237, [1994]
1 WLR 52, 91 LGR 655, 25 HLR 534, CA 72, 74
Bradley v Chorley Borough Council (1985) 83 LGR 623, 17 HLR 305, [1985]
2 EGLR 49, 275 Estates Gazette 801, CA 358
Bradshaw v Baldwin-Wiseman (1985) 49 P & CR 382, 17 HLR 260, [1985] 1
EGLR 123, 274 Estates Gazette 285, CA 178
Brent London Borough Council v Carmel (1995) 28 HLR 203, CA 359
Brickfield Properties Ltd v Hughes (1987) 20 HLR 108, [1988] 1 EGLR 106,
[1988] 24 EG 95, CA 174
Brikom Investments Ltd v Seaford [1981] 2 All ER 783, [1981] 1 WLR 863,
42 P & CR 190, 1 HLR 21, 258 Estates Gazette 750, 125 Sol Jo 240,
CA 350
Bristol City Council v Lovell [1998] 1 All ER 775, [1998] 1 WLR 446, 96
LGR 308, 30 HLR 770, [1998] RVR 133, [1998] NPC 31, [1998] NLJR
329, 142 Sol Jo LB 116, HL 73
Bristol City Council v Mousah (1997) 30 HLR 32, CA 141
Bristol Corpn v Sinnott [1918] 1 Ch 62, [1916-17] All ER Rep Ext 1179,
82 JP 9, 15 LGR 871, 62 Sol Jo 53, 117 LT 644, CA 409
British Anzani (Felixstowe) Ltd v International Marine Management (UK) Ltd
[1980] QB 137, [1979] 2 All ER 1063, [1979] 3 WLR 451, 39 P & CR
189, 250 Estates Gazette 1183, 123 Sol Jo 64 357
Brown v Brown. See B v B [1994] 2 FCR 228
Brown v Liverpool Corpn [1969] 3 All ER 1345, CA 351
Bruton v London and Quadrant Housing Trust [1999] 3 All ER 481, [1999] 3
WLR 150, 31 HLR 902, [1999] 2 EGLR 59, [1999] 30 EG 91, [1999]
NLJR 1001, 78 P & CR D21, HL 103
Burrows v Brent London Borough Council [1996] 4 All ER 577, [1996] 1
WLR 1448, [1997] 2 FCR 43, [1997] 1 FLR 178, 29 HLR 167, [1996]
43 LS Gaz R 26, [1996] NLJR 1616, 140 Sol Jo LB 239, HL 148
Burton v Camden London Borough Council [1998] 3 FCR 254, [1998] 1 FLR
681, [1998] Fam Law 322, 30 HLR 991, [1998] 04 LS Gaz R 33, 142 Sol
Jo LB 37, CA 259
Buswell v Goodwin [1971] 1 All ER 418, [1971] 1 WLR 92, 69 LGR 201, 22
P & CR 162, 218 Estates Gazette 562,115 Sol Jo 77, CA 350

PAGE

Butler, Re, Camberwell (Wingfield Mews) No 2 Clearance Order 1936 [1939]
1 KB 570, 108 LJKB 487, 103 JP 143, 37 LGR 315, 160 LT 255, 55
TLR 429, sub nom Re Camberwell (Wingfield Mews) No 2 Clearance
Order 1936, Butler's Application [1939] 1 All ER 590, 83 Sol Jo 256,
CA 380
Butterworth v Supplementary Benefits Commission [1982] 1 All ER 498,
2 FLR 264 237

C

Calabar Properties Ltd v Stitcher [1983] 3 All ER 759, [1984] 1 WLR 287,
47 P & CR 285, 11 HLR 20, 268 Estates Gazette 697, 127 Sol Jo 785,
[1983] LS Gaz R 3163, CA 358
Calthorpe v McOscar. See Anstruther-Gough-Calthorpe v McOscar
Camberwell (Wingfield Mews) No 2 Clearance Order 1936, Re, Butler's
Application. See Butler, Re, Camberwell (Wingfield Mews) No 2
Clearance Order 1936
Camden London Borough Council v Alexandrou (1997) 30 HLR 534, 74
P & CR D33, CA 268
Camden London Borough Council v Gilsenan (1998) 31 HLR 81, CA 143
Camden London Borough Council v Gunby [1999] 4 All ER 602, [1999] 44
EG 147, [1999] 29 LS Gaz R 30, [1999] NLJR 1146 409
Camden London Borough Council v Hawkins (1988) Legal Action (March)
p 18 140
Camden London Borough Council v McBride [1999] 1 CL 284, Cty Ct 138
Camden London Borough Council v Marshall [1996] 1 WLR 1345, 74 P & CR
107, 30 HLR 173, 140 Sol Jo LB 154 449
Camden London Borough Council v Oppong (1996) 28 HLR 701, CA 136
Camden Nominees Ltd v Forcey (or Slack) [1940] Ch 352, [1940] 2 All ER
1, 109 LJ Ch 231, 84 Sol Jo 256, 163 LT 88, 56 TLR 445 357
Campden Hill Towers Ltd v Gardner [1977] QB 823, [1977] 1 All ER 739,
[1977] 2 WLR 159, 34 P & CR 175, 13 HLR 64, 242 Estates Gazette
375, 121 Sol Jo 86, CA 351
Cannock Chase District Council v Kelly [1978] 1 All ER 152, [1978] 1 WLR 1,
142 JP 113, 76 LGR 67, 36 P & CR 219, 121 Sol Jo 593, CA 135
Canterbury City Council v Bern (1981) 44 P & CR 178, [1981] JPL
749 .... 440, 442
Carpenter v Carpenter [1988] 1 FLR 121, [1988] Fam Law 56, CA 155
Carr v Hackney London Borough Council (1995) 160 JP 402, 93 LGR 606, 28
HLR 749 407
Central YMCA Housing Association Ltd v Saunders (1990) 23 HLR 212,
CA 102, 131
Central YMCA Housing Association Ltd and St Giles Hotel Ltd v Goodman
(1991) 24 HLR 109, CA 102, 131
Charles v Charles (1984) Legal Action (July) p 81 306
Charsley v Jones (1889) 53 JP 280, 5 TLR 412 347
Chiodi's Personal Representatives v De Marney (1988) 21 HLR 6, [1988]
2 EGLR 64, [1988] 41 EG 80, CA 359
City of Westminster v Mavroghenis (1983) 11 HLR 56 439
Clarke v Taff Ely Borough Council (1980) 10 HLR 44 345
Cocker v Cardwell (1869) LR 5 QB 15, 34 JP 516, 10 B & S 797, 39 LJMC
28, 18 WR 212, 21 LT 457 410

PAGE

Cole v Harris [1945] KB 474, [1945] 2 All ER 146, 114 LJKB 481, 89 Sol Jo
477, 173 LT 50, 61 TLR 440, CA 131
Coleen Properties Ltd v Minister of Housing and Local Government [1971]
1 All ER 1049, [1971] 1 WLR 433, 135 JP 226, 69 LGR 175, 22 P &
CR 417, [1971] RVR 489, 218 Estates Gazette 1163, 115 Sol Jo 112,
CA 382
Community Housing Association v Hoy (1988) Legal Action (December) p
18 253
Conron v LCC [1922] 2 Ch 283, [1922] All ER Rep 643, 91 LJ Ch 386, 87
JP 109, 20 LGR 131, 66 Sol Jo 350, 126 LT 791, 38 TLR 380 58
Cookson v Walsh (1954) 163 Estates Gazette 486, CA 181
Coventry City Council v Cartwright [1975] 2 All ER 99, [1975] 1 WLR 845,
139 JP 409, 73 LGR 218, 119 Sol Jo 235, DC 406, 412
Coventry City Council v Cole [1994] 1 All ER 997, [1994] 1 WLR 398, 92
LGR 181, 25 HLR 555, [1994] 1 EGLR 63, [1994] 06 EG 133, [1994]
12 LS Gaz R 38, CA 86
Coventry City Council v Doyle [1981] 2 All ER 184, [1981] 1 WLR 1325, 79
LGR 418, 125 Sol Jo 639, DC 412, 413
Coventry City Council v Finnie (1996) 29 HLR 658 154
Crago v Julian [1992] 1 All ER 744, [1992] 1 WLR 372, [1992] 2 FCR 387,
[1992] 1 FLR 478, [1992] Fam Law 294, 63 P & CR 356, 24 HLR 306,
[1992] 1 EGLR 84, [1992] 17 EG 108, [1992] 3 LS Gaz R 32, 135 Sol
Jo LB 212, CA 268
Crawley Borough Council v Sawyer (1987) 86 LGR 629, 20 HLR 98, CA 132
Crawley Borough Council v Ure [1996] QB 13, [1996] 1 All ER 724, [1995]
3 WLR 95, [1996] 1 FCR 6, [1995] 1 FLR 806, [1995] Fam Law 411,
71 P & CR 12, 27 HLR 524, CA 255
Crédit Suisse v Allerdale Borough Council [1995] 1 Lloyd's Rep 315; affd
[1997] QB 306, [1996] 4 All ER 129, [1996] 3 WLR 894, [1996] 2
Lloyd's Rep 241, CA 208
Crédit Suisse v Beegas Nominees Ltd [1994] 4 All ER 803, 69 P & CR 177,
[1994] 1 EGLR 76, [1994] 11 EG 151, 12 EG 189 347
Croydon London Borough v Buston and Triance (1991) 24 HLR 36, CA 268
Cunard v Antifyre Ltd [1933] 1 KB 551, [1932] All ER Rep 558, 103 LJKB
321, 148 LT 287, 49 TLR 184 340
Cunningham v Birmingham City Council (1997) 96 LGR 231, 30 HLR 158,
[1998] Env LR 1 408
Curtis v London Rent Assessment Committee [1999] QB 92, [1997] 4 All
ER 842, [1998] 3 WLR 1427, 30 HLR 733, CA 227

D

Daiches v Bluelake Investments Ltd (1985) 51 P & CR 51, 17 HLR 543,
[1985] 2 EGLR 67, 275 Estates Gazette 462 356
Dance v Welwyn Hatfield District Council [1990] 3 All ER 572, [1990] 1
WLR 1097, 88 LGR 812, 22 HLR 339, CA 73
Davenport v Walsall Metropolitan Borough Council (1995) 28 HLR 754,
[1996] Env LR D33 414
Davies v Peterson (1988) 21 HLR 63, [1989] 1 EGLR 121, [1989] 06 EG 130,
CA 359
De Falco v Crawley Borough Council [1980] QB 460, [1980] 1 All ER 913,
[1980] 2 WLR 664, [1980] 1 CMLR 437, 78 LGR 180, 124 Sol Jo 82,
CA 303

PAGE

Delahaye v Oswestry Borough Council (1980) Times, 29 July 307
Demetri v Westminster City Council [1999] 45 LS Gaz R 32, 143 Sol Jo LB
    277, CA 327
Demetriou v Robert Andrews (Estate Agencies) Ltd (1990) 62 P & CR 536, sub
    nom Demetriou v Poolaction Ltd [1991] 1 EGLR 100, [1991] 25 EG 113,
    CA 350
Desmond v Bromley London Borough Council (1995) 28 HLR 518 448
Devenport v Salford City Council. See R v Salford City Council, ex p Devenport
Dickinson v Enfield London Borough Council (1996) 29 HLR 465, [1996] 2
    EGLR 88, [1996] 49 EG 108, CA 74
Din v Wandsworth London Borough Council [1983] 1 AC 657, [1981] 3 All
    ER 881, [1981] 3 WLR 918, 80 LGR 113, 1 HLR 73, 125 Sol Jo 828,
    HL 303
Dinefwr Borough Council v Jones (1987) 19 HLR 445, [1987] 2 EGLR 58,
    284 Estates Gazette 58, CA 349
DPP v Carrick District Council (January 1985, unreported) 460
Doe d Aslin v Summersett (1830) 1 B & Ad 135, 8 LJOSKB 369 254
Doherty v Allman (or Allen) (1878) 3 App Cas 709, 42 JP 788, 26 WR 513,
    39 LT 129, HL 152
Douglas-Scott v Scorgie [1984] 1 All ER 1086, [1984] 1 WLR 716, 48 P &
    CR 109, 13 HLR 97, 128 Sol Jo 264, 269 Estates Gazette 1164, CA 352
Dover District Council v Farrar (1980) 2 HLR 32 407
Dover District Council v Sherred and Tarling (1997) 29 HLR 864, CA 364
Dudley Metropolitan Borough Council v Bailey (1990) 89 LGR 246, 22 HLR
    424, [1991] 1 EGLR 53, [1991] 10 EG 140, CA 136
Duffy v Pilling (1977) 75 LGR 159, 33 P & CR 85, 241 Estates Gazette 607: 427
Dun Laoghaire UDC v Moran [1921] 2 IR 404 .... 150, 182
Dyson v Kerrier District Council [1980] 3 All ER 313, [1980] 1 WLR 1205,
    144 JP 447, 78 LGR 603, 124 Sol Jo 497, CA 303, 312

E

Ealing Corpn v Ryan [1965] 2 QB 486, [1965] 1 All ER 137, [1965] 2 WLR
    223, 129 JP 164, 63 LGR 148, 17 P & CR 15, 109 Sol Jo 74 427
Ealing Family Housing Association v Taylor (1987) Legal Action (December)
    p 15 140
East Staffordshire Borough Council v Fairless (1998) 31 HLR 677, [1998]
    41 LS Gaz R 46, [1998] EGCS 140 412
Eastleigh Borough Council v Betts [1983] 2 AC 613, [1983] 2 All ER 1111,
    [1983] 3 WLR 397, [1984] FLR 156, [1984] Fam Law 25, 81 LGR 721,
    127 Sol Jo 537, 133 NLJ 893, HL 310, 312
Edwards (Inspector of Taxes) v Bairstow and Harrison [1956] AC 14, [1955]
    3 All ER 48, [1955] 3 WLR 410, 36 TC 207, 34 ATC 198, 48 R & IT
    534, [1955] TR 209, 99 Sol Jo 558, HL 226
Edwards v Thompson (1990) 60 P & CR 222, [1990] 2 EGLR 71, [1990]
    29 EG 41, CA 180
Electricity Supply Nominees Ltd v IAF Group plc [1993] 3 All ER 372,
    [1993] 1 WLR 1059, 67 P & CR 28, [1993] 2 EGLR 95, [1993] 37 EG
    155 357
Elmcroft Developments Ltd v Tankersley-Sawyer (1984) 15 HLR 63, [1984]
    1 EGLR 47, 270 Estates Gazette 140, CA 353
Elvidge v Coventry City Council [1994] QB 241, [1993] 4 All ER 903, [1993]
    3 WLR 976, [1994] ICR 68, 26 HLR 281, CA 133

PAGE

Enfield Borough Council v French (1984) 83 LGR 750, 49 P & CR 223, 17
   HLR 211, CA 137, 181
Enfield London Borough Council v B (a minor) (1999) Times, 7 September,
   CA 155
Enfield London Borough Council v McKeon [1986] 2 All ER 730, [1986] 1
   WLR 1007, 85 LGR 24, 18 HLR 330, 130 Sol Jo 504, [1986] LS Gaz R
   2243, [1986] NLJ Rep 631, CA 73
Ephraim v London Borough of Newham (1992) 91 LGR 412, 25 HLR 207,
   [1993] 10 LS Gaz R 34, 136 Sol Jo LB 13, CA 312, 459
Epping Forest District Council v Pomphrett and Pomphrett (1990) 22 HLR
   475, [1990] 2 EGLR 46, [1990] 35 EG 60, CA 271
Ezekiel v McDade [1995] 2 EGLR 107, [1995] 47 EG 150, 10 Const LJ 122,
   CA 359

F

Family Housing Association v Jones [1990] 1 All ER 385, [1990] 1 WLR 779,
   60 P & CR 27, 22 HLR 45, [1990] 1 EGLR 82, [1990] 24 EG 118,
   [1989] NLJR 1709, 134 Sol Jo 233, CA 102
Fernandes v Parvardin (1982) 5 HLR 33, [1982] 2 EGLR 104, 264 Estates
   Gazette 49, CA 178
Fitzpatrick v Sterling Housing Association Ltd [1999] 4 All ER 705, [1999] 3
   WLR 1113, [1999] 43 LS Gaz R 34, HL 270
Foster v Day (1968) 208 Estates Gazette 495, CA 359
Francis v Cowlcliffe (1976) 33 P & CR 368, 239 Estates Gazette 977 355
Fredman v Minister of Health (1935) 100 JP 104, [1935] All ER Rep 916, 34
   LGR 153, 80 Sol Jo 56, 154 LT 240 381
Freeman v Wansbeck District Council [1984] 2 All ER 746, 82 LGR 131, 10
   HLR 54, 127 Sol Jo 550, [1983] LS Gaz R 2444, CA 72

G

Garlick v Oldham Metropolitan Borough Council. See R v Oldham Metropolitan
   Borough Council, ex p Garlick, and R v Tower Hamlets London Borough
   Council, ex p Ferdous Begum
Gateshead County Borough (Barn Close) Clearance Order 1931, Re [1933] 1
   KB 429, 102 LJKB 82, 97 JP 1, 31 LGR 52, 77 Sol Jo 12, 148 LT 264,
   49 TLR 101 381
Gay v Enfield London Borough Council [1999] 3 All ER 795, [1999] 2 FCR
   705, [1999] 2 FLR 519, [1999] Fam Law 619, [1999] 30 LS Gaz R 29,
   CA 241, 251
Gay v Sheeran [1999] 3 All ER 795, [1999] 2 FCR 705, [1999] 2 FLR 519,
   [1999] Fam Law 619, [1999] 30 LS Gaz R 29, CA 241, 251
Giddens v Harlow District Auditor (1972) 70 LGR 485, DC 215
Gillick v West Norfolk and Wisbech Area Health Authority [1986] AC 112,
   [1985] 3 All ER 402, [1985] 3 WLR 830, [1986] 1 FLR 224, 2 BMLR
   11, [1986] Crim LR 113, 129 Sol Jo 738, [1985] LS Gaz R 3551, [1985]
   NLJ Rep 1055, HL 281
Gloucester City Council v Miles. See R v Gloucester City Council, ex p Miles
Goddard v Minister of Housing and Local Government [1958] 3 All ER 482,
   [1958] 1 WLR 1151, 123 JP 68, 57 LGR 38, 10 P & CR 28, 102 Sol Jo
   860 381

PAGE

Goodrich v Paisner [1957] AC 65, [1956] 2 All ER 176, [1956] 2 WLR 1053,
100 Sol Jo 341, HL 427
Gordon v Selico Co Ltd (1986) 18 HLR 219, [1986] 1 EGLR 71, 278 Estates
Gazette 53, CA 340, 348
Gosling v Secretary of State for the Environment (1974) 234 Estates Gazette
531, [1975] JPL 406 382
Gould v Times Square Estates Ltd [1975] LAG Bulletin 147 412
Graddage v Haringey London Borough [1975] 1 All ER 224, [1975] 1 WLR
241, 139 JP 282, 29 P & CR 441, 118 Sol Jo 775 372
Gravesham Borough Council v Secretary of State for the Environment (1982)
47 P & CR 142, [1983] JPL 307 56
Great Western Rly Co v Bishop (1872) LR 7 QB 550, 37 JP 5, 41 LJMC 120,
20 WR 969, 26 LT 905 408
Greater London Council v Tower Hamlets London Borough Council (1983) 15
HLR 54 407
Green (HE) & Sons v Minister of Health (No 2) [1948] 1 KB 34, [1947] 2 All
ER 469, 111 JP 530, 45 LGR 590, [1948] LJR 1 213
Greenfield v Berkshire County Council (1996) 73 P & CR 280, 28 HLR 691,
CA 133
Greenwich London Borough Council v McGrady (1982) 81 LGR 288, 46 P &
CR 223, 6 HLR 36, 267 Estates Gazette 515, CA 252
Greg v Planque [1936] 1 KB 669, [1935] All ER Rep 237, 105 LJKB 415,
154 LT 475, CA 352
Griffin v Pillet [1926] 1 KB 17, 95 LJKB 67, 70 Sol Jo 110, 134 LT 58 349
Guinan v Enfield London Borough Council (1996) 29 HLR 456, CA 81

H

H (minors) (sexual abuse: standard of proof), Re [1996] AC 563, [1996] 1 All
ER 1, [1996] 2 WLR 8, [1996] 1 FCR 509, [1996] 1 FLR 80, [1996] Fam
Law 74, 140 Sol Jo LB 24, HL 240
Habinteg Housing Association v James (1994) 27 HLR 299, CA 341
Hackney London Borough v Ezedinma [1981] 3 All ER 438 .... 432, 445
Hackney London Borough v Lambourne (1992) 25 HLR 172, [1993] COD 231,
CA 331
Hall v Howard (1988) 57 P & CR 226, 20 HLR 566, [1988] 2 EGLR 75,
[1988] 44 EG 83, CA 349
Hall v Kingston upon Hull City Council [1999] 2 All ER 609 412
Hall v Manchester Corpn (1915) 13 LGR 1105, 79 JP 385, 84 LJ Ch 732,
113 LT 465, 31 TLR 416, HL 363, 365
Hamilton District Council v Lennon 1990 SC 230, 1990 SLT 533 270
Hammersmith and Fulham London Borough v Harrison [1981] 2 All ER 588,
sub nom Harrison v Hammersmith and Fulham London Borough Council
[1981] 1 WLR 650, 79 LGR 634, 44 P & CR 131, 125 Sol Jo 200, CA . 176
Hammersmith and Fulham London Borough Council v Hill (1994) 92 LGR 665,
27 HLR 368, [1994] 2 EGLR 51, [1994] 35 EG 124, [1994] 22 LS Gaz
R 35, CA 149
Hammersmith and Fulham London Borough Council v Monk [1992] 1 AC 478,
[1992] 1 All ER 1, [1991] 3 WLR 1144, [1992] 2 FCR 129, [1992] 1
FLR 465, [1992] Fam Law 292, 90 LGR 38, 63 P & CR 373, 24 HLR 206,
[1992] 1 EGLR 65, [1992] 09 EG 135, [1992] 3 LS Gaz R 32, 136 Sol Jo
LB 10, HL 252
Haringey London Borough Council v Jowett [1999] EGCS 64, 78 P & CR
D24 406

PAGE

Haringey London Borough Council v Stewart and Stewart (1991) 23 HLR 557,
 [1991] 2 EGLR 252, CA 150
Harrison v Hammersmith and Fulham London Borough Council. See
 Hammersmith and Fulham London Borough v Harrison
Harrison v Lewis [1989] FCR 765, [1988] 2 FLR 339, [1988] Fam Law 477,
 CA 237
Harrogate Borough Council v Simpson [1986] 2 FLR 91, [1986] Fam Law 359,
 17 HLR 205, [1985] RVR 10, CA 270
Harrow London Borough Council v Johnstone [1997] 1 All ER 929, [1997] 1
 WLR 459, [1997] 2 FCR 225, [1997] 1 FLR 887, [1997] Fam Law 478,
 29 HLR 475, [1997] 15 LS Gaz R 26, [1997] NLJR 413, HL 255
Harrow London Borough Council v Tonge (1992) 91 LGR 81, 25 HLR 99,
 [1993] 1 EGLR 49, [1993] 09 EG 109, [1992] 44 LS Gaz R 36, CA 72
Hart v Emelkirk Ltd [1983] 3 All ER 15, [1983] 1 WLR 1289, 9 HLR 114,
 267 Estates Gazette 946, 127 Sol Jo 156 356
Havant and Waterloo UDC Compulsory Purchase Order (No 4) 1950, Re, Re
 Watson's Application. See Watson v Minister of Local Government and
 Planning
Hazell v Hammersmith and Fulham London Borough Council [1992] 2 AC 1,
 [1991] 1 All ER 545, [1991] 2 WLR 372, 89 LGR 271, [1991] RVR 28,
 HL 208
Heglibiston Establishment v Heyman (1977) 36 P & CR 351, 246 Estates
 Gazette 567, 121 Sol Jo 851, CA 181
Hemsted v Lees and Norwich City Council (1986) 18 HLR 424 .... 213, 215
Herbert v Lambeth London Borough Council (1991) 156 JP 389, 90 LGR 310,
 24 HLR 299, 13 Cr App Rep (S) 489 414
Hereford City Council v O'Callaghan [1996] CLY 3831 270
Hewitt v Rowlands (1924) 93 LJKB 1080, [1924] All ER Rep 344, 131 LT
 757, CA 358
Hillbank Properties Ltd v Hackney London Borough Council [1978] QB 998,
 [1978] 3 All ER 343, [1978] 3 WLR 260, 76 LGR 677, 37 P & CR 218,
 3 HLR 73, [1978] RVR 209, 247 Estates Gazette 807, [1978] JPL 615,
 122 Sol Jo 401, CA 372
Hollis v Dudley Metropolitan Borough Council [1998] 1 All ER 759, [1999] 1
 WLR 642, 30 HLR 902, [1998] 2 EGLR 19, [1998] 18 EG 133 414
Holloway v Povey (1984) 49 P & CR 196, 15 HLR 104, [1984] 2 EGLR 115,
 271 Estates Gazette 195, [1984] LS Gaz R 1603, CA 182
Honig v Islington London Borough [1972] Crim LR 126 449
Hopwood v Cannock Chase District Council [1975] 1 All ER 796, [1975] 1
 WLR 373, 73 LGR 137, 29 P & CR 1256, 119 Sol Jo 186, CA 351
Horgan v Birmingham Corpn (1964) 63 LGR 33, 108 Sol Jo 991, CA 449
Horrex v Pidwell [1958] CLY 1461 363
Hounslow London Borough Council v Hare (1990) 89 LGR 714, 24 HLR 9 73
Hounslow London Borough Council v Pilling [1994] 1 All ER 432, [1993]
 1 WLR 1242, [1993] 2 FLR 49, [1993] Fam Law 522, 91 LGR 573, 66
 P & CR 22, 25 HLR 305, [1993] 2 EGLR 59, [1993] 26 EG 123, [1993]
 15 LS Gaz R 40, 137 Sol Jo LB 87, CA 253
Hughes v London Borough of Greenwich (1992) 65 P & CR 12, 24 HLR 605,
 CA; affd sub nom Hughes v Greenwich London Borough Council [1994]
 1 AC 170, [1993] 4 All ER 577, [1993] 3 WLR 821, [1994] ICR 48, 92
 LGR 61, 69 P & CR 487, 26 HLR 99, [1993] 46 LS Gaz R 38, [1993]
 NLJR 1571n, 137 Sol Jo LB 244, HL 132
Humberside County Council v B [1993] 1 FCR 613, [1993] 1 FLR 257,
 [1993] Fam Law 61 240

PAGE

Hungerford (Dame Margaret) Charity Trustees v Beazeley (1993) 26 HLR 269,
    [1993] 2 EGLR 143, [1993] 29 EG 100, [1993] 23 LS Gaz R 41, CA ...353
Hussain v Lancaster City Council [1999] 4 All ER 125, [1999] 2 WLR 1142,
    96 LGR 663, 77 P & CR 89, 31 HLR 164, [1998] 23 LS Gaz R 27, 142
    Sol Jo LB 173, 76 P & CR D31, CA 143
Hussey v Camden London Borough Council (1994) 27 HLR 5, CA 132
Hyde Housing Association Ltd v Harrison (1990) 23 HLR 57, [1991] 1 EGLR
    51, [1991] 07 EG 131, CA 133

I

Irvine v Moran (1990) 24 HLR 1, [1991] 1 EGLR 261 351
Islam, Re. See R v Hillingdon Homeless Families Panel, ex p Islam
Islam v Hillingdon London Borough Council. See R v Hillingdon Homeless
    Families Panel, ex p Islam

J

J, Re [1995] 1 FLR 660, [1995] Fam Law 300 237
Jackson v Knutsford Urban Council [1914] 2 Ch 686, 84 LJ Ch 305, 79 JP 73,
    58 Sol Jo 756, 111 LT 982 376
Jennings and Jennings v Epping Forest District Council (1992) 25 HLR 241,
    [1992] NPC 93, CA 132
Jones v Jones [1997] Fam 59, [1997] 2 WLR 373, [1997] 1 FCR 1, [1997]
    1 FLR 27, [1997] Fam Law 164, 29 HLR 561, CA 266

K

Kelsey Housing Association v King (1995) 28 HLR 270, CA 135
Kenny v Kingston upon Thames Royal London Borough Council (1985)
    17 HLR 344, [1985] 1 EGLR 26, 274 Estates Gazette 395, [1986] JPL
    352, CA 371
Kensington and Chelsea Royal London Borough Council v Simmonds [1996] 3
    FCR 246, 29 HLR 507, CA 140
Khan v Islington London Borough Council [1999] EGCS 87, CA 383
King v South Northamptonshire District Council (1991) 90 LGR 121, 64 P &
    CR 35, 24 HLR 284, [1992] 1 EGLR 53, [1992] 06 EG 152, CA 348
Kingston and Richmond Area Health Authority v Kaur [1981] ICR 631,
    [1981] IRLR 337 111
Kingston-upon-Hull District Council v University of Hull [1979] LAG Bulletin
    191 449
Kingston upon Thames Royal London Borough v Prince [1999] 1 FLR 593,
    [1999] Fam Law 84, 31 HLR 794, [1999] 02 LS Gaz R 28, 143 Sol Jo
    LB 45, CA 267, 270
Kirklees Metropolitan Borough Council v Field (1997) 96 LGR 151, 162 JP
    88, 30 HLR 869, [1997] 45 LS Gaz R 28, 141 Sol Jo LB 246 409
Kotecha v Manchester City Council (4 October 1982, unreported), Cty Ct ...355

L

Lake v Bennett [1970] 1 QB 663, [1970] 1 All ER 457, [1970] 2 WLR 355, 21 P
    & CR 93, [1970] RVR 56, 213 Estates Gazette 633, 114 Sol Jo 13, CA .. 56

Lally v Kensington and Chelsea Royal Borough (1980) Times, 27
   March 287, 312
Lambert v Ealing London Borough Council [1982] 2 All ER 394, [1982] 1
   WLR 550, 80 LGR 487, 2 HLR 58, 126 Sol Jo 228, CA 304
Lambeth London Borough Council v Stubbs (1980) 78 LGR 650, 255 Estates
   Gazette 789, [1980] JPL 517 413
Lee v Lee [1984] FLR 243, [1984] Fam Law 243, 12 HLR 114, 127 Sol Jo
   696, [1983] LS Gaz R 2678, CA 240
Lee-Parker v Izzet [1971] 3 All ER 1099, [1971] 1 WLR 1688, 22 P & CR
   1098, 115 Sol Jo 641 356
Leeds v Islington London Borough Council (1998) 31 HLR 545, [1998] Env
   LR 657,[1998] 07 LS Gaz R 33 412
Leeds Corpn v Jenkinson [1935] 1 KB 168, 104 LJKB 182, 98 JP 447, 32
   LGR 416, 78 Sol Jo 734, 152 LT 126, 51 TLR 19, CA 215
Leicester City Council v Aldwinckle (1991) 24 HLR 40, CA 149
Lewis v Lewis [1985] AC 828, [1985] 2 All ER 449, [1985] 2 WLR 962,
   [1985] FLR 994, [1985] Fam Law 328, 50 P & CR 231, 17 HLR 459,
   129 Sol Jo 349, [1985] LS Gaz R 2167, HL 249
Lewis v North Devon District Council [1981] 1 All ER 27, 124 Sol Jo 742,
   sub nom R v North Devon District Council, ex p Lewis [1981] 1 WLR
   328, 79 LGR 289 300
Lewisham London Borough v Simba-Tola (1991) 24 HLR 644, CA 153
Lillieshall Road Housing Co-operative Ltd v Brennan and Brennan (1991) 24
   HLR 195, CA 133
Lipson v Secretary of State for the Environment (1976) 75 LGR 361, 33 P &
   CR 95, 242 Estates Gazette 1049 427
Lismane v Hammersmith and Fulham London Borough Council (1998) 31 HLR
   427, [1998] 31 LS Gaz R 36, 142 Sol Jo LB 219, CA 292
Little v Borders Regional Council 1990 SLT (Lands Tr) 2 133
Liverpool City Council v Irwin [1977] AC 239, [1976] 2 All ER 39, [1976] 2
   WLR 562, 74 LGR 392, 32 P & CR 43, 13 HLR 38, 238 Estates Gazette
   879, 963, 120 Sol Jo 267, HL 347
Living Waters Christian Centres Ltd v Conwy County Borough Council and
   Fetherstonhaugh (1998) 77 P & CR 54, 31 HLR 371, [1999] 2 EGLR 1,
   [1999] 28 EG 121, CA 430, 431
London Housing and Commercial Properties Ltd v Cowan [1977] QB 148,
   [1976] 2 All ER 385, [1976] 3 WLR 115, 31 P & CR 387, 120 Sol Jo
   383 226
Loria v Hammer [1989] 2 EGLR 249 348
Lowe v South Somerset District Council (1997) 96 LGR 487, [1998] Env LR
   143 409
Lubren v London Borough of Lambeth (1987) 20 HLR 165, CA 359
Luby v Newcastle-under-Lyme Corpn [1964] 2 QB 64, [1964] 1 All ER 84,
   [1964] 2 WLR 475, 128 JP 138, 62 LGR 140, 107 Sol Jo 983; affd
   [1965] 1 QB 214, [1964] 3 All ER 169, [1964] 3 WLR 500, 128 JP
   536, 62 LGR 622, [1964] RVR 708, 191 Estates Gazette 121, 108 Sol Jo
   541, CA 215
Luganda v Service Hotels Ltd [1969] 2 Ch 209, [1969] 2 All ER 692, [1969]
   2 WLR 1056, 20 P & CR 337, 210 Estates Gazette 113, 113 Sol Jo 206,
   CA 102
Lurcott v Wakely and Wheeler [1911] 1 KB 905, [1911-13] All ER Rep 41,
   80 LJKB 713, 55 Sol Jo 290, 104 LT 290, CA 85

M

McAuley v Bristol City Council [1992] QB 134, [1992] 1 All ER 749, [1991] 3 WLR 968, 89 LGR 931, 23 HLR 586, [1991] 2 EGLR 64, [1991] 46 EG 155, [1991] NPC 81, CA 345
McCarrick v Liverpool Corpn [1947] AC 219, [1946] 2 All ER 646, 111 JP 6, 45 LGR 49, [1947] LJR 56, 91 Sol Jo 41, 176 LT 11, 62 TLR 730, HL 349
McClean v Liverpool City Council (1987) 20 HLR 25, [1987] 2 EGLR 56, 283 Estates Gazette 1395, CA 354
McDougall v Easington District Council (1989) 87 LGR 527, 58 P & CR 201, 21 HLR 310, [1989] 1 EGLR 93, [1989] 25 EG 104, CA 352
McEwan v Annandale and Eskdale District Council 1989 SLT (Lands Tr) 95 . 133
McGreal v Wake (1984) 13 HLR 107, [1984] 1 EGLR 42, 269 Estates Gazette 1254, [1984] LS Gaz R 739, 128 Sol Jo 116, CA 349
McIntyre v Merthyr Tydfil Borough Council (1989) 88 LGR 1, 21 HLR 320, CA 80
McLean v Burke (1980) 3 FLR 70, CA 237
McNerny v Lambeth London Borough Council (1988) 21 HLR 188, [1989] 1 EGLR 81, [1989] 19 EG 77, [1989] NLJR 114, CA 341
Mallon v Monklands District Council 1986 SLT 347 331
Malton Board of Health v Malton Manure Co (1879) 4 Ex D 302, 44 JP 155, 49 LJMC 90, 27 WR 802, 40 LT 755 .... 407, 408
Manchester City Council v Cochrane [1999] 1 WLR 809, 31 HLR 810, 143 Sol Jo LB 37, CA 129
Manchester City Council v Lawler and McMillan (1998) 31 HLR 119, CA ... 139
Manchester City Council v McCann [1999] 2 WLR 590, 31 HLR 770, [1998] 48 LS Gaz R 31, CA 157
Manchester City Council v Worthington (1999) Housing Law Monitor (August) p 8 155
Mandeville v Greater London Council (1982) Times, 28 January 215
Marcroft Wagons Ltd v Smith [1951] 2 KB 496, [1951] 2 All ER 271, 95 Sol Jo 501, CA 242
Marshall v Rubypoint Ltd (1997) 29 HLR 850, [1997] 1 EGLR 69, [1997] 25 EG 142, CA 354
Martin v Motherwell District Council 1991 SLT (Lands Tr) 4 147
Meravale Builders Ltd v Secretary of State for the Environment (1978) 77 LGR 365, 36 P & CR 87 58
Mickel v M'Coard 1913 SC 896 355
Middleton v Hall (1913) 77 JP 172, 11 LGR 660n, 108 LT 804 349
Milford Properties v London Borough of Hammersmith [1978] JPL 766, DC: 432
Miller v Wandsworth London Borough Council (1980) Times, 19 March 305
Mills v Allen [1953] 2 QB 341, [1953] 2 All ER 534, [1953] 3 WLR 356, 161 Estates Gazette 736, 97 Sol Jo 505, CA 184
Milne-Berry and Madden v Tower Hamlets London Borough Council (1995) 28 HLR 225, [1995] EGCS 86; affd (1997) 30 HLR 229, CA 80
Minchburn Ltd v Peck (1987) 20 HLR 392, [1988] 1 EGLR 53, [1988] 15 EG 97, CA 359
Mint v Good [1951] 1 KB 517, [1950] 2 All ER 1159, 49 LGR 495, 94 Sol Jo 822, 66 (pt 2) TLR 1110, CA 344
Mirza v Bhandal (1999) Housing Law Monitor (June) p 4 343
Monmouth Borough Council v Marlog (1994) 27 HLR 30, [1994] 2 EGLR 68, [1994] 44 EG 240, CA 103, 243

PAGE
Morgan v Liverpool Corpn [1927] 2 KB 131, [1926] All ER Rep 25, 96
    LJKB 234, 91 JP 26, 25 LGR 79, 71 Sol Jo 35, 136 LT 622, 43 TLR
    146, CA 364
Morley v Knowsley Borough Council (1988) Legal Action (May) p 22 345
Morris v Liverpool City Council (1987) 20 HLR 498, [1988] 1 EGLR 47,
    [1988] 14 EG 59, CA 354
Mossop v Mossop [1989] Fam 77, [1988] 2 All ER 202, [1988] 2 WLR 1255,
    [1988] 2 FLR 173, [1988] Fam Law 334, 132 Sol Jo 1033, [1988] NLJR
    86, CA 236
Mountain v Hastings (1993) 25 HLR 427, [1993] 2 EGLR 53, [1993] 29 EG
    96, CA 178
Muir Group Housing Association Ltd v Thornley (1992) 91 LGR 1, 25 HLR
    89, [1993] 1 EGLR 51, [1993] 10 EG 144, [1992] 43 LS Gaz R 31, CA .. 74
Mullaney v Maybourne Grange (Croydon) Management Co Ltd [1986]
    1 EGLR 70, 277 Estates Gazette 1350 353
Mullen v Hackney London Borough Council [1997] 2 All ER 906, [1997]
    1 WLR 1103, 29 HLR 592, CA 355
Murray v Birmingham City Council (1987) 20 HLR 39, [1987] 2 EGLR 53,
    283 Estates Gazette 962, CA 353

N

Nacion, ex p [1999] 11 LS Gaz R 69, CA 328
Nairne v Camden London Borough Council [1999] 1 All ER 450, [1999]
    1 WLR 384, 31 HLR 349, CA ' 328
National Coal Board v Neath Borough Council [1976] 2 All ER 478, 140 JP
    436, sub nom National Coal Board v Thorne [1976] 1 WLR 543, 74
    LGR 429, 120 Sol Jo 234, DC 408
Neale v Del Soto [1945] KB 144, [1945] 1 All ER 191, 114 LJKB 138, 89
    Sol Jo 130, 172 LT 65, 61 TLR 145, CA 131
Network Housing Association v Westminster City Council (1994) 93 LGR 280,
    27 HLR 189, [1995] Env LR 176 409
Newham London Borough v Patel [1979] JPL 303, CA 354
Newlon Housing Trust v Alsulaimen [1999] 1 AC 313, [1998] 4 All ER 1,
    [1998] 3 WLR 451, [1998] 3 FCR 183, [1998] 2 FLR 690, [1998] Fam
    Law 589, 30 HLR 1132, [1998] NLJR 1303, 142 Sol Jo LB 247, HL ...256
Nolan v Leeds City Council (1990) 89 LGR 385, 23 HLR 135, CA 445
Northampton Borough Council v Lovatt [1998] 2 FCR 182, 96 LGR 548, 30
    HLR 875, [1998] 1 EGLR 15, [1998] 07 EG 142, [1998] 10 LS Gaz R 28,
    CA 140
Northumberland and Durham Property Trust Ltd v Chairman of London Rent
    Assessment Committee [1998] 3 EGLR 85, [1998] 43 EG 138 227
Norwich City Council v Secretary of State for the Environment. See R v
    Secretary of State for the Environment, ex p Norwich City Council
Notting Hill Housing Trust v Etoria [1989] CLY 1912 174
Notting Hill Housing Trust v Rakey Jones (1999) Housing Law Monitor
    (February) p 8 267
Nottingham Corpn v Newton [1974] 2 All ER 760, sub nom Nottingham
    City District Council v Newton, Nottingham Friendship Housing
    Association v Newton [1974] 1 WLR 923, 72 LGR 535, 118 Sol Jo
    462 .... 384, 410

O

Oakley v Birmingham City Council (1999) Times, 8 January 408
O'Brien v Robinson [1973] AC 912, [1973] 1 All ER 583, [1973] 2 WLR 393,
   25 P & CR 239, 117 Sol Jo 187, HL 349
Ojutiku v Manpower Services Commission [1982] ICR 661, [1982] IRLR 418,
   CA 111
Okereke v Brent London Borough Council [1967] 1 QB 42, [1966] 1 All
   ER 150, [1966] 2 WLR 169, 130 JP 126, 64 LGR 72, 109 Sol Jo 956,
   CA 56, 431
O'Leary v Islington London Borough (1983) 9 HLR 81, CA 143
Orakpo v London Borough of Wandsworth and Secretary of State for the
   Environment (1990) 24 HLR 370, CA 453, 454
O'Rourke v Camden London Borough Council [1998] AC 188, [1997] 3 All
   ER 23, [1997] 3 WLR 86, 29 HLR 793, [1997] 26 LS Gaz R 30, 141 Sol
   Jo LB 139, HL 331
Osei-Bonsu v Wandsworth London Borough Council [1999] 1 All ER 265,
   [1999] 1 WLR 1011, sub nom Wandsworth London Borough Council v
   Osei-Bonsu [1999] 3 FCR 1, [1999] 1 FLR 276, 31 HLR 515, [1999] 1
   EGLR 26, [1999] 11 EG 167, [1998] 42 LS Gaz R 34, [1998] NLJR
   1641, 143 Sol Jo LB 12, CA 257
Our Lady of Hal Church v Camden London Borough Council (1980) 79 LGR
   103, 40 P & CR 472, 255 Estates Gazette 991, CA 370, 371

P

Paddington Churches Housing Association v Sharif (1997) 29 HLR 817, CA . . 182
Panayi v Secretary of State for the Environment (1985) 50 P & CR 109,
   [1985] JPL 783 428
Parker v Camden London Borough Council [1986] Ch 162, [1985] 2 All ER
   141, [1985] 3 WLR 47, 84 LGR 16, 17 HLR 380, 129 Sol Jo 417, [1985]
   LS Gaz R 2334, CA 356
Parr v Wyre Borough Council (1982) 2 HLR 71, CA 320
Parsons v Parsons [1983] 1 WLR 1390, 47 P & CR 494, 269 Estates Gazette
   634, 127 Sol Jo 823, [1984] LS Gaz R 43 254
Passley v Wandsworth London Borough Council (1996) 30 HLR 165, CA . . . 351
Patel v Mehtab (1980) 5 HLR 78 408
Patterson v Greenwich London Borough (1993) 26 HLR 159, CA 309
Payne and Woodland v Barnet London Borough Council (1997) 76 P & CR
   295, 30 HLR 295, CA 77
Peabody Donation Fund (Governors) v Higgins [1983] 3 All ER 122, [1983]
   1 WLR 1091, 47 P & CR 402, 10 HLR 82, 127 Sol Jo 596, CA 267
Peabody Housing Association Ltd v Green (1978) 38 P & CR 644, 122 Sol Jo
   862, CA 61, 187
Pearshouse v Birmingham City Council (1998) 31 HLR 756 412
Pembery v Lamdin [1940] 2 All ER 434, CA 352
Phillips v Phillips [1973] 2 All ER 423, [1973] 1 WLR 615, 117 Sol Jo 323,
   CA 239
Pidduck v Molloy [1992] 1 FCR 418, [1992] 2 FLR 202, [1992] Fam Law 529,
   CA 245
Pocklington v Melksham UDC [1964] 2 QB 673, [1964] 2 All ER 862, [1964]
   3 WLR 233, 128 JP 503, 62 LGR 427, 190 Estates Gazette 593, 108 Sol
   Jo 403, CA 374

PAGE

Pollway Nominees Ltd v Croydon London Borough Council [1987] AC 79,
  [1986] 2 All ER 849, [1986] 3 WLR 277, 85 LGR 1, 18 HLR 443,
  [1986] 2 EGLR 27, 280 Estates Gazette 87, [1987] JPL 121, [1986] LS
  Gaz R 2654, [1986] NLJ Rep 703, 130 Sol Jo 574, HL 56, 430
Pollway Nominees Ltd v Havering London Borough Council (1989) 88 LGR
  192, 21 HLR 462 409
Polychronakis v Richards and Jerrom Ltd [1998] JPL B35, [1998] Env LR
  346 411
Porter v Jones [1942] 2 All ER 570, 112 LJKB 173, CA 363
Portman Registrars and Nominees v Mohammed Latif [1987] CLY 2239 270
Preston Borough Council v Fairclough (1982) 8 HLR 70, CA 148
Puives v Midlothian District Council 1986 SCOLAG 144 331

Q

Quick v Taff-Ely Borough Council [1986] QB 809, [1985] 3 All ER 321,
  [1985] 3 WLR 981, 84 LGR 498, 18 HLR 66, [1985] 2 EGLR 50, 276
  Estates Gazette 452, [1985] NLJ Rep 848, 129 Sol Jo 685, CA 353
Quiltotex (or Quillotex) Co Ltd v Minister of Housing and Local Government
  [1966] 1 QB 704, [1965] 2 All ER 913, [1965] 3 WLR 801, 63 LGR 332,
  18 P & CR 50, 109 Sol Jo 393 380

R

R v Ashford Borough Council, ex p Wood (1990) Legal Action (December)
  p 16 322
R v Barking and Dagenham London Borough Council, ex p Okuneye [1995]
  3 FCR 311, 28 HLR 174, 160 LG Rev 381 284
R v Barnet London Borough Council, ex p Grumbridge (1992) 24 HLR 433 ..103
R v Basingstoke and Deane Borough Council, ex p Bassett [1984] FLR 137,
  [1984] Fam Law 90, 10 HLR 125 304
R v Basingstoke and Deane Borough Council, ex p Webb (1989) Legal Action
  (December) p 15 288
R v Bath City Council, ex p Sangermano (1984) 17 HLR 94 297
R v Beverley Borough Council, ex p McPhee [1979] JPL 94, 122 Sol Jo 760,
  DC 332
R v Birmingham City Corpn, ex p Sale (1983) 82 LGR 69, 48 P & CR 270,
  9 HLR 33 .... 376, 384
R v Birmingham City Council, ex p Mohammed [1998] 3 All ER 788, [1999]
  1 WLR 33, 31 HLR 392 397
R v Brent London Borough Council, ex p Awua [1996] AC 55, [1995] 3 WLR
  215, [1995] 3 FCR 278, [1996] Fam Law 20, 93 LGR 581, 27 HLR 453,
  160 LG Rev 21, [1995] 32 LS Gaz R 32, [1995] NLJR 1031, 139 Sol Jo
  LB 189, sub nom Awua v Brent London Borough Council [1995] 3 All
  ER 493, [1995] 2 FLR 819, HL 284, 303, 316, 320
R v Brent London Borough Council, ex p Blatt (1991) 24 HLR 319 .... 162, 217
R v Brent London Borough Council, ex p Macwan [1994] 2 FCR 604, 26 HLR
  528, CA 282, 320
R v Brent London Borough Council, ex p Omar (1991) 23 HLR 446 321
R v Brent London Borough Council, ex p Sawyers (1993) 26 HLR 44 106
R v Bristol City Council, ex p Bradic [1995] 3 FCR 189, 27 HLR 584, 160
  LG Rev 1, [1995] 32 LS Gaz R 32, CA 296

PAGE

R v Bristol City Council, ex p Browne [1979] 3 All ER 344, [1979] 1 WLR
1437, 78 LGR 32, 123 Sol Jo 489, DC 309
R v Bristol City Council, ex p Everett [1998] 3 All ER 603, [1999] 1 WLR
92, 96 LGR 531, 77 P & CR 216, 31 HLR 292, [1998] 3 EGLR 25,
[1998] 42 EG 166, [1998] 23 LS Gaz R 26, [1998] NLJR 836, 142 Sol
Jo LB 173; affd [1999] 2 All ER 193, [1999] 1 WLR 1170, [1999]
NLJR 370, [1999] 13 LS Gaz R 31, 143 Sol Jo LB 104, CA 407
R v Bristol City Council, ex p Johns (1992) 25 HLR 249 107
R v Bristol Corpn, ex p Hendy [1974] 1 All ER 1047, [1974] 1 WLR 498,
72 LGR 405, 27 P & CR 180, 117 Sol Jo 912, CA 420
R v Broxbourne Borough Council, ex p Willmoth (1989) 22 HLR 118, CA ... 284
R v Camden London Borough, ex p Gillan (1988) 21 HLR 114 286
R v Camden London Borough, ex p Pereira (1998) 31 HLR 317, CA 297
R v Camden London Borough Council, ex p Adair (1996) 29 HLR 236 125
R v Camden London Borough Council, ex p Mohammed (1997) 30 HLR 315,
[1997] 35 LS Gaz R 34 329
R v Camden London Borough Council, ex p Wait [1987] 1 FLR 155, [1986]
Fam Law 366, 85 LGR 297, 18 HLR 434 321
R v Canterbury City Council, ex p Gillespie (1986) 19 HLR 7 107
R v Cardiff City Council, ex p Barry (1990) 22 HLR 261, [1990] COD 94,
CA 332
R v Cardiff City Council, ex p Cross (1982) 81 LGR 105, 6 HLR 1, [1982]
RVR 270, [1983] JPL 245, CA 416
R v Chesterfield Justices, ex p Kovacs [1992] 2 All ER 325, 154 JP 1023 459
R v Chief Constable of Merseyside Police, ex p Calveley [1986] QB 424,
[1986] 1 All ER 257, [1986] 2 WLR 144, 130 Sol Jo 53, [1986] LS
Gaz R 124, CA 327
R v Chiltern District Council, ex p Roberts (1990) 23 HLR 387 288
R v Christchurch Borough Council, ex p Conway (1987) 19 HLR 238 304
R v City of Westminster, ex p Khan (1991) 23 HLR 230 302
R v Crown Court at Inner London Sessions, ex p Bentham [1989] 1 WLR 408,
153 JP 262, 21 HLR 171, [1989] Crim LR 450, 133 Sol Jo 785 ... 408, 414
R v Crown Court at Knightsbridge, ex p Hobin Abdillahi (1998) Legal Action
(May) p 24 415
R v Crown Court at Liverpool, ex p Cooke [1996] 4 All ER 589, [1997]
1 WLR 700, 29 HLR 249, [1997] 1 Cr App Rep (S) 7 415
R v Croydon London Borough, ex p Easom (1992) 25 HLR 262 304
R v Croydon London Borough Council, ex p Toth (1987) 20 HLR 576,
CA 305, 307
R v Dacorum Borough Council, ex p Brown (1989) 21 HLR 405 287
R v Dacorum Borough Council, ex p Taverner (1988) 21 HLR 123 288
R v Dacorum Borough Council, ex p Walsh (1991) 24 HLR 401 288
R v Devon County Council, ex p Baker (1992) Times, 20 October; on appeal
[1995] 1 All ER 73, 91 LGR 479, 11 BMLR 141, CA 163
R v Durham County Council, ex p Curtis and Broxson [1995] 1 All ER 73,
91 LGR 479, 11 BMLR 141, CA 163
R v Ealing London Borough, ex p Denny (1995) 27 HLR 424, CA 321
R v Ealing London Borough Council, ex p Fox (1998) Times, 9 March 310
R v Ealing London Borough Council, ex p Lewis (1992) 90 LGR 571, 24 HLR
484, CA 212, 215
R v Ealing London Borough Council, ex p McBain [1986] 1 All ER 13,
[1985] 1 WLR 1351, [1986] 1 FLR 479, [1986] Fam Law 77, 84 LGR
278, 18 HLR 59, 129 Sol Jo 870, [1985] NLJ Rep 120, CA 307, 321

R v Ealing London Borough Council, ex p Sidhu (1982) 3 FLR 438, 80 LGR
   534, 2 HLR 45, 126 Sol Jo 155 .... 263, 286
R v Ealing London Borough Council, ex p Sukhija (1994) 26 HLR 726, CA .. 303
R v East Devon District Council, ex p Robb (1988) Legal Action (June)
   p 15 310
R v East Hertfordshire District Council, ex p Hunt [1986] 1 FLR 431, [1986]
   Fam Law 135, 18 HLR 51 .... 304, 320
R v East Hertfordshire District Council, ex p Smith (1991) 23 HLR 26, CA .. 420
R v East Northamptonshire District Council, ex p Spruce (1988) 20 HLR
   508 300
R v Eastleigh Borough Council, ex p Beattie (No 2) [1984] Fam Law 115, 17
   HLR 168 302
R v Enfield Justices, ex p Whittle (1993) Legal Action (June) p 15 414
R v Enfield London Borough Council, ex p Akbas (1999) Housing Law
   Monitor (March) p 9 320
R v Epping (Waltham Abbey) Justices, ex p Burlinson [1948] 1 KB 79,
   [1947] 2 All ER 537, 112 JP 3, 46 LGR 6, [1948] LJR 298, 92 Sol Jo 27,
   63 TLR 628 412
R v Epsom and Ewell Corpn, ex p R B Property Investments (Eastern) Ltd
   [1964] 2 All ER 832, [1964] 1 WLR 1060, 128 JP 478, 62 LGR 498,
   108 Sol Jo 521, DC 374
R v Exeter City Council, ex p Gliddon [1985] 1 All ER 493, 14 HLR 103 304
R v Fenny Stratford Justices, ex p Watney Mann (Midlands) Ltd [1976] 2 All
   ER 888, [1976] 1 WLR 1101, 140 JP 474, 75 LGR 72, 238 Estates
   Gazette 417, 120 Sol Jo 201, DC 409
R v Forest Heath District Council, ex p West and Lucas (1991) 24 HLR 85,
   [1991] RVR 216, CA 107
R v Forest of Dean District Council, ex p Trigg (1989) 22 HLR 167, [1990] 2
   EGLR 29, [1990] 30 EG 95 369
R v Gateshead Metropolitan Borough Council, ex p Lauder (1996) 29 HLR
   360 125
R v Gloucester City Council, ex p Miles (1985) 83 LGR 607, 17 HLR 292,
   [1985] LS Gaz R 1415, sub nom Gloucester City Council v Miles [1985]
   FLR 1043, [1985] Fam Law 259, CA 286
R v Gravesham Borough Council, ex p Winchester (1986) 18 HLR 207 305
R v Greater London Council, ex p Royal Borough of Kensington and Chelsea
   (1982) Times, 7 April 215
R v Hackney London Borough Council, ex p Asilkender (1990) Legal Action
   (December) p 15 286
R v Hackney London Borough Council, ex p Evenbray Ltd (1987) 86 LGR
   210, 19 HLR 557 430
R v Hackney London Borough Council, ex p K (1997) 30 HLR 760, CA 292
R v Hackney London Borough Council, ex p Thrasyvoulou (1986) 84 LGR
   823, sub nom Thrasyvoulou v Hackney London Borough 18 HLR 370,
   CA 430, 432
R v Hammersmith and Fulham London Borough Council, ex p Beddowes
   [1987] QB 1050, [1987] 1 All ER 369, [1987] 2 WLR 263, 85 LGR 270,
   18 HLR 458, [1987] RVR 189, 130 Sol Jo 696, [1986] LS Gaz R 3001,
   CA 90, 163
R v Hammersmith and Fulham London Borough Council, ex p Fleck (1997)
   30 HLR 679 329
R v Hammersmith and Fulham London Borough Council, ex p Lusi and Lusi
   (1991) 23 HLR 260 303

PAGE

R v Hammersmith and Fulham London Borough Council, ex p M (1997) 30
HLR 10, [1997] 1 CCL Rep 85, CA 293
R v Hammersmith and Fulham London Borough Council, ex p O'Brian (1985)
84 LGR 202, 17 HLR 471 321
R v Hammersmith and Fulham London Borough Council, ex p O'Sullivan
[1991] EGCS 110 305
R v Hammersmith and Fulham London Borough Council, ex p Quigley (1999)
Housing Law Monitor (May) p 8 .... 148, 258
R v Haringey London Borough Council, ex p Erdogan (1998) Legal Action
(August) p 23 330
R v Haringey London Borough Council, ex p Garner (1991) Legal Action
(September) p 16 266
R v Harrow London Borough Council, ex p Carter (1992) 91 LGR 46, 26
HLR 32, [1992] 43 LS Gaz R 30 311
R v Harrow London Borough Council, ex p Fahia [1998] 4 All ER 137,
[1998] 1 WLR 1396, [1998] 3 FCR 363, 30 HLR 1124, [1998] NLJR
1354, 142 Sol Jo LB 226, HL 303, 307
R v Harrow London Borough Council, ex p Hobbs (1992) Times, 13 October: 287
R v Harrow London Borough Council, ex p Holland (1982) 4 HLR 108 287
R v Hertsmere Borough Council, ex p Woolgar [1996] 2 FCR 69, 27 HLR 703,
160 LG Rev 261 322
R v Highbury Corner Magistrates' Court, ex p Edwards (1994) 26 HLR 682,
[1995] Crim LR 65, DC 406, 412
R v Hillingdon Homeless Families Panel, ex p Islam (1981) Times, 10 February;
affd sub nom Re Islam [1983] 1 AC 688, sub nom R v Hillingdon London
Borough Council, ex p Islam [1981] 2 All ER 1089, [1981] 3 WLR 109,
79 LGR 534, 125 Sol Jo 443, CA; revsd sub nom Re Islam [1983] 1 AC
688, [1981] 3 WLR 942, 1 HLR 107, sub nom Islam v Hillingdon
London Borough Council [1981] 3 All ER 901, 80 LGR 141, 125 Sol Jo
809, HL 287, 305
R v Hillingdon London Borough, ex p Thomas (1987) 19 HLR 196 288
R v Hillingdon London Borough Council, ex p H (1988) 20 HLR 554 307
R v Hillingdon London Borough Council, ex p Islam. See R v Hillingdon
Homeless Families Panel, ex p Islam
R v Hillingdon London Borough Council, ex p Slough Borough Council (1980)
130 NLJ 881; affd [1981] QB 801, [1981] 1 All ER 601, [1981] 2 WLR
399, 79 LGR 335, 11 Fam Law 87, 125 Sol Jo 98, CA 310
R v Hounslow London Borough Council, ex p R (1997) 29 HLR 939 302
R v Ilkeston County Court, ex p Kruza (1985) 17 HLR 539 148
R v Islington London Borough, ex p Aldabbagh (1994) 27 HLR 271 107
R v Islington London Borough Council, ex p Adigun (1986) 20 HLR 600 309
R v Islington London Borough Council, ex p B (1997) 30 HLR 706 289
R v Islington London Borough Council, ex p Byfield (1991) Legal Action
(March) p 14 322
R v Islington London Borough Council, ex p Hinds (1995) 28 HLR 302, CA . 323
R v Islington London Borough Council, ex p Rahman and Cox (1989) Legal
Action (December) p 15 285
R v Islington London Borough Council, ex p Trail [1994] 2 FCR 1261 323
R v Kensington and Chelsea Royal Borough, ex p Ben-El-Mabrouk [1995]
3 FCR 812, 27 HLR 564, CA 283
R v Kensington and Chelsea Royal Borough, ex p Kassam (1993) 26 HLR 455,
CA 307
R v Kensington and Chelsea Royal Borough Council, ex p Byfield (1998)
Legal Action (March) p 16 330

PAGE
R v Kensington and Chelsea Royal Borough Council, ex p Ghebregiogis (1994)
27 HLR 602, [1994] COD 502 332
R v Kensington and Chelsea Royal Borough Council, ex p Halonen (1995)
Legal Action (December) p 20 332
R v Kensington and Chelsea Royal Borough Council, ex p Westwoods Ltd
(1995) 28 HLR 291 432
R v Kensington and Chelsea Royal London Borough, ex p Amarfio [1995]
2 FCR 787, 27 HLR 543, CA 296
R v Kensington and Chelsea Royal London Borough, ex p Minton (1988) 20
HLR 648 285
R v Kensington and Chelsea Royal London Borough Council, ex p Hammell
[1989] QB 518, [1989] 1 All ER 1202, [1989] 2 WLR 90, [1989] FCR
323, [1989] 2 FLR 223, [1989] Fam Law 430, 87 LGR 145, 20 HLR
666, 133 Sol Jo 45, [1989] 3 LS Gaz R 43, CA 306, 332
R v Kerrier District Council, ex p Guppy's (Bridport) Ltd (1975) 74 LGR 55,
30 P & CR 194, 119 Sol Jo 577; on appeal (1976) 75 LGR 129, 32 P &
CR 411, [1976] JPL 695, 120 Sol Jo 646, CA 415
R v Kerrier District Council, ex p Guppys (Bridport) Ltd (1985) 17 HLR 426,
274 Estates Gazette 924, CA 56, 430
R v Kingswood Borough Council, ex p Smith-Morse [1995] 3 FCR 655, [1995]
2 FLR 137, [1995] Fam Law 549, 159 LG Rev 469 298
R v Knowsley Metropolitan Borough Council, ex p O'Toole [1999] 22 LS
Gaz R 36 409
R v Lambeth London Borough, ex p Campbell (1994) 26 HLR 618 321
R v Lambeth London Borough, ex p Sarbrook (1994) 27 HLR 380, 159 LG
Rev 569 375
R v Lambeth London Borough Council, ex p Ashley (1996) 29 HLR 385 125
R v Lambeth London Borough Council, ex p Barnes (1992) 25 HLR 140,
[1993] COD 50 331
R v Lambeth London Borough Council, ex p Carroll (1987) 20 HLR 142 297
R v Lambeth London Borough Council, ex p Pattinson [1995] 3 FCR 692,
28 HLR 214 289
R v Lambeth London Borough Council, ex p Vagliviello [1991] Fam Law 142,
22 HLR 392, CA 297
R v Leeds City Council, ex p Adamiec [1992] 1 FCR 401, 24 HLR 138 302
R v Lewisham London Borough Council, ex p D [1993] 2 FCR 772, [1993]
Fam Law 277, 91 LGR 224, 25 HLR 68, [1992] 39 LS Gaz R 34, 136 Sol
Jo LB 274 321
R v Local Comr for Administration for the North and East Area of England,
ex p Bradford Metropolitan City Council [1979] QB 287, [1979] 2 All
ER 881, [1979] 2 WLR 1, 77 LGR 305, [1978] JPL 767, 122 Sol Jo 573,
CA 192
R v London Borough of Barnet, ex p O'Connor (1990) 22 HLR 486 300
R v London Borough of Merton, ex p Ruffle (1988) 21 HLR 361 ...... 285, 304
R v London Borough of Wandsworth, ex p Lindsay (1986) 18 HLR 502: 313, 320
R v London Borough of Wandsworth, ex p Nimako-Boateng [1984] FLR 192,
[1984] Fam Law 117, 11 HLR 95 306
R v London Rent Assessment Committee, ex p Hanson [1978] QB 823,
[1977] 3 All ER 404, [1977] 2 WLR 848, 34 P & CR 158, 120 Sol Jo
837, CA 227
R v Mabbott [1988] RVR 131, CA 430
R v Manchester City Council, ex p Harcup (1993) 26 HLR 402 316
R v Medina Borough Council, ex p Dee [1992] 2 FCR 691, 24 HLR 562 284
R v Merton London Borough Council, ex p Sembi (1999) Times, 9 June: 320, 329

PAGE

R v Mr Referee McCall (1981) 8 HLR 48 311
R v Mole Valley District Council, ex p Burton [1989] Fam Law 64, 20 HLR
    479 302
R v Mole Valley District Council, ex p Minnett (1983) 12 HLR 49 305
R v Newham Borough Council, ex p Bones (1992) 25 HLR 357 282
R v Newham Justices, ex p Hunt [1976] 1 All ER 839, [1976] 1 WLR 420, 74
    LGR 305, 120 Sol Jo 131, DC 408
R v Newham London Borough, ex p Laronde (1994) 27 HLR 215 314
R v Newham London Borough, ex p Watkins (1993) 26 HLR 434 106
R v Newham London Borough Council, ex p Campbell [1994] Fam Law 319,
    26 HLR 183, [1993] NLJR 1295 .... 148, 299
R v Newham London Borough Council, ex p Dada [1996] QB 507, [1995]
    2 All ER 522, [1995] 3 WLR 540, [1995] 2 FCR 441, [1995] 1 FLR 842,
    [1995] Fam Law 410, 27 HLR 502, 160 LG Rev 341, CA 319
R v Newham London Borough Council, ex p Gorenkin (1997) 30 HLR 278,
    [1997] 23 LS Gaz R 27, 141 Sol Jo LB 138 293
R v Newham London Borough Council, ex p Idowu (1998) Legal Action
    (August) p 22 329
R v Newham London Borough Council, ex p McIlroy and McIlroy (1991)
    23 HLR 570 302
R v Newham London Borough Council, ex p Miah (1995) 28 HLR 279 313
R v Newham London Borough Council, ex p Ojuri (No 3) (1998) 31 HLR
    452 .... 282, 295
R v Newham London Borough Council, ex p Tower Hamlets London
    Borough Council [1992] 2 All ER 767, [1991] 1 WLR 1032, 23 HLR 62,
    CA 308, 309
R v North Devon District Council, ex p Lewis. See Lewis v North Devon
    District Council
R v Northampton Borough Council, ex p Carpenter (1992) 25 HLR 349,
    [1993] COD 133 323
R v Northampton Borough Council, ex p Clarkson (1992) 24 HLR 529 307
R v Northavon District Council, ex p Palmer [1996] 2 FCR 389, [1996]
    1 FLR 142, [1996] Fam Law 21, 27 HLR 576, CA 331
R v Northavon District Council, ex p Smith [1994] 2 AC 402, [1994] 3 All
    ER 313, [1994] 3 WLR 403, [1994] 2 FCR 859, [1994] 2 FLR 671,
    [1995] Fam Law 16, 92 LGR 643, 26 HLR 659, [1994] 38 LS Gaz R
    42, [1994] NLJR 1010, 138 Sol Jo LB 178, HL 333
R v Oldham Metropolitan Borough Council, ex p Garlick [1993] AC 509,
    [1993] 2 WLR 609, [1993] 2 FCR 133, [1993] 2 FLR 194, 91 LGR 287,
    25 HLR 319, [1993] 26 LS Gaz R 38, [1993] NLJR 437, sub nom Garlick
    v Oldham Metropolitan Borough Council [1993] 2 All ER 65, HL 289
R v Oxted Justices, ex p Franklin [1976] 1 All ER 839, [1976] 1 WLR 420,
    74 LGR 305, 120 Sol Jo 131, DC 408
R v Paddington and St Marylebone Rent Tribunal, ex p Bell London and
    Provincial Properties Ltd [1949] 1 KB 666, [1949] 1 All ER 720, 113
    JP 209, 47 LGR 306, 93 Sol Jo 219, 65 TLR 200 227
R v Parker (1994) 26 HLR 508, CA 401
R v Peterborough City Council, ex p Carr (1990) 22 HLR 206 305
R v Poole Borough Council, ex p Cooper (1994) 27 HLR 605 288
R v Port Talbot Borough Council, ex p Jones [1988] 2 All ER 207, 20 HLR
    265 .... 107, 114
R v Port Talbot Borough Council, ex p McCarthy (1990) 23 HLR 207,
    CA 297

PAGE

R v Preseli District Council, ex p Fisher (1984) 17 HLR 147 299
R v Reigate and Banstead Borough Council, ex p Di Domenico [1989] Fam Law
    69, 20 HLR 153 297
R v Reigate and Banstead Borough Council, ex p Paris [1985] FLR 123, [1985]
    Fam Law 28, 17 HLR 103 304
R v Rent Officer for the London Borough of Camden, ex p Felix (1988) 21
    HLR 34, [1988] 2 EGLR 132, [1988] 45 EG 110 231
R v Rochester-upon-Medway City Council, ex p Williams (1994) 26 HLR 588,
    [1994] NPC 25, [1994] EGCS 35 . . . . 302, 304
R v Royal Borough of Kensington and Chelsea, ex p Bayani (1990) 22 HLR
    406, CA 288
R v Royal Borough of Kensington and Chelsea, ex p Cunha (1988) 21 HLR 16,
    [1989] COD 197 307
R v Royal Borough of Kensington and Chelsea, ex p Kujtim [1999] 4 All ER
    161, [1999] 31 LS Gaz R 41, 143 Sol Jo LB 157; affd (1999) Times, 5
    August, CA 293
R v Ryedale District Council, ex p Smith (1983) 16 HLR 66 320
R v Salford City Council, ex p Devenport (1983) 82 LGR 89, 127 Sol Jo 306,
    sub nom Devenport v Salford City Council 8 HLR 54, CA 300, 301
R v Secretary of State for Health and Social Security, ex p City of Sheffield
    (1985) 18 HLR 6 215
R v Secretary of State for the Environment, ex p Camden London Borough
    Council (1995) 28 HLR 321 214
R v Secretary of State for the Environment, ex p Harrow London Borough
    Council (1996) 29 HLR 1 167
R v Secretary of State for the Environment, ex p London Borough of
    Greenwich (1990) 22 HLR 543 213
R v Secretary of State for the Environment, ex p Norwich City Council [1982]
    QB 808, [1982] 2 WLR 580, 80 LGR 498, 126 Sol Jo 119, sub nom
    Norwich City Council v Secretary of State for the Environment [1982]
    1 All ER 737, CA 89
R v Secretary of State for the Environment, ex p Walters (1997) 30 HLR 328,
    CA 92
R v Secretary of State for Wales, ex p Rozhon (1993) 91 LGR 667, CA 332
R v Sefton Metropolitan Borough, ex p Healiss [1994] 2 FCR 659, 27 HLR
    34 288
R v Sefton Metropolitan Borough Council, ex p Cunningham (1991) 23 HLR
    534 316
R v Singh (Gurphal) [1999] Crim LR 582, CA 459
R v Slough Borough Council, ex p Ealing London Borough Council [1981]
    QB 801, [1981] 1 All ER 601, [1981] 2 WLR 399, 11 Fam Law 87,
    79 LGR 335, 125 Sol Jo 98, CA 308
R v Slough Borough Council, ex p Khan [1996] 1 FCR 774, 27 HLR 492,
    160 LG Rev 306 310
R v South Herefordshire Borough Council, ex p Miles (1983) 17 HLR
    82 . . . . 286, 288
R v Southampton City Council, ex p Ward [1984] FLR 608, 14 HLR 114 287
R v Southend Stipendiary Magistrate, ex p Rochford District Council [1994]
    Env LR D15, (1994) Times, 10 May 414
R v Southwark London Borough, ex p Anderson (1999) Housing Law Monitor
    (March) p 9 320
R v Southwark London Borough, ex p Cordwell (1994) 27 HLR 594, CA 367
R v Southwark London Borough, ex p Davies (1993) 26 HLR 677 301

PAGE

R v Southwark London Borough, ex p Lewis Levy Ltd (1983) 8 HLR 1, 267
     Estates Gazette 1041, [1984] JPL 105 .... 372, 430, 452
R v Southwark London Borough Council, ex p Melak (1996) 29 HLR 223 ... 125
R v Sutton London Borough Council, ex p Alger (1992) Legal Action (June)
     p 13 107
R v Swansea City Council, ex p John (1982) 9 HLR 56 300
R v Swansea City Council, ex p Thomas (1983) 9 HLR 64 300
R v Swansea District Council, ex p Evans (1990) 22 HLR 467 304
R v Tower Hamlets London Borough, ex p Ali (1992) 25 HLR 158, CA 311
R v Tower Hamlets London Borough, ex p Khalique [1994] 2 FCR 1074, 26
     HLR 517, 159 LG Rev 141 .... 313, 321, 331
R v Tower Hamlets London Borough, ex p Spencer (1995) 29 HLR 64 125
R v Tower Hamlets London Borough, ex p Uddin (1999) Housing Law
     Monitor (June) p 9 107
R v Tower Hamlets London Borough Council, ex p Ali (1993) 25 HLR
     218 .... 112, 322
R v Tower Hamlets London Borough Council, ex p Byas [1993] 2 FLR 605,
     [1993] Fam Law 624, 25 HLR 105, CA 333
R v Tower Hamlets London Borough Council, ex p Camden London Borough
     Council (1988) 87 LGR 321, 21 HLR 197 308
R v Tower Hamlets London Borough Council, ex p Commission for Racial
     Equality (1991) Legal Action (June) p 16 .... 266, 322
R v Tower Hamlets London Borough Council, ex p Ferdous Begum [1993] AC
     509, [1993] 2 WLR 609, [1993] 2 FCR 133, 91 LGR 287, 25 HLR 319,
     [1993] 26 LS Gaz R 38, [1993] NLJR 437, sub nom Garlick v Oldham
     Metropolitan Borough Council [1993] 2 All ER 65, HL 289
R v Tower Hamlets London Borough Council, ex p Hoque (1993) Times,
     20 July 282
R v Tower Hamlets London Borough Council, ex p Mahmood (1993) Legal
     Action (March) p 12 282
R v Tower Hamlets London Borough Council, ex p Monaf (1988) 86 LGR 709,
     20 HLR 520, CA 307
R v Tower Hamlets London Borough Council, ex p Rouf (1989) 21 HLR 294;
     affd (1991) 23 HLR 460, CA 288, 303
R v Tower Hamlets London Borough Council, ex p Saber (1992) 24 HLR
     611 288
R v Tower Hamlets London Borough Council, ex p Subhan (1992) 24 HLR
     541 321
R v Tunbridge Wells Justices, ex p Tunbridge Wells Borough Council (1995)
     160 JP 574, [1996] Env LR 880 411
R v Tynedale District Council, ex p McCabe (1991) 24 HLR 384 306
R v Tynedale District Council, ex p Shield (1987) 22 HLR 144 288
R v Wandsworth Borough Council, ex p Banbury (1986) 19 HLR 76 297
R v Wandsworth County Court, ex p Munn (1994) 26 HLR 697, [1994] COD
     282 355
R v Wandsworth London Borough, ex p Onwudiwe (1993) 26 HLR 302,
     CA 301
R v Wandsworth London Borough Council, ex p Crooks (1995) 27 HLR 660: 304
R v Wandsworth London Borough Council, ex p Hawthorne [1995] 2 All ER
     331, [1994] 1 WLR 1442, [1995] 1 FCR 539, [1995] 2 FLR 238, [1995]
     Fam Law 608, 93 LGR 20, 27 HLR 59, [1994] 37 LS Gaz R 50, 138 Sol
     Jo LB 178, CA 301
R v Wandsworth London Borough Council, ex p Henderson and Hayes (1986)
     18 HLR 522 287

PAGE

R v Wandsworth London Borough Council, ex p Lawrie (1997) 30 HLR
153 125
R v Wandsworth London Borough Council, ex p Wingrove [1997] QB 953,
[1996] 3 All ER 913, [1996] 3 WLR 282, [1996] 3 FCR 289, 29 HLR
801, 140 Sol Jo LB 158, CA 284, 304
R v Waveney District Council, ex p Bowers [1983] QB 238, [1982] 3 All ER
727, [1982] 3 WLR 661, 80 LGR 721, 4 HLR 118, 126 Sol Jo 657,
[1982] LS Gaz R 1413, CA 286, 297
R v West Dorset District Council, ex p Phillips (1984) 17 HLR 336 299
R v West Kent Housing Association, ex p Sevenoaks District Council (1994)
Inside Housing, 28 October, p 3 ....61, 187
R v Westminster City Council, ex p Ali (1983) 11 HLR 83 305
R v Westminster City Council, ex p Augustin [1993] 1 WLR 730, 91 LGR 89,
CA 332
R v Westminster City Council, ex p Bishop [1994] 1 FCR 720, [1993] 2 FLR
780, [1993] Fam Law 626, 91 LGR 674, 25 HLR 459, [1993] 27 LS
Gaz R 34, CA 307
R v Westminster City Council, ex p Iqbal (1990) 22 HLR 215 287
R v Westminster City Council, ex p N'Dormadingar (1997) Times,
20 November 299
R v Wheatley, ex p Cowburn (1885) 16 QBD 34, 55 LJMC 11, 50 JP 424,
34 WR 257, 54 LT 680, 2 TLR 137, DC 409
R v Wimborne District Council, ex p Curtis [1986] 1 FLR 486, [1986] Fam
Law 137, 18 HLR 79 305
R v Wirral Metropolitan Borough Council, ex p B [1994] 2 FCR 1113, 27
HLR 234 322
R v Woking Borough Council, ex p Adam (1995) 28 HLR 513, CA 374
R v Wolverhampton Metropolitan Borough Council, ex p Watters [1997]
3 FCR 747, 29 HLR 931, CA 122
R v Woodspring District Council, ex p Walters (1984) 16 HLR 73 287
R v Wycombe District Council, ex p Hazeltine [1994] 1 FCR 115, [1993]
2 FLR 417, [1993] Fam Law 523, 25 HLR 313, CA 314
R v Wycombe District Council, ex p Homes (1988) 22 HLR 150 284
R v Wyre Borough Council, ex p Joyce (1983) 11 HLR 73, DC 287
Rainbow Estates Ltd v Tokenhold Ltd [1999] Ch 64, [1998] 2 All ER 860,
[1998] 3 WLR 980, [1998] 2 EGLR 34, [1998] 24 EG 123, [1998] 15
LS Gaz R 30, 142 Sol Jo LB 117 355
Ravenseft Properties Ltd v Davstone (Holdings) Ltd [1980] QB 12, [1979]
1 All ER 929, [1979] 2 WLR 898, 37 P & CR 502, 123 Sol Jo 320, 249
Estates Gazette 51 352
Reading Borough Council v Ilsley [1981] CLY 1323 ....269, 270
Reed v Hastings Corpn (1964) 62 LGR 588, 190 Estates Gazette 961, 108 Sol
Jo 480, CA 56, 430
Reston Ltd v Hudson [1990] 2 EGLR 51, [1990] 37 EG 86 353
Reynolds v Sevenoaks District Council (1990) 22 HLR 250, CA 287
Richards v Richards [1984] AC 174, [1983] 2 All ER 807, [1983] 3 WLR 173,
147 JP 481, [1984] FLR 11, 13 Fam Law 256, 12 HLR 73, 127 Sol Jo
476, [1983] LS Gaz R 2134, 133 NLJ 725, HL 239, 245
Riddle v Secretary of State for the Environment [1988] 2 EGLR 17, [1988]
42 EG 120, CA 454
Rimmer v Liverpool City Council [1985] QB 1, [1984] 1 All ER 930, [1984]
2 WLR 426, 82 LGR 424, 47 P & CR 516, 12 HLR 23, 269 Estates
Gazette 319, 128 Sol Jo 225, [1984] LS Gaz R 664, CA 341
Robb v Dundee City Council [1999] 11 ELM 24 407

PAGE

Robbins v Jones (1863) 15 CBNS 221, [1861-73] All ER Rep 544, 33 LJCP 1,
10 Jur NS 239, 3 New Rep 85, 12 WR 248, 9 LT 523 340
Rogers v Islington London Borough Council [1999] 37 EG 178, [1999] 34
LS Gaz R 33, CA 434
Rogers v Lambeth London Borough Council [1999] 45 LS Gaz R 33, [1999]
EGCS 128, CA 148
Rowntree (Joseph) Memorial Trust Housing Association Ltd v A-G [1983]
Ch 159, [1983] 1 All ER 288, [1983] 2 WLR 284, 127 Sol Jo 137 62
Royal British Legion Housing Association Ltd v East Midlands Rent Assessment
Panel (1989) 21 HLR 482, [1989] 1 EGLR 131, [1989] 23 EG 84 227
Rushcliffe Borough Council v Watson (1991) 24 HLR 124, CA 148
Ryall v Kidwell & Son [1914] 3 KB 135, 83 LJKB 1140, 78 JP 377, 12 LGR
997, 111 LT 240, 30 TLR 503, CA 349
Rye (Dennis) Pension Fund Trustees v Sheffield City Council [1997] 4 All
ER 747, [1998] 1 WLR 840, 30 HLR 645, CA 400

S

Saddleworth UDC v Aggregate and Sand Ltd (1970) 69 LGR 103, 114 Sol Jo
931, DC 417
Salford City Council v McNally [1976] AC 379, [1975] 2 All ER 860, [1975]
3 WLR 87, 139 JP 694, 73 LGR 408, 236 Estates Gazette 555, 119 Sol
Jo 475, HL 384, 406, 412
Sanctuary Housing Association v Campbell [1999] 3 All ER 460, [1999]
1 WLR 1279, [1999] 2 FCR 657, [1999] 2 FLR 383, [1999] Fam Law
449, [1999] 2 EGLR 20, [1999] 18 EG 162, 78 P & CR D15,
CA 132, 236, 249, 258
Sarson v Roberts [1895] 2 QB 395, 65 LJQB 37, 59 JP 643, 14 R 616, 43 WR
690, 73 LT 174, 11 TLR 515, CA 347
Second WRVS Housing Society Ltd v Blair (1986) 19 HLR 104, CA 183
Selwyn v Hamill [1948] 1 All ER 70, 92 Sol Jo 71, CA 181
Sevenoaks District Council v Emmott (1979) 78 LGR 346, 39 P & CR 404,
CA 135
Sharpe v Manchester Metropolitan District Council (1977) 5 HLR 71 341
Sheffield City Council v Green [1993] EGCS 185, (1993) Times, 25 November,
CA 138
Sheffield City Council v Jepson (1993) 25 HLR 299, CA 138
Sheldon v West Bromwich Corpn (1973) 25 P & CR 360, 13 HLR 23, 117
Sol Jo 486, CA 349
Shelley v LCC [1949] AC 56, [1948] 2 All ER 898, 47 LGR 93, 113 JP 1,
[1949] LJR 57, 93 Sol Jo 101, 64 TLR 600, HL 106
Shepherds Bush Housing Association Ltd v HATS Co-operative (1991) 24 HLR
176, CA 102
Short v Tower Hamlets London Borough Council (1985) 18 HLR 171, CA . . . 163
Shrewsbury and Atcham Borough Council v Evans (1997) 30 HLR 123, CA . 143,
144
Siddiqui v Rashid [1980] 3 All ER 184, [1980] 1 WLR 1018, 40 P & CR 504,
256 Estates Gazette 169, 124 Sol Jo 464, CA 181
Silbers v Southwark London Borough Council (1977) 76 LGR 421, 122 Sol Jo
128, CA 431
Simmons v Pizzey [1979] AC 37, [1977] 2 All ER 432, [1977] 3 WLR 1,
141 JP 414, 75 LGR 583, 36 P & CR 36, 121 Sol Jo 424, HL 431, 446
Sleafer v Lambeth Borough Council [1960] 1 QB 43, [1959] 3 All ER 378,
[1959] 3 WLR 485, 57 LGR 212, 103 Sol Jo 599, CA 347

PAGE

Smedley v Chumley & Hawkes Ltd (1981) 44 P & CR 50, [1982] 1 EGLR 47,
261 Estates Gazette 775, 126 Sol Jo 33, CA 347
Smith v Bradford Metropolitan Council (1982) 80 LGR 713, 44 P & CR 171,
4 HLR 86, 126 Sol Jo 624, [1982] LS Gaz R 1176, CA 344
Smith v Cardiff Corpn (No 2) [1955] Ch 159, [1955] 1 All ER 113, [1955] 2
WLR 126, 119 JP 128, 53 LGR 176, 99 Sol Jo 76 215
Smith v Marrable (1843) Car & M 479, 12 LJ Ex 223, 7 Jur 70, 11 M & W
5 347
Smith v Scott [1973] Ch 314, [1972] 3 All ER 645, [1972] 3 WLR 783, 116
Sol Jo 785 143
South Glamorgan County Council v Griffiths (1992) 24 HLR 334, [1992] 2
EGLR 232, [1992] NPC 13, CA 133
South Holland District Council v Keyte (1985) 84 LGR 347, 19 HLR 97,
CA 331
South Shields (D'Arcy Street) Compulsory Purchase Order 1937, Re,
Bainbridge's Application. See Bainbridge, Re, South Shields (D'Arcy
Street) Compulsory Purchase Order 1937
Southwark London Borough Council v Ince and Williams (1989) 153 JP 597,
21 HLR 504 407
Southwark London Borough Council v Logan (1995) 29 HLR 40, CA 127
Southwark London Borough Council v Mills [1999] 4 All ER 449, [1999] 45
EG 179, [1999] 42 LS Gaz R 41, [1999] NLJR 1618, 143 Sol Jo LB 249,
sub nom Southwark London Borough Council v Tanner [1999] 3 WLR
939, HL 340, 407
Southwark London Borough Council v Williams [1971] Ch 734, [1971] 2 All
ER 175, [1971] 2 WLR 467, 69 LGR 145, CA 277
Spath Holme Ltd v Greater Manchester and Lancashire Rent Assessment
Committee (Chairman) (1995) 28 HLR 107, [1995] 2 EGLR 80, [1995]
49 EG 128, CA 227
Springett v Harold [1954] 1 All ER 568, [1954] 1 WLR 521, 118 JP 211,
52 LGR 181, 98 Sol Jo 197 406
Stalybridge (Castle Hall No 7) and (Acres Lane and Lawton Street) Compulsory
Purchase Order 1963, Re, Ashbridge Investments Ltd v Minister of
Housing and Local Government. See Ashbridge Investments Ltd v
Minister of Housing and Local Government
Steele v Minister of Housing and Local Government and West Ham County
Borough Council (1956) 6 P & CR 386, 168 Estates Gazette 37, CA 365
Stent v Monmouth District Council (1987) 54 P & CR 193, 19 HLR 269,
[1987] 1 EGLR 59, 282 Estates Gazette 705, CA 353
Stockdale v Haringey London Borough Council (1989) 88 LGR 7, [1989] RVR
107, CA 208
Stockley v Knowsley Metropolitan Borough Council [1986] 2 EGLR 141, 279
Estates Gazette 677, CA 351
Street v Mountford [1985] AC 809, [1985] 2 All ER 289, [1985] 2 WLR
877, 50 P & CR 258, 17 HLR 402, [1985] 1 EGLR 128, 274 Estates
Gazette 821, 129 Sol Jo 348, [1985] LS Gaz R 2087, [1985] NLJ Rep
460, HL 101
Sturolson & Co v Mauroux (1988) 20 HLR 332, [1988] 1 EGLR 66, [1988]
24 EG 102, CA 354
Summerfield v Hampstead Borough Council [1957] 1 All ER 221, [1957] 1
WLR 167, 121 JP 72, 55 LGR 67, 168 Estates Gazette 698, 101 Sol Jo
111 215
Summers v Salford Corpn [1943] AC 283, [1943] 1 All ER 68, 112 LJKB 65,
107 JP 35, 41 LGR 1, 86 Sol Jo 391, 168 LT 97, 59 TLR 78, HL 365

PAGE

Summers v Summers [1986] 1 FLR 343, [1986] Fam Law 56, CA 239
Surrey County Council v Lamond [1999] 1 EGLR 32, [1999] 12 EG 170, 78
  P & CR D3, CA 132
Surrey Free Inns plc v Gosport Borough Council (1998) 96 LGR 369, [1999]
  Env LR 1, [1998] Crim LR 578, [1998] JPL B86, [1998] 06 LS Gaz R 25,
  142 Sol Jo LB 84 410
Sutton Housing Trust v Lawrence (1987) 55 P & CR 320, 19 HLR 520, CA .. 138
Sutton London Borough Council v Swann (1985) 18 HLR 140, CA 74, 148
Swansea City Council v Hearn (1990) 23 HLR 284, CA 136

T

Taggart v Leeds City Council (1998) 31 HLR 693 368
Targett v Torfaen Borough Council [1992] 3 All ER 27, 24 HLR 164, [1992]
  1 EGLR 275, [1991] NLJR 1698, CA 341
Taylor v Liverpool Corpn [1939] 3 All ER 329 340
Taylor v Newham London Borough Council [1993] 2 All ER 649, [1993]
  1 WLR 444, 25 HLR 290, [1993] 1 EGLR 54, [1993] 23 EG 126, CA ... 81
Taylor v Walsall and District Property and Investment Co Ltd (1998) 30
  HLR 1062, [1998] 06 LS Gaz R 24, 142 Sol Jo LB 75 414
Thai Trading Co (a firm) v Taylor [1998] QB 781, [1998] 3 All ER 65,
  [1998] 2 WLR 893, [1998] 2 FLR 430, [1998] Fam Law 586, [1998]
  15 LS Gaz R 30, 142 Sol Jo LB 125, CA 419
Thompson v Arkell (1949) 99 LJ 597, Cty Ct 365
Thompson v City of Glasgow District Council 1986 SLT (Lands Tr) 6 131
Thompson v Elmbridge Borough Council [1987] 1 WLR 1425, 86 LGR 245,
  19 HLR 526, 131 Sol Jo 1285, [1987] LS Gaz R 2456, CA 148
Thornton v Kirklees Metropolitan Borough Council [1979] QB 626, [1979]
  2 All ER 349, [1979] 3 WLR 1, 144 JP 15, 77 LGR 417, 123 Sol Jo 285,
  CA 331
Thrasyvoulou v Hackney London Borough. See R v Hackney London Borough
  Council, ex p Thrasyvoulou
Thurley v Smith [1984] FLR 875, [1985] Fam Law 31, CA 239
Tickner v Clifton [1929] 1 KB 207, 98 LJKB 69, 93 JP 57, 72 Sol Jo 762,
  140 LT 136, 45 TLR 35, DC 150
Topping v Hughes [1925] NI 90, 58 ILT 156 181
Torridge District Council v Jones (1985) 18 HLR 107, [1985] 2 EGLR 54,
  276 Estates Gazette 1253, CA 136
Tower Hamlets London Borough v Ayinde (1994) 26 HLR 631,
  CA 103, 243
Tower Hamlets London Borough Council v Abadie 22 HLR 264 .... 145, 149
Tower Hamlets London Borough Council v Abdi (1992) 91 LGR 300, 25 HLR
  80, [1993] 1 EGLR 68, [1993] 06 EG 102, CA 331
Tower Hamlets London Borough Council v Miah [1992] QB 622, [1992]
  2 All ER 667, [1992] 2 WLR 761, 90 LGR 151, 24 HLR 199, [1992] 1
  EGLR 39, [1992] 18 EG 147, 136 Sol Jo LB 11, [1992] 4 LS Gaz R 33,
  CA 102, 134
Travers v Gloucester Corpn [1947] KB 71, [1946] 2 All ER 506, 115 LJKB
  517, 110 JP 364, 44 LGR 333, 90 Sol Jo 556, 175 LT 360, 62 TLR
  723 340
Truman Hanbury Buxton & Co v Kerslake [1894] 2 QB 774, 63 LJMC 222,
  58 JP 766,10 R 489, 43 WR 111, 10 TLR 668, DC 370

V

Vandermolen v Toma (1981) 9 HLR 91, CA 184
Victoria Square Property Co Ltd v London Borough of Southwark [1978] 2
All ER 281, [1978] 1 WLR 463, 142 JP 514, 76 LGR 349, 34 P & CR
275, [1978] RVR 10, 121 Sol Jo 816, CA 376

W

Wandsworth London Borough v Bowes (1989) 23 HLR 22, [1990] COD
167 449
Wandsworth London Borough Council v Brown (1987) Legal Action
(September) p 13 252
Wandsworth London Borough Council v Fadayomi [1987] 3 All ER 474,
[1987] 1 WLR 1473, [1988] 1 FLR 381, [1988] Fam Law 131, 86
LGR 176, 19 HLR 512, 131 Sol Jo 1285, [1987] LS Gaz R 2535,
CA 136, 257
Wandsworth London Borough Council v Osei-Bonsu. See Osei-Bonsu v
Wandsworth London Borough Council
Wandsworth London Borough Council v Sparling (1987) 152 JP 315, 20
HLR 169 439
Wandsworth London Borough Council v Winder [1985] AC 461, [1984] 3
All ER 976, [1984] 3 WLR 1254, 83 LGR 143, 17 HLR 196, 128 Sol Jo
838, [1985] LS Gaz R 201, [1985] NLJ Rep 381, HL 217
Wandsworth London Borough Council v Winder (No 2) (1987) 19 HLR 204,
[1987] NLJ Rep 124; affd (1988) 20 HLR 400, CA 215
Wainwright v Leeds City Council (1984) 82 LGR 657, 13 HLR 117, 270
Estates Gazette 1289, [1984] LS Gaz R 2000, CA 352
Wallace v Manchester City Council (1998) 30 HLR 1111, [1998] 3 EGLR 38,
[1998] 41 EG 223, CA 359
Waltham Forest London Borough Council v Thomas [1992] 2 AC 198,
[1992] 3 All ER 244, [1992] 3 WLR 131, [1993] Fam Law 67, 90 LGR
385, 24 HLR 622, [1992] 2 EGLR 40, [1992] 30 EG 87, [1992] 28 LS
Gaz R 32, [1992] NLJR 1005, 136 Sol Jo LB 200, HL 270
Wansbeck District Council v Marley (1987) 20 HLR 247, CA 145, 180
Warner v Lambeth London Borough Council (1984) 15 HLR 42 409
Warren v Keen [1954] 1 QB 15, [1953] 2 All ER 1118, [1953] 3 WLR 702,
97 Sol Jo 742, CA 354
Warsame v Hounslow London Borough Council (1999) Times, 21 July, CA .. 329
Warwick v Warwick (1982) 12 Fam Law 60, 1 HLR 139 .... 239, 306
Watson v Minister of Local Government and Planning [1951] 2 KB 779, 49
LGR 738, 95 Sol Jo 578, [1951] 2 TLR 503, sub nom Re Havant and
Waterloo UDC Compulsory Purchase Order (No 4) 1950, Re Watson's
Application [1951] 2 All ER 664, 115 JP 519 58
Webb v Ipswich Borough Council (1989) 88 LGR 165, 21 HLR 325, CA 454
Wells v Barnsley Metropolitan Borough Council (1999) Times, 12 November: 419
West Kent Housing Association Ltd v Davies (1998) 31 HLR 415, [1998]
EGCS 103, CA 183
Westminster City Council v Basson (1990) 62 P & CR 57, 23 HLR 225,
[1991] 1 EGLR 277, CA 103, 131, 132, 243
Westminster City Council v Clarke [1992] 2 AC 288, [1992] 1 All ER 695,
[1992] 2 WLR 229, 90 LGR 211, 24 HLR 260, [1992] 16 LS Gaz R 32,
[1992] NLJR 196, 136 Sol Jo LB 82, HL 102

PAGE

White v Exeter City Council [1981] LAG Bulletin 287 302

Wilson v Finch Hatton (1877) 2 Ex D 336, 46 LJQB 489, 41 JP 583, 25 WR
537, 36 LT 473 347

Wincentzen v Monklands District Council 1988 SC 329, 1988 SLT 847, 1989
SCLR 190 303

Wirral Borough Council v Smith (1982) 80 LGR 628, 43 P & CR 312, 4 HLR
81, 262 Estates Gazette 1298, CA 269

Woking Borough Council v Bystram [1993] EGCS 208, [1994] CLY 2297,
CA 140

Wolkind v Ali [1975] 1 All ER 193, 233 Estates Gazette 759, 119 Sol Jo 84,
sub nom Ali v Wolkind [1975] 1 WLR 170, 73 LGR 75, 29 P & CR 196,
DC 430

Woodspring District Council v Taylor (1982) 4 HLR 95, 133 NLJ 556, CA .. 148

Wookey v Wookey [1991] Fam 121, [1991] 3 All ER 365, [1991] 3 WLR
135, [1991] FCR 811, [1991] 2 FLR 319, CA 155

Wroth v Tyler [1974] Ch 30, [1973] 1 All ER 897, [1973] 2 WLR 405, 25
P & CR 138, 117 Sol Jo 90 236

Wycombe Health Authority v Barnett (1982) 47 P & CR 394, 5 HLR 84,
[1982] 2 EGLR 35, 264 Estates Gazette 619, CA 354

Y

Yelland v Taylor [1957] 1 All ER 627, [1957] 1 WLR 459, 101 Sol Jo 228,
CA 183

Z

Zaitzeff v Olmi (1952) 160 Estates Gazette 154, 102 L Jo 416 461

CHAPTER ONE

A brief history of social housing

Introduction

The principal purpose of this text is to provide law students and practitioners with a clear and comprehensive guide to current public sector housing law – by which term we mean the law relating to housing as provided and administered by local authorities, registered social landlords (previously 'housing associations') and one or two other agencies, such as local housing companies and the few housing action trusts that exist. It is apparent that in this field, as in many others, the relationship between the legal foundations in statute and case law and the wider policy environment are closely bound together, perhaps increasingly so. Law cannot be read and fully understood in isolation and policy analysis lacks clarity and depth unless it takes account of the legal context. The purpose of this chapter is to preface the description of public sector housing law with a discussion of the historical foundation and development of public housing in Britain. It is hoped that in this way the legal core of the book can be read more purposefully and with greater insight by law students and practitioners but also that the legal framework will be made more accessible to students of public and social policy. They too increasingly need a detailed knowledge of the relationship between law and policy in the sphere of public housing. But the main purpose of 'Public Sector Housing Law' is to expound the statutes and case law on social housing. It is not, therefore, an equal blend of law and policy but in this chapter and in shorter references throughout the book the policy context is etched in order to sharpen the focus of the legal material.

This chapter gives an account of the origins of public sector housing and how it evolved through over a century of development. It is a chronological account which is built around a discussion and evaluation of the major statutes that gave life to 'council housing'. Particular attention is paid to its origins and the early decades spanning the period up to the early 1920s for this is the time when the die was cast for much of what was to come. The decision that local authorities were to receive subsidy to build 'council' housing was taken during the 1914–18 war. It was not inevitable that this would be the case and most authorities did not seek nor want such a duty. The weave of this story also includes the circumstances in which the privately rented sector declined and in which home ownership began to come to prominence. The main focus, however, is on the progress of council housing, beginning with the relatively small and discretionary but, at the time, radical provisions contained in Part III of the Housing of the Working Classes Act 1890, to its peak in the mid-1970s when nearly one third of the population lived in it, to the decades of decline and residualisation that followed.

Council housing was reduced by nearly one third of its 1979 level during the course of the three Thatcher governments and the Major government. This demise was due to the right to buy provision of the Housing Act 1980 (and subsequent amendments), the decimation of public investment in social housing and a variety of other measures which allowed authorities to dispose of their housing stock. After 1980 a reduced programme of new building in the public sector was channelled mainly through housing associations although partnerships with the authorities have been a common feature of this form of provision.

The smaller stock of council houses (although still well over 4 million dwellings) now contains proportionately more flats than in 1979, fewer larger houses and more inner-city properties. It is a residual housing stock containing the poorest quality properties and is, moreover, much more geographically confined than in the past. Its social composition has also undergone a rapid metamorphosis. Much higher proportions of unemployed, workless and low income households live in council housing than historically was the case, and there are far fewer two-parent families with children. It contains a disproportionately high number of single parents and certain sections of the ethnic minority population, especially Afro-Caribbeans. The number of 're-lets' in the stock remains almost as high as it was in the pre-1979 period, suggesting that there is a great deal more movement of people into, out of, and within council housing now than previously. Thus the image of council housing has changed and has become regarded by many people as a less permanent solution to their housing needs than in the past, especially among younger households. Looked at in broad terms it is clear that both the structure and purpose of public sector housing has changed considerably and is very different now compared to even a few decades ago. The point is that it is difficult to understand or position the development of social housing law without some knowledge of this context and background. Following the 1997 General Election 'New Labour' brought a halt to the absolute decline of previous years but as we face the new millennium, a number of new issues have emerged requiring urgent policy responses.

The prominence of housing associations since 1979 is witnessed by the expanding number of their properties, which has doubled in just over two decades, growing from just over 2% of the national dwelling stock to five percent at the present time. The ratio of council houses to housing association properties has changed in the same period of time from 1: 15 to 1: 3.5. During the 1990s when new council housing could be counted in mere hundreds each year housing associations were putting in place tens of thousands of additional dwellings through schemes of new building and renovation of existing properties. In 1995 when the authorities completed only 770 houses the associations built over 31,000. However, much of this work was done in partnership with authorities, often on their land, leading to allocations policies that increasingly converged, the logical outcome of which has been common waiting lists. Voluntary stock transfers, by which an authority sold all its properties to associations, often specially set up for the purpose, accounted for an additional loss to council owned stock in excess of 250,000 properties.

Expansion of housing association activity, however, was bought literally at a price. Following the Housing Act 1988 associations had to operate within a much more rigorous funding régime based on a predetermined level of grant which needed to be 'topped up' by private finance, borrowed at market levels of interest. These higher costs were inevitably passed onto tenants in the form of higher rents. This new financial system effectively undermined the traditional, small-scale voluntary organisations which had been the backbone of the housing association movement because they were unable or unwilling to raise expensive private finance for new projects. As a result the 1980s and 1990s witnessed a pattern of mergers and transfers of stock leading to the development of a significant group of large, business-orientated associations which had little in common with traditional associations. Problems rather similar to those experienced on some council housing estates began to emerge during the period of the Major government (1992–97) and the fortunes of even the expansionary, business-orientated associations began to falter. Evidence of 'difficult-to-let' housing and even outright abandonment of inner-city properties appeared in many towns and cities, especially in the old industrial areas in the north.

It should be noted that the Housing Act 1996 created a new official category of landlord – registered social landlord. This term embraced housing associations, and non-profit making private agencies set up by local authorities, such as housing companies and a variety of voluntary bodies involved in the provision of 'social' housing. Thus although the main focus of the book is on council housing it is apparent that during the

1980s and 1990s there was a considerable blurring of the division between the authorities and the associations leading to stock transfers, to development partnerships, common waiting lists and so on. The administration and governance of British social housing has become more complex than at any time in its century long history. Note, for example, a recent change in the administration of Tai Cymru (the Welsh equivalent of the English Housing Corporation) which has been taken over by the Welsh Assembly.

In addition there has been a revolution in recent decades in the legal position of tenants following the introduction of secure tenancies in the Housing Act 1980. However, the strengthening of these legal rights occurred at a time when the emphasis politically was on individuality, the ultimate tenant's right being, therefore, the 'right to buy', to cease to be a tenant. Those tenants remaining in the public sector increasingly began to be spoken of as 'customers' or 'consumers' and therein lay a great deal of conceptual confusion because whatever politicians might have thought, in legal terms, the relationship of landlord and tenant remained paramount, as expressed in the terms of tenancy agreements. Arising from the same political context and motivation at this time little attention was paid to the development of tenants' collective rights. Such rights, which are inherent in the status and purpose of council housing, received scant attention through weak consultation procedures and duties to inform and little more than that. It is clear in this kind of debate that 'law' and 'policy' are closely entwined. Being treated as a 'customer' may express willingness by a company or agency to provide high quality services (although it may not) and the exchange of cash for a service or goods does carry legal obligations on both sides of the transaction, notably in English law for the purchaser to be careful before parting with their money! (*caveat emptor*). But in the case of public housing being a tenant of a landlord remains the fundamental reality and legal foundation of the relationship with rather different sets of rights and obligations, historically weighted in favour of landlords.

Also, in a wider sense, tenant and landlord law is clearly demarcated from political interference, at least in theory. For example, challenges made by tenants in the courts to rent increases have always failed because the law's concern is not with the level of rent but whether the administrative structure (in this case, the housing revenue account) is lawful. An important lesson from all of this is that, despite the major changes to social housing outlined above, there are some highly significant continuities and 'givens' arising from fundamental legal foundations, particularly via tenant and landlord law and administrative law. Such issues are crucial to understanding the relationship between law and policy and both lawyers, policy makers and housing managers need to know about them and where the boundaries lie.

We turn now to the principal aim of this chapter which is to set this discussion and the evolution of case and statute law on public sector housing into its historical context. The chapter will show how the statutory framework evolved and the extent to which it was shaped by the events and personalities of the day. Underneath this chronological account lie a series of seminal questions, the answers to which have shaped the pattern of housing provision in contemporary Britain. These questions take us into conceptual territory which in truth is beyond the boundaries of this text but the main lines of debate need to be sketched. The first issue concerns the origins of public sector 'housing' policy, particularly the point at which it became distinct from Victorian sanitary and public health policy. The second issue concerns the very fundamental question of why it was that local authorities became the almost exclusive provider of state subsidised, rental housing – 'council' housing – when almost everyone in the nineteenth century, in all social classes, lived in the privately rented sector. Intriguingly the council housing solution was a quite different turn to what happened on the Continent where social housing was provided (and still is) by a greater plurality of agencies, including subsidised *private* landlords.

The explanation in Britain hinges on what happened to the dominant privately rented sector and the way private landlords were treated in the policy process at this time (in the years before and after World War One). Although not for this text it should be noted *en passant* that these events also sow the seeds of the 'home owning' society (through the division of the rental sector into two completely separate tenures, public and private, leaving owner occupation to come, as it were, through the middle). In short, the rise of council housing as the almost exclusive provider of 'working class' state rental housing needs to be read in the wider context of the dramatic restructuring of the British housing tenure system during the course of the twentieth century. The story turns on what happened to classical nineteenth century private landlordism. In many ways these early decades were seminal to what was to follow and so it is necessary to dwell on this period at the outset.

Why 'council housing'?

Since 1919 Britain, unlike any other comparable European nation, has developed a large-scale public sector of housing based almost exclusively on local authority provision and management. At its peak in the mid-1970s one third of all households in the country lived in council houses. In other comparable north and west European societies state housing was provided through a plurality of agencies including non-profit co-operative societies, housing associations, trade unions, local societies, national agencies as well as local authorities. Of great significance is the fact that in most of these countries private landlords have been to a greater or lesser extent subsidised from the national exchequer, a position rarely enjoyed by British private landlords, and so have survived as major contributors to the supply of housing. It is the collapse of private landlordism in Britain that arguably more than any other factor accounts for the surge of local authority involvement in the provision of rental housing after the First World War.

Thus, at the outset of this brief history, we need to stand back from our familiarity with 'council housing' as the principal source of public sector housing in Britain and ask why this is the case. It has to be explained and certainly, by comparison with our European neighbours, cannot and should not be assumed. Indeed most local authorities took a lot of persuading and, above all, a guarantee of major central government subsidy before they would tackle the job. The second vital strand to the early part of the story is the fact that, after decades of prevarication, it was finally recognised that such subsidies were a necessary component of the new concept of 'housing policy'. Moreover, despite most accounts of the origins of council housing beginning with the Addison Act of 1919, it is clear from recent research that the need for large scale subsidised local authority provision of 'working class' housing was decided before the outbreak of the 1914–18 War. As Morton argues,

'... it was to authorities, from as early as 1914, that the Government was looking for a crash building programme to produce some 120,000 additional houses.'[1]

This realisation, however, was painfully slow to develop.

The public health origins

The nineteenth century was, of course, a period of dynamic change with very rapid urbanisation taking place in the wake of the Industrial Revolution. The population doubled between 1801 and 1851 from 9,000,000 million to 18,000,000 and the rate of increase never fell below 10% per annum until the early 1930s. The vast majority of this expansion took place in industrialised towns and cities. The abolition in 1834 of poor relief under the Speenhamland System, which subsidised from local rates the wages of virtually destitute agricultural labourers, swelled the ranks of those families who now turned to the industrial cities in the hope of finding work and a better life.

What they in fact found in many cases was a life characterised by appallingly high morbidity and mortality, poverty and slum housing. The housing problem was caused by the already poor quality of the stock and

1   Morton, J 'The 1890 Act and its aftermath – the era of the "new model dwellings"' in S Lowe and D Hughes (eds) *A New Century of Social Housing* (Leicester University Press, 1991), p30.

its very scarce supply. Consequently overcrowding was rife and rents were very high in relation to average industrial earnings. At the heart of this, and really the most enduring of 'the housing questions', was a contradiction between the relatively high costs of building compared to the return available to the developers and landlords. During the 19th century the vast majority of housing (over 90% up to the 1914–18 War) was provided by private landlords, mainly through small investments made by the urban middle class, small businessmen or industrialists. Production of low cost working class housing entailed a difficult financial equation. Employers, for example, needed a workforce near the factories; but they dare not set rent levels too high for fear of putting pressure on wages. It was, however, further assumed that rental housing would produce a profit and for many decades the idea of state intervention to assist the urban poor was a political and philosophical anathema. Housing standards were therefore often extremely poor as Enid Gauldie describes in her seminal book *Cruel Habitations*,[2] and anyone who has read the novels of Dickens will get a whiff of the Victorian slum.

In an obvious sense one source of housing policy was in the attempt to deal with the public health problems which were endemic to the slums. Indeed, some historians have read into this the notion that the origins of council housing are to be found in the Victorian public health legislation.[3] A brief examination of the issue suggests this is not really the case but that the adverse impact of these measures on the profitability of private landlordism is significant. We are mindful also that this legislation is the foundation of the modern public health system which includes various duties which local authorities have in relation to housing standards – now often shared in joint public or environmental health and housing departments.

Up to almost the close of the century there were basically three sets of public health powers conferred on local authorities which had a 'housing' dimension:

(1) powers to close and demolish insanitary dwellings;
(2) powers to clear areas of insanitary housing;
(3) powers over new building and the prevention of unhealthy use of existing houses.

The powers over individual insanitary dwellings were granted initially under the Artisans' and Labourers' Dwellings Act of 1868, popularly known as the 'Torrens' Act after its parliamentary sponsor. These powers were entirely discretionary and placed no obligation on the local authority to re-house the occupants following demolition.

The Artisans' and Labourers' Dwellings Improvement Act 1875 was rather more important because its sponsor, Cross, was the Home Secretary

2   Gauldie, E *Cruel Habitations* (Allen and Unwin, 1974).
3   Wohl, A S *The Eternal Slum: Housing and Social Policy in Victorian London* (Edward Arnold, 1977).

in Disraeli's government. His seniority is important because it enabled the accusations of 'socialist' interference in the rights of freeholders to be more effectively deflected. Local authorities were empowered, but not obliged, to clear whole areas of unfit housing and, significantly, were allowed to enable the re-housing of displaced families on the same site. Compensation was paid to the owners. The test of unfitness was whether the property could be brought up to a 'sanitary' standard, so that this is still very firmly public health and not housing legislation. Re-housing under the Cross Act was undertaken mainly by 'model dwelling companies' and philanthropic trusts, the local authorities having sold the sites to the trustees of the companies. There was certainly no question of subsidies to the tenants through rents set at below cost and the assumption was for the companies to achieve at least a 5% return on the investment. Model dwelling companies were important in providing low cost, good quality housing to the relatively well-to-do working classes in the period before the 1914–18 War. Indeed by that time they had built over 50,000 dwellings, twice as many as the local authorities themselves. There were many such companies – the Peabody Trust (set up by a wealthy American), the Improved Dwellings Company, The Guiness Trust – all run by businessmen aiming not to replace the market, but to show how the market could be made to operate more effectively.[4]

Even though cheap loans were available to them from the Public Works Loans Board and the sites, already cleared, were sold at below market price, these companies were never able to provide for the poorest social strata. Rents were simply too high. Furthermore, the management of these new dwellings – often tenements much criticised for being not dissimilar in appearance to workhouses – was exceedingly paternalistic and thoroughly imbued with the Poor Law morality of the 'deserving' and 'undeserving' poor. Having passed tests of eligibility for housing, tenants' behaviour was tightly controlled; for example, evening curfews were imposed. This tradition of housing management is very important in the subsequent history of public housing which was to unfold after 1919 and council housing has never entirely shed the accusation of paternalism in its organisation and management.

Although the Torrens and Cross legislation was amended at the end of the 1870s it remained largely ineffective and in fact created more problems than it solved. For low income households in particular it is clear that the situation was made considerably worse by the clearance of slum dwellings and was, indeed, the cause of further overcrowding problems. More substantial, longer-term benefits accrued from the Public Health Act 1875 which consolidated previous public health legislation and had a specific housing content through the grant to local authorities of powers to make byelaws. Byelaws regulating the width and layout of streets, the air spaces

4   Merrett S, *State Housing in Britain* (Routledge and Kegan Paul, 1979).

above houses, areas of windows etc had existed as an indirect consequence of the Local Government Act 1858. These derived from model powers in an accompanying Form of Byelaws. They helped in particular to control the 'back-to-backs'. This was a form of dwelling, built by speculative developers, in which a terrace of houses shared a back wall, each dwelling facing away from each other and having windows and access only at the front. Their advantage was that they were cheap to build and contained a high density of population and, although better in some ways than tenements, they frequently did not have internal water or sanitation and lacked proper ventilation. By ensuring that each dwelling had a separate area of open space, usually meaning a back yard, byelaws gradually eradicated back-to-backs, although they were still being built in Leeds well into the 1930s even though it was illegal to build them for the 'working classes' from 1905 onwards. Byelaws were not required to be in place in local authority areas in Victorian England because it was believed that they infringed the rights of freeholders. Nevertheless as Burnett suggests,

'... (they) acted as a useful guide to the more progressive towns and, at the same time, created an important precedent for national involvement in housing matters.'[5]

The 1875 Act consolidated the previous law and many local authorities did subsequently adopt model byelaws issued by the Local Government Board in 1877 which considerably extended and also clarified the 1858 powers. Local authorities were empowered to compel developers to deposit plans for inspection and amendment if necessary and could also inspect construction sites and change work which contravened their byelaws.

Although real progress was being made through this fairly mundane route the usefulness of the byelaws was limited because they were permissive only and not mandatory. Towns which already had laws in place did not need to amend them to the higher standard and, of course, the model byelaws could apply only to new dwellings, leaving untouched the vast mass of slums. Byelaw housing built between the late 1870s and 1914 was undoubtedly progressive in design and amenity standards. It was particularly appropriate for construction on green field sites which increasingly came into play with developments in public transport in the last three decades of the century. By 1905, for example, the London County Council estimated that 820,000 workmen were making extensive daily journeys from the new suburbs to work. Cheap travel by electric trams was responsible for the rapid growth of suburban areas in many towns and in progressive cities, such as Sheffield, was the basis of some of the earliest

5   Burnett, J *A Social History of Housing 1815–1985* (Methuen, 1986), p158.

examples of local authority housing provision under the terms of the Housing of the Working Classes Act 1890.[6]

But there is no doubt that the additional costs engendered in the construction of such housing tipped the affordability equation well beyond the pockets of low paid workers. Byelaw housing thus tended to intensify the differences between the 'better class of poor' and desperately low paid workers. Real incomes had grown by up to 50% between 1850 and 1900 and for large sections of the working class in the late century decades, despite periodic economic recession, there was marked improvement in housing and consumer standards. It is also abundantly clear that the inner cities still contained a mass of poor working people whose situation was getting worse. The new building standards, the sanitary controls and the clearance powers all acted to reduce the profitability of private landlordism. The majority of private landlords in the 19th century were individual middle class people, and some better-off artisan workers, who were quite content to harbour their savings in housing. It had been a generally safe investment. With the clearances and stricter building standards many private landlords began to look for alternative investment opportunities. These were not difficult to find and overseas investment was becoming particularly attractive. The extension of the franchise during the 1880s also served to damage the interests of private landlords because property taxes, particularly in the form of local rates, increased as new demands were placed on authorities to provide better and more services to satisfy public demand. So it was that in the decades before the First World War landlords' profits were being squeezed from a variety of sources while new investment opportunities were opening up.

Thus the origins of state intervention in housing do have a 'public health' dimension but it should not be read as a logical progression guided by enlightened reform. Rather this influence helped to shape the investment crisis which was a significant contributor to the beginning of the long decline of private landlordism in Britain. A major factor in the long-term development of council housing was its role in filling the vacuum left by the historic failure of private landlords to continue supplying low rent dwellings for working class families.[7]

'... the sty that made the pig'

These words, taken from the Report of the Royal Commission on the Housing of the Working Classes published in 1884, are a graphic expression of the gathering realisation, in a society dominated by utilitarian principles

---

6   Pollard, S *A History of Labour in Sheffield* (University of Liverpool Press, 1959).
7   Merrett S *State Housing in Britain* (Routledge and Kegan Paul, 1979).

and habits, and a laissez-faire market economy, that the squalor of Victorian slumdom was a *housing* problem and not the consequence of feckless and undeserving inhabitants. This shift in perception in part arose from the evidence collected for the Royal Commission itself. It was of a measurable deterioration of conditions, in inner London in particular, caused by an acute shortage of affordable housing. It is important because it recognised in a way unusual for the day the relationship between demand and supply in the housing market. Attention was particularly focused on the incomes of certain types of workers – dockers, costermongers and others – and the rents they were paying. It was found that incomes among such people were well below Charles Booth's poverty line and, moreover, they were paying a very high percentage of this income in rent. Booth's independent study of the inhabitants of the East End of London was a pioneering work of social investigation conducted between 1888 and 1901 and published in seven volumes of his *Life and Labour of the People of London.*[8] One of his most startling findings, published in 1889, was that 30.7% of the population of London (over one million people) lived below his scientific measure of poverty, with disastrous results for health and industrial efficiency. The problem for the Royal Commissioners was not difficult to evaluate. The property boom of the 1870s ended in the early 1880s and there was a major supply and demand problem. Their analysis is summed up neatly by Morton,

'The inner urban poor were being driven outwards by a of city centres to public and commercial uses but were being halted in their tracks by lack of access to newer, cheaper housing further out ...'[9]

Lord Salisbury's short-lived government of 1885 put through a somewhat obscure Housing Act which drew in a few of the Commission's recommendations and redefined the term lodging house to include individual dwellings, later to be an important change. There was no question yet of local authorities generally being involved as it was clearly thought that the market would eventually adjust. It was, however, recognised that the state did have an obligation to ease the situation in the meantime and especially for families affected by clearances arising from municipal activity and also where conditions were very poor.

It was not until Salisbury returned to power in 1886 with a programme to reform local government that the housing crisis was addressed. The Local Government Act 1888 put in place a unified system of local government by the creation of county and county borough authorities across the whole

8   Booth, C *Life and Labour of the People of London* (!st Series Poverty, 1902).
9   Morton, J 'The 1890 Act and its aftermath – the era of the "new model dwellings"' in S Lowe and D Hughes (eds) *A New Century of Social Housing* (Leicester University Press, 1991), p14.

country. The previous framework for the *ad hoc* provision of urban services was gradually incorporated into a system of local administration which lasted more or less intact until the major local government reforms of the mid 1970s. With housing supply tightening and some local authorities already experimenting with building projects the Housing of the Working Classes Act was passed by Parliament in July 1890. This was key legislation because it provided the context in which local authorities could intervene positively to address the housing crisis. In this sense it can be understood as the first statement of the need for a national 'housing policy'. The Act was very largely consolidating legislation and Parts I and II brought together the Torrens and Cross Acts, but in Part I there was provision for local authorities to redevelop a site directly if no other agency came forward, and in Part III they were empowered to build and also to renovate and improve 'working class lodging houses', defined (from the 1885 Act) to mean individual dwellings. Thus after 1890 as Gauldie points out, '... it was legally possible for an enlightened local authority to pursue an enlightened housing policy'[10]

The assumption remained that housing schemes should be self-financing and at first a rate of return was even stipulated and, as before, this certainly meant that authorities were not going to cater for low income households. It was still generally assumed that the model dwelling companies were the main source of 'social' housing. Authorities had to obtain the permission of the Local Government Board, and in the case of the London County Council the Home Secretary, in order to build. Despite innovative projects, notably those by the LCC which set high design and quality standards, the rents charged were very similar to the model dwelling companies. The problem of finance had not been solved. The use of local rate funds to support building was severely constrained by the political influence of the local ratepayers.

A new slump in the building industry took hold about 1905 and opinion, largely shaped by the experience of the more progressive local authorities, began to veer towards the need for some kind of subsidy to make rents for new housing affordable for working class families living on average incomes. It was clear that despite the growing interest of local authorities in building under Part III of the 1890 Act there was very little direct benefit for the really poor, although there was some evidence of filtering down. Nevertheless local authorities did respond to the new housing crisis and by the outbreak of the war in 1914, 316 councils had built using Part III permissions and between 1910 and 1914 over 11,000 council houses were built. By the outbreak of the war the total local authority provision was about 28,000 new dwellings nationally, about 90% of which had been built since the 1890 Act. This was a much smaller contribution than the model dwelling

10   Gauldie, E *Cruel Habitations* (Allen and Unwin, 1974), p294.

companies and the charitable trusts who had a combined total of about 50,000 dwellings.[11] Despite this numerical superiority it was to the local authorities that the government turned to provide what amounted to a crash programme of building. In the context of the times it is not difficult to see why. In the first place the model dwelling companies were private companies and, with notable exception, mainly focused their activities on London. Almost always their interest was to provide for the 'better class of poor'. Becoming anything more was not a role for which they were suited and neither, as Best points out, was it one they sought.[12] Secondly, as Morton shows, '... the sheer quality of council-house building' was incomparably superior to anything that had been built in the voluntary sector. As such it provided a model for the future and, despite an element of subsidy in their developments, authorities had demonstrated what could be done using limited finances.

In addition, harking back to achievements in the public health field, it should not be underestimated that virtually every authority now contained a body of professional inspectors. Their role in the interpretation and implementation of standards in local byelaws had given the profession a prestige and authority.[13] Local authorities had shown that they were capable of building and all over the country had delivered, albeit in small quantities, 'council houses'. They had officers with development experience and a well established body of inspectors familiar with the technical standards and design principles of housing.

Here, then, is the specific answer to the question 'why council house?' Even before the outbreak of war in 1914 it was widely recognised that the building slump had to be addressed by some form of temporary intervention. The government was looking to a programme of 120,000 dwellings and it was clear that they could not find a programme of this magnitude through the reliance on the philanthropic trusts and model dwelling companies. Reluctant actors as they might be authorities were waiting in the wings. The traumatic events of the 1914–18 war determined that it was not long before they would be thrust centre stage.

Subsidies and the private landlords

Thus far the explanation for the rise of state housing provision in Britain has focused on explaining why authorities came to play such a significant role.

11 Morton, J 'The 1890 Act and its aftermath – the era of the 'new model dwellings' in S Lowe and D Hughes (eds) A New Century of Social Housing (Leicester University Press, 1991), p29.
12 Best, R 'Housing Associations 1890 – 1990' in S Lowe and D Hughes (eds) A New Century of Social Housing (Leicester University Press, 1991).
13 Holmans A E *Housing Policy in Britain* (Croom Helm, 1986), p56.

We have suggested that limited and temporary use of authorities to build rental housing was widely acknowledged before 1914. We also suggested earlier that private landlordism was under considerable pressure in the latter decades of the 19th century due in large measure to the new byelaws and public health controls. A number of historians have also pointed to the additional factor that housing was increasingly subject to taxation at this time, particularly through the local rates, and private landlords were adversely affected by this. Profits were squeezed and capital values eroded.[14] Rather than opting for council housing one possible solution to the problem might, therefore, have been to improve the tax position of the private landlords, restore their profitability, and so ameliorate the need for state housing.

Before we arrive at the point in 1919 when the mechanism for the first large scale, nationally mandated and highly subsidised council house programme was put in place one further piece in the jig-saw needs to be fitted. Why were landlords not protected from high taxation and, eventually, from rent controls, and why did they not become the recipients of state subsidy? Was this, therefore, the beginning of the end for private landlordism in Britain being, in effect, the early stages of a permanent, structural collapse?[15] If the latter position is generally affirmed then there is a further crucial factor which underpins the rise of the municipal alternative. This argument carries forward the point made above that the main consequence of public health legislation for private landlordism was not the administrative response, although as we have seen that was important, but is found in the supply and demand pressures created by inner city clearances and by the inability of poor families to escape to the new suburbs. It helps explain the exceptionally large quantity of council housing eventually to be built in Britain over an extended period of time (1919–1979). Moreover, uniquely in the wider European context, it explains the concentration of the provision of state sponsored social housing on the local authorities. Why it was to authorities that the government looked for its crash building programme in 1919 is closely related to the specific character of British political culture.

Two very useful points are made here by Daunton. First, that compared to their European counterparts private landlords in Britain were a relatively powerless social and political force. As local ratepayers they certainly wielded influence but they were politically disorganised and certainly did not have the powerful voice enjoyed by, for example, the German private landlords. Daunton sums up the point,

'One factor (in the Anglo-German contrast) was the lack of political power of small property owners within the British political system,

---

14 Daunton M J *Housing the Workers* (Leicester University Press, 1990), p23.
15 Ball, M *Housing Policy and Economic Power* (Methuen, 1983).

both at local and national level. There was in Britain nothing equivalent to the three-class voting system of the Prussian state and municipal government which gave more weight to property owners.'[16]

As a result municipal housing was not tolerated in Germany where, instead, non-profit co-operatives and trade union based associations organised themselves autonomously. Even these were opposed but, even more surely, so was the large scale municipal alternative. On the continent generally, and not just in Berlin, – in Paris, Brussels, Budapest – the municipal route was not a preferred option and as a result there was a more diverse response to the problem of working class housing, including the subsidisation of private landlords by various means. The British lower middle class, which was the cradle of 19th century landlordism, was to an extent on the fringes of both main political parties. The Liberals sought to tax landowners, which in many cases meant urban landlords, out of existence and yet the Conservatives, with their roots firmly planted in rural landed interests, were not entirely at ease with small urban property investors.

Daunton's second point concerns the character of the Labour movements in the early years of the twentieth century and follows closely from his analysis of the contrasting nature of the political systems in European societies. In Germany, for example, the trade unions and Labour movement regarded the state as politically biased and treated it with a great deal of suspicion. In Britain, however, after a century of struggle and, it may be added of defeats, the British working class movement was essentially reformist in character. The Labour Party came into existence essentially to represent the trade unions in Parliament. The state was regarded as being class-neutral both nationally and locally. Moreover, Labour made quick gains through the local political route in some cities and were able to use the powers of the Housing of the Working Classes Act to experiment with 'council' housing. In Sheffield, for example, a design competition led to one of the earliest garden suburbs being built; the so called 'flowers' estate at Tinsley because all the streets were named after well known flowers. As a result the idea of the co-operative alternatives failed to take root and the British Labour movement looked squarely to the municipalities for solutions to their housing problems.

The 1914–18 war and 'Homes Fit for Heroes'

As in so many aspects of social and political life the traumatic events of the First World War jolted Britain out of its Edwardian complacency. The

16 Daunton M J *Housing the Workers* (Leicester University Press, 1990), p24.

horrific military campaign was compounded by the threat seemingly posed by Bolshevism. It was a time of turmoil, and individual and social trauma. In the housing context it is indeed a seminal point in time. At the close of hostilities, large-scale central Exchequer subsidies were introduced through the Housing and Town Planning etc Act 1919. This legislation turned council housing from a small, somewhat experimental form of housing provision into a major sector. Although it was not to be, at the time Addison Act housing (named after the parliamentary sponsor) was regarded as a one-off expedient to cope with the major shortages of housing resulting from the war; it is estimated that household numbers grew by over 1 million during the war and the 1921 Census revealed that 1,150,000 households out of a total of just under 8,000,000 were sharing accommodation, that is to say over one-eighth of all households.

The significant legislation in the war era was the Restriction of Rent and Mortgage Interest Act 1915 which controlled rents and mortgages at their 1914 levels. In the face of social unrest in some cities resulting from a crisis in landlord-tenant relations the government had no real alternative but to control the market. The focal point of civil unrest was Glasgow, an important centre of munitions production, where profiteering by landlords was intense and led to a collapse of already fragile relations between tenant and landlord. In Scotland the basis of the contract between landlord and tenant was significantly different from England. Up to 1911 most tenancies were annual with a single date of renewal agreed through an annual 'missive'. Rents were paid quarterly in arrears but in cases of late payment landlords were able to recover the whole year's payment through seizure of property to the value of the annual rent. After 1911 tenancies were put onto a monthly footing which gave tenants more flexibility but landlords were able to evict tenants at 48 hours' notice who were only seven days in arrears of payment. Relations especially at the bottom of the market were very strained and litigious. The opportunity to recoup profits, which had declined in Glasgow due to surpluses in the market prior to the war, caused an outrage because the landlords tried to force up rents, not only at the bottom end of the market, by using powers of summary eviction.[17] It is clear that in Scotland, and especially on Clydeside, landlord-tenant relations were very tense and already highly political well before the outbreak of The First World War. In the summer of 1915 the situation boiled over into a series of rent strikes and this civil unrest threatened to engulf the munitions factories.

In England the situation was less fraught because tenancies were invariably based on weekly lets which allowed flexibility for tenants although little security. Powers of summary eviction, however, were rarely used because it took at least 28 days to secure an eviction, with a probable loss of rent. The events of the summer of 1915 in Glasgow were a major

17 Daunton M J *Housing the Workers* (Leicester University Press, 1990), p21.

contributory factor to the introduction of rent controls which in turn led to a further reduction in the profitability of private landlordism. It became increasingly clear by the middle of the war that a large programme of council housing would have to be a main part of the solution to the housing problem. As a result of rent restriction rents were forced down in real terms so that at the close of hostilities not only were shortages very grave indeed but effective demand was much higher than it had been before the war. This problem also had a political dimension to it, as Bowley observes,

'Increases in rents staved off in deference to public opinion during the war could scarcely be regarded as an appropriate form of peace celebration.'[18]

As we have argued above a subsidy to encourage the return of private landlords was not a likely strategy in Britain given the weak political position of landlordism, and the behaviour of the landlords during the war did nothing to suggest that they could become the focus of a popular and sustained building programme. The shortages were too great and politically sensitive to be left to them. In any case, they had virtually abandoned building working class housing before the war and seemed unlikely to return under the prevailing conditions. Apart from anything else building costs and interest rates after the war were high. The rent freeze further limited the profitability of the private landlords.

Thus the First World War transformed the nature of the housing question in Britain, and faced with massive shortages of rental housing, social unrest, a system of private landlordism that was failing and discredited the government had no real alternative than to intervene. The decision to engage local authorities to provide the crash building programme, as we have seen, pre-dates the events of the war so that what happened during the war made the outcome almost inevitable.

The election of November 1919 resulted in a reduced coalition of Liberals and Conservatives led by Lloyd George. They won the campaign principally on the famous slogan of 'Homes Fit for Heroes'. In order to appease the ratepayers and to persuade reluctant local authorities to build the subsidy under the 1919 Act was very generous. The finance was variable to take account of local conditions, particularly variations in building costs which were high at this time. Authorities for their part were in a strong bargaining position because it was certain that only they could see such a large scheme through. Their co-operation was obtained by limiting their liability to the product of an annual penny rate with the whole of the balance made up from the Exchequer. The scale of this programme was in a completely different league to pre-war council housing. When the Addison Act programme was

18 Bowley, M *Housing and the State 1919–1944* (Allen and Unwin, 1945), p9.

aborted by the government in July 1921 there were 170,000 houses built or contracted. The programme ended because the Conservative section of the coalition opposed the escalating costs and because at the outset the programme was conceived as a temporary measure arising from the special post-war circumstances.

Apart from marking the beginning of mass council housing the Addison legislation is important because it established a basic administrative, legal and financial framework for the production of a large-scale national programme of municipal housing. Council housing was to be paid for out of rents, central subsidy and rate fund contributions with the local authority as the developer-landlord. They would borrow money at market cost and rates of interest (later on the problem of interest charges on loans became a major problem). More or less all the council house programmes from 1919 to the end of the 1960s were built under this basic system, the only differences being the variations in the levels of subsidy, for what purpose they were granted (typically general needs or slum clearance housing) and the length of time over which the subsidy would be paid. The legalities of local authority housing finance are considered in more detail in Chapter 4 but we should not miss at this point the importance of the 1919 Act in setting the agenda for what was, unknown at the time, to be the conventional pattern for the financing, production and management of British council housing.

The premature withdrawal of the subsidy is argued by some historians to demonstrate that the local authority building programme was initiated mainly to quell the threat of civil unrest. Once the threat had receded there was no need to continue the programme. As Swenarton, for example, argues money spent on housing was as much '... an insurance against Bolshevism and revolution' as it was a programme to provide 'homes fit for heroes'.[19] There is some truth in this but it does not do justice to the case outlined above that the need for a large scale programme of state rental housing was widely supported even before the war and neither, as Kemp points out, does it explain why the Conservative Government reintroduced subsidies for private and local authority building through their Housing Act of 1923.[20] The fact of the matter was that 'normal' housing market conditions were not returning and that the underlying logic of private landlordism was in abeyance. When circumstances improved for housing investment, as they did in the 1930s, there *was* a temporary return to investment in private renting. Some 900,000 houses were built for letting in the inter-war period, mostly in the 1932–37 period when building costs were very low and house

19 Swenarton, M *Homes Fit For Heroes: the Politics and Architecture of Early State Housing in Britain* (Heinemann, 1981), p71.

20 Kemp, P 'From solution to problem? Council housing and the development of national housing policy' in S Lowe and D Hughes (eds) *A New Century of Social Housing* (Leicester University Press, 1991), p46.

prices were declining. The proportion of houses built for rent as opposed to purchase by owner occupiers grew from 11% to 30% at that time.[1] Through the '20s and early 1930s economic conditions were generally, however, unfavourable even though rent controls did not apply to new houses. It should not, by the same token, be assumed that council housing was widely or enthusiastically embraced. It was accepted out of necessity due to the continuing and persistent shortages of housing which is the backdrop to most of the inter-war period. This position would certainly seem to explain the Housing Act of 1923 introduced by the Conservative Minister of Health, Chamberlain. It also helps account for why the rate of council house building through the inter-war period fluctuated very considerably and was never positively embraced except by the short-lived Labour Government of 1924. Merrett shows how the council house programme was persistently subject to cuts in subsidy rates and cost cutting reductions in building standards.[2] Even before the Addison Act subsidy was axed the average floor space of the model three-bedroomed dwellings had fallen.

The equivocal position of council housing through the inter-war period can also be explained by the important role played by the scale of private house-building (for sale) which enjoyed a period of unprecedented growth from the mid-1920s to the outbreak of the Second World War. Output rose from a 100,000 per annum to peak at over 250,000 in the five years before the war. Private construction thus overshadows the municipal building programme in scale of production. The growth of 'home ownership' was encouraged by several factors at work in the wider economy of the 1920s and '30s. First of all despite mass unemployment during the Depression years the number of people in secure, mainly white collar salaried posts increased very sharply. – jobs in banking, insurance. At the same time an increase in marriages led to a rapid growth in new household formations and there was a strong trend for households generally to be smaller because of a declining birth rate and more single person households resulting from the ability of people such as widows and widowers to live alone. Holmans argues that house prices were also at an historically low point in relation to other prices influenced by low building costs, cheap land on suburban greenfield sites and very weak planning controls allowing 'urban sprawl'.[3] There was in addition a readily available source of finance through the rapidly expanding building societies.

That having been said the build and design standards of 1920s council housing were mainly very good and superior to most private sector speculative housing. The influence of the seminal design standards and ideas of Raymond Unwin, the architect of the Rowntree garden suburb

1 Merrett S *State Housing in Britain* (Routledge and Kegan Paul, 1979), p13.
2 Ibid, p248.
3 Holmans A E *Housing Policy in Britain* (Croom Helm, 1986).

village at New Earswick in York, Letchworth New Town, and Hampstead Garden suburb is particularly noteworthy. Significantly Unwin was a member of the Tudor Walters Committee which was set up during the 1914–18 war by the Local Government Board to '... consider questions of building construction ... of dwellings for the working classes.' Their Report was published in November 1918 and as Burnett suggests,

> '... the Tudor Walters Report on the standards of post-war local authority housing were revolutionary, constituting a major innovation in social policy and in the future character of working-class life.'[4]

The Design Manual for local authorities which accompanied the report was largely drawn by Unwin himself and became a blue print for the now familiar styles of council housing built during the 1920s and 1930s. Gone were the Victorian tenements and the monotonous byelaw terraces and in came the working class cottage style epitomised by Unwin's New Earswick designs, an estate built very early on in the century in the first flush of the garden suburb movement.

Under the Conservatives' legislation council housing indeed played an entirely subordinate role to the private builders. The 'Chamberlain' Housing Act of 1923 provided building subsidies to both the public and the private sectors. The Treasury offered local authorities only £6 per dwelling over 20 years with no requirement for rate fund contributions. The aim was to limit the scope and scale of local authority housing programmes and encourage private builders to supply housing for sale to the working classes. Central controls were more stringent than under the Addison legislation and to begin with local authorities had to demonstrate to the Ministry that the private sector was not supplying the housing needs of the area before they were given permission to build. The 1923 Act was not repealed until 1929 but only 75,900 council houses had been built under its terms compared with 362,000 subsidised private sector dwellings.

The equivocal position of council housing at this time is further demonstrated in the vigorous programme of rehabilitation and reconditioning of properties in the privately rented sector. This was regarded as an alternative to new building and also slum clearance in the public sector; between 1919 and 1930 about 300,000 houses were made fit for habitation by statutory improvement orders made against private landlords.

The first Labour Government, 1924

There was no equivocation in the attitude of John Wheatley the Minister of Health in the first Labour Government which came to power for only nine months in 1924. Wheatley was a 'Red-Clydesider', a Glaswegian, Catholic socialist hardened by years of campaigning in Clydeside local politics who by some astute manoeuvring found himself responsible for the housing programme in the Labour Cabinet. His ideal was to use municipal construction to replace the privately rented sector but he stopped short of outright nationalisation because he was a pragmatist. Instead he opted to build on the existing system using a much improved level of subsidy. Wheatley's intention, through the Housing Act 1924, was to establish a long-term investment programme in high quality council houses. His vision was that council housing would be a socially and geographically ubiquitous housing tenure. Authorities no longer had to demonstrate 'housing need' to get building permission. The private rental sector showed few signs of reviving and so, according to Wheatley, could not be relied on to build working class housing. The subsidy was significantly increased and was to be payable over 40 years, instead of 20 years under the 1923 legislation, and the rate fund contribution to council house building was restored. The private sector was also able to benefit from this subsidy so long as it could be shown they were building for working class households.

Wheatley used the terms of this legislation and his Labour Movement credentials to negotiate a deal with the trade unions in the building industry which removed many of the trade's restrictive practices. This facilitated the housing drive in the public sector but also spilled over into the private sector where de-skilling in the construction industry accompanied by large-scale unemployment helped to create the conditions for the boom in house building in the 1930s. Wheatley also forced up the rate of construction by setting production targets for authorities and withheld subsidy unless they met their quotas.

Wheatley's was a long-term, strategic view of council housing and is very different, therefore, to the housing legislation of his Coalition and Conservative predecessors. The 1924 Act restored the general needs role for this sector of housing which had been abandoned to a residual role in the 1923 legislation and also re-established the debate about housing standards, arguing very strongly in favour of high quality. Although the Labour Government was quickly replaced by a new Conservative administration the Wheatley Act subsidies continued in place until 1933 by which time over 500,000 houses had been built under its terms. Thus for several years both the Chamberlain and the Wheatley subsidies operated in tandem. The Conservatives very reluctantly retained the Wheatley subsidy because investment in the privately rented sector at this time was minimal. There was no other source of large-scale building for rent. The subsidy needed to be generous to persuade some of the more reluctant authorities, of whom there were many, to build. Although the central government was able to give direction to the public housing programme, for example, the impending switch to slum clearance, authorities were fairly autonomous bodies at this time and this led to a considerable variation in provision of council houses across the country. Conservative-controlled authorities were quick to utilise both the Chamberlain and Wheatley subsidies to channel central government finance into the private building industry. The vast majority of housing whether in the public sector or built for sale in the private sector was built by private companies.[5]

Housing for the poor?

Council housing built in the 1920s under the terms of the Addison, Chamberlain and Wheatley subsidies varied very considerably in size and standard. The output figures fluctuated from year to year in response to the cuts in subsidies, building costs, labour shortages and also uncertainties about the relationship between subsidy levels and rents. There was no smooth progressive growth in council housing and with the exception of the few months of the Labour Administration support from central government for the progress of council housing was unstable and extremely hesitant. The growing number of Labour-controlled local authorities after the mid-1920s ensured more progress than would otherwise have been the case. And, in the main, the standards of building were far superior to any previous working class housing and the best Addison and Wheatley dwellings were better than any comparable housing in the private sector. For millions of people this was the beginning of a new life on 'council estates' built very broadly in the cottage garden vernacular style based on Unwin's Design Manual. What was happening, as Burnett describes it, was '... a minor revolution in the standards of working-class housing and living.'[6]

There need, however, be no hesitancy about one crucial point. This housing was not the solution to the problems of poor working class families. Even with the high level of subsidy under the 1919 Act rents were well out of range of the poor. Rents were meant to be set in line with controlled rents in the privately rented sector but authorities tended to set higher rents than those in the private sector. Rents under the Chamberlain Act were higher still because the level of subsidy was considerably reduced. Wheatley housing was supported by rate fund contributions and was specifically designed to reduce rent levels. But at this time council housing was occupied as Bowley suggests by, '... better-off families, the small clerks, the artisans, the better-off semi-skilled workers with small families and fairly safe jobs.'[7] Studies of tenants in London and Liverpool both revealed a

5   Finnigan, R 'Council houses in Leeds, 1919–39: social policy and urban change' in Daunton (ed) *Councillors and Tenants: Local Authority Housing in English Cities, 1919–39* (Leicester University Press, 1984), p109.

6   Burnett, J *A Social History of Housing 1815–1985* (Methuen, 1986), p234.

7   Bowley, M *Housing and the State 1919–1944* (Allen and Unwin, 1945), p129.

similar pattern in the social composition of council housing. Burnett cites research in Liverpool which showed that 20% of the occupants were non-manual workers.[8] There were, of course, variations in this situation.

Once subsidy contributions became fixed amounts (they were variable under the Addison finances) central government was generally uninterested in local authority rent setting policies, so some authorities tried to allocate to poorer households but at the cost of reducing building standards. There is no question, however, that it was not until the slum clearance programme of the 1930s that poor working class households accessed council housing in large numbers. The affordability problem for the mass of poor and, increasingly unemployed, working classes was not solved by council housing in the 1920s.

Slum clearance

The absence of any sustained support for council housing is clearly apparent in the abandonment of general needs building in the 1930s. Against a background of economic crisis and mass unemployment (3,000,000 by 1931) the second Labour Government was increasingly limited in its ability and will to continue the provision of general needs council housing. As we have suggested standards were already falling and at the very least were variable across the country well before the shift in policy made by Labour to tackle the slum problem, which was now urgent. The new government defended the Wheatley subsidies from the threatened termination and through the Housing Act 1930 introduced a new subsidy to encourage local authorities to clear slums and rebuild. The clear intention was to upgrade the conditions of the millions of slum dwellers so far untouched by 'general needs' council housing. Local authorities were required to submit plans for their slum clearance programme to be achieved in five years. The subsidies were related to the number of people being displaced, and this was useful in helping larger families to be re-housed. Budgetary constraints and the low incomes of these households meant that such a programme was going to be of limited scope and was achieved only at the expense of further reducing the design and building standards, which included the more widespread use of flats – a significant departure from the Tudor Walters Manual.

The 1930 Act also required local authorities to set 'reasonable' rents with powers to set up rent rebate schemes. The aim here was to enable authorities to charge lower rents to poor families at the expense of the better off. Subsidies would thus be more focused on the less well-off. Rent rebates

8 Burnett, J *A Social History of Housing 1815–1985* (Methuen, 1986), p238.

were not popular with the tenants who saw them as divisive and degrading (they were means-tested by the Public Assistance Boards). Indeed, a large and successful rent strike was mounted by tenants in Birmingham against such a scheme. Local authorities were not, in any case, particularly motivated to let to poor tenants. As Malpass and Murie suggest, '... from the point of view of a landlord, better-off tenants are an easier proposition.'[9] The introduction of housing revenue accounts through the 1935 Housing Act sought to compel local authorities to use rebate schemes – subsidies under the different Acts were pooled into a single account and rents were related to the use-value of different types of dwellings – thus, in theory, enabling councils to charge differential rents irrespective of the origins of the subsidy for particular houses. But very few authorities had schemes running by the outbreak of war in 1939.

The commitment to generally subsidised council housing continued for a while through the reduced Wheatley Act subsidies, but the Labour Prime Minister, Ramsey MacDonald, sabotaged his own party over the issue of expenditure cuts, and joined a Conservative-dominated 'National' Government – which held office from 1931 until the end of the war in 1945. This government abolished the Wheatley subsidies in 1933 so that the only subsidy for council housing between 1933 and 1939 was for slum clearance. The long-standing trend to reduced standards was confirmed in what in effect was a 'residual' role for council housing not dissimilar to its pre-1919 position. Housing policy for most of the 1930s thus abandoned the notion of general responsibility for supporting working class housing beyond the commitment to slum clearance. Between 1932 and 1935 council housing fell from about one third of new building to only one eighth. It was argued that, in addition to the public expenditure crisis, the boom in private housing construction, mostly for sale to owner occupiers, was such that government no longer needed to provide for general housing. As the new middle classes moved out to the private suburbs so their vacated byelaw terraces would filter down. The slum clearance subsidy would provide for the needs of those in the very worst housing and unable to move in the market. In practice the Greenwood subsidies (Greenwood was Labour's Minister of Health and responsible for the Housing Act 1930) provided nowhere near enough new dwellings to meet the need of the millions of families living in the squalid inner cities of Britain, trapped by the grip of economic depression. By 1939 a total of only 265,000 new council houses had been built under the slum clearance programme. The limited achievement is revealed by the fact that during the same period (1933–39) the number of houses built in the privately rented sector was more than the total council house programme.[10] Investors

9   Malpass P and Murie A *Housing Policy and Practice* (2nd edn) (Macmillan, 1987), p64.

10   Kemp, P 'From solution to problem? Council housing and the development of national housing policy' in S Lowe and D Hughes (eds) *A New Century of Social Housing* (Leicester University Press, 1991), p50.

took advantage of the very favourable conditions for building, stimulating a temporary but significant revival in private renting. Between 1934–35 and 1938–39 about 66,000 houses per annum were built for new private renting.[11] This revival further supports our view that the collapse of the privately rented sector was not principally a function of rent controls, although the economic position of private landlords was impaired by controls. New houses to rent were not subject to rent controls. It is the decline in the long-term investment potential of this sector of housing that is the root of the problem.

The situation in 1939

The overall picture of change in the inter-war years is dramatic. By 1939 very nearly one third of the housing stock was new. The local authority contribution to this was substantial and since 1919 councils had built 1,112,000 houses and flats, representing one quarter of new construction and accommodating one in ten households. But this achievement is highly qualified as we have seen by the prevarications about the role of council building, its financing, its standards and above all by the fact that until well into the 1930s very few poor working class families benefited, and even then by lower quality dwellings. The Poor Law principle of 'less eligibility' is close to the surface of housing policy at this time. Malpass and Murie argue that these lower standards were part of the drive to establish home ownership as the normal housing tenure for all but the poorest left as an 'undeserving' class of people in a residual public sector.[12]

Indeed, in the 20 years before 1939 the private builders had put in place very nearly 3 million dwellings, 430,000 of which were built with state aid. Moreover, so poor was the investment return that over one million privately rented dwellings were sold by landlords, commonly to sitting tenants.[13] The net effect, including losses through slum clearance, was that the privately rented sector lost about half a million dwellings. Owner occupation grew by 2.9 million dwellings by the combination of new building (60%) and sales from private renting (40%) and was clearly in the ascendant. By 1939 the owner occupied housing stock accounted for 32% of total dwellings. Although private renting remained the majority tenure (58% of dwellings) it was being eclipsed by home ownership and by council housing, a pattern of tenure restructuring that was to accelerate after 1945. Indeed, the polarisation between public housing for rent and private housing for sale was to become a feature of the post-1945 era. For the working class poor very

11 Merrett, S *Owner Occupation in Britain*, London, Routledge and Kegan Paul 1982, p14.

12 Malpass P and Murie A *Housing Policy and Practice* (2nd edn) (Macmillan, 1987), p64.

13 Merrett, S *Owner Occupation in Britain* (Routledge and Kegan Paul, 1982), p62.

little had changed through the 1920s and '30s and those that had not escaped to the suburbs continued to live in adequate but comfortless 'byelaw houses' and many millions more in the downwardly spiralling sub-standard conditions of the inner city. There was still much to be done.

After World War Two

It was, indeed, some time before the needs of low income households living in the Victorian slums were seriously addressed and for more than a decade following the end of the war the main emphasis in housing policy was to address the chronic problem of shortages of supply. The solutions adopted were not significantly different from those of the inter-war period and the role of public sector housing continued to be, in essence, to fill the gap left by the continued decline of the privately rented sector. Housing output contracted rapidly after 1939 as the nation went onto a war footing. Any new works had to be licensed by ministerial order and the number of workers in the building industry fell dramatically. Very little new construction took place for the duration and normal repair and maintenance was severely constrained. Repair of war damaged property was, however, quite considerable and was aided by a system of war damage compensation. The Blitz in 1940 and the 'doodlebug' attacks in 1944 destroyed or rendered uninhabitable 475,000 dwellings and damaged a further 3.5 million.

More important than this was the dramatic increase in the number of new household formations arising from early marriages (two million during the six war years) and also from an increase in family dissolutions. Holmans estimates that there was a shortfall of two million dwellings by 1945 including a large number of concealed households, people living with families and friends.[14] In addition the condition of the slums remained untouched and deteriorating. At the time even the Ministry of Reconstruction estimated a figure of half a million new dwellings to cater for replacement slums and overcrowding. During the war years the birth rate grew very sharply and by 1946 the population of Britain, despite the war casualties, had grown by over a million. There was, thus, a severe shortage of housing supply caused mainly by a massive increase in demand and this problem was the context for the housing policies of the next two decades.

The 1945 Labour Government

The Labour Party won the July 1945 election on a tide of popular belief that the sacrifices of the war years should lead to a renewal in Britain's social

14 Holmans A E *Housing Policy in Britain* (Croom Helm, 1987), p92.

and economic life. The disparity in supply and demand, the shortages of manpower and materials in the construction industry and the dangers of an inflationary explosion were formidable. The immediate response was to continue building controls and the private sector was controlled through a system of licensing. The minister in charge of the emergency situation was Aneurin Bevan, Minister of Health. Bevan was vociferously opposed to the role of the private sector saying that he refused to let the private developers, '... suck at the teats of the state' and that they were essentially an '... unplannable instrument.'[15] The programme of reconstruction was to focus on the needs of working class families and would operate through authorities. His vision was similar to that of John Wheatley, arguing forcefully for a housing policy that was not socially divisive. In essence Bevan argued that local authority housing should provide for all social classes and that the speculative building industry should supply under a system of licences to complement wider policy objectives. Unlike Wheatley, Bevan was not concerned to nationalise the privately rented sector but war-time rent controls were retained in order to allow control of that sector in the overall strategy. The control of land and speculative gain was additionally limited through the Town and Country Planning Act 1947 which, while stopping short of the election manifesto commitment to, '... work towards land nationalisation' introduced a 100% betterment levy on the changed value of land arising from the granting of planning permission.

In the event the Labour Government oversaw the building of 1,017,000 dwellings before it was defeated in the election of 1951. 146,000 of these were 'pre-fabs' built in 1946–47 but nevertheless this scale of programme was impressive and was the first large-scale positive investment in public housing since the Wheatley legislation. 80% of dwellings completed during Labour's terms of office were built in the authority sector. It should be noted that the high quality of both 'Wheatley' and 'Bevan' housing reflects the vision of two socialist politicians who both held Ministerial office at a time of national political crisis following wars. It is this, as Malpass and Murie suggest, that answers the question '... of why governments should choose to build the best houses at the most difficult times, and to reduce standards later on.'[16]

Nevertheless the 1945 Labour Government fell considerably short of what might have been achieved and what, indeed, was needed. This was largely to do with the inability of the government to exert sufficient control over its development programme due to reliance on private companies to undertake most of the construction. The problem was that authorities had to rely on the response of the companies for the fulfilment of their projects.

15 Quoted in Foot, M *Aneurin Bevan* (Granada, 1975), Vol 2, p71.
16 Malpass P and Murie A *Housing Policy and Practice* (2nd edn) (Macmillan, 1987), p73.

Labour and materials shortages compounded this problem and the very severe winter of 1946–47 also held up the building programme. These difficulties led to restrictions being imposed on tender approvals in 1947 and a further round of constraints were implemented following the economic crisis of 1948. Local authorities achieved a level of 100,000 dwellings in 1948 but the government fell very far short of its target – by as much as 240,000 units per annum – and one of the main causes of Labour's defeat in the 1951 election was dissatisfaction with its record on housing. Despite the high quality of the 'Bevan' houses the quantity of production was seriously lagging given the massive scale of demand.

The Conservative Party's pledge to build 300,000 houses by a combination of public and private provision was a major plank of their election victory. Moreover in the thirteen years of Conservative government public sector housing completions never fell below 100,000. Harold Macmillan, the Minister for Housing and Local Government, outlined a strategy which favoured the expansion of owner occupation but accepted the need for authorities to make up any deficits in production targets. Initially this meant that the council house programme was in the ascendant and council starts increased sharply from 171,000 in 1951 to 231,000 in 1953 during which year the Conservative's pledge to build 300,000 houses was redeemed. This, however, was achieved by decimating the building and design standards insisted on by Bevan and, although numerically dominant for a few years, the slashing of standards shows the essentially residualist policy for the public housing sector that was the intention of national housing policy throughout the period of Conservative government to 1964. In the private sector licensing was gradually phased out and abolished in November 1954. The Town and Country Planning Act 1953 abolished the betterment levy and the combination of the ending of controls on building and land supply created the conditions for the second 20th century boom in construction for owner occupation. Building starts in the private sector broke the 100,000 barrier in 1954 and accelerated year on year to peak at 247,000 in 1964 and was never far short of 200,000 up to the mid-1970s. Advances by building societies grew in conjunction with this boom era in home ownership. Personal disposable income grew from £377 per annum in 1948 to £581 in 1965. Inflation was modest and unemployment by the standards of the 1930s and the 1980s and 1990s was very low. Macmillan was not far short of the truth when he told the nation that 'they had never had it so good'. It was by no means the whole truth as the evidence of the growth of homelessness in the early 1960s was to demonstrate.

Once the private sector boom took hold, during 1954, the basic function allotted to the public sector became clear. As private building accelerated so the programme of council house building declined. Thus by 1961 local authorities built the relatively modest total of 105,000 dwellings, less than half their 1954 output. At this time the surging output of the private sector convinced the government that the problem of the slums could now be tackled once again, having been held in abeyance since 1939. This development further served to underpin the essentially residual role of public housing. The policy was stated unequivocally by Macmillan, 'Local authorities and local authorities alone can clear and rehouse the slums, while the general housing need can be met, as it was to a great extent before the war, by private enterprise.'[17] The Housing Repair and Rents Act 1954 restarted the slum clearance programme and encouraged private sector improvement. It was made increasingly clear that authorities had no general needs function and it was no surprise that in the 1956 Housing Subsidies Act the general needs subsidy was all but abolished. Subsidy was retained only for slum clearance and for the construction of one-bedroomed flats for the elderly.

Two other elements in the reorientation of policy in the mid-1950s were important. First, rent policy from 1955 began to compel local authorities to increase their rents towards market levels, called 'realistic rents', and to protect low income households by the increased use of rent rebate schemes. This policy intensified over the years and gradually lead to the ending of 'bricks and mortar' subsidies in favour of targeted means-tested benefits for low income families. Housing subsidies in other words became more closely attached to, and for a while paid by, the social security system.

The high-rise era

The second innovation was contained in the 1956 Act and concerns the encouragement given through the subsidy system to local authorities to build high-rise flats. The era of mass council house building was about to take on a very literal form. Experiments with prefabricated technologies by a number of the major construction companies made it appear that high-rise building, particularly in inner city slum clearance areas where space was limited and land relatively expensive, would solve the problem of high output combined with low cost. Le Corbusier's vision of 'machines for living in' suddenly found support, particularly in Labour controlled local authorities in London and some north of England cities, as the answer to mass housing. It is clear that this 'solution' played into the hands of a resurgent building industry dominated by relatively few giant companies and that a high proportion of high-rise blocks were built by only half a dozen companies.[18] The grandiose vision of architects and politicians incurred great cost to working class social and community life and further damaged

17 Quoted in Samuel et al 'But nothing happens', in *New Left Review,* 1962.
18 Dunleavy, P *The Politics of Mass Housing in Britain 1945–75* (Clarendon Press, 1981).

the already fragile legitimacy of public housing. This housing was out of touch with the shape and pattern of working class life which it replaced and architects and politicians rarely lived in it. To an extent the new mass housing did offer a home and haven for millions of people away from the Victorian slums but the social cost was very great and many of the worst and most gargantuan schemes were out of date and spiralling downwards into housing estates typified by social deprivation almost before they were complete. At the peak of the high-rise boom in 1966 blocks of flats over five storeys high accounted for over a quarter of public sector building approved for construction by central government and in some places a much higher share. For example, in the GLC area 91% of completions in 1967 were flats and two-thirds of these were high-rise blocks.[19]

Financial packages were offered which tied local authorities into huge debt repayment costs and undermined rent systems as tenants were called on to pay a higher and higher share of their rent in effect as interest payments to the financial institutions. This was not after all a cheap solution, and in the wake of the Ronan Point disaster in 1967 – when a tower block in the London Borough of Newham partially collapsed following a gas explosion, killing 13 people – and arriving at a point in time when the worst of the post-war shortages appeared to have been dealt with, the era of high-rise construction terminated abruptly. The construction of prefabricated maisonettes and low-rise blocks of flats persisted into the 1970s, accounting for nearly 40% of approvals in 1970.

The 1957 Rent Act

Earlier in the chapter we argued that the structural decline of the privately rented sector was a key to understanding the need for and the expansion of public housing. The revival of private renting was an additional feature of Conservative housing policy in the 1950s and continued to follow the logic of Chamberlain in the 1920s, that private landlordism was really in temporary abeyance until 'normal' circumstances returned. The Rent Act 1957 was the new incarnation of this belief and was the third strand in the web of Conservative housing policy. The principal emphasis was on private sector solutions to general needs housing supported by a residual role for public housing. The latter was focused on slum clearance and housing for the elderly, neither of which could be achieved at the minimum acceptable standard within the profit margins of the private construction industry. The significance in an account of public sector housing of the 1957 Act relates, as we shall see, to its failure to revive the privately rented sector. This failure compelled the Conservatives to re-think their strategy towards council

19 Power A *Property Before People* (Allen and Unwin, 1987), p45.

housing in the early 1960s leading to the reintroduction of general needs housing subsidies for local authorities. A new housing crisis emerged at this time with increasing evidence of the growth of homelessness.

As we argue above, it was the poor economic return available to private landlords that led over the long term to the demise of the privately rented sector. Within this general situation one of the contributory factors to its decline was rent control and the associated guarantees of security of tenure for tenants. Various modifications to the blanket controls introduced in 1915 were enacted in the 1920s particularly an element of decontrol introduced in the Housing Act 1923. Some tightening followed in 1933 but newly built private rental housing was not subject to control at any time. This patchwork of controls over rents in the private sector was put on ice in 1939 when all rents were frozen at their September levels for the duration of the conflict, and, in fact, this level of control remained virtually untouched until the Rent Act 1957. The aim of the 1957 Act was to allow landlords greater freedom in rent setting by the decontrol of tenancies of certain rateable values and new tenancies. The intention here was to establish a creeping decontrol of the sector and so bring about the expected revival of private landlordism. In fact there is no evidence that this happened and on the contrary in so far as tenants had to pay higher rents they were induced into owner occupation, and as house prices began to accelerate landlords were encouraged to sell into the market, preferably on vacant possession. The spectre of Rachmanism (so named after a large-scale private landlord in London who induced tenants through unscrupulous harassment into new agreements or sometimes to vacate property) haunted the 1957 Act: the image of private landlordism was tarnished further by Rachman and the seedier elements in the sector. Private landlordism did not 'revive' as had been forecast by the government and, as Kemp suggests, 'Decontrol thus proved to be a necessary, but not a sufficient, condition for the return of the private investor in rented housing.'[20]

The new housing crisis

By the early 1960s the government was forced to reconsider its *laissez-faire* strategy in the face of the evidence on homelessness and the further decline in private renting following the 1957 Act. The Housing Acts of 1961 and 1964 gave authorities considerably enhanced powers to compel landlords of multiply-occupied houses to undertake repair and improvement of the property. Renewal policy was no more successful than attempted

20 Kemp, P 'From solution to problem? Council housing and the development of national housing policy' in S Lowe and D Hughes (eds) *A New Century of Social Housing* (Leicester University Press, 1991), p53.

deregulation and from about this time it was recognised that housing renewal in the private sector was not going to be achieved through reliance on landlords. Grants to owner occupiers were, by contrast, up to 70,000 per annum in the early 1960s and in order to avoid the further degeneration of the housing stock it became apparent that the promotion of home ownership and renewal were inter-dependent. More important here is the point that the continuing failure of private landlords to supply general needs rented housing and evidence of an increase in homelessness forced the government to reconsider the role of authorities. They published a White Paper, (*Housing in England and Wales*, HMSO, 1961) and in the following legislation, Housing Act 1961, general needs subsidies were reintroduced, although at two rates and in a complex system of local calculations. In order to demonstrate that private renting could be made to work and in the absence of any significant return on investment the 1961 Act made loans available for establishing cost-rent housing societies, now called 'associations'. With the election approaching the Conservatives pushed further in this direction and in the Housing Act 1964 set up the Housing Corporation aimed at encouraging housing associations to build for letting at cost rents and with powers to borrow up to £100 million a year from the Treasury. The encouragement of a so called 'third arm' of provision through the revival of housing associations was held in check, however, as a result of the 1964 election which returned a Labour Government under Harold Wilson.

'The party of council housing'?

Housing was a key issue in the 1964 general election and Labour under Harold Wilson won on a manifesto which included a commitment to build 500,000 houses. This period of Labour government, however, was not to be a return to the visionary years of Wheatley or Bevan. In the 13 years since 1951 the Conservatives had sustained the role of the local authorities albeit reluctantly. Indeed far more council houses had been built under Conservative or Conservative dominated coalition governments than under Labour. Labour nevertheless were known as the 'party of council housing' but during the 1960s they began to distance themselves from this image and at some considerable pace. When they returned to power in 1964 their policy stance, compared to the 1945 government, was radically different. Merrett probably overstates the position when he says that, 'The main shift was to accept the residualist principle of Toryism.'[1] The evidence needs to be evaluated with care. In the Housing White Paper 1965 council housing is pigeon-holed into a number of defined roles,

---

1   Merrett, S *Owner Occupation in Britain* (Routledge and Kegan Paul, 1982), p42.

'The Expansion of the public programme now proposed is to meet exceptional circumstances; it is born partly out of short-term necessity, partly out of the conditions inherent in modern urban life. The of building for owner occupation *on the other hand is normal.*' (emphasis added)[2]

It seems most probable that this statement reflects several somewhat contradictory processes which were inherent in the circumstances of the mid-1960s. Principal among these was that the nation was reaching the period which marked the end of the post-war shortages. There was, for example, significant weakening in demand for council housing illustrated in the emergence of so called 'difficult to let' estates.

Initially, however, the expansion referred to above took place under Labour's 'National Housing Plan' and the rate of council house building accelerated for several years reaching a post-war peak of 180,000 in 1967. This programme was reined back following the devaluation of the pound in November 1967 and never really recovered its former pre-eminence at any subsequent stage. The planned 500,000 dwellings was dropped quietly from the policy statements as the economic crisis bit very deeply into Labour's social programme.

An indication of Labour's approach can be seen in the improved building standards which were made mandatory in 1969 with the adoption of the 1961 Parker Morris Report – which recommended an optional standards yardstick. The report argued for increased space standards so that modern families could experience greater privacy, have more storage room and, noting changing social habits, advocated larger kitchens where families could sit to eat meals and a generally more flexible use of living space which at the time was quite radical and certainly anticipated and encouraged new perceptions of the home'. Technical issues were also highlighted in the report, particularly the need for better heating standards. In fact a high proportion of local authority dwellings built in the mid-1960s already met these standards. The mandatory adoption of Parker Morris standards is, however, illustrative of Labour's pragmatically supportive approach to council housing.

Nevertheless, the use of this standard became tangled into the need to reduce the building programme due to economic crisis. The Parker Morris standard caused a significant increase in building costs (Burnett suggests evidence of up to 15%)[3] and so itself became a cause of the reduced building programme. More important, a cost yardstick was introduced in 1963 by the Ministry of Housing. It involved a sliding scale of subsidies which compared house size with number of occupants – higher densities attracted

2   *The Housing Programme 1965–70* (Cmnd 2838, HMSO, 1965).
3   Burnett, J *A Social History of Housing 1815–1985* (Methuen, 1986), p309.

more subsidy – and was controlled, within Parker Morris minimum standards, by central government. In effect the yardstick operated as a mechanism for regulating tender approvals and so the rate of building output. Labour was thus still supportive of council housing and good quality production but increasingly were enmeshed in financial problems. Good intentions tempered by financial realities seems to sum up their position and it is clearly not the case that they saw no future role for council housing or that their attitude was 'residualist'; seeing council housing as a last resort for people unable to access the market.

From redevelopment to rehabilitation

Community action was also a feature of the major change in the direction of housing policy this time announced in a White Paper 'Old Houses into New Homes'[4] signalling the switch away from slum clearance and general re-housing towards the private rehabilitation of the housing stock through the voluntary take-up of improvement grants. Resistance had built up to the most excessive mass slum clearance 'rolling programmes' now threatening to engulf areas which by no stretch of the imagination could be considered to be slums. Residents' associations and community action groups sprang up nationwide to resist the onslaught of the bulldozer.[5] Because slum clearance was specifically an authority role the era of local authority housing as the agency for this task was drawing to a close. As Kemp observes, 'The switch to rehabilitation removed a significant part of the demand for new local authority housing.'[6]

As we pointed out earlier in the chapter this is also the period which coincided with the growing dissatisfaction and disillusionment with high rise housing. Families with children and elderly people found this form of living difficult and even dangerous. Costs were much higher than initially forecast by the construction companies and were causing authorities severe problems with their housing revenue accounts because debt charges were consuming an increasingly large share of their resources. Some city councils with large building programmes found that the whole of their rental income was spent on interest repayments. This issue underlay a gathering tide of resentment among the tenants themselves and the period was marked by a series of rent strikes culminating in the overthrow of Labour councils

4   *Old Houses into New Homes* (Cmnd 3602, HMSO, 1968).
5   Lowe S G *Urban Social Movements: the city after Castells* (Macmillan, 1986).
6   Kemp, P 'From solution to problem? Council housing and the development of national housing policy' in S Lowe and D Hughes (eds) *A New Century of Social Housing* (Leicester University Press, 1991), p55.

in several cities, notably Sheffield which fell to the Conservatives in 1968–69 for the first time since Labour took control of the city council in 1926.[7] So it was that the disillusionment with high rise housing, community action of various sorts, the severe economic crisis facing the mid-term Wilson government and declining demand saw public sector housing, now responsible for housing nearly a third of the population, reach a significant turning point. Labour's National Housing Plan was in tatters and private rehabilitation of the existing housing stock gradually supplanted public redevelopment as the principal plank of housing policy and marked the end of the high out-put era.

The Housing Act 1969 accordingly introduced General Improvement Areas and the Housing Act 1974 added Housing Action Areas in which grants for house improvement were supplemented by environmental improvements. This policy, pursued by the second Wilson and then the Callaghan Government (1974–79), in fact conceals a significant withdrawal of state expenditure on housing. By 1977 public sector completions had fallen to a post-war low of only 88,000. The withdrawal of investment in the development programme, often associated with the Thatcher governments after 1979, was in fact a well established trend under Wilson and Callaghan. These cuts were closely connected to the worsening economic situation in the country and were a direct consequence of restrictions on state expenditure imposed by the International Monetary Fund in December 1976. This changed environment for housing finance led to a stricter system of cash limited controls on local authority capital expenditure, administered through an annual housing investment programme.

Thus the dominant theme during this period was the problem of housing finance. It was a confusing picture and the general thrust of housing finance was unclear with controls on rent increases, interest rates rising sharply and the scale of tax reliefs to owner occupiers generating an increasingly regressive system of housing finance, by which high income owner occupiers gained compared to standard rate tax payers because relief was obtained at the highest tax threshold of the mortgagor. Subsidy was also being clawed back from the public sector and so financial gain accrued to better-off households both within the home ownership sector and between home owners and council tenants. A major review of housing finance was accordingly established, but events moved quickly and when the Housing Policy Review Green Paper appeared in 1977 a general pattern of all party consensus had emerged and spending controls on local authorities were already well established. For historians of housing policy this document is of more than passing significance for it encapsulates Labour's thinking on housing policy at this time and is generally regarded as a conservative paper, particularly regarding their advocacy of home ownership.[8]

7   Lowe S G *Urban Social Movements: the city after Castells* (Macmillan, 1986), p89.
8   *Housing Policy: A Consultative Document* (Cmnd 6851, HMSO, 1977).

Let it be clear, however, that the 1977 Housing Policy Review argued quite strongly for the continuation of the public sector as a major supplier of housing, albeit it at lower levels of output than in the past and more targeted at locally identified needs rather than large scale national plans. The Green Paper emphasised the need for a more pluralistic approach to these smaller scale needs incorporating housing associations and the private sector as main providers in such circumstances. There can be no doubt that Labour sought to narrow the scope and role of public housing, and sustain the existing trends in the tenure structure focused on the expansion of owner occupation. But, as we have suggested at several points in our account, the document needs to be read carefully and within the context of the longer term trends. Forrest and Murie's characterisation of the 1977 Green Paper as, '... Labour's capitulation to owner occupation and acceptance of a limited, residual role for council housing.'[9] is an exaggerated position. The Green Paper described the historic role local authorities across the country had in ameliorating the squalor of the Victorian slums and demonstrated the impact council housing had had in raising housing standards. Labour still regarded authorities as bastions of this long campaign and that they still had an important future role to play, albeit in new circumstances and in a more pluralistic housing system.

Labour and owner occupation

Before turning to discuss the approach of the Conservative governments (Heath, Thatcher and Major) in this new era of reduced shortages there remains the as yet unanswered question of Labour's attitude to home ownership. Labour's advocacy of owner occupation was, by the late-1970s, well established. In that sense the 1977 Green Paper is a statement of a long-standing position and not a 'capitulation'. It was never supposed that council housing would be the only form of provision and that under normal circumstances owner occupation would be the principal form of supply. Indeed, later on, in the 1965 White Paper, Labour described home ownership as 'a long-term social advance' and contrasted the public housing programme (which it was argued should focus on short-term necessity and on exceptional needs) with the more normal 'expansion of building for owner-occupation'.[10] Richard Crossman, the Labour Housing Minister at this time was keenly aware of the need to limit his party's identification as the party of council housing, partly out of sheer electoral necessity. Owner occupiers were by the mid-1960s nearly a majority of voters. In his famous Diaries Crossman

9   Forrest R and Murie A *Selling the Welfare State: The Privatisation of Public Housing* (Routledge, 1990), p32.
10   *The Housing Programme 1965–70* (Cmnd 2838, HMSO, 1965).

wrote that, '... we only build council houses where it is clear they are needed' and he went on to say that the main aim of Labour's housing policy should be to encourage owner occupation.[11] Labour was thus firmly committed to reforms in all the main housing tenures, but by the mid-1960s had a clear vision of home ownership as a symbol of social advance.

During the period of the first Harold Wilson government the fiscal advantages of owner occupation were further enhanced, following the abolition of Schedule 'A' taxation on the imputed rental income of the home owner in 1963 by the Conservatives. Home owners were exempted from paying capital gains tax on the sale of their principal dwelling, tax relief was retained for home improvements, and mortgage interest tax relief was retained when most other forms of tax reliefs were abolished. In the light of the abolition of Schedule 'A' taxation this meant that owner occupiers with mortgages were in effect being subsidised for the purchase of the dwelling as consumers and because they paid no capital gains tax reaped a considerable financial gain as investors. In order to widen the social base of home ownership a system of 'Option Mortgages' was introduced in the Housing Subsidies Act 1967 and allowed both local authorities and building societies to offer mortgages at 2% lower than the standard rate for households on low incomes. Option mortgages thus enabled lenders to increase the amounts they loaned or reduce monthly payments of people of 'modest incomes'. The main form of subsidy to owner occupiers, through tax relief on their mortgage payments, was not available to non-taxpayers who by default were excluded from fiscal subsidy. This series of measures considerably enhanced the position of owner occupiers but caused, as we have shown, imbalances in housing subsidies which now favoured home owners against public tenants and was generally regressive.

There was, in short, no doubting Labour's commitment to owner occupation. Neither should it be doubted that their view of council housing was quite distinctive from that of the Conservatives. They saw it as a necessary contribution to meeting the housing needs of the nation and this was as much the case in 1979 as it was in 1945. However, in a period which was no longer dominated by the shortages issue and where the worst slums had been demolished there was a considerable degree of agreement between the two parties in the mid-1970s about the general drift of housing policy with home ownership and provision through the market as its cornerstone. The idea that there was a major reversal in Labour's position at this time is not a wholly justifiable case because home ownership had always been recognised by them as a central feature of British housing. Where the two major parties most sharply diverged was over the treatment of the privately rented sector, with Labour at this time looking to housing associations as an alternative to private renting.

11 Cited in Boddy, M *The Building Societies* (Macmillan, 1980), p19.

The last important housing measure taken before the advent of the Thatcher governments was the Housing (Homeless Persons) Act of 1977. It may be thought ironical that at a time when council building had reached a post-war low this measure was enacted. In it local authorities were given duties to house very specifically defined groups of 'deserving' homeless people – households with dependent children, 'vulnerable' people such as the elderly, and people made homeless due to an emergency such as a flood or fire (see Chapter Six). As we saw earlier in the chapter there had been mounting evidence of a growing problem of homelessness through the 1960s and 1970s but this was not seen as a 'housing' problem, rather one arising from the isolated difficulties of individual families in local housing markets. The main housing related issue was regarded as the continued decline of private renting. The attempted decontrol of the privately rented sector under the Conservative administrations was halted by Labour through the Rent Act 1965, which gave security of tenure in unfurnished accommodation and introduced a 'fair rents' system, through which rents were set by rent officers according to the type and quality of the property but excluding consideration of local market conditions. This allowed for a controlled increase in rent levels in the private sector.

Housing subsidies under the Conservatives

One of the consequences of this new system of rent setting was that very soon private sector rents were accelerating away from those in the public sector and as a result there was some concern about this disparity and the role of subsidies in the public sector. With the return to power of the Conservatives under Edward Heath in 1970 this issue became a major focal point of policy in which the aim was to reduce the distorting effect created by the disparity between the two sectors. The apparent advantage enjoyed by the public sector was to be terminated, although it should be added that alternative approaches which built on the historic cost subsidy system were never on the policy agenda. This subsidy reduced the debt burden on the properties and in turn led to lower rents. Once development capital had been paid off at the end of the loan period the houses were debt free and, in theory, rents needed only to cover management and maintenance costs. The maturing in this way of the rental structure in public housing had been used in other countries, notably in Scandinavia, to decease rents in the whole rental system both public and private. The response to this in Britain was rather different with anxieties expressed about the threat such a declining public sector rent structure might have on the private rental market (ie the public sector would become more popular). In effect this was politically unacceptable particularly at a time when market economics was in the ascendant. The issue of what to do with public sector rents was resolved by linking their calculation to prices in the private sector, with an implication of much higher rents supported by means tested rent rebates. Eventually council house rents were pegged to local house prices, although with a need for considerable 'dampening' in high house price areas. The resolution of the issue in this way was a reassertion of the standard Conservative view which was always reluctant to accept a large and growing public housing sector, even though the failure of the privately rented sector to revive made such an expansion inevitable.

In a similar vein the government removed restrictions on the sale of council houses to sitting tenants which had been in force since 1968. Converting council housing to owner occupation and drawing the rents in the public sector closer to the market were different strands of a common policy stance. The aim was both to reduce public expenditure on subsidies to council housing and to make council housing more expensive, with protection for worse off tenants through a mandatory rent rebate system.

The legislative instrument for dealing with public sector rents was the Housing Finance Act 1972. Local authority discretion in rent setting was largely removed and council rents were linked to the 'fair rent' system operating in the privately rented sector since the Rent Act 1965. To protect poorer tenants from the consequences of increasing rents a mandatory rent rebate system was also introduced. The significance of this was that it foreshadowed the system of housing finance which was to become a feature of Thatcherite housing policy; an emphasis on means-tested targeted subsidies to individuals – operated through the social security system – rather than 'bricks and mortar' subsides for housing construction. This had been inherent in the housing finance system since the adoption of rent pooling in the mid-1950s, but the 1972 Act, although short-lived, signalled the direction of future policy and is an important juncture in the history of public housing because it established a clear break from the 'historic cost' system of public housing finance which had operated since 1923. As Malpass points out the 1972 Act breached at least three long established conventions by providing that: existing subsidies should be phased out; rents should be set in relation to current incomes and house prices, and general subsidy should now be set on a deficit basis. Notional rents were to be calculated in advance, based on market principles, with the (lower) subsidy then paid in relation to the total of higher rental income and management and maintenance costs. When subsidies became fixed it was rent levels that were the flexible element in the calculation, and this led to considerable variations round the country depending on the quantity and age of the housing stock. Accordingly the 1972 Act introduced, for a while, a new logic which, as Malpass suggests, established a new way of thinking about rent setting and subsidy.

'The 1972 Act was too controversial and too flawed to, but it stands as a major landmark in the development of public sector housing finance.'[12]

In practice the economic climate was unfavourable to this change because interest rates were increasing sharply, construction costs and land prices were also accelerating and house prices rose. These conditions actually led to a slump in the private sector building industry and to many potential purchasers being unable to enter the market. Council house waiting lists grew. Thus although the purpose of the 1972 Act was to make public sector tenants pay higher, more market determined, rents and so reduce central subsidies the outcome once again was completely different from the intention. Subsidies grew by nearly 100% between 1972 and 1974 and although some Labour controlled authorities mounted a (largely unsuccessful) political campaign against the 'Fair Rent Act' – mostly focused on the rebate system and the centralisation of rent setting – many authorities were helped through a difficult financial period due to the protection afforded to low income tenants by the rebate system. Almost the first action of the incoming Labour government following the 1974 General Election was to abandon fair rents for council housing and the market orientation of the now curiously distorted subsidy system. A rent freeze was announced, with a return in law to the concept of 'reasonable rents', and Labour's National Housing Plan reinstated the general needs building programme via the '500,000' target.

The rise of housing associations

Although overshadowed by the political turmoil caused by the 1972 Act the fair rent system also applied to the tenants of housing associations and the Housing Corporation was given wider powers and increased resources to lend to associations. The Housing Corporation thus widened the scope of their activity away from the co-ownership projects and the so-called 'third arm' of provision of rental housing was set to emerge. Housing associations enjoyed all-party support at the national level, although continuing to be opposed by some mainly Labour local councillors who saw their growing role and funding as competition to the democratically mandated role of authorities. In principle, however, Labour's stance was to support the associations as an alternative to the privately rented sector while the Conservatives saw them as an alternative to the local authorities.

The introduction of Housing Association Grant (HAG) in the Housing Act 1974 gave the associations a completely different financial regime from

12   Malpass, P 'The financing of public housing' in S Lowe and D Hughes (eds) *A New Century of Social Housing* (Leicester University Press, 1991), p70.

the historic cost approach which had typified council house finance. Since the 1923 Housing Act authorities had been paid a subsidy per dwelling over a set number of years. This amount was predictable and, once paid, the burden of any expenditure increases or inefficiencies were the liability of the local authority. Under the HAG system associations were enabled to build schemes or renovate property and enjoy an almost complete write-off of the development costs at the beginning of the life of the project. Through the Housing Corporation and its accountancy controls central government was able to exert a considerable influence over what housing associations did and, as Best suggests, '... an important linkage had been created between the state and the voluntary sector.'[13] They were certainly more open to control than were authorities and it is largely for this reason that they grew in importance during the 1980s. Indeed the Housing Act 1980 further tightened the auditing and performance monitoring of associations. Thus, for example, in the period from the 1974 Act to the early 1980s their role was strongly redirected to rehabilitation, so that by 1979–80 nearly 40% of their completed schemes were of this type compared to only 6% in 1974–75.[14] The speed with which associations were able to move was also a factor in their new status and from a base of only 170,000 properties in 1970 they had grown by 1990 to over 600,000 homes, including 50,000 hostel places and shared housing schemes.

The Thatcher years

The Conservatives returned to their themes on housing subsidies with a vengeance after the election of the Thatcher government in 1979, although their agenda on housing ran much deeper than merely reforming the subsidy system. An important strand of Thatcherism was premised upon the belief that council housing was an inherently inferior form of housing provision compared to owner occupation and represented a stumbling block to the creation of a nation of home owners. It was council housing above all else that was the anathema of modern British society. At the end of three governments lead by Mrs Thatcher council housing had been radically changed both in the quantity of housing stock, the geography of its distribution and, above all in its social purpose. The long tradition of council housing established in 1919 and which by the 1970s catered for the housing needs of very nearly a third of the population came to an abrupt end. While the Labour governments under Wilson and Callaghan had both re-focused the emphasis of housing policy towards owner occupation these

---

13 Best R 'Housing Associations: 1890–1990' in S Lowe and D Hughes (eds) *A New Century of Social Housing* (Leicester University Press, 1991), p153.
14 Malpass, P and Murie, A *Housing Policy and Practice* (Macmillan, 1987), p170.

governments were not openly hostile to the council housing sector. Under Mrs Thatcher's influence the post-1979 era undoubtedly initiated a 'new era', because with almost unprecedented reforming zeal, the aim of Conservative housing policy was to break up council housing as a mainstream housing tenure. This policy turn was innovative even by the standards of post-war Conservative Party politics, which had never been positively supportive of council housing but had accepted its important role in the provision of rental accommodation given the seemingly inexorable decline of the privately rented sector. As we have seen far more council houses were built under Conservative administrations than under Labour and generally they had accepted that council housing had a distinctive purpose and role in meeting certain types of housing need and making provision for slum cleared families. In the 1980s and 1990s, however, the number of council houses fell year by year mainly as a result of the right to buy policy enacted in the Housing Act 1980. This gave secure tenants a statutory right to purchase their dwelling after three years occupancy with an immediate 33% discount and a 1% per annum sliding scale discount up to 50% on the market value of the property.

Sales of council houses had been permissible for long periods of time throughout the inter-war and post-war years. Indeed, as we saw earlier in the chapter, the very first 'council' housing, built under the terms of the Housing of the Working Classes Act 1890, incorporated the requirement that authorities should sell the properties into the private sector within ten years of their completion. In practice relatively few were sold because as time went by there was a general acceptance that municipally owned rental housing was a desirable, indeed, competitive form of provision. Sales of council houses in the inter-war period required Ministerial consent with a condition that authorities obtain the highest possible price for the property. After the Second World War sales policy had a chequered history, generally being more favourably treated under Conservative governments than Labour. A number of Conservative dominated local authorities, notably Birmingham, consistently promoted the idea. They were stalled in the late-1960s by a Labour government circular (42/68) which argued against sales on the grounds that it was unjustifiable to sell public assets for private gain. The circular was withdrawn by the Conservative government elected in 1970 and support for a positive sales policy grew with moves to increase the discount for what increasingly became known as 'right to buy' (RTB) sales from 20% to 30% of the property value. The boom in house prices, however, blunted the edge of this drift in policy because even at the higher level of discount prices were simply unaffordable for most tenants. During the Conservative government of 1970–1974 100,000 council houses were sold but most of them were replaced by newly built council properties. During the Wilson/Callaghan governments (1974–1979) the general consent to sell at 20% discount was retained and sales increased quite sharply, largely due to Conservative Party successes in local elections. In 1975 only 2,700 houses were sold but this rose steadily to over 30,000 in 1978. By now the Conservatives had adopted a housing policy which was overtly centred on the right of tenants to buy their dwelling and the Manifesto commitment for the 1979 election was clear and unequivocal in this regard.[15]

The Housing and Building Control Act 1984 reduced the qualifying period for 'the right to buy' to two years and enhanced the size of the discounts; tenants of flats, for example, were allowed up to a 70% discount. Within the decade well over a million houses had been sold and the share of council housing in the overall stock of dwellings had fallen from 31.5% to 23.6%. Sales of council housing subsequently accelerated, especially in south of England where house prices were high and the investment potential of home ownership was greatest.

Between 1980 and 1998 the housing stock in the United Kingdom increased by over three million dwellings and there was a radical redistribution in the balance of housing tenures. Owner occupation expanded by over 10% while council housing declined, mainly due to the right to buy, by almost two million properties. In 1980 local councils provided rental accommodation for nearly 31% of the nation's households. By 1998 the figure was only 18%. This dramatic quantitative decline has led simultaneously to a radical re-shaping of the social composition of the sector and to its social purpose. A brief résumé of the most important features of this will suffice to indicate the dramatic nature of this change. Generally sales have been of the most valuable, high quality suburban-style properties leaving the core stock disproportionately represented by high rise flats and low amenity inner city and peripheral estates. A much high proportion of sales has been in the south of England than elsewhere in the country. Its is also clear that in the two decades since the 1980 Act these properties have had a high re-sale value and have become integrated fully into the mainstream housing market. Research shows that former council houses have become attractive purchases for first time buyers and also to families moving *from* an owner occupied house. As Murie and Malpass suggest, 'Former council houses as a whole cannot be said to be at the bottom end of the owner-occupied market.'[16]

Most council house purchasers were middle-aged, white collar or skilled manual workers with grown up children. There is also clear evidence in the research studies that RTB purchasers were much better off than council tenants as a whole. This was especially the case in the south of England

---

15 A detailed account of the history of the 'right to buy' can be found in Malpass, P and Murie, A *Selling the Welfare State – The Privatisation of Council Housing* (Routledge, 1988).
16 Malpass, P and Murie, A *Housing Policy and Practice* (5th edn, Macmillan, 1999), p256.

where house prices had been and remain considerably higher then elsewhere. Conversely those households entering the public sector during this period were much more likely to be lone parents or young couples who generally regarded council housing as a temporary form of accommodation. Analysis of income and employment indices have shown a marked trend for the poorest households to be concentrated very disproportionately in council housing. For example 65% of households in the lowest three income deciles live in council housing compared to 16% of owner occupiers. It follows that the proportion of households with no earners or whose head of household is unemployed is also high. In 1991 63% of council tenants were non-earners and 20% of heads of households were unemployed (compared to 26% and 5% respectively for owner occupiers). In 1996/7 47.6% of council tenants derived their income from social security payments compared to 9.1% of owner occupiers (including outright owners who by definition tend to be older, having paid off their mortgages). In short council housing contains a very high percentage, by any measure, of our nation's poorest and most marginalised citizens. Moreover, the gap between the incomes of council tenants and owner occupiers has widened considerably since 1980. Average incomes of council tenants have grown from £68 per week to £131 between 1980 and 1996. For owner occupiers the figures are £111 and £302; the percentage change shows that in 1980 tenants' incomes were 61% of those of owner occupiers but by 1996 this figure had fallen to only 43%.[17]

There is also striking recent evidence that despite the fall in the size of the council housing sector the number of re-lets of vacant properties remains as high as it was in the 1980s. Pawson concludes that such high rates of turnover imply growing residential instability and a weakening of social cohesion.[18] We will comment further on the implications of this in the conclusion to this chapter but for now it is clear that the context in which public sector housing law is currently read has been radically re-shaped during the last twenty years compared to the long historical view.

The second strand of the housing strategy of the Thatcher governments was to prevent the replacement of properties sold under RTB. This was relatively easily achieved in line with the general strategy of public expenditure cuts. However, the axe fell with particular severity on the housing programme, initially through restraining the Housing Investment Programme (HIP) system. Capital spending on housing was cut by over 75% between 1979–80 and 1986–87. Rather perversely from the central government's point of view local authorities were accruing large amounts of capital receipts from the sale of council houses. As time went by the policy

17 *Housing Finance Review 98/99* (Joseph Rowntree Foundation), Table 34, p124.
18 Pawson, H 'The growth of residential instability and tenancy turnover' in Lowe, S, Spencer, S and Keenan, P (eds) *Housing Abandonment in Britain: studies in the causes and effects of low demand for housing* (Centre for Housing Policy, University of York, 1998).

instrument used for implementing the reduced capital programme (HIPs) became less effective. Even though capital spending was strictly controlled after 1980 to an extent authorities were able to circumvent the system by creative use of the proportion of capital receipts available to them and interest that was accruing. However, the 'new financial regime' introduced through the Local Government and Housing Act 1989 re-asserted the influence of central government. The fundamental point is that the role of local authorities as developers of large quantities of public housing came to an end, and councils looked to others, mainly housing associations but also private developers, to join with them in 'partnerships'.

The 'enabling role' and beyond

During the mid-1980s the government intensified its attack on local authorities as inefficient and overly bureaucratic managers. William Waldegrave, one of several Housing Ministers during this phase said that he saw no future role for council housing and that '... the next big push should be to get rid of the state as a big landlord and bring housing back to the community.'[19] Two reports by the Audit Commission severely criticised the performance of housing management and the local authorities' record on housing maintenance. This seemed to signal a new stage in the development of policy that was positively hostile to the very existence of council housing. This new phase, while continuing the promotion of owner occupation as the core policy, also included a growing recognition that the housing system needed a revived privately rented sector, if nothing else, in order to facilitate labour mobility during a period of considerable and growing disparities in regional house prices. This new phase was formalised after the 1987 General Election in a White Paper 'Housing Policy: the Government's Proposals'[20] and put on the statute book via the Housing Act 1988 and the Local Government and Housing Act 1989.

Key developments here concerned the role of authorities as 'enablers' and the determination of the government to 'demunicipalise' council housing by dispersing it in large chunks to other landlords in the private sector and to quasi-private housing associations. This package of legislation also enacted a 'new financial regime' for all providers of housing in the public sector and was the next stage in the enduringly complex web of local finance. Important changes to the basis of the calculation of subsidy were made in Part VI of the 1989 Act. In essence the system was simplified so that

19 Quoted in Malpass, P 'Housing Policy and the Housing System Since 1979' in Malpass, M and Means, R (eds) *Implementing Housing Policy* (Open University Press, 1993), p 30.
20 DoE (Department of the Environment) *'Housing Policy: the Government's Proposals'*, (Cmnd 214, 1987).

the three main sources of subsidy payment – general subsidy, rent rebate subsidy and local rate fund contributions – were amalgamated into one subsidy. The net effect was to bring most authorities back into subsidy and to re-establish a considerable degree of influence over local rents. The 1989 legislation marked the government's attempt to re-assert control by the centre with the aim of pushing rents towards fully market-related levels. However, because the calculation of rent was now related to local capital values in the private housing market there were considerable implementation difficulties. For example, guideline rents were much higher in the south of the country than in the north where some authorities had to reduce rents. In fact a complex system of 'dampening' smoothed out the peaks and troughs with the implication that tenants in low house price areas (generally in the north) paid higher rents than forecast by the model.

At the heart of the 1988 Act was an intention to redefine authorities as enablers, giving them a more strategic and co-ordinating role and at the same time reviving the private rental sector – by then reduced to a fragmented shell accounting for only about 7% of households – and considerably strengthening the role of associations as the main direct providers of social housing. At the time it was planned that the remaining council housing, still numbering well in excess of four million households, despite the right to buy, would be sold or transferred to alternative landlords. The government itself would facilitate some transfers through the establishment of Housing Action Trusts (HATs) and so would by-pass the authorities and in theory demunicipalise some council stock by taking them out of local authority control. Estates were to be specially designated by the Secretary of State as HAT areas and it was hoped that the promise of additional public funds and an injection of private finance would 'turn round' the fortunes of downwardly spiralling communities. Central to these plans, therefore, was the vision of market forces and private finance in conjunction reviving the private and quasi-private rental sectors of housing while 'council' housing would whither on the vine of commercial enterprise.

None of these measures accomplished its specific aim, although the consequences of the attempt to implement them was considerable, particularly for the tenants of housing associations and the character of the housing association movement itself. As we have shown throughout the chapter, the outcome of a policy is often at variance with its intention. Key issues in the implementation of the 1988 Act illustrate this. The 'revival' of the privately rented sector through the traditional mechanism of deregulation of the rent system largely failed, although there was an expansion of the sector in the early 1990s due to the availability of housing benefit on an equal basis to both public and private tenants. Of their own accord the 'assured' tenancy and the 'assured shorthold' tenancy, which allowed landlords to set market level rents on a change of tenancy, were unable to induce substantial new investment into the privately rented sector. At a time when house prices fell sharply, after the peak of the boom in the summer of 1988, households able to afford assured rents for the small quantities of reasonable quality private rental housing available could generally afford a mortgage for properties at the lower end of the market. The revival of private renting also reflected the slump in house prices between 1989 and 1994 as developers were forced to rent out newly built dwellings as a temporary measure until profitability and turnover in the property market improved. The programme of tax reliefs announced for investors in the Business Expansion Scheme (BES) in the 1988 Budget (not part of the 1988 Act), also failed to produce general affordable rental housing but did have a limited impact in the south of the country providing good quality rental accommodation for more affluent, younger and upwardly socially mobile tenants.[1] Some housing associations and universities saw the BES as a way of securing new loans at relatively low cost and universities in particular have made use of BES to build student accommodation.

The measure in the 1988 Act to introduce Housing Action Trusts (HATs) was rejected in every area where a HAT was initially proposed. As announced in a White Paper[2] in September 1987, there was to be no participation by tenants themselves in the arrangements for setting up a HAT or its ultimate transfer to another landlord – which specifically would not be the local authority. But a vociferous campaign by tenants' associations around the country against these procedures forced the government to revise this proposal. It has been suggested that Lord Caithness, the Minster of Housing at the time, was cornered by David Dimbleby in a BBC television interview and '.. blurted out that tenants in HAT estates would get a ballot.'[3] Ironically this concession to tenants' demands made the first wave of HATs impossible to implement. The ballots were unsuccessful and none of the original six targeted estates went forward. By early 1994 only four HATs were operating (Waltham Forest, Liverpool, Castle Point and Hull), and in each case with the support of massive injections of public subsidy and the co-operation of authorities. As a vehicle for displacing council housing into the private sector by the wholesale declaration of HAT estates the policy has failed. It was superseded by somewhat more subtle incentives via the regeneration of inner city and peripheral housing estates, for example, through schemes such as City Challenge.

1   Crook, A D H, et al *Tax Incentives and the Revival of Private Renting* (Cloister Press, 1991).
2   DoE (Department of the Environment) *'Housing Policy: the Government's Proposals'* (Cmnd 214, HMSO, 1987).
3   Cited in Karn, V 'Remodelling a HAT', in Malpass, M and Means, R (eds) *Implementing Housing Policy* (Open University Press, 1993), p.78

The new world for housing associations

The 1988 Act intended to draw the housing association movement firmly in the direction of a private and 'independent' rental forms of provision. It was supposed that greater exposure to the disciplines of market forces would lead to greater cost efficiencies and thereby increase housing output relative to a given public subsidy. Allocation of funding was to be based on associations' ability to meet unit cost targets. The key change introduced in the legislation was to abandon the old 1974 HAG system and replace it with a funding mechanism based on a *fixed* level of grant. Previously grant had written off most of the capital cost of a scheme at the beginning of the life of the dwellings but under the new regime a high proportion of funding was derived from private finance and a much greater share of the financial risk was borne by the associations.

Here we note that the Housing Act 1988 changed the face of the traditional housing association movement from a diverse set of mainly small scale providers specialising in people with special housing needs and with a strong record of inner-city housing renovation, towards a larger scale, more homogeneous style of development mounted mainly by a few very large national associations. In 1984 the National Federation of Housing Associations had 3,500 member organisations but by 1997 there were only 2,500 RSLs registered with the Housing Corporation. In England, for example, 30,200 properties were owned by the 1,700 smallest associations (owning 100 properties or less) whereas 70,500 units were owned by only 112 associations (owning over 2,500 properties). The significantly higher financial risks and liabilities have undermined the voluntary movement and produced a commercial ethos which has changed the services they offer, the type of people catered for and the kind of housing being built. Serious problems on some of the new large estates has opened up a new seam of criticism which is not far removed from those levelled at local authorities in the past – their administrative inefficiencies, the over-large scale of estates, the poor record of management, and a potent sense of being a residual housing tenure.

The Major Government

The Conservatives came to power for a fourth consecutive term in May 1992 under the leadership of John Major who had succeeded Margaret Thatcher as Prime Minister in 1991. The period is perhaps best characterised as one of continued experimentation with the restructuring of social rented housing, which was an extension of the Thatcherite project, but also a growing recognition of the problems of inner-city estates and the dangers to social stability of the social and economic collapse of these communities. By the mid-1990s the language of 'regeneration' was common currency with a new emphasis on the need to take a strategic approach which cut across the institutional boundaries of social security, education, health and housing. The neo-liberal agenda was, however, very much in place in the determination of the government to tackle the so called 'fast-track' route into public housing (via homelessness procedures) which was alleged to be increasing to the detriment of ordinary waiting list applicants. The behaviour of young single mothers was particularly highlighted and the government signalled its intention in a consultation paper to abandon the longstanding commitment to provide permanent accommodation for the statutorily homeless, untouched throughout the Thatcher period.[4] Despite many thousands of highly critical responses to the consultation document a White Paper was subsequently published (June 1995)[5], incorporating most of the Consultation Paper proposals and, in due course, these became incorporated into Part VII of the Housing Act, 1996.

The main thrust of this was, indeed, to abandon the 1977 duty (as consolidated in Part III of the Housing Act, 1985) to provide permanent accommodation and replace it with a duty to provide only temporary accommodation, not in council housing, for a period of only two years. Moreover, application procedures changed with the introduction of new eligibility criteria and a new test; the availability in the area of 'suitable alternative accommodation'.

Other areas of housing policy continued to emphasise market solutions, including the sale of council houses. But given that there were still four and a half million council properties still remaining the next best solution for 'bringing the benefits of the market' to public sector housing was the privatisation of the management systems. A prime example of this was the move to extend compulsory competitive tendering (CCT) into the delivery of housing services. CCT was introduced in Part III of the Local Government Planning and Land Act 1980 and further extended by the Local Government Acts of 1988 and 1992. Under the 1988 Act authorities had to subject their housing management system to 'market testing'. This involved a basic division of the 'client' functions from the 'service' functions with tenders invited from the private sector for the service functions. The precise activities which had to be put out to tender were listed under powers exercised by the Secretary of State. The experience of CCT was very patchy simply because the range of agencies in a position to compete with and win contracts against existing providers was limited. Indeed one of the first measures taken by the New Labour government when it came to office in June 1997 was to put the brakes on any further CCT projects, allowing existing tenders to proceed, but proposing in future a system based on the idea of 'best value.' The law relating to best value is dealt with in detail in Chapter Three.

4   Department of the Environment *Access to Local Authority and Housing Association Tenancies* (DoE, 1994).
5   Department of the Environment *Our Future Homes: Opportunity, Choice and Responsibility* (Cm 2901, HMSO, 1995).

The schemes arising from the Housing Act 1988 to facilitate the continued break up of council housing – compulsory stock transfer via Tenants' Choice and HATs made relatively little impact and were quietly dropped or absorbed into new programmes. In fact the main source of stock transfer occurred through the response of some authorities to the 'new financial regime', particularly that they could not spend the bulk of their capital receipts from right to buy sales. Large Scale Voluntary Stock transfer (LSVT) emerged in the late 1980s when some authorities explored the possibilities of transferring their entire stock to an existing or a newly created housing association. It was not government policy although there was a permissive legislative framework for it in the Housing Act 1985, which gave authorities powers to dispose of housing and land. The initiative often arose from officers of authorities anxious about the future of their housing stock in the new financial era. Between 1988 and 1998 nearly 250,000 properties were transferred involving nearly 60 local authorities, mainly in rural authorities in the south of England. A system of 'trickle down' transfer – whereby individual houses were transferred when a tenancy terminates – was adopted by some larger, urban authorities. A statutory 'rent to mortgage' scheme under the Housing and Urban Development Act 1993 enabled tenants to buy part of their home by converting their rent into a mortgage payment. Apart from LSVT these schemes have had only a limited impact. Problems with the funding of LSVT slowed this development considerably as the government sought to limit the scale of private finance being tied up in these transfers. Clearly, however, in its heyday the LSVT system took a considerable bite out of the local authority housing stock.

From the mid-1990s a range of new initiatives were introduced designed to transfer inner-city and poor quality stock to new landlords. The Estates Renewal Challenge Fund offered limited resources for this purpose and the idea of Local Housing Companies emerged to facilitate transfers as alternatives to housing associations. The 1995 White Paper 'Our Future Homes' clearly envisaged housing companies taking over council housing as well, so placing these new agencies squarely in the private sector. But the establishment of Challenge Funding reflected a new line of thinking which emphasised the idea that urban renewal and inner-city problems could not be treated only as a 'housing' issue but required a co-ordinated strategy which linked up different tiers and departments of government. This line of thinking was enhanced by a review of urban renewal policy published in 1994 which spoke of the drag on the economy caused by the decline of the old urban centres, both because of the underlying economic causes of these problems and the costs of dealing with their symptoms.[6]

6   Robson, B, Bradford, M, Dean, I, Hall, E, Harrison, E, Parkinson, M, Evans, R, Garside, P Harding, A, Robinson, F *Assessing the Impact of Urban policy* (HMSO, 1994).

Arising from the review new Regional Offices were set up by the government in the six major regions and a new Single Regeneration Budget (SRB) was introduced to incorporate the previous housing programmes (including HATs and Estate Action). As a result resources became increasingly less targeted at 'housing' and more at strategies that were joined up to training, employment, and education initiatives. The idea of 'housing policy' even began to be spoken of as at an end as this more holistic approach gathered in importance.

One of the underlying causes of inner-city decline was a very significant imbalance between the regions in the supply and demand for housing. This problem was beginning to become apparent in the mid-1990s although the scale of the problem only came to light after the Labour government took office. In the old industrial heartlands of the north and in the mining communities surpluses of council housing and RSL property began to inflame the general difficulties caused by unemployment. Housing needs studies, which were now required by the DoE so that proof of need could be documented, increasingly showed areas of considerable housing surplus. Indeed some northern local authorities were quietly embarking on programmes of demolition in order, as it were, to cut out the cancer. It became increasingly apparent that 'difficult-to-let' property was in many cases a consequence of local and regional economic collapse not of poor quality housing management or poor quality property. But at this stage the issue of low demand was kept under wraps, particularly by the authorities worst affected because applying for SRB and City Challenge funding was not helped, in a very competitive environment, by evidence of surpluses of housing. Following a conference in York during the summer of 1998 a series of papers were published which for the first time aired many of these concerns.[7]

New Labour

The need to place 'housing' in the wider economic context and the realisation that inner city housing problems could not be treated in isolation was a central part of the New Labour agenda. One of the very first innovations of the government was to set up a Social Exclusion Unit (SEU) inside the Cabinet Office, personally overseen by the Prime Minister. The SEU quickly identified the 3,000 so called 'worst estates' and in its first major report, *Bringing Britain Together*, highlighted the need for integrated, cross-departmental and locally focused solutions to the problems of the

---

7   Lowe, S, Spencer, S and Keenan, P *Housing Abandonment in Britain: studies in the causes and effects of low demand for housing* (Centre for Housing Policy, University of York, 1998).

worst estates.[8] The report emphasised problems of economic restructuring over the last few decades, notably the collapse of manufacturing industry, and the close relationship between urban deprivation, housing and the economy.

At the time or writing (late summer 1999) there had been no major housing legislation during Labour's term of office. Positive features of the 1996 Act continue to be pursued and the notorious Part VII, dealing with changes to the treatment of homeless people, in effect had its teeth drawn. As before authorities continued to exercise considerable discretion but many still offered permanent accommodation to families unintentionally homeless. Technically the government went a long way to redeem its election manifesto commitments with regard to housing. CCT was more or less dropped. The government moved quickly to release capital receipts from the sale of council houses (which had been frozen and much of which had already been used in paying off local authority historic debts). As a result of the comprehensive spending review in July 1998 £3.6 billion was provided over three years for local authorities to develop their renovation programmes. Welcome as it was critics of the government saw this as not enough to tackle the back-log of repair work on council housing and as signalling a housing policy based around renovating existing stock rather than investment in new building. New Labour clearly had no intention of going back to the days when local authorities were major builders and innovators in housing construction. But as Malpass and Murie observe this spending package did in effect fulfil the election pledge to release £5 billion of accumulated capital receipts for housing purposes. However, as they observed, '…after five years of Labour government overall annual capital spending on housing will remain below the levels achieved by the Conservatives in the early 1990s.'[9]

The key to the future, however, is found only partly in such comparisons, even though they are important in measuring relative financial performance and commitments. It is clear that New Labour is unlikely to try to spend its way out of the inner-city crisis. Rather the message is that they are seeking new ways of tackling old problems. This is signalled in the Social Exclusion Unit's report and the structure of integrated departmental and agency arrangements which have been put in place. It clearly is sensible that housing policy should take its place within this more 'joined up' approach. Inner-city and 'worst estates' problems self-evidently cannot be solved only by 'housing' policy initiatives. The fundamental economic base of

8   Social Exclusion Unit *Bringing Britain Together: a national strategy for neighbourhood renewal* (Cm 4045, The Stationery Office, 1998).
9   Malpass, P and Murie, A *Housing Policy and Practice* (5th edn, Macmillan, 1999), p277.

these areas is indeed the root of the problem and has to be tackled. This requires the further development of *regional* economic policies and systems of governance.

Almost certainly the most far-ranging development which will impact on the formulation and delivery of social housing policy is contained in the White Paper on the reform of local government.[10] The White Paper in essence asks local authorities to move out from the provision of 'their' traditional services to become leaders of more open communities. They are urged to embrace inter-agency partnerships in delivering services and to modernise their internal structures in a very radical way. The traditional committee system of local councils is to be abolished and replaced by a 'political executive' with elected mayors or cabinets. Much greater emphasis is to be placed on the views and needs of the local population rather than party political agendas. The White Paper proposes the expansion of the idea of 'best value' to improve the quality and effectiveness of services. Some local authorities are already experimenting with the use of best value and the delivery of housing services are very much part of these (see Chapter Three for detailed discussion of the law on best value). The aim of best value is to set out clearly what the authority is trying to achieve and to find the most effective way of doing it and not necessarily using in-house services of the authority. New technologies, greater involvement of voluntary and private services, new management systems and groupings of services are all part of this new vision. The local authority thus becomes a more dynamic and proactive agency for co-ordinating, commissioning and reviewing how services are delivered. The aim gradually is to extend a greater sense of community involvement and for local people to be more in touch with what is going on and why.

There are also significant opportunities in this context to reaffirm the role that the law has in defending and enhancing the basic fairness and equivalence in treatment of tenants in the public sector. The secure tenancy introduced in the Housing Act 1980 was in theory a considerable advance. In reality the greatest threat to security, namely the suspended possession order in rent arrears cases, still largely go through on the nod in the county courts. Tenants still do not know their rights sufficiently well and even when they do changes to the legal aid system inhibit their ability to make progress through legal redress. The potential raft of new rights arising from the secure tenancy was enacted ironically at a time when the entire rental sector was in decline (more rights but fewer tenants) and when the stress politically was on individual rights rather than those of a more collective nature. Much still rests on how good landlords are at encouraging tenants to enjoy their rights. But collective right are evolving, notably in case law with an

10 Department of the Environment, Transport and the Regions *Modern Local Government – In Touch with the People* (HMSO, 1998).

emphasis on the interests of authorities in keeping the peace and preserving the tranquillity of estates against 'nuisance' tenants. A further development of rights to consultation and participation in decision-making and management would surely fit with New Labour's vision of a more participatory and responsive local government system. Taken together these more collective rights would undoubtedly help to underpin the creation once again of council estates as desirable and safe places to live.

Conclusion

The latter part of the chapter has shown that one hundred years after the inception of state housing policy there has been rapid change to the sector during the last two decades. The radical New Right agenda from the 1980s and through most of the 1990s has had a dramatic impact. The stock of council properties has declined by almost a third and the social composition of the sector is significantly different than at any stage throughout the long history of municipal housing. Many people do not now regard it as a settled end to their housing needs but a temporary staging post. This process of residualisation has lead to a situation in which the social purpose of council housing provision has changed dramatically. No longer is council housing sought after by a wide variety of people spanning a broad band of the social class spectrum, no longer is it an expanding sector, and no longer is it a beacon for high standards in design and building quality. Council housing used to be all these things as this 'brief history' has shown. Nevertheless, all the house building estimates indicate a continuing need for the provision of a significant programme of social housing for the foreseeable future. It is unlikely that this will be met in the traditional manner as described in this chapter. Such a policy would almost certainly be inappropriate and the future is much more likely to encompass compacts and partnerships between a plurality of providers, albeit with the authorities playing a proactive role. It is against this long view, as well as the more immediate concerns, that public sector housing law needs to be read. One thing is certain. Redressing the inequities and mistakes of the past for new generations of public sector tenants requires that their legal rights, both individual and collective, are constantly developed and improved.

Further reading

History of housing

Burnett, J *A Social History of Housing 1815 – 1985* (Methuen, 1986)
Holmans, A *Housing Policy in Britain: a History* (Croom Helm, 1987)

Lowe, S and Hughes, D (eds) *A New Century of Social Housing* (Leicester University Press, 1991)

Merrett, S *State Housing in Britain* (Routledge and Kegan Paul, 1979)

Swenarton, M *Homes Fit For Heroes* (Heinemann, 1981)

Housing policy

Burrows, R, Pleace, N and Quilgars, D (eds) *Homelessness and Social Policy* (Routledge, 1997)

Clapham D, Kemp, P and Smith, S *Housing and Social Policy* (Macmillan, 1990)

Lund, B *Housing Problems and Housing Policy* (Addison Wesley Longman, 1996)

Malpass, P and Means, R (eds) *Implementing Housing Policy* (Open University Press, 1993)

Malpass, P and Murie A *Housing Policy and Practice* (5th edn, Macmillan, 1999)

Marsh, M and Mullins, D *Housing and Public Policy* (Open University Press, 1998)

CHAPTER TWO

The provision and disposal of social housing

What is social housing and who provides it?

A number of provisions in the Housing Act 1985 define 'house', 'flat', and 'dwelling' for a variety of purposes, but there is no one unified definition, and the approach of the courts seems to be to take a common sense view in deciding whether as a matter of fact any given set of premises can be reasonably called, for example, a 'house' and then to decide further, as a matter of law, if it falls within the particular provision of the legislation in question[1]. In *Gravesham Borough Council v Secretary of State for the Environment*[2] McCullough J pointed out, in a case under planning law, that an important factor to consider is whether any given set of premises provides facilities required for daily private domestic existence[3]. As a general rule premises constructed as a house will continue to be treated as such unless they are drastically reconstructed, as for example, where premises are reconstructed as a block of self-contained flats[4], though whether the process of reconstruction goes far enough in any given case to warrant holding that the character of the original house has been lost must be a question of fact[5].

1   *Reed v Hastings Corpn* (1964) 62 LGR 588 and *Okereke v Brent London Borough Council* [1967] 1 QB 42, [1966] 1 All ER 150.
2   (1982) 47 P & CR 142.
3   See also *Lake v Bennett* [1970] 1 QB 663, [1970] 1 All ER 457.
4   *R v Kerrier District Council, ex p Guppys (Bridport) Ltd* (1985) 274 Estates Gazette 924.
5   *Pollway Nominees Ltd v Croydon London Borough Council* [1987] AC 79, [1986] 2 All ER 849.

So far as flats are concerned, in many cases they are treated as the equivalents of houses, but in particular instances there are distinctions made, for example with regard to the Right to Buy, see further below. The most important point to remember is that it is not the 'label' a particular owner or occupier puts on a building which determines what might pass in everyday language as a definition of 'house' or 'flat'. The task of definition is for the law.

The housing authorities

Outside Greater London in the English shires the principal local housing authorities are the district councils, see section 1 of the Housing Act 1985. In addition certain areas have 'unitary' authority status under the Local Government Act 1992. Many of these, eg Leicester, were formerly districts, but at least one, Herefordshire, is a former county. Unitary authorities have housing functions within their areas. County councils have only limited powers – such as to provide homes for persons employed or paid by them, for example school caretakers – under section 29 of the Housing Act 1985. In the Metropolitan areas Metropolitan District Councils are the housing authorities. In the Greater London area the Common Council is the housing authority for the City of London. In the rest of the metropolis the London Boroughs are, under section 1 of the Housing Act 1985, the principal housing authorities within their areas. In Wales the position is governed by the Local Government (Wales) Act 1994 under which local government functions are entrusted to 'principal areas', ie counties (largely corresponding to the old historic counties of Wales before the changes made by the Local Government Act 1972) together with a number of large urban areas given county borough status, see section 1 and schedule 1 of the 1994 Act. Section 17 and schedule 8 of the 1994 Act transfer housing functions to the new Welsh counties and county boroughs.

The local authority duty to provide housing

This duty is contained in Part II of the Housing Act 1985. (All references hereafter are to this Statute unless otherwise stated.)

Section 8 provides that it shall be the duty of every local housing authority to consider the housing conditions in their district *and* the needs of their district with respect to the provision of further housing accommodation. 'Conditions' must be reviewed annually for that refers to the state of properties in an area. This may result from surveys carried out by their own officers, or from information otherwise received, see particularly section 605. 'Needs' are to be reviewed from time to time, and include the needs of residents in an area, and also those of persons who might conveniently be housed in it[6]. Authorities must also consider the needs of chronically sick and disabled persons[7].

Under section 9 accommodation may be provided by erecting houses or by converting buildings into houses, on land acquired by the authority, or by the acquisition of existing houses. These powers may also be used where the houses to be provided are subsequently to be disposed of, and housing land may also be disposed of to persons intending to provide housing on it, see section 9(3).

Supplementary powers to fit out and furnish section 9 accommodation are granted by section 10, and powers to provide meals, refreshments, including the sale of alcoholic liquors for consumption with meals, laundry facilities and services are granted by section 11 together with power to provide Welfare Services, under section 11A, in connection with housing. However, under section 9(5), as inserted in 1989, authorities are *not* required to hold any housing land or stock, and a number of semi-urban and rural districts have in fact divested themselves of their stock, see below. They remain, of course, housing authorities for a variety of purposes, for example with regard to homelessness, and have to make appropriate arrangements for this purpose.

Section 12 provides that the local authority may, with ministerial consent, provide alongside housing accommodation, shops, recreation grounds and other land or buildings which the minister considers would benefit the occupants of the housing provided, a power wide enough, according to the opinion of Peterson J in *Conron v LCC*[8], to cover the provision of public houses so long as they are 'conducted on the most improved lines'.

Section 23 permits the making of byelaws with respect to the use of any land held under section 12, and *not* covered by buildings or within the curtilage of a building or forming part of a highway, and for the management and regulation of local authority housing. Little use appears to have been made of this power in the past. Greater use could be made of this power by authorities to regulate activities such as the repairing and purchasing of cars on their estates – matters which can frequently lead to inter-neighbour disputes. The process of making such byelaws is, however, slow consequent on the need for ministerial approval.

The London Boroughs also have powers to provide and maintain commercial premises along with housing accommodation, under section 15(1). Section 13 grants powers to lay out public streets, roads and open spaces on land acquired for housing purposes. In *Meravale Builders Ltd v Secretary of State for the Environment*[9] it was held that this power only

6   *Watson v Minister of Local Government and Planning* [1951] 2 KB 779, [1951] 2 All ER 664.
7   Section 3, Chronically Sick and Disabled Act 1970.
8   [1922] 2 Ch 283 at 297.
9   (1978) 36 P & CR 87.

empowers a local authority to build such roads as fairly and reasonably relate to the provision of housing accommodation, and not to create new major roads, interchanges and extensions which have a purpose independent of housing. Section 607 requires local authorities to have regard to 'the beauty of the landscape or countryside, the other amenities of the locality, and the desirability of preserving existing works of architectural, historic or artistic interest' when proposing to provide housing. As a matter of strict law authorities enjoy considerable powers to acquire land for housing purposes under section 17, either by agreement, or, subject to ministerial approval, by compulsion. In practice of late these powers have been very little used because of the move in housing policy away from authorities as *providers* of housing and towards their being overall strategic enablers of others to undertake this task.

Provision of housing by housing associations, and other 'registered social landlords'

Housing Associations, as will be discussed in detail below, are voluntary bodies having a number of legal forms, but all with the purpose of providing housing of one sort or another either generally or for those with particular needs. They have their own representative organisation in the form of the National Federation of Housing Associations (NATFED) which does much by the promotion of training and the circulation of 'best practice' guidance to ensure that the association movement is highly self regulating. However, because associations are generally in receipt of public funds central statutory agencies are required to ensure, inter alia, accountability.

The Housing Corporation (HC)

From 1988 there were two corporations, one for England, and one (Housing for Wales) covering Wales. The functions of Housing for Wales were transferred to the Secretary of State for Wales under section 140 et seq of the Government of Wales Act 1998 and SI 1998/781. For ease of understanding in this work 'HC' refers to the English Corporation and the Welsh successor. The HC exists under Part III of the Housing Associations Act (HAA) 1985. The HC must, under section 76 of the HAA 1985, act in accordance with directions given by the Secretary of State. Section 78 imposes a duty on the HC to make an annual report. Under section 75 the HC is to promote, assist, register and regulate registered social landlords.

The HC (the detailed organisation of which is contained in Schedule 6 of the HAA 1985) has power to lend money to registered landlords under section 79 of the HAA 1985, and may lend to individuals for the purpose of assisting them to acquire dwellings for their occupation from the HC or a registered social landlord. Section 83 gives a power to guarantee, with the Secretary of State's consent, the repayment of the principal and interest on sums borrowed by registered social landlords. The aggregate amount of loans guaranteed must not exceed £300 million, though the Secretary of State may increase this up to £500 million, prorata arrangements are made in respect of Wales. Section 92 of the HAA 1985 empowers the HC to borrow from the Secretary of State, and from other sources including the European Investment Bank or the Commission of the European Communities, or on the open money market, but these powers are subject to an aggregate limit under section 93 of £2,000m, which may be increased to up to £3,000m with Treasury consent (prorata arrangements are made for Wales). The Treasury may, under section 94, guarantee in such manner or on such conditions as they think fit, the repayment of the principal or interest on any sums borrowed by the HC from any source other than the Secretary of State. The HC may invest portions of its funds, see section 96 of the HAA 1985, and may, under section 98, acquire stocks and shares etc in companies. Proper accounts and audits are required by section 97, and grants in aid of administrative expenses may be paid to the HC by the Secretary of State under section 95. Despite the range of its powers, the HC is not, as its annual reports make clear, a trading body seeking to make a return on its capital. Money advanced to registered social landlords as loans is charged at a rate of interest sufficient to meet that on its own borrowings.

Section 88 of the HAA 1985 empowers the HC to acquire land by agreement, or compulsorily if so authorised by the Secretary of State, for the purpose of selling or leasing it to registered social landlords, or to provide hostels or dwellings for rent or sale itself. The procedure for compulsory acquisition is that under the Acquisition of Land Act 1981. Section 89 further empowers the HC to provide or improve dwellings or hostels on its land. They may insure and repair their buildings and manage them, doing all such things as are conducive to facilitating the provision or improvement of dwellings or hostels on the land, including the provision of ancillary developments for commercial, recreational or other non-domestic purposes. Section 90 authorises the disposal of land on which no dwellings have been provided to a limited range of bodies, principally registered social landlords or subsidiaries of the Corporation. Where dwellings have been provided, they may be disposed of to, inter alia, registered social landlords. The HC may sell or lease individual dwellings to persons for their occupation. Certain disposals require the consent of the Secretary of State, see section 90(3) to (6) of the HAA 1985. In the context of the HAA 1985 generally 'hostel' is defined by section 106(1) as a building in which is provided for persons generally, or for classes of persons, residential accommodation *not* in separate and self-contained sets, *and* either board, *or* facilities for the preparation of food adequate to the needs of those persons, or both.

Under section 46 of the Housing Act 1988 relevant functions in respect of Wales were transferred to Housing for Wales (Tai Cymru). As stated above, however, these functions were subsequently transferred to the Secretary of State for Wales, and have since been further transferred to the Welsh Assembly under the terms of the Government of Wales Act 1998. (The equivalent body in Scotland is Scottish Homes, but the law of housing in Scotland is outside the scope of this work.) The HC has considerable powers of oversight over registered social landlords, including the power to monitor them by requiring production of their books, accounts, and documents and to demand explanations of them, see Schedule 1 of the Housing Act 1996. For further supervisory functions of the Corporation see Chapter Three below.

The types and structures of registered social landlords: housing associations

As associations are voluntary bodies, they are not generally subject to the rules of judicial review, so that even where they receive public funds which they are obliged to apply in particular ways, that does not turn *their normal and essential functions as landlords* into the exercise of a reviewable statutory power, see *Peabody Housing Association Ltd v Green*[10] , though the HC as a statutory regulatory agency is open to judicial review. The position *may* be different where an association has been formed to take over all the authority provided housing in an area, see *R v West Kent Housing Association, ex p Sevenoaks District Council*[11].

Housing associations (a generic term) are further defined by section 1 of the HAA 1985. They are societies, bodies of trustees or companies established for the purpose of providing, constructing, improving, managing, *or* facilitating or encouraging construction or improvement of housing accommodation, *and* which do not trade for profit, or whose constitution or rules prohibit the issue of capital with interest of dividend exceeding such a rate as may be prescribed by the Treasury. This covers a multiplicity of forms.

Associations which are 'societies' will in general exist under the terms of the Industrial and Provident Societies Act 1965. They will be run by a Committee of Management and may have charitable status, depending on their constitution, or they may be self-help bodies such as co-operative or self-build organisations. Charitable status applies to those associations who act to relieve 'aged, impotent and poor people'. These words must be read disjunctively, for the aged need not be necessarily also impotent or poor, nor the poor aged etc. What is required is that the body alleviates need

10 (1978) 38 P & CR 644.
11 (1994) 'Inside Housing' 28 October, p 3.

attributable to the aged, impotent, or poor condition of the recipient of relief, and that that need is one which those persons could not alleviate, or would find it hard to alleviate, from their own resources, see *Joseph Rowntree Memorial Trust Housing Association Ltd v A-G*[12] . The rules of a '1965 Act' society determine its legal entity, its powers, and the internal relationships of its members. Such societies may only do what their rules permit them to do.

Associations which are charitable trusts derive their powers from their trust deeds and will come under the jurisdiction of the Charity Commissioners under the Charities Act 1960. '1965 Act' societies are outside this jurisdiction, whether or not 'charitable', as they are supervised generally by the Registrar of Friendly Societies and the Housing Corporation. An association which is a company will derive its powers and functions from its memorandum and articles of association under the terms of the Companies Acts.

Associations which are 'fully mutual' are those with rules that restrict membership to persons who are tenants or prospective tenants of their association and which preclude granting or assigning tenancies to persons other then members. Co-operative housing associations are those that are both fully mutual and societies registered under the 1965 Act.

The next point is that an association may be registered or unregistered with the HC under Part I, Chapter 1 of the Housing Act 1996. Registered associations, along with other registered social landlords, are eligible for loans and grant aid, but, of course, are supervised by the HC. Before considering registration it is, however, convenient to consider other bodies which also may be registered social landlords.

Local housing companies

It became policy under John Major, and has remained so under Tony Blair, to widen the range of social landlords beyond authorities and associations, and in particular to encourage the formation of non-profit making 'local housing companies' to whom the ownership of authority housing may be transferred. As will become apparent later, though few such bodies were initially created, from 1999 onwards they have become rather more common. There are a number of permutations of structure such a company can take, but the *basic* notion is that the company is an independent legal person, while the relevant local authority and the company's tenants are involved in its running. One common 'model' for such a company is that it is managed by a board of directors one third drawn from the local authority, one third elected by tenants and one third who represent the wider local community and financial institutions who lend to the company. The local authority may

12 [1983] Ch 159, [1983] 1 All ER 288.

only have a minority financial interest in such a company and must not control it. Such companies are considered to have a degree of accountability to the local authority, their tenants and the community via their directors, while they are because of their corporate structure able to seek finance for housing development and improvement in the financial market place.

The term 'registered social landlord' is thus also, like 'housing association' a generic one, covering a number of different types of body. Both local housing companies and housing associations may be 'registered social landlords', however, and it is to bodies falling into that class that the powers of the HC now apply.

The process of registration

Under section 1 of the 1996 Act the HC is to maintain a register (open to inspection at all reasonable times) of 'Registered Social Landlords' to which all the previously registered housing associations automatically belong. Under section 2 bodies are eligible for registration if they are registered charities which are housing associations, societies registered under the Industrial & Provident Societies Act 1965, a company registered under the Companies Act 1985 *provided they do not trade for profit* or their constitutions/rules prohibit the issue of capital with interest or dividend exceeding a rate prescribed by the Treasury under section 1 (1)(b) of the Housing Associations Act 1985, and have amongst their objects housing provision, construction, improvement of housing with a view to keeping it available for letting, and the provision of hostels. Such bodies can have additional supplementary objects, eg providing land, amenities or services for residents of housing, acquiring property etc for repair, etc with a view to sale, lease or shared ownership disposal, constructing houses for shared ownership, managing blocks of flats and houses let on leases or other lettings by other bodies, providing general services for those who occupy houses – eg repairs. The fact that these ancillary powers include powers to acquire commercial properties, repair, improve or convert them on a basis incidental to the provision etc of housing, does not render the body in question ineligible to be a registered social landlord.

The HC under section 3 of the 1996 Act may register any eligible body, though application for registration is not free and has to be made in a prescribed form, while under section 4 a registered social landlord may only be de-registered in certain circumstances, ie

(a) if the HC concludes the landlord is no longer 'eligible';
(b) if the HC concludes the landlord has ceased to exist or is no longer operating.

The HC must erase the registration after giving the registered body 14 days' notice.

Registered social landlords may, however, under section 4(4) request de-registration, though here before complying with the request the HC must consult with relevant local authorities, ie those in whose areas the landlord operates.

Under section 5 of the 1996 Act the HC is required to establish (and may vary) criteria for registering social landlords. Similarly, criteria must be established for deciding applications for voluntary deregistration. These criteria are subject to consultation with representatives of such landlords and must be published and appropriately publicised. A body aggrieved by a HC decision on non-registration or removal may appeal under section 6 to the High Court.

Schedule 1 of the 1996 Act provides for the detailed regulation of registered social landlords. In particular the HC has power to remove persons as directors, trustees or committee members of such a body where they are bankrupt, disqualified, incapable of acting through mental disorder, or have disappeared. New directors and trustees may be appointed, as may new committee members by the HC either where a person has been removed, or where there are no such persons, or where the HC considers it necessary for the proper management of affairs.

The HC continues to have the powers previously available under the Housing Associations Act 1985 to determine accounting requirements for registered social landlords under Part III of Schedule 1, while Part IV grants powers for the HC to inquire into the affairs of such bodies, to obtain relevant information, to carry out audits for inquiry purposes, to suspend persons and transactions on an interim basis while inquiries are carried out where there is reason to suspect misconduct or mismanagement and where immediate action is needed to protect the interests of the body's tenants. Long term there are further powers following a *finding* of misconduct, etc to remove persons from office and to take over and direct transactions. Thus the HC is able to intervene in the affairs of a registered social landlord where it appears to them there may have been misconduct or mismanagement. Clearly some objective evidence would be needed before such powers can be exercised.

The 1996 Act re-enacts the powers formerly in the Housing Associations Act 1985 which are largely repealed in consequence. However, it should be remembered that eligibility for registration is extended to *non-profit, non-charitable companies* provided they in effect otherwise meet the criteria laid down for registered associations. Thus provision is made for diversification of the social landlord structure. Companies may be set up which have a freedom to borrow and trade somewhat akin to ordinary plcs, and they need not have charitable objects – ie they will be able to supply *general* housing needs – but they must not distribute a profit to shareholders.

Chapter III of the 1996 Act gives the HC power to give 'social housing grants'. Under section 18 these may be made to *any* registered social landlord. Total control over the determination and allocation procedure for such grants is vested in the HC, who may impose conditions on grants. Under section 22 local authorities may promote the formation of bodies as registered social landlords, and may give such a body grant aid. Though in the past authorities had power to promote housing associations, the chief use of this provision now is likely to be in the creation of local housing companies.

Provision is also made by section 23 of the 1996 Act for the Public Works Loans Commissioners (a quango) to lend money to registered social landlords – in the past this was the classic way of financing construction by authorities. All money borrowed from whatever source has, however, to be repaid at a rate of interest, and this will be reflected in rent levels charged. Provision is also made under section 27 for the HC to reduce or claw back grants paid in accordance with principles to be determined by the HC itself.

The general regulatory powers of the HC and registered social landlords

Section 30 of the Housing Act 1996 continues the general powers of the HC, previously found in the 1985 Act to obtain information relevant to their functions concerning registered social landlords from such landlords, past/ present officers, etc of such a body, subsidiaries of such a body and their officers etc, and any other relevant person. Under section 31, it is an offence to fail to do anything required by a notice under section 30. Section 32 empowers government departments, local authorities, constables and other public or regulatory bodies to disclose relevant information to the HC, while section 33 enables the HC to disclose any information it has received relating to a registered social landlord to government departments, authorities, constables, etc for the discharge of HC functions, or for the discharge of the informee's functions.

Section 34 of the 1996 Act enables the HC to determine performance standards (and arrange for their publication) from time to time for registered social landlords, after consultation, and with the possibility that standards will vary from landlord to landlord. Information on achieving performance targets is to be collected under section 35 from time to time by the HC and a yearly obligation to provide specified performance information is laid on landlords. It is an offence for a registered body to fail to comply with this obligation.

Section 36 of the Housing Act 1996 continues the power of the HC to issue guidance to registered social landlords on housing management, in particular with regard to:

(a) housing demand to be met and means of meeting it;
(b) allocation;
(c) terms of tenancies and principles for fixing rent;

(d)   maintenance and repair standards and how to meet them;
(e)   services to be provided to tenants;
(f)   procedures adopted to deal with tenants' complaints about the landlord;
(g)   consultation and communication with tenants;
(h)   devolution to tenants of decisions concerning management of housing
        accommodation.

Such guidance is to be issued after consultation with representative
bodies and is subject to the Secretary of State's approval. Such guidance
may be withdrawn/revised and may make different provision for different
areas, different descriptions of housing and different types of landlord.
Compliance with guidance is to be taken into account by the HC in
determining whether to take steps to secure proper management of landlords'
affairs. Section 37 further grants powers of entry for the HC to any premises
where it appears the registered social landlord is failing to maintain them in
accordance with guidance under section 36 – it is an offence to obstruct
such an entry: see section 38.

Section 39–50 of the Housing Act 1996 make *new* provision with regard
to the insolvency etc of a registered social landlord – clearly a possibility
should such a body take on a rather more risk-oriented housing provision
role than has been the case in the past with housing associations. First of
all a number of sections give the HC interventionist powers: eg sections 42
and 43 which impose a moratorium on the disposal of land; sections 44 and
45 concerning proposals as to future ownership of land, and provisions
relating to appointing a manager to a registered body (sections 46–48),
giving assistance by the HC (section 49), and securing compliance in court
(section 50).

Secondly *before* any one of a specified number of persons can take any
one of a number of specified actions against a registered social landlord the
HC has to be given notice under section 40 of the 1996 Act. This enables
the HC to decide whether to exercise any of the powers outlined above. The
specified steps include: attempting to enforce a security (eg a mortgage)
against a registered social landlord, or to wind up such a body, or a voluntary
resolution by the body to wind up itself. Similarly, such notice has also to
be given to the HC as soon as may be *after* any one of a number of specified
steps (similar to the foregoing) has been taken: see section 41. There are then
a number of consequential events. First under sections 42 and 43 a
moratorium is placed automatically on the disposal of any of the landlord's
land and housing which can then only be disposed of with the HC's consent
– any disposal made without consent being void. Though the moratorium
is initially quite short (28 days) it may be extended by agreement with the
registered social landlord's creditors – obviously this gives the HC time to
work out a rescue package – where possible – and this may involve the HC
itself providing the necessary financial resources under section 49. Also
while the moratorium is in force the HC may, under section 44, make

proposals as to the future ownership and management of land held by the registered social landlord, though only after consultation with the landlord and the tenants, and on taking into account the interests of all creditors. Where agreed by the creditors the proposals then become binding under section 45 on relevant parties. Section 46 empowers the HC to appoint a manager to implement the proposals as agreed, and that manager has total and extensive powers of management, sale, insurance, agency, payment etc – in short everything necessary to do the job of transferring the housing to another registered body at an appropriate price: see sections 47 and 48. Section 49, further empowers the HC to step in and assist a registered social landlord pending the making and agreement of proposals in order to preserve the position, though assistance by way of grant requires the Secretary of State's consent.

Much of Chapter IV of the 1996 Act repeats and simply updates provisions formerly in the Housing Associations Act 1985, but note in particular the new powers relating to transfer orders which will apply if a registered social landlord becomes, or appears likely to become insolvent.

THE DISPOSAL OF SOCIAL HOUSING

Introduction

Sale of *council* housing has been an issue ever since municipalities first began to provide housing. Central and local policies have varied greatly from time to time and place to place. It has been the subject of fierce and often bitter controversy. This chapter is concerned with individual disposals under the 'right-to-buy' (RTB) (a central plank of government policy on housing since 1980) and block disposal under the Housing Acts 1985 and 1988. When speaking of disposal of social housing one is referring to disposal of council houses. The law is principally concerned with reducing the role of authorities as active landlords while boosting that of associations. Before that law is examined, however, some examination of the development and impact of disposal policies must take place.

The sale of council houses

The sale of council houses has always been a matter of some controversy. Before 1980 local authorities had a power, subject to the consent of the Secretary of State, to sell houses. Individual tenants could thus become owner-occupiers – sometimes at a discounted price. The Secretary of State's consent was generally given and was contained in a number of circulars over the years. The *form* of the consent, however, varied from time to time, usually being more restrictive in its terms under Labour as opposed to Conservative governments. Local authorities also made varying use of the power, some – usually Conservative controlled – being more ready to use the power than others. In 1980 all this changed when, in addition to the power to sell, the Housing Act of that year imposed on local authorities a *duty* to sell at a discount to certain qualifying secure tenants. The sales policy thus initiated was extended throughout the 1980s, with enhanced discount levels, and has led to the disposal of over one million council dwellings on an individual basis – truly the 'Sale of the Century' as Mr Michael Heseltine the initially presiding Secretary of State described it.

Further changes were made in the Housing Act 1988 which introduced legal measures to ensure the block disposal of council housing to new landlords. The 'pick a landlord' and Housing Action Trust (HAT) provisions were, however, conspicuous failures in practice with very little use being made of them. Indeed in the case of the latter the 1988 Act's provisions were subsequently amended to enable housing taken over by a HAT to be returned to its original local authority. Of much more significance was the general move on the part of local authorities to use their *powers* to sell housing to dispose of estates – in some cases their entire stock – on a voluntary basis – Large Scale Voluntary Transfer (LSVT). These transfers became so popular that statutory controls over them had to be introduced. Nevertheless they continue today, with some transfers taking place to housing associations (many of them purpose created to receive the transfer) and some to local housing companies – the latter being the minority. The legal mechanism for achieving LSVT will be examined in due course. It should also be remembered that since 1989 there has been no legal obligation on an authority to own any housing. So far as housing associations were concerned the Right to Buy (RTB) introduced in 1980 in general applied to them as their tenants had 'secure' status under the Housing Act of that year. Post 1988, of course, *new* housing association tenants had 'assured tenant' status and so did not generally enjoy RTB. The Housing Act 1986 addressed that problem.

The Right to Acquire (RTA)

Section 16 of the 1996 Act gives to assured tenants (not assured shorthold tenants) of registered social landlords, where they are tenants of dwellings built or acquired after the commencement of section 16, the right to acquire the dwellings of which they are tenants, provided:

(i)   the dwelling was provided with *public* money, ie as a result of a social housing grant paid by the HC to a registered social landlord under section 18 of the 1996 Act (largely new build properties) or as a result of applying or appropriating sums under section 25 of the Act (funds

acquired in consequence of RTA sales), or as a result of acquisition by the landlord after the commencement of the 1996 Act from a public sector landlord, eg by LSVT;
(ii) the acquiring tenant satisfies the conditions otherwise applicable to RTB sales (see further below).

Thus certain tenants of registered social landlords are generally re-equated with their local authority fellows, but only where their dwellings have been publicly funded. The HC, however, has powers under sections 9–15 of the 1996 Act to consent to other disposals of housing owned by registered bodies (see further below on voluntary disposals).

Section 17 of the 1996 Act contains supplementary provisions relating to RTA, including the power of the Secretary of State to specify discount rates at which sales are to take place, and to designate rural areas – generally settlements with a population of less than 3000 – in which RTA will not apply. See further SI 1997/619, the general regulations on RTA, SI 1998/2014, the general discount provisions, SI 1999/620–625 setting out the various rural areas where RTA does not exist. It may be noted that a tenant having RTA does not enjoy RTB on rent to mortgage terms, nor Preserved Right to Buy (see further below), and while RTA and RTB are generally similar in effect certain types of dwellings are excluded from RTA which are not excluded from RTB, eg dwellings in designated rural areas.

Voluntary disposals by registered social landlords

Such landlords have general powers to dispose of housing under section 8 et seq of the Housing Act 1988, and under these powers there is a Voluntary Purchase Scheme which is operated by most registered social landlords, including ones formed to take voluntary transfers of authority stock. Eligible tenants include *secure* and *assured* tenants occupying self-contained accommodation. Where such a person already enjoys a *right* of purchase he/she must opt for which scheme to pursue. The landlord must not be merely a manager of the property, and the tenant must have been a public sector tenant for two years in total, and furthermore must be solvent, not in arrears, nor facing possession proceedings. Eligible dwellings are those in a local authority area where the registered landlord has an allocation of Voluntary Purchase Grant from the Corporation, and the dwelling must not otherwise be excluded from the statutory Right to Buy (see below). Certain dwellings may be excluded at the landlord's discretion, and the landlord may also allow the tenant to purchase a property other than that actually occupied. Discounts are available on properties purchased under the scheme. The basic mechanism here is that registered landlords have an allocation of money to enable them to make purchase grants to enable tenants to acquire dwellings. If, however, such a body finds that demand for grants exceeds the number allocated by the Corporation, it has to prioritise the applications. (See further James Driscoll *A Guide to the Housing Act 1996* (Butterworths, 1996), pp 29–31 to which indebtedness is acknowledged).

The 'right to buy' under the Housing Act 1985 (as amended)

RTB is enshrined in Part V of the 1985 Act, and unless otherwise stated all subsequent references are to that legislation.

Section 118 grants secure tenants (see Chapter Three for the definition of 'secure tenant') the right to acquire the freehold of their dwellings where they are houses, and the landlord owns the freehold, or, where the dwelling is a flat, or where the landlord does not own the freehold, to take a long lease of it. Dwelling-houses and flats are defined by section 183 so that:

(a)   where a building is divided horizontally the units into which it is divided are *not* houses;

(b)   where a building is not structurally detached from its neighbours it is *not* a house if a material part of it lies above or below the remainder of the structure (this covers maisonettes and flats built over shop developments) however, each one of a row of terraced houses is 'a house';

(c)   where a building is divided vertically the units may be houses so a dwelling in a terrace is a house, provided it is otherwise a structure reasonably so called.

Any dwelling which is not a house must be treated as a flat for sale purposes. Any land used for the purposes of the dwelling may be included in the disposal by agreement between the parties (section 184(2)) and land let with a dwelling is to be treated as part of the dwelling unless it is agricultural land exceeding two acres (section 184(1)).

RTB only arises after the *secure tenant* has enjoyed the status of a *public sector tenant* for a period of not less than two years, or for a number of shorter periods amounting together to two years. During that period neither the landlord nor the dwelling-house need have been the same throughout so a secure tenant can build up entitlement to buy, for example, during a time in which he/she moves from one secure tenancy with one authority to another, see section 119 and Schedule 4.

A 'public sector tenancy' is one where the landlord is, inter alia, a local authority, a new town corporation, a housing action trust, an urban development corporation, or a registered housing association which is not a co-operative association, or such other landlord as is specified by the Secretary of State, see SI 1992/1703 as amended by SI 1996/2651 which brings government departments and ministers, amongst a host of other bodies, into the list of relevant landlords.

A period qualifies towards exercise of RTB, under Schedule 4 paras 2–5A, where the secure tenant, or his/her spouse (provided they are living together at the relevant time) or a deceased spouse of his/hers (provided they were living together at the time of death) was a public sector tenant, or was the spouse of such a person and occupied the house of which that person was the tenant as his/her only or principal home. Joint tenants are deemed to fulfil these requirements provided they occupied the dwelling as their only or principal home. Likewise where the public sector tenant of a dwelling has died, or has otherwise ceased to be a public sector tenant of the relevant dwelling, and thereupon a child of that tenant who before occupied the dwelling as his/her only or principal home becomes the new public sector tenant of the dwelling, a period during which that new tenant, since reaching the age of 16, occupied as his/her only or principal home a dwelling-house of which a parent was sole or joint public sector tenant, counts towards qualifying to exercise RTB, *provided* that that period was the portion of time at the end of which the new tenant became the public sector tenant or it was a portion of time ending not *more* than two years before that date. Time spent by the secure tenant, or his/her living or deceased spouse, in accommodation provided for regular armed forces also counts towards qualification. Similar provisions apply in respect of periods during which the tenant enjoyed the Preserved Right to Buy, see further below. The periods may be aggregated together where applicable and necessary. The essential point is that though RTB attaches to the dwelling of which a qualifying person is the tenant, it is those periods spent as a public sector tenant in the circumstances outlined above that qualify the tenant to exercise the right.

Where a secure tenancy is a joint tenancy, irrespective of whether each of the joint tenants occupies the dwelling as his/her 'only or principal home' RTB belongs jointly to all of them, or to such one as they may agree. Such an agreement is only valid if the person who is to exercise RTB occupies the dwelling as his/her 'only or principal home', see section 118(2). In any case a secure tenant may, under section 123, join up to three members of his/her family in RTB even if they are not joint tenants provided those members occupy the dwelling as their only or principal home, and:
(a) they are either the tenant's spouse, or
(b) they have been residing with the tenant throughout the period of 12 months preceding the notice claiming RTB, or
(c) the landlord consents.

The claim to join members of a family in the purchase must be made in the notice claiming to exercise RTB.

By virtue of section 186 a person is a member of a tenant's family if he/she is his/her spouse, parent, grandparent, child, grandchild, brother, sister, uncle, aunt, nephew or niece: relationships by marriage count as relationships by blood; half-blood counts as whole blood, and step-children count as ordinary children, with illegitimate children being treated as legitimate, and also treating persons living together as man and wife as being members of a family. Once a section 123 notice is effective RTB belongs to the tenant and the 'joined' persons and they are to be treated as joint tenants. Such a deemed joint tenant has sufficient security to be able to press a sale to completion even where otherwise not qualified to be a successor tenant under section 87 (see Chapter 5 below), see *Harrow London Borough Council v Tonge*[13]. Contrast, however, *Bradford Metropolitan City Council v McMahon*[14] where a tenant began the process of purchase and died without completing it, but did *not* join any family member in the transaction.

Section 120 and Schedule 5 (as amended) lay down certain exceptions where RTB does not apply. These are:

(a)   Where the landlord is a housing trust or is a housing association *and* a charity.

(b)   Where the landlord is a co-operative housing association.

(c)   Where the landlord is a housing association which at no time received public funding under certain specified statutes.

(d)   Where the landlord does not own the freehold or some other interest sufficient to grant a lease, in the case of a house, for a term exceeding 21 years, or, in the case of a flat, for a term of not less than 50 years.

(e)   Where the dwelling-house is comprised in a building held by the landlord mainly for non-housing purposes *and* consisting mainly of non-housing accommodation, or is situated in a cemetery, *and* the dwelling was let to the tenant or a predecessor in consequence of the tenant's or that predecessor's employment by the landlord or the local authority, etc.

(f)   Where the dwelling has features substantially different from ordinary dwellings designed to make it suitable for occupation by physically disabled persons, *and* it is part of a group which it is the landlord's practice to let for occupation by such persons, *and* social services or special facilities are provided in close proximity to assist those persons.

In this context note that in *Freeman v Wansbeck District Council*[15] the Court of Appeal held that the special features referred to above comprise matters such as ramps instead of staircases, special doors, cooking surfaces at special heights, etc, and *not* facilities such as additional downstairs lavatories. The special features will be 'designed' to make a dwelling suitable for occupation by a disabled person where the building is designed and built with those features; merely to add special features to an ordinary dwelling with the *intention* of having a disabled person reside there is not enough.

(g)   Where the dwelling is one of a group of houses which it is the landlord's

13   (1992) 25 HLR 99.
14   [1993] 4 All ER 237, [1994] 1 WLR 52.
15   [1984] 2 All ER 746.

practice to let for occupation by persons who are suffering, or have suffered, from mental disorder, *and* social services or special facilities, are provided to assist those persons.

(h) Where the dwelling is one of a group particularly suitable, having regard to location, size, design, heating systems and other features for occupation to elderly persons, and which it is the landlord's practice to let for occupation by persons aged 60 or more or for occupation by such persons *and* physically disabled persons, *and* special facilities consisting of, or including, warden alarm and common room facilities are provided for such persons in close proximity.

(i) Where the dwelling is particularly suited having regard to its location, size, design, heating system and other features for occupation by elderly persons, *and* it was let to the tenant (or his/her predecessor in title) for occupation by a person aged 60 or more. But in determining suitability no regard is to be had to features provided by the tenant. Matters of dispute arising under this exception are to be determined by the Secretary of State provided they are raised by the tenant. The exception only applies to dwellings first let before 1 January 1990.

(j) Where the dwelling is held by the landlord on a Crown tenancy, subject to certain exceptions.

A sale in contravention of an exception though technically void may still pass the property to a purchaser *provided* the sale has been registered. The title will be protected by the Land Registration Act 1925, and the court may decline to rectify the register[16].

Under section 121 RTB cannot be exercised where either:

(a) the tenant is, or will be, obliged to give up possession of the house in pursuance of a court order, or

(b) where a bankruptcy petition is pending against the person to whom RTB belongs, or where he/she is an undischarged bankrupt, or has made a composition with creditors. Where a possession order in respect of a council house or flat is obtained by the landlord *after* the tenant has served notice claiming to exercise RTB, the tenant is precluded from continuing with the purchase, because exercising RTB is a continuing process until the sale is completed, and so the tenant can be prevented from exercising the right if any of the circumstances mentioned above occur[17].

---

16 *Hounslow London Borough Council v Hare* (1990) 24 HLR 9.

17 *Enfield London Borough Council v McKeon* [1986] 2 All ER 730, [1986] 1 WLR 1007. Contrast, however, *Dance v Welwyn Hatfield DC* [1990] 3 All ER 572, [1990] 1 WLR 1097, CA, where a sale was allowed to proceed because *all* matters relating to the sale were agreed or determined and so section 138 (see below) applied. *Dance* was, however, overruled in *Bristol City Council v Lovell* [1998] 1 All ER 775, [1998] 1 WLR 446 where the House of Lords held it is up to the court's discretion whether to allow a possession action claim to supersede action by the tenant to force completion of RTB. In such cases the seriousness of the allegations made by the landlord must be taken into account.

The position is similar where a secure tenant loses that status before a purchase is completed, for example by quitting the property[18], or by moving out to take up a residential job and sub-letting the house in breach of tenancy condition[19], or by dying before completion[20].

The price to be paid for the house or flat

By section 126(1)(a) the price is the 'value at the relevant time' which, under section 127, is the price the dwelling would fetch on the open market at that time, that is the date, under section 122(2), on which the tenant's notice claiming to exercise RTB was served, on a willing vendor basis but subject to certain assumptions:

(a) the vendor was selling for an estate in fee simple, or was granting a lease, for the appropriate term defined in Schedule 6 paragraph 12, *generally* 125 years, at a ground rent of not more than £10 per annum *with vacant possession*;

(b) neither the tenant nor a member of his/her family residing with him wished to acquire the property;

(c) any improvements made by the tenant or his/her tenant predecessors in title together with any failure by them to keep the property in good internal repair are to be disregarded[21];

(d) that the conveyance, or grant of the lease, is on the terms laid down in Part V of the Housing Act 1985;

(e) that any service charges or improvement contributions payable will not be less than the amounts to be expected in accordance with notices served under section 125 (see below).

This price must be discounted according to section 126(1)(b). The discount is, under section 129 as amended, in the case of a house, 32% plus 1% for each complete year by which the qualifying period of entitlement exceeds two years up to a maximum of 60%, and, in the case of a flat, 44% plus 2% for each complete year by which the qualifying period exceeds two years, up to a maximum of 70%. Under section 129(2A) the Secretary of State may order maximum and minimum discounts and the amount of percentage increase per annum to be *increased*, and, under section 129(2B) such orders may make different provision with respect to different cases or types of case. The qualifying period for discount entitlement is calculated, as is the period for determining qualification to exercise RTB, by reference to Schedule 4

18 *Sutton London Borough Council v Swann* (1985) 18 HLR 140.
19 *Muir Group Housing Association Ltd v Thornley* (1992) 91 LGR 1.
20 *Bradford Metropolitan City Council v McMahon* [1993] 4 All ER 237, [1994] 1 WLR 52, CA.
21 'Improvement' is to be defined by reference to section 187, see *Dickinson v Enfield London Borough Council* (1996) 29 HLR 465.

(see above). Thus discount entitlement is built up where the secure tenant, or his/her spouse (provided they are living together at the relevant time, see section 122(2) supra), or a deceased spouse of his/hers (provided they were living together at the time of death) was a public sector tenant (see above) or was the spouse of a public sector tenant and occupied as his/her only or principal home the dwelling of which spouse was such a tenant. A person who, as a joint tenant under a public sector tenancy, occupied a dwelling house as his/her only principal home, is treated as having been the public sector tenant under that tenancy. Likewise entitlement will be built up by the child of a public sector tenant of a dwelling where that tenant has died or otherwise ceased to be such a tenant, and thereupon the child, having occupied the dwelling as his/her only or principal home becomes the new public sector tenant. A period during which that new tenant, since reaching the age of 16, occupied as his/her only or principal home a dwelling house of which a parent of his/hers was the public sector tenant, provided that period was the period at the end of which the child became the new public sector tenant *or* it was an earlier period ending *two years or less* before that period, is to be treated as a period during which the child was a public sector tenant.

The legislation is retrospective so that time spent, for example, as an authority or association etc, tenant before 1980 counts towards discount entitlement and qualifying to exercise RTB.

Where two joint tenants exercise RTB, Schedule 4 is applied so that for the secure tenant is substituted that one of the joint tenants whose discount entitlement is greatest.

There is to be deducted, under section 130, from the discount an amount equal to any previous discount qualifying because it was given before the relevant time on a conveyance or lease by a public sector landlord, *and* was given to the person, or one of the persons exercising RTB, *or* to the spouse of that person (provided they are living together at the relevant time) or to a deceased spouse of that person (provided they were living together at the time of death). *Furthermore*, under section 131 as amended, except where the Secretary of State so determines, the amount of discount may *not* reduce the purchase price below the amount which, in accordance with his determination, represents so much of the costs incurred in respect of the dwelling in the period of eight years before the tenant claimed to exercise RTB. If the price before discount is below that amount there is no discount. *Furthermore* discount may *not* reduce the price by more than such a sum as is prescribed from time to time by the Secretary of State. From 1989 onwards a maximum discount of £50,000 was set. However, under SI 1998/2997 (England) and SI 1999/292 (Wales) maximum discount levels have been dramatically reduced on a regional basis. The greatest discount is now £38,000 in London and the South East, while the lowest is £24,000 in Wales and East Midlands, for example. The changes are based on 70% of the average value of council properties by region—65% in London.

Where the price is discounted section 155 requires the purchaser to covenant to repay *on demand* a specified amount of discount, if within a period of three years he/she further conveys, leases, or assigns, as the case may be, the dwelling acquired. The amount of discount repayable is the discount reduced by one-third for each complete year elapsing after the date of transfer to the purchaser. Liability to repay discount is, under section 156, a charge on the premises.

Liability to repay arises in respect of 'relevant disposals' as outlined above, see further section 159 and later material on restrictions on the resale of dwellings in rural areas. However, liability to repay does not arise if the disposal is 'exempted' under section 160 (as amended). This will be considered in greater detail below, but note that it exempts disposals under wills and intestacies, under the terms of the family provision and inheritance legislation, certain disposals within families and disposals of dwelling houses under section 23, 24 or 24A of the Matrimonial Causes Act 1973 (property adjustment orders in connection with matrimonial proceedings), orders under section 2 of the Inheritance (Provision for Family and Dependants) Act 1975, orders under section 17 of the Matrimonial and Family Proceedings Act 1984, and orders under paragraph 1, Schedule 1 of the Children Act 1989.

Exercising RTB

Under section 122(1) the tenant must serve on the landlord written notice claiming to exercise RTB. If this notice is not withdrawn the landlord must, under section 124, serve written counter notice *generally* within four weeks either admitting the right, or denying it, stating the reasons why, in the landlord's opinion, it does not exist. Disputes as to RTB are determined by the county court, see section 181. Once RTB has been established the landlord must serve, under section 125, as amended, within eight weeks where the right is to acquire the freehold, or within twelve weeks where it is to acquire a leasehold interest, a further notice on the tenant. This will describe the dwelling-house and state:

(a) the price at which the tenant is entitled to purchase, and further stating the value of the dwelling at the relevant time, and any improvements disregarded under section 127 in determining value;

(b) the appropriate discount, and the discount period taken into account under section 129;

(c) the provisions which should be included in the conveyance/lease;

(d) where the notice states provisions which would enable the landlord to recover service charges or improvement contributions, it must also contain estimates and other information required by sections 125A (service charges) and 125B (improvement contributions);

(e) a description of any structural defect known to the landlord affecting the dwelling or the building in which it is situated;

(f) rights to have the value of the dwelling fixed by the district valuer, and rights under sections 125D and 125E (see further below).

It appears there is no duty of care owed at common law in addition to the duties imposed under section 125, eg as to the price of the property[1].

Under section 125A the landlord's section 125 notice must state as regards service charges the estimate of average annual amounts (at current prices) which would be payable in respect of each head of charge in the 'reference period' and the aggregate of those estimated amounts, and shall also contain a statement of the reference period adopted for estimate purposes. For the purposes of sections 125A and 125B (see below) the 'reference period' is effectively five years beginning on a date specified reasonably by the landlord as a date by which the conveyance/lease etc will be completed, such date not to be more than six months after the section 125 notice is given. With regard to *flats* certain charges must be separately itemised under section 125A(2), which provides that the notice must, as regards service charges in respect of repairs (including works to make good structural defects) contain:

(i) in respect of works itemised in the notice, estimates of the amount (at current prices) of the likely cost of, and of the tenant's likely contribution in respect of, each item, and the aggregates of those costs and contributions;

(ii) for non-itemised works, an estimate of average annual costs (at current prices) which the landlord considers likely to be payable by the tenant;

(iii) a statement of the reference period adopted for the purpose of the estimates;

(iv) a statement of the effect of paragraph 16B of Schedule 6 (see below) and

(v) a statement of the effect of section 450A (see below).

Paragraph 16B of Schedule 6 provides that where the lease of a flat requires the tenant to pay service charges in respect of repairs (including works to make good structural defects) liability to pay in respect of costs incurred in the 'initial period' (see below) is restricted, so that the tenant is not required to pay in respect of works itemised in the estimates contained in the section 125 notice any more than the amount shown as the tenant's estimated contribution in respect of that item, together with an allowance for inflation. In respect of works not itemised the tenant is not required to pay at a rate exceeding:

1 *Payne v Barnet London Borough Council* (1997) 30 HLR 295 and *Blake v Barking and Dagenham London Borough Council* (1996) 30 HLR 963. Furthermore, the duty to give notice of defects is dependant on knowledge of those defects, not mere suspicion they exist. The relevant defects are those which are structural *and* inherent, and which require the structure to be made good.

(a) as regards parts of the 'initial period' falling within the reference period (see above) for estimates contained in the section 125 notice the estimated average amount shown in the estimates;

(b) as regards parts of the initial period falling outside the reference period, the average rate produced by averaging over the reference period all works for which estimates are contained in the notice, together with, in each case, an allowance for inflation. Such inflation allowances are to be calculated according to methods prescribed by the Secretary of State under paragraph 16D of Schedule 6. The 'initial period' of a lease is effectively five years from the date of its grant.

Section 450A provides that the Secretary of State may provide by regulations that where the lease of a flat has been granted in pursuance of RTB and the landlord is the *housing authority (which generally includes a registered social landlord) who granted the lease, or another housing authority*, the tenant shall have the 'right to a loan', to be charged on the security of the flat, see section 450C, in respect of certain service charges. These are charges in respect of repairs (including works for making good structural defects) payable in the period beginning with the grant of the lease, and ending, generally, with its tenth anniversary. The right may be specified by the regulations only to arise in respect of specified amounts of a service charge. Where the landlord *is a housing association* the right is to a loan from the Corporation. In any other case it is a right to leave the whole or part of the service charge outstanding. (Section 450B creates a *power* to grant loans etc in circumstances falling outside the right to a loan.) See further SI 1992/1708 and DoE Circular 21/92.

'Service charges' are defined by section 621A to be amounts payable by purchasers or lessees of premises which are payable directly or indirectly for services, repairs, maintenance or insurance or the vendor/lessor's costs of management, and the whole or part of which may vary according to 'relevant costs'. These latter are the costs or estimated costs incurred, or to be incurred, in connection with the matters for which the charge is payable, including overheads.

Under section 125B the landlord's notice in respect of a flat will also, as respects 'improvement contributions', contain a statement of the effect of paragraph 16C of Schedule 6 (see below) and estimates for works in respect of which the landlord considers that costs may be incurred in the reference period (see above). The works must be itemised, and estimates must show the amount (at current prices) of the likely cost of, and the tenant's likely contribution in respect of, each item, and the aggregate of costs and contributions. Section 187 (as amended) provides that 'improvement' means any alteration in or addition to a dwelling, including additions or alterations to a landlord's fixtures and fittings or to ancillary services, the erection of wireless or television aerials and carrying out external decoration. 'Improvement contribution' means a sum payable by a tenant of a flat in respect of improvements carried out to the flat, the building in which it is situated, or any other building or land, other than works carried out in discharge of obligations under paragraph 16A of Schedule 6 to repair or reinstate property etc.

Paragraph 16C of Schedule 6 provides that where the tenant of a flat is required to pay such contributions, liability in respect of costs incurred in the initial period (see above) of the lease is restricted so that he/she is not required to make any payment in respect of works for which no estimate was given in the landlord's section 125 notice, and he/she is not to pay in respect of works for which an estimate was given in that notice any more than the amount of the estimated contribution in respect of that items with an allowance for inflation.

The section 125 (as amended) notice must further inform the tenant of the right under section 128 to have the value of the dwelling determined by the district valuer. The tenant must follow the procedure laid down in section 128 and serve written notice within three months of having received the section 125 notice, requiring the district valuer to determine the value of the property at the 'relevant time', that is the date on which notice claiming to exercise RTB was served. The three month period is extended if there are proceedings pending on the determination of any other question arising under Part V of the 1985 Act. In such a case the notice may be served at any time within three months of the final determination of those proceedings. Where such proceedings are commenced *after* a determination made by the district valuer, a redetermination may be required under section 128(3) of the Act by either of the parties within four weeks of the conclusion of the proceedings. The district valuer must consider any representations made to him by either landlord or tenant within four weeks from the service of a notice under section 128. It is the duty of the authority under section 128(5) to inform the tenant of the outcome of any determination or redetermination made by the district valuer. The jurisdiction of the district valuer is exclusive.

In addition the section 125 notice, under changes introduced by the Leasehold Reform, Housing and Urban Development Act 1993, must also inform the tenant of the effects of sections 125D, 125E, 136(2), 140 and 141, the effect of Part II, Chapter I of the 1993 Act (Rent into Mortgage) and 143B.

Sections 125D and 125E (which were inserted to take account of the new 'rent into mortgage' scheme – see below) provide that where a section 125 notice has been served, the tenant must, within 12 weeks of service of that notice, serve written notice of intention to proceed with RTB on the landlord, or notice of withdrawal of the claim, or notice of intention to acquire on rent to mortgage terms under section 144 (as substituted). Where the tenant neglects to do this in time the landlord may, by a further written notice, require the tenant to serve notice as to his/her intentions within 28 days, and stating the effect of section 125E(4) which is that failure to comply with the landlord's notice leads to the claim to exercise RTB being deemed withdrawn. There is, however, discretion to extend the time periods within which a response is required where it would be unreasonable to expect the tenant to comply with the notice.

Miscellaneous points

Where a former secure tenant has given notice claiming to exercise the right to buy and is superseded by a new secure tenant under the same secure tenancy (otherwise than on assignment made as an exchange under section 92), or under a periodic tenancy arising after the end of such a tenancy under section 86, the new tenant is in the same position *as if the notice had been given by him/her*; see section 136. For the purposes of entitlement to exercise RTB and also discount entitlement it is, however, the former tenant's circumstances that must be considered, see *McIntyre v Merthyr Tydfil Borough Council*.[2]

Where there is a change of landlord, by transfer of the freehold, after the service of notice claiming to exercise RTB, section 137(1) lays down that all parties shall be in the same position as if the acquiring landlord had been landlord before the notice was given and had taken all steps which the former landlord had taken. However, if any of the circumstances after the change differ in any material respect, as where, for example, an exception to RTB becomes applicable, section 137(2) requires that all concerned must, as soon as possible, take such steps as are necessary for securing that the parties are, *as nearly as may be*, in the same position that they would have been in had those circumstances previously obtained.

Under section 140, as amended, the landlord *may* at any time serve written notice on the tenant requiring him/her, if all relevant matters concerning the grant and finance have been agreed or determined, to complete the transaction within a specified reasonable period of at least 56 days, *or*, if any relevant matter is outstanding, to serve on the landlord a written notice specifying the matter to be settled. This is the 'first notice to complete' and it must inform the tenant of the effect of the notice, and of the landlord's power to serve a 'second notice to complete'. Such a 'first notice' may not be served earlier than 12 months after service of the landlord's notice under section 125 (see above) *or* where a notice under section 146 has been served (see below) the service of that notice. Minor misdescriptions in this notice may be of no effect, provided a reasonable person could not have been misled by them[3].

Under section 141 where the tenant does not comply with the first notice to complete, the landlord *may* serve a second notice requiring completion within a specified reasonable period of at least 56 days, and informing him/

2   (1989) 21 HLR 320.
3   *Milne-Berry v Tower Hamlets London Borough Council* (1995) 28 HLR 225.

her of the effect of the notice. Where the tenant fails to comply the notice claiming to exercise RTB is deemed withdrawn at the end of the specified period.

Conversely under section 153A, as amended in 1993, where a secure tenant has claimed to exercise RTB and the landlord is guilty of delay by, for example, failing to admit/deny the existence of the right, an 'initial notice of delay' may be served which specifies the last action taken by the landlord and specifies a period of not less than one month within which the landlord may serve a counter notice to cancel the initial notice of delay – which can only be done if the landlord has taken requisite steps or does so contemporaneously with the counter-notice. A failure by the landlord to serve a counter-notice enables the tenant to serve under section 153B, an 'operative notice of delay' after which any payment of *rent* is to be treated additionally as a payment on account of the purchase price. Counter-notices must state the basis on which they are served, but a notice served in good faith will be sufficient to prevent the operation of section 153B, even if a sale subsequently goes ahead on terms disputed by the landlord, but required of them by the court[4].

Completing the transfer

Once all the above steps have been taken, the matters relating to the transfer and the arrangements as to mortgage finance, etc, have been completed, section 138(1) binds the landlord to convey or lease, as the case may be, the dwelling to the tenant. On completion the secure tenancy comes to an end: section 139(2). The landlord is not bound to complete while the tenant is found to be in arrears with the rent or other tenancy outgoings for a period of four weeks after the money due has been lawfully demanded from him (section 138(2)). If there are no impediments to the transfer the landlord must go ahead with it. The duty is enforceable by way of an injunction (section 138(3)) and the court has no discretion to refuse an injunction, for example, on the ground of hardship to third parties[5].

The actual transfer takes place according to the registered conveyancing procedure under section 123 of the Land Registration Act 1925.

Rent into mortgage

To assist purchasers of dwellings under RTB there was in the legislation from 1980 a concommittant 'right to a mortgage' (for details of which see

4   *Guinan v Enfield London Borough Council* (1996) 29 HLR 456.
5   *Taylor v Newham London Borough Council* [1993] 2 All ER 649, [1993] 1 WLR 444, CA.

Hughes, *Public Sector Housing Law*, 2nd edition 1987 pp 61–64). However, under the Leasehold Reform, Housing and Urban Development Act 1993, this right was abolished as from 11 October 1993, along with the right to defer completion and the right to be granted a shared ownership lease, which, it appears, had been very little used (for details see Hughes, op cit, pp 72–75, and for transitional provisions see DoE Circular 13/93). In their place was introduced the right to acquire on rent to mortgage terms ('Rent into mortgage' or RIM). Under this a secure tenant who wishes to exercise RTB but who cannot afford to pay the full purchase price in 'one go' may transmute the rent he/she pays to the discounted purchase price of a 'share' of his/her dwelling along with a right to purchase the remainder at some future time; ie he/she may make an 'initial payment' out of money otherwise payable as rent while the rest of the purchase is financed by a mortgage to be redeemed at a future date. Whether this will dramatically increase the numbers of sales remains to be seen: many tenants will be excluded because they are 'on' housing benefit, while those entitled to a RIM purchase are probably likely to be able to raise the full purchase price from the ordinary mortgage market.

A new section 143 provides that where a claim to exercise RTB has been made, established and remains in force, RIM also applies, *save where*, under section 143A it is determined that the tenant is or was entitled to housing benefit, or an outstanding claim for housing benefit has been made by or on behalf of the tenant during the 'relevant period', ie the period beginning 12 months before the claim to acquire on RIM terms and ending on the day on which the transfer of the property to the would-be purchaser is made. Acquisition under RIM is also excluded under section 143B if the minimum initial payment (see below) in respect of the dwelling *exceeds* the maximum initial payment, which is 80% of the price the tenant would pay on exercising RTB. Minimum initial payment (MIP) varies from case to case. In a case, for instance, where the weekly rent at the time the landlord admits the RIM claim under section 146 (see below) does not exceed the relevant amount (ie a sum declared from time to time by the Secretary of State), MIP is determined as $P = R \times M$, where $P = MIP$, $R =$ weekly rent and M is the Secretary of State's specified multiplier. The object of the equation as declared by section 143B(6) is that 'the relevant amount and the multipliers ... shall be such that ... they will produce a minimum initial payment equal to the capital sum which, in the opinion of the Secretary of State, would be raised on a 25 year repayment mortgage in the case of which the net monthly mortgage payment was equal to the rent at the relevant time calculated on a monthly basis'.

Thus where MIP is *less* than 80% of the price otherwise payable under RTB, acquisition on RIM terms is generally available. The tenant may calculate what 'share' he/she would be able to buy if the present rent level was a monthly mortgage repayment, though a larger 'share' may also be acquired. The 'share' is then acquired and financed by a mortgage.

Under section 144 (as substituted) where a tenant wishes to acquire on RIM terms, written notice to that effect must be served on the landlord, whereupon any notice served by the landlord under sections 140 or 141 (see above) are deemed withdrawn, and no further such notices may be served while the section 144 notice remains in force. Under the new section 146 of the 1985 Act the landlord must as soon as practicable serve a notice either admitting or denying the tenant's claim. Where the claim is admitted the notice must also set out the terms and consequences of a RIM acquisition. Section 146A then requires the tenant to serve a further written notice on the landlord, within 12 weeks of service of the section 146 notice, stating that the tenant intends to proceed with the RIM acquisition and stating the amount of the initial payment proposed (which must be not *less* than the minimum initial payment or *more* than the maximum), *or* that the RIM claim is withdrawn in order to pursue a 'standard' RTB purchase, *or* that the tenant is withdrawing from acquisition. Once the 12 week period has elapsed the landlord may, under section 146B, serve on a tenant who has failed to respond a written notice requiring a response and stating the consequences of failure. Where there is a failure to respond within 28 days the RIM claim is deemed withdrawn. Where, however, the tenant pursues the RIM claim the new section 147 requires the landlord to serve another written notice stating the landlord's 'share' and the initial discount available. These figures are calculated under a substituted section 148 which provides that the landlord's 'share' will be calculated by the formula:

$$S = \frac{P - IP}{P} \times 100$$

where S is the landlord's share, P is the price payable on a 'standard' RTB sale, and IP is the amount of the tenant's initial payment. The initial discount (ID) is determined by the formula:

$$ID = \frac{IP}{P} \times D$$

where IP and P have their above meanings and D is the amount of discount available on a 'standard' RTB sale.

A substituted section 149 provides that where the interest of the landlord in the dwelling passes to another body (eg on a transfer of stock from an authority to a registered social landlord) *after* a secure tenant has given notice claiming the right to a RIM acquisition, all the parties shall, in general, be in the same position as if the 'other' body was the landlord *before* the tenant's notice was given and had been given that notice and had taken all the steps the landlord had taken.

Where all formalities relating to a RIM acquisition have been completed, section 150, as substituted, requires the landlord to make a transfer of the *freehold* of the dwelling (where it is a house and the landlord owns the freehold) or (where the dwelling is a flat or the landlord does not own the freehold) to grant a lease of the property. Section 151, as substituted, then provides for the terms and effect of the transfer to conform with Schedule 6 of the 1985 Act (see below), subject to certain modifications to ensure that on a leasehold transfer where a service charge is payable that charge is abated to take account of the 'shared' nature of the transaction.

After the transfer, of course, there is a somewhat strange legal 'beast'. The purchaser has acquired the freehold/leasehold, but that is subject to the landlord's 'share' and that share at some time has to be 'redeemed'. Provision for that is made by section 151A and Schedule 6A of the 1985 Act as introduced in 1993. A *right* to redeem at any time is guaranteed by Schedule 6A, para 2, while an *obligation* to do so is imposed by para 1 on the happening of particular events. These are: making a relevant disposal which is not otherwise 'excluded', and the expiry of one year beginning with a 'relevant death'. Disposals of the property thus attract the obligation *unless* they are transfers between spouses, or take effect under a will or intestacy, or under the terms of sections 23A, 24 or 24A of the Matrimonial Causes Act 1973, section 2 of the Inheritance (Provision for Family and Dependents) Act 1975, section 17 of the Matrimonial and Family Proceedings Act 1984, or paragraph 1 of Schedule 1 of the Children Act 1989. Similarly the obligation will arise within one year of the death of the acquiring tenant, or the survivor where there was a joint acquisition. Schedule 6A also makes provision for the value of the landlord's share to be determined for redemption purposes, and also for redemption to take place on a staged *or* interim payment basis at any time. Where the *obligation* to redeem arises, under section 151B, introduced in 1993, the liability is secured by mortgage on the property. For the purposes of completeness note that sections 152 and 153 of the 1985 Act, as amended, supply powers to landlords to 'hurry along' a dilatory purchaser with regard to RIM acquisitions similar to those with regard to RTB sales under sections 140 and 141 supra.

The terms of the freehold sale or long lease

Section 139(1) and Schedule 6 contain the terms on which transfers take place.

Leasehold terms: Schedule 6, Parts I and II

(1)   The lease must be, *in general*, for a term of not less than 125 years at a ground rent of not more than £10 per annum. But if in a building containing two or more dwellings one has already been sold on a 125 year lease since 8 August 1980, any subsequent long lease granted under RTB provisions may be made for a term of less than 125 years so as to expire at the same time as the initial 125 year term.

(2) Following transfer the purchaser will continue to enjoy common use of any premises, facilities or services enjoyed previously as a secure tenant unless both parties agree otherwise.

(3) The landlord is made subject to quite onerous repairing covenants:

    (a) to keep in repair the structure and exterior of the dwelling, and also of the building in which it is situated (including drains, gutters and external pipes) and to make good any defect affecting that structure;

    (b) to keep in repair any other property over or in respect of which the tenant has any rights by virtue of Schedule 6, for example any common parts;

    (c) to ensure, so far as practicable, that any services which are to be provided by the landlord and to which the purchaser is entitled are maintained at a reasonable level, and also to keep in repair any installation connected with provision of such services;

    (d) to rebuild or reinstate the dwelling and the building in which it is situated in the case of destruction or damage by fire, tempest, flood or any other normally insurable risk.

It will be seen that these covenants are extensive, but liability will not be absolute. Landlords are not liable for any breach of covenant unless they are given notice of the defect, and the standard of repair required will depend on the age, character and locality of the dwelling[6].

Under paragraph 16A of Schedule 6 a lease may require a tenant to bear a reasonable part of the landlord's costs in discharging, or insuring against, obligations to repair, make good structural defects and also to provide services mentioned above, or in insuring against the obligation to rebuild or reinstate. Where the lease requires a tenant to contribute towards insurance, the tenant is entitled to inspect the policy at reasonable times. Where the landlord does not insure against the obligations imposed by the covenant to rebuild or reinstate, the lease may require the tenant to pay a reasonable sum in place of the contribution otherwise required if there were insurance. Paragraph 16A has effect subject to paragraph 16B which, as we have seen, limits certain costs payable by a tenant during the initial period of the lease.

Paragraph 18 of Schedule 6, as substituted, makes it clear that a provision in a lease, or an agreement collateral thereto, is void in so far as it purports either to authorise the recovery of contributions in respect of those repairs, etc, mentioned in paragraph 16A otherwise than in accordance with paragraphs 16A and 16B, or to authorise the recovery of any charge in respect of the landlord's costs incurred in discharging the obligation to rebuild or reinstate, or the recovery of an improvement contribution otherwise than as allowed by paragraph 16C.

Schedule 6 also makes void any term of the lease purporting to prohibit or restrict assigning or subletting the dwelling.

---

6 *Lurcott v Wakely and Wheeler* [1911] 1 KB 905.

Those who purchase *long leasehold* interests in flats may also rely on the provisions of sections 18 to 30 of the Landlord and Tenant Act 1985 as amended. These are particularly concerned with further regulating service charges.

A 'service charge' is an amount payable by a tenant as part of, or in addition to, the rent, in respect of services, repairs, maintenance or insurance or the landlord's costs of management and which amount varies or may vary according to the costs or estimated costs incurred or to be incurred in any period by the landlord in providing the service. These costs are known as 'the relevant costs' and include overheads. See section 18 of the Landlord and Tenant Act (LTA) 1985 and also section 621A of the Housing Act 1985. Irrespective of the wording used to describe it, a charge which does not match the statutory requirements is not a 'service charge' for the purposes of the Landlord and Tenant Act 1985[7].

Section 19 of the LTA controls the extent to which costs can be recovered as service charges by a test of reasonableness. The tenant will only have to pay where costs can be shown to have been reasonably incurred and where they are for services or works only if the services or works themselves are of reasonable standard.

Section 20 of the LTA, as substituted, goes further than section 19 and places a limit on costs incurred in carrying out works on buildings which can be recovered without getting estimates and complying with other requirements. This amount is £25 multiplied by the number of flats in the building or £500 whichever is the greater. The Secretary of State may specify other figures. Any costs incurred in excess of this amount cannot be regarded as relevant costs unless these requirements are satisfied in the case of a tenant *not* represented by a recognised tenants' association:

(a) at least two estimates for works must be obtained, one from a person wholly unconnected with the landlord;

(b) a notice with copies of the estimates must be forwarded to the tenant concerned or displayed in the building and, if one exists, forwarded to the relevant tenants' association. The notice must describe works to be carried out and invite observations by a date not earlier than one month after the date of service or display of the notice;

(c) the landlord must consider observations received and must not commence works before the date specified in the notice unless required urgently.

In proceedings relating to a service charge, the county court, if satisfied that the landlord acted reasonably, may dispense with all or any of the requirements set out above.

The requirements applying to tenants who *are* represented by a recognised tenants' association are similar, though here some communications may take place via the association's secretary.

7   *Coventry City Council v Cole* [1994] 1 All ER 997, [1994] 1 WLR 398, CA.

The landlord must, under section 21 of the LTA, supply, on written request by a tenant or secretary of a relevant tenants' association, a written summary of costs incurred and from which service charges are determined. This information must be provided, under section 21(4) within six months of the end of the previous accounting period or within one month of the request whichever is the later.

Terms common to freehold and leasehold sales

Schedule 6, paragraph 2(1) provides, inter alia, that as regards any rights to support or access of light and air, the passage of water, or sewage or of gas or other piped fuel smoke and fumes, to the use or maintenance of pipes or other installations for such passage, or to the use or maintenance of cables or other installations for the supply of electricity, are subject to certain conditions. These are that purchasers will acquire rights of usage and maintenance equivalent to those enjoyed under secure tenancies or under any collateral agreement or arrangement on the severance of the dwelling from other property then comprised in the same tenancy, and second that dwellings will remain subject to all such rights for the benefit of other property *as are capable of existing in law* and are necessary to secure to persons interested in other properties as nearly as may be the same rights against purchasers as were available when they were secure tenants, or under any collateral agreement or arrangement made on severance.

Restrictions on resale, etc

One of the chief fears of those opposed to indiscriminate sales of social housing has been that the most attractive houses only will be purchased leaving landlords with less desirable homes. This argument has also been heard in relation to *areas* of houses. There is a danger that houses in rural areas may be purchased by their tenants and then sold to wealthy city dwellers looking for second or holiday homes, thus further eroding the already limited stock of dwellings available to people living and working in rural areas. Section 157 goes some way towards allaying such fears by placing restrictions on the resale of certain houses.

Where a transfer is made by, inter alia, a district council, a London Borough council, or a housing association, of a dwelling situated in a National Park, an area designated under section 87 of the National Parks and Access to the Countryside Act 1949 (area of outstanding natural beauty) or an area designated by order of the Secretary of State as a rural area, covenants may be imposed limiting the freedom of the purchaser and his/her successors in title to dispose of the dwelling.

The limitation is that until such time as is notified by the landlord to the tenant, there may be no 'relevant disposal' which is not an 'exempted disposal' without the landlord's written consent, though such consent may not be withheld if the disposal is to a person who has throughout the period of three years immediately preceding the application for consent had his/her place of work in a region designated by order of the Secretary of State which is wholly or partly comprised in the National Park or area, *or* has had his/her only or principal home in such a region *or* has had the one in part or parts of that period and the other in the remainder, though the region need not have been the same throughout the period. This enables rural workers and dwellers to move from one designated region to another over a short period and yet retain the ability to purchase houses otherwise subject to resale restrictions. Similarly there may be no disposal by way of tenancy or licence without the landlord's written consent, unless it be to a person satisfying the foregoing condition, or *by* a person whose only or principal home is, and throughout the duration of the tenancy, etc, remains the dwelling house in question: see section 157(2)(b). This prevents purchasers letting out their homes for holidays, etc. A 'relevant disposal' is, under section 159, a conveyance of the freehold or assignment of the lease, or the grant of a lease for more than 21 years, otherwise than at a rack rent. An 'exempted disposal' is under section 160:

(a) a disposal of the whole of the dwelling and a further conveyance or assignment to a 'qualifying person', ie a person, or one of the persons, by whom the disposal is made, or the spouse or former spouse of that person, or one of those persons, or a member of the family of that person(s) who has resided with him/her throughout the period of 12 months ending with the disposal; or

(b) a vesting of the whole dwelling under a will or on an intestacy; or

(c) a disposal under section 23, 24 or 24A of the Matrimonial Causes Act 1973 or section 2 of the Inheritance (Provision for Family and Dependents) Act 1975, or section 17 of the Matrimonial and Family Proceedings Act 1984, or paragraph 1 of Schedule 1 of the Children Act 1989;

(d) a compulsory disposal, as under a compulsory purchase order;

(e) a disposal of property consisting of land let with or used for the purposes of the dwelling house.

Disposals in breach of covenant are void.

With the consent of the Secretary of State *or the Corporation where the landlord is a housing association* the covenant may be that until the end of the period of ten years beginning with the initial disposal there will be no further sale or long lease, etc other than an exempted disposal, unless:

(a) the tenant or his successor in title first offers to re-transfer the dwelling to the original landlord, and

(b) they refuse the offer or fail to accept it within one month of its being made.

The purchase price to be paid in such cases will be, under section 158, the price agreed or determined by the district valuer, reduced to take account of any liability to repay discount.

The powers of the Secretary of State

The sale of social housing, particularly council houses, to sitting tenants was a fundamental plank of government housing policy under the Conservatives from 1980 to 1997, and has not been ended under the Blair government. To assist tenants the Secretary of State has extensive powers under sections 164 to 170.

Where it appears to the Secretary of State, presumably on reasonable evidence, that a tenant or tenants of a particular landlord, or landlords, are finding it difficult to exercise RTB effectively and expeditiously, he may, by giving written notice of intention to do so, intervene in the given situation, under section 164. Once such notice is in force, and it is deemed to be given 72 hours after it has been sent, he may do *all* such things as appear to him necessary or expedient to enable the exercise of RTB, etc. The Secretary of State's notice has the effect of preventing further action by a vending landlord with regard to RTB, and nullifies any previous action taken. The rights and obligations of the landlord are vested in the Secretary of State though he is not bound to follow the exact sales procedure required of a landlord in the exercise of RTB. See on this provision *R v Secretary of State, ex p Norwich City Council*[8].

For the purpose of making a transfer section 165 empowers the Secretary of State to make a Vesting Order which has the effect of:
(a) vesting the property in the tenant on the appropriate tenurial basis; and
(b) binding landlord and tenant, and their successors in title, by the covenants it contains.

A vesting order, on presentation to the Chief Land Registrar, requires the registration of the tenant as proprietor of the title concerned.

Under section 166 where the Secretary of State receives money due to a landlord in consequence of using his powers, he may retain it, while the section 164 notice is in force, and the interest thereon. He may furthermore recover costs, with interest, as a debt from the landlord, and may do this by withholding any sums due from him to the landlord. Section 167 gives the Secretary of State power to direct landlords not to include certain covenants in conveyances or grants of dwellings where inclusion of such covenants would lead to inconformity with the requirements of Schedule 6. Such a direction can have a retrospective effect under section 168, to such extent or in such manner as the notice provides. Section 169 grants the Secretary of State extensive powers to obtain documents, and other information

8   [1982] QB 808, [1982] 1 All ER 737.

where that appears necessary or expedient for the purpose of determining whether powers under section 164, 166, 167 or 168 are exercisable, or for, or in connection with, exercising those powers. This power is exercised by written notice to the landlord. Any officer of the landlord designated in the notice or having custody of documents or possessing information must, without instructions from the landlord, take all reasonable steps to ensure that the notice is complied with. Finally section 170 gives the Secretary of State powers to grant assistance to a party to proceedings in connection with RTB, etc, other than valuation proceedings, who applies to him for assistance. Assistance may be granted on grounds that the case raises issues of principle, or that it is unreasonable, having regard to the complexity of the issues, to expect the applicant to deal with the matter unaided. The assistance may take the form of giving advice, or procuring, or attempting to procure, a settlement, arranging for legal advice and/or representation, or any other form of aid considered appropriate.

GENERAL POWERS OF DISPOSAL

RTB is not the only plank in sales policy. Not every tenant will wish to buy the house he/she occupies, and there may be individuals or organisations who wish to purchase houses offered for general sale.

Section 32 of the Housing Act 1985 empowers authorities to dispose of housing land and stock. In general disposals other than by way of a secure tenancy or under RTB require the consent of the Secretary of State. It appears, however, that it is not unlawful for an authority to have a general policy of progressive disposal of their stock[9], and, of course, by virtue of section 161 of the Local Government and Housing Act 1989 authorities are not bound to have a housing stock at all. Section 34 (as amended) makes provision for the giving of either general or individual consents. In giving consent the Secretary of State must consider the extent to which the proposed transferee is likely to be subject to influence from the authority. Ministerial consent may also be required for disposals *by* the transferee under section 133 of the Housing Act 1988.

Sales may also take place at a discount as provided for by section 34(4). The provisions in section 35 relating to the payment of discount on an early disposal mirror those of section 155 of the 1985 Act.

Section 33 allows authorities only limited freedom to impose such covenants or conditions as they think fit on a disposal. Certain covenants and conditions may only be imposed with ministerial consent.

---

9   *R v Hammersmith and Fulham London Borough Council, ex p Beddowes* [1987] QB 1050, [1987] 1 All ER 369, CA.

Section 37 applies similar restrictions on resale of houses situated in National Parks, areas of outstanding natural beauty and other designated rural areas, to those contained in section 57.

The Secretary of State, in exercise of powers under section 34, has issued general consents that equate, in so far as possible, disposals of individual houses under the power of sale with those under RTB; see the Ministerial Letters of 31 August 1994 and 27 March 1995.

Voluntary stock transfers

Voluntary stock transfer using the foregoing powers commenced in the 1980s, with 53 recorded transfers comprising 6,000 empty houses and 3,000 tenanted dwellings having centrally recorded: by the summer of 1994 31 authorities had transferred housing on a voluntary basis. These authorities were mainly in the south of England and had disposed of their council housing to an association or a group of associations through the LSVT process. After a flurry of LSVTs at the end of the 1980s the government moved to regulate this form of disposal because of the implications for the wider housing association movement of the large amounts of private finance tied up in LSVTs.

Apart from the constraints imposed by the availability of private finance these transfers are subject to a degree of consultative control by virtue of section 106A of the 1985 Act, inserted in 1986.

Section 106A and Schedule 3A regulate the duties of authorities proposing to dispose of *dwellings subject to secure tenancies* and those of the Secretary of State in considering whether to give consent to disposals. These provisions, which replace the normal consultation requirements of section 105 of the 1985 Act in relation to questions of disposal, require regard to be had to the views of tenants likely to lose secure tenant status in consequence of the disposal. Where an authority disposes of an interest in land as a result of which a secure tenant of theirs will become the tenant of a person *other than* a body falling within section 80 of the 1985 Act, the Secretary of State must not entertain an application for consent to the disposal unless consultation requirements have been complied with. These are that the authority must, first, have served written notice on the affected tenant giving appropriate details of the proposed disposal, including the identity of the person to whom disposal will take place, the likely consequence of the disposal *for the tenant* the preservation of RTB and the effect of the consultation provisions of Schedule 3A. The tenant must also be informed of the right to make representations to the authority within a specified reasonable time. Secondly, any representations received must be considered, and, thirdly, the authority must then serve a further notice on the tenant stating any significant changes to the proposal, and the right to object to the Secretary of State. The tenant must also be informed that consent must be withheld if it appears that a majority of relevant tenants oppose the proposal. The Secretary of State may require further consultation to take place, but *must not* give consent if it appears a majority of relevant tenants do not wish the disposal to proceed, though he may refuse consent for other reasons. In coming to a decision the Secretary of State may have regard to any information available to him. In *R v Secretary of State for the Environment, ex p Walters*[10] the effect of these provisions was examined, and the following propositions were made:

- the purpose of the consultation exercise is to enable tenants to have their say about the likely consequences of disposal for them before being placed in a position which, as individuals, they might regard as worse than their current situation;
- Parliament has clearly required authorities to explain to tenants the likely consequences of disposal for them not just in general but in relation to the specific terms of any given proposed disposal – eg what effect will the proposed scheme actually have on RTB;
- Paragraph 6 of Schedule 3A provides that the Secretary of State's consent to a disposal is *not* invalidated by any failure to comply with the requirements of the Schedule, including the requirement of paragraph 5 that he must not give his consent if it appears to him a majority of tenants do not wish the disposal to proceed. Consent would not be vitiated if the Secretary of State mistakenly believed *as a matter of fact* that a majority of tenants were not opposed to transfer. However, the court may still upset the Secretary of State's decision if it is made on the basis of a misunderstanding of the law – ie if the Secretary of State has proceeded on a basis which shows he has misunderstood what the Act requires;
- The court will not lightly condone by-passing statutory consultation requirements, but may exercise its discretion not to grant a remedy where tenants opposed to a transfer are in a very clear minority, *and* have delayed in exercising the right to seek judicial review and where a scheme overall is manifestly beneficial.

The consultation provisions cover in effect only secure tenants in occupation. They could not apply where housing had already been *cleared* of tenants. See also DoE Circular 6/88. Further guidance was given in a DoE paper: 'Large Scale Voluntary Transfers of Local Authority Housing to Private Bodies' (June 1988), supplemented since 1993 by the DoE's 'Large Scale Voluntary Transfers – Guidelines'. This identified suitable transferees as those which are:

(a)   independent of the authority; in this connection council membership or shareholding should be *clearly* in a minority (under 20%), and there

10   (1997) 30 HLR 328.

should be a minimum of commercial agreements between the transferee and the authority; retention of nomination rights and waiting lists by the authority was not then considered acceptable, and neither would a power to specify staff from the authority to be transferred to the new landlord;

(b) able to demonstrate stability and responsibility with long term commitment to providing rented housing, ie those who take account of housing demand and conditions in lettings policies and who normally relet property falling vacant at rent levels affordable by those in lower paid employment;

(c) committed to providing a good service to tenants.

The Secretary of State also indicated unwillingness then to see authority monopolies of rented accommodation turned into private monopolies, and hoped that disposals would take place to a number of transferees, even in the area of small authorities. This would not seem to have been borne out in practice. Early disposals seem to have fallen within the 5,000–10,000 limits for disposal to a single purchaser.

The Secretary of State also indicated that authorities seeking to transfer should be able to demonstrate ability to discharge statutory obligations *after* transfer, particularly with regard to homelessness. This *can* be done by contractual arrangements with other landlords in their areas, including transferees of council stock.

The terms of transfers should be that sales are at market value subject to tenancies with an allowance for necessary repairs. Purchasers should seek private sector funding for sales. The 1993 guidelines repeated the 5,000 unit figure and indicated that only transfers to associations approved by the Secretary of State and the Housing Corporation were likely to be approved.

(The Ground of Possession, paragraph 10A in Schedule 2 to the Housing Act 1985 (as amended) allows for recovery of possession of dwellings subject to re-development schemes centrally approved under Part V of Schedule 2, following due tenant consultation, see Chapter Three.)

Central powers over local authority stock disposal

Controls over the rate at which LSVTs can occur are operated centrally to ensure that, inter alia, sufficient private finance is available, and as this problem is overcome it seems probable that there will be an increased flow of transfers, including larger urban authorities, as it clearly is government policy to encourage voluntary stock disposal. Section 135 of the Leasehold Reform, Housing and Urban Development Act 1993, as amended, provides that 'qualifying disposals' may only take place within a financial year if they have been included in a central 'programme' of disposals for that year. A qualifying disposal is one which requires the consent of the Secretary of

State (see above) *and* the aggregate number of dwelling houses included in the disposal (ie the number at that point to be disposed of, *plus* the number previously disposed of *by* the authority *to* the disponee within the five years ending with the date of the disposal) exceeds 499. Authorities may apply for disposals to be included in a programme, but in drawing a programme up the Secretary of State is to take into account, inter alia, any costs to the Exchequer of the disposal (eg housing benefit costs), and whether or not a particular disposal is likely to be opposed by affected tenants. Programmes have to be made in the form of a statutory instrument, and different programmes may be drawn up for different types of authority. Section 136 further provides that where stock is disposed of under a programme a levy is to be paid by relevant authorities to the Secretary of State, the rate to be fixed by a formula whose elements will be largely centrally determined. The purpose of this levy is to compensate the Treasury for the greater expenditure it has to bear on housing benefit in respect of increased rents charged by 'new' landlords following stock transfer.

Block disposals may involve the rehabilitation of existing stock, units of which are subsequently sold for owner occupation, and may be on the basis that the person/organisation acquiring housing land and stock from an authority does work on other authority housing as consideration rather than making a capital payment.

The programme of voluntary disposal has continued under the Blair Government. Thus on 11 March 1999, the 1990/2000 housing transfer programme involving some 140,000 dwellings was announced, subject to tenant approval. The overall capital receipts were predicted to be £822m, though nine of the transfers had to be supported by central funding under the Estates Renewal Challenge Funding scheme to facilitate transfer. Even with that support two authorities involved still expected to retain historic debt on the transferred housing because the capital receipts received would not cover these debts. Two of the proposed transfers were above DETR limits for transfer to a single landlord (though these limits have 'stretched' to allow transfers in the 7,000 dwellings range – in one case up to 13,000) and the practice in such cases is for 'group structure landlords' to be set up, ie there will be more than one registered social landlord to whom transfers will be made, but each of them will be in a group.

The majority of transfers consented to by tenants in the year beginning January 1999 appear to have been to local housing companies or housing trusts, which, of course, provide for tenant representation in their management structures. This was particularly noticeable in urban areas. Nevertheless some transfers to housing associations were also consented – usually in rural or semi-urban areas. Transfers are approved by the DETR subject to the giving of guarantees for tenants that rent increases will normally be limited by not more than inflation plus 1% for a period of five years.

The effect of transfer on RTB

RTB will, however, continue to apply to dwellings transferred out of the public stock as Preserved Right to Buy (PRTB) by virtue of section 171A to 171H (as amended) of the Housing Act 1985. The RTB provisions continue to apply where a person ceases to be a secure tenant by reason of the disposal (a 'qualifying disposal') by the landlord of *an interest* in the dwelling to a person who is *not* an authority or other body within section 80. The provisions accordingly refer to the 'former secure tenant' and the 'former landlord'. PRTB does not apply where the former landlord was a body falling within Schedule 5, paragraphs 1,2 and 3 to the 1985 Act, that is charities and certain housing trusts and associations, against whom RTB could not be exercised, *or in any other case provided for by order of the Secretary of State.* Under section 171B former secure tenants have PRTB so long as they occupy 'relevant dwellings', see below, as their only or principal homes, but this is subject to, inter alia, the requirements of paragraph 6 of Schedule 9A whereunder PRTB is a registrable interest under the Land Registration Act 1925, and so requires registration to be protected, such registration to be effected by the Chief Land Registrar on the disposal of relevant housing stock, the disposing body to ensure that the Chief Land Registrar is informed of all necessary particulars.

PRTB is exercisable only by a 'qualifying person', that is the former secure tenant, a person to whom a tenancy of a dwelling is granted jointly with a person having PRTB in relation to that dwelling, and a 'qualifying successor', that is either:

(a) a member of the former secure tenant's family who has acquired the dwelling under the will or intestacy of the former secure tenant, or to whom the former secure tenant has assigned the property, *provided* immediately before the death/assignment, as the case may be, the former secure tenant was an assured tenant of the dwelling in question (transfer of a dwelling from an authority to a registered social landlord will, of course, result in a tenant becoming 'assured'); or

(b) a person who becomes the tenant of the dwelling in place of the former secure tenant by virtue of orders under matrimonial legislation; or

(c) a person who was a member of the former secure tenant's family, to whom that tenant assigned the assured tenancy of the dwelling in question.

PRTB is also exercisable *only* in respect of a qualifying or 'relevant' dwelling. Such are:

(a) in relation to former secure tenants, dwellings subject to the disposals under which they ceased to be secure;

(b) in relation to qualifying successors, the dwellings of which they became the tenants; and

(c) in relation to persons to whom tenancies of dwellings are granted
      jointly with persons who have PRTB in relation to them, those
      dwellings.

However, if a person having PRTB becomes the tenant of another
dwelling, *and* the landlord is the same as the landlord of the previous
dwelling, *or*, where the landlord is a company, is a connected company, the
new dwelling is the relevant dwelling for PRTB. 'Connected companies' are,
under section 736 of the Companies Act 1985, subsidiary or holding
companies. PRTB is accordingly not lost on transfers between dwellings
of the same landlord.

Section 171C empowers the Secretary of State to make regulations to
modify the provisions of the 1985 Act with regard to PRTB, see currently
SI 1993/2241.

Part III of the 1988 Act (HATs)

The 1987 White Paper on Housing, Cm 214 (para 6.1 et seq) was the John
Major Government's attempt to address the problem of run-down inner
urban council estates. Housing Acting Trusts (HATs) were proposed to:
improve housing; provide other community needs such as shops, workshops
and advice centres; encourage local enterprise, *and* to give authority
tenants a greater diversity of landlords. HATs were seen as intermediate
bodies to take over housing, improve it, and then to pass it on to others. A
DoE consultation paper expanded this. Areas suitable for HAT treatment
were identified as those containing large numbers of poor quality public
sector dwellings etc in deprived environments with high vandalism rates
and other social problems such as unemployment, a high proportion of
residents in receipt of state benefits, poor estate design, and general decay.
The task of a HAT was to reverse such decline.

Part III of the Housing Act 1988 contained the new law.

Section 60 enables the Secretary of State to designate a HAT area which
may comprise two or more areas of land which need not even be contiguous
or situated in the same district. This discretion is extremely wide, but
particular regard may be had to the proportion of housing in a proposed
HAT area in authority ownership, its physical state and design type, its
housing management record, the living conditions of residents and their
social and general environment.

The Secretary of State must consult with affected authorities, see section
61, and must also notify all secure or other classes of prescribed tenants of
the proposal. He must make arrangements for a poll to be conducted, by
independent persons, of notified tenants with a view to establishing their
view, *or* otherwise hold a ballot or poll of those tenants to ascertain their
views. However, a ballot in some form has to be held, a far cry from the initial

proposal that tenants should merely be consulted – something which sparked fierce tenant resistance to the entire notion. He may *not* make the designation if it appears a majority of those who expressed an opinion oppose designation. Where there is majority support the designation *may* be made by order laid before, and approved by Parliament.

HATs are created under section 62 and Schedules 7 and 8 of the 1988 Act. Each HAT has a chairman and between 5 and 11 other members. The Secretary of State must have regard to the desirability of appointing local people to HATs, and must consult the authority before making an appointment. HAT members must not have any financial or other interest that could prejudice their membership function.

HATs' primary objectives are laid down in section 63:

(a) to secure improvement and repair of their stock;
(b) to secure proper housing management;
(c) to secure diversity of housing tenure and a diversity of landlords of tenanted property;
(d) to improve social and general environmental conditions.

To this end they may:

(a) provide and maintain housing and shops, and other community facilities;
(b) acquire, reclaim and dispose of land, and carry out operational development;
(c) ensure provision of main services;
(d) carry on businesses etc.

Under section 64 as soon as practicable after establishment a HAT is to draw up proposals for its area. It must consult with every affected housing authority, and must publicise its proposals within the affected area and give those likely to be affected an opportunity to make representations, which must be taken into account by the HAT. The Secretary of State must be kept informed of the HAT's work in this respect.

Section 65 empowers the Secretary of State to grant to a HAT extensive housing powers.

A HAT, under section 67, may be designated as a planning authority for its area, even, in specified instances to the exclusion of other authorities.

The Secretary of State has a general power to give directions to HATs under section 72. Thus, for example, ministers indicated HATs would be required in general to hold their meetings in public, and would also be required to set up tenants' advisory groups.

Section 74 empowers the Secretary of State to transfer housing and ancillary land from an authority to a HAT on such terms *as he thinks fit*, including financial terms, which may include payments *from* an authority to a HAT. Transfers of housing stock to HATs do not take place on the basis that the HAT will assume responsibility for the entire debt and loan charges incurred in relation to provision of the houses. Instead the basis is that the

'price' of the housing is the *estimated market value of the houses* subject
to existing tenancies. That 'price' may well be lower than the debt and loan
charges figure. Before making the transfer the Secretary of State must, under
section 75, consult with affected authorities and must publicise the proposal
so that persons such as secure tenants may know what is proposed, there
is, however, no obligation to *consult* with them.

HATs were not destined to be permanent bodies, and were always
intended to dispose of areas revived. Section 79 gives them wide land
disposal powers, subject to ministerial direction. Houses subject to secure
tenancies may (subject to section 84, which grants authorities powers of
pre-emption in respect of housing disposals by HATs), be disposed of to
a person or body approved by the Housing Corporation (who may not
approve 'public sector' landlords, or other persons or bodies *not*
independent of such institutions). Subsequent disposals by such 'approved'
persons or bodies are also subject to ministerial consent under section 81.
Some disposals are exempt, eg the granting of an assured tenancy. Likewise
subsequent disposals are subject to consultation requirements involving
relevant tenants. It should, however, be noted that RTB disposals are not
caught by the various requirements outlined above, see sections 79(2),
81(8)(a), and 83 of the 1988 Act.

The rights of tenants in HAT areas

Initially the transfer of housing from authority to HAT has no immediate
effect on tenants. They continue to be 'secure'. However, the Conservative
government's intention was that a HAT should seek to pass on improved
dwellings to new owners. Much housing could thus be transferred to other
bodies, eg associations. Section 84 imposes obligations on HATs in respect
of secure tenants affected by such disposals. A HAT may only dispose of
land with ministerial consent (section 79).

Section 84 of the 1988 Act (as amended in 1993) further, however, applies
where a HAT proposes to dispose of one or more dwellings let on secure
tenancies where the consequence would be that a secure tenant would
become the tenant of 'another person' which is not an authority. Before
applying for ministerial consent, the HAT must serve written notice on the
relevant local housing authority informing them of the proposed disposal
and requiring them, within not less than 28 days, to serve notice on the HAT
informing the HAT in respect of relevant houses of the likely consequences
for each affected tenant if the authority were to acquire the houses.
Thereafter, but before ministerial consent is applied for, the HAT must
inform affected tenants of the proposed disposal, together with: the name
of the disponee; the likely consequences of the disposal for secure
tenancies; the likely effect of acquisition by the authority, if they have so

indicated; the right of tenants to make representations in connection with becoming an authority tenant (see further below), and the right to make general representations about disposal. Any representations generally made must be taken into account. Where, however, tenants represent that they (or even one of them) wish to become authority tenants, that triggers action under section 84A (inserted in 1993). The Secretary of State, the authority and the tenant(s) have to be served with notice of this fact by the HAT which must also amend its disposal proposal so as to exclude property made subject to representations. The Secretary of State must then transfer the dwellings, by order, from the HAT to the authority – note that in the case of a flat block such an order is to be made if the *majority of tenants* in that block *making representations* represent that they wish to be authority tenants. This important change in the law, effectively ensuring a return to authority ownership at the end of a HAT designation, had to be inserted to make the policy in any way workable and acceptable to tenants.

HATs in practice

Tenant resistance to the very notion of HATs was considerable. Between July 1988 and November 1989 seven HATs were proposed (Lambeth, Leeds, Sandwell, Southwark, Sunderland, Tower Hamlets, Waltham Forest – NB all urban areas where RTB and voluntary transfers would make little impact). Apart from the Waltham Forest HAT which was actually *requested* by tenants (and where £150m over ten years in resources was promised) all were decisively rejected by ballot. Only one HAT proceeded rapidly towards fruition, that in North Hull. The North Hull HAT (which was promoted by the local authority) was put to a ballot in March 1991, £50m over ten years in resources being promised. The North Hull HAT was very active, issuing its own newsletter to tenants detailing the very considerable progress made in renovating properties. Tenants were involved in redesigning their houses. The HAT 'team' were principally seconded officers from Hull City Council housing department.

The Waltham Forest HAT came into operation on 9 December 1991, while there are also HATS in Liverpool, Hull, Castle Point and Tower Hamlets. The most recently designated HAT is at Stonebridge in Brent (SI 1994/1987) in the London Borough of Brent. HATs were one fairly small part of a package of measures at the disposal of the government for the regeneration of inner cities and peripheral estates – in many ways the most difficult and least subtle of these provisions. Schemes such as City Challenge have yielded more fruitful and rather less controversial results. Purely in terms of the strict focus of this chapter– the disposal of council houses – HATs have been one of the least successful policies, dogged, as is clear, by implementation problems. It is unlikely that more HATs will be designated under the Blair

Government. The other disposal initiative promoted by the Conservatives and implemented by Part IV of the Housing Act 1988 namely the, so-called, 'Tenants' Choice' or 'Pick-a-Landlord' scheme was a total non-starter in practice, and the provisions were repealed by the Housing Act 1996.

Further reading

Audit Commission *Who Wins? Voluntary Housing Transfers* HMSO, 1993

Department of the Environment *Housing Action Trusts. A Consultation Document* DoE/HMSO, 1987

English, J (Ed) *The Future of Council Housing* Croom Helm, 1982

Evans, A 'Voluntary Transfer: Weighing up the Pros and Cons' *Housing and Planning Review* Vol 44, No 1 February 1989, p 14

Forrest, R and Murie, A *Right to Buy? Issues of Need, Equity and Polarisation in the Sale of Council Houses* Working Paper No 39, University of Bristol, School of Advanced Urban Studies, 1984

Forrest, R and Murie, A 'If the Price is Right', *Roof*, March/April 1986, p 23

Forrest, R and Murie, A *Selling the Welfare State: The Privatisation of Public Housing* Routledge, 1988

Jones, P and Hillier, D 'Privatising Local Authority Housing', *Housing and Planning Review*, Vol 41, No 4, August 1986, p 20

Karn, V 'Remodelling a HAT: the implementation of the Housing Action Trust legislation 1987–92', in *Implementing Housing Policy* (eds) Malpass, P and Means, R, Open University Press, 1993

Knight, M 'When Owning Becomes a Nightmare', *Roof*, November/December, 1983, p 23

Lynn, P *The Right to Buy: A National Follow-Up Survey of Tenants of Council Homes in England*, London, DoE/HMSO, 1991

Owens, R 'If the HAT fits', *Roof*, January/February, 1992, p 17

Woodward, R 'Mobilising opposition: the campaign against Housing Action Trusts in Tower Hamlets', *Housing Studies*, Vol 6, No 1, 1991, p 44

CHAPTER THREE

Social housing: its allocation, the rights and status of its tenants

THE STATUS OF HOUSING OCCUPATION

This chapter is primarily concerned with the rights of secure and assured tenants (STs and ATs respectively). But before those rights can be enjoyed a person must have the status of 'tenant'. All forms of social landlords operate in situations where, for a variety of reasons, 'clients' are not tenants, but licensees.

The basic distinction between a tenancy and a licence is that, as a general rule, the former is a legal estate in land which, though limited in time, confers a package of rights on its holder, the most basic being the right to have exclusive possession of relevant property, i e the right to exclude the whole world, including the landlord, even if only for a limited period of time. The latter is a purely personal right which simply allows its holder to be on or in a property and which may be terminated simply by giving reasonable notice. This, however, should be read subject to the more detailed discussion below of recent case law developments. A person may be a licensee either because of the quality of premises occupied – some premises are effectively incapable in certain modes of occupation of supporting a tenancy – or because of the nature of the legal relationship between the parties. In all cases it is for the law to decide the nature of the right of occupation: the matter is not to be decided on the basis of the claimed intention of the parties. Since *Street v Mountford*[1] generally a situation where a person has exclusive occupation of premises for *a term* (which may be on a fixed time or periodic basis, eg a week) at *a rent* is a tenancy. The courts normally lean

---

1   [1985] AC 809, [1985] 2 All ER 289.

in favour of finding a tenancy when there are disputes as to the residential status of an occupier. Indeed in *Family Housing Association v Jones*[2] it was doubted whether *in ordinary circumstances* it is possible to create a licence which gives exclusive occupation of a self-contained, separate residential unit in return for a money payment. Even so there have been, and in some cases still are, exceptional cases:

(1) where a person is accommodated in a long stay hotel[3];
(2) where accommodation is provided in an old person's home[4];
(3) where the licensor is itself only a licensee of the premises[5] (this exception must now be considered no longer to be good law, see further below);
(4) where the occupier is only a lodger whose contract allows the licensor to have total access to and use of the premises in order to provide the attendance and services;
(5) where the occupier is living in a hostel and does not live in separate accommodation within that hostel. In *Westminster City Council v Clarke*[6] C was placed in temporary hostel accommodation as a vulnerable homeless person as the first stage of discharge of homelessness duties. The hostel was used to accommodate single homeless men, including some with personality disorders or physical disabilities. There was a resident warden with a resettlement team of social workers. C was given a 'licence to occupy' and paid a weekly accommodation charge. His licence gave him no right of exclusive occupation of a particular room or accommodation which might be allocated to him. The licence gave the authority power to change allotted accommodation and to require C to share accommodation with any other person. The House of Lords took into account the need of the authority to retain total control over all rooms in the premises in order to discharge their homelessness duties, the very considerable limitations on the occupier's ability to enjoy any room allotted to him, the need for him to obtain approval before he could entertain guests, and for him to comply with instructions from resident staff and concluded his occupation could only be as a licensee[7];

2   [1990] 1 All ER 385, [1990] 1 WLR 779, CA.
3   *Luganda v Service Hotels Ltd* [1969] 2 Ch 209, [1969] 2 All ER 692.
4   *Abbeyfield (Harpenden) Society Ltd v Woods* [1968] 1 All ER 352n, [1968] 1 WLR 374.
5   *Shepherds Bush Housing Association Ltd v HATS Co-operative* (1991) 24 HLR 176, CA and *Tower Hamlets London Borough Council v Miah* [1992] QB 622, [1992] 2 All ER 667, CA.
6   [1992] 2 AC 288, [1992] 1 All ER 695.
7   See also *Central YMCA Housing Association Ltd v Goodman* (1991) 24 HLR 109 and *Central YMCA Housing Association Ltd v Saunders* (1990) 23 HLR 212, both cases where a bedroom with en suite washing but no cooking facilities were concerned.

(6) where a licence is granted as a temporary expedient to a squatter or where a person stays on in a property where he/she lived with the tenant after that tenant moves out, even where a charge is levied, *provided* it is made clear that no intention to create a tenancy ever exists, *Westminster City Council v Basson*[8] and *R v Barnet London Borough Council, exp Grumbridge*[9]. Informal arrangements whereby secure tenants share their accommodation with others will generally not give rise to any rights for those others vis a vis the landlord. This will be so even where those others occupy parts of the property and pay a contribution towards costs. The court will be slow to infer in such cases that the tenant intended to create a sub-tenancy[10]. However, authorities can be caught by their own inaction. In *Tower Hamlets London Borough Council v Ayinde*[11], a secure tenant invited the defendant into a council flat, and later wrote to the authority stating a decision to leave and not return and requesting a transfer of the flat to the defendant, who thereafter paid rent which was accepted. The Court of Appeal found the letter from the original tenant to be a surrender which the authority had accepted and a new tenancy had been granted from the authority's knowledge of the situation and its acceptance of rent from the defendant.

The foregoing categories must now, however, be read subject to the House of Lords' decision in *Bruton v London and Quadrant Housing Trust*.[12] A local authority had acquired a block of flats, and being unable to redevelop it at once, licensed it to a charitable housing trust to provide short term accommodation for homeless people. One of these people was Mr Bruton who in 1989 entered into occupation of one of the flats under a licence agreement which specifically stated:

• the property was 'short life;'
• as had been explained to Mr Bruton, he was to have only a weekly licence from 6 February 1989;
• the Trust held the property only on a licence itself on a 'pending' basis until the block was demolished;
• Mr Bruton's occupation was conditional upon his agreeing to vacate on being given 'reasonable' notice from the Trust – normally not less than four weeks;
• Mr Bruton agreed to allow access to the flat during normal working hours to the Trust's staff, the local authority and their agents for all purposes connected with the Trust's work;

8   (1990) 23 HLR 225.
9   (1992) 24 HLR 433.
10   *Monmouth Borough Council v Marlog* [1994] 2 EGLR 68, CA.
11   (1994) 26 HLR 631.
12   [1999] 3 All ER 481, [1999] 3 WLR 150.

- Mr Bruton further agreed to allow the Trust, its agents, surveyors or consultants to enter the flat at all reasonable hours in order to inspect its state of repair and cleanliness;
- Mr Bruton agreed to pay £18 pw for the flat.

The local authority's intention to redevelop appears subsequently to have been abandoned, and the question of the legal nature of Mr Bruton's occupation of the flat arose when he subsequently claimed to be owed repairing obligations appropriate to a tenancy under the Landlord and Tenant Act 1985 – see Chapter Seven below.

Lord Hoffman delivered the principal judgement in the case and, basing himself on *Street v Mountford*, argued that:

> 'a "lease" or "tenancy" is a contractually binding agreement, not referable to any other relationship between the parties, by which one person gives another the right to exclusive possession of land for a fixed or renewable period or periods of time, usually in return for a periodic payment in money. An agreement having these characteristics creates a relationship of landlord and tenant to which the common law or statute then attach various incidents.'

It is the *conduct and agreement* of the parties that creates the relationship, and once a right to *occupy* land exclusively has been given for a period of time, and (usually) at a rent the clear presumption is that the relationship of landlord and tenant exists. Once these identifying characteristics are present it is irrelevant that the parties use language more appropriate to some other form of transaction such as the creation of a licence.

Lord Hoffman appears to have removed the distinction between 'exclusive possession' and exclusive occupation' and to have made the two concepts one, whereas previously the latter, as a question of fact, had been thought to be good evidence (no more) of the existence in law of the former.

He furthermore went on to argue that:

- the character of the landlord is irrelevant to whether the relationship of the landlord and tenant exists, for no Act of Parliament states that what would be a tenancy if granted by one landlord will be something else if granted by another;
- Mr Bruton's own agreement was irrelevant, because he could not contract out of the terms of the Landlord and Tenant Act 1985;
- the fact that if the Trust had created a tenancy that action placed the Trust in breach of its own licence agreement with the local authority was irrelevant. There was nothing in the Trust's constitution to make the granting of tenancies beyond its powers. Indeed Lord Hobhouse also made the same point rather more explicitly: 'it is correct that both parties knew that the Housing Trust was a mere licensee of the Council and, in so far as they may have thought about it, should have realised

that for the Housing Trust to grant Mr Bruton the exclusive possession of the flat probably amounted to a breach of the Housing Trust's obligations to the Council. But this cannot contradict what was actually agreed between the Housing Trust and Mr Bruton or its legal effect as between them ... The Housing Trust had the requisite capacity to make the agreement with Mr Bruton (as for that matter had the Council – section 44(1) of the Housing Act 1985).'

Lord Hoffman also stated:

'the term "lease" or "tenancy" described a relationship between two parties who are designated landlord and tenant. It is not concerned with the question of whether the agreement creates an estate or other proprietary interest which may be binding on third parties. A lease may, and usually does, create a proprietary interest called a leasehold estate, or technically a "term of years absolute". This will depend upon whether the landlord had an interest out of which he could grant it ... But it is the fact that the agreement is a lease which creates the proprietary interests.'

That is a quite revolutionary change in the law. *An agreement can create a tenancy which has implications for the parties to the agreement without creating a legal estate which binds third parties*. That is so even if the granting party has in itself no legal estate in the land in question.

The House of Lords thus affirmed the decision in *Family Housing Association v Jones* (Supra) and cast doubts on whether *Shepherds Bush Housing Association Ltd v HATS Co-operative (Supra)* and *Tower Hamlets London Borough Council v Miah* (Supra) are still good law, though the latter may survive on the basis of a specific point of the law relating to homelessness.

The implications of *Bruton* appear to be:

- the nature of an agreement for the occupation of land is to be determined by the law and not the parties – their words and intentions are seemingly irrelevant;
- agreements for the exclusive occupation of land by a person for a period, and (normally) in return for a rent will, except in highly special circumstances such as those in *Clarke's* case where a hostel was involved, give rise to the relationship of landlord and tenant, and this will be the case even if the grantor has no legal estate in the land;
- the agreement being a tenancy will have implications for the parties to it, even if third parties are not bound by it;
- one such consequence is that repairing covenants apply as between the parties;
- another is that the tenancy cannot be brought to an end by the grantor by mere reasonably notice, but only in due legal form;

•   short life agreements nationwide are now at risk of being classified as tenancies and not licenses, which must hamper the freedom of authorities and charitable bodies to use that type of agreement to assist homeless persons.

It is arguable, of course, that the degree of security enjoyed by people in Mr Bruton's position is not all that great. Following this case those in short life property before 28 February 1997 will have assured tenancies – though only as against the immediate grantor, while those entering after that date will, under section 19A of the Housing Act 1988 as inserted in 1996 have no more than assured shorthold tenancies which have effectively no real security of tenure. Even so the main problem in such cases is the existence of repairing obligations which could involve the expenditure of unbudgetted sums of money.

It remains to be seen how courts will deal with circumstances where it is the actual owner of the property in question who is involved in proceedings against, or issued by, the occupant in circumstances such as the above. There is in such a circumstance no contractual relationship between the owner and the occupant, and so it is hard to see how the occupant could resist a claim for possession should the owner revoke the head licence agreement. Nevertheless we may find ourselves venturing ever further into legal *terra incognita* in relation to such matters.

However, it should be noted that when an authority grant an exclusive right to occupy certain living accommodation, eg a 'bed sitter', with cooking facilities (even with shared toilet facilities) that is likely to be, even if not a tenancy, a *secure licence* falling within section 79(3) of the 1985 Act and so subject to statutory protection.

To obtain the status of 'tenant' a person must also be allocated a property.

ALLOCATION POLICIES (COUNCIL HOUSING)

Section 21 of the Housing Act 1985 vests the general management, regulation and control of local authority housing in the local authority. Historically this has meant that the general selection and allocation powers of local authorities have been subject to very little legal supervision, see per Lord Porter in *Shelley v LCC*[13]. Though the courts have intervened in allocation decisions by way of judicial review, they have been loath to do so, but would, for example, where an authority is clearly failing to do its reasonably practicable best for applicants for housing or where there is clear unlawfulness affecting the whole of an allocation scheme[14].

13   [1949] AC 56 at 66, [1948] 2 All ER 898 at 900.
14   *R v Newham London Borough Council, ex p Watkins* (1993) 26 HLR 434 and *R v Brent London Borough Council, ex p Sawyers* (1993) 26 HLR 44.

This did not mean that authorities had total *carte blanche* to allocate at their will: for many years now it has been established that authorities must behave reasonably, and are subject to the general principles of administrative law. In *R v Canterbury City Council, ex p Gillespie*[15] a woman and her child lived in overcrowded and unsatisfactory situations following a relationship breakdown. The authority refused for almost three years to rehouse her, or even place her on a housing 'waiting list' unless she relinquished the joint tenancy she held with her former cohabitee. But the landlord authority for that tenancy would not accept the surrender because of rent arrears, and she could not take proceedings against the man as that could render their other child living with him homeless. It was held that the authority were rigidly adhering to a policy of not rehousing a person who had a share in a joint tenancy, and had fettered their discretion in not considering the applicant's peculiar circumstances. Similarly a rigid rule whereby tenants with rent arrears are not considered for rehousing, even where they have a good medical case for a transfer, is illegal[16] Where a policy is adopted it must be operated flexibly, so that, for example it is unlawful to operate a scheme which allocates points for medical need without considering *all* the persons in a household who may have medical needs[17].

Authorities must not allocate homes for arrantly political reasons to enable a person to develop a residence into a 'power base' for a ward election[18], and should not refuse to house persons who owe them money particularly where other means of obtaining that money are available[19], nor should they *automatically* exclude from consideration for rehousing all owner occupiers *irrespective of need*[20].

These principles continue to be applicable even following the legislative changes made by the Housing Act 1996, and, as will be seen, apply additionally to transfers and exchanges by tenants. However, the remedy by way of judicial review is discretionary; can only serve to quash the authority's decision, and is only available to someone with a 'sufficient interest' in the issue, for example the prejudicially affected person, but not a person merely concerned over illegality, unless in a particular position of responsibility, as in *R v Port Talbot Borough Council, ex p Jones* where the applicant was the leader of the council.

---

15 (1986) 19 HLR 7.
16 *R v Islington London Borough Council, ex p Aldabbagh* (1994) 27 HLR 271.
17 *R v London Borough of Tower Hamlets, ex p Uddin* (1999) Housing Law Monitor, June p 9.
18 *R v Port Talbot Borough Council, ex p Jones* [1988] 2 All ER 207, 20 HLR 265.
19 *R v Forest Heath District Council, ex p West and Lucas* (1991) 24 HLR 85.
20 *R v Sutton London Borough Council, ex p Alger* (1992) Legal Action, (June) p 13 and *R v Bristol City Council, ex p Johns* (1992) 25 HLR 249.

Reform

The Government's 1994 consultative paper *Access to Local Authority and Housing Association Tenancies* proposed radical changes in the legal basis of selection and allocation schemes for social housing organisations. So far as authorities are concerned it proposed replacing section 22 of the 1985 Act with a provision requiring *all* authorities to maintain a housing waiting list, with *all* allocatees to secure tenancies and nominees to association tenancies being drawn from those lists, while allocation policies should be subject to terms and conditions laid down by Parliament. It was made clear that social housing should be targetted primarily at low income groups, while in allocating tenancies housing authorities would have to take account of individuals' housing circumstances, and the length of time they had been waiting to be rehoused. The new principles of allocation would:

(i)   require authorities generally to grant secure tenancies and make nominations to registered social landlords' tenancies solely by reference to a 'nominated housing waiting list' held by authorities or their agents;

(ii)   lay down principles in accordance with which priority for rehousing would be determined;

(iii) lay down limits to the discretion of authorities to prescribe who might/ might not appear on the waiting list, eg by way of residence or age requirements;

(iv)   require publication of allocation rules *and* adherence to the rules once published;

(v)   take as a determinant of allocation policy the need to balance time spent on a waiting list against intensity of need for rehousing;

(vi)   empower the Secretary of State to issue guidance to authorities on detailed local application of allocation principles.

In the outcome, not all of these principles made it to the statute book.

In July 1994 the Government announced its intention to proceed with the proposal that for *new* applicants authorities should *only* allocate secure tenancies, or exercise nomination rights to association stock, through a waiting list. Authorities were only to have discretion over allocation policies to the extent allowed by law, but it appeared that the law would *not* involve itself in detailed regulation of allocation policies. What was to be outlawed were practices generally regarded as discriminatory such as requiring five years' minimum residence qualifications before rehousing can take place. The object of the law was to secure fairness and consistency.

In the event the Housing Act 1996 introduced rather different rules for allocations – some of them particularly detailed. At the same time little was done to curb the discriminatory practices on which action was promised in 1994.

Before examining the legislative changes made in 1996, it is, however, necessary to consider other legislation which affects the allocation decisions of *all* social landlords.

Discrimination in housing allocation on racial and sexual grounds

Black people, by which term is meant all non-white ethnic groups, have fared badly in relation to housing in both sectors. The Commission for Racial Equality's (CRE) 1984 report *Race and Council Housing in Hackney* found in particular that white applicants were more likely to be housed in houses and maisonettes than blacks, who were more likely to be placed in flats, very often on the sixth floor or higher. White applicants were also much more likely to receive new properties from the local authority than blacks. The inequality of treatment could only be attributable to racial discrimination. The earlier report *Allocation of Council Housing with Particular Reference to Work Permit Holders* (CRE, November 1982) found discriminatory practices in providing housing for short stay foreign workers on work permits by the Greater London Council and two London Boroughs.

Note also the 1989 Central Government report on housing discrimination *Response to Racial Attacks and Harassment* (HMSO).

Black people have suffered for a variety of reasons: language problems and a lack of knowledge, experience and negotiating ability in applying for public sector housing; poor existing housing leading to low expectations of what the public sector can offer, both factors tending to lead landlords to offer less desirable housing; allocations systems disadvantaging ethnic groups, for example rules barring owner-occupiers from eligibility for rehousing which can operate against those who live in small, poor quality houses in inner city areas; the housing construction system which provides units apt for western 'nuclear' families, but not the larger units found in the Asian Community.

In a multi-racial society, both the law and administration of housing must operate to promote equal housing opportunities. Section 71 of the Race Relations Act 1976 makes it the general duty of *authorities* to work towards the elimination of discrimination and to promote good race relations and equal opportunities for all. Under section 75(5) of the Housing Associations Act 1985 the Housing Corporation has a similar duty. Other provisions are also relevant to housing. Section 21 of the 1976 Act provides:

'(1) It is unlawful for a person, in relation to premises...of which he has power to dispose, to discriminate against another –
(a) in terms on which he offers those premises; or

(b)   by refusing his application for those premises; or
(c)   in his treatment of him in relation to any list of persons in need
of premises of that description.

(2)   It is also unlawful for a person, in relation to any premises
managed by him, to discriminate against a person occupying the
premises –
(a)   in the way he affords him access to any benefits or facilities, or
by refusing or deliberately omitting to afford him access to them;
or
(b)   by evicting him, or subjecting them to any other detriment'

Unlawful discrimination can happen in two ways.

Direct racial discrimination

This is the act of treating another less favourably on grounds of colour, race,
nationality or ethnic or national origins, see sections 1(1)(a) and 3(1) of the
Race Relations Act 1976, for example to refuse an applicant's name for
rehousing because he/she is black.

Good housing practice will reflect the requirements of the non-
discrimination notice issued by the CRE to Hackney London Borough
Council under section 58 of the 1976 Act:
(1)   landlords should record the ethnic origin of all applicants for housing,
and those they house, and monitor records regularly in relation to the
quality, type, age and location of properties offered to applicants;
(2)   there should be a review of procedures, practices and criteria used in
allocation and transfer matters, and such procedures, etc, should be
clearly relevant to housing need and applied equally;
(3)   housing staff should be trained to avoid discriminatory practices, to
inform applicants of all options available to them, to consider the
special needs and preferences of applicants, and to apply only criteria
relevant to housing need in allocation decisions, particularly where a
number of applicants are effectively competing for an available dwelling.
It is also wise for landlords to know the racial composition of the
communities within their areas, provide facilities for communicating with
members of ethnic minority groups in their own languages, understand the
cultural and family patterns of such groups, and where possible, to provide
appropriate accommodation within their housing stock for extended families.
Similarly it should not be assumed that all black people will wish to live in
the same area.

However, though direct discrimination is suffered by black people in
housing, it is, perhaps, more common to encounter indirect discrimination
which unintentionally leads to housing disadvantage.

Indirect racial discrimination

This is the act of applying to a person a requirement or condition which applies equally to persons of *other* racial groups but which is:

(1) such that the proportion of persons of the *same* racial group as that of the person affected who can comply with the condition is considerably smaller than the proportion of persons not of that group who can comply;

(2) not *justifiable* irrespective of the colour, race, nationality or ethnic or national origins of the persons to whom it applies; and

(3) is to that person's detriment because he cannot comply with it. See section 1(1)(b) of the 1976 Act.

The following are examples of indirectly discriminatory practices:

(1) a requirement that applicants for authority housing must have been resident in an authority area for a specified period because fewer numbers of ethnic minority groups could comply with the residence requirements than could members of the host community, or;

(2) a requirement that housing points can only be given for children actually living with an applicant, as this works to the detriment of immigrants part of whose families have yet to join them;

(3) use of racial stereotypes;

(4) steering particular people to particular areas on racial assumptions;

(5) applying criteria which result in single parent families being accorded low priority on housing waiting lists.

Those authorities who apply residence qualifications should certainly review them to ensure that they do not result in indirect discrimination. Indeed it is arguable that a landlord operating a residence requirement might have to justify it under the terms of the legislation; in other words show that it is supported by adequate reasons which would be accepted by right thinking people as sound and tolerable[1]. It is not enough to argue a practice is needed because it is practically convenient or preserves a particular image of a service[2]. Landlords should consider carefully whether residence requirements result in recognisable discrimination, and assess how serious is that effect.

They should ask what purpose they seek to achieve by the requirement and whether that could be achieved by non-discriminatory or less discriminatory means. Then they must weigh and balance all these issues and ask whether residence requirements can be objectively considered to be reasonable and equitable.

Section 47 of the Race Relations Act 1976, as amended by section 137 of the Housing Act 1988, provides for the introduction of Codes of Practice

---

1   *Ojutiku v Manpower Services Commission* [1982] ICR 661, [1982] IRLR 418.
2   *Kingston and Richmond Area Health Authority v Kaur* [1981] ICR 631, [1981] IRLR 337.

to eliminate *racial* discrimination and promote equal *racial* opportunities in housing, such codes are admissible as evidence in proceedings under the Race Relations legislation, and must be taken into account in deciding whether unlawful discrimination has taken place where relevant provisions of the Code are not adhered to. The Race Relations Code of Practice begins by outlining the relevant general law and gives examples of good equal opportunity practices. It then exhorts housing organisations to pursue declared equal opportunities policies with regard to access to, and *quality* of housing, and the delivery of housing services, and to keep practices and procedures under constant review so as to eliminate any form of discrimination by way of record keeping and monitoring. Training should thus be given to staff to ensure they understand equal opportunities policies and the needs of minorities. The policy should further extend to combating racial harassment and the support of victims of such harassment. Monitoring records should be undertaken and the unmet needs of minority groups considered so that action may be taken in respect of them. Organisations are further counselled to adopt clearly non-discriminatory selection and allocation procedures and to avoid practices that smack of racial discrimination – eg asking a person to produce a passport as a means of identification. The delivery of services to tenants should also be non-discriminatory so that repairs and housing advice are not provided for the host community faster than for tenants from a minority group.

If it can be shown that an allocation/transfer/exchange scheme is being operated by an authority in a way that is less than even handed from a racial point of view, judicial review may be sought.[3]

For provisions relating to sex discrimination see sections 1 and 30 of the Sex Discrimination Act 1975, for women of all races suffer particular discrimination in housing.

For an exhaustive treatment of the issue of racial and sexual discrimination in housing see Handy, *Discrimination in Housing*, 1993.

Discrimination and disability

Sections 22 and 24 of the Disability Discrimination Act 1995 apply the same basic anti-discrimination concepts encountered under the race relations and sex discrimination legislation to the letting of property. Disabled persons under section 1 of the 1995 Act are those having physical or mental impairments which have substantial and long term adverse effects on their ability to carry out normal day-to-day activities. It is thus unlawful to discriminate against a disabled person by refusing to let to that person, or by virtue of the terms of any letting to such a person, or in relation to any

3   *R v Tower Hamlets London Borough Council, ex p Mohib Ali* (1993) 25 HLR 218.

list of persons need of premises of the sort in question. Discrimination arises where a person treats a disabled person less favourably than non disabled persons for reasons related to that person's disability, and where such treatment cannot be justified. Justification can be shown only where (i) the action results from a reasonable opinion on behalf of the discriminator, and (ii) such an action is necessary in order not to endanger the health or safety of *any* person, *or* the disabled person is incapable of entering into an enforceable agreement or giving an informed consent. Thus a landlord could refuse to let a particular property to a disabled person where either that person's physical disabilities would prevent him/her from using the property safely, or where the person is incapable of understanding the nature and consequences of a tenancy. Note, however, that there is no general duty on a landlord to make reasonable adjustments to a dwelling in order for it to be accessible to a disabled person.

The statutory rules on allocation

The Housing Act 1996 repealed section 22 of the Housing Act 1985 which gave very considerable discretion to authorities in the allocation of housing and replaced it with new provisions designed to ensure consistency, fairness, transparency and challengeability in allocation practices – at least up to a point. The legislation is also supplemented by a Code of Guidance issued under section 169 of the Act to which authorities are 'to have regard', though, of course, they need not slavishly adhere to it. This Code also contains guidance on homelessness functions.

The prime objective of the 1996 Act here is to ensure a single route of entry into social housing, whether that be by application or by virtue of homelessness, with all entrants being subject to registration, and fair assessment of their needs according to consistently applied principles. However, the 1996 principles do not apply to those already in social housing whose rights to transfer and exchange are still governed by the Housing Act 1985 and the general principles of administrative law as laid down in case law. Thus the new system applies where a person is:

- selected to be a secure or introductory tenant of an authority's housing;
- nominated to be a secure or introductory tenant of housing held by another person – for example another authority;
- nominated to be an assured tenant of a registered social landlord (RSL): see section 159 of the 1996 Act. Furthermore the provisions on allocation do not apply:
- where an introductory tenancy (see further below) becomes secure;
- where a secure/introductory tenancy vests on succession following the death of a tenant;

- where such a tenancy is assigned to a person who would be qualified to succeed on the tenant's death;
- where such a tenancy vests or is disposed of under matrimonial legislation;
- where a *secure* tenancy is assigned under section 92 of the 1985 Act;
- in those other cases prescribed by the Secretary of State – see the Allocation of Housing Regulations 1996, SI 1996/2753 which apply to people who are already either secure tenants in Northern Ireland or Scotland, or are assured tenants of certain Scottish Housing Associations.

There are a number of other general duties under the 1996 Act, performance of which could be compelled by a person with a 'sufficient interest' in the matter seeking an order of mandamus on judicial review. It might also be possible for such a person to seek certiorari to quash an allocation decision made in breach of an authority's statutory duties. It is, however, questionable who would have such a 'sufficient interest'. In *R v Port Talbot Borough Council, ex p Jones*[3a] to which earlier allusion has been made the Leader of the Council was considered to have a 'sufficient interest' to entitle him to intervene in a case of irregularity by his authority, particularly as the allocation in that case was in breach of the authority's own published rules. However, would an applicant for housing be able to challenge an illegal allocation to another person? Perhaps only if the applicant had been promised a house then let to someone else whose priority according to the council's scheme of allocation was less.

The duties of authorities in brief are:

- section 159(1) – to comply with the 1996 Act;
- section 161(1) – to allocate housing only to 'qualifying' persons
- section 162(1), (4) – to establish and maintain a housing register;
- section 164(5) – to notify decisions and rights of review, etc to applicants;
- section 165(5) – to notify review decisions, with reasons;
- section 167(1) – to have an allocation scheme;
- section 167(7) – to consult with other social landlords where major policy changes to the scheme are proposed – what is 'major' is not defined in the 1996 Act;
- section 167(5) – to allocate housing only in accordance with the scheme;
- section 168 – to publicise the scheme;
- section 169(1) – to have regard to guidance from the Secretary of State.

The obligations of local authorities

Under section 161 of the 1996 Act a housing authority may allocate a house

3a [1988] 2 All ER 207.

only to someone who 'qualifies'. 'Qualifying persons' are, first, those people who fall within classes determined by the Secretary of State, and, secondly, those who are determined to be in a 'qualifying' class according to the authority's decision. There is thus room for local variation as to who 'qualifies'. However, as a general rule if one or more of a pair of joint applicants qualifies there can be a joint allocation to both.

'Qualifying Persons' – the Secretary of State's classes

These are to be found in the Allocation of Housing Regulations 1996, SI 1996/2753, as amended by SI 1997/631, and SI 1999/2135. The key to understanding this complex scheme is that it is first of all based on a broad general *exclusion* of a particular group of people, namely those who are subject to immigration control, but then certain classes of persons who are subject to that control are specifically *reincluded* by the regulations, ie those persons do qualify. Next there are two classes of homeless persons who are specifically declared to be 'qualifying' by the regulations. Finally there are particular groups of people who are *not* subject to immigration control who are further specifically excluded while particular provision here had to be made to *reinclude* certain of these groups who have rights under EC Law.

The initial exclusion

Persons subject to immigration control under the Immigration Act 1971 and the Asylum and Immigration Act 1996 are generally incapable of 'qualifying'. These are all those who require leave from the Home Office to enter or to remain in this country, irrespective of whether such leave has been given. Such persons are those who have no 'right of abode' here, in other words they are *not* UK citizens connected with this country by way of birth, adoption, naturalisation or registration. In addition a person will have a 'right of abode' if he/she has a parent connected with this country by birth, etc, *or* if he/she has (a) been lawfully settled in this country and (b) ordinarily resident here for the last five years, *or* if he/she is a Commonwealth citizen with a parent born in the UK. Thus to take an example, Raminder is a Leicester born and bred male of Asian extraction; he has a right of abode: his cousin Bhalvinder was born in and lives in India; he does not have such a right.

Re-included from the broadly excluded class are five categories of 'excepted immigrants':

A – persons having the status of refugees;

B – persons granted 'exceptional' leave outside the immigration rules to enter or remain in this country where that leave is not subject to conditions as to maintenance and accommodation – but note only rarely will there be an absence of such conditions;

C   –   persons granted current leave to enter or remain in the UK not subject to any limitation or condition – but again note only rarely will this be the case, and the reinclusion does *not* apply to persons who have been given leave to enter on an undertaking from another person (the sponsor) to be responsible for the immigrant's maintenance and accommodation, and who have been resident in the UK for less than five years, and whose sponsor is still alive, (this largely excludes overseas students from qualifying);

CA   –   persons who are nationals of states who have signed the European Convention on Social and Medical Assistance, or the Council of Europe Social Charter, *provided* those persons are habitually resident in the 'Common Travel Area' (CTA – ie the UK, the Channel Islands, the Isle of Man and the Republic of Ireland);

CB   –   persons who left the territory of Monserrat after 1 November 1995 because of the volcanic eruption there.

Then there are classes of persons who are specifically required to be 'qualifying':

D   –   persons owed duties because they are homeless or threatened with homelessness unintentionally and have priority need, under Section 194(3) of the 1996 Act;

E   –   persons aged 18 or more who in the previous two years have fallen within Sections 192(2) or 197(2) of the 1996 Act as unintentionally homeless persons who do not have priority need.

(Further provision is also made here for displaced residents of Montserrat).

There then follows a second general exclusion with specific reinclusions. The exclusion is of *all* persons not 'habitually resident' in the Common Travel Area, then there are reinclusions of 'European Workers', ie those nationals of member states of the EC who travel between states as workers, and other EC nationals who have a right to reside in the UK under certain EC Council Directives. However, even here such persons may fail to 'qualify' where they are required to leave the UK by the Home Secretary.

'Habitual Residence' is a concept not defined in the 1996 Act, however, decisions taken under the law of immigration indicate that the issues to be considered in determining whether or not someone is 'habitually resident' are the person's family ties with the UK, or lack of them, where the person has spent most of his/her life, whether the person has employment permanently in the UK, and what the nature of that job is – eg a seasonal job is unlikely to provide a basis for 'habitual residence', the reasons why the person came to this country, how long that person has been resident elsewhere, and what the person's intentions are with regard to staying here.

This foregoing complexity is perhaps best understood by a series of worked examples.

1.   Bhaljinder was born in Amritsar in India and has lived there all his life. He is thus subject to immigration control. He obtains clearance,

however, from the Home Office under the immigration rules to come to England to work for his Uncle Raminder, but there are conditions attached as to his maintenance and accommodation. Bhaljinder does not qualify, though he would have done had his entry been free of conditions and 'exceptional'.

2. Pierre was born in Paris, France, and is thus subject to immigration control and has come under EC rules to work as a waiter in a French restaurant in London. Pierre does qualify, though he would cease to if he was required to leave the country by the Home Office upon conviction for dealing in drugs.

3. Mary was born in Manchester some 55 years ago and thus is not subject to immigration control; but she moved with her entire family to Venezuela shortly thereafter. She has now returned alone, without friends, family or a job in the country simply 'on the off-chance' of getting a house here but with no other settled plans. Mary will not qualify.

Other qualifying persons

Each local authority is able to determine other classes of qualifying and non-qualifying persons. The Code of Guidance, while urging authorities not to be rigidly over prescriptive indicates they may retain restrictions as to, inter alia, age, marital status, ownership of residential accommodation, length of time spent within an area, rent arrears' records, past creation of neighbour nuisances. Even so this discretionary power must always be exercised according to law; in other words in a procedurally correct fashion, without bias or oppression, without taking into account irrelevant considerations, and with noimposition of rigid fetters in the form of absolute exclusions. Even so the 1998 Shelter Report 'Access Denied' argued that a number of authorities have adopted rigorous exclusion policies, sometimes excluding people who are 'believed' to be responsible for acts of anti-social behaviour in the absence of formal proof. While it was also found that authorities would consider the cases of individuals otherwise caught in 'excluded' categories if an advice worker or solicitor took up the case, Shelter remained concerned that the practical effect of exclusionary policies would be most hard felt by individuals not able to access such aid. There was further evidence that many authorities (over 50% of those surveyed) do not monitor those whom they exclude so their numbers are unknown. The Shelter figures indicate inter alia:

- 63% of authorities surveyed would exclude a person for rent arrears;
- authorities may exclude people who are owner occupiers, or whom they consider to have insufficient length of residence in their area;
- exclusion for anti-social behaviour accounts for only 3% of instances,

but in some cases the bad behaviour can be that of a member (or even former member) of the would-be applicant's family;

• even where people fall within a group who qualify according to an authority's policies, individuals may find their applications 'suspended' for unlimited periods of time, and the legislation gives no right of appeal or internal review in such cases, though judicial review in theory would be available if an individual suspension could be shown to be utterly unreasonable.

So far as exclusion for rent arrears is concerned the present author's experience of authorities in the East Midlands indicates that many exclude for arrears owed to either themselves or other social landlords, but not for arrears in the private sector. The justification for this is often given as mutual interdependence by social landlords and the need to ensure that a culture of letting arrears build up amongst potential tenants is discouraged. Some registered social landlords have similar policies, while others will exclude for arrears owed to any landlord. The pattern of policy is one of enormous diversity, and indeed change, for landlords do change their policies on this issue.

Housing Register

Section 162 of the 1996 Act requires *each local housing authority to establish and maintain a 'housing register'* of qualifying persons. This must contain such 'prescribed information' about the people on it as is prescribed by the Secretary of State. Otherwise authorities may decide what information to register, and the form in which the register is to be kept. In particular it may be kept as part of a register held for other purposes or as a register maintained in common with other landlords – eg a joint list held with registered social landlords of all people seeking housing in an area, *provided* it is clear which of them is registered by the authority: *entries constituting the authority's register must be distinguishable.*

The 'prescribed information' is defined by SI 1996/2753 (The Allocation of Housing Regulations), and is: the name of the qualifying person; the numbers of persons normally residing with him/her or who could reasonably be expected to, and amongst those – persons who are under 10, pregnant or over 60; the person's current address, date of registration and the most recent date on which an entry was amended.

A person may be placed on the register under section 163 provided:
i.   he/she applies;
ii. he/she 'qualifies' (see above).

However, an authority may put any person on the register without any application provided he/she 'qualifies' and provided he/she is notified.

Registrations can be amended by the authority 'as they think fit' but they must inform the person affected.

Section 163 of the Act further provides that registrations *must* be erased if the registered person requests *and* is *not* owed a homelessness duty *or* is not a 'qualifying person' and *may* be erased in such other circumstances as an authority thinks fit. However, before erasure the authority must comply with the Secretary of State's requirements as to notification of the person and as to any other matters.

SI 1996/2753 lays down the relevant requirements. Before de-registering someone an authority must give to that person a notice which (a) requires the person to provide them with such information as the authority *reasonably* require to enable them to take the deregistration decision, (b) specifies a minimum period of 28 days running from the date of receipt of the notice during which that information must be supplied and (c) informing the person that they may be de-registered if the authority does not receive the information in due time, *or* where the authority consider in the light of information received in due time that there are reasons for removal from the register. Such a notice has to be in writing and if not received by the person is treated as given if made available for a reasonable period for collection by that person at the authority's office.

Section 164 of the 1996 Act applies to refusals of applications and removals of names from the register.

Where an authority decide either *not* to register a person (other than at that person's request) they must notify that person in writing, with reasons. This notification must inform the person of the right to seek a review of this decision, and the time within which review must be sought, which is 21 days from the notification, though a longer period *may* be allowed. Note that there is no *right* to request a further review of a decision reached on an earlier, review. Notices may be made available via the authority's office. The Allocation of Housing and Homelessness (Review Procedures and Amendment) Regulations 1999, SI 1999/71 provide the framework for reviews.

The decision taker on review

Authorities have a choice:
(i) where the review decision is to be made by an officer of the authority, that officer must be someone not involved in the original decision, and senior in rank to the officer who made the original decision;
(ii) alternatively members of the authority may be involved.
The 'senior officer' route is that normally followed, but the Shelter Report 'Access Denied' which has already been referred to calls for reviews to be heard by a board containing an independent member.

Review procedures

One a 'duty made request' for a review has been received the authority must notify the applicant, or that person's representatives, of the right to make written representations in connection with the review and (if this has not already been done) of the review procedure. Authorities must consider representations made. Reasonable periods should be given for representations to be made, received and considered – but what these could be might be a subject for debate and conflict!

Time limits

Under section 164, and SI 1999/71 reg 5, the period within which authorities must notify applicants of decisions is *8 weeks* from the day on which a request for a review was made, *or* such longer period as may be agreed in writing – another point at which there could be room for conflict.

The Secretary of State's Code of Guidance on allocations etc, indicates that authorities should, in effect invite the person to state his/her grounds for requesting a review and to give any new information he/she wishes to put forward. Authorities *may* also point out that where no representations are duly received an authority is entitled to decide the matter on the basis of the facts then known to them. They may indicate representations from representatives are acceptable and may draw attention to the time period of the review. Further enquiries may be made during the progress of the review to elicit the most recent facts. The Code advises authorities to be flexible about allowing further exchanges. Where this may lead to a delayed decision the applicant may agree an extension of the time period. Agreements for extensions of time should be obtained as early as possible where a significant delay is anticipated.

The regulations make no provision for oral hearings but the Code of Guidance indicates these may be desirable where applicants could be disadvantaged if required to put all their case in writing. There may here also be time implications and thus a need for agreed time extensions.

A failure to observe good administrative practise during a review (for example by excessive delay or inefficiency) could lead to a maladministration investigation by the Commission for Local Administration. A failure to observe the general principles of administrative law could result in a judicial review application. The only way to challenge a review decision in court is by way of judicial review. No right of appeal to the county court exists.

Rights of information

Where persons are on the register under section 166 they are entitled to see their entries and to have a free copy of them, *and* to be informed *generally* of the state of the register so as to be able to assess their general chances of re-housing compared with other persons. But the fact that a person is on a register, and the information about them thereon, may not be divulged to any other member of the public. Where a registered person makes an enquiry misleading information must not be given, nor should any undertaking or promise appear to be made. Enquirers are entitled only to information which enables them to assess how long they will have to wait before accommodation appropriate to their needs becomes available for allocation to them. Only general information has to be given; furthermore the information is that which enables the making of an assessment of the likely period of waiting in relation to accommodation appropriate to the enquirer's needs. This, according to the Code of Guidance is information giving enquirers an indication of their place in the queue for housing; and an indication of the likely property supply during the next twelve months.

The Allocation Scheme

Under section 167 of the Housing Act 1996 every Local Housing Authority is required to have an 'allocation scheme' for determining priorities and to lay down allocation procedures. 'Procedure' here includes all aspects of the allocation process, including the persons by whom decisions are taken. *No authority is able to allocate housing except in accordance with their scheme*. That scheme, under section 168 of the Act has to be published in summary form and copies of this made freely available. The full scheme itself has to be available at the authority's principal office, and copies made available at reasonable cost. Should the scheme be altered in that a major change of policy occurs, the authority must within a reasonable period of time notify all those on the register, who must be informed in general terms of the effect of the change. Further guidance on operating schemes is contained in the Code of Guidance issued by the Secretary of State.

The 1996 Act did not lay down too many prescriptive rules on the functioning of schemes, but note that under section 167 it is statutorily required that allocation schemes *must be* so framed as to secure that 'reasonable preference' is given to:
(i)   people living in unsanitary/overcrowded or otherwise unsatisfactory housing;
(ii) people living in temporary/insecure tenancies – this is the only provision *in the Act* under which any consideration its to be given to the homeless, see, however, further below;
(iii) families with dependent children and households consisting of or including someone who is expecting a child;
(iv) households with a member having an identified need for settled accommodation eg a physically or mentally disabled person, or having

such a need on some other welfare ground, with 'additional preference' given to a household with a member with particular need who cannot be expected to find accommodation for themselves in the foreseeable future.

(v)   households with limited opportunities to secure settled accommodation, such as those on low incomes, ie those whose social or economic circumstances are such that they have difficulty in securing accommodation.

Category (i) supra existed previously under section 22 of the 1985 Act, the rest are new categories. However, all must be given, in general 'reasonable preference'.

The meaning of this expression was considered in *R v Wolverhampton Metropolitan Borough Council, ex p Watters*[3b] 'Reasonable preference' does *not* mean 'absolute preference', and indeed it is rather a process than an entitlement, for it requires authorities to balance the applicant's needs against other relevant factors, such as a history of rent arrears or anti-social behaviour. This may lead to an authority concluding in any given case that an applicant's 'reasonable preference' may be rendered of no account, and, provided they have acted reasonably and not in a vindictive or oppressive fashion, a court would be loathe to intervene.

'Additional preference' has not been judicially defined. Those to whom it applies must be prioritised over other 'reasonable preference' categories. This category would apply to groups of people such as the elderly, those with physical or learning disabilities, severe mental illness or degenerative diseases. Even so an authority would not be required to give absolute preference to a person in such a group, but would still need to consider whether any given property is suitable to that person's needs or might reasonably be offered to some other person to whom it is more suited. In coming to such a decisions authorities should act in concert with other relevant bodies such as social services authorities and health authorities, and voluntary sector agencies. As a general principle it should be assumed that priority should be given to those needing long-term social housing, such as those with disabilities or chronic illnesses.

Further reasonable preference categories

The Allocation of Housing (Reasonable and Additional Preference) Regulations 1997, SI 1997/1902 made under section 167(3) of the 1996 Act created further classes of persons to whom a reasonable preference has to be given. These are:

3b   (1997) 29 HLR 931.

(i)   homeless persons falling within the 'Main Housing Duty' for the homeless under section 193 and 195(2) of the Housing Act 1966;
(ii)   homeless persons kept in accommodation at an authority's discretion after the initial two year 'Main Housing Duty' has ended;
(iii)   homeless people who have been given advice and assistance to obtain other suitable accommodation and who have, in consequence, obtained it.

The Secretary of State has further powers under section 167 to make regulations to specify other groups of persons to whom preference is to be given, or to take preference from any mentioned group.

Regulations could in theory be made to prevent consideration of specified factors in the allocation of housing. Section 167(5) empowers the Secretary of State to specify procedural principles to be followed in the framing of an allocation scheme. Thus under the Allocation of Housing (Procedure) Regulations 1997, SI 1997/483 an elected member is excluded from making an allocation decision where the accommodation in question is in his/her ward, or where an applicant has his/her sole or main residence in a particular member's ward.

The type of scheme adopted

Authorities are able to take into account a very wide range of factors in drawing up their schemes, but all criteria used must be made patent in the scheme. The legislation does not specify what sort of scheme an authority should adopted, and thus in theory a number of models are available.
(i)   *'Date Order' schemes*, ie 'First come, first served';
(ii)   *Points schemes*, ie where homes are allocated on the basis of 'points' assessed for satisfying certain stated criteria – eg so many for size of family, or bedrooms needed, so many for length of time on the list, etc;
(iii)   *Combined schemes*, which are a combination of the above.

Other types of selection schemes, historically existed, very often to supplement the broad types of schemes outlined above. These included: (a) allocation of houses only to slum dwellers; (b) entry of an applicant's name on list only after a period of residential qualification; (c) allocation of housing proportionally to different groups in need.

The practice adopted by some authorities in the past of allocating accommodation entirely at the discretion of officers and or members no longer appears legal as this practice could hardly amount to a 'scheme'.

The preferred option of most advanced authorities is for a sophisticated points scheme which is:
•   open to all who may reasonably wish to live in the authority's area;
•   gives points on the basis of recognised need such as family size, insecurity, or lack of, current accommodation;

- further takes account of the statutory priority need and additional preference groups;
- make particular provision for special needs groups; and
- retains a publicly declared residual allocation discretion to be exercised by identified officers as a 'special allocations category' thus enabling a flexible response to be made to applications out of the ordinary.

Whatever the scheme adopted, however, it must be operated even-handedly, promptly and efficiently if the authority is to escape allegations of maladministration, and fairly, reasonably, procedurally correctly and without rigidity if judicial review is also to be avoided. Even so it must always be remembered that no scheme can allocate accommodation that does not exist, and that much will therefore depend on what stock an authority has available at any given moment and what its suitability is, given the needs of particular persons and groups of applicants. Thereafter the scheme will have to make provision to determine priorities *between and within* groups, and a points scheme seems best suited to achieved this.

Section 167(7) requires that before an authority adopts or alters an allocation scheme in a material way they must send a copy of their draft to every registered social landlord with whom they have nomination rights and give them a reasonable opportunity to comment thereon.

Other allocations and relocation

Allocations to those who are already tenants of authorities but who wish to move for a variety of reasons, for example health, employment or family commitments, fall outside the terms of the 1996 legislative scheme and instead are governed by section 106 of the 1985 Act. This requires authorities to have rules for determining allocation priorities in such cases and to publish summaries of them – the actual rules themselves available for public inspection at their principal offices during reasonable hours. Existing tenants who have applied for relocation may under section 106(5) obtain copies of any details they have supplied about themselves and their families and which have been recorded as relevant to their applications.

Case law makes it clear that while the courts are unwilling to sit as appellate bodies from the decisions of authorities, they will intervene where there is clear illegality in the way an authority has operated. Thus the courts will intervene where policies are phrased, or operated, in rigid ways. Schemes must be patently flexible *and* must be operated in a flexible fashion.[3c]

3c   *R v Gateshead Metropolitan Borough Council, ex p Lauder* (1996) 29 HLR 360; *R v London Borough of Tower Hamlets, ex p Spencer* (1995) 29 HLR 64; *R v Camden London Borough Council, ex p Adair* (1996) 29 HLR 236; *R v Southwark London Borough Council, ex p Melak* (1996) 29 HLR 223; *R v Lambeth London Borough Council, ex p Ashley* (1996) 29 HLR 385; *R v Wandsworth London Borough Council, ex p Lawrie* (1997) 30 HLR 153.

ALLOCATION POLICIES (REGISTERED SOCIAL LANDLORDS)

Though the constituent documents setting up a registered social landlord such as a housing association may restrict it to housing only certain sorts of people, for example the elderly, the housing corporation under section 36A of the Housing Associations Act 1985 issued HC Circular 36/94 in, inter alia, allocation policies. This continued in force under Section 36 of the Housing Act 1996, see HC Circular 36/96, and stressed the general need for allocation policies to be open, fair and based on need.

Housing Corporation Circular RI–01/98 now stresses the need for such landlords to have fair and accountable allocations policies which, in general, provide assess to housing for those in the greatest need, (especially those mentioned in section 167(2) of the Housing Act 1996) though allowing for other objects to be given priority where appropriate. Lettings policies are in this way harmonised in general terms, with those of local authorities and the same overall policy objectives are imposed by *administrative* reference to the *statutory* requirements laid on authorities. Thus the lettings policy should:

- reflect the landlord's governing instrument;
- be reached, and only varied, after consultation with relevant local authorities and should reflect any obligations owed to them;
- where possible participate in a 'common housing register' with other relevant landlords, but not to the extent of joining a common allocations policy, save where that would *not* threaten the landlord's aims and objectives;
- be made available in full and in summary to the public, with a copy sent to the Housing Corporation and relevant local authorities;
- kept under regular review with the aim, inter alia, of creating stable communities and sustainable tenancies;
- provide, where appropriate, for different letting schemes for different types of development.

The Housing Corporation has indicated it will check compliance with the foregoing by, inter alia, asking relevant local authorities whether they have been consulted on changes to the policies of landlords.

With regard to allocation itself landlords should have clear systems indicating who is responsible for making lettings and how applications are received and priorities. In relation to this matter landlords must, of course, comply with the legislation on race, sex and disability discrimination already considered. As a compliance test the Corporation will monitor the percentage of lettings to ethnic minority households in relation to the proportion of such households within relevant local authority districts, and landlords are expected to comply with the Commission for Racial Equality's 1991 Code of Practice for rented accommodation on the elimination of discrimination and the promotion of equal opportunities.

As part of the requirement that landlord should assist wherever possible those in the greatest need the housing corporation have made it clear they will monitor the average income of new tenants.

Lettings policies are further expected to make provision for transfers and exchanges and to give reasonable preference to those having priority need where this makes the best use of the stock available or contributes to stable communities. Furthermore in general landlords are expected to participate in national and local mobility schemes to enable tenants to move from one part of the country to another: the current national scheme is known as HOMES. Furthermore when a local housing authority makes a request under section 170 of the Housing Act 1996 for co-operation from a landlord the Housing Corporation's understanding is that at least 50% of vacancies (both new and relet) becoming available should be made available to nominees from the authority – this being 'reasonable' co-operation as required by the statute.

This requirement will be monitored by checking the proportion of new lettings going to local authority nominees, and by asking authorities if they are happy with the proportion of a landlord's new tenants who are nominees.

Finally it should be noted that Housing Corporation Circular 36/94 also laid particular stress on: *not* requiring more rent in advance than is due in respect of the initial rental period; no deposits or premiums on the grant of a tenancy – ie a capital payment, nor references from bankers etc; compliance with residential qualifications, save where inescapable under the constituent rules or a restriction under planning law.

THE REQUIREMENTS FOR THE COMMENCEMENT OF A TENANCY

It is easy to forget, given all the statutory overlay, that the relationship of landlord and tenant between landlord and their tenants is essentially a common law matter based on principles of contract.

Though the overwhelming majority of lettings are on a weekly basis and so do not require the legal form of a documentary lease under the Law of Property Act 1925, nevertheless there are basic requirements.
(i)   The landlord must agreed to let a particular property to the tenant in return for a specified rent.
(ii)   The tenant must agree to take that property at the set rent – in other words there must be offer, acceptance, consideration and intention to create legal relations.
A person cannot 'wish' him/herself on a landlord as a tenant simply by occupying property, see also Chapter 5.

This issue is, however, well illustrated by *Southwark London Borough Council v Logan*[3d]. L had lived in a particular house since 1985 with her four

3d   (1995) 29 HLR 40, CA.

children. Before then she had lived with her husband and children in a 2-bedroom 1st floor council flat of which she had been tenant since 1975. Serious racial violence had occurred at this flat which was in any case inadequate accommodation, and in 1979 L's name was placed on the transfer list. In 1985 the authority adopted a policy whereunder victims of racial harassment were transferred to homes of equal or better standard, and L was then offered a 4 bed-roomed flat, but this was withdrawn as she needed 5. At this time the former Greater London Council was developing housing near to L's home, and she and her family, illegally, moved into one property. The house in question had been intended for another family but L would not leave. Possession proceedings were taken against her, and were successful, though an order to leave obtained on 8/5/86 was not enforced. A council official then wrote to L confirming her registered need of 5 bedrooms and her priority following racial harassment for a transfer, and undertaking not to enforce the possession order. Then in 1991 the authority took further proceedings to obtain possession which were finally heard in 1994, and resulted in a further possession order against L, which L appealed arguing she either had some sort of contractual right to be in the house, or that the authority were estopped from seeking possession because of the letter from the council official.

The argument as to a contractual right failed completely because there was clearly no contract as there was no agreement as to any terms of payment for the dwelling. Similarly the estoppel argument failed because L had voluntarily given up her original flat long before the letter from the council official was sent to her and could not therefore be said to have acted to her detriment in reliance on it.

INTRODUCTORY TENANCIES

This notion was introduced by Part V Chapter 1 of the Housing Act 1996. In the White Paper leading to the legislation 'probationary tenancies' were mentioned, but this expression was perhaps a little pejorative. Nevertheless it is clear that where an introductory tenancy is granted it can easily be brought to an end by the landlord on account of the tenant's misbehaviour. Whether it can properly be otherwise terminated is not made explicit in the 1996 Act, though see further below on this issue.

Headed 'Conduct of tenants', Part V of the legislation gives power to authorities and Housing Action Trusts to 'elect to introductory tenancy scheme – ie no one has to.

Under section 124 of the 1996 Act where such a scheme is in force *every* (NB – *every*) periodic tenancy of a dwelling granted by the landlord shall, if it would otherwise be secure, be an 'introductory tenancy', *unless immediately before* the tenancy was entered into the tenant (or one of them where there are joint tenants) was a secure tenant of the same or another dwelling *or* was an assured tenant of a registered social landlord (otherwise than under an assured shorthold tenancy) in respect of the same/another dwelling *or* the tenancy is entered into under a contract made before the landlord elected to introduce an introductory scheme. Once the election is made it can be withdrawn – without prejudice to remaking a further election later.

Under section 125 of the 1996 Act a tenancy remains 'introductory' until the end of the 'trial period' unless a 'specified event' occurs before the end of that period. The 'trial period' is one year beginning with the date on which the tenancy was entered into, or, if later, the date on which the tenant was entitled to take possession,

A tenancy will cease to be 'introductory' if *before* the end of the trial period:

(i)   the circumstances are such that the tenancy would not otherwise be secure – eg the tenant ceases to occupy as his/her 'only or principal home';

(ii)   a person or body other than a local authority or Housing Action Trust becomes the landlord;

(iii) the landlord's election to operate the scheme is revoked;

(iv)   the tenancy ceases to be introductory by virtue of succession but there is on-one qualified to succeed (see below).

On ceasing to be 'introductory' in the foregoing circumstances a tenancy continues, all other things being equal, but it cannot become 'introductory' again. Quite what sort of tenancy it is will depend on the circumstances. For example if the tenant ceases to occupy the dwelling the tenancy would presumably exist only at common law. Of course, *at the end* of the trial period an introductory tenancy will become 'secure'.

But note that under section 130 of the 1996 Act where possession proceedings are begun and the trial period ends or the tenancy would otherwise cease to be 'introductory' the tenancy is prolonged as an introductory tenancy until the issue is determined.

Security of tenure for introductory tenancies

Under section 127 et seq, the landlord may only bring an introductory tenancy to an end by court order, but the court *must* make such an order and the tenancy will come to an end on day on which the tenant gives up possession in accordance with the order. However, the court may not entertain possession proceedings unless the landlord has served notice on the tenant stating:

(i)   the Court will be asked to make an order for possession;

(ii)   the reasons for seeking possession – see section 128(3);

(iii) a date after which proceedings may be begun – which must not be earlier than the date on which the tenancy could be brought to an end by notice to quit: see section 128(4). The court may not entertain proceedings unless they are begun after that date specified in the notice.

The tenant may request a review of the landlord's decision to seek possession under section 129, and must in the notice of proceedings be informed of this right. The right must be exercised by the tenant serving notice on the landlord to that effect 14 days of receipt of the landlord's notice. Note the need for the tenant to be proactive. In effect the right is for an internal appeal. Regulations may provide for the review to be conducted by a person of appropriate seniority. The reviewer must not have been involved in the original decision. They may provide for oral hearings and for representation of the tenant. The landlord is then to notify the tenant of the result of the review, and if the decision is confirmed reasons must be given. Such review must be carried out and the tenant notified before the date specified in the notice of proceedings as the date after which proceedings may be begun – note the need for timely action. See further the Introductory Tenant (Review) Regulations 1997 SI 1997/22.

Provided the landlord complies with the procedure laid down in sections 127 and 128 of the 1996 Act the county court *must* grant a possession order. That court cannot entertain a defence to possession proceedings based on a denial of allegations of breach of the introductory tenancy agreement – for example an allegation of causing a nuisance – neither may that court grant a stay of the proceedings. Should a tenant who is disappointed with the outcome of a review decision wish to challenge the decision, for example on the basis that the review failed to comply with the requirements of the rules of natural justice, the only mode of challenge is to seek judicial review in the High Court on a point of law. Should the tenant do that, however the County Court may adjourn the possession proceedings until the judicial review is concluded.[3e]

Succession and introductory tenancies

Under section 131 et seq of the 1996 Act there can be succession under an introductory tenancy by a 'qualified person', ie someone who occupies the dwelling as his/her only/principal home at time of the tenant's death and is either:

(i) the tenant's spouse; or

3e *Manchester City Council v Cochrane* [1999] 1 WLR 809, 31 HLR 810, CA.

(ii) another member of the tenant's family who has resided with the tenant thoughout the 12 months prior to the death; unless in *either* case the original tenant was a successor ie, under section 132

    (a) the tenancy vested in him/her by succession under section 133 (ie only one succession is possible) or

    (b) the original tenant was a joint tenant who became a sole tenant, or

    (c) the original tenant became the tenant on an assignment, or

    (d) the original tenant became the tenant on the tenancy being vested in him on death of previous tenant.

Under section 133 when a tenant under an introductory tenancy dies and there is a 'qualified person' (as described above) the tenancy will vest in that person – or, where there is more than one qualified to succeed, in the spouse in preference to all others, and if there is no spouse, in such one of those qualified as they may decide, or, in the event of no agreement, such one as is chosen by the landlord. Where no one is *qualified* to succeed, the tenancy ceases to be introductory, when it is vested during the course of administration of the estate. On ceasing to be introductory the tenancy becomes one at common law and can be ended by NTQ.

Introductory tenancies cannot be assigned save within the matrimonial context, or to a person who would otherwise be qualified to succeed if the tenant died immediately prior to the assignment. 'Member of the family' for the foregoing proposes is defined by section 140 and is the traditional definition under Housing Act 1985: see further Chapter 5.

Miscellaneous

Under Section 136 of the 1996 Act every landlord letting dwellings on introductory tenancies is to publish information about its tenancies from time to time in form suited to explain in simple terms their express terms, the relevant legal provisions and the landlord's repairing obligations. A copy of this information is to be supplied to every introductory tenant along with a written statement of the terms of the tenancy. Under section 137 consultation arrangements similar to those for secure tenancies under section 105 of the Housing Act 1985 have to be maintained for introductory tenancies.

Comment

Though early evidence suggested many authorities were considering adopting introductory tenancies it is far from clear whether they have become popular. More authorities might adopt them if they could choose which tenancies were to be introductory, but that would surely invite challenge on the grounds of bias. Some authorities, about 31% at the time of writing, though this may rise to over 40%, have adopted such tenancies, while others argue the time and expense of setting up a scheme are better devoted to dealing with actual cases of bad behaviour by tenants. It may also be asked why no such scheme was introduced on a mandatory basis for registered social landlords. Guidance from the Housing Corporation in the form of Circular RI–01/98 indicates that registered social landlords may utilise the form of the assured shorthold tenancy (for the details of which see below) to operate a type of introductory or 'starter' tenancy scheme. Such a tenancy confers no real security of tenure on its holder but can be transformed into a more secure form of assured tenancy after it has run its initial course. At the time of writing only 13% of registered social landlords utilised this, but the figure could rise to over 30%.

The most that can be said so far about introductory tenancy schemes is that their use is far from uniform and their value as yet unproven. In fact it appeared by the end of 1999 that where introductory tenancies are brought to an end by eviction, the most common reason is rent arrears, *not* bad behaviour by tenants.

Tenure of council dwellings

The rights of secure tenants are contained in Part IV of the 1985 Act, as amended. These rights belong to *tenants*, not their spouses, children, partners, nor people whom they leave behind them in their dwellings if, for example, they choose to abscond without paying rent[4]. Sections 79 to 81 define tenancy as secure where the following conditions are satisfied:

(1) the dwelling must be let as a separate dwelling-house; there must be no sharing of 'living accommodation' (for example kitchens, but *not* bathrooms or lavatories) with other households, see *Neale v Del Soto*[5], *Cole v Harris*[6] and *Thompson v City of Glasgow District Council*[7] where a single bedroom in a multi-storey block run for single men which had no cooking or washing facilities and where the occupant did not carry out all his 'living' was held *not* to be 'separate';[8]

(2) the landlord must be a local authority, eg a county, unitary or district council, a London Borough council, an urban development corporation, or a housing action trust.

---

4   *Westminster City Council v Basson* (1990) 62 P & CR 57, CA.
5   [1945] KB 144, [1945] 1 All ER 191, CA.
6   [1945] KB 474, [1945] 2 All ER 146, CA.
7   1986 SLT (Lands Tr) 6.
8   See also *Central YMCA Housing Association Ltd v Saunders* (1990) 23 HLR 212 and *Central YMCA Housing Association Ltd v Goodman* (1991) 24 HLR 109.

Authorities may, however, find themselves with unexpected tenants as in one case where part of premises let on a non-residential basis were converted into a flat and sublet. On the surrender of the head lease the sublessee of the flat became a direct tenant of the local authority and was held to have a secure tenancy[9].

NB Until 15 January 1989, secure tenancies could also be granted by registered associations and the Housing Corporation. Such tenancies granted before that date remain secure;

(3)　the tenant must be an individual, or in the case of a joint tenancy each joint tenant must be an individual, and he/she, or in the case of joint tenants at least one of them, must occupy the dwelling as his/her only *or* principal home; a tenant may thus have more than one home, but only a *principal* home, which is an issue of fact in each case, can be the subject of a secure tenancy; furthermore a tenant need not be physically present in a dwelling provided there is an intention to return and to retain possession which may be evidenced by the presence of furniture, *Crawley Borough Council v Sawyer*[10].

Though secure tenant status may be lost by a failure to occupy a dwelling as one's only or principal home, thus rendering the tenant liable to dispossession by ordinary Notice to Quit, security can be regained by moving back in before Notice to Quit is served[11].

(4)　the tenancy must not fall within the excepted classes as laid down in Schedule 1. These include:

(a)　long tenancies, that is a tenancy granted for a term certain exceeding 21 years, nor, of course, Introductory Tenancies, see above, and Schedule 1, para 1A of the 1985 Act;

(b)　premises occupied by the tenant as a requirement of a contract of employment directed to the better performance of his/her duties; it is for the landlord to show the exemption exists, *Hughes v London Borough of Greenwich*[12]; there is no presumption automatically arising from the mere fact of employment, a distinction must be made between cases of *necessity* and those of mere *convenience*, equally someone may continue to live in a property

---

9　*Basingstoke and Deane BC v Paice* [1995] 2 EGLR 9, CA, contrast *Westminster City Council v Basson* [1991] EGLR 277, CA, where the secure tenant abandoned the home, thereby losing secure tenant status and left behind another person, who acquired no status at all – a situation reinforced by letters from the landlord refusing to treat any payment made as rent. See also *Sanctuary Housing Association v Campbell* [1999] 3 All ER 460, [1999] 1 WLR 1279, CA.

10　(1987) 20 HLR 98.

11　*Hussey v Camden LBC* (1995) 27 HLR 5; note also *Jennings v Epping Forest DC* (1992) 25 HLR 241 where tenants moved out of a house and it was sublet, with consequent loss of their rights.

12　(1992) 24 HLR 605, CA; affd [1994] 1 AC 170, [1993] 4 All ER 577, HL, see also *Surrey County Council v Lamond* [1999] 12 EG 170, CA.

originally subject to a service tenancy and yet do another job which does not require residence, in which case the exemption ceases to apply, *Little v Borders Regional Council*[13] and *McEwan v Annandale and Eskdale District Council*[14]. In any given case much will depend on questions of distance between the dwelling and the place of work, and the nature of the job involved. Conversely where a person takes a tenancy of a dwelling and subsequently accepts employment in consequence of which residence in that dwelling is a contractual requisite, the exemption applies, *Elvidge v Coventry City Council*[15]. Retirement *may* not, however, automatically destroy the exemption, once it applies, *South Glamorgan County Council v Griffiths*[16], but where a person is made *redundant* from a job yet is allowed to stay on in the *former* tied accommodation pending a move to a further tied house, the exemption from security may be destroyed[17];

(c) where the house stands on land acquired for development and is only being used as temporary housing accommodation, it will, however, be a question of fact in any given case whether an intention to redevelop land survives an extended period during which no action is taken and at the end of which there is little prospect of redevelopment, *Lillieshall Road Housing Co-operative Ltd v Brennan and Brennan*[18]; however, a simple change in planned development will not be enough to destroy the exemption, *Attley v Cherwell District Council*[19], neither does the *immediate* landlord have to have an intention to develop, provided that is the owner's intention, *Hyde Housing Association Ltd v Harrison*[20];

(d) where a tenancy has been provided under any duty pursuant to Part VII of the Housing Act 1996 for a homeless person, the tenancy cannot be secure until the local authority inform the tenant that the tenancy is to be regarded as secure, at which point, of course, the authority has, in effect, made an allocation of a secure tenancy to the one time homeless person;

(e) accommodation *specifically* granted to a person who was *immediately before the grant not resident* in the district, *and having employment or the offer thereof, within the district* or its

13 1990 SLT (Lands Tr) 2.
14 1989 SLT (Lands Tr) 95.
15 [1994] QB 241, [1993] 4 All ER 903, CA.
16 [1992] 2 EGLR 232, CA.
17 *Greenfield v Berkshire County Council* (1996) 28 HLR 691, CA.
18 (1991) 24 HLR 195, CA.
19 (1989) 21 HLR 613.
20 [1991] 1 EGLR 51, CA.

adjoining districts, *to meet a need for temporary accommodation in order to work* there, *and also to enable him/her to find permanent housing*, cannot be subject to a secure tenancy before the expiry of one year from the grant unless the tenant is otherwise notified within that period;

(f) where the landlord has taken only a short term lease from a body incapable of granting secure tenancies, for example a private individual, of a dwelling for the purpose of providing temporary accommodation, on terms including one that the lessor may obtain vacant possession on the expiry of a specified period or when he requires it, there is no secure tenancy for *their* lessees, and the position is the same where the property has been *licensed* to the landlord, *Tower Hamlets London Borough Council v Miah*[1] ;

(g) a tenancy is not secure if it is of a dwelling made available for occupation by the tenant while works are being carried out at his/her own former home, *and* provided the tenant was *not* secure in that home;

(h) where the tenancy is of an agricultural holding and the tenant is a manager;

(i) where the tenancy is of licensed premises;

(j) where the tenancy is one granted specifically to a student to enable attendance on a designated course at a university or further education establishment;

(k) where the tenancy is of business premises falling within Part II of the Landlord and Tenant Act 1954;

(l) where the licence to occupy the dwelling was granted by an almshouse charity.

NB Once acquired secure tenant status can only be lost by:

(i) exercise of the right to buy: see section 139(2) of the 1985 Act;

(ii) change of landlord where the new one does not fulfil the landlord conditions;

(iii) death of fixed term tenant, unless the lease passes to someone who qualifies as a successor (see section 91) – the *death of a periodic tenant* means the tenancy ceases to be secure because the tenant ceases to occupy – (the case may, however, fall within the succession provisions) – there will still however, be a contractual tenancy to end by notice to quit;

(iv) tenant ceasing to occupy the dwelling as his 'only or principal home' (above);

(v) sub-letting of the whole premises: see section 93 of the 1985 Act (below);

(vi) tenant giving notice to quit: see below;

1   [1992] QB 622, [1992] 2 All ER 667.

(vii) possession being granted to the landlord by the court: see below.

All tenancies excluded from 'secure' status simply exist at common law and, in general, may be terminated by four weeks' written notice to quit, *Cannock Chase District Council v Kelly*[2] and *Sevenoaks District Council v Emmott*[3].

Security of tenure

The basic rule contained in section 82 of the Housing Act 1985 is that a secure tenancy cannot be brought to an end at the landlord's behest without an order from the court (that is the county court by virtue of section 110).

NB *Tenants* may bring tenancies to an end by simply giving notice to quit in due form, and, generally, section 5 of the Protection from Eviction Act 1977 will require there to be four weeks' notice in writing to expire at the end of a tenancy period, see further Chapter Five below. Landlords may allow a lesser period of notice, either by an express tenancy term – a 'break clause' – or by parol agreement in particular cases. But neither of these will satisfy the requirements of a 'notice to quit' where one of two joint tenants wishes to depart, and here the formalities have to be complied with.

The Housing Act 1996 inserted a new section 83 in the 1985 Act. The court cannot entertain proceedings unless the landlord has served a notice of possession proceedings (NOPP) *or the court considers it just and equitable to dispense with such a notice.* In this connection note *Kelsey HA v King*[4] where the court allowed dispensation with notice in a nuisance case and took into account (i) events happening since the proceedings started and (ii) the fact that the tenant only raised the notice point at a late stage in the proceedings. The general line of authority is that the court may allow dispensation with written notice where clear oral notice has been given, but too much reliance should not be placed on this. The notice must: be in a form prescribed by the Regulations made by the Secretary of State, and must specify the ground on which the possession is sought; give particulars of the case and specify a date after which proceedings may be commenced, in which case the notice will then have a currency of 12 months[5] *But* in the case of a periodic secure tenancy where possession is sought on Ground 2 of Schedule 2, ie the so-called 'nuisance grounds', the NOPP *must state that possession proceedings may be begun immediately and must also specify the date sought by the landlord as the date on which*

2   [1978] 1 All ER 152, [1978] 1 WLR 1.
3   (1979) 39 P & CR 404.
4   (1995) 28 HLR 270.
5   The Secure Tenancies (Notices) Regulations 1987, SI 1987/755.

the tenant is to give up possession, and that the notice will cease to have effect 12 months after the date specified by the landlord.

The date specified in either case (ie nuisance and non-nuisance cases) must not be earlier than the date on which the tenancy could, apart from section 83, be brought to an end, ie 4 weeks' minimum notice is required ending on an anniversary date of the initial grant. However, in 'nuisance cases' the court can entertain the proceedings once the NOPP has been served, though it must still remain in force: in non-nuisance cases the possession action cannot be brought until *after* the specified date has passed, though, again, the notice must still remain in force: see section 83A.

The changes made in 1996 were designed to speed up possession proceedings in 'nuisance' cases: in practice the changes may be more cosmetic than real as the actual hearing date may well depend upon the state of the local county court calendar.

A notice not containing all requisite information will be defective leading to dismissal of proceedings, *Swansea City Council v Hearn*[6]. Note also the requirements of section 48 of the Landlord and Tenant Act 1987 that *landlords* generally must furnish tenants with an address at which notices may be served on the landlord by the tenant – a requirement relevant to the inception of possession proceedings.

The court may not, however, grant a possession order outside the parameters fixed by the legislation, even if the parties agree to it[7]. Furthermore, the Notice of Possession Proceedings must make it clear to its recipient what is needed to amend the situation leading to an action, eg by specifying the level of arrears in question, but a mere minor error in these particulars will not invalidate the notice[8].

The grounds on which possession is sought may be altered or added to with the leave of the court; see section 84(3) of the 1985 Act. This extends to allowing alteration of particulars of the claim[9]. But a possession order cannot take effect earlier than the date specified by the landlord in the NOPP, see Section 84(4).

The grounds on which possession may be given are found in Schedule 2 of the 1985 Act.

6   (1990) 23 HLR 284.
7   *Wandsworth London Borough Council v Fadayomi* [1987] 3 All ER 474, [1987] 1 WLR 1473.
8   *Torridge DC v Jones* (1985) 18 HLR 107, but contrast *Dudley Metropolitan Borough Council v Bailey* (1990) 22 HLR 424 where the landlord had stated the ground for possession and given particulars at the time notice was served and had acted in good faith, so that a minor error did not invalidate the notice.
9   *Camden London Borough Council v Oppong* (1996) 28 HLR 701.

GROUNDS FOR POSSESSION (INITIAL ISSUES)

Section 84 provides that possession will only be obtained on stated grounds, and that in addition one or both two further preconditions must be satisfied:

(i) (for grounds 1–8) it must be reasonable to make the order.
(ii) (for grounds 9–11) suitable alternative accommodation will be available (Schedule 2 Part IV Housing Act 1985 see below).

NB for grounds 12–16 *both* conditions must be satisfied.

Suitable alternative accommodation

The Housing Act 1985 was based on existing Rent Act provisions, though with different wording in places and the significant omission of any reference to the 'character' of the offered premises. This has the consequence of eliminating the need to consider general environmental factors affecting the property. To be 'suitable' the premises offered must be:

(i) let as a separate dwelling under a secure or assured tenancy, though *not* an assured shorthold tenancy, nor one where the landlord might recover under Grounds 1 to 5 of Schedule 2 of the Housing Act 1988 (certain mandatory grounds for possession); and
(ii) reasonably suitable, in the court's opinion, to the tenant's and tenant's family's needs and means, having particular regard to:
   (a) nature of accommodation which the landlord normally allocates to those with similar needs;
   (b) distance from place of work;
   (c) distance from the home of the members of the tenant's family where proximity is essential for the well being of the tenant;
   (d) needs of the tenant and family, eg as to extent;
   (e) the terms on which the accommodation is available;
   (f) any furniture to be provided.

In *Enfield Borough Council v French*[10] it was held that property that is otherwise suitable may qualify as alternative accommodation even where the particular need regarded as important by the tenant – in this case a garden – cannot be satisfied by the property offered.

Ground 1

This applies where any rent lawfully due from the tenant has not been paid, or where any obligation of the tenancy has been broken or not performed.

10 (1984) 17 HLR 211.

The use of possession action to deal with arrears of rent will be considered below. Note that an authority may apply for a mandatory prohibitory injunction to enforce a negative covenant (eg a 'no pets' clause) in a tenancy agreement. Such a remedy is discretionary and the tenant may resist on the basis that greater hardship would flow from granting the order than would follow from denying it, *Sutton Housing Trust v Lawrence*[11]. Some authorities, however, make use of their power to prohibit racial harassment by means of a tenancy obligation and possession has been obtained in cases of breach. Where a breach of covenant is admitted, and there is clearly an intention to continue the breach the court will only rarely refuse to grant a possession order, *Sheffield City Council v Green*[12]. Clauses forbidding harassment by tenants are the most common methods used by authorities to prevent racist, sexist, homophobic, or criminal behaviour on estates, coupled with well publicised policies on violence and harassment. Indeed the tenancy agreement *should be* the most effect means of dealing with a wide range of 'bad behaviour' including noise, unruly children and pets, dumping rubbish, repairing vehicles to an excessive degree and domestic violence. A majority of authorities are now prepared to at least threaten possession proceedings against tenants who perpetrate such incidents, though many authorities are also prepared to move victims of such abuse as a matter of priority – this may be seen as 'rewarding' a perpetrator whose desire was to drive away a neighbour. For further details see Love and Kirby *Racial Incidents in Council Housing: The Local Authority Response* (HMSO, 1994). Landlords should, however, avoid phrasing tenancy obligations subjectively – eg 'conduct in the council's opinion which is a nuisance' as that may be an unfair contract term[13].

Ground 2

Section 144 of the Housing Act 1996 amended the 1985 Act so that possession may be sought where the tenant or a person residing in (eg the tenant's child) *or visiting* the dwelling:

(a) has been guilty of conduct *causing or likely to cause* a nuisance or annoyance to *a person residing, visiting or otherwise engaging in a lawful activity in the locality of the dwelling*;

(b) has been convicted of using the dwelling or allowing it to be used for immoral or illegal purposes; or

---

11 (1987) 19 HLR 520, contrast *Sheffield City Council v Jepson* (1993) 25 HLR 299 where a dog was kept in deliberate and flagrant breach of a tenancy condition and possession was granted.

12 [1993] EGCS 185.

13 See SI 1994/3159 Regulation 4, and *Camden London Borough Council v McBride* [1999] 1 CL 284, Cty Ct.

(c) *has been convicted of an arrestable offence committed in or in the locality of the dwelling house* ie offences under section 24 Police and Criminal Evidence Act 1984, including all offences with fixed penalties at law, and offences for which adults may be imprisoned for five years or more, taking a car without the consent of the owner ('TWOC') and offences under section 22 and 23 Sexual Offences Act 1956, such as causing prostitution and procuring girls under 21. It also includes theft, burglary and drug trafficking.

In the foregoing passages the expansion of the previous law is indicated by italics. A number of other points should also be noted.

(1) Note the need 'to cause' – is an element of intention required, or is there an objective standard of behaviour? It appears to be the latter.

(2) The current law is much wider than the old ground 2 – behaviour within the locality of a tenant's dwelling will now be caught. Nuisance or annoyance to authority officers going about their lawful business would be caught, as would acts of racial harassment against local shopkeepers who would not been classified as 'neighbours' under the old law.

(3) What does 'locality' mean? It is clearly less wide than authority's entire 'district'. Guidance from the DETR indicates it extends to the 'common parts' of an estate in question. It is furthermore open to authorities and other social landlords to include a clause in their tenancy agreements that tenants shall not indulge in criminal or abusive or threatening behaviour anywhere in *the district*. Breach of such a condition would be relied on in a possession case. DETR Circular 2/97 gives further guidance.

The courts have also given guidance on certain issues.

The issue of locality

Manchester City Council v Lawler[14] gives some guidance on the meaning of 'locality'. L and her ten-year-old son had 60 visits from the police during the course of her tenancy, and in August 1997 the authority sought possession. L gave six undertakings not to cause a nuisance, not to use, or to threaten use of, violence, not use abusive, insulting or threatening words or behaviour 'in the locality' of her home. The authority subsequently claimed she had broken the undertakings in particular by threatening a child with a knife in a shopping area three streets from where L lived. They applied for her to be imprisoned (breach of undertaking is contempt of court). L argued that the undertaking was too vague to be binding as 'in the locality'

14 (1998) 31 HLR 119, CA.

had no meaning. The Court of Appeal held that the meaning of the phrase had to be determined as a matter of fact in each set of circumstances. As a matter of common sense a shopping precinct three streets away from L's home was clearly 'in the locality', and hence L had been quite properly punished for breach of undertaking.

Northampton Borough Council v Lovatt[15] provides further guidance. L and his family had been dispossessed following a 'reign of terror' on the Spencer Estate, Northampton. L and his wife had failed to control their family, and his sons had 11 convictions for offences against persons or property on the estate. Mrs L had a conviction for a breach of the peace on the estate and L had used the house for running a car maintenance and repair business. They appealed against the order arguing that acts of 'nuisance or annoyance' committed away from their home could not be 'nuisance or annoyance' for the purposes of Ground 2, as the victims were not 'neighbours'. The Court of Appeal rejected this. *'Neighbour' covers all persons sufficiently close to the source of conduct complained of to be adversely affected by it.* The court then went on to hold that *the conduct complained of need not emanate from the dwelling in question but can be conduct in the neighbourhood.* What needs to be shown is a *link between the bad behaviour in question and the fact of residence in the area.* That – and this is novel – is provided by the legitimate interest of the authority in requiring their tenants to respect the neighbourhood and the interests of other residents. In other words, to obtain an order an authority needs to show that their interests *as a landlord* have been affected. But those interests are affected if a tenant disrupts a local authority estate.

The type of behaviour

In relation to this issue remarkable developments in judicial attitudes have taken place. Ten years or so ago the courts were unwilling to order possession against long-standing tenants whose children had committed acts of nuisance[16], even where there was ample confirmatory evidence[17]. That judicial reluctance to act has now been swept away.

Thus in *Woking Borough Council v Bystram*[18] foul language, and menacing and abusive behaviour led to the granting of a suspended possession order. More judicial activism was displayed in *Kensington and Chelsea Royal London Borough Council v Simmonds*[19]. S was the tenant

---

15   [1998] 2 FCR 182, CA.
16   *Camden London Borough Council v Hawkins* (1988) Legal Action, March p 18.
17   *Ealing Family Housing Association v Taylor* (1987) Legal Action, December p 15.
18   [1993] EGCS 208.
19   (1996) 29 HLR 507.

of a council flat. She lived there with her son (aged 13). Above them lived a Pakistani family. The tenancy agreement forbade misuse of the property or annoyance to neighbours whether by the tenant or any member of the tenant's household, or visitors, and specifically forbade the tenant to commit (or allow) offence to other tenants on grounds of race, colour, ethnic origin or nationality. However, the Pakistani family complained of racist abuse from S's son, and the authority sought possession under Schedule 2 of the 1985 Act, Grounds 1 and 2. It was found S's son and his friends had abused the neighbours, though it was also established that S found it hard to control her son. Nevertheless it was found reasonable to make an order which was suspended on condition there was no further nuisance.

S appealed arguing she was not in breach of the tenancy as she could not be said to have 'allowed' her son to commit acts of nuisance. It was also, she argued, not reasonable to make an order under Ground 2 against a tenant who was not at fault. The court held:

(1) as it had been found that the abuse had continued over a period of time it was quite open to the trial judge to find that S had 'allowed' her son to continue – one act of nuisance alone, however, would not have been enough;

(2) in determining whether to make an order, the extent of a tenant's personal blame is a relevant consideration. If a tenant has tried to control a child and failed an order may still be made. The court must not only consider the interests of the tenant, but also those of neighbours. It would be intolerable for neighbours to be deprived of relief merely because a tenant was incapable of controlling his/her household.

The interesting points about this case are:

• the signal failure of S to control her son's behaviour over a number of months was considered sufficient to find she had 'allowed' him to indulge in conduct amounting to a breach of the tenancy agreement;

• there is no 'mileage' in an argument that a child is too old to control and yet is too young to be put out of his/her home;

• the fact that a parent tries to exercise control and fails similarly is not of itself enough to protect the parent from dispossession. A lack of personal blame is no automatic defence.

It may, however, also be relevant for the court to consider any undertaking given by the tenant in respect of future behaviour.

The greatest advance in what we may call 'judicial control of bad behaviour' however, came in *Bristol City Council v Mousah*[20].

In November 1993 Bristol let a property to M. By March 1994 there were complaints of noise and nuisance from the premises, and on 10 April 1994

20 (1997) 30 HLR 32, CA.

they served notice of proceedings on M. The police had already raided the property under the drugs legislation and had found six persons using cocaine, this incident was later repeated. On 10 June 1994 the authority sought possession. After this drug taking again occurred on the property and on 10 November 1994 Bristol issued a summons claiming possession on the basis that M owed rent, and secondly that he, or a person living in the dwelling, had committed acts of nuisance. In this they relied on a clause in their tenancy agreement forbidding the use of premises for the supply of drugs and making tenants liable for any relevant misconduct by their household, lodgers or visitors.

In defending the possession action M pleaded:
1.   a considerable period of time had elapsed since the last drug incident, and it would not be reasonable for an order to be granted;
2.   he was vulnerable, being schizoid, and would be substantially prejudiced by being evicted – he was assisted in this by medical evidence.

At the trial it was established the premises had been used for the supply of drugs, though M had not been at the premises on any occasion when they had been searched, and asserted he did not know what was going on. It was, however, established by the judge that he did know. The judge further found that a clear breach of the conditions of tenancy. He considered, however, it would not be reasonable to make an order. He thought that an attempt was being made to make an example of M. Furthermore if an order was granted M could be likely to become homeless which would affect his condition, and though there was a public interest that property should not be used for the supply of drugs, equally there was a public interest that people who might become dangerous in consequence of illnesses they have should be kept off the streets. Additionally his chances of being reaccommodated under homelessness legislation would be slight.

The Court of Appeal reiterated that only rarely will the discretion of the trial judge be disturbed on appeal in a possession case. However, if incorrect matters have been taken into account they would intervene and that was the case here.

•   The trial judge had become too embroiled in a consideration of what M's chances would be under homelessness legislation if he applied as a homeless person. There was ample evidence from the authority that his case would be properly dealt with on its merits. That was all the judge needed to know.
•   Too liberal an approach had been adopted with regards to M's claim that a long period of time had elapsed between the last recorded drug incident and the commencement of the proceedings – much of that delay was the consequence of M's own spinning out of the preliminary proceedings. Furthermore this was not a case in which there was only an isolated case involving a small quantity of a Class B drug.

- *In a case where there is such a serious breach of a tenancy condition it is only in exceptional cases that it can be said it is not reasonable to make a possession order.*
- The medical evidence did not support the judge's conclusion that M would, if dispossessed, become a public danger – M had said in evidence he wanted to move to another part of Bristol and could from there keep in touch with his doctors.

This decision was followed by *Camden London Borough Council v Gilsenan*[1] G had been a secure tenant since August 1983. In the period 1994–96 she incurred rent arrears and had, allegedly, frequently caused or permitted her visitors to cause severe nuisance to her neighbours in the flats where she lived by virtue of loud music, drunkenness, deposition of rubbish and violence involving a machete. It was further alleged that G had verbally abused an estate co-ordinator and had locked that person in a boiler room. The authority took various steps to prevent the nuisances and ultimately commenced possession proceedings, going so far as to obtain an 'unless' order. (This is a procedural device which requires as a condition of defending a case that the defendant should abstain from a certain course of behaviour). G failed to comply with the 'unless' order and was debarred from defending the possession proceedings, but nevertheless sought to, promising to give undertakings of good behaviour. Nevertheless possession was granted. G appealed, but the Court of Appeal held that on the facts it was perfectly reasonable to grant possession.

Surely here we see a line of judicial policy. The nature and character of the wrong doing is a major issue in determining whether to grant possession. In cases of serious wrong doing it will *normally* be reasonable to grant possession.[2]

It should however, be noted that authorities are not normally liable for nuisances committed by their tenants,[3] nor is there an implied term in tenancy agreements that a landlord will act to restrain acts of nuisance[4]. Neither does a failure to act amount to negligence.[5] The use of injunctions to restrain bad behaviour by tenants will be considered below.

[Ground 2A inserted in 1996 relates to domestic violence and is dealt with in Chapter Five.]

---

1   (1998) 31 HLR 81, CA.
2   See also *Shrewsbury and Atcham Borough Council v Evans* (1997) 30 HLR 123.
3   *Smith v Scott* [1973] Ch 314, [1972] 3 All ER 645.
4   *O'Leary v Islington London Borough Council* (1983) 9 HLR 81.
5   *Hussain v Lancaster City Council* [1999] 4 All ER 125, [1999] 2 WLR 1142, CA.

Ground 3

Where the condition of the dwelling or any common parts of a building comprising the dwelling have deteriorated as a result of the tenant's waste, neglect or default or as a result of the acts of any person residing in the dwelling-house whom the tenant (if that person is a lodger or sub-tenant) has unreasonably failed to remove from the dwelling.

Ground 4

Where the condition of any furniture provided by the landlord for use under the tenancy (or in any common parts of a building as the case may be) has deteriorated as result of ill treatment by the tenant or any person residing in the dwelling.

Ground 5

Where the tenant obtained the tenancy knowingly or recklessly by false statements[6].

Ground 6

Where the tenancy was assigned to the tenant, or to the tenant's predecessor in title being a member of the tenant's family and residing in the dwelling, by virtue of exchange under section 92 *and* a premium was paid in connection therewith.

Ground 7

Where the dwelling is comprised within a building held by the landlord mainly for non-housing purposes and consisting mainly of non-housing accommodation, *and* the dwelling was let to the tenant in consequence of employment by the landlord, or the local authority etc, *and* the tenant, or a person residing in the dwelling, has been guilty of conduct such that, having regard to the purpose for which the building is used, it would be wrong for the tenant to remain in occupation.

---

6   See *Shrewsbury and Atcham Borough Council v Evans* (1997) 30 HLR 123 where the court indicated the nature and degree of untrue statements and whether they were made deliberately or recklessly should be considered.

Ground 8

Where the tenant, being a secure tenant of another dwelling which is his/her home and which is subject to works, has accepted the tenancy of the dwelling of which possession is sought on condition that he/she would move back to the original home on completion of the works in question, and where the works have been completed. *Tower Hamlets London Borough Council v Abadie*[7] indicates that a tenant may defend under this ground by showing the original accommodation is not being offered.

Ground 9

Where the dwelling-house is illegally overcrowded.

Ground 10

Where the landlord intends within a reasonable time to demolish, or reconstruct or carry out works on the dwelling, etc, and cannot do so without obtaining possession. Here a mere desire simply to remove a particular person from a particular dwelling is not enough: the landlord must show a clearly defined and settled intention to do major works which cannot be done without possession being obtained, *Wansbeck District Council v Marley*[8].

Ground 10 A (Introduced by the Housing and Planning Act 1986)

Where the dwelling is in an area subject to a ministerially approved re-development scheme under Part V of Schedule 2 and the landlord intends to dispose of the dwelling under the scheme within reasonable time of obtaining possession.

Under Part V of Schedule 2 approval may be given for schemes of disposal and redevelopment of areas of dwellings. Landlords must first serve notice on affected tenants stating the main features of the scheme, that they intend to apply for approval, the effect of approval in relation to possession proceedings, and giving the tenants at least 28 days to make representations. Landlords must not apply for approval before considering representations made. In considering whether to approve a scheme the Secretary of State must particularly consider the effect of the scheme on

7   [1990] EGCS 4.
8   (1987) 20 HLR 247.

housing accommodation in the area, the proposed time scale of the scheme, the extent to which housing to be provided under the scheme is to be sold or let to existing tenants and other representations made to him or brought to his notice. Approval may be given subject to conditions. Suitable alternative accommodation must be available.

Ground 11

Where the landlord is a charity and continued occupation by the tenant would conflict with its objects.

Ground 12

Where the dwelling is sited in a building held by the landlord mainly for non-housing purposes and consisting of mainly non-housing accommodation, *and* the dwelling was let to the tenant in consequence of employment by the landlord, or the local authority etc, *and* that employment has ceased *and* the landlord reasonably requires the dwelling for some other employee.

Ground 13

Where the dwelling has features which are substantially different from those of ordinary houses so as to make it suitable for occupation by a physically disabled person, and where there is no longer such a disabled person living in the house, while the landlord requires the dwelling for occupation by such a person.

Ground 14

The landlord is a housing association or trust which lets dwellings to persons whose non-financial circumstances make it difficult for them to satisfy their housing need, and *either* there is no longer such a person residing in the dwelling, *or* the tenant has received an offer of a secure dwelling from a local authority, *and* the landlord requires the dwelling for occupation by a person with special needs.

Ground 15

Where the dwelling is one of a *group* which it is the practice of the landlord

to let for occupation by persons with special needs, and also:
(1) a social service or special facility is provided in close proximity to the dwellings in order to assist those with the special needs;
(2) there is no longer a person with those needs residing in the house, and
(3) the landlord requires the house for someone with those needs.

Note that a *'group'* cannot be made up of a number of dispersed properties all of which have the special features in question[9].

Ground 16

Where the tenant, being a successor (other than a spouse successor), by virtue of being a member of the deceased previous tenant's family, is under occupying the dwelling, in that it is too large for reasonable requirements. Notice of intention to commence possession proceedings must be served *more* than six months, but *less* than twelve months, after the date of death of the original tenant. In determining whether to make an order under this ground the court must consider, inter alia, the tenant's age, the period of occupation of the dwelling and any financial or other support given by the tenant to the previous tenant.

The court is not to make a possession order on Grounds 1 to 8 unless it considers it reasonable to do so; on Grounds 9 to 11 unless it is satisfied that suitable accommodation will be available for the tenant on the order taking effect, and on Grounds 12 to 16 unless *both* conditions are satisfied.

General considerations affecting discretionary grounds of possession

Under section 85 of the 1985 Act the court has extended discretion as to ordering possession.

Where possession proceedings are brought under Grounds 1 to 8 and 12 to 16 above, the court may adjourn the proceedings for such periods as it thinks fit. Where a possession order is made under any of the above grounds its execution may be stayed, suspended or postponed for such period as the court thinks fit. Where the court exercises this discretion it must impose conditions with regard to the payment of any arrears of rent, etc, unless it considers that to do so would cause exceptional hardship to the tenant or would be otherwise unreasonable. Other conditions may be imposed. Where these conditions are fulfilled the court may rescind or discharge the order. In those cases where the court must be satisfied that

9   *Martin v Motherwell District Council* 1991 SLT (Lands Tr) 4.

it is reasonable to make a possession order, it is for the landlord to show why it would be reasonable to grant possession[10].

Landlords should not assume that a tenant vacating a dwelling while owing rent is evidence of surrender of the tenancy, *Sutton London Borough Council v Swann*[11]. In such circumstances landlords should seek possession on the statutory grounds, *Preston Borough Council v Fairclough*[12]. The court may also take into account the homelessness consequences of making a possession order, *Rushcliffe Borough Council v Watson*[13].

It is also possible to seek judicial review of a decision to seek possession on the basis that a relevant factor has not been taken into account, such as the possibility that an absentee tenant may be willing to assign the tenancy to an estranged partner still living in the dwelling and caring for children there[14].

Where a suspended possession order is granted failure by the tenant to meet its conditions means the tenancy is ended, *Thompson v Elmbridge Borough Council*[15], though even here the county court retains jurisdiction to suspend execution of the order[16]. *R v Newham London Borough Council, ex p Campbell*[17] indicates, however, that once a tenancy is lost by breach of a suspended order, making a further suspension does *not* revive the tenancy: the tenant simply has a personal status of irremovability while the terms of the suspension are complied with (and until they are discharged). Even where the former tenant stays on with the landlord's agreement and makes payments, the attitude of the courts is that the landlord in forbearing from executing the order, not granting a tenancy; this makes the occupier a 'tolerated trespasser'[18]. This is a most untidy situation, and many landlords – let alone tenants – are unlikely to understand the consequences of breach of a suspended order.

It is possible to set a suspended order aside or to appeal against the making of such an order, see County Court Rules Ord 37, r 1 and r 2. Even after an order has been executed it may still be set aside on appeal provided

10 *Woodspring District Council v Taylor* (1982) 4 HLR 95.
11 (1985) 18 HLR 140.
12 (1982) 8 HLR 70.
13 (1991) 24 HLR 124.
14 *R v London Borough of Hammersmith and Fulham, ex p Quigley* (1999) Housing Law Monitor, May p 8.
15 (1987) 19 HLR 526, [1987] 1 WLR 1425.
16 *R v Ilkeston County Court, ex p Kruza* (1985) 17 HLR 539.
17 [1994] Fam Law 319, 26 HLR 183.
18 *Burrows v Brent London Borough Council* [1996] 4 All ER 577, [1996] 1 WLR 1448, HL. But if the broken order is subsequently discharged under section 85 the tenancy will revive , and with it all its repairing obligations, even on a retrospective basis: *Rogers v Lambeth London Borough Council* [1999] 45 LS Gaz R 33, CA.

the landlord is not prejudiced, and the tenant has an arguable case to defend the actions: *Tower Hamlets London Borough Council v Abadie*[19].

Once a possession order has been granted the landlord may proceed to execute it by obtaining a county court warrant, and no need exists to inform the tenant of an application for warrant, this was the subject of criticism in *Leicester City Council v Aldwinckle*[20]. Once the order has been executed, the warrant for possession may not be set aside or suspended unless: (a) the possession order itself is set aside; (b) the warrant has been obtained by fraud, or (c) there has been some abuse of process or oppression during execution, see *Hammersmith and Fulham London Borough Council v Hill*[1].

Where the court makes a possession order on grounds where the reasonableness of the issue is not a deciding factor, discretion is limited by section 89 of the Housing Act 1980 (still in force). So far as secure tenancies are concerned this provision is relevant where recovery of possession is sought under Grounds 9 to 11. In such circumstances the giving up of possession cannot be postponed (whether by the order itself, or any variation, suspension or stay) to a date later than 14 days after the making of the order unless it appears to the court that exceptional hardship would be caused by requiring possession to be given up by that date. In such cases the giving up of possession may be suspended for up to six weeks from the making of the order but for no longer. The provision also applies to non-secure tenancies.

Use of possession proceedings in cases of arrears

The great majority of possession actions brought by authorities are brought to ensure payment arrears of rent. Such actions may frequently go through the county court 'on the nod'. The tenant rarely attends, and if there is unlikely to be represented, particularly following the 1999 changes to court procedures and eligibility for legal aid. Suspended orders are often granted in such cases, but they have the disadvantage of putting the tenancy at risk. Where arrears of rent are the basis for an action they must be specified in the NOPP and proved in court, *and* the landlord must still convince the court it is reasonable to make a possession order taking into account the conduct of both parties and the public interest in the matter. The arrears must exist at the date proceedings commenced, and a refusal to accept rent tendered will mean there are no arrears, while a tender of arrears

19 (1990) 22 HLR 264.
20 (1991) 24 HLR 40.
1   [1994] 2 EGLR 51, CA – here local authority staff deterred a tenant from seeking legal assistance with regard to applying to stay execution of a warrant.

after the commencement of proceedings is likely to persuade the court against making an order save where the tenant has a history of persistent late payment, see *Bird v Hildage*[2], *Haringey London Borough Council v Stewart and Stewart*[3]. The arrears must have been run up by the tenant in question[4], while disputes as to the amount of rent owed may reduce the likelihood of an order being made[5]. The court will also consider the nature of the arrears, eg are they recent, and the reason for their existence, and whether the landlord is itself in breach of any of its obligations.

However, how does the law work in practice? The research study *'Taking Tenants to Court'* Leather & Jeffers (DoE 1989) discovered that orders are most often sought for rent arrears, and that authorities have evolved their own procedures for such cases involving:

(1)   identification of the problem;
(2)   issuing a NOPP;
(3)   allowing a minimum period of 28 days before seeking a county court summons;
(4)   the setting of the hearing date, and finally
(5)   the judgement – which, if for an order, is usually suspended.

On average the number of NOPPS served as a percentage of housing stock was 8.7%, though the figures varied from a high of 21% to a low of 3%. There is an enormously wide variation in the numbers of court cases as a percentage of NOPPS. On average that percentage was 29.7%, but the high was 74% and the low 8% – clearly there is a wide variation in practice between authorities as to what happens after a NOPP has been served and before action starts. Equally there is variation as to what level of rent arrears will lead to a case being taken to court, with the figure for one authority being as low as £169 while the highest figure was £988. Most authorities are generally successful in gaining orders where they seek them.

Though some suspended orders are discharged, many tenants do not comply with conditions and discharge their debts, which suggests limited effectiveness for such orders. However, an application for a warrant to evict tends to produce a flurry of response, either in the form of some payment, or with the tenant leaving voluntarily – often with no forwarding address. This suggests that from the authority's point of view possession proceedings are not truly effective as a means of dealing with arrears. Certainly from the tenant's point of view they are unsatisfactory. It has a long been argued, and the 1989 survey confirms this, that most tenants in arrears served with a NOPP do not realise their tenancies are in danger. Tenants rarely know how to respond in such circumstances, lack independent advice on how to act,

2   [1948] 1 KB 91, [1947] 2 All ER 7, CA.
3   (1991) 23 HLR 557.
4   *Tickner v Clifton* [1929] 1 KB 207.
5   *Dun Laoghaire UDC v Moran* [1921] 2 IR 404.

are intimidated by courts, and especially by public hearings. Many tenants reach an informal agreement that the authority should have a suspended order in return for 'so much off the arrears each week'; from which has grown the myth of the 'consented possession order'.

Other criticisms can be made on the basis that under the new civil procedure rules (CPR) cases where arrears are below £5,000 can now be treated as 'small claims' where no costs are awarded and legal aid is usually unavailable, thus increasing tenants' lack of representation problems.

Distress is the other remedy for arrears of rent. It was characterised as 'archaic' by Lord Denning in *Abingdon RDC v O 'Gorman*[6], and is subject to severe restrictions in relation to assured tenancies under the Housing Act 1988. In 1986 the Law Commission, in an interim report recommending its abolition, concluded the remedy was riddled with inconsistencies, uncertainties, anomalies and archaisms. However, in 1978 105 authorities used distress regularly as a remedy and 32 used it exceptionally. In 1986 CIPFA concluded from its postal survey of all 405 English and Welsh authorities (which received a 68% response) that amongst English shire districts use of distress was evenly matched by non-use. Further research carried out for the Certificated Bailiffs' Association in the late 1980s revealed a total then of 102 English and Welsh authorities using distress – 1 inner London Borough, 7 outer London Boroughs, 2 Metropolitan districts, 86 shire districts and 6 Welsh districts. Not all authorities using distress in 1978 were still using it in 1986–88. Authorities may take up use of distress and then refrain from it over a period of time. The pattern of use is not necessarily connected with the party 'colour' of an authority.

However, what is distress? Very briefly it is a remedy which allows the landlord to obtain satisfaction of rent in arrears by the seizure and sale of certain goods found on the premises in respect of which rent is due. Only certain goods may be the subject of distress – clothing and bedding are, for example, exempt up to certain values. Survey evidence suggests the sort of goods usually taken are easily transportable and saleable items, such as electrical goods, and luxury items such as cameras and jewellery. The actual procedure for levying distress is exceptionally technical. Those levying distress may not break into a house or enter by force, though they may enter by a door which is closed but not fastened. Once inside, however, inner doors may be broken open during the levying process. Bailiffs may also enter via *open* windows, and may climb over walls and fences from adjoining premises – these are merely some of the minutiae of the technical rules. However, these detailed rules are, it has been repeatedly alleged, often overlooked. Many complaints have been made of the behaviour of bailiffs.

DoE Circular 18/87 did not counsel against the use of distress, however, and it is unlikely that the government will take up the Law Commission's

6   [1968] 2 QB 811, [1968] 3 All ER 79.

1991 final proposal to abolish the remedy. Nevertheless of all the legal remedies for arrears considered it is the most unsatisfactory.

(1) It is discriminatory in that it is effectively available only against authority tenants.
(2) Its use is geographically uneven.
(3) Where authorities do use it there seems to be little concern as to how and when. Some are long term users, adopting it as a well publicised part of a managerial stance on arrears, others resort to it only rarely, perhaps as a short, sharp shock, others use it as a threat.
(4) The amounts levied by distress often bear no resemblance to the amounts owed.
(5) There is no long term evidence to suggest that distress prevents the build up of arrears where these are caused by misfortune and poverty.
(6) Bailiffs are subject to weak regulation, and yet the evidence suggests they can act in an abusive, intimidatory and illegal manner.

If distress is to continue in use as a remedy for arrears measures need to be taken to remove at least the worst abuses. These could include stricter guidance from the DETR on the use of distress, if necessary backed up by legislation; the use of distress only after a policy decision to that end has been taken by the full council, who thereupon become democratically answerable for their decision; and a stricter regulation and examination of the qualifications of bailiffs to act. Failing these steps it is hard to see how the continued use of an arcane, medieval remedy can be countenanced.

Alternative remedies to seeking possession

Landlords may seek an injunction to restrain the behaviour of tenants, but it must be stressed that the grant of injunctive relief is always at the discretion of the court.

The contractual injunction

Landlords can seek an injunction (an order of the court ordering cessation of particular behaviour) where a breach of tenancy conditions is committed, even though the landlord has suffered no damage as a result of the breach, according to obiter dicta in *Doherty v Allman*[7].

It must, however be noted that:

(1) the only terms that can be enforced are those specifically in the contract – no "re-writing" is allowed in/by the court;

7   (1878) 3 App Cas. 709.

(2) only a party to the contract can be injuncted, but it is possible to phrase a tenancy condition in such a way that a tenant is forbidden to allow third parties to behave in particular ways on the premises.

The advantage of injunctive proceedings are as follows.

Injunctions are flexible:

- they may be permanent/interlocutory (ie an interim order);
- where the latter, they can be obtained *ex parte* (post the Woolf reforms 'without notice') (ie on the basis of the landlord's evidence);
- where sought *ex parte/without notice*, they can be obtained on affidavit evidence;
- there is a need, however, for a serious issue to be shown before relief is granted.

Injunctive relief can be combined with PO proceedings, which is useful where the possession action is defended – offensive conduct can be injuncted while possession proceedings continue – that can be enough in itself to end the problem.

Other advantages of injunctions are:

- they can be rapidly obtained (within 24 hours);
- their object is to change behaviour;
- they can have the effect of protecting witnesses;
- they can provide a 'breathing space' within which it can be seen whether the offender will amend his/her ways;
- an undertaking to modify behaviour pending trial can be given;
- a failure to respond to an injunction can make the court more likely to award a possession order.

The disadvantages of injunctive proceedings:

- interlocutory injunctions are short term remedies only;
- where combined with possession proceedings the court may conclude only an injunction is needed;
- punishment for breach of injunction *may* not be particularly condign;
- contractual injunctions can only be used to enforce contractual terms, and are therefore, limited to what the terms say. Thus in *Lewisham London Borough v Simba-Tola*[8] there were tenancy terms not to commit nuisance 'against other people' on or around the tenant's home or its surrounding estate, or 'around any other housing property of the council'. It was held this did not extend to allow a nuisance committed by the tenant in the council's central offices to be restrained by an injunction.

8   (1991) 24 HLR 644, CA.

Section 222 Local Government Act 1972 injunctions

Local housing authorities have a wider power enabling them to seek injunctions generally by virtue of their general ability to pursue legal action *for the benefit of their areas*. It is possible, and has been done, eg in Hackney, to seek an injunction against individuals who, for example, by criminal activity are disturbing the peace of a particular estate. Such injunctions are normally only encountered in situations where bad behaviour affecting an entire area is encountered.[9]

New injunctive powers under the Housing Act 1996

Section 152 of the 1996 Act provides that a *local authority* (NB not a registered social landlord) may apply to *either* the High Court or the county court for an injunction *prohibiting any person* from:

(i)   engaging in or threatening to engage in conduct *causing* or *likely to cause* a nuisance or annoyance to a person residing in, visiting or otherwise engaging in a lawful activity in *residential premises* (see below) or in their locality; *or*

(ii) using or threatening to use such premises for immoral or illegal purposes; *or*

(iii) entering such premises or being found in their locality.

The premises in question are dwellings held under secure tenancies, or used to provide accommodation in homelessness cases. But the injunctee need not be the actual tenant, it could be a spouse/partner or a child, for example.

The discretion to grant an injunction lies with the court, which, however, *may not* grant an injunction unless it considers:

(a)   that the respondent has used, or threatened to use violence to persons residing in a relevant dwelling or visiting or otherwise engaging in lawful activities in such a dwelling *and*

(b)   there is a *significant risk of harm* to that person, or to a person of a similar description if the injunction is not granted. 'Harm' is defined as ill treatment or the impairment of health in the case of an adult and also extends to impairment of development in the case of a child.

Where an injunction is granted it may relate to particular acts or conduct or types of conduct or both, and may relate to particular premises or a particular locality. It may also be made for a specified period or until varied or discharged – which may occur if the respondent makes an application, or the authority makes such an application. A power of arrest may be

---

9   See generally *Coventry City Council v Finnie* (1996) 29 HLR 658.

attached to one or more of the provisions of such an injunction. In any case where the court considers it just and convenient the court may grant/vary an injunction even though the respondent has not been given the normally required notices, though here the court must give the respondent the chance to make representations as soon as convenient at hearing of which all parties have been given notice. Where an injunction is granted and broken, in the subsequent proceedings the authority are entitled to be heard on the background to the case and the gravity of the breach; it is not enough for the court to hear only the respondent's side of the story.[10]

The new power does not introduce a housing utopia for authorities wishing to seek injunctions. There is a considerable deal of proof of particular circumstances required before the court may grant an injunction. There may be situations where someone is engaging in menacing conduct which is short of violence or its threat – eg simply carrying an air gun around. Such a situation would not be caught by the new law. Furthermore it appears that as section 152 injunctions are civil in nature, not criminal, their breach is not a criminal matter and thus they cannot be made against a minor[11], nor can a power of arrest be attached if the respondent gives an undertaking to honour the injunction.[12]

Serious limitations on the use of section 152 appear to flow from the unsatisfactory Court of Appeal decision in *Enfield London Borough Council v B (a minor)*.[13] Here a violent incident had occurred in a district housing office situated in a council owned shopping centre, within 300m of which were council properties let out on residential tenancies. It was clear the defendants had perpetrated violence, and a common law injunction prohibiting further tortious activity was granted by the county court, but no remedy was given under section 152 which would have carried with it an automatic power of arrest for any breach.

It was agreed in the Court of Appeal by Waller and Buxton LJJ that section 152 does not apply to protect persons who are engaging in a lawful activity in a place unconnected with residential premises. It would appear that the fact that the premises in question were used for housing management and were in the locality of residential premises is not enough to supply that connection, compare the *Simba-Tola* case above. There must be a nexus between residential premises and the person it is sought to protect.

What was not agreed is whether section 152 applies only to allow injunctions against local authority *tenants* and not other persons. The problem arises from the wording of section 152(1)(a), which must be contrasted with the changes made to the 1985 Act by section 144. The former

10 *Manchester City Council v Worthington* (1999) Housing Law Monitor (August) p 8.
11 See *Wookey v Wookey* [1991] Fam 121, [1991] 3 All ER 365, CA.
12 *Carpenter v Carpenter* [1988] 1 FLR 121.
13 (1999) Times, 7 September.

refers to persons 'engaging in or threatening to engage in conduct causing or likely to cause a nuisance or annoyance to a person residing in, visiting or otherwise engaging in a lawful activity in residential premises to which this section applies or in the locality of such premises.' The latter refers to persons 'guilty of causing or likely to cause a nuisance or annoyance to a person residing, visiting or otherwise engaging in a lawful activity in the locality'. Are the slight differences of wording intended to lead to differences of interpretation and application? Waller LJ thought so, Buxton LJ did not. Clearly, however, section 152 needs to be reformulated so that it mirrors section 144 and applies to all persons, irrespective of tenancy status, whether as perpetrators of injuncted activity or as someone protected by an injunction. Some thought also needs to be given to defining 'in the locality', for this present case is out of line with the authorities considered above on the issue.

Attaching a power of arrest to an 'ordinary' injunction

Section 153 of the 1996 Act empowers the High Court/county court to attach a power of arrest to one or more provisions of an injunction it intends to grant in relation to a breach/anticipated breach *of the terms of a tenancy* where the applicant is, inter alia:

i.   a local housing authority;
ii.   a registered social landlord.

However, there are conditions relating to this power:

• the applicant must be acting in its capacity as landlord of the premises;
• the respondent must be the tenant or a joint tenant under a tenancy agreement;
• the tenancy must be a secure or assured tenancy, *or* accommodation provided in respect of homelessness;
• the breach in question must consist of the respondent engaging/threatening to engage in conduct which is/likely to be a nuisance to a person residing, visiting or otherwise engaging in a lawful activity in the locality, *or* the respondent is using/threatening to use the premises for illegal/immoral purposes, *or* the respondent is *allowing* any sub tenant or lodger of his or any other person residing (temporarily or otherwise) on the premises, or visiting them to commit acts of nuisance etc. or illegal/immoral use.

Furthermore the court must consider that the respondent or any subtenant/lodger etc, has used or threatened violence against a person residing, visiting or otherwise engaging in a lawful activity in the vicinity of the premises *and* there is significant risk of harm to that person *or* to a person of similar description if the power of arrest is not attached.

Note, however, that nothing prevents the grant of 'ordinary' injunctions in which no power or arrest is attached: see section 153(7) of the 1996 Act.

Contempt of court

It is, of course, contempt of court to ignore an injunction and imprisonment may be consequence of contempt. The contempt power is wider in its application than this, however, and covers, for example, threats and wilful insults made to witnesses in possession actions, either on their way to court, or returning from it, by the tenant subject to those proceedings. In such circumstances the landlord may bring the issue before the court, which has jurisdiction under section 188 of the County Courts Act 1984.[14]

Anti social behaviour orders

Under section 5 of the Crime and Disorder Act 1998 *local authorities*, which in the present context means local housing authorities, are classified as 'responsible authorities' along with chief officers of police, to create and adopt a crime and disorder strategy for their areas. Though this will obviously relate to a far wider range of problems than those of troublesome tenants, tenancy relations issues will obviously need to be addressed as part of the overall strategy for an area, if only to deal with the question of *which* body is best suited to take *what* sort of action to deal with a particular trouble maker. In addition section 17 of the 1998 Act requires authorities to exercise all their functions with due regard to their effect on the prevention of crime and disorder, and further obligates them to do all they reasonably can to prevent crime and disorder. This requirement clearly has implications for, inter alia, allocation policies and practices, for a housing authority should, arguably, refrain from housing persons in an area where they are likely to cause crime or disorder.

Rather more specifically as a 'relevant authority' a housing authority, in consultation with the chief constable for its area, may under section 1 of the 1998 Act apply to the magistrates for an 'Anti Social Behaviour Order' (ASBO). The application may be made in respect of any person aged ten or more, and must show that the respondent has acted in an 'anti social manner', ie that he/she has caused, or is likely to cause, *harassment, harm or distress* to one or more persons not of the same household as him/herself, *and* that an order is *necessary* to protect persons in the local government area in which the bad behaviour occurred from further anti social acts. The magistrates have discretion to make an ASBO prohibiting the respondent from doing anything prescribed in the order, provided that is 'necessary' to protect persons against anti social behaviour. It is an offence to contravene an order without a reasonable excuse, and an order once made will general last for two years, though it may be made for longer.

14 *Manchester City Council v McCann* [1999] 2 WLR 590, 31 HLR 770, CA.

ASBOs may become attractive alternatives, on grounds of cost and ease of procedure, to injunctions or possession proceedings in respect of bad behaviour by tenants, their spouses, partners and families, particularly where it is not considered appropriate to put a tenancy at risk. However, it should be remembered that a registered social landlord cannot seek an ASBO, in respect of one of their badly behaved tenants, etc – they would have to rely on the local authority to do that for them. Furthermore where an authority does obtain an ASBO the enforcement of that order will depend upon the police. It may well be that some authorities will prefer to resort to possession and injunctive proceedings which they can enforce themselves.

One matter is, however, clear. The 1998 Act gives to authorities a very defined role as agents of social control. They must adopt an overall strategic view of their tasks and must exercise all their functions in the light of their strategic responsibilities. They must further determine which of the variety of powers available to them they are best advised to use to deal with any given incident of bad behaviour by a tenant.

OTHER INDIVIDUAL RIGHTS OF SECURE TENANTS

Subletting and assignment

Section 93(1)(a) of the Housing Act 1985 makes it a term of secure tenancies that tenants may allow any persons to reside as lodgers. Section 93(1)(b) goes on to state the tenants must not, without written consent, sublet or part with possession of a part of their dwelling-houses. Such consent is not to be unreasonably withheld, see section 94. In any dispute over consent it is for the authority to show refusal was not unreasonable. The county court has jurisdiction in such matters. Possible overcrowding, and also any proposed carrying out of work on the house in question may be taken into account when determining whether a refusal was unreasonable. Consent may not be given conditionally. If a tenant applies for consent in writing the authority must give consent within a reasonable time or it is deemed withheld. If they withhold consent they must give a written statement of reasons.

Secure tenancies *cannot be assigned*. (Neither can a secure tenant part with possession of or sublet the whole of a dwelling let on a secure tenancy, without the tenancy *ceasing to be secure*.) See sections 91 and 93(2) of the Act of 1985. To this there are three exceptions:

(1)   where the tenancy is assigned under section 23A or 24 of the Matrimonial Causes Act 1973, section 17(1) of the Matrimonial and Family Proceedings Act 1984, Schedule 1, para 1 of the Children Act 1989; or

(2)   where the assignment is to a person who would be qualified to succeed the tenant if the tenant had died immediately before the assignment; or

(3) where the assignment is by way of exchange, or is part of a chain of assignment, under section 92.

Secure tenants may, with the landlord's consent, assign tenancies to another secure tenant or to an assured tenant of the Housing Corporation, its Welsh successor, a registered social landlord or Housing Trust which is a charity (see section 92 (2A), provided that other has his/her landlord's written consent to the operation. Consent, which may not be given conditionally (save as to conditions requiring the payment of rent arrears or the performance of tenancy obligations) may only be withheld on the grounds set out in Schedule 3 of the 1985 Act. These are that the tenant or proposed assignee is subject to a possession order; possession proceedings under Grounds 1 to 6 of Schedule 2 have begun; the proposed assignee would unreasonably under-occupy the dwelling; the dwelling is not reasonably suitable in extent to the assignee's needs; the dwelling is comprised within a building held mainly for non-housing purposes and was let to the tenant in consequence of his being in the landlord's (etc) employment; the assignee's occupation of the dwelling would conflict with the landlord's charitable status; the dwelling has features substantially different from ordinary dwellings designed to make it suitable for occupation by a physically disabled person, and the result of the assignment would be that such person would no longer reside there; the landlord is a housing association or trust letting dwellings to persons whose non-financial circumstances make it difficult for them to satisfy their housing needs, and if the assignment were made such a person would no longer reside; the dwelling is one of a group normally let for occupation by persons with special needs and close to a social service or special facility provided therefor, and if the assignment were made such a person would no longer reside; the dwelling is subject to a management agreement with a qualifying tenants' association and the proposed assignee is unwilling to be a member of the association. To rely on any of these grounds the landlord must serve notice specifying and particularising the ground in question on the tenant within 42 days of the tenant's application for consent.

See further on assignments Chapter Five below.

Improvements

It is a term of secure tenancies under section 97 that a tenant may not make any improvement without the landlord's written consent, though such consent is not to be unreasonably withheld. 'Improvement' covers any alteration in, or addition to a dwelling and includes additions to or alterations to the landlord's fixtures and fittings, and alterations, etc, to the services to the house; the erection of wireless or television aerials, and the carrying out of *external* decoration. If a dispute arises over the withholding of consent it is for the landlord to show (section 98) that it was reasonable. The county court may take into account in disputes:

(1) whether the improvement would make the dwelling or any other premises less safe for occupiers;

(2) whether it would be likely to involve landlords in otherwise unlikely expenditure, or

(3) whether it would be likely to reduce the price of the house if sold on the open market, or the level of the rent at which it could be let.

Where a tenant applies in writing for the necessary consent the landlord must give it within a reasonable time, otherwise it is deemed withheld, and must not give it subject to an unreasonable condition, otherwise consent is deemed unreasonably withheld. A refusal must be accompanied by a written statement of reasons for refusal. Consent *unreasonably* withheld is treated as given.

Consents may be given retrospectively to work already done, and may be given conditionally, though it is for the landlord to show the reasonableness of conditions. Under section 99 failure to comply with reasonable conditions is treated as breach of a tenancy obligation. This may render the tenant subject to possession proceedings, as will carrying out improvements without consent.

Section 99A of the 1985 Act, inserted in 1993, applies prospectively to work where the landlord, being an authority, gave written consent to an improvement, or is treated as having done so, *and* at the time the tenancy comes to an end it is secure and the landlord is an authority. The section gives the Secretary of State power to make regulations *entitling* 'qualifying persons' at the time when the tenancy ends to be paid compensation by the landlord. It is generally for the landlord to determine the amount of compensation (see below).

Particular provision is made as to when a secure tenancy shall be *treated* as coming to an end by section 99A(8). Such will be the case where the tenancy ceases to be secure because the landlord condition is no longer satisfied, or where it is assigned with the consent of the landlord to another secure tenant under section 92, or to a secure tenant under section 92(2A). But *no* compensation is payable under the regulation (see below) where a tenancy comes to an end on possession being ordered, or on exercise of RTB etc.

To be a qualifying tenant under section 99B a person must fit one of a number of definitions. Thus a person must be the tenant at the time the tenancy comes to an end *and* either the improving tenant, or a joint tenant with that person, or a successor to the improver by succession, devolution or assignment, or a transferee under matrimonial legislation.

The detailed rules on this right to compensation are contained in SI 1994/613. A formula provides for calculation of compensation whereby the cost of listed qualifying improvements are to be 'written down' in value over a specified number of years and the written down value is to be deducted from the actual cost to produce a compensation figure at the time compensation is payable. No compensation less than £50 or more than £3,000 is payable, and compensation may be further reduced in specified cases, eg where the tenant owes the landlord money.

Where a secure tenant begins and makes an improvement to a dwelling after 3 October 1980 and this (a) has received the landlord's consent, and (b) has added materially to the dwelling's sale or rental value, section 100 of the Act gives the landlord *power* to make such payments to the tenant as they consider appropriate at the end of the tenancy. The amount payable must not exceed the cost or likely cost of the improvement *after* deducting the amount of any grant paid under Part XV of the Housing Act 1985. Under section 101 of the Housing Act 1985 the rent of a dwelling let on a secure tenancy is not to be increased on account of a tenant's improvements where the tenant has borne the *whole* cost, or would have so borne that cost but for a grant paid under Part XV of the Act. If, irrespective of grant aid, only part of the cost is borne by the tenant, a pro rata increase in rent can be made. (For the 'right to repair' see Chapter Seven below.)

The distinction between sections 99A and B and 100, is of course, that the former create a *right* to compensation for improvement, the latter now provides merely a residual discretion to cover cases outside its predecessors' scope.

THE COLLECTIVE RIGHTS OF SECURE TENANTS

The rights described above are 'individual' in the sense that their exercise by a tenant affects only the relationship of landlord and tenant between the parties on a one to one basis. The rights that follow are those where the exercise of powers by a landlord affects *all* their tenants, or where it is the sum total of exercises of options *or* rights by tenants, or a group of them, which has an effect on the landlord.

Variation of terms and publicity

Under section 102 of the 1985 Act the terms of a secure tenancy, other than those implied by statute, and *other* than with regard to rent etc, may be varied, deleted or added to by agreement between the parties. In the case of a secure periodic tenancy terms may also be varied under section 103 by the landlord serving notice on the tenant. The notice must specify the variation, and the date on which it takes effect. The period between service and the coming into effect of the change must not be shorter than the rental period of the tenancy, nor shorter than four weeks. Before notice of variation is served, the landlord must serve a preliminary notice on the tenant stating the proposed changes and effects and inviting comments within a specified time. Comments received must be considered. When the variation is made it must be explained to the tenant. A variation will not take effect where the tenant gives a valid notice to quit before the arrival of the date specified in the notice of variation. A change in premises let under a secure tenancy is *not* a variation. For variation of rents see Chapter Four below. Note also that the statutory power to vary tenancy terms supersedes the terms of tenancies created before the passing of the relevant legislation.[15]

Section 104 of the 1985 Act imposes duty to publish, and thereafter to up-date, information about secure tenancies. This must explain in simple terms the effect of the express terms (if any) of secure tenancies, the provisions of Parts IV and V of the Housing Act 1985, and of sections 11 to 16 of the Landlord and Tenant Act 1985 (implied covenants of repair). Every secure tenant must be supplied with a copy of this information, and also with a written statement of the terms of the tenancy so far as not expressed in a lease or tenancy agreement or implied by law. This written statement must be supplied on the grant of the tenancy or as soon as practicable afterwards. Note also section 104 (3), inserted in 1993, which imposes yearly obligation to supply secure tenants of authorities with copies of current information published under section 104. See also section 106 on requirements for publication of information about allocation systems. These, of course, are now supplemented by the provisions of the 1996 Housing Act which were considered earlier.

Tenant participation in housing management

Section 105 of the 1985 Act requires that landlord authorities shall maintain such arrangements *as they consider appropriate*, to enable secure tenants who are likely to be substantially affected by matters of housing management to be informed of proposed changes and developments, and also to ensure that such persons are able to make their views known to the authority within a specified time. Matters of 'housing management' are defined by section 105 to include matters which, *in the opinion of the authority,* relate to management, maintenance, improvement, or demolition of municipal dwellings, or are connected with provision of services or amenities to such dwellings, *and* which represent new programmes of maintenance, improvement or demolition, or some change in the practice or policy of the authority, *and* which are likely to affect substantially all an authority's secure tenants or a group of them. A 'group' is defined as tenants forming

15   *R v Brent London Borough Council, ex p Blatt* (1991) 24 HLR 319.

a distinct social group, or those who occupy dwelling-houses which constitute a distinct class, whether by reference to the kind of dwelling, or the housing estate or larger area in which they are situated. However, see *Short v Tower Hamlets London Borough Council*[16] where the Court of Appeal held that a decision taken 'in principle' to market the sale of certain council properties was not a matter of 'housing management' requiring consultation. Neither is the identity of a possible purchaser a consultative issue at such a stage[17]. The obligation to consult arises where there is a real question of *implementing* a change.

A matter is *not* one of housing management in so far as it relates to rent payable or to any charge for services or facilities provided by the authority. It is the duty of an authority to *consider* any representations made by secure tenants before making any decisions on a matter of housing management.

Landlord authorities must publish details of their consultation arrangements. A copy of any published material must be made available for free public inspection at their principal offices during reasonable hours. Copies must also be available for sale at reasonable charges. 'Landlord authorities' for the purposes of this provision *include* district and London Borough councils.

Duties to consult tenants and licensees generally may arise outside the context of section 105 where the law considers it would be procedurally unfair to allow an authority to proceed with a proposal without taking into account the view of occupiers likely to be affected by it – such instances are likely to be rare[18].

Practice varies greatly as to the involvement of tenants in management. Some authorities have joint estate management committees (JEMS) to transfer a measure of power to tenants, or have created area or district committees of tenants, members and officers to discuss relevant housing issues. Consultation rights and procedures may or may not be mentioned in tenancy agreements or tenants' handbooks.

It was possible from 1975 to transfer authority housing management powers to housing co-operatives, but little use was made of this power, so that by 1993 there were only 62 estates under tenant management organisations. Section 27 of the 1985 Act, as amended, allows authorities to transfer specified management functions over specified properties to 'another person' subject to ministerial consent. Such devolutions are made by 'management agreements' which must contain any provisions specified in regulations made by the Secretary of State. Ministerial approval is needed

16 (1985) 18 HLR 171.
17 *R v London Borough of Hammersmith and Fulham, ex p Beddowes* [1987] QB 1050, [1987] 1 All ER 369, CA.
18 *R v Devon County Council, ex p Baker* (1992) Times, 20 October; *R v Durham County Council, ex p Curtis and Broxson* [1995] 1 All ER 73, CA.

for such devolutions, but that may be given on a block basis to authorities generally or on an individual basis.

The rise and fall of compulsory competitive tendering

Before, however, considering the mechanics of transferring management, some mention must be made of attempts *to force* authorities to make such transfers. Compulsory Competitive Tendering (CCT) was introduced generally under the Local Government Act 1988. This broadly required where an authority wished to allow its own staff to carry out a particular activity they had first put that activity out to tender, ie authority staff had to compete for contracts to provide particular services. Section 2(3) of the Local Government Act 1988 empowered the Secretary of State to list activities subject to CCT, and housing management was a candidate for inclusion in the CCT process from April 1994, while some authorities had already put their estate management out to tender from the private sector on a voluntary basis using their section 27 powers.

The Secretary of State exercised these powers by the Local Government Act 1988 (Competition) (Defined Activities) (Housing Management) Order SI 1994/1671 which laid down that certain housing management activities could only be carried out by authorities provided they had previously been put out to competitive tender. See also SI 1994/2297 which required authorities to subject specified proportions of housing management work to competitive tendering.

Though there were fears that CCT could lead to a large scale disposal of housing management functions, the process, which began in 1994 and was designed to have a phase-in time of three years proved to be less drastic in its outcome. By the end of the first phase of tendering in 1996 95% of the services required to be put out to tender remained in-house with local authority housing departments 'winning' the contracts to provide the services they had traditionally been responsible for.

The effective end of CCT came in May 1997 with the election of a Labour government who were opposed to *compulsory* tendering for services. CCT is now to be replaced under the terms of the Local Government Act 1999. This will abolish CCT (see section 21 of the 1999 Act) repealing the relevant portions of the Local Government, Planning and Land Act 1980, and the Local Government Acts 1988 and 1992. In its place Part 1 of the new legislation will, from Spring 2000, subject English and Welsh authorities to a duty to achieve 'best value' in the performance of their functions – including housing management. The duty, which is not exhaustively defined in the legislation, will under section 3 of the 1999 Act require authorities to make a continuous improvement in the performance of management functions by taking into account the principles of economy, efficiency and effectiveness, and in this context to consult, inter alia, representatives of persons likely to use the service in question – ie tenants. Guidance will be issued centrally on this consultative duty, including the persons to be consulted and the form, timing and content of consultations. The Secretary of State also has powers, under section 4, to specify 'performance indicators' according to which authorities' performance in exercising their functions can be measured, and 'performance standards' which they will be required to meet. In discharging this function the Secretary of State will be advised by the Audit Commission which functions now under the Audit Commission Act 1998, and which will analyse data on performance from relevant authorities.

Authorities will further be required, by section 5, to conduct best value reviews of their functional performance at prescribed intervals, probably every five years. Factors to be considered in the review will be centrally prescribed and will include the level at which a function should be performed – eg is there a need for more than basic provision of a service – and the extent to which a service is meeting performance indicators and targets. From these reviews will emerge action plans and targets, under section 6, which will feed into yearly Best Value Performance Plans (BVPPs) required of each authority, and these will form the basis for local accountability on the provision of services. This will be achieved by requiring plans to provide local people with: a summary of the extent to which their authority was successful in meeting the previous year's targets and objectives and a comparison of its performance with other relevant authorities; a statement of targets to be set for the following and future years; a statement of the outcome of any review carried out, for example by way of a revision of targets and the programme for achieving them. The Secretary of State will also be able to prescribe the content of BVPPs. BVPPs will be subject to local audit under section 7 as to their accuracy and with a view to recommending remedial action. The initial audit will be carried out by each authority's own auditor, but may give rise to later action undertaken by a central inspectorate or the Secretary of State. In response to an auditor's report on its BVPP each authority will be obliged by section 9 of the 1999 Act to respond where the circumstances are that the report has identified serious deficiencies in the BVPP *and* the auditor has recommended that the Secretary of State should intervene. The response must be made as soon as practicable and must state what action the authority proposes to take and the proposed timetable for action. This response must be forwarded to the Secretary of State and incorporated in the next edition of the BVPP.

Inspection powers

The new legislation gives to the Audit Commission powers under sections

10 and 11 to inspect authorities with a view to check how they are complying with best value policy, for example to check whether authorities have reviewed their performance as required, and whether they have set sufficiently challenging performance targets to obtain 'best value' in future years. Such inspections will be carried out on a programmed basis; but provision is also made for non programmed ad-hoc or 'spot check' inspections where an authority's performance is considered to be falling well below required levels and the authority in question have no immediate plans to review the function in question. The Secretary of State has power, under section 10(2)-(4) to issue guidance to the Audit Commission in this connection, and may direct them to carry out an inspection of an individual authority. In carrying out inspections the Commission will have extensive powers to obtain papers and other relevant information.

Following an inspection the commission will issue a report to the authority concerned. If the conclusion is that the authority is failing in its functions, but not sufficiently seriously for referral to the Secretary of State, the authority will be required to record its failure and the action taken to remedy the situation within the next BVPP: see section 15.

Where serious failures are detected the Commission will also send its report to the Secretary of State. This will be one potential 'trigger' for the Secretary of State to utilise enforcement powers under section 15 to require an authority to prepare or amend a BVPP, or to follow specified procedures with regard to such a plan, to carry out a review of the performance of specified functions, or to take such other action as is considered requisite by the Secretary of State to meet 'best value' criteria. The Secretary of State may further hold a local inquiry into the performance of specified functions of an authority, and may further, after giving the relevant authority an opportunity to be heard on the issue, direct that a specified function shall be taken over by him or by some other nominated person, for a specified period, or for so long as he considers appropriate.

Serious mismanagement of an authority's housing stock could thus lead to the authority losing housing functions to commissioners appointed by the Secretary of State. This is a very considerable extention of central powers with regard to local government; however, it is a move away from the compulsory privatisation of services. At the time of writing 35 English and 3 Welsh authorities had been identified to undertake pilot 'best value' schemes to run for a period of 3 years from 1998. (See further below on consultation exercises undertaken with regard to central guidance in connection with the implementation of the foregoing legislative scheme.)

It is now appropriate to consider the mechanisms still in place for transferring housing management functions, and then to consider a different style of tenant involvement developing under the terms of the new Local Government legislation.

Transfer arrangements

As the law stood from 1993 where an authority proposed to make a management agreement under section 27 it had to follow the procedure laid down in section 27AA which required consultation with tenants as to the proposal. This was replaced in 1996 with new provisions contained in section 27AB of the 1985 Act. This empowers the Secretary of State to make regulations to require authorities to consult tenants generally – or to consider tenant representations – with regard to the exercise of their housing management functions. This provision clearly supplements section 105, see above, but also has a clear applicability to proposals to transfer management functions, for the regulations may require consultation in relation to, inter alia, specifications of functions proposed for exercise by an authority or 'another person', the identity of 'any person' the authority proposes to invite to bid for the exercise of management functions; standards of service to be achieved by any such persons; proposals to enforce standards of service under management agreements. Provision may be made as to the identity of consultees, the means by which consultation is to take place, arrangements for making representations, and the action to be taken when representations from tenants are received. The regulations once made are to supersede the provisions of section 105 where relevant.

Where consultation with tenants is required the prime responsibility for conducting it lies with the authority, and the Secretary of State may only intervene where that consultation process is flawed.[19]

Proactive tenant management

Though section 27 of the 1985 Act permitted delegation of housing management functions, authorities were for many years apparently reluctant to transfer functions to tenants – even though a tenant's organisation could clearly fall within the concept of 'another person' in the Act. Thus by 1993 a transfer of management had taken place on only 62 estates. Changes to the law were introduced in 1993 to force the pace of change.

Section 27AB of the 1985 Act, as inserted in 1993, empowers the Secretary of State to make regulations requiring authorities to take steps to respond where any tenant management organisation (TMO) serves written notice proposing that the authority should enter into a management agreement with the TMO. Those regulations are the Housing (Right to

19 *R v Secretary of State for the Environment, ex p Harrow London Borough Council* (1996) 29 HLR 1.

Manage) Regulations 1994, SI 1994/627. (See also DoE Circular 6/94.) These regulations supersede any other consultation requirements under section 27BA or section 105. Under these a TMO may serve a right to manage notice (RMN) on an authority where it is a representative and accountable body, eg it must be open to any tenant of a relevant dwelling to joint the TMO and the TMO must pursue an equal opportunity policy. It must serve a defined geographical area and have a membership of at least 20% of *both* secure tenants and of *all* tenants of houses, flats, hostels etc belonging to the authority within the designated area. The TMO must take a democratic decision to serve a RMN by delivering a copy to each affected dwelling, and authorities are able inter alia, to refuse a RMN relating to fewer than 25 dwellings let on secure tenancies. Only members of the TMO can vote, and a majority of members must back the proposal. If a notice is accepted the TMO will select a training agency and the authority is expected to support the TMO with accommodation and office facilities, and the TMO will select a training agency (an 'approved person') from a list maintained by the DETR and a feasibility study funded by a grant under section 429A of the 1985 Act by the Secretary of State will be undertaken. This study will be in two parts, the full study can only proceed if the initial study indicates to the approved person it is reasonable to proceed, and at that point the authority will arrange for a ballot or poll of *all* affected tenants. (It is not reasonable to proceed where it is concluded a TMO is unlikely to progress towards full tenant management, or where it appears a TMO is not representative of its community and will not reform itself.) If the ballot is in favour by a majority of all tenants and a majority of all secure tenants, the full study proceeds. A further training agency *then* selected by the TMO from the DETR list will proceed to develop a programme of management skills for the TMO by reference to the range of functions the TMO wishes to assume: a training programme – *Preparing to Manage* – has been developed for this purpose. 75% of these development costs will be met by section 429A grants, the rest will come from authorities (see also the TMO Modular Management Agreement, HMSO 1994).

If, however, the training agency concludes the development programme is unlikely to result in the TMO assuming a range of management functions, a timely report should be made to the TMO, the authority and the Secretary of State, and if the TMO accepts the conclusion its proposal is deemed withdrawn and no further similar proposal can be put forward for two years. But when a programme is successful the TMO will need registration as a company or an individual or provident society so as to provide a legal 'person' with whom the management agreement can be made. Only when the training agency certifies a TMO has reached the requisite level of competency for the functions it wishes to discharge can matters proceed. If the agency decides against the TMO on this point, the TMO may submit the issue to arbitration. If, however, the TMO is certified to proceed then within two months the authority must inform affected tenants of the terms of the proposed management agreement with the TMO, *and a ballot will then be held in prescribed form*: all tenants of affected dwellings must be given the chance to vote and a vote must be given to each tenant. If the TMO gains a majority vote from all tenants including a majority of secure tenants, the proposed management agreements must be entered into; a failure to obtain a majority result is the deemed withdrawal of the proposal and a moratorium of two years on similar proposals.

Note, however, that it is also possible for authorities to enter into management agreement with TMOs voluntarily, provided the Secretary of State approves the form of the agreement and the requirements of section 27 are complied with. It is also possible for a TMO to invite an authority to nominate one or more people to be directors/officers of the TMO where the authority have entered into or propose to enter a management agreement with the TMO.

Individual TMO agreements were, by April 1994, in place for 11 estates with a further 67 well advanced. It was then government policy that authorities should divest themselves of direct housing management by 1996 and it was considered likely that large scale voluntary transfer of management (LSVT) to associations or TMO transfers would be the preferred means for authorities to achieve this.

As so often happens with housing policy, however, the reality was different from the expectation. In the first place TMOs have taken on a variety of forms. Some are Tenant Management Coops (TMCs) with a management committee elected by tenants which have delegated management tasks; some are Estate Management Boards (EMBs) with a mixture of elected tenant representatives and authority nominees, again having delegated responsibilities for a particular estate; some (a few) are Par Value Coops (PVCs) which were effectively registered as housing associations totally controlled as co-operatives by their members, and which have provided new housing.

The Price Waterhouse study for the DoE 'Tenants in Control: an Evaluation of Tenant led Housing Management organisations' (HMSO 1995) concluded that TMOs in general have flourished where groups of tenants have perceived a need to safeguard and sustain improved housing conditions on their estates, and where an incentive has existed to obtain the finance needed to carry out improvement and modernisation of housing. It was found that each form of TMO outlined above could be effective in securing improved conditions and management for tenants, but those which were most successful were: small in scale; driven by the desire of residents for improved management services and greater control over their delivery; characterised by continuing high levels of resident involvement; effectively controlling their budgets; able to call upon specialised outside agencies for particular services; supported by their authorities with practical and financial help. TMOs are best suited to areas where they can be 'mission driven', and will enjoy a high level of tenant involvement with consequent autonomy for residents over how their homes are managed. They are generally unsuitable for large areas of housing having no common focus, or where they will be tightly constrained as to budgetary or policy changes, or where the tenants are disadvantaged in terms of low income, poor employment or lack of amenities. The conclusion of the Price Waterhouse study was thus that small scale community based TMOs are best able to deliver superior value for money in management terms. That may well explain why their use has not spread so fast as was the desire of the Conservatives between 1993 and 1997.

One cautionary note

Some authorities, particularly smaller, largely rural ones, have made section 27 management agreements with registered social landlords (ie housing associations) for the exercise of management functions. These agreements create a triangular arrangement with the authority 'purchasing' services from the association which are then provided for tenants. This does not free the authority of responsibilities, however, for there is a need to monitor service provision. Furthermore problems can arise for tenants as their prime contractual and tenurial relationship is not with the service provider and they may be unaware of procedures for voicing complaints about the level of service provision.

Further developments – moving towards 'best value', consultation on central guidance

On 25 January 1999 the government unveiled proposals to take forward the concept of 'best value' in housing management, already alluded to above, in the form of a consultation paper 'Tenant Participation Compacts.' The core notion of these proposals is to ensure that all council tenants have a central role in planning, managing and delivering housing services. Under these new proposals, authorities will have to negotiate council-wide and neighbourhood-level agreements with their tenants, and have them ready to implement by April 2000. These compacts will set out clearly how tenants will be involved collectively in shaping local decisions on housing issues.

What are these tenant participation compacts?

They will be locally-negotiated agreements between each authority and its tenants, setting out how tenants will be involved *collectively* in taking local decisions on housing issues which affect them. These local agreements will be based upon core standards published in the 'National Framework for

Tenant Participation Compacts' which form part of the consultation paper. The National Framework set, for the first time, *national core standards* for tenant participation aimed at offering equal opportunity for involvement to all council tenants, to bring the performance of all councils up to that of the best. The national standards are those which the Government believes are fundamental to building sustainable and real tenant involvement. It is expected that councils and tenants may add to these in developing their compacts, to meet local needs and priorities.

The core standards bring together issues on which the Government believes tenants should 'have their say', including:

- developing an authority's housing policy and strategy;
- drawing up capital and renovation programmes;
- developing and implementing regeneration and improvement programmes;
- allocations and letting policies;
- management of housing services;
- tenancy conditions and agreements;
- budgets, finance and rent-setting.

It may be asked, however, whether these 'compacts' will be legally binding, or will they be mere 'gentlemen's agreements' or so vaguely phrased as to be meaningless in practice. Authorities certainly will be expected to report each year, in consultation with tenants, on their achievements in tenant involvement, and set targets for continual improvement. Each compact will need to be open-ended. The implementation of the core standards needs to be recognised by all as *laying the foundation* for *developing* a strategy of good quality, effective tenant participation. Official emphasis is laid on a *continuous process of review and evolution*, as the arrangements for participation settle down and participants become attuned to their new roles. However, it is also stressed that a basic principle of compacts generally is that tenants themselves must decide how they wish to be involved so that local decisions will reflect local priorities. Thus while each authority will have to have a scheme of compacts, those compacts may well vary between authorities – subject to compliance with national core standards – and even between estates of the same authority. It was furthermore centrally recognised that tenants will need to be empowered to take up their role. They may need training to develop skills, technical knowledge and confidence, and capacity-building to enable them to be better prepared and organised to make an effective contribution on a truly equal basis.

Further key points about the policy

- Compacts should deliver real benefits to all parties, by ensuring that local services are efficient and responsive, while decisions should

reflect local needs and priorities;
- development and implementation of compacts will be a partnership between authorities and tenants;
- tenants need to be involved at an early stage in decision-making;
- commitment to joint working must be publicly stated by all parties;
- tenant participation should be properly budgeted for and supported in other ways, for example, through tailored training and provision of facilities and advice;
- authorities will need to set aside a budget specifically to implement compacts;
- arrangements for communicating with tenants and feedback should be designed to meet tenants' needs, so that they can make a full input to decision-making *and* can see how their views have influenced final decisions;
- tenants' groups will be empowered to take part in decision-making by meeting standards for formal recognition. Good quality decision-making should build on representative and accountable tenant structures;
- authorities and tenants will together draw up systems to enable progress on implementing the compact to be measured;
- a national benchmark for successful tenant participation will be established;
- the range of housing services to which compacts will apply will be specified;
- authorities and tenants will develop internal systems to deal with complaints and disputes on the operation of compacts;
- tenants and authorities will need to review, monitor and, where necessary, change existing polices and systems for tenant involvement to meet compact requirements;
- Compacts should be fully negotiated and implemented by 1 April 2000.

On 1 June 1999 the DETR published the results of the responses to the above consultative exercise. This reported general support for the 'best value' concept, and for the argument that communities should be involved in setting objectives and that tenants should be involved in performance review, with the general need for performance indicators being accepted. Against this, however, there were concerns over resource implications, and concerns that there could be 'consultation overload', and too much concentration on *reviewing* services as opposed to actually providing them. It was argued that a 'best value' in housing policy should be equally applied to both authorities and registered social landlords, while strong views also emerged on the need to ensure flexibility on the timetabling of reviewing performance, though the performance indicators could be standardised across *all* providers of social housing. Overall the general view seemed to be there should be a small core of national performance indicators complemented by locally defined ones locally agreed and taking account of the aspirations of local service consumers. There was less agreement over external inspection of housing services. While there was general acceptance of some form of external auditing of performance, there was no consensus whether an entirely new inspectorate is needed, with some arguments being made about duplication of existing accountability systems. Once again there were concerns about the resource implications of setting up an inspectorate – who is to pay for it, and who is to be part of it? It was, however, felt that the Inspectorate if created should be composed of experts in local authority housing management, with support also for the argument that tenants should be included in inspection teams.

It would, however, appear clear that we are moving in terms of both the law and management of housing towards an era of much greater accountability in which the principal concept is not '*who owns the house*', but '*who lives in the house?*' (See further below on the accountability issue.)

TENURE OF HOUSING ASSOCIATION DWELLINGS AND DWELLINGS OF OTHER REGISTERED SOCIAL LANDLORDS

Consultation papers issued by the DoE before the Housing Bill 1987 was published made it clear that *existing* association tenants would continue to enjoy statutory security of tenure and the other rights enshrined in the Housing Act 1985. Future association tenancies would be on the new assured tenancy basis. Some 70,000 new lettings are made by associations each year and these new lettings are virtually all on the 'assured' basis.

After the commencement of the 1988 Act the fair rent provisions of the Rent Act 1977 Part VI do not *generally* apply to new tenancies granted by associations. Furthermore association tenancies entered into after commencement are not *generally* secure. *New* tenants do not have the rights of secure tenants (including the right to buy) instead they are *Assured Tenants* under Part 1 of the 1988 Act. A tenancy entered into after commencement is not a 'housing association tenancy' as previously defined by Part VI of the Rent Act 1977 *unless:*

(a) entered into by virtue of contract made *before* commencement, *or*
(b) granted to a person who (solely or jointly) was a housing association tenancy holder immediately before grant, *and* is granted by a person who was landlord under that tenancy, *or*
(c) it is granted to a person who prior to grant was previously in possession of a dwelling subject to a possession order subject to section 84 (2) (b) or (c) of the Housing Act 1985, *and* the grant is of premises which are suitable accommodation for the purpose of those provisions, *and* in the possession order the court directed the tenancy to be a housing association tenancy.

Assured tenancies: the basic position

Under section 1 of the 1988 Act a dwelling (including a flat) is let on an assured tenancy (AT) if it is let (ie the relationship of landlord and tenant must exist) as a separate dwelling (ie a unit capable of supporting the functions of living such as eating and sleeping). 'Separate' bears the meaning it has in the corresponding provisions of the 1985 Act, see above, *save* that under section 3 of the 1988 Act where a tenant enjoys exclusive occupation of some accommodation with persons *other* than the landlord, and that is the *only* reason why assured status would be denied, the accommodation the tenant has is deemed to be a dwelling let on an AT. The tenant, or if there are joint tenants, each of them, must be an individual, and *must* occupy the dwelling as his/her only or principal home. This may, however, be satisfied if the tenant is absent by an intention to return plus physical indications in the dwelling evidencing that intention, eg the presence of furniture. Occupation of some other dwelling as the only or principal home will cost a tenant his/her security.[20] The requirement of residence may be satisfied by one of a number of joint tenants. The dwelling must also not fall within the excepted classes of Part 1, Schedule 1 of the 1988 Act, ie tenancies:

(a)   entered into before, or pursuant to a contract made before, 15 January 1989;

(b)   at high rents, ie £25,000 per annum;

(c)   at *no* or low rents, ie £1,000 per annum in Greater London or £250 elsewhere;

(d)   within the provisions of Part II of the Landlord and Tenant Act 1954 (business lettings);

(e)   of licensed premises;

(f)   of agricultural land or agricultural holdings;

(g)   granted to students intending to follow specified courses of study by specified educational bodies;

(h)   which are holiday lettings, ie those where the purpose is to confer on the tenant the right to occupy the dwelling for the purpose of a holiday;

(i)   granted by resident landlords, ie in general tenancies where the landlord, who must be an individual, has granted a tenancy of a dwelling which forms only part of a building which is *not* a purpose built block of flats, *and* the landlord resided in some other part of the building as his/her only or principal home at the time of the grant and has so resided ever since and the tenancy must *not* have been granted to a

---

20   See *Brickfield Properties v Hughes* (1987) 20 HLR 108 and *Notting Hill Housing Trust v Etoria* [1989] CLY 1912 where the tenant who was in prison retained furniture in his home, and had his brother living there, which was enough to preserve his rights in the property.

person who immediately previously was an assured tenant of the same dwelling or of another dwelling in the building, *and* the landlord is the same in relation to each; but such an exemption is not available to a company landlord, even where a director resides in the building, and would be unavailable to an association[1];

(j)   which are granted by the Crown or a local authority.

Where the tenancy is excluded from AT status *and no other legislation applies*, it will be a tenancy at common law, and subject only to control under section 3 of the Protection From Eviction Act 1977 which requires that possession can only be obtained by court order.

The great majority of tenancies granted by associations since 1989 were thus 'assured'. However, in some cases an association could decide to grant an 'assured shorthold tenancy' (AST), for example of short life property it wished to have occupied on a temporary basis. An AST is an AT in all respects (eg as regards recovery of possession) save that its creation was historically subject to certain formalities which had to be complied with before a prospective tenant was allowed into possession and its security was limited to a great degree. Thus before the amendments made by the Housing Act 1996, an AST was a tenancy falling within section 20 of the 1988 Act, ie one:

(a)   for an initial *fixed* term of not *less* than six months;

(b)   where the *landlord* has no power to end the tenancy earlier than six months from the start of tenancy, and

(c)   where due notice in prescribed form giving certain information, and clearly stating the tenancy is to be an AST, has been served by the landlord on the tenant *before* the tenancy is entered into.

Though the position of tenants holding ATs and ASTs prior to the coming into force on 27 February 1997 of the relevant provisions of the Housing Act 1996 was preserved, that Act made a revolutionary change which, however, is likely to be of consequence to tenants of private landlords rather than those of housing associations and other registered social landlords. Thus under section 19A of the 1988 Act, inserted in 1996, new ATs are *automatically to be ASTs* – with considerable implications for security of tenure as will become apparent below – unless they fall within the provisions of Schedule 2A of the 1988 Act. This provides, inter alia, that landlords may still grant fully assured tenancies where they serve notice on tenants before their tenancies are entered into stating that the tenancy is *not* to be an AST, and is to be an assured periodic tenancy.

Acting under its powers under section 36A of the Housing Associations Act 1985 and section 36 of the Housing Act 1996 the Housing Corporation issued to all registered social landlords Circular R3 – 36/96 – 'The Tenants Guarantee, Policy on Tenure, "Code of Practice on Tenure" and "Rights and

---

1   *Barnes v Gorsuch* (1981) 43 P & CR 294.

Responsibilities" leaflets'. This stated that landlords should utilise a periodic AT as the normal tenancy for their housing, and should therefore ensure that correct notice is issued before the tenancy commences. ASTs are only to be utilised in particular circumstances, ie for housing whose use is time limited (eg 'short life' properties) or which is 'tied' accommodation, for special needs accommodation, or for those tenants in general needs housing with agreed programmes of care – where a special code of practice in any case applies, and where the letting is to a person who is a homeless applicant by virtue of assistance rendered to a housing authority under section 213 of the Housing Act 1996. In this latter case section 209 of the 1996 Act requires the letting to be an AST. It should also be noted in this connection that under section 19A of the 1988 Act there is no longer any requirement for an AST to have an initial fixed term of six months.

Security of tenure

ATs have a degree of security of tenure, for under sections 5(1), 7(7) and 9(3) the basic rule is that the tenancy can only be brought to an end by a court order following service of Notice of Possession Proceedings (NOPP). Thus if an AT is for an initial fixed term a periodic tenancy arises under statute, see section 5(2) of the 1988 Act, on its expiry, while a periodic AT will continue until terminated in legal form, and a mere notice to quit *from the landlord* will have no effect, though the tenant may exit via this route.[2]

The application of the rules of security is thus dependent upon whether the AT is initially periodic or fixed term. It should, however, be remembered that registered social landlords should normally grant only periodic ATs.

Periodic tenancies

The position here is that the AT can only be brought to an end by means of a NOPP and a court order, see sections 5(1) and 7(1).

Fixed term tenancies

Here the tenancy can come to an end by:
(a) surrender (including clear long term abandonment) by the tenant;
(b) where the tenancy contains a break clause ie a power for the landlord to determine it in certain circumstances, the exercise of that power *followed* by NOPP and court order – mere exercise of power to

2   *Harrison v Hammersmith and Fulham London Borough Council* [1981] 2 All ER 588, [1981] 1 WLR 650, CA.

determine alone is not enough, but note that exercise of a break clause *by the tenant* will be effective to end the tenancy;

(c) by effluxion of time, ie the tenancy runs out, *and* there is a NOPP and a court order.

A number of points need to be noted.

(1) In the case of a fixed term AT which is still current provided there is a 'break clause' enabling the landlord to determine in particular circumstances, exercise by the landlord of that clause in those circumstances will bring the AT to an end but the tenant will remain in possession under the statutory periodic tenancy which automatically arises under section 5(2). To gain actual possession the landlord will then need to proceed by the NOPP route and will thus have to prove that one of the statutory grounds for possession applies.

(2) In the case of a fixed term AT which is still current where the tenant is in breach of obligations, *and* tenancy conditions make provision for it to be brought to an end – by way of re-entry, forfeiture, determination by notice or otherwise – on the basis of facts falling within Grounds 2 or 8 (mandatory) or Grounds 10 to 15 (discretionary) of Schedule 2 to the 1988 Act (see below, but effectively serious rent arrears or breach of condition) the court may, under section 7, entertain possession proceedings. In other situations the AT will subsist until its contractual expiry.

(3) Where a fixed term AT expires, provided the landlord follows, and can follow, the NOPP route, the court's power to order possession will bring to an end any statutory periodic tenancy as from a specified date.

Though registered social landlords may only rarely grant fixed term ATs it is clearly crucial that their terms are carefully drafted so as to comply with the above requirements.

Where a fixed term tenancy expires and there is *no* NOPP and a court order the tenant will be entitled to stay in possession of the dwelling by virtue of the statutory periodic tenancy. This, as stated, takes effect immediately on the end of the fixed term and is deemed granted by the landlord to the tenant in respect of the dwelling on broadly comparable terms, save that the only means of obtaining possession is NOPP and a court order: see sections 5(1) and (2). Not later than one year after the former tenancy is succeeded by a statutory periodic tenancy either party may serve on the other notice in prescribed form proposing terms for the statutory periodic tenancy different from those implied under the 1988 Act, see section 6.

Procedure for obtaining possession

The county court is the appropriate forum (see section 40 of the 1988 Act) and the NOPP procedure *must* be used, see section 8. The landlord must serve notice in prescribed form (see SI 1988/2203) informing the tenant that:

(a) the landlord intends to begin proceedings for possession on one or more of the grounds specified in the notice (which may be added to or altered only with the leave of the court), and

(b) proceedings will not begin *earlier* than a date specified in the notice, and will also not begin *later* than 12 months from the date of service of the notice. The *general rule* is that proceedings may not begin *earlier* than two weeks from the date of service of notice, however, where possession is sought on the basis of Grounds 1, 2, 5, 6, 7, 9 and 16 (for which see below) proceedings may not begin *earlier* than two months from date of service of notice nor, in the case of a periodic tenancy, earlier than the date the tenancy could have been ended by notice to quit. Where, however, possession in sought under Ground 14 (Nuisance) the tenant is to be informed proceedings will be begun not earlier than the date of service of the notice itself. The requirement for a NOPP may be relaxed if the court considers it just and equitable, though this dispensing power does not exist where the landlord is relying on Ground 8. The courts' ability to dispense with the need for a NOPP has only been tested in private rented sector cases, and even there was exercised only where it was clear the tenant was under no illusion as to what was happening so there could be no injustice[3]. What is clear is that the NOPP *must* fully set out the substance of the landlord's case or be declared defective[4].

The actual grounds for possession are specified by section 7 and Schedule 2 of the 1988 Act. Two types of grounds are provided, mandatory and discretionary. Part 1 of Schedule 2 contains the mandatory possession grounds. If the ground is made out and all other requirements are complied with the court here has no option but to order possession.

Ground 1

Not later than the beginning of the tenancy (ie the day it was entered into) the landlord gave the tenant *written* notice that possession might be required *and* some time before the tenancy the landlord occupied the dwelling as his/her only or principal home, *or* the landlord *requires* the dwelling as his/her or his/her spouse's only or principal home, *and* the

3   *Fernandes v Parvardin* (1982) 5 HLR 33, CA; but see also *Bradshaw v Baldwin-Wiseman* (1985) 17 HLR 260, HL, and *Boyle v Verrall* [1997] 1 EGLR 25, CA, for different views.

4   *Mountain v Hastings* (1993) 25 HLR 427.

landlord did *not* acquire the dwelling for value over the sitting tenant's head. Clearly this ground is inapplicable to an assured tenancy granted by a registered social landlord.

Ground 2

The dwelling is subject to a mortgage granted before the commencement of the tenancy and the mortgagee is entitled to exercise the power of sale and desires possession to exercise that power. Again notice must be given before the tenancy commences if this ground is to be relied on, though the court, as with the requirements for a NOPP, has a dispensing power if, for example, an adequate verbal warning has been given.

Ground 3

The tenancy is for a fixed term of not more than eight months, and written notice was given before commencement that this ground might be relied on *and* at some time within the period of 12 months ending with the beginning of the tenancy the dwelling was occupied for holiday purposes, again this ground is unlikely to be relevant to the lettings of registered social landlords.

Ground 4

The tenancy is for a fixed term not exceeding 12 months *and* written notice that possession might be sought was given before commencement, *and* some time within the period 12 months ending with commencement the dwelling was let as student accommodation by specified educational bodies or persons. This provision facilitates vacation lettings of student accommodation, yet again likely to be irrelevant to registered social landlords.

Ground 5

The dwelling is held for the purpose of being available for occupation by a minister of religion as a residence from which to perform clerical duties *and* written notice that possession might be sought was given *and* the court is satisfied that the dwelling is required for occupation by such a minister, again unlikely to be relevant to a registered social landlord.

Ground 6

The landlord who is seeking possession, or, where that landlord is a registered social landlord or charitable housing trust, a superior landlord must intend to demolish or reconstruct the whole or a substantial part of the dwelling, or to carry out substantial works on the dwelling or any part of it, or any building of which it forms part, *and* in addition:

(a) the intended work must be incapable of being carried out unless possession is obtained , *and* either
    (i)   the tenant is unwilling to agree access to enable the work to be done, *or*
    (ii) the nature of the work is such that granting access alone would be insufficient to enable it to take place, *or*
    (iii) the tenant is unwilling to forgo possession of that part of the dwelling as would allow the landlord to carry out the work reasonably, *or*
    (iv) the nature of the work is such that it is not practicable for the tenant to be left with a tenancy of part only of the dwelling.

(b) It is further required that landlords must demonstrate a settled intention to do works of demolition/construction and that they have reasonable prospect of carrying them out. This must be established at the date of the possession hearing[5], when the landlord must demonstrate both the means and the ability to carry out the entire redevelopment[6]. (See above the similar Ground 10A under the Housing Act 1985.) Where possession is ordered under Ground 6 the tenant's reasonable removal expenses must be reimbursed by the landlord, see section 11(1). This ground will be of relevance to registered social landlords, for example where they own short life property they seek to redevelop, or where they are themselves 'head tenants' of such property.

Ground 7

The tenancy is *periodic* (including a SPT) and has devolved by will or intestacy on the death of the previous tenant, *provided* proceedings are begun not later than 12 months after the death of the former tenant. The acceptance by a landlord of rent from a new tenant after the death of the former tenant is not to be regarded as creating a new periodic tenancy unless the landlord agrees to a change, in writing with regard to rent, the period of the tenancy, the premises or the terms of the tenancy. This ground of

5   *Wansbeck District Council v Marley* (1987) 20 HLR 247.
6   *Edwards v Thompson* (1990) 60 P & CR 222, CA.

possession does *not*, however, affect any statutory succession rights given by the Act itself, see below Chapter Five.

Ground 8

To rely on this ground *both* at the date of service of the NOPP *and* at the date of the hearing there must be substantial rent in arrears, ie:
(a) where the rent is payable weekly or fortnightly, at least 8 weeks' arrears;
(b) where payable monthly, at least 2 months' arrears are owed;
(c) where payable quarterly at least one quarter's rent is more than three months in arrears;
(d) where payable yearly at least three months' rent must be more than three months in arrears.

Discretionary grounds

Ground 9

Suitable alternative accommodation is or will be available by the time the possession order takes effect, and available to the tenant in question[7] – this is further defined in Schedule 2, Part III as either:
(a) a certificate from the local housing authority that they will rehouse;
(b) premises which are to be let as a separate dwelling on an assured basis (but not as an AST or any dwelling subject to such notice as would allow mandatory recovery of possession), or
(c) premises which will afford security equivalent to that of an AT.
  The premises must also be reasonably suitable to the needs of the tenant and his/her family as regards proximity to place of work and must also be *either* similar as regards rent and extent to authority properties in the area provided for persons with needs similar to those of the tenant, *or* reasonably suited to the means and needs of the tenant and his/her family as regards extent and character. A property is not suitable if occupation would result in statutory overcrowding. Indeed shared property generally will not qualify[8]. Suitability will be determined by considering the tenant's *housing* needs, as opposed to cultural and spiritual matters see *Siddiqui v Rashid*[9]. These 'needs' will however, include the nature of the property in question, and the personal needs of the tenant[10].

---

7 *Selwyn v Hamill* [1948] 1 All ER 70 and *Topping v Hughes* [1925] NI 90.
8 *Cookson v Walsh* (1954) 163 Estates Gazette 486, CA.
9 [1980] 3 All ER 184, [1980] 1 WLR 1018.
10 *Enfield LBC v French* (1984) 17 HLR 211 ('need' for a garden?) and *Heglibiston Establishment v Heyman* (1977) 246 EG 567 (need to avoid an estranged wife).

Ground 10

Some rent lawfully due must be unpaid on the date on which possession proceedings are begun and must have been in arrears at the date of service of the NOPP though an order is unlikely to be made where there is a genuine dispute over the amount of money owed[11].

Ground 11

Whether or not there are arrears, this applies where the tenant has persistently delayed paying rent lawfully due. What constitutes 'persistent delay' will be a question of fact in each case – but the delay may arise for reasons outside the tenant's control – eg as a result of delayed housing benefit, and this would make it unreasonable to grant an order. It is also unlikely that an order will be made where the arrears have been paid off by the date of the hearing, unless the tenant has a persistent history of 'brinkmanship' in relation to payment[12].

Ground 12

There has been a breach of a tenancy obligation (see the similar ground above in relation to secure tenancies).

Ground 13

Where the condition of the dwelling, or of any common parts, has deteriorated owing to acts of waste by, or the neglect or default of, the tenant or of any other person residing in the dwelling, provided in this latter case the tenant has failed to take such steps as he/she should to remove the wrongdoer. This ground can extend to cover failure to tend the garden of the house so that it becomes wholly uncontrolled[13].

Ground 14

Where the tenant or any other person residing in, or visiting, the dwelling has been guilty of conduct which causes or is likely to cause a nuisance or

11 *Dun Laoghaire Urban District Council v Moran* (1921) 2 IR 404.
12 *Paddington Churches Housing Association v Sharif* (1996) 29 HLR 817.
13 *Holloway v Povey* (1984) 15 HLR 104.

annoyance to a person residing, visiting, or otherwise engaging in a lawful activity in the locality, *or* has been convicted of using the dwelling, or of allowing it to be used, for immoral or illegal purposes; or has been convicted of an arrestible offence committed in the locality of the dwelling-house, see the similar ground above in relation to secure tenancies.

Ground 14A

Domestic violence: see Chapter Five, below.

Ground 15

Where the condition of furniture provided under the tenancy has deteriorated owing to ill treatment by the tenant or by residents in the house whose wrong-doing the tenant has failed to prevent by removing them from the dwelling.

Ground 16

Where the dwelling was let to the tenant in consequence of employment by the landlord and that employment has ceased.

The discretionary grounds require both the factual basis of the ground(s) relied on and the reasonableness of granting possession to be made out by the landlord[14] – as with secure tenancies – and the court will then take into account all the factors in the case – eg the length of time the tenant has resided in the dwelling. The court will consider the interests of both parties, and the public interest in the matter. The conduct of the tenant will be a generally relevant issue[15], particularly so where bad behaviour is concerned, as is the willingness and ability of the tenant to make amends[16]. Also in relation to the discretionary grounds, section 9 of the 1988 Act grants the court extended discretion to adjourn for such period as it thinks fit any proceedings for possession. Likewise where an order is made under the discretionary grounds the court may stay or suspend its execution or postpone the date of execution. However, conditions are to be imposed with regard, inter alia, to the payment of any arrears of rent, unless the court considers that such an imposition would cause *exceptional* hardship to the

---

14　*West Kent Housing Association Ltd v Davies* (1998) 31 HLR 415, CA.
15　*Yelland v Taylor* [1957] 1 All ER 627, [1957] 1 WLR 459.
16　*Second WRVS Housing Society Ltd v Blair* (1986) 19 HLR 104.

tenant or would otherwise be unreasonable. Where these conditions are complied with the court may then rescind or discharge a possession order. There is a presumption, however, against indefinite suspensions of possession orders, and even against a lengthy suspension[17]. The better course of action is for the tenant to be warned that further default will lead to an order for outright possession being made[18].

Security of tenure: ASTs

Where an AST, granted before 28th February 1997, expires under section 20(4) and, for example, the tenant 'holds on' a new AST will arise. While in relation to ASTs granted after that date *any* new tenancy will be no more than an AST under section 19A. There is little long term security for the holder of an AST.

(1) All the mandatory and discretionary grounds applicable to ATs also apply.
(2) Note the special ground for obtaining possession provided by section 21 of the 1988 Act as amended.

Once the end of an AST *which was for an initial fixed term* has come, the court *must* make a possession order if satisfied:

(1) that the initial AST has come to an end and that no further assured tenancy (whether shorthold or not) is for the time being in existence (*other* than an assured shorthold periodic tenancy) see section 21(1*a*), and
(2) the landlord has given the tenant not less than two months' written notice stating that he/she requires possession of the dwelling.

The court has no discretion in the matter once satisfied of the foregoing matters, see section 21(1) of the 1988 Act. Note also that the notice may be given once the initial fixed term has expired, or before or on the expiry date, even though a statutory periodic tenancy would arise on that date, for where possession is ordered any such tenancy ends automatically the day the possession order takes effect, see sections 21(2) and (3).

Likewise the court *must* make a possession order in respect of a dwelling let on a AST which is a periodic tenancy following the initial fixed term AST under section 20(4) where satisfied:

(a) that the landlord has given the tenant a notice stating that after a specified date (such a date marking the end of a period of the tenancy, and not being earlier than two months after the date of the notice) that possession of the dwelling will be required, *and*
(b) that the date specified in the landlord's notice is not earlier than the earliest day on which at common law the tenancy could have been brought to an end following notice to quit.

17 *Vandermolen v Toma* (1981) 9 HLR 91.
18 *Mills v Allen* [1953] 2 QB 341, [1953] 2 All ER 534, CA.

In relation to ASTs granted under Section 19A of the 1988 Act there are particular requirements relating to possession orders, for in relation to these 'new' ASTs there is, as stated above, no longer a requirement for an initial fixed period of at least six months. Section 21(5)–(7) as added in 1996 now provides that possession of an AST cannot be ordered before a period of six months from the granting of the initial tenancy has elapsed, not from the starting date of any replacement tenancy, no matter whether this arises by virtue of the statute, or by agreement with the landlord. However, once again it should be remembered that the provisions restricting security of tenure for holders of ASTs are only likely to be of peripheral significance for registered social landlords.

Only one notice to gain possession under section 21 need be served. The court, it must be remembered has no discretion in relation to such issues, save as provided by Section 89 of the Housing Act 1980 – ie power to postpone a possession order for only 14 days save in cases of exceptional hardship where postponement for up to 6 weeks is allowed.

Modification of the assured tenancy regime for association, etc, tenants

With the introduction of assured tenancies for new association tenants as from 15 January 1989, it was clearly necessary to ensure their position was not radically different from existing association *secure* tenants, and also to make provision to ensure a measure of continuity for *authority secure* tenants becoming *association assured* tenants on any transfer.

Section 49 of the Housing Act 1988 inserted section 36A into the Housing Associations Act 1985, which enabled the issue of guidance by the Housing Corporation on the management of housing by registered associations, either generally or more specifically. The power to give guidance to registered social landlords was continued by section 36 of the Housing Act 1996. Particular guidance may be given on housing demand for which provision should be made, selection and allocation procedures, tenancy terms, principles for determining rent, maintenance and repair standards and practices, services to be provided to tenants, complaints procedures, devolution of housing management decisions and consultation and communication with tenants. Such guidance may be issued from time to time, but before issue or revision consultation must take place with bodies representing registered social landlords, and a draft of the advice submitted to the Secretary of State for approval. In deciding whether a registered social landlord being well (or badly) managed the Corporation may consider whether they are (or are not) complying with section 36 advice.

Under section 36A of the 1985 Act the Housing Corporation issued 'The Tenants' Guarantee', whose object was to create additional rights for association ATs. Extra rights were conferred in respect of: repairs; in relation to complaints procedures; rents; exchanges, taking in of lodgers, carrying out of improvements; being consulted about changes in management. None of this caused any legal problems; the rights given (in addition to those given by the 1988 Act to ATs) are similar to those of STs, and are given by contract, see the model tenancy, initially drawn up in consultation with the NATFED.

The guidance initially issued in 1988 was revised in 1991 and again in 1994. It was supplemented by further guidance, for example in relation to hostels and special needs housing. The 1994 guidance began a period of revision in 1996 so that there should be up to date material on ATs and ASTs, where these were considered appropriate. These were initially supposed to be in place, along with a newly revised Model Assured Periodic Tenancy Agreement from the National Federation of Housing Associations, in 1997. However, revised performance standards for registered social landlords were issued as Housing Corporation Circular RI – 01/98, and this guidance superseded that previously provided by the Tenants' Guarantees, though '*charters*' for residents of and applicants to registered social landlords were also provided.

In particular guidance is given on 'Social Housing Standards' including lettings policies, residents' rights, management services, repairs, maintenance and improvements.

In the present context it is pertinent to examine this guidance in relation to tenants' rights though the guidance speaks of 'residents' who are clearly a wider group than simply 'tenants'.

The basic principle is that registered social landlords should give to their tenants the most secure form of tenancy compatible with the purpose of the housing. This will normally be an assured periodic tenancy, though, as already stated, ASTs may be used in particular circumstances. One such of these is where a registered social landlord wishes to operate a form of introductory tenancy parallel to those which authorities may operate. In such a case an AST may be granted on the understanding that at the end of the first year if the tenant is satisfactory the necessary statutory notices are given under Schedule 2A, paragraph 2 of the Housing Act 1988 to convert the tenancy to fully assured status. In addition contractual rights above and beyond the requirements of the 1988 Act should be given to assured tenants. These rights should include those to exchange, to take lodgers, to have repairs, to be consulted on changes in housing management, to carry out improvements and to be compensated for improvements made, to be able to refer complaints to a housing ombudsman, to homelessness and disturbance payments, to 24-hour access to their home and communal areas; to succession rights for those not having rights of succession under the Housing Act 1988, eg a same sex partner (see also Chapter Five) provided that person has been living with the tenant for one year before the tenant's death, or has been looking after the tenant for a period, or has accepted responsibility for the tenant's dependants. Tenancies should also, inter alia, permit an increase of rent once only each year and state the right of the tenant to refer such an increase to a rent assessment committee, should state services to be provided and how service charges are calculated, and define repairing responsibilities.

Tenancy agreements should make it clear what the rights and responsibilities of both landlords and tenants are, and there should be published explicit and fair procedures relating to dealing with tenancy breaches. Registered social landlords should only seek possession of a property in a case of breach once all other reasonable steps have been taken.

The terms of tenancies must all be in writing and should comply with statutory requirements on unfair contractual terms.

Tenancies should also provide residents and recognised residents' organisations with opportunities to influence policy on accountability to residents, while residents should also be given clear information about the services they may expect to receive, and this extends to services for which a service charge is made. There must also be consultation arrangements laid down with regard to housing management and residents and residents' associations should be consulted along with those who are specifically tenants. Consultations arrangements should give residents reasonable opportunities to participate in or to influence the design and management of housing and related services. Residents' associations should be set up, encouraged and supported, and there must be effective complaints procedures.

THE ACCOUNTABILITY OF SOCIAL LANDLORDS

There are a variety of methods to ensure that social landlords are accountable to their tenants. In the most extreme cases of illegal activity (and such cases are very rare) a local authority landlord may be made subject to judicial review[19]. Housing associations and other registered social landlords are subject to the very considerable investigative and monitoring powers of the housing corporation under section 30 et seq of the Housing Act 1996.

The Housing Corporation's regulatory powers in practice

The way in which the Corporation exercises its powers was examined by Day, Henderson & Klein in *Home Rules: Regulation and Accountability in Social Housing* (Rowntree Foundation, 1993). (These powers formerly

19 A *housing association* was generally not thought open to judicial review: see *Peabody Housing Association v Green* (1978) 38 P & CR 644. That may, however, no longer be tenable with regard to an association *specifically created* to take over and run an authority's stock: see *R v West Kent Housing Association, ex p Sevenoaks District Council* (1994) 'Inside Housing' 28 October, p 3.

existed under section 28 of the Housing Associations Act 1985.) They discovered that since 1988 the Corporation had radically revised its operating procedures so that, for example, there was much greater scrutiny of associations applying for registration. This resulted in the number of new registrations declining; but 'sifting' would-be registrees had become an essential part of the regulatory system designed to ensure that inexperienced organisations are prevented from getting themselves into problems. Once registered every major registered body is inspected by corporation staff in detail every three to four years. Some of these landlords receive an 'update' visit once a year when some specific aspect of policy is examined. Medium sized organisations are given a 'partial, management only visit' every four years and other visits if needed. The programme of visits is drawn up by the corporation's regions and time is left free to deal with emergencies or to visit landlords causing alarm by their performance. Newly registered bodies are regularly checked and visited. Since 1993 the Corporation has received quarterly financial returns from all registered bodies which are actively developing housing and any others deemed to need regular scrutiny: these returns enable the Corporation to identify any body 'at risk' and therefore in need of inspection.

The Corporation has further used its powers to ensure that registered bodies maintain adequate standards of service provision for their tenants, and that national social policy objectives are implemented, and a number of documents have been issued to further this objective. Current guidance will be examined in due course.

When a corporation inspector has visited a registered body the practice has been to grade it on a four (A–D) point scale – the lowest positions indicating a good or generally satisfactory performance needing a few minor improvements. Other grades have indicated either the need for major change or that Corporation intervention is needed. Where major change is needed a realistic time scale (between three and six months) for improvement has normally been allowed. If, however, the Corporation has had to intervene its practice has been first draft in new committee members to strengthen the body and oversee to its workings. Where, however, a body continues to act badly, generally illegally or unconstitutionally, the Corporation will use its 'last resort' powers and order an inquiry.

Section 30 and Schedule 1 Part IV empowers the Corporation to conduct inquiries into the affairs of registered social landlords. They may require the production of books, accounts and other documents relating to a landlord's business for the purpose of conducting the inquiry. A special audit of accounts for the inquiry may be undertaken under Schedule 1 Part IV, paragraph 22. Where the Corporation are satisfied that there has been misconduct or mismanagement in a body's affairs, they may, under Schedule 1, Part IV, paragraph 24, remove or suspend those responsible from membership and/or office, order banks or others holding the body's money or securities not to part with them without Corporation approval, and generally restrict the powers of the registered body to enter into transactions. Due notice (at least 14 days) of an intention to remove a person from office, etc must be given to the person and the registered body and the person has rights of appeal to the High Court.

Where an inquiry or audit has uncovered mismanagement or misconduct in the administration of a registered social landlord, *or* the management of the body's land would be improved if transferred, the Corporation may direct such a transfer. Where the mismanaged body is a charity the transfer can only be to another similar charity, otherwise it may be to another registered social landlord.

In practice corporation visits have historically concentrated on the quite small number of associations which collectively provide most of the stock. Most have been given a clean bill of health, though in 1990/1 37% of those inspected were graded C or D. There were, however, regional variations in ratings with some areas having no 'Ds' while others had up to 17% – this *may* have reflected differences in regulatory style encountered by Day, Henderson and Klein in the survey, or local differences in the composition of associations. The survey evidence indicated 'management only' associations as being more likely to be graded unsatisfactory especially with regard to equal opportunity policies, while larger associations tended to receive the most satisfactory gradings. On the other hand new 'developing' associations were most likely to be lowly graded with regard to finance and management control.

The objects of the Corporation are to ensure that registered social landlords are publicly accountable for the money they are given, that they are good stewards of their assets and that they fulfil social policy objectives. Financial viability is a precondition to achieving these objects, but not all viable bodies will otherwise reach required standards. Day, Henderson and Klein concluded that the device of concentrating most inspection effort on the largest associations meant most of the stock is subject to effective oversight at low cost, but this could result in less than effective supervision of smaller bodies. It was also discovered that most effort was devoted to inspecting managerial structures and processes by looking at files and minutes as opposed to physical investigation of actual properties.

The issue has been raised of whether some form of common public regulatory system for both registered social landlords and authorities is desirable. One suggestion has been the creation of National Housing Agencies, which would fund *all* social housing, and a new Standards Agency to assess and ensure quality of management amongst social landlords. Such bodies would, however, be non-elected which could result in a diminution in tenant participation. Common standards, performance indicators and publicity requirements for *all* social landlords could, however, be developed. In this context it will be interesting to note the development of 'best practice' requirements for authorities under the terms of the Local Government Act 1999.

However, on a day-to-day basis something less drastic than these powers outlined above is needed to ensure that social landlords always bear in mind the fact that while the freehold of units of accommodation they provide is legally theirs, those dwellings are other people's homes. What is provided to achieve this is a range of measures some of which are adjudicatory, some provide channels of complaint while others are informatory.

Adjudicatory systems

These are the various ombudsmen systems and arbitration. It is convenient to deal with arbitration first. A tenancy agreement may provide for tenants to be able to refer disputes with their landlords to independent arbitration under the terms of the Arbitration Acts 1950 and 1979. The procedure can be cheap, speedy and less risky than litigation, and allows tenants to conduct their own cases. However, arbitration is only available in respect of those matters dealt with by the arbitration agreement and there is no legal obligation on any landlord to provide such an agreement.

Ombudsmen

Local government has been subject to the supervision of the Commission for Local Administration (the 'Local Ombudsman' or LO) since the Local Government Act 1974, see especially section 25(1)(a).

The 1974 Act section 34(3) provides that nothing in the Act authorises or requires the LO to question the *merits* of a decision taken without maladministration by an authority in the exercise of a discretion vested in it. This does not prevent the *investigation* of the merits of a decision, but it prevents the LO from criticising a decision as *wrong in substance* when there was no procedural flaw in the process leading up to the decision. The maladministration must, by virtue of section 26(1) of the 1974 Act, arise 'in connection with action taken *by or on behalf of* a local authority'. This is wide enough to cover the acts and decisions of members, officers and other employees, and also agents of an authority.

'Maladministration' is an elusive concept, which certainly has a procedural aspect, seeming to extend, penumbra like, from cases where an authority has clearly behaved illegally, for example by fettering its discretion, to instances of excessive delay in dealing with matters, biased or hearsay influenced decision-making, victimisation or oppression of those subject to administrative powers, bad or non-existent procedures, making misleading statements about policy or practice, breaking promises, failing to respond to justifiable complaints, imposing harsh requirements on applicants for housing, and generally behaving in an inappropriate and heavy handed way.

The complaint must also claim to have sustained injustice in consequence of maladministration. 'Injustice' is not legislatively defined but covers a wide range of matters from loss consequent upon refusal to make a financial grant through to annoyance, disturbance or frustration caused by maladministration. No financial loss need be proven.

There are certain sorts of failings and practices that regularly result in findings of maladministration causing injustice. Authorities should beware of:

(1) delay in taking appropriate action, for example, with regard to processing grant applications, or applications for housing benefits, or claims to exercise the right to buy, or in transferring anti-social tenants to other accommodation or otherwise failing to deal with nuisances caused by such tenants, or in pursuing programmes of repair and modernisation;

(2) failure to comply with legal requirements or otherwise to keep promises or implement undertakings given in relation to housing matters, or to compensate tenants for damage suffered as a result of an authority's fault in relation to their obligations;

(3) not making adequate information or advice available or failure to explain policies on housing issues clearly, or failing to make clear the effect of obtaining alternative accommodation on a waiting list application;

(4) failing to investigate matters properly or to consider medical or overcrowding evidence in relation to rehousing applications, similarly taking incorrect action or failing to take appropriate action;

(5) general inefficiency in processing housing applications etc, or in providing services where stipulated in a contract of letting, or in failing to give a tenant an opportunity to reply to complaints made about his behaviour by other tenants;

(6) failing to maintain adequate records, or to secure liaison between various departments, or to respond to letters from tenants and other similar inquiries, or failing to comply with their own policy, practice or procedures, or failing to provide adequate guidance for staff. A very full list of 'failings' can be found in the Annual Report of the Local Government Ombudsman 1996/97 at p 39.

Procedure

There is a strict procedure, laid down in section 26 of the 1974 Act, to be followed before a complaint will be entertained. Though there has been direct access to the LO since 1988, the LO will not investigate any complaint until it has been brought to the attention of the authority complained against, either by the person aggrieved or by a member of the authority on behalf of that person, and until the authority has had a reasonable time in which to reply to the complaint. Since June 1992 this provision has been particularly strictly applied. A complaint intended for reference should be made in writing to a member of the authority complained against with a request that it should be sent to the LO. It should state the action which it is alleged constitutes maladministration. If the member does not refer the complaint to the LO, the person aggrieved may ask the LO to accept the complaint direct. In 1996 it was further suggested that the LO should become the 'ultimate rung' on the ladder of complaint, with complainants being required to exhaust all local complaints systems before the LO will interfere.

The current operating procedures were laid down in 1991.

(1)   Complainants complete forms which are sent to the LO's office. If the LO decides a complaint cannot be investigated the complainant is told, with reasons, in writing. If an investigation is to take place the complainant is also told.

(2)   The LO communicates with the Chief Executive of the authority in question and asks for comments on the matter.

(3)   Officers of the authority will then usually supply details of the matter to the Chief Executive who will then respond with the authority's view.

(4)   A decision is then taken whether to investigate further; a decision to proceed indicates suspicion of maladministration and injustice.

(5)   An investigating officer will speak to the complainant and also visit the authority to carry out a detailed investigation which will involve studying files and interviewing appropriate members and officers.

(6)   A decision and report will then be made and issued.

The effectiveness of the LO in providing a remedy

Certain matters are excluded from the ambit of the LO's investigations; for example there cannot normally be an investigation of a matter if the complainant has or had a right of appeal or a right to go to the courts but has not used it, Local Government Act 1974, section 26(6). Similar exclusions apply where there is a right of appeal, reference or review to any statutorily constituted tribunal, or where there is a right of appeal to a minister. These exclusions are subject to the proviso that the LO may conduct an investigation if satisfied that in the particular circumstances it was reasonable for the complainant not to have used other legal remedies, for example, because the cost of pursuing a remedy in the High Court would be prohibitively high. The Commission has a general discretion to investigate complaints, the exercise of which was considered by the Court of Appeal in *R v Local Comr for Administration for the North and East Area of England, ex p Bradford Metropolitan City Council*[20].

The decision confirmed:

20   [1979] QB 287, [1979] 2 All ER 881.

(1) although the LO cannot question the merits of a decision taken without maladministration, a complaint about the decision can be investigated to see whether there was maladministration in the process of making it;

(2) the fact that a complaint is about the exercise of 'professional judgement' does not prevent investigation by the LO;

(3) a complainant should not have to specify any particular 'piece' of maladministration. It is enough to specify the action of the authority in connection with which the complaint arises;

(4) because the complainant might be able to voice the complaint in court proceedings, the LO is not barred from investigating questions of injustice and maladministration which will not be directly at issue in those proceedings.

A perceived weakness of the LO's work is that there is no obligation on authorities made subject to a report of maladministration to implement recommendations, though authorities must report to the LO any action taken or to be taken. Where no such report is received, or where it is unsatisfactory, the LO may issue a second or 'further' report indicating what would be an appropriate response. From 1990/91 to 1996/97, 2,078 reports finding injustice caused by maladministration (*not* just in housing cases) were issued, 131 further reports, were issued. A satisfactory settlement was achieved in 1,852 cases, 154 were still awaiting an outcome in 1997, while an unsatisfactory result had been the outcome in only 72 cases. Since 1988, authorities have been under an obligation to make reports of action they propose in response to further reports, and, under section 26 of the Local Government and Housing Act 1989, where no satisfactory response to a further report is made, the authority in question is under an obligation to issue public statements as to the LO's recommendations and, if they wish, a statement of why they do not intend to implement them; this can cost more than putting right the initial injustice, and it remains a feature of the office that a number of authorities fail to implement specifically recommended remedies.

The evidence to hand suggests that most cases where maladministration causing injustice was found were remedied satisfactorily. The general rarity of further reports indicates that the activities of the LO have *some* effect on authorities and *may* contribute to the better administration of discretion. Against this it should be said that some authorities have from time to time been made the subject of multiple complaints by numbers of individuals. The evidence here suggests that there may be pockets of resistance to the introduction of good administration policies.

Remedial action is likely to fall under one, or more, of the following four headings: giving an apology; redressing the actual grievance; a compensatory payment; and improvement of administrative procedures. Steps taken to redress the cause of a complaint will satisfy the complainant. However, there are times when correcting one wrong may well cause the other problems, for example where rehousing a complainant raises allegations of unfair treatment in relation to other persons awaiting accommodation. In such circumstances an authority is justified in considering the wider issues and their implications before deciding what response to make.

In some cases making a monetary payment may be the best course of action. Section 1 of the Local Government Act 1978 allows authorities to make payments to or provide other benefits for persons who have suffered injustice because of maladministration. It may not, however, always be easy to quantify the loss caused by maladministration. Some authorities have resorted to the services of an independent expert to quantify the amount of the payment to be made. In 'Local Authority Response to the Local Ombudsman' [1979] JPL 441 Christine Chinkin revealed that sums of up to £20,000 have been paid as compensation. Over the years the LO has become more willing to make specific suggestions in reports as to the best way to ensure that the act of maladministration has been remedied.

The receipt of a finding of maladministration may, of course, lead to a change or improvement in an authority's administrative workings so as to minimise the risk of future complaints. Some authorities now have schemes to monitor their further performance in relation to their statutory functions, and others have created special subcommittees to deal with specific problems.

The LO is generally agreed to be quite effective in securing a means of redress for *some* grievances on the part of authority tenants, but the procedures adopted act as a sieve through which only a certain number and type of complaints pass. In addition, the level of public awareness of the LO's service generally remain low. Many tenants are simply unaware of its existence, and even where tenants have heard of the service most will not know how to contact it, while some potential complainants perceive the LO as 'too important' to approach. Knowledge of the LO's service, and of how to contact it is markedly higher in 'advantaged' areas than in 'deprived areas'. To improve access the LO service has its own website on the internet and has arranged for information about how to complain to be made electronically accessible. It also publishes Digests of Cases illustrating good practice for authorities.

It is not, however, simply authority tenants who may utilise an ombudsman service.

An Ombudsman for tenants of registered social landlords

In the first annual report on the Citizen's Charter, Ministers declared an intention to create an ombudsman service for association tenants to:
(1) provide an accessible, fair and effective means of resolving complaints against associations by those they serve;
(2) *seek* redress where a complaint is found justified;

(3) identify deficiencies in service delivery and to improve associations' quality of service; clearly a point of distinction from the Commission for Local Administration.

After consultation the Housing Corporation set out its proposals for the Housing Association Tenants Ombudsman Service (HATOS) in 1993, and the service became operational in 1994. The service was non-statutory and was established by the Housing Corporation. However, to underscore the independence of HATOS the corporation undertook to: restrict their power to remove the ombudsman within the first three years of service; set up an independent expert panel to advise the ombudsman; allow direct access for the ombudsman to the Chairman of the Corporation; locate the service in a building not occupied otherwise by the corporation or any association. HATOS had no power to *enforce* its recommendations, but derived its powers from the Corporation's extensive investigative and other regulatory powers.

The HATOS scheme was subsumed under the mandatory provisions of Chapter V of the Housing Act 1996.

By virtue of section 51(2) of the 1996 Act registered social landlords are subject to the jurisdiction of a 'Housing Ombudsman' under Schedule 2 in accordance with a scheme approved by the Secretary of State with regard to the investigation of complaints by tenants and other individuals.

Schedule 2 of the 1996 Act goes on to provide that all registered social landlords, must be members of an 'approved scheme' for dealing with housing complaints – clearly more than one scheme may in theory be 'approved' but in aggregate all a relevant body's housing must be covered by one or more schemes. This is a duty enforceable by an order obtained from the High Court by the Secretary of State. *But note* such schemes do not need to be restricted to registered bodies for their membership – a scheme could thus conceivably cover private landlords and/or local authorities – though the latter are unlikely members as they remain subject to the powers of the Commission for Local Administration under the Local Government Act 1974.

All 'approved schemes' must make provision for:
(a) establishment/appointment of an independent scheme administrator;
(b) criteria for bodies to be accepted as members of scheme;
(c) manner of becoming/ceasing to be a member;
(d) matters about which complaint may be made;
(e) grounds on which matters may be excluded from investigation (including that the matter is subject to court proceedings or has proceeded to judgement);
(f) description of who may complain;
(g) appointment of an independent 'housing ombudsman' for the scheme;
(h) appointment of assistant staff and terms of office;
(i) duty of housing ombudsman to investigate any complaint duly made and to make a determination of it;

(j)   power to propose alternative methods of dispute resolution – eg mediation;
(k)   powers of the ombudsman for investigative purposes, and procedures to be followed;
(l)   powers on making a decision;
(m)   making of an annual report by ombudsman;
(n)   manner of communicating decisions to complainant and the subject of the complaint and manner of publication;
(o)   defraying expenses of the scheme by members;
(p)   keeping of accounts – and their submission to the Secretary of State;
(q)   making of annual administration reports;
(r)   mode of amending the scheme.

Schemes must be approved by the Secretary of State and submission for approval is to take place according to his determination, and shall be accompanied by such information as he requires. The Secretary of State must approve a scheme if it covers the prescribed matters and is otherwise 'satisfactory'. An approved scheme may have approval withdrawn, but notice of proposed withdrawal of approval must be given to the scheme administrator who must be informed of reasons and given a chance to make representations which must be taken into account before a decision is made.

Where a registered social landlord becomes a member of an approved scheme, or is a member of a scheme which becomes approved, notice of that fact must be given to the Housing Corporation by the registered body and the Corporation must record it. Similarly a registered body wishing to withdraw from a scheme must inform the Corporation specifying housing activities which may be investigated under the scheme, the scheme(s) of which member is or *will be* after withdrawal, and what arrangements will be made after withdrawal for investigation of complaints on matters covered by arrangements under the scheme which is to be left. Confirmation of withdrawal by the Corporation can only be given where they are satisfied withdrawal will not lead to failure to comply with the duty to be a member of an approved scheme. If the Corporation withholds approval the registered body will continue to be a member of, and be bound by, the initial scheme.

Schemes that are approved by the Secretary of State must be registered with the Corporation and the register must be open to the public.

Particular powers and obligations relating to the determination of investigations

These include:
(i)   the duty to investigate according to the terms of the scheme and to determine the complaint by reference to what is in the opinion of the ombudsman fair in the circumstances of the case;
(ii)   to make an order that compensation shall be paid to a complainant;

(iii) to order that either the member or the complainant shall not exercise or shall not require the performance of any contractual or other obligation;

(iv) where there is a failure by a member to comply with a determination in a reasonable time the ombudsman may order the registered body to publish in such manner as is determined, the reasons for non-compliance – note the parallel with the Commission for Local Administration here. The original Bill preceding the 1996 Act provided that the housing ombudsman might seek an order from the High Court to direct a scheme member to comply with a determination – but that order's award would be at the discretion of the High Court. This would have been a distinction from the Commissions's powers; but this provision was *not* included in the 1996 Act;

(v) determinations on complaints may be published, as may supplementary reports on the discharge of the ombudsman's functions. Such reports etc may contain material obtained in the performance of functions, however, regard shall be had to excluding so far as possible material relating to the private affairs of individuals where publication would cause prejudicial affectation, similarly any material relating specifically to the affairs of a scheme member, save where inclusion of the material is necessary for the purposes of the determination/report;

(vi) communication with the housing ombudsman on a relevant issue by complainants/complainee will be absolutely privileged for the purposes of the law of defamation, as will determinations and publication of reports;

(vii) the administration of an approved scheme *may* be in the hands of a body corporate (eg a company) and where they appoint the ombudsman the appointment is subject to approval by the Secretary of State. Where a scheme does not make such provision the Secretary of State will appoint an ombudsman for the purpose of the scheme;

(viii) housing ombudsmen are not servants or agents of the Crown;

(ix) members of approved schemes must pay a subscription determined by the scheme, though the Secretary of State and the Corporation may also fund such schemes.

It will be noted that the word 'maladministration' does *not* appear in the 1996 Act. HATOS never *expressly* confined itself to such a limiting notion, though *in practice* there was a concept of maladministration applied.

HC Circular RS – 03/97 gives guidance on 'The Responsibilities of a Social Landlord with Respect to the Independent Ombudsman Scheme Approved by the Secretary of State for the Environment'. It points out, inter alia, that in addition to the requirements of the Housing Act 1996 that such a landlord must be a member of an approved ombudsman scheme, failure to join such a scheme is deemed to be a failure to meet the HC's own regulatory standards, and may lead to their regulatory intervention in the landlord's affairs.

HATOS also followed a number of paths in seeking to resolve disputes laid before the service.

Mediation is a technique overseen, but not provided by HATOS, and is encouraged as a way of resolving disputes by communal arrangement between the parties as opposed to an imposed third party solution. The 'mediation route' is an entirely private arrangement between the parties and the end result is not binding on either.

Arbitration again depends upon the agreement of the parties, though here the decision of the arbitrator is binding in law, and once the process has begun neither party may abandon it unilaterally.

Registered social landlords – further guidance on accountability

Housing Corporation Circular RI – 01/98 gives further guidance on this issue. It indicates that being properly structured with the presence of appropriate skills and experience is fundamental to true accountability – as is adherence to the terms of the landlord's constituent instrument, and commitment to openness of action and equality of opportunity. Decision-making procedures should be regularly reviewed – generally on a triennial basis – and they will be reviewed by the Housing Corporation to ensure compliance. Landlords must be independent bodies and should be so structured as to ensure that single interest groups do not unduly influence the decision-taking procedure. As a general rule at least one third of such a landlord's governing body should be independent members – even where a landlord is so constituted that there are a majority of tenants on the governing body. In the Corporation's view it is not appropriate to have a majority of tenant representatives where the landlord was formed by a whole stock transfer from a particular authority, or where the landlord will be the dominant landlord within an authority's area. Similarly local authority representation on the landlord's board should not normally be more than one third of the membership.

All aspects of a landlord's activities should be under the direction and control of the governing body which must act in an effective and accountable way. They should be open in their activities and should normally make information generally publicly available, responding positively to reasonable requests for information relating to their policies and activities. In particular there should be annual reports on activities, annual reports to residents on the landlord's performance, and provision of information to residents and applicants about policy issues. In these respects the *requirements* of the Corporation mirror similar legal *obligations* placed on authorities.

Furthermore landlords should have in place arrangements enabling them to show they have appropriate levels of accountability, both to those to whom they have contractual obligations, and to those to whom they have a responsibility to account for their actions. It is clearly easier to ensure the latter because of the investigative and monitoring powers enjoyed by the Housing Corporation. Indeed it is arguable that the 'accountability' of landlords is largely 'vertical' in this respect, with 'horizontal' accountability to tenants and other residents being largely consequential. In the case of accountability to tenants (as a group to whom such a landlord will have a contractual obligation) the detailed rules on accountability are best laid down in tenancy agreements if tenants are to know and pursue their rights.

Complaints mechanisms

The LO service has not been simply concerned with investigating individual allegations of maladministration, but also with promoting overall good practice amongst authorities. Thus in 1978 the Local Authority Associations and the Local Commission issued a Code of Practice on complaints, urging all authorities to have a written procedure for dealing with all complaints about their activities. In their 1988/89 annual report the Local Commission expressed their expectation that all authorities would have an internal complaints procedure, and stated a failure to have such a procedure, or reliance on a faulty procedure, would be itself good evidence of maladministration. Further guidance on such procedures was issued by the service in 1992, and members of the public are in general expected to utilise their authorities' internal procedures before taking allegations to the LO. Since then there has been widespread adoption of local complaints systems by authorities. It is further a feature of the 'Citizens Charter' approach to public administration that not only should management be open and co-operative in nature but that there should be a complaints service with provision for compensation to be paid in cases where complaints of a serious nature are shown to be justified and loss has been suffered. However, in 1996 the Government declined to impose a statutory obligation on authorities to maintain a complaints procedure meeting specified requirements, preferring instead a voluntary system which can be tailored to meet local needs.

The basic hallmarks of a complaints system are that it should be 'user friendly', it should possess clearly defined stages through which complaints should proceed, and should be promptly responsive to problems. The service should also be objective, confidential and comprehensive in operation. All complaints mechanisms should have definitions of what constitutes a complaint, who is able to complain, when and how complaints may be made, how they are to be processed and who is charged with taking appropriate action, see further, Hughes, Karn, Leabeater, Lickiss, and Ward *Housing Complaints Procedures: Principles of Good Practices for Social Landlords*, National Consumer Council, 1991.

A number of authorities currently operate a complaints service – some under the terms of their tenancy agreements, others as a free standing service or 'guarantee' thereof. There is no one national standard model complaints mechanism.

So far as tenants of registered social landlords are concerned the Tenants' Guarantee, see above, (reinforced by Circular R1-01/98) indicated that such bodies should have complaints procedures, and there is evidence to suggest the Housing Corporation expects monitoring of complaints to be part of overall self assessment of their service by registered bodies. Certainly such bodies are expected to be responsive to tenants' complaints. There is no reason why the principles applicable to authority mechanisms should not apply equally to registered social landlords.

Informatory systems: reports to tenants

Tenants of authorities receive annual reports from their landlords detailing housing managerial performance which must be sent to them within six months of the end of the previous financial year – effectively by the end of September in each calendar year. A copy of such a report must also be sent to the Secretary of State, see Section 167 of the Local Government and Housing Act 1989. The philosophy here is that publicity is a form of accountability and the objectives for reports are that they should provide up-to-date information about housing performance to promote tenant interest and involvement, and thus to enhance management standards by stimulating customer demand and interest. Though specific management targets do not have to be set under the statute, ministers *expect* authorities to do so, and thus the system is designed to be a form of self discipline, see DoE Circular 10/94.

The content of reports is determined by ministers by direction under section 167(1) of the 1989 Act and the current direction is contained in Circular 10/94. Currently authorities are required to report on: the status of the housing stock, including the number of dwellings and those that are houses, flats or maisonettes, and the numbers of dwellings by number of bedrooms; rents, including average weekly rents and the percentage of those owing over 13 weeks' arrears; repairs including priority cases, target response times and compliance with such times; allocations, including those to new tenants, nominations to associations, allocations to priority homelessness cases, dwellings empty and available for letting, or awaiting only minor repairs and average re-let times of such dwellings, average weekly management costs per dwelling per year. This is the minimum content of reports, authorities may provide more information if they wish, and may set it in the context of local circumstances.

Reports should provide information in understandable forms, and may be in languages other than English where appropriate. Information should be given on qualitative as well as quantitative matters – eg on the delivery of services. Reports should be simple and inexpensive and authorities are urged by ministers to disaggregate information on an estate by estate basis whereever possible. For similar requirements imposed on registered social landlords see Housing Corporation Circular R1—01/98.

CONCLUSION

Despite a long historical tradition of English Law which has allowed the ownership and control of property to be 'parcelled out' among a number of persons in the form of the trust and the settlement of land, the dominant position with regard to the provision of rented housing has been to vest both ownership and control in the landlord. How to modify that, particularly in relation to social housing, has been a matter of legal and policy concern since the 1960s. It was then recognised that, as the private rented sector declined, society was becoming polarised in housing terms, between owner occupiers (the larger group) and (then) authority tenants, with the tenurial position of the latter being, in terms of legal rights, very weak. Strengthening that position, and that of the increasing number of association tenants, has led legislators down a variety of paths. From 1980 onwards the position of authority tenants was legally revolutionised – that term is not too strong – by the introduction of the secure tenancy. However, that package of rights was primarily individual in nature in that the rights conferred affected most of all the relationship between *individual tenants and their landlords*. Furthermore the principal right, namely to buy, was a right to *cease* to be a tenant.

Collective rights where the sum total of tenants' exercises is what affects a landlords' behaviour were scarcely well developed in the 1980 legislation. The Callaghan Government's 1979 Housing Bill, on which the Thatcher Government's 1980 Housing Act was largely based in so far as it created the notion of a secure tenancy (though not with the right to buy), did contain the notion of the Joint Estate Management Committee (JEM). These would have been required nationwide within authorities, and would have ensured a measure of representative tenant democracy in housing. Some authorities have set up JEMs on a voluntary basis: some have encouraged the development of vigorous and local tenants' associations, but there is no single national mechanism for enabling tenants' views even to be ascertained, apart from the weak requirements of section 105 of the 1985 Act.

Thus since 1980 there has been a diverse search to find means whereby landlords may be made more responsive generally to their tenants; but the search has not produced an even pattern across the sectors. Arguably within the local authority sector the chosen 'model', under the Citizen's Charter and Council Tenant's Charter, has been that of a company where an authority is like a board of directors making reports to, and seeking the views of, tenants who are thus likened to shareholders. Turning to registered social landlords the model is rather more that of a public utility where the Housing Corporation has increasingly adopted the role of an external regulator such as OFGAS or OFWAT. In the meantime some authorities have followed another model, namely that of a retailer offering a complaints mechanism as a service to tenant 'consumers' or 'customers'.

It may be asked whether any of these models is appropriate to the world of housing coming as they do from commerce and industry. None of them address the fundamental issue of how to divide ownership and control so that the landlord's ownership of 'the house' and the tenant's possession of 'the home' are held in an equitable balance which further recognises the landlord's need to intervene from time to time to ensure harmonious neighbour relationships and tenants' collective wishes for the future of their local environments.

It remains to be seen how far the 'best practice' initative under the Local Government Act 1999 will affect this issue in the years to come.

Further reading

In addition to the books and articles noted in the text, the following should also be consulted.

General policy

Donnison, D and MacLennan, D (eds) *The Housing Service of the Future* (Longman/Institute of Housing, 1991)
Cole, I and Furbey,R *The Eclipse of Council Housing* (Routledge, 1994 Chapters 5 and 6)
Balchin, P *Housing Policy* (Routledge, 1995) Chapters 6 and 7

Racial discrimination

Race Relations and Housing Cmnd 6252 (HMSO)
Housing in Multi Racial Areas (Community Relations Commission, 1976)
Handy, C *Discrimination in Housing* (Sweet & Maxwell, 1993)
Love, A-M and Kirby, K *Racial Incidents in Council Housing: The Local Authority Response* (HMSO, 1994)
CRE 'Homelessness and Discrimination: Report of a formal investigation into Tower Hamlets' (CRE, 1988)
CRE 'Housing Allocation in Oldham: Report of a formal investigation' (CRE, 1993)

Dhooge, Y and Barelli, J *Racial Attacks and Harassment: the Response of Social Landlords* (HMSO, 1996)

Allocation policies

DETR *Code of Guidance for Local Authorities on the Allocation of Accommodation and Homelessness* (HMSO, 1999)
Hughes, D and Jones, S 'Bias in the Allocation and Transfer of Local Authority Housing' (1979) *Journal of Social Welfare Law* 273
Lewis, N 'Council Housing Allocation: Problems of Discretion and Control' (1976) 54 *Public Administration* 147

Tenants' rights

Chinkin, C 'Local Authority Response to the Local Ombudsman' [1979] JPL 441
Chinkin, C 'The Power of the Local Ombudsman Re-examined' [1980] JPL 87
Hoath, D C 'Council Tenants' Complaints and the Local Ombudsman' (1978) 128 NLJ 672
Hughes, D Karn, V Leabeater, D Lickiss, R and Ward, F *Housing Complaints Procedures* (National Consumer Council, 1991)
Luba, J Madge, N and MaConnell, D *Defending Possession Proceedings* (Legal Action Group, 1992)
Karn, V Lickiss, R Hughes, D and Crawley, J *Neighbour Disputes* (Institute of Housing, 1993)
Ward, C *Tenants Take Over* (Architectural Press, 1974)
Williams D W 'Social Welfare Consumers and their Complaints' (1979) *Journal of Social Welfare Law* 273
Karn, V, Lickiss, R and Hughes, D *Tenants' Complaints and the Reform of Housing Management* (Dartmouth, 1997)

Reports

Centre for Housing Research *The Nature and Effectiveness of Housing Management in England*, DoE, HMSO, 1989
DETR *Developing Good Practice in Tenant Participation* (DETR, 1999)
Institute of Housing *Tenant Participation in Housing Management* (IOH/ Tenants' Participation Advisory Service, 1989)
Maclenna, D and Kay, H *Moving On, Crossing Divides* DoE (HMSO, 1994)

CHAPTER FOUR

The legalities of housing finance, rents and subsidies

The financing of social housing has undergone major change over the last 20 years, broadly speaking reflecting its transition to a more overtly residual function within the housing system as a whole. This period of change culminated in the introduction of a 'new financial regime' in the Local Government and Housing Act 1989. This chapter examines in turn the capital and the revenue sides of the financial arrangements for both authorities and registered social landlords, although it will rapidly become apparent that the elements of capital and revenue (current expenditure) are very closely connected, not least because, in the case of the authorities, a large share of current spending is the repayment of loans and debt charges arising from past capital projects.

Local authority capital spending

Capital spending generally refers to investment programmes in housing infrastructure particularly for new building. However the renovation and rehabilitation of *existing* older housing stock which thereby lengthens its life span can also be considered as capital spending. Such works might, however, also be regarded as essential for landlords to keep their houses lettable and thus in reality are *current* expenditure, the cost of which should properly fall on the revenue accounts drawn from rental income. Whether repair work was capital investment or recurrent revenue expenditure was, as we shall see, an issue of considerable controversy between central and local government in the 1980s in relation to spending capital receipts raised from the sale of council houses.

There were some controls on the use of capital f*or housing improvement* introduced under the Housing Act 1974 and this is indicative of the increasing need of governments of all political complexions to control public spending. In 1976 this system of central 'allocations' was extended to all housing investment programmes (HIPs) and from 1977/78 each authority was required to submit an annual HIP to the DoE based on an assessment of local housing needs and costed capital programmes. Permission to borrow necessary capital was then given on the basis of HIPs, see further below. The original aim of the HIP system was to strength central control over the capital programme at a time of financial constraint, but also with the intention of giving authorities greater freedom in forward planning and allowing them to set priorities for spending locally. In practice the most important feature of the HIP process has been to control borrowing on a year by year basis which has severely curtailed the development programme and made forward planning *more* difficult. In retrospect it is clear that the aims of the original HIP process were somewhat contradictory and, although established during a period of Labour government, were used to constrain and then virtually eradicate municipal house building under the Conservatives. Following restrictions on HIP allocations from the early 1980s the level of spending on new building by the end of the decade was down to very low levels and the share of public sector building was less than 30% of total housing construction (see Chapter One). In this respect the policy instrument was very effective. Moreover in the 1980s when the receipts from the sale of council houses began to accrue to authorities the HIP system became the instrument for restricting the use and reinvestment of these massive capital receipts (amounting to nearly £20 billion since 1980).

Under the post-1977 system the total capital spending programme was allocated in theory according to an assessment of local needs, said to be captured in a set of indices which together formed the General Needs Index (GNI), and by reference to previous years' spending. This system was never very satisfactory because the indices were themselves subject to considerable local variations which reflected individual authorities' policy stances. For example, one index was a count of statutorily homeless households but this figure could be low in areas which had a liberal policy which aimed to assist families in housing need before they became actually homeless. There was also a very large element of discretion in the final allocation of borrowing permission for capital projects which reflected the central government's own prorities rather than the GNI measurement.

During the 1980s the practice of 'top-slicing' the capital programme was also increasingly influential in asserting support for favoured central programmes. Money was taken out of programmes and re-allocated elsewhere, for example, into the Priority Estates Initiative and Estate Action projects designed to revive inner cities and regenerate 'difficult to let' estates. This form of targeted spending clearly further reduced local control and is now an overt mechanism for making authorities compete against each other for borrowing permissions under the HIP system.

In making a HIP bid an authority sought permission to borrow money– the 'net allocation' – but also was able to spend a certain proportion of the receipts from the sale of council houses and other assets such as land. The capital programme was financed from these two sources and during the 1980s the rapid increase in the receipts from the sale of council houses had a considerable impact on the balance of advantage between the centre and the local level.

Under arrangements made through the Local Government, Planning and Land Act 1980 authorities were, however, permitted to spend only a fixed proportion of their capital receipts. Following the introduction of the RTB in the 1980 Act this was set at 50% of receipts but was subsequently reduced as receipts built up. After 1985/86 the proportion was reduced down to only 20%. Nevertheless, the expenditure rules allowed authorities to spend during each year the same proportion of remaining accumulated receipts and under this so called 'cascade' effect authorities in England and Wales would eventually have been able to spend all their receipts. One of the main purposes of the reform of the 1980s system in the Local Government and Housing Act 1989, was to deal with this issue by compelling authorities to use their accumulated receipts to pay off historic debts.

The use of capital receipts was one of the most bitterly fought and controversial features of housing policy in the 1980s with many authorities critical of government control over what they regarded as their own money. On the other hand the centre did not wish to do anything which detered council house sales. A total prohibition on the use of receipts would have inhibited the sales programme – particularly sales on a voluntary basis – which by the mid 1980s was already past its initial peak. As receipts built up and the cascade effect developed many authorities were able to undertake a considerable programme of capital spending, often not on building houses but in renovating their existing stock. Although not technically considered to be 'capital' spending, this system of 'capitalising repairs' was widespread and caused central government concern that public spending limits were being breached by creative accountancy and the redefinition of what were or were not capital works. It should be remembered, however, that many authorities did not wish to build new houses so this apparent defiance of central policy did not amount to a breach of core political doctrine. It does, though, illustrate that the balance between central and local levels was not at all one-sided through most of the 1980s.

The accumulation of capital from receipts varied very considerably from authority to authority, and where large numbers of council house sales took place the balances were so great that the *interest* received on this deposited money became a significant source of income to the Housing Revenue

Accounts (HRAs). 12% of total HRA income was derived from this source in 1988/89[1].

Housing Revenue Accounts (HRAs)

Authorities have been required to maintain a HRA since 1935 and that is a unified account in respect of subsidies, if any, rents and capital receipts relating to their housing. The scale of capital receipts caused distortions in the revenue side of the financial system. Moreover due to the distribution of sales this system tended to favour already affluent areas, particularly suburban authorities in South East England, where housing needs were relatively less acute. The DoE's strategy for distributing borrowing permissions through the HIP proposals and the GNI was also very much distorted by the uneven distribution in the volume of RTB sales and the whole logic of a national distribution of resources, including weightings towards areas of particular housing stress, fell apart. In 1980/81 HIP allocations accounted for over 80% of expenditure while capital receipts accounted for less than 20%. By the late 1980s this position was completely reversed with only 28% of total spending accounted for by HIP borrowing permission[2].

It is against this background of faltering central control due to the 'cascading' of receipts, the uneven patterns of expenditure round the country, and the problem of what to do with the massive accumulation of capital receipts that the government moved in the late 1980s to reform the housing finance system and thereby strengthen their grip over local authority investment programmes and to re-establish their policy instruments on the revenue side which they had progressively lost, as many authorities by this time received no central subsidy.

The new regime for capital spending

The Local Government and Housing Act 1989, which came into effect in April 1990, introduced very considerable changes in both the capital and the revenue sides of funding arrangements.

The new regime for capital spending restricted the definition of 'capital' to prohibit the capitalisation of repairs, although improvement of property to enhance its life expectancy was within the definition. The system controls much more tightly the ability of authorities to spend capital receipts. The major change to the 1980's system was that only 25% of capital receipts could be spent on capital projects and all the rest must be used to pay off debt charges or, if sufficient capital was available, to pay the interest on an

1   Gibb, K and Munroe, M *Housing Finance in the UK* (Macmillan, 1991) p 73.
2   Gibb and Munro, op cit.

equivalent amount of debt. Either way the new regime effectively ended the 'cascading' of resources and stopped authorities from spending three quarters of capital receipts.

Rules for capital controls over local authority house building

The detailed rules on borrowing generally are now found in Part IV of the Local Government and Housing Act 1989, see particularly section 43(8). Section 428 of the Housing Act 1985 (which must be read subject to the terms of the above Act) is also relevant in this context. Section 428 grants a general power to authorities to borrow in so far as that relates to the execution of repairs and works by them, and also with regard to clearance and re-development. Local authorities also have power to borrow for the purposes of providing housing accommodation, housing grants and mortgages.

Approval for loan finance may be withheld or given subject to restrictions whenever central government feels it necessary to reduce or contain public spending, and also to reduce the housing provision role of authorities. However, as described above, not only is borrowing capital subject to control, the expenditure of other capital derived for example from RTB receipts is also stringently centrally controlled.

Part IV of the 1989 Act aims generally to keep the total amount of net authority capital spending in a given financial year within central government expenditure plans, to enable central government to target allocations of spending and borrowing allocations, having considered the resources authorities have; further to ensure that some capital generated by the sale of assets goes to repay existing debts, and to require authorities to make provision for repayment of debt.

Housing authorities fall under the post 1989 Act system by virtue of section 39, while housing capital expenditure is 'caught' generally by virtue of section 40, borrowing powers, as already noted, are brought within the system under section 43, further limits on powers to borrow apply under sections 44 and 45. Section 44 imposes an external limit on borrowing determined by the Secretary of State by means of the 'aggregate credit limit' system, and an authority may not exceed this limit by 'internal' borrowing, eg from its superannuation funds.[3] Section 43 requires each authority to set an annual 'overall borrowing limit' for itself beyond which it may not borrow.[4] Section 62 of the 1989 Act provides for the calculation of an 'aggregate credit limit' for each authority, and powers to borrow may not be generally used so that the aggregate credit limit is exceeded. Section 53

---

3   *Stockdale v Haringey London Borough Council* (1990) 88 LGR 7.
4   *Hazell v Hammersmith and Fulham London Borough Council* [1992] 2 AC 1, [1991] 1 All ER 545, HL; and *Crédit Suisse v Allerdale Borough Council* [1995] 1 Lloyds Rep 315.

empowers the Secretary of State to issue annually 'basic credit approvals' (BCAs) to authorities which are, inter alia, the base authority for capital spending purposes. They further have the effect of limiting authorities' borrowing powers. Indeed, the 'amount' of a BCA for any given year may be nil. Sections 55 and 56 lay down the criteria to be used in issuing BCAs, making the system very much subject to the discretion of the Secretary of State; likewise the way in which authorities are to use BCAs have been allocated. In addition to the annual BCAs the government indicates the likely limits for the next two years so that an element of forward planning can occur and under section 54 such Supplementary Credit Approvals (SCAs) can be set for specific purposes as decided by the government. Section 58 proceeds to control the capital receipts an authority may receive – for example from RTB sales. Section 59(2) particularly provides that where council dwellings are sold 75% of the receipts must be 'reserved' to meet 'credit liabilities', ie to redeem past debts. This clearly is a major limitation on the powers of authorities to reinvest RTB receipts in the provision of new housing.

Under the 1989 system – which was described in full in DoE Circular 11/90 – authorities now have very limited annual capital programmes.

Current expenditure

The new regime for current expenditure also developed out of the system that was put in place by the Housing Act 1980 and a brief explanation of the 'old' system is a prerequisite to the discussion of the 1989 Act. The 1989 regime represents a tightening of control by central government over the revenue side of local authority finance to mirror constraints on capital spending.

The 1980s system

The 1980 Act implemented a set of arrangements designed to achieve control over the level of local authority housing subsidy, but in this case without giving the appearance of destroying local autonomy. The innovation in the 1980 Act was to base HRAs on a centrally controlled model, a so called 'notional HRA', rather than the actual income and expenditure as before. This notional HRA was based on central government's own ideas of annual costs and notably the expected income from rent. Authorities were still able to use their own locally generated rate funds to keep down rents if they wished, and could spend in theory whatever they wanted on management and maintenance costs, but the government gradually withdrew general exchequer subsidies hitherto paid into each authority's HRA, and so rents were forced up to compensate for the shortfall on the notional HRA.

The main impact of this system was felt largely on the income side of the HRA. Expenditure in the new system remained much as it had been and continued to form the basis of the 'new financial regime' in the 1990s. The main expenditure items within the HRAs are loan charges in respect of past capital borrowing, capital expenditure (a very small amount), management costs on such items as staff and offices, repairs and maintenance, covering planned programmes and small works and a variety of other smaller costs.

The main source of income to the HRA is rents for which in the 1980s there were two sources; the rents paid in cash directly by tenants (net rents) and the rent paid in the form of a rent rebate under the housing benefit system to low income households. Together these sources of rent accounted for nearly 65% of HRA income by the end of the 1980s. Other sources of income were interest from deposited capital receipts – the second largest source of HRA income in 1988/89 – and rate fund contributions.

One other main source of income under the 1980s system was the general subsidy referred to above paid by the centre to authorities. Each authority was in effect given notional HRA figures while the housing subsidy was a sum to balance such accounts annually. The calculation of subsidy was based on the rather simple mechanism of taking last year's subsidy payment and adding on estimates for changes in expenditure on debt charges and the cost of management and maintenance (M and M). This amount was then adjusted according to the central government's calculation of the expected increase in income from rents, the rate fund and the rent rebate subsidy. The notional HRA and subsidy calculation drawn up by central government was thus a mixture of actual costs, estimates of some costs and a series of assumptions about the level of income to be generated, particularly from rents. By 1989, because the changes wrought in 1980 led to rent increases, the average authority rent in England and Wales was £20.64 compared to only £7.71 in 1980[5]. The problem, however, from the point of view of central government, was that with the rapid withdrawal of subsidy the leverage over authorities to increase rents was gradually lost. Indeed by 1988 only 95 authorities (out of over 400 in England and Wales) received housing subsidy into their HRAs and in total this was only 5% of total HRA income.

One of the consequences of the increase in rents was a further differentiation between different types of authority, and against the steeply upward trend of rents considerable variations emerged between individual authorities, as exemplifed by the London Boroughs of Redbridge and Tower Hamlets where average rents in 1989 were £35.90 and £20.97 respectively. Authorities varied quite considerably in their response to the 1980 Act system with some authorities driving up rents in order to create surpluses on their HRAs (then transferred into the rate fund) while others resisted

5   Gibb and Munroe, op cit, p 90.

pressure to increase rents by the risky strategy of transferring money *from* the rate fund to support the HRA. It was also discovered that some authorities still in subsidy at the end of the 1980s were *transferring* money *from* the HRA *into* the rate fund suggesting that the system was extremely poorly targeted in terms of housing needs. The government thus needed to improve targeting and above all from their point of view to regain control of what happened at the local level.

The new financial regime (revenue)

The Government announced their reform of public housing finance in a 'consultation' paper (*New Financial Regime for Local Authority Housing in England and Wales*, DoE, 1988). It was argued that the subsidy system needed to be simpler, more equitable between authorities and tenants, and to encourage improved management practice. As with the 1980 system entitlement to subsidy is based on notional calculations about levels of expenditure and on rents and the so called 'deficit' on this account is met by a new combined Housing Revenue Account subsidy.

HRA subsidy, introduced in section 79 et seq of the 1989 Act, replaces not only the old housing subsidy but also rent rebate (now housing benefit) subsidy and excluded contributions from the rate fund. A crucial part of this realignment of HRA subsidy is that the new unified subsidy includes an estimate for rent rebate payments for the following financial year. By bringing rent rebates into the new HRA subsidy the government in effect changed the definition of how HRAs balance. Rent rebates instead of being an item of income along with net rent are now in effect counted as expenditure against net rental income. As a result virtually all authorities instantly come back 'into subsidy' and by this very simple mechanism the government solves its problem of how to exert leverage on rents which they lost during the 1980s. One effect of this is that any surplus made on the HRA by increases in net rents will be offset against rent rebates. Thus tenants paying full net rent will be paying some of the housing benefit of those of their neighbours who are in receipt of the benefit.

The overall effect of the new regime has been to re-establish government control over HRAs. Income to HRAs is limited to net rents and the unified HRA subsidy with rate fund contributions eliminated as a source of balancing the account. Expenditure is much the same as before, but it is now no longer permissible to draw on the rate fund to help balance the HRA which *must* balance and on a yearly basis a *planned* deficit cannot occur, see section 76 of the 1989 Act. Unforeseen circumstances may result in an unplanned deficit in any given year and such a deficit has to be carried forward to the next year as a debit. (The detailed rules on maintaining HRAs will be examined below.)

Thus the revenue side is completely self-regulating, an arrangement sometimes referred to as 'ring-fencing'.

The Local Government and Housing Act 1989: the detailed rules

Section 74 of the 1989 Act continues to impose on authorities a duty to keep a HRA of sums 'to be credited and debited' in respect of their housing stock, even where an authority no longer possess any stock, unless exempted by the Secretary of State, see section 74(4). Though six classes of property are capable of being 'stock' for HRA purposes, the most important are: houses and other buildings provided under Part II of the 1985 Act, ie council houses and flats and ancillary shops and other buildings; buildings and housing purchased but not yet in use, land required or appropriated for Housing Act use, houses which have been purchased as unfit under section 192 of the 1985 Act but which are repairable at reasonable expense and any other land, houses or buildings specified centrally. For further guidance see DoE Circular 8/95.

Section 75 and Schedule 4 of the 1989 Act lay down the rules for keeping a HRA. As we described above the account is 'ring-fenced' from other authority accounts, ie it must internally balance itself, and cannot be generally subsidised by the authority. Authorities have very little discretion as to what can or cannot be excluded save where an item is on the borderline of a definition. Even then the Secretary of State has powers under section 87 of the 1989 Act to give directions on the issue. See generally *R v Ealing London Borough Council, ex p Lewis*[6].

As credits to the HRA authorities must include rents and charges (eg for heating) in respect of houses etc within the account. 'Rent' includes notional amounts for those dwellings where the actual cost of the rent is met by housing benefit. Any HRA subsidy (HORAS) payable under section 79 of the Act of 1989 is also to be credited to the HRA, likewise any subsidy for rent rebates on HRA dwellings under the Housing Benefit Scheme. Credit may be given to the HRA from the Housing Repairs Account which authorities have a discretion to keep under section 77 of the 1989 Act; however, only exceptionally may credit be given from authorities' general funds, and then only at the direction of the Secretary of State.

Debits to the HRA remain much as they were under the 1980 Act system; costs of repair, maintenance, supervision and management of HRA properties, though not all 'housing related work' will qualify, for example initial work done on assessing a homelessness application.[7] (But see below

6   (1992) 24 HLR 484. See also section 78 on the Secretary of State's power to give directions on HRA accounting practices.
7   *R v London Borough of Ealing, ex p Lewis* (1992) 24 HLR 484.

on 'special cases'.) Also included are rents, rates and other taxes an authority may have to pay on relevant property, as are rent rebates paid to tenants. Any sum paid to a Housing Repairs Account must also be a debit, as must unpaid rents, etc, considered to be 'bad' or 'doubtful' debts.

In certain 'special cases' sums may be credited to the HRA, for example sums received by an authority in respect of facilities such as shops, recreation centres etc, provided by them under housing powers (such as section 12 of the 1985 Act). Such facilities confer benefits not just on tenants but on the community as a whole, and an amount to reflect the community's share of that benefit is to be credited to the HRA, see generally *Hemsted v Lees and Norwich City Council*[8] . Also included is income from certain welfare services provided in connection with housing, eg housing advisory services, warden services, etc, under section 11A of the 1985 Act, see section 127 of the Leasehold Reform, Housing and Urban Development Act 1993. The cost of providing the services is also debited to the HRA as a 'special case'.

Under the current system the Secretary of State has, under section 80 of the 1989 Act, virtually total discretion as to drawing up formulae from which subsidies for each financial year are calculated – even to the extent of fixing a negative amount of subsidy for given authorities: in which case an equivalent positive amount has to be taken from the HRA and placed in another fund (usually the authority's general fund) but the HRA must still be made to balance after the debit, meaning increases in the credits to it, ie rents. Before making a determination the Secretary of State must consult such representatives of local government and relevant professional bodies as seem appropriate to him, and if he makes, as he has power to, an individual determination for an individual authority, he must consult them, see section 87. The matters taken into account in determining HORAS include: the fixed sum the Secretary of State will receive from the Treasury in respect of the subsidy fixed under central government's spending rules[9] ; any actual loan charges on capital borrowing an authority has, and changes therein; numbers of tenants receiving rebates; changes in the size of the housing stock. The Secretary of State may also make assumptions annually about rent levels and management and maintenance costs and fix subsidies accordingly. Section 80A of the 1989 Act inserted in 1996 requires the Secretary of State to make a final decision as to the amount of HORAS payable to an authority *after* a financial year is ended. This enables underpayments to be corrected and overpayments to be recovered by

8   (1986) 18 HLR 424, and see also *HE Green & Sons v Minister of Health (No 2)* [1948] 1 KB 34, [1947] 2 All ER 469.
9   *R v Secretary of State for the Environment, ex p London Borough of Greenwich* (1990) 22 HLR 543.

central government.[10] Once the decision is notified in writing to the authority it is conclusive and is not to be questioned in any legal proceedings – an apparent attempt to exclude legal challenge. Where money is recoverable from an authority it may be done by withholding or reducing subsidy payments: see also section 86 of the 1989 Act.

HRAs – future changes

Under changes announced on 22 June 1999 (and following a 1998 DETR Consultation exercise) as from the financial year 2001–02, and subject to Parliamentary approval of the necessary legislation, rent rebates will no longer form part of HRAs; the cost of rebates will be reimbursed to authorities via a different channel. HRAs will thus become 'pure landlord accounts'. Authorities will also receive directly into their HRA a major *repairs allowance* which will reflect the cost of maintenance of housing, rather than being given credit approvals for borrowing with subsidies granted to reflect the financing costs of borrowing. This will be calculated following further consultation.

At this point it is necessary to consider what sums an authority may charge by way of 'reasonable rents' to tenants.

Reasonable rents

The notion of 'reasonable rent' goes back to the Housing Act 1935, the same legislation that introduced HRAs. Attempts had been made before to equate rents for council houses with those prevailing in the private rental sector but there were several problems. New council dwellings were very different in age and character from the mainly pre-1919 urban housing stock, while authority 'cost' rents were far higher than anything at the lower end of the private sector. Moreover rent control was still in place for much of that sector and this also caused problems when making comparisons between the private and public rental systems. The 1935 Act introduced the idea of a 'reasonable' rent which authorities were to charge, but it was not defined in the Act and in practice authorities were given very wide discretion to charge a rent which suited the type and age of property. There has been no successful legal challenge to the basic concept, and reasonable rents have come to mean nothing more than the actual rents set by authorities having regard to the subsidies from the centre, rate fund contributions to HRAs and latterly rent rebate subsidies; though an

10 *R v Secretary of State for the Environment, ex p Camden London Borough Council* (1995) 28 HLR 321.

authority abusing the system may be challenged.[11] The current position in law regarding reasonable rents is outlined below.

Reasonable rents – the current legal framework

Under section 24 of the Housing Act 1985 authorities may make such reasonable charges for the occupation of their houses as they determine, but must from time to time review their rents. This does not give an absolute discretion as to fixing rents. See generally *Belcher v Reading Corpn*[12]. Authorities are entitled to pursue social policies in fixing rent levels, provided they do not behave unreasonably[13]. The courts will intervene in the rare cases where an authority comes to a clearly perverse decision on its policies and considers immaterial policy matters. An authority can, however, consider the existence of a subsidy when fixing rent levels, see *R v Secretary of State for Health and Social Security, ex p City of Sheffield*[14]. The courts thus exercise little effective supervision over the day-to-day administration of authority rent policies, and will only intervene in certain unusual circumstances. This remains true even after the 'ring fencing' of housing revenue following the 1989 legislation, though that does limit an authority's ability to decide what ranks as 'housing expenditure'[15]. Thus authorities may charge different rents for different houses in the same area, or different rents for the same type of houses. They may thus charge differential rents, or may decide not to. They may reduce rents payable by tenants who take on themselves certain repairing tasks. They may phase increases in rent but do not have to.[16] It would appear, however, that 'relevant considerations' in determining a reasonable rent include: relevant legislation, the duty to balance the HRA, housing costs, inflation, subsidies to be received, costs of taking a tenancy relative to other housing tenure costs, the way in which an increase in rent is to be

---

11 *Backhouse v Lambeth London Borough Council* (1972) 116 Sol Jo 802, where an authority fixed a ridiculous rent on only one property in an attempt to evade provisions of the Housing Finance Act 1972.

12 [1950] Ch 380, [1949] 2 All ER 969.

13 *Mandeville v Greater London Council* (1982) Times, 28 January and *R v Greater London Council, ex p Royal Borough of Kensington and Chelsea* (1982) Times, 7 April.

14 (1985) 18 HLR 6.

15 *R v Ealing London Borough Council, ex p Lewis* (1992) 24 HLR 484 and *Hemsted v Lees and Norwich City Council* (1986) 18 HLR 424.

16 *Leeds Corpn v Jenkinson* [1935] 1 KB 168; *Summerfield v Hampstead Borough Council* [1957] 1 All ER 221, [1957] 1 WLR 167; *Smith v Cardiff Corpn (No 2)* [1955] Ch 159; *Luby v Newcastle-under-Lyme, Corpn* [1964] 2 QB 64, [1964] 1 All ER 84; *Giddens v Harlow District Auditor* (1972) 70 LGR 485; and *Wandsworth London Borough Council v Winder (No 2)* (1987) 19 HLR 204.

implemented and the speed and progress of implementation. The weight to be given to each factor is, of course, a matter for the decision-taker. It would not appear, however, to be a relevant consideration for an authority to assume that circumstances do not change from year to year so that what is an appropriate matter for one year must inevitably remain so in the following year. In other words, a proper determination is required, and it is generally thought this should happen on an annual basis.

The general lack of a statutory method of fixing rents for authority dwellings has also been somewhat addressed by section 24(3) and (4) of the 1985 Act inserted in 1989. Authorities are required in fixing their rents to have regard to the principle that the rents of houses/flats of any class or description should bear broadly the same proportion to private sector rents (ie rents under assured tenancies) as the rents of other houses of any other class or description. This somewhat unclear provision introduces the notion of 'relative desirability' which is a device to ensure that rents for the various types authority dwellings should bear some comparison with those for comparable dwellings subject to assured tenancies.

Such comparisons are very difficult to sustain in practice because of the different characteristics of the stocks of dwellings. In general the idea seems to have been to let the market define the difference in cash terms between rents on dwellings on, say, difficult-to-let estates and those in more desirable areas. However, with such a high proportion of tenants in receipt of housing benefit such logic is meaningless because the tenant response is to seek the most desirable properties irrespective of rent because that, to them, is a zero marginal cost. In addition the level of rents now charged for more desirable properties, because it partly depends on geographical area, equates very closely to levels of mortgage repayment for the discounted prices of RTB dwellings. This convergence of the levels of rents and mortgage repayments seems likely to have the effect of stimulating an increase in RTB sales rather than the stabilisation of a 'market' based rental system. Alternatively the provision may require no more than some recognition in rent levels of the fact that a privately let three bedroomed house with a garden is likely to be let at a higher rent than a three bedroomed tower block flat also privately let.

Increasing rents

By section 24(2) of the Housing Act 1985 'the authority shall from time to time review rents and make such changes, either of rents generally, or of particular rents, as circumstances may require'.

With regard to *secure* tenancies sections 102 and 103 of the Housing Act 1985 allow variations of rent to be made *either* by agreement between landlord and tenant *or* in accordance with any terms in the lease or the agreement creating the tenancy.[17] In the case of periodic tenancies variations may also be effected by the landlord serving a notice of variation on the tenant. (This method of variation also applies to introductory tenancies: see section 111A of the 1985 Act.) This notice must specify the variation it makes and the date on which it takes effect; and the period between the date on which the notice is served and the date on which it takes effect must not be shorter than the rental period of the tenancy nor in any case shorter than four weeks. Where such a notice is served and, before the arrival of the date specified in it, the tenant gives a valid notice to quit, the notice will not take effect unless the tenant, with the landlord's written consent, withdraws the notice to quit before the relevant date.

Tenancies which are not secure or introductory tenancies fall to be dealt with under section 25 of the Housing Act 1985. This provision gives authorities power to increase rents for their houses let on weekly or other periodical tenancies by means of the service of a 'notice of increase'.

Challenging rents

The normal mode of challenge to a decision on rent fixing by an authority will be by way of judicial review, provided a breach of public law principles can be shown, and the remedy sought will be a declaration that the scheme of rents is unreasonable, coupled with an injunction to prevent implementation of the scheme. A tenant has a 'sufficient interest' in such a matter to bring an action by virtue of being an affected rent payer. Alternatively where a tenant is the subject of possession proceedings for arrears of rent, the validity of the rent may be questioned as a defence[18].

Rent arrears

Despite the existence of a statutory housing benefit scheme many authority tenants still get into arrears with their rents either because of an unforeseen financial problem, such as unemployment, desertion by a spouse, illness, or general poverty, or, much less probably, because of unwillingness or incapacity to manage their financial affairs in a satisfactory way.

As long ago as 1983 Duncan and Kirby's *Preventing Rent Arrears* pointed out that *serious* rent arrears, ie at 1980/81 levels, £50 or more, affected one in twenty authority tenants, but arrears were not evenly distributed among authorities. Serious arrears are found in cases where

17 See also *R v London Borough of Brent, ex p Blatt* (1991) 24 HLR 319.
18 *Wandsworth London Borough Council v Winder* [1985] AC 461, [1984] 3 All ER 976.

there is a low income, a sudden income drop, eg as a consequence of unemployment, or unexpected heavy demand on finances. Families with dependent children and single parent families are the most likely households to be in arrears, with a crisis, such as the departure of a wage earner, precipitating arrears. Tenants in arrears often live in flats and maisonettes and are dissatisfied with their housing, and the highest rates of arrears are often found on unpopular 'difficult to let' estates, especially where rents are above average. Tenants in arrears frequently experience other budgeting problems, experiencing other forms of debt, yet rarely do such tenants live extravagantly or possess cars and other expensive commodities.

A more recent study commissioned by the DoE confirms these earlier findings (DoE, *Rent Arrears in Local Authorities and Housing Associations in England* 1994). Rent arrears are very widespread and almost half the relevant tenants were 'behind with their rent'. One in seven authority tenants owed more than four weeks' rent. The research found that households with dependent children and single adults are most likely to be in rent arrears. It suggested a number of closely associated problems which cause a propensity to fall into arrears – living in areas of multiple social deprivation, other debts, and the age of the head of household (with young heads being most at risk). The tenants themselves identified unemployment, changes in domestic circumstances and having other debts as the reasons for their arrears problem.

The study was critical of authority handling of arrears cases with legal remedies often being invoked far too early. The research recommended the establishment of specialist teams of housing department officers to deal with arrears problems by better counselling of tenants and better information systems so that arrears problems can be identified at an early stage and before the problem gets out of hand. They should ensure that all tenants who are entitiled to housing benefit are receiving it and that tenants are fully aware of the authority's policy on arrears and the ultimate consequences of withholding rent.

The Duncan and Kirby Report, the Audit Commission's 1986 Report *Managing the Crisis in Council Housing* and the recent DoE study between them recommended:

(1) authorities should ensure, by campaigns and other informative processes, that tenants take up as many benefits as possible and that monetary counselling is available for tenants with many debts, with housing staff receiving training to identify those in need of such counselling;

(2) authorities should consider using door-to-door collection of rent (which has been abandoned in many areas for security reasons), as this reduces arrears, and consider tenant representations about methods of rent payment, trying to ensure that, consistent with economy, it is as easy as possible for tenants to pay;

(3) use of 'rent-free' weeks helps to prevent arrears, as tenants in arrears can be visited then and back rent collected;

(4) there is a need to identify tenants with mounting arrears in respect of whom action is, or ought, to be taken: tenants should be clearly told how much they owe;

(5) accounting practices should be examined to prevent the creation of 'technical arrears', eg accounting periods which close mid-week when many tenants pay on Fridays, and rent collecting and accounting should be undertaken by one department;

(6) authorities should fix specific levels at which action in respect of arrears is taken, allocate sufficient staff to deal with arrears, should give tenants more information about rent payment options, and how to cope with arrears, should monitor performance in dealing with and reducing arrears: members should set clear policy guidelines on control of arrears;

(7) good staff training in dealing with arrears and those in arrears is most important: specialist staff may be needed;

(8) effective liaison with the courts and local DSS offices can help in dealing with tenants against whom action has to be taken;

(9) early, firm and fair action over arrears is useful in reducing arrears, though no action should be threatened that an authority is not prepared to follow up; interviews with tenants in serious arrears are also useful;

(10) policies on the allocation of dwellings and on transfers should reflect the need to prevent, or reduce existing arrears, with tenants informed in advance of the likely cost of running a dwelling, and the least well off not being placed, or required to stay, in the most expensive housing.

It is the general tenor of central advice that distress for rent and actions seeking possession from those in arrears, see Chapter Three, are remedies of last resort.

Financial arrangements of registered social landlords[19]

The focus of this portion of this chapter is on the funding arrangments introduced in the Housing Act 1988 and subsequent developments. As with authorities the order is first the capital and then the revenue elements of this 'new financial regime'. Once again a brief survey of the old funding system is a prerequisite to the discussion. The consequences of the new regime were, however, dramatic and the housing association movement

19 NB. Throughout this portion of this chapter the word 'landlord' will be used to refer to those bodies that before 1996 were known as 'housing associations' and those others, such as Local Housing Companies, which are now known collectively with them as 'registered social landlords'.

underwent a fundamental transformation in character as a result, with a further transformation in 1996.

The 1988 Act stated the government's intention to establish a much expanded 'independent' rented sector in which associations were to play a central role. The Act reflected the anxiety that associations had become too identified with the mainstream public sector of housing and sought by introducing greater 'market' disciplines to create a more efficient and revitalised supply of rented accommodation. The 1988 Act also restructured the Housing Corporation (HC) and set up two new agencies, Housing for Wales ('Tai Cymru') and Scottish Homes to organise housing west of Offa's Dyke and north of the border.

Mirroring the withdrawal of subsidy from authorities the government also sought progressively to withdraw subsidy from associations and thereby encourage a more business-like and 'risk' oriented ethos. A principal feature of this policy was to replace public subsidy under the system created in the Housing Act 1974 with increasing amounts of private finance in the capital programmes.

The pre-1989 HAG system

Under the old system a high proportion of development costs was written off by a once and for all central government subsidy, Housing Association Grant (HAG). The calculation was based on the Rent Officer's 'fair rent' assessment of the properties in the scheme at the end of the development process. In this process the Rent Officer utilised the methods of arriving at a rent more usually encountered in the private rental sector under the Rent Act 1977, see further below. The fair rent income was then used to pay management and maintenance charges with any residual amount used to sponsor, ie repay principal and interest only, that share of the outstanding loan it was capable of supporting. Until 1989 this would result in HAG payments which typically covered 80%–90% of the costs of the scheme, and cases of 100% HAG were not uncommon. This flexible approach meant that associations could develop projects in the knowledge that there was no risk involved because the HAG calculation was done at the end of the project and the vast majority of the borrowing would be written off by the subsidy (an approach to public subsidy quite different from that for authorities).

Each year the HC would announce the framework for the capital programme in its Approved Development Programme (ADP). Associations bid for a share of the ADP to support their projects, although the ADP was very indicative of the types of development it would support. The funds were distributed through the regional offices of the HC to which associations made bids. The regional offices received their share through a modified version of the DoE's General Needs Index for authorities.

The '1988' capital regime

The main ideas behind the '1988' regime – increased numbers of mixed funded schemes, increased value for money and more business-like management through higher risks and incentives – were announced in a consultation paper *Finance for Housing Associations, the Government's Proposals* 1987 (DoE). Following the 1988 Act the number of mixed funded schemes was to be increased so that by 1994/95 over 90% of HAG funded projects would be required to draw in private finance through the new 'fixed' HAG regime. At the same time the proportion of private finance was increased, beginning in 1989/90 with HAG set at an average of 75% of initial costs (a proportion that was planned to decline, and was by 1994/95 65%). Landlords had to make up the remaining share from private financial sources and had to bear the whole risk of increases in costs as the scheme progressed. Rents for new lettings were deregulated from 15 January 1989 in line with the assured tenancy regime in the PRS. The logic of this regime was that the flexible element in the system was the ability of landlords to increase their rents to meet their higher loan costs, while the financial risks were borne by those landlords and ultimately their tenants. Under the old system, it was HAG that was the flexible element but this became a fixed proportion of the intial cost of the scheme.

A new part of the capital regime require landlords to fund major repair works from a sinking fund which they must set up. Instead of using HAG for this purpose as was the case under the old system landlords were required to set aside 0.8% of their current income to cover future major repairs. The system divided relevant property into two categories; Block A and Block B. As the sinking fund builds up landlords were gradually to reclassify their properties from A to B categories. 'B' properties are those which are deemed most likely to need major repair work. Landlords therefore had little control over how their sinking funds could be used, and it was considered quite likely that a significant share of their properties would remain in Block B and therefore could only be repaired using the difficult route of new fixed HAG funding.

Under the '1988' regime, because private investment was not counted as public spending, there appeared to be the possibility of a considerable increase in housing output for less public spending. However, in the event the expected boom in output did not materialise. This was partly to do with an initial transitional cash crisis during the first year of the new regime which was unforeseen by the HC. The problem appears to have been caused by changes in the rules on the HC's approvals procedures in order to speed up the administration of grants. In the the first year HAG was claimed by associations more quickly than had been anticipated and the HC ran out of money before the end of the financial year. In January 1989 the government had to allow £120 million from the 1990/91 allocation to be brought forward and the expected expansion of production was stalled.

In the financial years 1989/90 and 1990/91 £1.4 billion of public subsidy was drawn down to the development programme with some £370 million of private loans. Private finance reduced average HAG payments from 85% to 75% of scheme costs and resulted in 4,700 more units being built than would otherwise have been provided. Mixed funded projects subsequently rose within the overall ADP for new houses to rent, but the 1990/91 approvals were lower than for the previous decade and the 1994/95 programme had a projected output of only 30,000 units which is similar to low output in the late 1970s under the old flexible HAG system and but a small fraction of the annual output achieved by local authorities year on year for over half a century.

The '1988' regime significantly increased the financial risk for landlords and this led to a series of mergers between smaller bodies trying to defend themselves from the dangers inherent in the new regime. More recently there was a strong trend for the bulk of the ADP to be taken up by a small number of very large landlords operating at the national level.

In order to achieve maximum 'value for money' landlords were forced to change the type of people housed from those they had traditionally catered for, and also the type of accommodation provided. They undertook less rehabilitation work (by 1994/95 less than 20% of the ADP compared to over 50% in 1988) and undertook few small schemes, and instead were developing large estates built by volume builders. It was found that there were considerable savings to be made by buying 'off the peg' housing from speculative builders rather than undertaking more costly 'design and build' schemes which were characteristic of development under the old flexible HAG system. As a result fewer flats and one-bedroom units were built in favour of 'family' housing. Moreover the space standards of these buildings were on average 10% lower than pre-1989 dwellings. Fewer older people and those with special needs were being catered for in favour of families with children and homeless households[20]. This lower risk type of development moved landlords away from their traditional involvement with inner-city renewal and created additional problems for them because of their relative inexperience of managing large estates.

One of the most worrying problems to emerge from the recent experience of the '1988' capital regime has been the disinclination of many of the major sources of private capital to invest in mixed funded schemes. This was a significant flaw in the logic of the system at a time when landlords were becoming much more dependent on this source of finance for their projects. Virtually no lending came from pension funds or insurance companies, and of the banks and building societies a very high proportion of lending was accounted for by only a handful of organisations: in the first two years of

20   Page, D *Building for Communities: A study of new housing association estates* (Joseph Rowntree Foundation, 1993).

the new financial regime 21 building societies were involved but three of these accounted for over 85% of total lending[1] .

The 1996 system of financial regulation of registered social landlords

Deficiencies in the '1988' system coupled with a desire on the part of the Conservative government in the early 1990s to further 'demunicipalise' social rented housing led to the growth of the notion of the local housing company (LHC) in which there should be both local authority and tenant participation, and which should emerge to stand alongside traditional housing associations. In addition it was policy, as announced in the 1995 White Paper *Our Future Homes* that companies and other bodies would be able to compete with traditional associations for finance in order to provide new social housing. To obtain this funding such bodies would be known as 'registered social landlords', while finance would be made available via 'the Corporation' meaning (see section 56 of the 1996 Act) in England the Housing Corporation and in Wales Housing for Wales – Tai Cymru – though in this work the abbreviation 'HC' will continue to be used to denote that funding body. All previously registered housing associations are automatically also registered social landlords by virtue of section 1(2) of the Housing Act 1996 which translates the new policy into law. Other bodies may of course be registered under sections 2 and 3 of the 1996 Act, see above Chapter 2 (and also on the fate of Housing for Wales).

It is Chapter III of the 1996 Act which governs the grants and financial assistance which the HC may give to relevant landlords – ie those that are registered.

Acting in accordance with principles it is to determine from time to time the HC *may* make grants to landlords in respect of expenditure incurred or to be incurred in connection with providing social housing and other housing activities, and may impose conditions on such grants: see section 18. Thus 'Social Housing Grants' (SHG) replace the '1988' system of HAG and revenue deficit grants. The 1996 Act grant will cover both new build and also conversion, alteration, enlargement, repair or improvement of existing housing: see further section 63(2) of the 1996 Act.

Acting under this provision the HC has made the Social Housing Grant (Capital) General Determination and the Social Housing Grant (Management Grants) General Determination of 1997 (HC Circular FI – 19/97), and see section 53 of the 1996 Act. Certain common law principles also appear arguably applicable to grant determinations; thus a grant paid in error should be recoverable by way of restitution on the basis of 'unjust

---

1   Randolph, B 'The re-privatization of housing associations' in Malpass and Mears (eds) *Implementing Housing Policy* (Open University Press, 1993), p 53.

enrichment'. Such a recovery could take place by way of deduction from a future grant.[2] SHG is not, however, payable to a landlord in respect of local authority housing managed by a relevant landlord: see section 19.

The HC may also under sections 20 and 21 of the 1996 Act make 'Purchase Grants' to relevant landlords in respect of discounts given by them to persons exercising the 'right to acquire' or otherwise, as tenants, acquiring their dwellings: see further Chapter Two above.

Section 23 of the 1996 Act continues the power of the Public Work Loan Commissioners to lend money to registered social landlords in order to construct, improve, facilitate or encourage the construction or improvement of dwellings, or to purchase dwellings with a view to their improvement, or for the purchase and development of land.

Where a grant has been received by a relevant landlord the HC has power to reduce *any* grant payable, or may suspend or cancel any instalment of such a grant, or may direct the landlord to apply or appropriate the grant to specified purposes, or to pay to the HC such sum as they specify. Such recovery can only take place in accordance with determinations made by the HC, and again these are those made in 1997: see section 27 of the 1996 Act.

The 1996 legislative scheme gives the HC as great a degree of control over grants as the 1988 Act did. It was clearly the intent of the framers of the legislation that registered social landlords should continue to have to look increasingly to non-governmental sources of funding, however, just as housing associations had been required to under the 1988 Act. The difference, of course, was that under the 1996 Act there could be rather more 'competitors' seeking SHG than there were for HAG under the 1988 Act.

What the HC can do, however, has to be set in the wider context of available public finance. On coming to power in May 1997 the Labour government undertook a major review of public spending, the results of this 'Comprehensive Spending Review' were announced on 9 July 1998 and indicated that preference was to be given to authorities over registered social landlords insofar as the provision of new homes is concerned. Further activities for registered landlords were, however, presaged on 15 February 1999 when the DETR announced a consultation exercise on proposals to enable such bodies to involve themselves in community regeneration projects via the provision of land, amenities or services or the provision, construction, repair or improvement of buildings for the benefit of residents in an area not just for those who are tenants of the landlord. It may thus be that financial arrangements for registered social landlords will point them in new policy directions.

2   *Auckland Harbour Board v R* [1924] AC 318.

Rents under registered social landlords

Existing secure tenants of those landlords who are housing associations continue to benefit from the 'old' rent system based on fair rent assessment and the detail of this entitlement is described below.

Rents for secure tenancies granted before 1989

Part VI of the Rent Act 1977 applied to 'housing association tenancies', and still does to tenancies granted before 15 January 1989, to ensure that their holders are charged only 'fair rents'. Section 87 lays down that there shall be a part of the register under Part IV of the 1977 Act in which rents may be registered for dwelling-houses let under housing association tenancies and that sections 67, 67A, 70, 70A, 71 and 72 and Schedule 11 apply to that part of the register. Under section 88 a rent limit exists for these association tenancies, excess rent above the limit being irrecoverable from the tenant. That limit is, where a rent is registered, the registered rent or, where there is no registered rent, whichever of the following applies is the limit:

(a) where the lease or agreement creating the tenancy was made prior to 1 January 1973, the rent recoverable thereunder;

(b) where the lease or agreement was made after 1 January 1973, and not more than two years before the tenancy began the dwelling was subject to another tenancy, the rent is that recoverable under that other tenancy's last rental period;

(c) otherwise the rent originally payable under the lease or agreement is that which is recoverable.

Under section 94 where a tenant has paid 'irrecoverable' rent, that tenant is entitled to recover the relevant amount from the landlord, and may do this by deduction from rent payable, though no such amount is recoverable at any time after the expiry of two years from the date of payment. Housing association periodical tenancy rents may, under section 93, be increased, without the tenancy being terminated, from the beginning of a rental period by a written notice of increase, specifying the date on which the notice is to take effect and given by the landlord to the tenant not later than four weeks before that date.

Under section 67 of the 1977 Act application for registration of a fair rent may be made to a rent officer by either landlord or tenant, or jointly. However, the pre-1989 practice was for associations to refer rent fixing on new developments to the rent officer at the end of the development process and the determination of the 'fair rent' then had implications for HAG. Applications (now, of course, limited to cases where it may be that the parties are not satisfied as to the 'fairness' of rent) must be in prescribed form, and must specify the rent it is sought to register, sums payable in respect of services and such other particulars as are prescribed. In general once a rent is registered, no application by *either party alone* for registration of a different rent for the dwelling may be entertained before two years have expired from the date on which a registered rent took effect, or, where a registered rent has been confirmed, the date on which its confirmation took effect, unless there has been such a change in the condition of the dwelling (including improvements), the terms of the tenancy, the quantity, quality or condition of furniture provided under the tenancy, or any other circumstances (save personal circumstances) taken into account when the rent was registered, as to make the registered rent no longer fair. This formula is wide enough to cover changes in methods of heating a property[3]. However, a *landlord* alone may make an application within the last three months of the period of two years.

The procedure in respect of determining a rent is laid down in Schedule 11. Where an application to register is received the rent officer may obtain information relevant to the application from the parties. On a joint application the rent officer may register the rent specified in the application without more ado if he/she considers it fair. In other cases the rent officer invites the parties whether they wish him/her, in consultation with them, to consider what rent ought to be registered. The party who did not make the application must be served with a copy of the application. Where no response is made in due form to the rent officer's invitation, he/she may consider what rent ought to be registered, and register a rent, or new rent, or confirm the existing as the case may be, or serve notice of intention to fix a rent. Where the officer's invitation results in a written response from either or both parties that they wish the rent to be considered, the officer must serve notice of the time and place at which he/she proposes in consultation with the parties, or such as appear, to consider what rents ought to be registered etc, for the dwelling. At the consultation the parties may be represented. Thereafter the officer may determine, or confirm, as the case may be, the rent and register it, informing the parties by notice. They then have 28 days in which to lodge an objection, and the matter is then referred by the officer to a rent assessment committee (RAC).

The RAC may obtain further information from the parties, and must allow them to make representations, either in writing or orally. It is the committee's duty to make such inquiries as they think fit and to consider information supplied and representations made, and then to determine whether the rent officer reached a correct fair rent, or whether the rent was not fair, in which case they determine the fair rent. Their decision is notified to the parties and the officer, who makes an appropriate entry in the register of fair rents. Appeals to the court from a RAC are governed by section 13 of the Tribunals and Inquiries Act 1971, and may only be on a point of law,[4] though they are

3   *London Housing and Commonwealth Properties Ltd v Cowan* [1977] QB 148, [1976] 2 All ER 385.
4   *Edwards v Bairstow and Harrison* [1956] AC 14, [1955] 3 All ER 48, HL.

also subject to judicial review[5], for example where they fail to observe the principles of natural justice and allow a landlord to argue the case for a higher rent in the absence of the tenant[6].

In determining a fair rent under section 70 regard has to be had to all the circumstances, other than personal circumstances, which includes in the case of a registered social landlord, the receipt of grant aid[7], and in particular to the age, character, locality and state of repair of the dwelling, and the quantity, quality and condition of any furniture provided under the tenancy. Certain matters may not, however, be taken into account, for example improvements or defects attributable to the tenant affecting the dwelling or furniture provided under the tenancy. Furthermore where demand for dwellings exceeds supply thus giving them a 'scarcity value' a discount of that element in the rent has to be made, see section 70(2). The amount to be registered as rent under section 71 must include any sum payable for the use of furniture or services, whether or not those sums are separate from the sum payable in respect to occupation of the dwelling, or are payable under a separate agreement. Where any sums payable include sums varying according to the cost from time to time of services provided by the landlord, or works of repair carried out by the landlord, the amount to be registered as rent may, where the rent officer, or RAC as the case may be, is satisfied that the terms as to variation are reasonable, be entered as an amount varying in accordance with those terms.

A number of decisions in the mid 1990s led to fears that 'fair rents' would be allowed to rise to the levels of market rents obtainable in respect of assured tenancies (see further below). Thus in particular *Spath Holme Ltd v Greater Manchester and Lancashire RAC*[8] stated that a 'fair' rent is not the same as a 'reasonable' rent, while *Curtis v Chairman of the London Rent Assessment Committee*[9] and *Northumberland and Durham Property Trust Ltd v London Rent Assessment Committee*[10] indicated that there were circumstances in which RACs should take into account existing market rents under assured tenancies before looking at existing registered fair rents. To meet concerns that this could lead to increases in fair rents in 1998 the DETR undertook a consultation exercise – 'Limiting Fair Rent Increases'. This has led to use of powers under section 31 of the Landlord and Tenant Act 1985 to make the Rent Acts (Maximum Fair Rent) Order 1996, SI 1999/6. This creates a formula for determining *maximum* fair rents, ie the *existing* fair rent plus the percentage difference between the UK Retail Price Index

---

5   *R v Paddington and St Marylebone Rent Tribunal, ex p Bell London and Provincial Properties Ltd* [1949] 1 KB 666, [1949] 1 All ER 720.
6   *R v London Rent Assessment Committee, ex p Hanson* [1978] QB 823, [1977] 3 All ER 404, CA.
7   *Royal British Legion Housing Association Ltd v East Midlands Rent Assessment Panel* (1989) 21 HLR 482.
8   (1995) 28 HLR 107.
9   [1999] QB 92, [1997] 4 All ER 842, CA.
10 [1998] 3 EGLR 85.

published during the month immediately preceding that month in which the new determination is made, and the published index for the month in which the previous rent registration was made *plus* 7.5% (for first applications made after 1 February 1999) or 5% (any subsequent applications). Thus rent increases are limited to price inflation plus a specified percentage amount.

Under section 72 the registration of a rent takes effect, where determined by the rent officer, from the date of registration, and, where determined by the committee, from the date of their decision, and similarly for confirmation of existing rents.

The new law of renting under the Housing Act 1988

Cm 214 promised the de-regulation of private sector lettings, and this policy was enshrined in the 1988 Housing Act, though this did not entirely translate into legal form the White Paper proposals. However, the basic philosophy of the White Paper is contained in the Act: higher rents *will call forth an increased supply of rented accommodation*. The ability of the new financial regime to deliver the hoped for gains in output and value for money hinges on the deregulated rent regime introduced in the 1988 Act. Under the new system rents were to be set by individual associations for most of their new lettings and there was no specific guidance from the HC about the principles behind this new form of rent setting. In HC Circular: HC 60/89 associations were urged to maximize rental income while at the same time keeping rents 'affordable' for people in low paid employment. These somewhat contradictory objectives were in fact resolved by increasing pressure on the housing benefit system and the income of tenants in new lettings.

Average weekly rents for new lettings increased in the first two years of the new system from £18 to nearly £33 (an increase of 81%) and rents for newly built homes increased by 104%. These figures compare with an increase in the Retail Prices Index of only 26% over the same period[11] . Thus rents in this new system were nowhere near being 'reasonably affordable' for the traditional tenants of housing associations and it was the social security system and an additional burden on the income of tenants themselves, paying excess rent *above the HB tapers*, that shored up the new system.

HC Circular 60/89 was replaced by Circular 5/93 and this indicated that landlords should 'set and maintain rents at levels which are within the reach of those in low paid employment' so far as assured tenancies were concerned. However, landlords were also told to take into account the need

11 Randolph, B 'The Re-Privatization of Housing Associations' in Malpass and Means (eds) *Implementing Housing Policies* (Open University Press, 1993), p 45.

to cover costs of loan charges, of management and maintenance, including making 'prudent' provision for future repairs, and that they should in setting a rent for each dwelling take into account its size, amenities, location and condition. The current guidance is found in HC Circular RI–01/98 which indicates that landlords should 'endeavour' to charge rents below equivalent private market levels, and that are affordable to those in low paid employment. Rents should be apportioned among individual properties by taking account of local market values, their relative sizes, amenities, location and condition. Neither rents nor service charges should make a distinction between those tenants who are in receipt of housing benefits and those who are not. This is an attempt to reflect government policy on securing a downward pressure on the rents of registered social landlords, and to constrain the cost of housing benefit. It must also be realised, however, that this policy is part of a wider one to discourage dependence on benefits and to encourage a move from welfare to work. Where people can get work, rents should be fixed at such a level that they are not discouraged from getting work whereby staying out of work they could secure a higher level of income because benefits would meet their rent commitments.

For existing stock not transferred from an authority the Circular indicates that landlords should endeavour to keep annual rent increases to guidelines to be set by the HC, ie the Retail Price Index percentage increase plus 1% (RPI+1%). The HC will investigate landlords to ensure compliance with this guideline and where significantly higher rent increases than regional averages are found the landlord in question will be asked to produce a plan for holding or reducing rents – regulatory action may be taken by the HC in default of such a plan.

Where properties were transferred from an authority before 1/4/98, rents for *existing* tenants should be limited to those specified for the guarantee period to tenants in the transfer arrangements (see further Chapter 2), while for new tenants, and for transferring tenants once the initial guarantee period has expired, rent increases should endeavour also to adhere to the 'RPI+1%' formula. In respect of properties transferred after 1 April 1998 rent increases should be limited to RPI formula applied by the transfer agreement – ie increases are to be in line only with retail price increases.

Assured tenancies (AT): rent provisions – the law

The basic law is contained in sections 13–14 of the 1988 Act and depends on the principle of sanctity of contract; both sides are bound by what they have agreed. There is no limit to what can be charged by way of the initial contract and the principle of market forces applies, save that where a tenancy is granted by a registered social landlord the principles of 'affordable rents' examined above apply. Nevertheless HC Circular 36/94 'The Tenants'

Guarantee' makes it clear that landlords should inform tenants of their right to rely on the provisions outlined below to refer rent increases to the RAC.

With regard to a fixed term AT there is no legal limit to what can be contractually charged, and no outside agency can interfere with the level of rent. The ability to increase rent will depend upon whether the tenancy agreement makes provision for this.

Where a statutory periodic tenancy has arisen (ie after the end of the initial assured contractual period) or where there is *no* rent review clause governing a periodic AT, the landlord may increase the rent by serving on the tenant a notice in prescribed form[12] proposing a new rent to take effect at the beginning of a 'new period' of the tenancy specified in the notice. That new period must be a period beginning not earlier than:

(a) in relation to yearly tenancies, six months;
(b) in relation to periodic tenancies of less than a month, one month, and
(c) in relation to any other case, the period of the tenancy, *but*:
   (i) the new rent period can *generally* only begin as from the end of the first anniversary of the date on which the first period of the tenancy began, and
   (ii) in a case where rent has previously been increased by the statutory method a further notice of increase can only be served once one year has expired from the taking effect of the new rent.

Effectively this means the landlord has a statutory right to increase the rent at the end of a fixed term tenancy, or at the end of the first year of a periodic tenancy provided there is no other rent review clause – it is likely that properly drafted tenancy agreements will contain such clauses, and they will then govern the situation, see section 13(1)(b). Indeed it is implicit in HC Circular 36/94 that there should be express provision on rent increases in tenancy documents. Notices of increase can generally only be served under the statutory system once every 12 months and the notice can only come into effect at the end of whatever is the appropriate minimum period. However, under section 13(5) the landlord and tenant may *agree* at any time to vary the rent.

Where a statutory notice is duly served the new rent will take effect *unless* before the beginning of the new period as specified in the notice the tenant refers the issue in prescribed form to the relevant Rent Assessment Committee (RAC), *or* the parties together agree on a variation of rent different from that proposed, or agree *not* to vary the rent. Notice that the onus is on the tenant to take action, a failure to act is taken as assent. The effect of a notice *not* in prescribed form is unknown. If the tenant accepts it and pays the revised rent there is no statutory right to recover any payment. On the other hand it may be possible to ignore notices not in due

---

12 See The Assured Tenancies and Agricultural Occupancies (Forms) Regulations 1997, SI 1997/194.

form. Where a tenancy is joint, any application to the RAC must be made by all, unless they have agreed to one acting as their agent.[13]

Where the matter is referred to the RAC under section 14 of the 1988 Act they are under a duty to determine the rent at which they consider the dwelling might reasonably be expected to be let on a willing landlord and AT basis in the open market. In particular they are to work on the basis, inter alia, that the AT will be periodic, having the same periods as the current tenancy, and will have the same terms as that tenancy. The RAC must, however, disregard:

(a) any effect on the rent attributable to the existence of a sitting tenant;
(b) any improvements carried out by the tenant which have increased the value of the dwelling;
(c) any failure on the tenant's part to act in accordance with the terms of the tenancy which has reduced the value of the dwelling.

The personal circumstances of the parties are irrelevant, and scarcity value will be relevant (contrast the position under the Rent Act 1977). To assist in their deliberations RACs may obtain information from the parties under section 41 of the Housing Act 1988. 'Rent' does *not* include any service charge but *will* include, inter alia, any payments made for use of furniture. The parties may under section 14(8) agree in writing to withdraw the reference from the RAC, and nothing in either section 13 or 14 affects the rights of the parties to vary any term of an AT (including terms as to rent) by agreement.

An appeal against the RAC's determination is available under section 13 of the Tribunals and Inquiries Act 1971, though only on a point of law, alternatively such a body is susceptible to judicial review.[14]

The rent as determined by the RAC will not be a rent limit for the dwelling as was the case with fair rents under the Rent Act 1977 and the parties may subsequently agree a higher rent in any case. The rent fixed by the RAC will come into effect on the date originally specified by the landlord in the notice to the tenant, unless the RAC decides a later date is, under section 14(7), justified on grounds of hardship to the tenant.

A duty is laid under section 42 of the 1988 Act on the president of every rent assessment panel to keep and publicise in a manner specified by the Secretary of State information about rents for ATs, which includes ASTs, which have undergone scrutiny by RACs (see SI 1988/2199 as amended by SI 1990/1474 and SI 1993/657). This may over time lead to the 'going rate' for market rents for ATs within any given area becoming known. Section 43 further empowers authorities to publish information about the AT

---

13 *R v Rent Officer for Camden LBC, ex p Felix* (1988) 21 HLR 34.
14 *Ellis and Sons Fourth Amalgamated Properties v Southern Rent Assessment Panel* (1984) 14 HLR 48, and *R v London Rent Assessment Panel, ex p Chelmsford Building Co* (1986) 278 EG 979.

system for the benefit of landlords and tenants. Apart from this authorities do not play a part in the rent fixing process as they could do under the Rent Act 1977.

Rents for assured shortholds (ASTs)

Again the basic principle is sanctity of contract, the tenant is bound by what he/she has agreed. However, the tenant under an AST may, by virtue of section 22 of the 1988 Act, as amended, refer the rent to the RAC for their determination of what the landlord could reasonably expect to receive by way of rent. The application must be made in due form, see SI 1997/194. Such a right will be of use to the tenant where the rent is 'significantly higher' than rents payable for similar tenancies of similar dwellings (whether on a shorthold basis or not) in the locality (an indeterminate area). However, there are a number of restrictions on the powers of the RAC and hence on the tenant's rights.

(a)   No application may be made if the rent is a rent previously determined under section 22 ie the right exists on a 'once only once' basis. Neither may an application be made in respect of a tenancy falling within section 19A of the Housing Act 1996 once more than 6 months have elapsed from its beginning. Such a tenancy is a tenancy not covered by Schedule 2A of the 1988 Act, ie cases where the landlord has told the tenant the tenancy *is* to be assured – remember tenancies now are *assured shorthold* unless stated to be *assured*: see Chapter Three, above.

(b)   No application may be made where the AST in question is a periodic one that has arisen at the end of the previous AST's initial fixed term.

(c)   The RAC may not make a determination unless they consider there is a sufficient number of dwellings in the locality let on ATs and ASTs to enable them to make a comparison, nor may they make a determination unless they consider the rent in question is significantly *higher* than what the landlord could reasonably expect to obtain having regard to comparable rents for comparable properties.

Where the RAC do determine a rent for an AST under section 22, the new rent, which may only be a reduction of that contractually agreed, will take effect from the date fixed by the RAC and will operate as a rent limit for the tenancy in question, any excess sums being irrecoverable from the tenant. However, the determination will *not* act as a rent limit for any other lettings of the dwelling, contrast the former position under the Rent Act 1977. Where a determination is made under this provision no notice of increase of rent may be served for one year from when the determination takes effect.

It will, of course, only rarely be the case that a registered social landlord will grant an AST: see Chapter Three, above.

Further reading

Balchin, P *Housing Policy* (Routledge, 1995) Chapters 2 and 10.
Driscoll, J (ed) *Butterworths Residential Landlord and Tenant Guide* (Butterworth, 1997), Chapter 3.
Reeves, P *An Introduction to Social Housing* (Arnold, 1996) Chapter 2.

CHAPTER FIVE

Housing and relationships

This chapter focuses on the legal framework which surrounds and regulates the housing rights of people in the context of their close personal relationships. The, historically, rather weak position of women is a salient issue. However, before we consider legal rights it is important to remember the most important of certain wider social developments.

- The rise in the divorce rate, particularly since the divorce reform legislation of 1969, so that about one third of all marriages are in danger of ending in divorce.
- The increase in the number of lone parent families to well over one million households by the early 1990s.
- Increasing numbers of remarriages, with many of these resulting in the birth of children, which creates an increased demand for 'family' accommodation.
- Legal and social policy stressing the need for both a child's natural parents to share responsibility, even though divorced/separated; again resulting in increased demands for suitable 'family' homes if children are to stay with both parents.
- A continued marked increase in the number of couples cohabiting, even after the birth of children, leading to pressures to harmonise wherever possible marriage and cohabitation.
- Continuing relative poverty amongst lone parent families, particularly where that parent is female. Such families predominantly look to the public sector for accommodation.

General housing rights within relationships

The law is concerned to regulate housing rights at a number of times within a relationship. While it exists and when it ends there will be legal consequences for a couple's home. These will not follow a common pattern. Everything depends on the mode of tenure of the dwelling, the nature of the relationship between the partners – married, unmarried, gay or lesbian ('same-sex' relationships) – the legal status of the tenancy held, and whether there are children involved.

Housing rights while a relationship subsists

English law recognises only two marital statuses, married and unmarried (including the bereaved and divorced). There is no such status as 'common law wife/husband' and use of that phrase will be avoided. In this chapter when the rights of those who are in an unmarried heterosexual relationship are discussed they will be referred to as 'partners' while married persons will be denoted as 'spouses'. The weak housing rights of those in same-sex relationships must also be considered where appropriate.

Freehold conveyancing practice tends to treat joint ownership of a house as the norm where property is to be occupied jointly. In municipal housing historic practice assumed where a married couple occupied a council house the husband would be the tenant. The 1976 National Consumer Council discussion paper Tenancy Agreements pointed out it cannot be assumed the male within a couple should automatically be the tenant. In 1977 the Housing Services Advisory Group (HSAG) in its report on tenancy agreements argued that prospective tenants should be given the opportunity to chose between joint and sole tenancies. By 1978 HSAG (report on the housing of one parent families) recommended use of joint tenancies in municipal lettings. It is now quite common for both spouses and heterosexual partners to be given joint tenancies. Practice still tends to vary rather more with regard to same-sex relationships, though both authorities and other social landlords are tending to grant more joint tenancies.

A joint tenancy gives both parties the right to occupy the home, irrespective of whether they are spouses or partners. The Housing Act 1985 recognises that authorities may grant joint tenancies. Joint assured tenancies may also be granted by associations under the Housing Act 1988.

Administrative practice should reflect the legal situation and communications from landlords should be sent to tenants jointly in both names. It should be made clear in the tenancy agreement that the authorisation of either joint tenant is sufficient for the doing of works and repairs by the landlord. Where a joint tenancy is not possible, a couple being allocated a house should be given a choice as to which will be tenant. Before a choice is made it is obviously a matter of good housing management for a landlord to explain the implications of tenancy types to intending tenants.

The rights of non-tenant spouses during the subsistence of a relationship

A wife who is not a tenant has the right to occupy and use the matrimonial home because at common law she is entitled to maintenance by her husband. Legislation goes further than this. However, even though legislation to some extent now harmonises the rights of spouses and cohabitants, marital status is still an important issue.

Section 30 of the Family Law Act 1996 confers 'matrimonial home rights' (MHR) on *spouses* only. Thus where one spouse has the right (eg as a sole tenant) to occupy a dwelling, while the other is not so entitled, that other has a MHR either, if in occupation, not to be evicted or excluded except by virtue of a court order, or, if not in occupation, a right with the leave of the court to enter and occupy the dwelling. Furthermore any payments made by the person enjoying the MHR in respect of liabilities on the dwelling will be treated as if made by the tenant spouse, likewise occupation of the dwelling by the person having the MHR as his/her 'only or principal home' shall be treated as sufficient occupation by the tenant spouse to satisfy the requirements of the Housing Acts 1985 and 1988 to keep in being secure/ assured tenancies. It must, however, be further noted that:

- the MHR only exists in relation to dwellings which are/were intended to be the matrimonial home of the spouses in question;
- the MHR exists only so long as the marriage subsists, *and* only so long as the spouse entitled by right to occupy the dwelling retains that right – eg while a sole tenant spouse retains the tenancy, though the court may under section 33(5) of the 1996 Act by order provide *during the marriage* that a MHR is not to be brought to an end *by the death* of the tenant *or the termination of the marriage*, a means of protecting a pending claim for the transfer of a tenancy: see further below;
- MHRs *cannot* arise where both spouses are joint tenants of the dwelling;
- a MHR is personal and non-assignable; it is a right not to be evicted while marriage subsists or until a court makes an appropriate order;[1]
- the MHR gives the non-tenant spouse rights to tender rent to the landlord, and to be joined in any possession proceedings in order to defend them;
- it appears *engaged* couples cannot enjoy MHRs as the court's powers exist where there is jurisdiction to make divorce, nullity or separation orders.[2]

---

1   *Wroth v Tyler* [1974] Ch 30, [1973] 1 All ER 897 and see *Sanctuary Housing Association v Campbell* [1999] 3 All ER 460, [1999] 1 WLR 1279, CA.
2   *Mossop v Mossop* [1989] Fam 77, [1998] 2 All ER 202, CA.

Occupation orders

Sections 33 to 38 of the 1996 Family Law Act replace the previous legislative tangle of ouster, occupation and exclusion orders, and again do much to harmonise the position of spouses and cohabitants, and in this connection section 62 of the 1996 Act defines 'cohabitants' as a man and a woman who, though not married, are living together as husband and wife, while 'former cohabitants' – who also have certain rights – are defined as men and women who previously so lived together, but *not* including any persons who subsequently married each other.

The following have been held by the courts to be relevant factors when determining cohabitant status:
- Do the parties live in the same household? This is fundamental; usually neither must have any other home where he or she normally lives – a mere sexual relationship alone is not enough;[3]
- Is the relationship stable, ie more than occasional or very brief?
- Do the parties provide financial support for each other?
- Is there a sexual relationship? Without that it is hard to find cohabitation.[4]
- Are there any children of the union?
- Have the couple held themselves out in public as partners?

Note that moving in a housekeeper to one's home does not usually give rise to a cohabitation.[5] However the fact that one partner still has a spouse elsewhere is not in itself a bar to a cohabitation.[6]

Under section 33 where a person is *entitled* to occupy a dwelling house – eg as a sole or joint tenant – *or* has a MHR in relation to the dwelling, *and* that dwelling is/has been the home of that person and of another person with whom he/she is 'associated' *or* was intended to be their home, that person may apply for an 'occupation order'. These are orders which may variously:
- enforce the applicant's entitlement to remain in the dwelling as against the other person (the respondent)
- require the respondent to the order to permit the applicant to enter and remain in the dwelling or part of it;
- regulate the occupation of the dwelling by either or both the parties;
- where the respondent is the person *entitled* to occupy, prohibit, suspend or restrict his/her entitlement;
- where the respondent has a MHR, prohibit, suspend or restrict that right;
- require the respondent to leave the dwelling, or part of it;
- exclude the respondent from an area around the dwelling;

3   *Harrison v Lewis* [1988] 2 FLR 339.
4   *Re J (Income Support Cohabitation)* [1995] 1 FLR 660.
5   *Butterworth v Supplementary Benefits Commission* [1982] 1 All ER 498.
6   *McLean v Burke* (1980) 3 FLR 70.

- declare that the applicant is entitled to occupy the dwelling or has a MHR over it;
- make provision (under section 33(5)) *during* the substance of a *marriage* that where the applicant has matrimonial home rights, those rights shall not be brought to an end by the death of the respondent spouse or the termination of the marriage.

This provision applies to engaged couples, but under section 33(2) where an engagement is terminated no application may be made by reference to it later than three years beginning with the date of termination. It will also be noted that section 33 applies to 'associated persons'. This is a very wide concept defined by section 62(3) of the 1996 Act.

'*Associated persons*' are those who:
- *are* married to each other;
- *have been* married to each other;
- are cohabitants;
- have been cohabitants with another;
- live/have lived, in the same household (though not merely as employees, tenants, lodgers or boarders);
- are relatives (see below);
- are the parents of a child, or who have parental responsibility in relation to any child;
- are parties to the same family proceedings;
- have agreed to marry one another (whether or not the agreement has been terminated);
- are connected by adoption.

This is a very large class of people covering not just husbands and wives, but also parents and children, children of one member of a household into which another person moves and that other person – eg, the daughter of a woman (whose husband has left) into whose home the woman's boyfriend moves and that boyfriend. Thus the class of 'associated persons' is wider than that of spouses and cohabitants.

Note also the very wide definition of 'relative' under the 1996 Act. Under section 63(1) relative *means* (a) fathers, mothers, stepparents, sons, daughters, stepchildren, grandparents, grandchildren of the person in question *or* of that person's spouse *or* former spouse, *or* (b) brothers, sisters, uncles, aunts, nieces, nephews (whether of the full blood or of the half blood or by affinity) of the person in question *or* of that person's spouse or former spouse *and* this includes in relation to a person who is living or who has lived with another as husband and wife *any* person who would fall within the foregoing list if the parties were to be married to one another.

This covers a vast range of persons, and the only omissions appear to be cousins and the former partner of a person's current partner. To obtain further guidance on this complex issue see Michael Horton's excellent study, *Family Homes and Domestic Violence: the New Legislation*,[7] to which indebtedness is acknowledged. It is, however, arguable that 'associated persons' extends to cover persons in same-sex unions where they fall within section 62(3)(c) where 'they live or have lived in the same household'. If this is so, then, for example, a gay man who is a sole or joint tenant (being 'entitled') could apply for an order requiring his partner to leave the dwelling. However, a gay man who is in a relationship but who has no entitlement as a tenant to the dwelling where he lives with his partner cannot apply for such an order for that man cannot have a MHR because he cannot be 'married' to his same-sex partner under English Law. Furthermore, as will be examined below, there is no jurisdiction to transfer tenancies as between persons in same-sex unions under the 1996 Act.

The exercise of the foregoing powers is discretionary (ie it must be 'just and reasonable' to act) and the court is to consider all relevant circumstances including (a) the housing needs and resources of the parties and relevant children, (b) the financial resources of the parties, (c) the likely effect of the orders or decisions to make orders on the health, safety or well being of the parties and any relevant child. The court is *required* to make an order where it appears the applicant/a relevant child would otherwise suffer significant harm, *save* where *more* harm would be suffered by the respondent/any relevant child on the making of such an order. It should be noted that 'housing resources' will include any likelihood of a party being rehoused by a local authority or other social landlord[8]. The court may also consider the conduct of the parties towards one another, and conduct will include any physical violence, jealous, strict and unyielding behaviour, and even the wish of one party not to stay in the same dwelling as the other.[9] The court may make an order even where violence has not yet broken out if it is clear the marriage cannot continue – though mere tension between parties is not enough.[10] Neither will a court make an order simply to assist a landlord in obtaining possession of a property to which it is clear one party will not return once the other is removed.[11] Orders should not be made to allow 'cooling off' periods, nor as 'routine' steps on the way to divorce.[12]

It will be noted that under section 33(7) the court *must* make an order where there is the likely risk of 'significant harm' to the applicant or a 'relevant child' – ie any child who is living with or who might reasonably be expected to live with either party, or any child subject to orders under the Adoption Act 1976 or the Children Act 1989 where the order is in

---

7   FT Law and Tax, 1996.

8   *Thurley v Smith* [1984] FLR 875.

9   *Brown v Brown* [1994] 1 FLR 233 and *Richards v Richards* [1984] AC 174, [1983] 2 All ER 807, HL.

10   *Phillips v Phillips* [1973] 2 All ER 423, [1973] 1 WLR 615.

11   *Warwick v Warwick* (1982) 1 HLR 139.

12   *Summers v Summers* [1986] 1 FLR 343.

question in the proceedings, or any other child considered relevant by the court. 'Harm' means ill treatment or impairment of health, including physical and mental health, in the case of an adult and further extends to harm to intellectual, emotional, social or behavioural development in the case of a child, thus embracing conduct such as sexual abuse. 'Significant' appears to mean 'considerable and important'[13]. Thus a court should certainly now make an order where a wife can prove allegations of indecency against his daughter by the husband.[14] However, each case will turn very much on its own facts. Thus even where one party has been violent towards another, forcing that other to leave and to seek homelessness assistance from the local authority, the court may decline to make an order where the violent party retains responsibility for providing a home for a child who may suffer greater harm if forced out of the dwelling than another child who has departed with the other party.[15] The 'likely' outcome that significant harm may be suffered is where such an outcome is a real possibility which cannot be sensibly ignored.[16]

Section 35 of the 1996 Act applies to *former spouses* who do not have entitlements to occupy, eg a non-tenant divorced wife, but *not* separated cohabitants or separated same-sex partners.

Where one *former* spouse is entitled to occupy a dwelling by virtue of a beneficial estate – eg a secure or assured tenancy – and the other is *not*, and the dwelling was at *anytime* their matrimonial home, or was intended to be, the non-entitled former spouse may apply to the court for an order against the order ('respondent') former spouse.

Where the applicant is actually in occupation any order granted must give that person the right not to be evicted or excluded from the dwelling or any part of it during a specified period, and must prohibit the respondent from evicting or excluding the applicant during that period. Where the applicant is not in occupation an order, if made, must give the applicant the right to enter and occupy for a specified period.

Orders *may* also under section 35(5) regulate occupation of the dwelling by either/both of the parties, prohibit, suspend or restrict the respondent's rights to occupy, require the respondent to leave the dwelling (wholly or in part) or exclude the respondent from the dwelling, or the area in which it lies.

In deciding whether to exercise its power the court, as under section 33, is to take into account particular issues such as the housing needs and resources of the parties, their financial resources, their conduct, the length of time they have been apart, the length of time that has elapsed since their

---

13   *Humberside County Council v B* [1993] 1 FLR 257.
14   *Lee v Lee* [1984] FLR 243.
15   *B v B (Occupation Order)* [1999] 2 FCR 251, CA.
16   *Re H (Minors) (Sexual Abuse: Standard of Proof)* [1996] AC 563, [1996] 1 All ER 1, HL.

divorce. The court must also consider the existence of any pending proceedings between the parties for a property adjustment order under the Matrimonial Causes Act 1973, or under the Children Act 1989. Orders may not be made after the death of either of the parties, and are only to be made for six months at a time (extendable).

As in the case of section 33 mandatory requirements are imposed on the court to regulate occupation of a dwelling by the respondent in cases where significant harm is likely to affect the applicant or a relevant child: see section 35(8).

Section 36 of the Family Law 1996 applies to cohabitants or former cohabitants with no existing right to occupy the property in question, but does not, of course, apply to same-sex partners.

Where *one cohabitant or former cohabitant* is entitled to occupy a dwelling which was the former home *or* intended home of the parties (eg as a sole tenant) and the other cohabitant/former cohabitant is not so entitled, the non-entitled person may apply for an occupation order.

Such an order, if made, must provide that where the applicant is actually in occupation of the dwelling the applicant is not to be evicted or excluded by the other party for a period specified in the order, *or* if the applicant is not in occupation permitting the applicant to enter and go into occupation. *In addition* the order may contain provisions similar to those relating to former spouses under section 35. The court must in deciding whether or not to exercise its powers take into account the housing needs and resources of the parties, their financial resources and the likely effect of orders made/not made and their conduct. *Additionally*, where the parties are cohabitants/former cohabitants *the court must consider the nature and length of their relationship, whether there are children of the parties* of whom they have had parental responsibility *and*, where the parties are *former* cohabitants or spouses *the length of time they have been apart, and* the existence of pending proceedings, an order for financial relief under the Children Act 1989, or relating to the legal/beneficial ownership of the dwelling. Once again provision to regulate occupation *has* to be made in cases of likely significant harm: see section 36(8).

Effectively this section largely equates the rights/procedures relating to cohabitants with those of spouses.

It appears that an occupation order under section 36 can be made in favour of a cohabitant still living in the dwelling who has ceased to cohabit with the former partner, and that an application does not have to be made immediately upon cessation of cohabitation. Such an order does not settle long term property rights, but it can be made as a short term holding operation to enable occupation to continue, though this has implications for landlords, eg as to rent etc, and may serve as a prelude to application for the transfer of the tenancy: see further below.[17]

17 *Gay v Sheeran, Gay v Enfield London Borough Council* [1999] 3 All ER 795, CA.

Sections 37 and 38 confer certain rights on spouses and cohabitants were *neither* party to the relationship has an entitlement to occupy the dwelling.

Where one spouse/former cohabitant *and* the other spouse/former cohabitant actually still occupy a dwelling in which they formerly had their joint home, *but* neither in fact has the legal right to remain in occupation, either may obtain a limited range of occupation orders against the other, *but* only for a period of up to six months – though this may be extended on further applications for up to six months at a time.

Again in both cases there are specific factors listed which the court will have to take into account in exercising its discretion, such as housing needs, etc.

It is most unlikely that sections 37 or 38 would ever be invoked in relation to any property belonging to a local authority or other social landlord. However, it is conceivable that the issue might arise in connection with a licensed squat.

Occupation orders have particular significance for landlords because they can have the effect of substituting an occupant for the person recorded as the tenant by the landlord. There may also be considerable implications for the payment of rent and entitlements to housing benefit. In this connection it is important to note the effect of section 40 of the Family Act 1996. Under this provision the court may on, or at any time after, making an occupation order under sections 33, 35 or 36, impose on either party obligations as to repairs, payment of rent, mortgage payments etc, and/or to order any party occupying the dwelling or any part of it to make periodical payments to the other, and/or grant possession/use of furniture/contents to either party.

In exercising this power the court, once again, is to take into account the financial needs and resources of the parties and their actual and prospective financial obligations.

Non domestic situations

What happens if a sole tenant takes in a lodger – may be even a casual lover – and then leaves, while the other person remains in occupation. The general attitude of the court towards such 'staying on' situations is that a new tenancy does not arise, even where the remaining partner pays money to the landlord claimed to be 'rent' see *Marcroft Wagons Ltd v Smith*[18]. However, the operative test appears to be whether the partner is staying on with the agreement of the landlord. Landlords should make clear their attitude to the creation of a new tenancy in such circumstances. In

18   [1951] 2 KB 496, [1951] 2 All ER 271.

Westminster City Council v Basson[19] , a couple were secure tenants and the defendant went to live with them. The couple gave notice to quit, handed in their keys and left the defendant in occupation. The Authority wrote to the defendant informing her of possession proceedings and stating a 'use and occupation charge' would be made, they also stated they did not intend to create a tenancy. It was found that no tenancy had been created. Landlords must, however, be very wary in such situations to ensure that no new tenancy is created.

This is illustrated by two more recent cases. In *Monmouth BC v Marlog*[20] , a woman had lived with – without cohabitation – a man in a council house. He was the tenant, and had his own rooms, while the woman and her family had the other bedrooms. The downstairs areas were shared: the contents of the house largely belonged to the man. The council commenced possession proceedings against the man, who gave notice to quit. The woman then tried to join in the possession proceedings, claiming she was a sub-tenant.

The court found that there had been no intention to create a legal relationship between the man and the woman. The case was simply one of sharing: a person who was a tenant had allowed another to have accommodation. The woman here had no rights against the man, and none against the landlord. The court indicated that judges should be slow to infer a tenancy relationship in such cases.

Contrast with this *Tower Hamlets LBC v Ayinde*[1] . Here a secure tenant invited another person into his council flat. He subsequently wrote to the local authority stating his decision to leave the property and not to return it. He further requested that the authority should transfer the flat to his sharer. The sharer paid rent, which the authority accepted.

The Court of Appeal found that the letter from the original tenant had operated as a surrender of the flat, which the Council had accepted. They had also created a new tenancy by conduct in favour of the sharer because (a) they had full knowledge of the situation and (b) in that knowledge had accepted payment as rent.

Housing rights on disintegration of a relationship

There is a need to distinguish between long and short term remedies. Historically the former were only available under matrimonial legislation to the married, though the Children Act 1989 and possession of a joint tenancy could result in entitlements for unmarried couples. This has been much changed by the Family Law Act 1996.

19   [1991] 1 EGLR 277, CA.
20   [1994] 2 EGLR 68, CA.
1   (1994) 26 HLR 631, CA.

A disintegrating relationship may also result in a couple being unable to live together under one roof. There may be inter party violence or violence to children. There are remedies in such circumstances available on a short term basis

Domestic violence

'Domestic violence' is the euphemism for spouse/partner battering, usually but not exclusively perpetrated by men on women. There are parallel problems where one partner to a relationship abuses children, both those to whom he/she is a biological parent, and those who are the biological children of the other partner. The Select Committee on Violence in Marriage Report[2] recognised this problem and recommended special refuges be set up where women could get away from violent men. Initial target provision should be one family place per 10,000 of the population. Authorities should assist in making this provision and the HSAG report *The Housing of One Parent Families* stated at pp 15–16:

> 'The refuge need not be in the form of a hostel. In fact in rural areas and small towns it will probably be more appropriate to have mutual arrangements between the police, probation services, social services and housing departments for the provision of emergency accommodation and social work support where and when the need arises. In cities, there may be a strong case for hostel-type provision, but this should be only for short stay emergency accommodation and more satisfactory family accommodation should be provided as quickly as possible, even if this is an intermediate step before permanent rehousing'

There were by the mid-1980s some 150 to 200 refuges nationwide (one refuge place per 70,000 of the population) some municipally provided and administered, others provided by various support groups, often run co-operatively. Recent research revealed that by the mid-1990s there had been very little improvement in the situation. A study by the London Housing Unit revealed that there were less than 1,700 places in refuges for women and their children in England whereas there was a demand for over 8,000 such places, estimated to require an additional 700 refuges. The research further revealed the poor standard of accommodation being provided with overcrowding, lack of privacy and limited facilities being common problems, sometimes resulting in women returning to a violent partner. (*Nowhere to*

2   HC 553, 1974–5.

Run: Underfunding of Women's Refuges and the Case for Reform, London Housing Unit, 1994.)

To protect women in the home the Domestic Violence and Matrimonial Proceedings Act 1976 was enacted. Previously a wife could commence assault proceedings against her husband, and this might result in him being bound over with, perhaps, some supervision by a probation officer. Likewise where a wife had commenced divorce or judicial separation proceedings she could also apply for an injunction excluding the husband from the home. But faster and simpler legal machinery was needed, and this was provided by the 1976 Act.

For unmarried persons the 1976 Act provided domestic violence remedies, married persons could use the route provided by section 1 of the Matrimonial Homes Act 1983 and indeed following *Richards v Richards*[3] they were expected to do so.

The 1976 Act only applied, furthermore, where partners were actually living with each other as if married at the time of the incident in question. Where partners were living separately the jurisdiction was not available[4]. The deficiencies of the 1976 Act were recognised in *Pidduck v Molloy*[5]. Here a man and woman had lived together and had a child. The woman began an action in trespass, assault and battery against the man from whom she had separated and had obtained an injunction against him restraining trespass on her property. The Court of Appeal pointed out the 1976 Act did not apply to former cohabiting couples who have parted and between whom violence then arises, and argued the law should be extended to protect ex cohabitees.

Section 16 of the Domestic Proceedings and Magistrates' Courts Act 1978 added to the tangle of remedies by empowering a magistrate's court to make a personal protection order prohibiting a spouse from threatening, or using violence against, the other spouse or any child in the family.

The new law under the Family Law Act 1996

The 1996 Act attempts to clear away the previous tangle of remedies, and to dispense with unnecessary distinctions between married and unmarried persons, while at the same time extending remedies to deal with situations such as that alluded to above where the violence or abuse exists not between spouses or partners but, for example, between one of them and the teenage daughter of the other.

---

3   [1984] AC 174, [1983] 2 All ER 807.
4   Contrast *Adeoso v Adeoso* [1981] 1 All ER 107, [1980] 1 WLR 1535 with *Ainsbury v Millington* [1987] 1 All ER 929, [1987] 1 WLR 379n.
5   [1992] 1 FCR 418, [1992] 2 FLR 202.

The detailed law on this issue is beyond the confines of this book, but a brief outline is given because the consequences of orders may have implications for the management and occupation of housing.

The 1996 Act replaced the Domestic Violence and Matrimonial Proceedings Act 1976; the relevant provisions of the Domestic Proceedings and Magistrates' Courts Act 1978 and the Matrimonial Homes Act 1983. The 1996 Act makes two basic sets of provision.

1.   To give a particular group of people – 'associated persons' – certain rights and remedies during *and* after, a relationship. These relate to the *occupation* of the home (already dealt with above) and personal safety;

2.   To provide for the *transfer* of certain tenancies on the break up of a marriage or a cohabitation relationship.

To whom does the new law apply?

Various remedies are available to a new class of people – *Associated persons* – while other remedies are still only be available to spouses and '*cohabitants*' (this new term in 1996 replaced 'cohabitees'). Indeed as has been argued the 1996 Act went a very long way towards equating the position of those who are formally married with those who have long term but informal unions. However, for some purposes it remains necessary to distinguish between those who are formally married (spouses) and those who are not.

Non molestation orders (NMOs)

Section 42 et seq of the 1996 Act enables the court to make such an order.

A NMO prohibits its respondent from molesting another 'associated person' (see above) or a 'relevant child' (again see above), and may be made either on specific application by another associated person, or where in any family proceedings (eg for an occupation order) to which the respondent is a party the court of its own motion thinks that such an order should be made. The court must have regard to all the circumstances of the case including the need to secure the health, safety and well being of the applicant and any relevant child. NMOs may be general or specific in their terms or both general and specific. They may be made for a specified time or until a further order is made. They may be granted on an ex parte ('without notice') basis in cases of 'significant risk of harm' (again see above), though in such cases the respondent must be given the opportunity to make representations as soon as just and convenient at a full hearing. Powers of arrest are generally to be attached in cases where the respondent has used or threatened to use violence against the applicant/a relevant child.

Supplemental points

NMOs are available between the full range of 'associated persons', eg they can apply to children, parents, spouses, former spouses, cohabitants, former cohabitants, persons in same-sex relationships.

A NMO is one containing either/both:

(i)   a provision prohibiting the respondent from molesting another with whom he/she is associated;

(ii) a provision prohibiting the respondent from molesting a relevant child.

Which courts have jurisdiction in relation to these matters?

The 1996 Act gave powers generally to the High Court, county court and magistrates court to make any of the orders outlined above in this Chapter. However:

*   an order for the transfer of a tenancy (see further below) can only be made by the High Court or county court;

*   Magistrates' courts may not deal with any application involving a disputed question as to a party's entitlement to occupy a property eg a dispute as to whether a person is a joint tenant;

*   the Lord Chancellor has power to specify that certain proceedings may be commenced only in a specified level of court.

Is a tangle of remedies re-emerging?

The 1996 Act reduced the clutter of the law, and it is therefore somewhat irritating to witness tangle and confusion re-emerging following the passage by Parliament of the Protection from Harassment Act 1997 and the Crime and Disorder Act 1998. Admittedly the former was passed to deal, ostensibly, with the phenomenon known as 'stalking' whereby celebrities – and others of course – are made subject to the pestering and unwanted attentions of another person. Thus where a person harasses another by a course of conduct, including alarming that other or putting the other in a state of distress, by speech or action a criminal offence is committed under sections 1 and 2 of the 1997 Act, in respect of which a civil remedy is also available under section 3. The 1998 Act was designed, inter alia, to deal with anti-social behaviour in general. Thus relevant authorities (local authorities and the police) are enabled to apply under section 1 of the 1998 Act for an 'anti-social behaviour order' where a person acts in a manner that has caused or is likely to cause harassment, alarm or distress to one or more persons not of his/her household, and such an order is needed to protect persons from further anti-social acts. (See further Chapter Three.)

It is not hard to conceive of a situation falling within the purview of all three Acts, with consequent confusion as to who is best placed to take which steps in respect of the conduct in question. One example must suffice.

Dilys, the former cohabitant of Donald, is a secure tenant of Ducktown DC. Donald used to live with Dilys but sometime ago left her and moved away. He has now returned to Ducktown and stands outside their former home repeatedly waiving placards saying: 'Come back to me, Ducky', while at the same time threatening to attack the property if Dilys does not have him back.

Such a situation, it is submitted could be subject of a NMO under the 1996 Act, either civil or criminal proceedings by Dilys or the police (for both are possible) under the 1997 Act, or anti-social behaviour proceedings by the local authority acting in concert with the police under the 1998 Act. Can this really have been the intention of Parliament; or is it yet another instance of legislation being made without due thought being given to the questions of what problems are we seeking to solve, and could these be dealt with under existing legislation, or do we really need new provisions?

The long term rights of the parties on the break-up of a relationship

Section 24 of the Matrimonial Causes Act 1973 granted the court extensive jurisdiction to adjust property rights of parties on the break up of a marriage, and to order one party to transfer property to the other. The assignment of a secure tenancy in pursuance of a property adjustment order made in connection with matrimonial proceedings was allowed under section 91 (3)(b) of the Housing Act 1985. In the case of a secure tenancy the court had wide powers to order transfer between the parties to a divorce, decree of nullity or judicial separation. The 1973 Act powers still technically exist in relation to named persons, but are now unlikely to be used in view of the more effective jurisdiction conferred by the Family Law Act 1996. Assured periodic tenancies, however, could, in general, only be assigned with the landlord's consent, see section 15 of the Housing Act 1988. The court, however, also had power to transfer, by its own order, secure and assured tenancies, see section 7 and Schedule 1 of the Matrimonial Homes Act 1983 (as amended).

Under section 22 of the Matrimonial and Family Proceedings Act 1984 the court had the same power to transfer a secure or assured tenancy as it had under the Matrimonial Homes Act 1983, Schedule 1 on the grant of a divorce etc, where leave was given to apply for an order for financial relief, provided the dwelling-house had at some time during the marriage been a matrimonial home.

The court may make an order under paragraph 5 of the schedule to direct who is to be responsible for what past debts in respect of the dwelling. It is therefore a dubious practice for a landlord to demand a transferee should discharge rent arrears incurred by a former sole tenant – and in Scotland it is specifically declared illegal, see section 20 (2) (a) of the Housing (Scotland) Act 1987. In England such a practice may be maladministration – see David Hughes's work with Stephen Jones at [1979] Journal of Social Welfare Law 273 at 286–287.

The above jurisdiction only applied to spouses. Save where the Children Act 1989 applied courts had no jurisdiction to alter property entitlements of partners. The 1989 Act allows courts to regulate where children can live and with whom they may have contract and to order the transfer of property (including housing) where this is in the interests of children.

Transfer orders

The Family Law Act 1996 makes provision now for transfers of tenancies on divorce *or* on the breakdown of a cohabitation relationship, but not on the ending of a same-sex union.

Section 53 and Schedule 7 of the Act provide that *the court* (effectively the county court but also technically the High Court) may transfer certain tenancies (including protected/statutory tenancies under the Rent Act 1977, secure or assured tenancies under the Housing Acts of 1985 and 1988) on the divorce of spouses or the separation of cohabitants – this latter power is a considerable development in the law.

Such a transfer may be made between tenants (whether previously solely or jointly entitled). In the case of *spouses* this may happened on divorce, or a decree of nullity, or judicial separation, or at any time thereafter. *In the case of cohabitants* it may occur after they have ceased to live together as husband and wife.

Such an order may only be made in respect of the dwelling where the parties made their home together, ie as their matrimonial home, or where they *lived together as husband and wife*. The power does not apply to *intended* homes, but the tenancy in question must still subsist at the date of the transfer application.[6]

The court's powers exist once the relationship of the parties (where married) has come to an end, also on application for divorce/separation or to convert a separation order into one for divorce, *or* where a separation order is in force or after a divorce order is in force. In the latter two cases the application for transfer must predate the making of the order, unless the leave of the court to do otherwise has been obtained. Transfer will not normally take effect before the making of the divorce/separation order unless in exceptional cases the court considers it just to allow prior transfer. In the case of cohabitants the court's powers exist where the parties cease

6   *Lewis v Lewis* [1985] AC 828, [1985] 2 All ER 449, HL, and see *Sanctuary Housing Association v Campbell* [1999] 3 All ER 460, [1999] 1 WLR 1279, CA.

to live together as husband and wife, ie they could still be under the same roof. Unless an application is made before remarriage, the remarriage of a former spouse bars a subsequent transfer. No such bar, however, exists in respect of cohabitants.

The order itself once made effects the transfer and there is no other conveyancing/assignment mechanism needed, *and the order will override any prohibition against assignment in the tenancy*.

Transfer orders are discretionary remedies

In exercising its powers the court is to have regard to all the circumstances of the case including the circumstances in which the tenancy was granted to either/both of the parties, or the circumstances in which either/both became tenants under the tenancy – eg by way of succession.

The court must also consider the housing needs and resources of the parties and of relevant children, their financial resources, and the likely effect of orders made/not made, *and, in the case of cohabitants where only one was entitled to occupy the dwelling under a tenancy, the nature of their relationship including, it appears, the fact they did not make the commitment of marriage, and the length of time they lived together, whether there are any children, and the length of time that has elapsed since they ceased to live together*. Finally the court must also in all cases consider the respective suitability of the parties as tenants – eg their records in paying rent etc. Presumably here landlords may be called upon to give evidence.

Orders that may be made (known colloquially as Part II Orders) will be effective to vest in the person to whom the tenancy is awarded the estate interest which the other person had previously, along with all the rights (eg RTB) and liabilities going along with it (eg to pay rent/arrears of rent). But where such an order is made, any obligation of the dispossessed party falling due to be exercised *after* a date specified in the order shall not be enforced against that person. Thus the dispossessed former tenant will have no future liability to pay rent in respect of the property.

However, the court *may* direct that both former spouses/cohabitants are to be jointly or separately liable to meet any liabilities or obligations which *have arisen* in respect of the dwelling up to the date of the order, and may further direct that either spouse/cohabitant must indemnify the other in whole or part in respect of meeting any such obligations. This allows the court to apportion liability for rent arrears.

This issue of liability to pay rent is a point to be carefully noted by all landlords. It is preferable from a landlord's point of view now for the court to make the order transferring property under the terns of the 1996 Act and to make provision for liability in respect of past and present rent, rather than to rely on the parties doing it themselves in response to an order from the court under the Matrimonial Causes Act 1973: see further below.

Where the dispossessed party (the transferor) was a successor tenant the person who is awarded the tenancy (the transferee) will also be deemed to be a successor. Furthermore where an order is made the court may direct the party to whom the transfer is made to compensate the one who is losing his/her interest, but only after considering the loss that that person is suffering, the financial needs and resources of both, their obligations and likely future obligations. It is not generally thought that compensation will often be ordered, and where it is it will not be on a generous scale, though, for example, it might cover a person's removal expenses. Whether or not a court might consider ordering compensation to be paid to a person who loses the RTB does not yet appear to be the subject of any reported case law. In any case in situations where the financial burdens on the transferee of making a compensation order would outweigh those to the transferor, the court may either order deferred payment of compensation, or payment by instalments.

Obviously the orders which can be made under Schedule 7 of the 1996 Act will apply to divorce or after cohabitants separate as the case may be, ie on dissolution. They are in addition to matrimonial home rights, and rights arising under occupation orders which, of course, arise while a married or cohabitation relationship subsists. It should be remembered that an occupation order may provide that a right of occupation conferred may not be brought to end even by the divorce of married parties, though see later notes on the effect of a notice to quit on a joint tenancy.

The effect of Schedule 7 was considered in *Gay v Sheeran, Gay v Enfield London Borough Council*[7] Here a man (S) and his partner (X) took a *joint tenancy* of a flat. A little later X moved out and another woman (G) moved in to cohabit with S. S later moved out, said he was not returning and asked G to tell the landlord, though she still lived in the flat, and the council did not become aware of the facts for some months until G applied for housing benefit. The council issued a notice to quit to S and X and G then applied for a transfer of S's interest to her. The Court of Appeal ruled that a transfer could not be made.

• A transfer can only be made where one cohabiting partner is entitled to occupy, and that meant, in the current context entitlement to occupy under a current secure tenancy. However, S's tenancy was not 'secure'

---

7   [1999] 3 All ER 795, CA.

as he had ceased to occupy the flat as his only or principal dwelling. The 'entitlement' condition has to be satisfied though it remains uncertain whether this has to be at the time the application for a transfer order is made or at the later time when the order actually is made.

• In any case a transfer could not be made to G of a joint tenancy held by S and X; the legislation does not allow such an order where the property in question is that of a cohabitant who is a joint tenant with a person other than the intended transferee; ie a transfer can only take place where either *both* cohabitants are jointly entitled to property or where one of them is solely entitled. G could not be 'foisted' as a joint tenant on X , even though she had long departed.

The joint tenancy issue

It was stated earlier that said landlords generally are making increasing use of joint tenancies in relation to married and cohabiting couples, and those in same-sex unions. This has the effect of conferring rights and liabilities on both parties. However, what if one gives a unilateral notice to quit?

In *Greenwich London Borough Council v McGrady*[8] it was held that notice to quit from one joint secure periodic tenant was sufficient to determine the rights of both. This ruling was subsequently accepted in *Hammersmith and Fulham London Borough v Monk*[9]. There the defendant and his partner were joint tenants of a council flat on a weekly joint tenancy, terminable by four weeks' notice. The partners quarrelled; the woman left and gave notice to quit in due form without the defendant's knowledge or consent. The House of Lords considered the ordinary rules of contract clearly indicated a joint periodic tenancy at common law may be terminated by one tenant irrespective of whether the other concurs. Notice to quit destroys the consensus necessary for the continued existence of the contract. Notice by one joint tenant (*provided it is in due form*) is, as a general rule, effective to bring a joint tenancy to an end. This is the rule concerning secure and assured tenancies. But the notice to quit must be in due form if the above principle is to be relied on. Thus in *Wandsworth London Borough Council v Brown*[10], notice to quit did not comply with section 5 of the Protection from Eviction Act 1977 which says notice must be in writing and must be given at least four weeks before it is due to take

8   (1982) 81 LGR 288.
9   [1992] 1 AC 478, [1992] 1 All ER 1.
10   (1987) Legal Action (September) p 13.

effect. The notice was ineffective to determine the tenancy. Note also *Community Housing Association v Hoy*[11]. On similar facts to the above the notice was ineffective. The departing tenant then served a second notice of correct length, but found the tenancy agreement forbade the unilateral ending of a joint tenancy and therefore, the notice remained ineffective.

Note further *Hounslow London Borough Council v Pilling*[12], which reinforces the necessity for care by landlords in such cases. An authority had granted a weekly secure joint tenancy to a man and a woman. The tenancy agreement was on a standard printed form, the couple were described as the 'tenant', and both were declared to have all rights and liabilities of the tenancy. Clause 14 of the agreement allowed tenants to give four weeks' written notice to quit, or 'such lesser period as the council may accept'. The tenancy commenced on Monday 22 April 1991 but, after making allegations of domestic violence, the woman left on Friday 6 December 1991, writing to the authority that she wished to terminate her tenancy 'with immediate effect'. The authority accepted this as notice to quit, informed the man he was no longer a tenant, and in due course sought possession against him.

Was the woman's letter a valid notice to quit? The court began by pointing out that, as the tenancy was weekly and had begun on a Monday, the earliest date on which a notice given on Friday 6 December could take effect was Monday 16 December. In response the Council relied on Clause 14 of the tenancy agreement which enabled them to accept a lesser period of notice than four weeks. The court considered that, though it was said in *Monk* that a secure joint tenancy could be terminated by an 'appropriate notice to quit' by one of two joint tenants, that also means it cannot be terminated by an inappropriate notice. A notice which did not give the period of notice required by the common law or by the terms of the tenancy was an inappropriate notice. But the council argued that the woman's notice was within the terms of Clause 14. That gave them the ability to accept a lesser period of notice. Not so, said the court. Clause 14 effectively allowed immediate termination by a tenant, even in the middle of a tenancy period. It was therefore a break clause. The woman's letter was not notice to quit at all but a letter operating the break clause.

The court added the council had to lose because any notice to quit to be effective under the rule in *Monk* must also comply with Section 5 of the Protection from Eviction Act 1977 ie it must be given for a minimum of four weeks before the date on which it is to take effect. The woman's letter did

11 (1988) Legal Action (December) p 18.
12 [1994] 1 All ER 432, [1993] 1 WLR 1242.

not comply with that rule and should not have been accepted by the council.

Where one of two joint periodic secure or assured tenants wishes to give notice to quit effective to end the rights of both, that notice must be:

(1) in writing;
(2) of a minimum period of four weeks given before the notice is due to take effect;
(3) expressed to take effect at the end of the appropriate contractual period, ie, in a weekly tenancy at the end of a week counting from the day of the week on which the tenancy began;
(4) of the minimum period which, apart from the rule in section 5 of the 1977 Act, is the minimum period required by common law, ie, the period of notice for any periodic tenancy greater in length than four weeks must be a period equal to the length of the tenancy, so for a two monthly periodic tenancy the period of notice is two months;
(5) given in accordance with a term of the tenancy which allows notice to quit only to be given in accordance with the due requirements of law.

Break clauses in tenancy agreements must not be used where it is wished to rely on the *Monk* principle, and it appears they should appear separately from ordinary 'notice to quit' clauses.

The foregoing rules do not apply where under a joint tenancy, either assured or secure, one of the joint tenants simply departs leaving the other occupying the dwelling as his/her 'only or principal home'. In such cases both the Housing Acts of 1985 and 1988 provide for the continuation of the assured/secure tenancy. The problem arises where the one who leaves then seeks unilaterally to serve *notice to quit*, (as opposed to a 'surrender' which requires consensus). The historic principle, as outlined above, was that the notice to quit determined the interests of both tenants for it destroyed the unity between them on which a joint tenancy depends.[13] This historic principle has now been reiterated, though for a while it appeared to be under question. For instance, where land is held jointly, even on a weekly joint tenancy, it is subject to an implied trust, and the tenants will be trustees for one another and also beneficiaries under the trust. However, under the Law of Property Act 1925 (see now section 11 of the Trusts of Land and Appointment of Trustees Act 1996) it is a general principle that trustees should consult beneficiaries before affecting the future of the property. Could that operate to frustrate the giving of notice to quit by one joint tenant

---

13 *Doe d'Aslin v Summersett* (1830) 1 B & Ad 135 *Parsons v Parsons* [1983] 1 WLR 1390.

who had not consulted with the other on the issue? The answer appears to be no, for in *Crawley BC v Ure*[14] it was held that such an obligation only arises where a trustee wishes to do something *positive* about a property. A desire to surrender a tenancy is *negative* and this is not subject to the obligation.

A rather more serious problem arose in *London Borough of Harrow v Johnstone*.[15]

In 1989 the parties took a joint tenancy of a council property. Clause 19 of the tenancy agreement specified four weeks' notice to quit (NTQ) in writing had to be given. In 1994 Mrs J left with her children and commenced divorce proceedings finalised in 1995. In 1994 Mr J obtained an order under the then current legislation which forbade Mrs J to use or threaten violence against him or to try to exclude or attempt to exclude him from the matrimonial home. Mrs J applied to the local authority for housing but was told she could not be helped as she technically had accommodation. She could be helped if she gave NTQ in due form ending her joint tenancy – this she did. The authority then told Mr J he had to leave, and he then told them of the court order against his wife, and used this in defending the possession order the authority then sought. At first instance the authority was found in contempt of court for commencing proceedings in view of the order against Mrs J. This was confirmed in the Court of Appeal. The House of Lords, however, reasserted the *Monk* principle, and also found that in the present case the terms of the actual order against Mrs J were insufficiently precise to prevent her from giving NTQ. More importantly they *doubted* whether a specific injunction requiring one joint tenant not to serve NTQ could actually invalidate such a notice. Thus it appears arguable that the unilateral termination of a joint tenancy will be effective even where there is a clear injunction to the contrary, and landlords can safely advise the giving of NTQ in relationship breakdown situations. This will continue to be the case under the Family Law Act 1996 as it was under the previous legislation.

At the time of the Court of Appeal decision in the above case it was considered that where an occupation order (see above) is in force *any* disposition of the dwelling by the respondent to such an order would not only be a breach of the order but would be ineffective, and furthermore where an injunction is obtained against the respondent, and this is known to the landlord, neither the respondent nor the landlord can rely on any NTQ. In view of the doubts expressed by the House of Lords, however, this argument cannot now be relied on. This conclusion is given support by

14 [1996] QB 13, [1996] 1 All ER 724, CA.
15 [1997] 1 All ER 929, [1997] 1 WLR 459, HL.

Newlon Housing Trust v Alsulaimen[16]. Here Mr and Mrs A had a flat owned by Newlon Housing Trust. In April 1995 Mrs A left Mr A and on 1 November 1995 she gave NHT NTQ to expire on 4 December 1995 – that effectively brought the tenancy to an end. Mr A stayed on and on 28 March 1996 NHT sought possession. Mr A tried to have the possession proceedings adjourned on the basis that he wished to make an application under section 24 of the Matrimonial Causes Act 1973 for a property adjustment order transferring the property into his sole name. Whether this could be done reached the House of Lords. Lord Hoffmann, giving the principal judgement, held that the joint tenancy had been terminated six months before Mr A had sought to make his application. However, could that tenancy be renewed by the application? Lord Hoffman argued that in English law rights of property in land are four dimensional, ie they are defined not just in three dimensions by reference to an area of land, but in a fourth ie by reference to the time for which they endure. Under the *Monk* principle where one joint tenant gives notice to quit that is an indication that he/she is not willing to consent to the continuation of the tenancy beyond the date at which it would otherwise expire. On the effluxion of that notice the property right ceases to exist and can not be revived and transferred. Mr A therefore had no answer to the possession order.

One question remaining open is whether an order under section 37 of the Matrimonial Causes Act 1973 – which is, of course, only available to married persons – could be used to restrain a *proposed* intention by one joint tenant to serve NTQ, on the basis that that amounts to 'dealing with' the tenancy which is then still in being. A partial answer was given in *Bater v Bater* [17]. Here the Court of Appeal held that no order can be made under section 37(2)(b) of the 1973 Act to set aside a unilateral notice terminating a joint tenancy held by a couple otherwise engaged in matrimonial proceedings as such a notice is *not* a 'disposition of property' within the statutory provisions. *However*, Thorpe LJ considered that under section 37(2)(a) the Court does have power to restrain a unilateral notice as that in 'otherwise [dealing] with any property', and can thus protect the claims of the other tenant until the matter can be sorted out by the court. Alternatively he thought the court has an inherent power to control acts or omissions by either spouse *after* or *immediately before* the issue of divorce proceedings if such acts, etc, could harass or molest the other party or adversely affect a child's welfare, or which could affect the power of the court to distribute assets to protect a child's welfare and to protect a financially dependent applicant. Family law practitioners should thus seek to protect their clients against unilateral termination by seeking an undertaking from the other side

16   [1999] 1 AC 313, [1998] 4 All ER 1, HL.
17   [1999] 4 All ER 944.

not to terminate, and that could then be notified to the landlord – this could be reinforced by an injunction if necessary. He further considered that a similar power applies to cohabitants who have children under the Children Act 1989. The other members of the court gave no opinion on this point.

There is nothing to prevent the tenant who gives notice to quit from being given a new sole tenancy of the former joint home, or another property. Nor is there anything to prevent the other joint tenant from being given a new tenancy.

Though landlords cannot prevent tenants from availing themselves of the principle in *Monk*, to accept unilateral notice to quit without giving warning to the other tenant may amount to maladministration.

Marital disputes may also have consequences for other proceedings between landlord and tenant.

In *Wandsworth London Borough Council v Fadayomi*[18] a husband and wife lived in a council flat which was in the husband's name. They lived there with their two children. The marriage broke down and divorce proceedings started. Before their conclusion, the council sought possession under Ground 10, Part II, Schedule 2 of the Housing Act 1985. The court had to decide whether suitable accommodation within para 1, Part IV, Schedule 2 of the 1985 Act would be available for the husband and his family if possession were granted. The wife wished to be joined as a party to the proceedings, but the county court registrar refused this. The wife appealed on the ground that, because of the divorce proceedings, 'suitable accommodation' in the context meant separate suitable accommodation for her and her children. The Court of Appeal considered every member of a tenant's family living in premises subject to possession proceedings has a potential interest in those proceedings. They may wish, for example, to object to alternative accommodation offered. In such circumstances it is appropriate to join them as defendants to the proceedings. In the present case the factors to be established before an order for possession could be made had not been established and the order would be set aside.

There may be further consequences also. Thus in *Osei-Bonsu v Wandsworth London Borough Council*[19] a local authority had granted a joint secure tenancy of a dwelling to a married couple in 1989. One year later the wife and their children left an account of the husband's alleged violence, seeking various orders against him, including one requiring him to leave the dwelling. He failed to comply and the wife commenced committal proceedings for contempt of the court's order. At that point the husband left, handing over his keys to his wife's solicitors and so no committal order was actually sought. The wife's solicitors returned the set of keys to the local authority,

18   [1987] 3 All ER 474, [1987] 1 WLR 1473.
19   [1999] 1 All ER 265, [1999] 1 WLR 1011, CA.

but the husband refused to surrender his tenancy. The local authority secured the dwelling against intruders and began to transfer the wife to other accommodation, and she served a notice to quit which was, however, of less than the 28 days required by both the tenancy agreement and section 5(1)(b) of the Protection from Eviction Act 1977. The local authority, however, mistakenly treated the notice as valid and accepted it, and in due course they formally repossessed the former matrimonial home. The husband then requested readmission to the dwelling but was refused as the property was proposed for reletting to another person. The husband commenced proceedings alleging he was still joint tenant of the dwelling, during the course of which the authority caused the wife to second notice to quit which gave the full 28 days' notice.

The Court of Appeal held that, even though the authority had acted under a mistake of law in accepting the wife's first notice to quit, nevertheless they had committed a wrong under section 27(8)(a) of the Housing Act 1988 in that they had unlawfully deprived the husband as a residential occupier of his occupation of the premises. Furthermore they could not in this case rely on a 'reasonable cause to believe defence' on the basis of the argument that they believed he had ceased to occupy the premises in question at the relevant time. They could not show that their belief was 'reasonable', for there were alternative court procedures open to them to gain possession of the dwelling, or a declaration as to the exact legal position which they could have employed. In such a case a tenant is entitled to one of two remedies, either the award of a declaration of a continuing right to possess the property in question, or an award of damages under the 1988 Act. The tenant cannot receive both awards and must elect which is wanted at the time of trial. Furthermore there is no additional right to damages at common law.

The need to maintain scrupulous operating procedures in such circumstances cannot be over stressed, especially in view of the fact that in the foregoing case the local authority had to pay £30,000 in damages.[20]

This is further emphasised by *R v London Borough of Hammersmith and Fulham, ex p Quigley*.[1] Here a man had been granted a tenancy of a property where he lived for about a year with his children. He then went abroad and Ms Quigley, apparently his estranged partner, moved into the property and cared for the children. The authority commenced possession proceedings, and subsequently claimed the tenancy had been in any case abandoned. The decision to seek possession was questioned on judicial review on the basis that the authority had failed to take into account the possibility of an assignment of the tenancy to the applicant.

---

20 See *Sanctuary Housing Association v Campbell* [1999] 3 All ER 460, [1999] 1 WLR 1279, CA on the much weaker position of a spouse who is not the tenant where the one who is gives notice.

1   (1999) Housing Law Monitor (May) p 8.

The deeds of release issue

What of a situation in which, without serving NTQ in due form, one joint tenant makes a deed of release to the other and that other then continues in occupation paying rent? This was the circumstance in *Burton v Camden London Borough Council*[2] . Here two women, B and H, took a joint weekly tenancy of a council flat in February 1994. In July 1996 B informed the housing department H had signed a deed of release of the tenancy to B and planned to leave. She also applied for housing benefit to cover the entire amount of the rent, and for a new sole tenancy of the property. Camden refused this, and further argued the deed of release had no effect on the joint tenancy, nor was an increase in housing benefit granted. This led to B falling into arrears and Camden sought possession of the property, a response to which she sought a declaration that she was the sole tenant of the flat. The Court of Appeal, relying on section 36(2) of the Law of Property Act 1925, argued that the common law rule that one tenant can release his/her interest to the other was effective in the present case. H had extinguished her interest and the secure periodic tenancy vested in B. It was further argued that in relation to periodic tenancies where there is a deed of release which vests the tenancy in one for no matter how short a time, if the landlord then renews the tenancy – which, of course, can arise by the landlord's conduct – the remaining former joint tenant becomes the sole tenant and the departing person is no longer liable for any rent. There could appear to be little a landlord can do in such circumstances. Acceptance of rent following notice of the deed of release is sufficient conduct to create a new tenancy on the foregoing facts, and if that rent is met in any case in whole or part by housing benefit how can the landlord not accept it? It might be possible to respond to notice of a deed of release by writing to the remaining tenant in terms that no new tenancy is being created and that any payments of rent made will be treated as referring solely to the joint tenancy which is kept in being under section 81 of the Housing Act 1985 by the continued occupation of the dwelling by the remaining tenant.

Further powers for social landlords

Section 145 of the Housing Act 1996 introduced a new ground for possession of a secure tenancy, Ground 2A, in Schedule 2 of the Housing Act 1985. This provides that where a dwelling was occupied (alone or with others) by a married *or* cohabiting couple *and*:
• one/both of them are tenants of the dwelling;

2   [1998] 3 FCR 254, CA.

- one has left because of violence or threats of violence by the other to him/her *or to a member of the family of the partner who has left* who was residing with that person immediately before he/she left, *and*
- the court is satisfied the person who has left is unlikely to return,

the landlord may seek possession.

This is a new ground for possession on grounds of domestic violence. There is in the legislation no requirement to show domestic violence *and* consequent underoccupation. The ground *does* not apply as between same-sex couples, nor where it is violence *from* a child which forces parents to leave a property. The landlord does have to show, however, that:

- the dwelling had been a home to the couple in question;
- the one who has left has done so *because* of violence etc, not some other reason;
- the one who has left is unlikely to return.

It should be noted that the violence (actual or threatened) could be directed to a member of the family of the one who has left – this includes that person's parents, grandparents, children, grandchildren, siblings, uncles, aunts, nephews, nieces, treating relationships by marriage as by blood, half blood as full blood, stepchildren as children and illegitimate children as legitimate (see section 113 of the Housing Act 1985). Where the landlord relies on Ground 2A and the partner who has left is not a tenant or a joint tenant, the landlord must serve a copy of the notice on that partner, or show the taking of 'all reasonable steps' to do so (see section 83A(3) Housing Act 1985 as inserted). The court may, however, dispense with this requirement where:

(a)   the landlord has also relied on Ground 2 (Nuisance) *and*
(b)   it is just and equitable to do so.

The reason for this requirement appears to be that the partner who has left should be given warning of possession proceedings so that he/she may make an application under the Family Law Act 1996 for appropriate occupation/transfer orders in time to forestall the loss of the tenancy.

Section 149 of the 1996 Act also inserts a similar ground (14A) into Schedule 2 of the Housing Act 1988 in respect of assured tenancies. A new section 8A is also added to the 1988 Act to provide that where the landlord relies on 14A to obtain possession of an assured tenancy and the partner who has left the dwelling is *not* a tenant of that dwelling, the court may not entertain proceedings for possession *unless* the landlord has served on the partner who has left a copy of the notice of possession procedures, or has taken all reasonable steps to serve a copy of the notice on that person, or the court considers it just and equitable to dispense with the requirements of such a notice.

This new ground of possession for assured tenancies is available to charitable housing trusts, and registered social landlords.

The housing consequences of relationship breakdown.

In the late 1970s and into the 1980s orthodox wisdom on rehousing following relationship breakdown was contained in the HSAG's *The Housing of One-Parent Families*.

(1) Authorities should remember that on the break-up of marriage two tenancies may be needed rather than one. This 'two for one' element should be remembered in computing future housing needs.

(2) Where a man is living in the former matrimonial home with a woman who is not his wife, following the breakdown of marriage, and the court makes an order against him in respect of that home, eviction leads to an increase in the number of homeless persons.

(3) Where the husband has developed no new relationship and is alone following marital breakdown, the authority should attempt to rehouse him bearing in mind the following factors:

   (a) will the man be living near enough his children to be able to see them;

   (b) will he need to be able to have them to stay;

   (c) is he expecting to remarry;

   (d) is he emotionally upset and unable to cope with eviction on top of losing his wife and children?

The general tenor of the HSAG's findings was that, wherever possible, housing should be provided for parties leaving the matrimonial home.

After marital break-ups where there are children the parent with whom they live will face other problems, in particular those of a financial nature. The HSAG also made recommendations with regard to local authority housing practices in relation to such one-parent families.

(1) The best policy, would be to house one-parent families in ordinary family housing in a mixed development, as such accommodation accords with their needs and helps prevent social stigmatism.

(2) Even where both former partners have been responsible for rent arrears, these may have arisen during a period of stress. Authorities should make arrangements for gradual repayment of arrears, but should not otherwise penalise the parties.

(3) Liaison between housing and social service departments is essential in order to provide all-round support for the one parent family. Though this is difficult where services are administered by different tiers of the local government system, such co-operation is essential if financial and emotional distress amongst one-parent families is to be reduced.

(4) A wife who retains, or is granted possession of, the former matrimonial home may not wish to stay there. Requests for transfers to housing closer to relatives, schools, places of work or nursery facilities, or to the area of another authority, should be treated sympathetically. A

transfer request should not be made conditional on a woman paying off arrears of rent for which her husband was solely responsible. Authorities should be prepared to make rapid housing exchanges in the case of any woman who fears violence from her former husband. Similar conclusions were reached in the Finer Report, Cmnd 5629.

The disposal of more than 1.5 million public sector dwellings under RTB and other disposals since 1979 has done much to deprive social landlords of the stock to meet demand for housing consequent on relationship breakdown. The dearth of appropriate rehousing properties is a problem compounded by the complexity of the legal issues involved, already examined above, and the lack of a clearly articulated central policy on family housing matters.

The issue of housing and relationship breakdown falls between departmental boundaries. Environment ministers regard the matter as one for the Lord Chancellor's department to deal with via matrimonial law. The Lord Chancellor tends to regard it as an issue in housing law. However, ministers are not prepared to make changes in the law simply to deal with a problem faced by social landlords, though they have at least in the Family Law Act 1996 taken some steps to harmonise the position of married couples and cohabitants.

The result of this dislocation between housing and matrimonial law is that housing and legal practitioners have had to 'cobble together' such solutions as they can. In this context the findings of Kay, A, Legg, C, and Foot, J, in *The 1980 Tenants' Rights in Practice* are of great interest.

Their report indicated only 20% of 140 responding authorities would rehouse a partner from a broken marriage who did not have custody of children and who did not otherwise qualify as a homeless person. This fell to 1% in relation to rehousing a childless former cohabitee. Where no children were involved, 85% of authorities would not rehouse both former marriage partners and 87% would not aid former cohabitees. Some authorities required legal evidence of separation or marriage breakdown. 34% of authorities surveyed required settlement of a divorce and associated property issues before a woman could obtain a tenancy. The concept of exclusive custody is now, of course, redundant following the Children Act 1989. Under legislation the paramount consideration is the child's welfare, while the basic notion is that parental responsibility for a child is not to be foregone, but is joint between a child's parents. The court may, however, make 'residence orders' which, for the time being, fix with whom a child is to live.

Women often have to show they have taken action under matrimonial legislation before they can receive aid from social landlords. The policies of some authorities in particular have been punitive against women and frequently have led to inappropriate demands for court orders. Women have had to occupy unsuitable temporary accommodation during lengthy court proceedings while authorities dealt with the issue of housing.

Authorities who have required tenants with broken relationships to take particular courses of legal action as pre-conditions to obtaining a tenancy, have sometimes been found guilty of maladministration. Tenants should not be required to regulate their private lives to suit the administrative convenience of landlords. If the law does not require the taking of a particular step, then neither should an authority, a practice that was, condemned in *R v Ealing London Borough Council, ex p Sidhu*[3].

Some authorities have attempted to have a pro-active role in regulating domestic violence. Kay, Legg and Foot discovered a number of authorities had imposed tenancy obligations dealing with and prohibiting actual or threatened domestic violence. Breach of such a condition could lead to possession proceedings being taken. The report, however, could give no instance of such a clause being tested in court. A court might require a considerable amount of proof of violence before accepting it would be reasonable to allow an authority to obtain possession under such a clause.

Otherwise, there is a considerable diversity of practice in relationship breakdown cases between authorities. This is further highlighted by Frances Logan's 1986 study *Homelessness and Relationship Breakdown*. One authority had a detailed written policy on relationship breakdown and housing which in part resulted from external pressure from a housing aid centre. The policy included rehousing both partners on breakdown. Another authority did not rehouse both partners because this would be at the expense of other priority groups. Instead there was an internal appeal system against housing decisions in relationship breakdown cases, but this did not appear to have been very well publicised. One authority with a policy of rehousing both partners had subsequently extended it to cover all cohabitees, couples in same-sex relationships and those living as a unit through other family ties, such as aunt and niece, for example. However, officers of that authority were concerned that implementing such a liberal policy would become increasingly difficult as housing resources became more limited.

Kay, Legg and Foot further discovered liberal policies on paper may not work in practice unless staff are adequately trained in applying the policies and tenants are informed of them. In one case an authority rehoused a woman's ex-partner close to her. She then suffered violence and the authority was found guilty of maladministration.

Some authorities have taken a much more resistant line in assisting those who lack accommodation following relationship breakdown. This is a consequence of the increasing use of the homelessness provisions as a device to ration the supply of housing. Women have been refused rehousing or assistance if they have an interest in their current home, or where the authority have instructed them to resort to their rights under matrimonial law. In some cases an offer of rehousing may not be made to a woman unless

---

3   (1982) 80 LGR 534, see further, Hughes, D, and Jones, SR [1979] JSWL 273.

she first obtains an order against the man who is abusing her. In other cases a woman forced from her home by violence may be adjudged intentionally homeless unless she obtains an order.

The general view, however, is that such orders should normally be used as temporary expedients. Their use is drastic and not routine, only to be used in emergencies. The court may be unwilling to exclude a violent man from the former home where the effect is to place the woman in the one spot where he knows she will be, thus making her particularly vulnerable. It may be unreasonable to expect a woman to stay in a dwelling in relation to which she has little chance of obtaining an order capable of giving her real and lasting peace and security.

McCarthy and Simpson's 1991 study *Issues in Post Divorce Housing* also cast light on the practice of authorities in discharging functions following homelessness relationship breakdown, and the responses of applicants in such situations. A number of applicants expressed dissatisfaction with accommodation offered by authorities. Women particularly voiced complaints over accommodation, especially where they feared for its effects on their children because of perceptions of high crime, weak parental discipline, poor schools, etc, in the area. There could also be adverse reactions to moving into accommodation which, though reasonable and suitable from a legal point of view, is dirty, ill-decorated and may be lacking in repair.

Men homeless following relationship breakdown also reported that, where they qualified for accommodation, properties offered were frequently of poor quality. This exacerbated already bruised feelings where a man claims he was the 'innocent' party in the divorce. The allocation of single person's accommodation in a stigmatised area of a district can affect the viability of a divorced man's access to his children.

Future argument on how social landlords may best respond to relationship breakdown may polarise. McCarthy and Simpson argued current approaches are fixated with a 'special needs' view of issues, seeing the single parent family as a group at whom particular resources are targetted, very often as a type of safety net to ensure recipients of benefits do not fall too far into poverty. They argued that children of divorced parents should have equivalent 'life chances' to their contemporaries whose parents do not divorce. (By analogy the argument can be extended to those whose parents never married in the first place.) McCarthy and Simpson's justification was that children are society's future, and they pointed to the enormously important, but generally hidden, role of women in producing this 'human capital' by their work in the home as mothers. The provision of a range of decent affordable accommodation, some of it by social landlords, to meet the needs of a society where relationship breakdown is increasingly common is thus justifiable, for it especially recognises the role of female parents in producing and caring for the next generation of economically active people.

Obviously, housing provision by itself is not enough. It must be accompanied by appropriate welfare and employment benefits. There would be considerable costs incurred in realising McCarthy and Simpson's proposals. Against McCarthy and Simpson's vision, however, is ranged a powerful and emotional, some would say emotive, argument that the family as an institution needs to be preserved and rejuvenated, and that individuals should learn that their actions have consequences for which they must take some responsibility. This latter argument remains attractive to many in the Conservative Party; it is not without Labour supporters. The arguments cut across races, sexes and social classes. There are many who view with dismay what is perceived as a decline in order in many inner urban areas, who find it disturbing that many young men grow up with no model of responsible male parenthood, and who do not find it desirable that society should encourage beliefs that relationship breakdown carries with it no adverse consequences, and that standards of living and lifestyles are not affected by it.

The long term outcome of this matter is beyond prediction. In the short term those who provide social housing must continue to palliate problems, and look to themselves for solutions. They need to establish policies on relationship breakdown and housing. Policies, should wherever possible, include the following principles:

(1) where resources permit both parties to relationship breakdown should be rehoused, either in the same district or by co-operation with other districts, in areas sufficiently separate to prevent recurrent incidents of violence;

(2) prohibitions on domestic violence should be included in tenancy agreements;

(3) women who are forced from their homes by violence should not automatically be regarded as intentionally homeless if they do not rely on domestic remedies;

(4) sympathetic handling is needed of those made homeless as a consequence of relationship breakdown;

(5) staff must receive appropriate training to implement policy efficiently and sensitively; this includes training in the legal issues, and appointment of specialist officers to ensure relationship breakdowns are appropriately dealt with;

(6) good practice requires that all homes known to be subject to matrimonial disputes should be recorded as such so that inappropriate action with regard to the property rights of the parties is not taken inadvertently;

(7) parties should not be required to take steps not legally required simply to suit the administrative convenience of landlords;

(8)   landlords' policies must be clearly spelt out to tenants and potential tenants;

(9)   in the provision of accommodation authorities must not discriminate on ground of race or sex,[4] neither may an authority plead impecuniousity as a reason for not fulfilling a duty to accommodate under homelessness powers.[5]

None of the foregoing will remove the need for other national legal and policy changes, but collectively they may alleviate stress locally.

In the meantime as an example of the problems outlined above consider *Jones v Jones*[6]. Mr J and Mrs J were both aged 52, without children and on income support. They were married for 15 months and lived in a council flat. This flat had been modified for a person under disability, and this suited Mr J as he had emphysema and a heart condition. Mrs J applied for a divorce, and under the then current legislation the initial order was that the flat should be transferred to her on the basis that Mr J's medical condition meant that he would in any case get priority rehousing treatment. The issue eventually reached the Court of Appeal. Phillips LJ reviewed the various arguments that had been in issue on the case: Mr J's medical condition; the fact that Mr J had been a tenant for 20 years whereas Mrs J was quite new to a council tenancy; public policy argues that it was wrong to rely on assumptions Mr J would be rehoused if dispossessed while Mrs J would not. He concluded in such circumstances the court must be guided by the effect of the decision on those who will be directly affected by it. This involves taking into account the fate of the dispossessed person, and local housing policy. Courts must therefore at least be aware of the way in which social landlords perform their functions, and this will have implications for the decisions of courts. In the present case the balance came down in favour of allowing Mr J to stay where he was, because further evidence indicated Mrs J could obtain finance to acquire accommodation in the private sector. It would surely have been perverse to dispossess Mr J simply because of his condition, on the basis that as a homeless person he would be better treated than his wife could have been.

Succession rights

In housing terms death is not 'the only true unraveller'; legal personality survives physical extinction: both secure and assured tenancies are 'property' which can descend to those related to a deceased tenant, while in some cases an inter vivos transfer is possible.

4   *R v Tower Hamlets London Borough Council, ex p Commission for Racial Equality* (1991) Legal Action, (June) p 16.
5   *R v Haringey London Borough Council, ex p Garner* (1991) Legal Action, (September) p 16.
6   [1997] Fam 59, [1997] 2 WLR 373, CA.

Secure tenancies

A secure periodic tenancy, or a secure fixed term tenancy granted after 5 November 1982, is not capable under section 91 of the 1985 Act, as amended, of being assigned save in three situations;

(1) under the 'right to exchange' provided by section 92 of the Housing Act 1985, see Chapter 3;

(2) pursuant to an order made under section 24 of the Matrimonial Causes Act 1973 (property adjustment), section 17(1) of the Matrimonial and Family Proceedings Act 1984 (overseas divorces), Schedule 1, paragraph 1 of the Children Act 1989 (financial relief against parents);

(3) where the assignment is to a person who would be qualified to succeed if the tenant had died immediately before the assignment. See section 91 of the 1985 Act.

Note that the 1973, 1984 and 1989 Acts mentioned above all permit the court to order the transfer of property owned by a parent/spouse to a minor child. Such a child would appear to gain security of tenure.[7]

It is possible for a secure tenant to pass on during life his/her home to someone otherwise qualified to succeed after the tenant's death, despite prohibition on assignment in the tenancy,[8] though such an assignment might give rise to a possession action for breach of tenancy condition. For example, an elderly tenant could transfer to a single daughter who has lived with him all her life in the house in question, the secure tenancy of a three bedroom council house. The new tenant could not then be subject to possession proceedings on grounds of under occupation following the former tenant's death; the tenancy would exist by way of assignment and not by way of succession.

Where an assignment under the 1973 Act takes place on divorce problems can arise as to liability for arrears of rent. In *Notting Hill Housing Trust v Rakey Jones*[9] following a divorce the former wife became the tenant of a flat of which her ex husband had been the tenant, and *subsequently agreed* to pay off his accumulated arrears week by week. She then failed in this obligation and possession was sought. The Court of Appeal, however, held that in such a case the wife *could not be said to 'inherit' the husband's liabilities*. Moreover, the tenancy had been acquired *before* she agreed to pay off the arrears so in no sense could the assignment count as consideration for the subsequent agreement. Thus the claim for possession failed. In such cases may landlords obtain an undertaking from the incoming tenant that he/she will be responsible for the outgoing tenant's arrears *before* the tenancy is transferred? This seems to happen from time to time informally

---

7   *Kingston upon Thames Borough Council v Prince* [1999] 1 FLR 593, CA.

8   *Peabody Donation Fund (Governors) v Higgins* [1983] 3 All ER 122, [1983] 1 WLR 1091.

9   (1999) Housing Law Monitor (February) p 8.

in practice, but its legality is open to question. So far as registered social landlords are concerned 'their' housing ombudsman regards such a practice as amounting to a demand for an illegal premium. In such circumstances of transfer consequent on relationship breakdown it is therefore clearly more desirable for all social landlords that the court must make the transfer under Schedule 7 of the Family Law Act 1996 because then provision may be made to the court for liabilities in respect of past arrears.

There are, however, technical requirements before assignment can be effective. In *Crago v Julian*[10] a married couple occupied a privately rented flat on a weekly tenancy. On divorce the man gave a written undertaking to do everything necessary to effect a transfer of the flat to his wife; in fact he did nothing. The woman continued to pay rent and dealt with the managing agents; they continued to issue new rent books in the husband's name. In 1987 the agents realised the former husband had given up all interest in the property. They refused to accept further rent and in 1988 commenced possession proceedings. The issue was whether the tenancy had been assigned. The Court of Appeal pointed out the creation and assignment of interests in land are governed by section 53(1) (a) of the Law of Property Act 1925 which required transfer in writing. To this there was only one exception, namely under section 54 (1) of the 1925 Act under which a lease not exceeding three years taking effect in possession at full market rent may be created by spoken words. But the assignment of any lease requires the written form of deed. As no such deed had been used in the present case no assignment had taken place.

The rule is the same in the social rented sector, see *London Borough of Croydon v Buston and Triance*[11] – a deed is required for an effective assignment of a secure tenancy. Deeds must comply with the requirements of the Law of Property (Miscellaneous Provisions) Act 1989 section 1. A deed need not be sealed, but must be: in documentary form; signed and witnessed as a deed; intended to be a deed, and delivered as a deed.

Note that where a fixed term tenancy granted before 5 November 1982 is assigned outside the three cases outlined above, the consequence is that it continues at common law but ceases to be 'secure', nor can it subsequently become 'secure'.

But who are those who are qualified to succeed to a secure tenancy, and how does succession operate ?

Section 89 provides that where a secure periodic tenant dies, and there is a person qualified to succeed (see below) the tenancy vests in that person. Where there is more than one qualified person the successor will be determined by the following rules:

(1) the tenant's spouse has priority.

10 [1992] 1 All ER 744, [1992] 1 WLR 372.
11 (1991) 24 HLR 36, and *London Borough of Camden v Alexandrou* (1997) 30 HLR 534, CA.

(2)   where there are two or more other qualified persons they may agree among themselves who is to succeed, otherwise the landlord selects.

Where there is no qualified successor under section 89(3) and (4), as amended, the tenancy ceases to be secure, save where the case may fall within section 24 of the Matrimonial Causes Act 1973, or Schedule 1, paragraph 1 of the Children Act 1989, or section 17(1) of the Matrimonial and Family Proceedings Act 1984 (overseas divorces) and cannot subsequently become secure. The effect of the provisions are explained in *Wirral Borough Council v Smith*[12]. On the death of a secure tenant, the secure tenancy comes to an end, but a contractual tenancy remains, and to bring that to an end notice to quit (NTQ) in proper form must be served whether by or on the personal representatives (PRs) of the deceased. If there are no PRs the notice should be served on the President of the Family Division at the Royal Courts of Justice.

Where a deceased tenant had a fixed term secure tenancy, the tenancy remains secure under section 90 of the Housing Act 1985 until vested or otherwise disposed of during the administration of the deceased's estate (save where that vesting etc is in pursuance of an order made under section 24 of the Matrimonial Causes Act 1973, or where the vesting etc, is in a person qualified to succeed, or where Schedule 1, paragraph 1 of the Children Act 1989 applies – orders for financial relief against parents – or where section 17(1) of the Matrimonial and Family Proceedings Act 1984 applies) or it is known that on vesting etc the tenancy will not be secure, eg it will vest in a person not qualified to succeed. A fixed term tenancy which ceases to be secure cannot become secure, but, of course, will otherwise continue for its contractual term etc.

Those qualified to succeed are identified by section 87 of the 1985 Act. Such a person is one who:
(1)   occupied the dwelling/house as his/her only or principal home at the time of the tenants' death; and
(2)   is either the spouse of the deceased tenant, or another member of the deceased's family who has resided with the deceased throughout the period of 12 months ending with the deceased's death, save, in either case, where the deceased was him/herself a successor (see further below).

A 'member of the family' is defined by section 113 of the 1985 Act to include those living together as husband and wife, and those who are the parents, grandparents, children, grandchildren, brothers, sisters, uncles, aunts, nephews and nieces of the deceased, treating relationships by marriage as by blood, the half blood as the whole, step-children as children and illegitimate children as legitimate children of their mothers and reputed fathers. There is doubt whether this extends to cover foster children always treated as the deceased's own, as the decision in *Reading Borough*

12 (1982) 262 Estates Gazette 1298.

Council v Ilsley[13] was not followed in *Hereford City Council v O'Callaghan*[14]. The latter, however, was only a county court decision.

A minor may, however, inherit a secure tenancy, though in such cases the minor will hold the equitable estate and will need a trustee to hold the legal estate until he/she is 18. This is in line with the practice of authorities, and indeed other registered social landlords, in granting tenancies to those under 18.[15] Note, however, the nature of the residence requirement. In *Waltham Forest London Borough Council v Thomas*[16], the defendant lived with his half brother for two and half years in property owned by the authority of which the brother was a secure tenant. On 11 April 1988 they moved to another council house, of which the brother also became a secure tenant. On 21 April the brother died. The defendant claimed to succeed to his brother's tenancy under section 87 of the Act of 1985. The plaintiffs disputed the claim on the ground that the defendant did not reside with his deceased brother in the same premises throughout the requisite 12 month-period. The House of Lords held that section 87 of the 1985 Act required the successor to a tenancy should have resided with the tenant during the period of 12 months ending with the tenant's death, but did not require the residence to have taken place for the whole of that period in the premises to which succession was claimed: and, accordingly, the defendant was entitled to succeed.

In this connection 'residence' connotes making one's home with the deceased. Even where a familial relationship exists, simply for a person to move in with a secure tenant does not automatically make that person a joint tenant with the original tenant, see *Hamilton District Council v Lennon*[17].

The definition of 'family' in section 113 of the 1985 Act appears not to extend to lesbian/gay relationships nor to an older man/woman living with a younger man/woman unless cohabitation exists between them: see *Harrogate Borough Council v Simpson.*[18] In the House of Lords' decision in *Fitzpatrick v Sterling Housing Association Ltd*[19] it was held that a homosexual partner could succeed on the death of a Rent Act protected tenant as a member of that deceased person's family. That is not to say that the position of same-sex relationship couples has been generally equated in law with spouses. Furthermore within the context of Fitzgerald type situations the would-be successor still has to prove a long-term relationship with the deceased, a passing affair is not enough, even if intimate, and mere

---

13 [1981] CLY 1323.
14 [1996] CLY 3831.
15 *Kingston upon Thames Borough Council v Prince* [1999] 1 FLR 593, CA, following *Portman Registrars and Nominees v Mohammed Latif* [1987] CLY 2239 on similar provisions under the Rent Acts.
16 [1992] 2 AC 198, [1992] 3 All ER 244.
17 1990 SLT 533.
18 (1986) 17 HLR 205.
19 [1999] 4 All ER 705, [1999] 3 WLR 1113.

cohabitation between friends in the sense of house sharing as a matter of convenience will not do either. In addition the minimum period of residence under the Rent Act has also to be satisfied. However, the rule in the public sector may not have changed. This is because under section 87 of the 1985 Act a person may succeed if he/ she is a member of the deceased's family, but 'family' is then defined by section 113 in highly specific terms, including persons who live together as husband and wife and various relationships by blood and affinity. Such an exhaustive list is not found in the Rent Act 1977 which is why the House of Lords in *Fitzpatrick* were able to come to the decision they reached. An aching gap may thus open up between the two sectors unless it is possible to argue that section 113 should not be read preclusively on the *expressio unius est exclusio alterius* basis, but only as a set of examples. This is unlikely, given the fact that the House of Lords confined their remarks very much to the special facts before them. In the light also of the impending human rights legislation there is a need for the law to be re-thought and clarified.

Note, however, Annex C of the Code of Guidance on Parts VI and VII of the Housing Act 1996 advising authorities to grant joint tenancies where members of a household have a long-term commitment, including sharing as friends or carers. In addition where a sole tenant dies and leaves behind someone not qualified to succeed but who has lived with the tenant for at least a year the normal practice should be to grant that person a tenancy of the dwelling or of suitable alternative accommodation.

With regard to secure tenancies there may be only one succession, and section 88 (1)–(3) of the 1985 Act provides a tenant shall be deemed to be a successor, inter alia, where:

(1) the tenancy vested by virtue of section 89;
(2) the tenancy was joint but has become sole;
(3) the tenancy vested on the death of the previous tenant;
(4) the tenancy was assigned, save that a tenant who was an assignee under section 24 of the Matrimonial Causes Act 1973 is a deemed successor only if the assignor was also a successor, and similarly a person who is a tenant by way of exchange under the right to exchange (see section 92 of the 1985 Act) is similarly a successor only if he/she was a successor in relation to the tenancy which he/she assigned under the exchange provisions.

Note also section 88(4) of the 1985 Act which provides that where within six months of the coming to an end of a secure periodic tenancy the tenant becomes possessed of another periodic secure tenancy, and the tenant was a successor under the former tenancy, and under the current tenancy either the dwelling house or the landlord, or both, are the same as before, the tenant is a deemed successor unless the tenancy provides otherwise.

It is not hard to mistake the effect of the foregoing rules as the cases show. In *Epping Forest District Council v Pomphrett and Pomphrett*[20], in

20 (1990) 22 HLR 475.

1948 Mr Pomphrett was granted a tenancy of a council house. In 1978 he died intestate and no letters of administration were taken out. The authority granted the tenancy to his widow in her name. She died intestate in 1985. No letters of administration were taken out, and her children applied to take over the tenancy. The authority claimed a single succession had already taken place. The court held that on Mr Pomphrett's death his tenancy had vested in the President of the Family Division who had no power to assign or vest it in someone else. When Mrs Pomphrett was allowed to stay on a new tenancy was created and she became the secure tenant when the Housing Act came into force. Her children were entitled to succeed to her tenancy. Likewise note *Bassetlaw District Council v Renshaw*[1] . Mr and Mrs Renshaw were joint tenants of a council house. Mr Renshaw terminated the joint tenancy and thereafter the authority granted a new sole tenancy to Mrs Renshaw. She lived in the house with her son and some years later died. The son claimed successfully to be a successor.

Succession to introductory tenancies

Where the tenant under an introductory tenancy (see further Chapter Three) dies there may be a succession under section 133 of the Housing Act 1996, where there is a person qualified to succeed, and if there is more than one of the tenant's spouse is to be preferred as successor, or, where there is no spouse, those qualified may agree amongst themselves, and if they fail to do so the landlord is to determine the succession. Where there is no person qualified to succeed the tenancy ceases to be 'introductory' once vested in the course of administration of the estate (unless the vesting falls within section 24 of the Matrimonial Causes Act 1973, section 17(1) of the Matrimonial and Family Proceedings Act 1984, or Schedule 1, paragraph 1 of the Children Act 1989). A person is qualified to succeed under section 131 where he/she occupied the dwelling house as his/her only or principal home at the time of the tenant's death and is either the tenant's spouse, or another member of the tenant's family who resided with the tenant throughout the period of twelve months ending with the tenant's death, unless the tenant was already a successor as defined in section 132. In this respect the rules for introductory tenancies mirror those for secure tenancies, see above. Similarly under section 134 an introductory tenancy is generally incapable of being assigned save under the matrimonial jurisdiction or that relating to children, or where the assignment is to a person otherwise qualified to succeed.

The Family Law Act 1996 makes no mention in Schedule 7 (transfer of tenancies) of introductory tenancies.

1   [1992] 1 All ER 925, CA.

Assured tenancies

Restrictions on assignment of assured tenancies exist under section 15 (1) of the Housing Act 1988. It is an implied term of every periodic assured tenancy that, save with the landlord's consent, the tenant may not assign the tenancy in whole or in part, nor sublet or part with possession of the whole or any part of the dwelling house. Nor is there any requirement that the landlord must not unreasonably refuse consent to a request to assign. This implied term is superseded under section 15 (3) if there is a specific provision dealing with the position concerning assignments, sub-letting, etc, and where a premium is required to be paid on the grant or renewal of the tenancy the implied restriction does not apply. Guidance issued by the Housing Corporation indicates that for registered social landlords assignment should only be permitted where required by an order of the court, or in execution of permitted contractual rights to exchange with other tenants of registered social landlords or authorities.

Section 17 of the 1988 Act provides for succession to an assured periodic tenancy by a spouse, which term includes a person living with the deceased tenant as his/her husband/wife, see section 17 (4). The conditions for succession are that immediately before the death of the sole assured tenant the spouse was occupying the dwelling as his/her only or principal home, and the deceased must not have been a successor, ie, under section 17 (2) someone in whom the tenancy had previously vested by virtue of section 17, or someone who became a sole tenant of the dwelling by survivorship following the death of the other joint tenant. If on the death, by virtue of section 17 (4), there is more than one person qualified to succeed as a spouse under the foregoing provisions, section 17 (5) states they may choose who is to be treated as the spouse; in default the county court shall decide.

Housing associations and other registered social landlords and succession

For association tenants having secure tenancies on 15 January 1989, the position concerning succession is as for authority tenancies. For other tenants the position is 'governed' by the guidance issued by the Housing Corporation as 'The Tenants' Guarantee' under section 36A of the Housing Associations Act 1985, and, to a lesser degree, the National Federation of Housing Association's (NATFED) model tenancy agreement annexed to the original version of the section 36A 'guarantee'. The Housing Corporation first issued its guidance as Housing Corporation Circular No 43/88; this was revised and reissued in 1991 as HC Circular 29/91. This was further reissued as HC Circular 36/94 and kept in force by Circular R3-36/96 after the Housing Act 1996.

As currently issued the 'guarantee' counsels registered social landlords to consider, in addition to the right of succession for spouses (including cohabitants) who immediately before the death of the relevant tenant were occupying the dwelling in question as their only or principal homes, whether they wish to grant, by contract, rights of succession to members of a tenant's family *or* to the same sex-partner of a deceased tenant who have been living with that tenant for the year before the tenant's death, or who have been looking after the tenant, or who have accepted responsibility for dependants of the tenant, or who would be made homeless if required to vacate the accommodation. Alternatively the offer of suitable alternative accommodation to people in these situations should be considered.

The guidance further counsels seeking possession against anyone entering a property by bequest from a deceased tenant or on an intestacy where no-one qualified to succeed wishes to assume the tenancy.

The future

The law relating to the housing rights of married and cohabiting couples has to a very considerable extent been harmonised by the Family Law Act 1996. What remains a point of contention is the position of same-sex relationships where currently English Law does not generally recognise the parties as a 'family', thus causing problems of succession where one only is the tenant and that one dies. A number of our partner states in the EC, for example the Netherlands, increasingly recognise as of equal legal validity marriages, registered cohabitations and registered same-sex unions. The UK may voluntarily decide to follow their example; or it may find itself required to do so under EC law. It is at least arguable that the freedom of movement allowed to workers between EC states will lead to couples in same-sex unions moving from states where their relationships are legally recognised and have succession consequences to those where they are not. Such workers might then argue under the EC's anti-discrimination provisions that the rights they enjoy in one member state should be upheld by all others. If that were to be established it would be hard to resist calls for a general recognition of both registered cohabitations and same-sex unions.

Further reading

Austerberry, H and Watson, S *Women on the Margins. A study of single women's housing problems* (The City University, 1983)

Bird, R *Domestic Violence and Protection from Harassment* (Family Law, 1997)

Bradshaw, J and Millar, J *Lone Parent Families in the UK* (HMSO, 1991)

Bull, J *Housing Consequences of Relationship Breakdown* (HMSO, 1993)

DETR *Relationship Breakdown: A Guide for Social Landlords* (HMSO 1999)

Horton, M *Family Homes and Domestic Violence: The New Legislation* (FT Law and Tax, 1996)

HSAG *The Housing of One Parent Families* (The Department of the Environment, 1978)

Hughes, D J and Jones, S R *Bias in the Allocation and Transfer of Local Authority Housing* (1979) Vol 1 *Journal of Social Welfare Law* 273

Kay, A, Legg, C and Foot J *The 1980 Tenants' Rights in Practice* (Housing Research Group, The City University)

Levison, D and Atkins, J *The Key to Equality* (1987, Institute of Housing)

Logan, F *Homelessness and Relationship Breakdown: How the Law and Housing Policy Affects Women* (National Council for One Parent Families, 1986)

McCarthy, P and Simpson, B *Issues in Post Divorce Housing* (1991, Avebury)

Smith, L *Domestic Violence: an overview of the literature* (HMSO, 1989)

Thornton, R 'Homelessness Through Relationship Breakdown: The Local Authorities' Response' (1989) Journal of Social Welfare Law 67

CHAPTER SIX

Homelessness

Historical context

Action on behalf of, or rather against, homeless people has been a feature of English local government since the Elizabethan Poor Law. Up to 1948 the Poor Law authorities attempted to curb homelessness by treating homeless people as an 'undeserving poor' and according to the Victorian Poor Law principle of 'less eligibility' the conditions in the workhouse were made deliberately harsh and degrading. Moreover, people not recognised as local could be ejected from the area under the Vagrancy Acts. These two important principles, of less eligibility and the local connection, figure very prominently in contemporary social policy and law and it is somewhat salutary to see how historically rooted are these themes. In the nineteenth century the number of people affected by Poor Law conditions was very considerable. Virtually everyone at that time lived in uncontrolled privately rented accommodation and eviction and homelessness were prevalent. It is very difficult to get a feel for the scale of the problem but even as late as 1911 a quarter of all single men over the age of 65 were living in casual wards of workhouse infirmaries[1].

Homelessness is thus a centuries-old phenomenon affecting millions of destitute families, but although a common enough experience, homelessness was only recognised officially as a *housing* problem in the Housing (Homeless Persons) Act 1977.

The aftermath of the Second World War marked an important turning point in the treatment of homeless people, as in so many aspects of national

---

1   See further Donnison and Ungerson, *Housing Policy* (Penguin, 1982).

social life. The National Assistance Act 1948 abolished the Poor Law, but continued much of the muddled thinking that characterised that law in failing to see homelessness as a problem in its own right, nor did it create a comprehensive institutional framework to deal with the issue. Section 2(1) of the 1948 Act created the National Assistance Board among whose functions was[2] the provision of reception centres for the unsettled. Responsibility for the *wandering* homeless was entrusted to a *national* authority, while the rest of the homeless came within the care of local authority welfare departments[3] : local *housing* authorities had no real responsibility for the homeless.

Administrative confusion was compounded by lack of resources and use of hostel accommodation, while the law gave rise to particular difficulties. Section 21(1)(b) of the 1948 Act created a statutory duty (since repealed) to provide: 'temporary accommodation for persons who are in urgent need thereof, being need arising in circumstances which could not reasonably have been foreseen or in such other circumstances as the authority may in any particular case determine'. In *Southwark London Borough Council v Williams*[4], it was held that this imposed no enforceable duty on local authorities.

Neither was there guidance about what constituted 'urgent need' or 'unforeseen circumstances' and local authority practice was highly variable, as it has remained to this day. Legal and administrative difficulties became 'confusion worse confounded' following the reorganisation of local government under the Local Government Act 1972. Section 195 and Schedule 23 of that Act converted the duty under section 21(1) of the 1948 Act into a discretion, though reserving power to the Secretary of State to re-impose the duty. The Department of the Environment issued joint circular No 18/74 *Homelessness*[5] . This stated that: 'suitable accommodation for the homeless should in future be undertaken as an integral part of the statutory responsibility of housing authorities ...' However, on 1 February 1974 the Secretary of State for Social Services issued DHSS Local Authority Circular No 13/74. This re-imposed the duty on social services authorities to provide temporary accommodation.

The results were chaotic. The existence of some sort of duty on *social services* authorities encouraged some *housing* authorities to ignore the exhortations of DoE Circular No 18/74. It was obvious urgent changes in the law were necessary, though it was left to a private member, Mr Stephen Ross, to introduce legislation. His Bill, partly drafted by Shelter was also in

---

2   Section 17, National Assistance Act 1948.
3   Section 21(1).
4   [1971] Ch 734, [1971] 2 All ER 175.
5   Department of Health & Social Security (DHSS) Circular 4/74, Welsh Office Circular 34/74.

part based on a draft already prepared by the Department of the Environment and it achieved a measure of all party support in Parliament. Even so the Bill was considerably amended in Parliament, largely as a result of fears of large numbers of homeless people moving themselves around the country with the object of jumping local authority housing queues.

The 1977 Act was codified with the rest of the housing legislation in 1985 and became Part III of the Housing Act 1985. Hardly was the ink dry before amendments were made by the Housing and Planning Act 1986. In November 1989 the Government published a review of the homeless legislation. This document proposed to keep the existing law broadly as it was. Managerial change was urged to make better use of existing housing stock, closer liaison with associations, preventative advice, and encouragement of those willing to provide lodgings. It was, however, recognised that enhanced central guidance was needed to ensure a greater degree of consistency between local authority homelessness practices.

Further legal changes came under the Children Act 1989 and the National Health Service and Community Care Act 1990. The result is that around the main body of the 1985 Act there was further legal provision under:

(1) Section 21(1)(a) of the National Assistance Act 1948 (as amended) *empowering* (and where the Secretary of State for Health directs, *requiring*) local social services authorities to provide residential accommodation for persons aged 18 or more who are in need of care and attention by reason of age, or other circumstances.

(2) Section 67(2) of the National Health Service and Community Care Act 1990 which, from 1 April 1993, under SI 1992/2975 extends the above duty to those in need of care by reason of illness or disability.

(3) Section 20(1) of the Children Act 1989 which requires social service authorities to provide accommodation for children in need within their areas in certain stated circumstances, while other authorities may be *required* to assist in providing accommodation under section 27 of the 1989 Act.

(4) Schedule 5 of the Supplementary Benefits Act 1976 (as substituted by the Social Security Act 1980) which requires the Secretary of State for Social Security to provide and maintain resettlement units at which those without settled ways of life are afforded temporary board and lodging, and under which the Secretary of State may require councils of counties, metropolitan districts and London boroughs to discharge this function.

By the mid 1990s we were thus in a situation comparable to that of 1972-77. Once again there are overlapping jurisdictions, and the potential for particular applicants to be shuttled between local authority departments. Furthermore no less than three Secretaries of State have an interest in homelessness. This, coupled with a continuing lack of resources, is guaranteed to cause confusion – at the very least.

The legal nature of homelessness

The duties originally given to local authorities under the 1977 Act remarked relatively unchanged until 1996, and that became coupled with a somewhat sceptical view of the function of the law, particularly with regard to the official statistics. The statutory definition of homelessness was, and is, essentially a rationing device which balances available supply of council tenancies with judgments about 'priority needs.' As a result, homeless people presenting at different local authorities will be faced with very different receptions depending on the policy stance of the particular authority.

Moreover, the statutory framework with its emphasis on families with children and the elderly not only excludes other groups of people but itself only recognises one form of homelessness. There is an important debate about what precisely constitutes homelessness. Without some consideration of this debate it will be difficult fully to appreciate the nature of the case law which follows. Is a woman having been driven from her marital home by a violent husband and now living in a women's refuge homeless? Is the accommodation provided by the refuge of such a poor standard as to render it uninhabitable? If so, despite the roof over her head, is she homeless? Does other suitable accommodation happen to be available in the area where she resides? Do the housing advisory services know of its existence and if so will they help her approach the hostel managers? Some of these issues have particular relevance for the interpretation and application of the law, but they also shade into other questions of housing administration and the provision of housing services.

The official statistics

The emergence of homelessness as a distinctively *housing* issue was triggered by the revelation of a sharp increase in the number of people living in temporary accommodation, particularly but not exclusively, in London in the early 1960s.

Although the problem has often been associated principally with London all the evidence shows that homelessness affects all authorities' areas, urban and rural. In 1990 nearly 80% of households accepted as homeless were recorded outside London and the place with the highest number of acceptances in relation to total population was Manchester.

In England and Wales homelessness acceptances grew from 53,000 in 1978 to nearly 148,000 in 1990. Taking all local authorities in Britain the figure for 1990 alone was nearly 170,000 involving about half a million people, 50% of whom were dependent children. Over the full decade 1980-1990 well over a million households were accepted by authorities as homeless and the number of acceptances doubled during the 1980s. These statistics referred only to households housed in some way by authorities and it should be noted that only about half those who applied were accepted and that 80% of these were families with children. None of these figures were in any case a rigorous measure of the total problem because the net total comprises the year on year additions to the total less those who move out of temporary accommodation.

The proportion of those families statutorily 'rehoused' but placed in 'temporary accommodation' rose dramatically from under 10,000 per annum in the early 1980s to over 50,000 per annum (140,000 individuals) in the early 1990s, and as the supply of council housing has declined during the decade so the number of those placed in temporary habitations has increased.

Homelessness continued to rise into the 1990's apparently faster in rural than in urban areas.

The current position

In the latter part of the 1990s homelessness acceptances were declining, while the numbers of people in bed and breakfast accommodation declined by 2/3 from 1991 levels. In the year ending September 1994 homelessness acceptances were down 9% on the previous year, 125,640 cases in all, the peak year being 1992. The numbers in temporary accommodation were 49,330, 13% down on the previous year, and the numbers in bed and breakfast were 4,740, 25% down on the previous year. More recent figures continue to show a decline in the number of households *accepted* as homeless. For the 2nd quarter of 1996 the figures for England were 28,160. The figure for the 2nd quarter of 1997 was 24,930, a decline of 11%. In England in the final quarter of 1997 there were 24,810 acceptances, a decline of 7% on the previous year's figures. Even so there were still 44,340 households in temporary accommodation – 4,240 in bed and breakfast, 9,330 in hostels and 30,860 'other' (ie interim housing).

In the 12 months between December 1997 and December 1998 local authorities in England accepted responsibility for accommodating 105,800 households – 26,500 of these were in London. While that was clearly lower than the peak year of 1992 it must still be compared with an acceptance figure of 53,000 for December 1978 to December 1979. The latest (June 1999) figures show a slow continuing decline in the numbers of persons accepted as being eligible, unintentionally homeless and in priority need, and, despite seasonal variations, the numbers are 25% lower than the peak year of 1992. There has been an increase in the number of households receiving bed and breakfast accommodation, or otherwise in hostels, but even so the figures are below the peak levels which in this case were in 1991. Homelessness nevertheless remains a problem, and it must also be remembered that the figures reflect acceptances only of those who apply – there are some, perhaps many, who do not.

The law

As stated above the Housing Act 1985 largely repeated the provisions of the 1977 homelessness legislation, and though a major revision had been expected in 1989, following minor changes in 1986, it was not until 1994 that a harder line on the issue was taken by ministers.

The outcome of the proposals of the Conservative Government was the Housing Act 1996. It was argued that the homelessness route into council accommodation had become a 'fast track' whereby the normal waiting list procedures were being evaded. The 1996 Act took away the priority right to accommodation previously enjoyed and replaced it with a temporary entitlement. It was, however, argued by ministers that during the temporary entitlement period otherwise homeless people, whose names would be placed on the housing register, would qualify for 'ordinary' allocations – but they would have to wait their turn in temporary accommodation. The Blair government, as we shall see later, has 'draw the teeth' of the 1996 Act to a degree by passing delegated legislation ensuring that homelessness persons have to be given 'reasonable preference' in housing allocations. However, the primary right to accommodation has not been reintroduced and seems unlikely to reappear.

The next section considers the definition in law of homelessness and its consequences. Here all references, unless otherwise stated, are to the Housing Act 1996. The legislation does not 'stand alone' and considerable guidance on implementation is given by a Code of Guidance (CoG) under section 182, which requires authorities to 'have regard' to the CoG in the discharge of their functions. A number of issues concerning the CoG are dealt with initially because they bear directly on the interpretation and implementation of the statute. The current version – *Code of Guidance for Local Authorities on the Allocation of Accommodation and Homelessness* – was issued on 12 April 1999, and is accessible via the Internet.

The CoG is *not* law: rather it is advice on how law should be implemented. Indeed if a statement in the CoG contravenes either the wording of legislation, or a judicial decision – whether made before or after the Code's introduction – then to that extent the CoG is unlawful and may not be applied, see *Gillick v West Norfolk and Wisbech Area Health Authority*[6]. The CoG is a relevant factor which has to be taken into account, though it need not be slavishly adhered to and authorities are technically free to depart from it. (On the other hand departure may be good evidence of

6   [1986] AC 112, [1985] 3 All ER 402.

maladministration should a complaint be made to the Commission for Local Administration.)

The *legal status of the current CoG is no different from that of its predecessors* – as a matter of strict law. However, what is different is:

(1) the number of the issues covered;

(2) the degree of detail – or specificity – in which those issues are covered.

It is in practice harder than it was for authorities to depart from the guidance of the CoG, and it may be easier to argue an authority has misdirected itself as to the law on any specific issue on which the CoG has given particular and detailed guidance. While there has been some judicial support for this view[7], clearly the CoG does not have the force of law and is not mandatory. On the other hand where as a matter of fact it is clear the CoG's provisions have been ignored a decision can be struck down[8]. It is certainly necessary for an authority's decision letter to show that the CoG has been taken into account[9]. Authorities should also rely only on the most recent version of the CoG because of the change in emphasis referred to above[10].

It is important to note that the CoG lays considerable emphasis on *prevention*. Preventive measures may, of course, involve liaison with other services and departments. See Chapters 7 and 8 of the CoG.

The 1996 Act also makes provision for preventive measures on homelessness, though there is no national legislative scheme of prevention, and authorities are left to make local ad hoc arrangements.

Under section 179 every local housing authority *must* ensure that advice and assistant about homelessness and its prevention is freely available to all persons in their districts, and they *may* give assistance to any person providing advice etc or help by way of a grant/loan, and may permit them to use their premises, along with the provision of furniture and goods and the services of authority staff.

Section 180 empowers the Secretary of State or a local housing authority to give financial assistance to voluntary bodies (ie those who seek no profit) concerned with homelessness and related matters and an authority may permit them the use of authority premises, furniture, goods and the services of authority staff.

Under section 181 the assistance given may be subject to conditions and undertakings *must* be given by recipients that they will use money, premises, furniture, etc for the specified purpose for which assistance is

---

7   Contrast *R v Tower Hamlets London Borough Council, ex p Hoque* (1993) Times, 20 July where the provisions of the CoG were regarded almost as rules, with *R v Brent London Borough Council, ex p Macwan* [1994] 2 FCR 604, 26 HLR 528 where the Court of Appeal doubted this.

8   *R v Newham London Borough Council, ex p Ojuri (No 3)* (1998) 31 HLR 452.

9   *R v Tower Hamlets London Borough Council, ex p Mahmood* (1993) Legal Action (March) p 12.

10   *R v London Borough of Newham, ex p Bones* (1992) 25 HLR 357.

given. In all cases there must be conditions imposed as to keeping of books and auditing of accounts, keeping records as to how money has been spent, and provision for inspection of books, etc by the aid donor. Where assistance etc is abused the grant donor must take steps to recover from the donee an amount equal to the assistance, but must first serve notice on the donee of that amount and how it has been calculated.

The homeless in law

Under sections 175–178 'homelessness' is a legal concept, which may be *actual* or *threatened*, and which centres on a person having 'no accommodation'. Thus, persons are homeless if they have no accommodation in the United Kingdom or elsewhere. They have no such accommodation if there is no accommodation they are entitled to occupy: by having an interest in it or under a court order; by express or implied licence; by virtue of any enactment or rule of law. Such persons are also homeless where they have accommodation but: cannot secure entry to it; or the accommodation is a movable structure vehicle or vessel and there is no place where it can be located for them to reside in it. Persons are 'threatened with homelessness' where it is likely they will become homeless within 28 days. Obviously the '28 day rule' should not be rigidly applied as an inflexible rule. See section 175(1), (2) and (4).

Persons are not to be treated as having accommodation unless it is accommodation which it would be reasonable for them to continue to occupy (see section 175(3)), and regard may be had, in determining the issue of reasonableness, to the general circumstances prevailing in relation to housing in the district of the authority applied to. Applicants should thus be classified as homeless if the accommodation they have is of such a condition that it would not be reasonable for them to continue to occupy it bearing in mind, inter alia, general housing circumstances in a district. However, if others are enduring similar housing conditions, it may be 'reasonable' to stay in the accommodation. Much will depend, it appears, on how bad conditions are. It may not be 'reasonable' to stay in a property that is unfit, prejudicial to health and a fire hazard where an authority having served notice on the owner of the property under the legislation relating to housing standards (see Chapters 7 and 8) then does nothing to enforce their action[11].

The CoG gives extended guidance on the definition of what constitutes homelessness (para 11.12 et seq). A list of criteria for determining 'reasonableness' is included, for example the seriousness of assaults suffered, the likelihood of further violence, physical conditions and

11 *R v Kensington and Chelsea Royal Borough Council, ex p Ben-el-Mabrouk* (1995) 27 HLR 564.

overcrowding[12]. Circumstances must be individually considered and investigated, not pre-judged according to rigid norms derived from other legislation. An illustrative case is *R v Medina Borough Council, exp Dee*[13]. The applicant had a tenancy of a prefabricated beach hut which was in such poor condition she claimed it was unfit. She was pregnant at the time and was given medical advice that the property would not be suitable for a new born baby. The local authority did not consider the hut statutorily unfit. After the baby was born the applicant joined a squat and applied as a homeless person. The authority, incorrectly, found her not homeless because they considered she had 'accommodation'.

Was it reasonable for the applicant to continue to occupy the accommodation she had? In determining this question the authority had to consider:

(1) the physical condition of the premises;
(2) its suitability for the mother and her new-born baby;
(3) the medical advice given to the applicant.

The 'core' of the definition, is, as stated, having 'no accommodation' but what is 'accommodation'?

It is 'a place which can fairly be described as accommodation', though short term or temporary accommodation may still qualify in this context[14], while the location and quality of the property in question are also clearly relevant factors to consider.[15] Note, however, that to be 'available' the accommodation must be available not only to the applicant but also, under section 176, to all those who normally reside with him/her as a family member, or who might reasonably be expected to. It is for the authority to decide what is 'reasonable' in this context. A mere *desire* to live together may not be enough.[16]

As already stated accommodation is also not 'available' unless it is such that it would be reasonable for a person to continue to occupy, and in particular, it is not reasonable to continue to occupy accommodation where occupation will lead to domestic violence from some '*associated person*', *or to threats of violence from such an associated person who is likely to carry them out*. It is also not reasonable to continue to occupy where there is domestic violence or threats of it to a person who normally resides with the homeless person as a member of his/her family, or against any other

12 See also *R v Broxbourne Borough Council, ex p Willmoth* (1989) 22 HLR 118.
13 [1992] 2 FCR 691, 24 HLR 562.
14 *R v Brent London Borough Council, ex p Awua* [1996] AC 55, [1995] 3 All ER 493, and see also *R v London Borough of Wandsworth, ex p Wingrove* [1997] QB 953, [1996] 3 All ER 913.
15 *R v Wycombe District Council, ex p Homes* (1988) 22 HLR 150.
16 *R v Barking and Dagenham London Borough Council, ex p Okuneye* (1995) 28 HLR 174. Accessibility must be taken into account in determining availability but mere travel problems do not mean an applicant cannot secure entry to otherwise available property: see *Begum (Nipa) v Tower Hamlets London Borough Council* (1999) Times, 9 November.

person who might reasonably be expected to live with him/her: see section 177(1).

Who is an associated person? This was a new categorisation in 1996 and covers, under section 178, persons who are/have been married, cohabitants, former cohabitants, those who live/have lived in the same household, those who are related, or have agreed to be married (whether or not the engagement has been terminated), those who are the parents of a child or have parental responsibility for a child. Special provision is also made for adoption situations, while a very wide meaning is given to 'relative' to include: parents, step parent, child, stepchild, grandparent, grandchild, whether by affinity or blood, siblings, uncles, aunts, nieces, nephews etc. In addition 'relative' covers persons brought into a relationship as a result of cohabitation who would have been relatives had the cohabitation been a marriage. There is no need for co-residence between the applicant for assistance and the violent person whose actions etc cause the applicant to lose accommodation.

A mere offer of a room is *not* in itself 'accommodation' as is shown by *R v Kensington and Chelsea RBC, ex p Minton*[17].

Mrs Minton was a live-in housekeeper who resigned and left the house. She applied as a homeless person, and the local authority contacted her former employer who indicated willingness to take her back. The council considered it was reasonable for her to return to the former residence and considered her not to be homeless. It was held she had *no accommodation*, as all she possessed was a mere offer of accommodation which did not amount to accommodation for the purposes of the Act.

These provisions thus define the classes of persons to whom the various obligations under the Act can be owed. These *include* those having no physical accommodation, those who have no accommodation which they have the *right* to occupy (for example as owners) or are allowed to occupy under some rule of law, or which they are allowed to occupy by some express or implied licence (for example persons living with relatives). Much in this last case depends on the attitude of individual authorities. Some interpret the Act liberally and classify such people as threatened with homelessness as they have no security of tenure. Where persons are living in premises on a 'grace and favour' basis and are asked to leave with no possibility of resisting the request legally, it would be incorrect for authorities to have rigid requirements that evidence of possession orders must be produced before assistance is given[18].

Case law shows how difficult it can be to decide whether a person has 'no accommodation'. A woman living in crisis accommodation provided by

---

17 (1988) 20 HLR 648.
18 *R v Islington London Borough Council, ex p Rahman and Cox* (1989) Legal Action (December) p 15 and *R v Merton London Borough Council, ex p Ruffle* (1988) 21 HLR 361.

a women's refuge was held to be homeless in *R v Ealing London Borough Council, exp Sidhu*[19] , as was a man whose only roof was that put over him nightly in a night shelter, see *R v Waveney District Council, exp Bowers*[20] . As authorities, under section 75 of the 1985 Act, must consider whether accommodation is available for occupation by the applicant along with a person who can be reasonably expected to reside with him/her, a person will have 'no accommodation' if what they have is uninhabitable or incapable of accommodating the number of people living in it.[1]

Initial contact with the local authority

When a homeless or potentially homeless person makes contact with an authority there are duties under section 184 to make inquiries. These arise under section 183 where a person makes an application *either* for accommodation *or* for assistance in obtaining accommodation in circumstances giving the authority reason to believe the applicant is or may be homeless or threatened with homelessness, though the application need not be formally made as one of homelessness. The initial duty is to make inquiries necessary to satisfy themselves as to the applicant's condition.

Authorities should have appropriately trained officers of both sexes responsible for these matters. The Act does not lay down specific rules for conducting inquiries, and there is no requirement to operate a 24 hour a day, seven days a week service. Cooperation with the social services authority is useful, and authorities should have '24 hour-a-day' arrangements, as recommended by the CoG (9.11 et seq). These may consist of telephone numbers of duty officers supplied to appropriate persons and agencies. Once an application is made it must be dealt with: authorities are under duties to take reasonable steps to receive and adjudicate upon applications. What is reasonable depends upon the facts of each case.[2] Authorities should ensure physical and geographical access to their homelessness services, see the CoG para 9.12.

The CoG also provides guidance as to how inquiries should be undertaken. They should be speedy, sympathetic and conducted in private, with applicants given the opportunity to state cases fully. The assistance of friends and/or interpreters or other intermediaries may be appropriate. The

---

19   (1982) 80 LGR 534.
20   [1983] QB 238, [1982] 3 All ER 727.
1   *R v South Herefordshire Borough Council, ex p Miles* (1983) 17 HLR 82 and *R v Gloucester City Council, ex p Miles* (1985) 17 HLR 292.
2   *R v Camden London Borough Council, ex p Gillan* (1988) 21 HLR 114, and *R v Hackney London Borough Council, ex p Asilkender* (1990) Legal Action, (December) p 15.

needs of those with inflexible working hours or young children must be borne in mind. Authorities should have standard systems for recording applications, and should adopt target timescales so that initial assessment of eligibility is made on the day of application, or, where application is made out of office hours, on the first following working day. Subsequent inquiries should normally be completed, in 30 working days, with a written decision being given within a further three working days. See CoG paras 9.9–9.17.

There has been considerable litigation on inquiry duties. In *R v Hillingdon Homeless Families Panel, ex p Islam*[3] Glidewell J held that correct inquiries are those necessary to satisfy the authority about the matter in question. It is for the authority to make inquiries and elicit all relevant facts.[4] They must generally behave fairly in doing this. Once told the applicant is homeless and the source of that information, an authority may not refuse to make inquiries, insisting that the applicant furnishes further confirmation of the facts.[5] An officer with delegated authority to make homelessness decisions may rely on interviews conducted by assistants, and does not personally have to interview the applicant, though this is desirable.[6] An authority is under no duty to make 'CID' type inquiries[7], but they must enable applicants to state their cases[8], and applicants should ensure the authority is informed of what they otherwise might be unable to find out[9]. A brief 10 minute interview is, however, unlikely to satisfy legal requirements with regard to fact finding.[10] Refusing to be interviewed may prejudice an applicant[11], though special provision may be required in respect of those with language difficulties.[12] In conducting inquiries authorities may accept hearsay, where reasonable to do so (though not obvious 'tittle-tattle') and are under no obligation to put any information received 'chapter-and-verse' to applicants, though they must be made aware of the substance of evidence discovered and given a fair chance to reply.[13] However, information received by an authority during the inquiry process is not confidential, and, it appears, has to be disclosed to the applicant where there is any matter

---

3   (1981) Times, 10 February.

4   *R v Harrow London Borough Council, ex p Holland* (1982) 4 HLR 108, and *R v Wandsworth London Borough Council, ex p Henderson and Hayes* (1986) 18 HLR 522.

5   *R v Woodspring District Council, ex p Walters* (1984) 16 HLR 73.

6   *R v Harrow London Borough Council, ex p Hobbs* (1992) Times, 13 October.

7   *Lally v Kensington and Chelsea Royal Borough* (1980) Times, 27 March.

8   *R v Wyre Borough Council, ex p Joyce* (1983) 11 HLR 73.

9   *R v Harrow London Borough Council, ex p Holland* (supra).

10 *R v Dacorum Borough Council, ex p Brown* (1989) 21 HLR 405.

11 *Reynolds v Sevenoaks District Council* (1990) 22 HLR 250.

12 *R v Westminster City Council, ex p Iqbal* (1990) 22 HLR 215.

13 *R v Southampton City Council, ex p Ward* (1984) 14 HLR 114.

which materially affects the applicant's case.[14] It is not a performance of the obligation to 'rubber stamp' another authority's findings.[15]

Where an applicants' evidence is inconsistent, that can be taken into account[16], for an authority is the judge of facts and is entitled to decide which version of varying facts it wishes to accept, provided this does not fly in the face of logic.[17]

The inquiry process is a matter for authorities: the courts will only intervene where that process is so defective, or attenuated, that it leads an authority to an unreasonable decision.[18] Authorities may not change their minds once they have issued a notice of a decision following inquiries unless further inquiries have led them to discover major changes in the circumstances of applicants.[19] The inquiry process, however, must be conducted independently of other housing processes, such as requests for transfers.[20]

The essential 'core' of the inquiry duty is that it should be a real fact finding exercise – deductions may not be made from inadequate inquiries[1] – while the process must also be fair, with any issue that may be decisive being put to the applicant, and not to some other person – even a spouse.[2]

What is an application, and who may apply?

As already noted an application need not be formal. An authority may be put 'on notice' via a department other than that which normally deals with homelessness. An application does not have to be made 'in person' by a homeless person; it can be made on a person's behalf, provided it is made clear what the issue is.[3] It may be that once conditions exist which trigger a duty to inquire, an authority is bound to proceed, even if it is possible to

---

14 *R v Poole Borough Council, ex p Cooper* (1994) 27 HLR 605.
15 *R v South Herefordshire Borough Council, ex p Miles* (1983) 17 HLR 82, and *R v Basingstoke and Deane Borough Council, ex p Webb* (1989) Legal Action, (December) p 15, and *R v Tynedale District Council, ex p Shield* (1987) 22 HLR 144.
16 *R v Hillingdon Borough Council, ex p Thomas* (1987) 19 HLR 196.
17 *R v Dacorum Borough Council, ex p Taverner* (1988) 21 HLR 123.
18 *R v Kensington and Chelsea Royal Borough Council, ex p Bayani* (1990) 22 HLR 406.
19 *R v Dacorum Borough Council, ex p Walsh* (1991) 24 HLR 401.
20 *R v Sefton Metropolitan Borough Council, ex p Healiss* [1994] 2 FCR 659.
1   *R v Tower Hamlets London Borough Council, ex p Rouf* (1989) 21 HLR 294.
2   *R v Tower Hamlets London Borough Council, ex p Nadia Saber* (1992) 24 HLR 611.
3   *R v Chiltern District Council, ex p Roberts* (1990) 23 HLR 387.

treat an application as one for a simple transfer to other accommodation.[4] However, not every *person* is qualified to be an *applicant.*

In *R v Oldham Metropolitan Borough Council, ex p Garlick*[5] the House of Lords had to deal with the issue of who is qualified to be an applicant in cases involving applications by two children aged four, and two disabled adults, one aged 24 but with a mental age of 10 to 13, the other profoundly deaf and with no ability to communicate outside the immediate circle of her family. The House of Lords decided the test for whether a child can be an applicant is to determine whether it is independent of parents/guardians, etc, and has the capacity to appreciate any offer of accommodation and make a decision on it. The House of Lords did not rule out a child aged under 16 being independent, though clearly a very young child is incapable of being independent.

In coming to a decision on a child applicant authorities should consider: whether the child can exercise choices in respect of offers of accommodation made; whether the child is able to act upon advice and assistance given; is of sufficient age and understanding to enter into effective contractual relations in respect of accommodation offered, and can fulfil the duties expected of an occupier.

With regard to adults under disability the test is whether an individual has the capacity to make an application him/herself, or to authorise another to make the application, and has the ability to comprehend and evaluate any offer of accommodation made so as to be able to respond to it.

It is for the authority applied to decide whether the applicant has sufficient capacity. That is a question of fact in each case which can only be challenged if the decision is based on erroneous considerations, or fails to take into account relevant matters, or is clearly unreasonable or perverse.[6]

Post-initial application inquiries

Once the initial application is made and the authority have reason to believe the applicant may be homeless section 184 places the authority under a further duty to make inquiries to satisfy themselves whether applicants are eligible for assistance (see further below) and if so whether any duty, and if so what duty, is owed under the Act, and, if they think fit, whether applicants have a local connection with the district of another local housing authority in England, Wales or Scotland. On completing their inquiries the

4   *R v Islington London Borough Council, ex p B* (1997) 30 HLR 706, but contrast *R v Lambeth London Borough Council, ex p Pattinson* (1995) 28 HLR 214 – the point remains open.
5   [1993] AC 509, [1993] 2 All ER 65.
6   *R v Tower Hamlets London Borough Council, ex p Begum* [1993] AC 509, [1993] 2 All ER 65.

authority must give the applicant notification in writing of their decisions, informing him of their reasons for any adverse decision: this will be returned to below in connection with challenging decisions.

The next matter to be established is whether the applicant is 'eligible for assistance'. This was a new provision in 1996.

Eligibility for assistance

It is not enough to be "homeless" *one also has to be eligible*. Section 185 initially defines the 'ineligible'. They are persons who are subject of immigration control under the Asylum and Immigration Act 1996 *unless* they are in a class of persons prescribed under Regulations made by the Secretary of State, who may also classify other persons as 'persons from abroad who are ineligible for housing assistance'. It should be noted that an ineligible person must be disregarded when determining whether any other person is either homeless/threatened with homelessness, or has a priority need for accommodation. The various classes of person who are thus either prevented from being assisted, or are specifically reincluded within the scope of assistance are laid down by the Homelessness Regulations 1996, SI 1996/2754 as amended by SI 1997/631, SI 1997/2046 and SI 1999/2135. Very extensive guidance is given on the issue by Chapter 20 of the CoG and Annexes 6–19.

As a general rule British citizens, Citizens of the European Economic Area (that is all EU states plus Iceland, Norway and Liechtenstein) and Commonwealth citizens otherwise having a right of abode in the UK will be eligible. Other persons, who are subject to immigration control, are generally not eligible. To make this initial distinction it is important that authorities should follow the model screening procedure laid down in Annex 6 of the CoG.

The following are the classes of persons who are eligible under the Act and the Regulations.

• British Citizens provided they are habitually resident in the common travel area (CTA – see below).
• Commonwealth Citizens with a right of abode in the UK who are habitually resident in the CTA.
• EEA Nationals who are either 'workers' (see below) or who have an EC right of residence (see below) provided they have not been required to leave the UK by the Secretary of State.
• EEA nationals other than those above who are habitually resident in the CTA provided they have not been required to leave the UK by the Secretary of State.
• Persons subject to immigration control who are on income related job seeker's allowance or in receipt of income support.

- Persons subject to immigration control who are non EEA nationals but whose country of origin is a signatory to the European Convention on Social and Medical Assistance (ECSMA) or the Council of Europe Social Charter (CESC), ie EU nations plus EEA nations plus certain Eastern European and Mediterranean states – (see CoG Annex 11) provided they are habitually resident in the CTA and are *not* asylum seekers with accommodation – no matter how temporary – in the UK.
- Persons subject to immigration control with indefinite leave to remain (ILR) which is not subject to any limit or condition *and* who are habitually resident in the CTA, *but not including* a sponsored person also has been in the UK for less than five years from the date of entry or the date of the sponsorship agreement, whichever is later, and whose sponsor is still alive, eg where an elderly person from abroad joins a family member here on that person's sponsorship undertaking to be responsible for maintenance etc.
- Persons with exceptional leave to enter or remain in the UK provided there is no condition attached requiring them to maintain and accommodate themselves (and dependants, if any) without recourse to public funds.
- Persons subjects to immigration control who have refugee status under the 1951 UN Convention on the Status of Refugees (generally stateless persons) – this will be determined and certified by the Home Office.
- Persons subject to immigration control who are asylum seekers (generally people fleeing from persecution in their homelands) who made a claim for asylum before 5 February 1996 *and* who were then in receipt of housing benefit, *and* where the decision on the claim has not yet been determined, or is subject to an appeal, *and* who have no accommodation no matter how temporary in the UK.
- Persons subject to immigration control who are asylum seekers where the claim for asylum was made at the point of entry or whose country of origin has been declared by the Home Secretary to have been subject to an upheaval and the claim is made within three months thereof.

It should be further noted that:
- the CTA is the UK, the Channel Islands, the Isle of Man and the Republic of Ireland;
- EU Workers are those falling within EC Council regulation No 1612/68 or 1251/70;
- persons with an EU right to reside in the UK are those falling within Council Directives No 68/360/EEC and 73/148/EEC; [Together these give rights to workers and their families – and to various classes of those who having worked in a member state have retired there, etc, also included are nationals of member states who are students, or who have self sufficient means];

- habitual residence is to be the subject of supplementary CoG guidance but *basically* means that the person in question satisfies tests such as, is the UK the centre of the person's interests, is the person in stable employment here, and what is the nature of that employment – eg is it by nature merely temporary, why did the person come to this country, how long and how continuous has been residence here, and what are the person's intentions about staying here?

The following are ineligible persons:

- persons not habitually resident in the CTA (*unless* EU workers, etc), eg a British citizen who has been living and working abroad for many years;
- EEA nationals required to leave the UK by the Secretary of State;
- persons subject to immigration control with only limited leave to enter or remain in the UK on the basis they will have no recourse to public funds, eg overseas students;
- persons with valid leave to enter or remain in the UK subject to no condition but who are not habitually resident in the CTA;
- sponsored persons who have been in the UK for less than five years from the date of entry etc, and whose sponsors are still alive;
- persons who have entered the UK illegally or who have overstayed their leave.

Asylum seekers or their dependants not otherwise falling within section 185, ie not excluded by that section from eligibility, are however, still *not eligible*, where they have any accommodation – *however temporary* – available for occupation in the UK: see section 186. That accommodation must still, however, be 'accommodation' for the purposes of the Act.

In *Lismane v Hammersmith & Fulham LBC*[7] L – a Latvian – arrived in the UK in 1997 claiming to have fled from persecution. She was allowed to enter and brought her son. They settled with her husband in a single room; L was at that time pregnant. Was the room 'accommodation?' The Court of Appeal held no – the room could not count as accommodation available for L's occupation. It was not reasonable that L should continue to occupy the accommodation, and so it was not 'accommodation', and thus L did not have any accommodation falling within section 186, and accordingly was not excluded from eligibility by that section.

It should also be noted that duties to asylum seekers arising before the commencement of the 1996 Act are not affected by its passage and coming into force.[8] Furthermore even where an asylum seeker falls outside the terms of eligibility, he/she may still be entitled to assistance under section 21(1) of the National Assistance Act 1948 if effectively destitute and in need of

---

7   (1998) 31 HLR 427, CA.
8   *R v Hackney London Borough Council, ex p K* (1997) 30 HLR 760.

care and attention.[9] There can thus arise a situation where an authority having both social service and housing functions can find themselves dealing with a person to whom they can offer no 'housing' assistance (as such) because he/she is excluded from eligibility while having to do what is in effect the same job by virtue of their social service functions.

In most cases an authority in this situation will have little choice but to accept a duty under section 21 of the 1948 Act once it has carried out an assessment of a relevant individual under section 47 of the National Health Service and Community Care Act 1990. Even so this does not mean there is a mandatory obligation to provide accommodation whatever the circumstances are. So where in *R v Kensington and Chelsea London Borough Council, ex p Kujtim*[10] a destitute asylum seeker had twice been provided with accommodation in the voluntary sector by the efforts of an authority, and had twice lost it through his violent behaviour, the court considered the authority could take such behaviour into account in deciding whether or not to conduct a further assessment under the 1990 Act – and, of course, without such an assessment the duty under the 1948 Act is not triggered. In such circumstances an authority are not bound to provide accommodation willy-nilly irrespective of a person's willingness to take advantage of it. Any duty in such a case presupposes some measure of co-operation from the recipient of the benefit, and furthermore the extent of any duty must reflect the resources an authority have to discharge it. They are entitled to impose requirements to ensure that those resources are not abused. An unreasonable refusal to accept accommodation offered, or a persistent and unequivocal refusal to observe reasonable conditions imposed by an authority entitle them to regard their duty as discharged, though due warning of this in writing should be given. It remains open to a person in this sort of situation to reapply under the 1990 Act, and then his/her case must be reconsidered in the light of his/her needs, willingness to behave, medical requirements etc.

The Immigration and Asylum Seekers Act 1999 seeks to make different provision in such circumstances for destitute Asylum Seekers. Section 91 et seq empower the Secretary of State to make arrangements to provide support in such cases where, inter alia, a person has no adequate accommodation or means of obtaining it. Whether accommodation is 'adequate' will be determined, inter alia, by whether the person has an enforceable right to occupy it, whether there is sharing, the temporary nature of the accommodation and its location. Local authorities are empowered to provide support under section 98 but only in accordance with the arrangements made by the Secretary of State under section 93, etc.

---

9   *R v Hammersmith and Fulham London Borough Council, ex p M* (1997) 30 HLR
     10 and *R v Newham London Borough Council, ex p Gorenkin* (1997) 30 HLR 278.
10   [1999] 4 All ER 161; affd (1999) Times, 5 August, CA.

Indeed local authorities and registered social landlords are to assist the Secretary of State under section 99 with the provision of accommodation if he requests that, but only to the extent of doing what is reasonable in the circumstances. However, under section 100 the Secretary of State is empowered, after consultation with affected authorities, to designate 'reception zones', and if an authority has suitable housing accommodation in that zone, the Secretary of State may direct the authority to make it available for a specified period (not exceeding five years) to enable him to discharge his section 93 functions. 'Suitable' accommodation in this context is that which is unoccupied and is likely to remain so for the foreseeable future, and is otherwise appropriate to accommodate relevant persons, or capable of being made appropriate with minor work. Particular responsibilities with regard to rent, maintenance, inspections of accommodation, etc, will be provided for under regulations to be made by ministers.

Section 114 of the Act further provides that persons subject to immigration control (see further above) are generally excluded from state benefits such as job seeker's allowances or income support, etc, and under section 115 section 21 of the National Assistance Act 1948 is then amended to provide that otherwise destitute persons falling within section 114 are excluded from assistance under the 1948 Act. Such persons also may not become 'prescribed persons' for the purposes of general housing allocation powers, nor for homelessness purposes, while provision is made for the repeal of section 186 of the 1996 Act. Section 117 imposes an obligation on local housing authorities to secure that so far as is practicable no tenancy or licence of accommodation is granted to a person subject to immigration control unless he/she is of a class specified by the Secretary of State, or the tenancy or licence is granted in accordance made with arrangements under section 93 of the 1999 Act. Furthermore any tenancy or licence provided for an asylum seeker under the 1999 legislation is excluded from even the minimal protection given by the Protection from Eviction Act 1977 with regard to the need to obtain court orders, and tenancies granted cannot be 'secure' under the Housing Act 1985, nor 'assured' under the Housing Act 1988.

The object of the new provisions is to remove from the main benefits system those subject to immigration control, including asylum seekers and to provide a new 'safety net' for them provided they are in genuine need, funded and administered nationally by the Home Office, and lifting the burden from local authorities. Accommodation provided will be without choice as to location.

The interim duty to accommodate

This duty is often known as 'the Friday night duty' because it frequently arises late and out of normal hours arises under section 188.

Where an authority have reason to believe that an applicant may be (1) *homeless*, (2) *eligible for assistance* and (3) *have a priority need* they must secure accommodation for that person pending a decision as to the duty (if any) owed. This duty arises irrespective of any referral to another authority, but continues *only until* the authority's decision is notified to the applicant, even *if the applicant requests a review of the decision* – though the authority *may* continue to secure accommodation pending a decision on a review.

Note that the *duty* is limited in point of time, the *power*, on the other hand, will have to be exercised according to the requirements of the *Wednesbury* principles – eg on the basis of relevant considerations and reasonably, etc.

Note also that for the first time, by virtue of section 205 and 206 the accommodation provided under the interim duty to accommodate must be 'suitable' – ie there is a need to avoid unfit, overcrowded or multiple-occupied premises, and see further below. Certainly the CoG argues bed and breakfast is not suitable for families with children. Thus in *R v Newham LBC, ex p Ojuri (No 3)*[11] O applied as a homeless person to Newham – he had a family. Pending the outcome of inquiries they were offered bed and breakfast accommodation, and Newham made it clear they thought O was 'lucky' to be offered that; the family might have found themselves placed even further away from their original home. It was argued that Newham had failed to consider the provisions of the CoG which indicate families should not be placed in bed and breakfast unless it is suitable, that the schooling of children should be considered so that they may stay in their existing school, if at all possible, and the medical condition of the family should be considered. While the CoG does not place a ban on the use of such accommodation if that is all that is available, authorities forced to utilise it should keep families so accommodated under review. Collins J found that on the facts it was clear Newham had not taken into account the needs of the Ojuri family and had not tried to match those needs with what was available as accommodation, hence their decision had to be struck down.

Priority need

Whether the section 188 duty is owed depends on whether the applicant is in 'priority need': this is defined in section 189. A number of persons may have such need: pregnant women, or persons with whom such a woman resides or might reasonably be expected to reside (eg the father of the unborn child); persons with whom dependent children reside, or might reasonably be expected to; persons vulnerable as a result of old age, mental illness or handicap or physical disability, or other special reasons, or with whom such a vulnerable person resides or might reasonably be expected to (eg a carer); persons homeless or threatened with homelessness as a result of emergencies such as floods, fires or other disasters.

The definition is far from clear, though considerable guidance is given in the CoG (Chapter 12). Priority arises on pregnancy, irrespective of its length, and a doctor's or midwife's letter is sufficient evidence of pregnancy. So far as dependent children are concerned the legal trend is to move away from highly formal notions of custody, and this is reflected in the CoG. It is the factual issue of which people, and how many of them, have actual 'care and control' rather than who is named in any order which is important. 'Dependent children', undefined by the Act, are those aged under 16, or 16-18 year olds in education or training, and dependency may exist even where a child is not living with an applicant at the time of application, for example because they are abroad. Authorities are to avoid, wherever possible, splitting up families with dependants.

Finally note that it appears that when an authority make an assessment of priority need for accommodation, a person on a youth training scheme is not considered a 'dependent child'.[12]

Priority need which arises as a result of vulnerability is also further explained by the CoG, with a list of indicators (not exhaustive) being included to aid authorities. With regard to old age, frailty as a result of age will not be the only criterion, and the age of 60 for both sexes is recommended as a 'bench mark' for determining the onset of old age though 60 is not an age at which vulnerability will inevitably arise, and below which it cannot occur: authority practice here historically varied considerably. In respect of mental/physical illness and disability the Code stresses:

(1) the need for *authorities* to seek necessary medical and social services opinions;
(2) the need for confidentiality;
(3) the need to make special provision for those discharged from psychiatric care;
(4) the desirability of having liaison arrangements with health authorities in respect of patients discharged from National Health Service care.

Priority need arising as a consequence of other 'special' reasons extends to cover young people at risk of, inter alia, violence or sexual abuse at home, prostitution, drug taking, etc. Youth alone is not an absolute indicator of vulnerability. It is those who are less well able to fend for themselves as a result of their youth who are contemplated. Also included are those suffering from chronic illnesses such as AIDs and HIV. So far as homelessness in consequence of an emergency is concerned, it appears that a person who has been unlawfully evicted does not qualify as being in priority need.[13]

---

12 *R v Royal Borough of Kensington and Chelsea, ex p Amarfio* (1995) 27 HLR 543.
13 *R v Bristol City Council, ex p Bradic* (1995) 27 HLR 584.

'Emergency' connotes accommodation being made uninhabitable by fires or floods, whether naturally caused or man-made.

The advice given is only a matter for consideration; nor does it go far enough. There is no proper statutory definition given to vulnerability by virtue of mental illness; for example, would this cover a homeless alcoholic? In *R v Waveney District Council, exp Bowers*[14] an elderly man who suffered from both alcoholism and the consequences of severe head injury was found to be 'vulnerable', and in *R v Bath City Council, ex p Sangermano*[15] it was said that where a person has mental subnormality, a record of incompetence, and no ability to articulate and communicate, there is evidence of vulnerability. Vulnerability arises where persons are less able to fend for themselves so that an injury can befall them in circumstances where others would be able to cope without ill effects. However, in *R v London Borough of Camden, ex p Pereira*[16] the Court of Appeal argued that the test is whether a person is less able to fend for him/herself in comparison to a less vulnerable homeless person. A person is not vulnerable if their weakness is simply an inability to find housing: vulnerability is that which leads to physical detriment or injury. However, self-imposed disabilities, such as drinking problems, do not generally constitute vulnerability, nor does the presence of vulnerability mean a person cannot be intentionally homeless: though a person *incapable* of managing his/her affairs through mental illness will be vulnerable and may be incapable of being intentionally homeless.[17]

What makes a person vulnerable is a question of fact and degree. Authorities should consider the frequency of any affliction affecting the applicant.[18] They should consult relevant experts in housing and social welfare, and not rely on the opinion of a single doctor who has neither seen nor examined the homeless person, and certainly should not 'rubber stamp' his assessment,[19] though a decision which has followed the taking of good medical opinion is hard to upset in court.[20]

Where priority need depends on the presence of dependent children, they need not live exclusively with the applicant, but mere staying access granted to one parent is unlikely to be enough to enable that parent to claim the presence of dependent children. It is for authorities to decide with whom children 'normally reside'.[1] Authorities should not try to decide the issue

14 [1983] QB 238, [1982] 3 All ER 727.

15 (1984) 17 HLR 94.

16 (1998) 31 HLR 317.

17 *Ex p B (Homelessness)* (1994) Times, 3 May.

18 *R v Wandsworth London Borough Council, ex p Banbury* (1986) 19 HLR 76.

19 *R v Lambeth London Borough Council, ex p Carroll* (1987) 20 HLR 142.

20 *R v Reigate and Banstead Borough Council, ex p Di Domenico* (1989) 20 HLR 153.

1   *R v Lambeth London Borough Council, ex p Vagliviello* (1990) 22 HLR 392 and *R v Port Talbot Borough Council, ex p McCarthy* (1990) 23 HLR 207.

by reference to a child's main residence, but by reference to residence with the applicant, considering past, present and future arrangements.[2]

The duties owed to the homeless

The provisions of the 1996 Act create a number of classes of person to whom a variety of housing duties are owed:

(1) A person who is homeless unintentionally and in priority need: see section 193(1) below;

(2) A person who is threatened with homelessness, and in priority need, and who has not become so threatened intentionally: see section 195(1) below;

(3) A person who is homeless, and who has priority need, but who is homeless 'intentionally': see section 190(1) below;

(4) A person who is homeless but who has no priority need: see section 192(1) below.

Much will therefore depend on whether the applicant for aid has committed an act of intentional homelessness.

Intentional homelessness

Where under section 190 the authority are satisfied the applicant is homeless and eligible but are also satisfied he/she is intentionally homeless,

(a) if they are also satisfied he/she has priority need, they must:

(i) secure accommodation for such period as they consider will give the applicant a reasonable opportunity of securing his/her own accommodation, *and*

(ii) provide him/her with advice and appropriate assistance in the attempt to seek such accommodation;

(c) if they are not satisfied as to priority need, the duty is limited to giving advice and appropriate assistance to help the person secure accommodation.

The definition of intentional homelessness is to be found in section 191(1).

'A person becomes homeless intentionally if he deliberately does or fails to do anything in consequence of which he ceases to occupy accommodation which is available for his occupation and which it would have been reasonable for him to continue to occupy'

2   *R v Kingswood Borough Council, ex p Smith-Morse* [1995] 2 FLR 137.

An act/omission in good faith on the part of a person unaware of any relevant fact is not 'deliberate': see section 191(2).

A matter will be 'relevant' in this context if, had the applicant been aware of it, he/she would have taken it into account in deciding whether or not to give up accommodation, but only clear and defined issues can be such relevant facts.[3]

The intentional provision was originally inserted in the 1977 legislation to quell fears that some might make themselves deliberately homeless with an intent to 'jump' the council house waiting list queue. In practice it has been applied to a much wider range of situations, and has been the subject of considerable litigation, with each 'ingredient' subjected to judicial attention. It is for the authority to satisfy themselves whether an applicant falls squarely within the requirements of section 191 before they can treat him/her as intentionally homeless. Applicants are entitled 'to the benefit of the doubt' where there is any.[4] Furthermore though an authority should look at all circumstances relating to an applicant's conduct and situation, its decision is most unlikely to be upset provided it can show it reasonably concluded the applicant's condition was *predominantly* intentionally self inflicted.[5]

Further the CoG, para 13.1, makes it clear decisions on intentionality must follow from inquiries made in individual cases: predeterminations purporting to define intentional homelessness in advance are unacceptable. Authorities do not have to have legal 'proof' on all the issues involved, their task is to come to a reasonable decision in the light of their inquiries.

Before the 'core' definition of intentionality is 'unpacked' two further instances of deemed intentionality added in 1996 must be noted.

A person *must* also be treated as becoming homeless intentionally under section 191(3) where:

(i)   he/she enters into an arrangement under which he/she is *required* to cease to occupy accommodation which it would have been reasonable for him/her to continue to occupy, *and*

(ii) the purpose of the arrangement was to enable him/her to be entitled to assistance as homeless, *and*

(iii) there is no other 'good reason' why he/she is homeless.

In other words the homelessness must arise as a result of the arrangement and for no other reason such as, eg the accommodation burning down before the arrangement 'bites'.

---

3   *R v Westminster City Council, ex p N'Dormadingar* (1997) Times, 20 November.
4   *R v Preseli District Council, ex p Fisher* (1984) 17 HLR 147, and *R v West Dorset District Council, ex p Phillips* (1984) 17 HLR 336.
5   *R v Newham London Borough Council, ex p Campbell* [1994] Fam Law 319, 26 HLR 183.

The object of this provision is to strike at *deliberate* 'doomed from the outset' schemes whereby an insecure short letting or licence is accepted simply to obtain the protection of the homelessness legislation.

Note also that under section 191(4) where a person is given advice or assistance in the circumstances of suitable alternative accommodation being available (see further below), and then fails to secure suitable accommodation in circumstances in which *it was reasonably to be expected* that he/she would, that person, if he/she makes a further application, is to be treated as having become homeless intentionally. This is a further instance of 'deemed' intentionality which will affect a subsequent application, and because of the use of the word 'reasonable' it needs careful application.

Whose act or omission is in question?

Usually the applicant's, it may be that of some member of the applicant's household in which he/she acquiesced;[6] especially where the applicant is a joint tenant with the party at fault and fails to defend possession proceedings brought in consequence of that other's acts.[7] Failure to control nuisances committed by members of the applicant's family or lodgers the consequence of which is a grant of possession against the applicant can amount to acquiescence in those acts rendering the applicant intentionally homeless.[8]

Two cases illustrate acquiescence. In *R v East Northamptonshire District Council, ex p Spruce*[9] the applicants were joint council tenants evicted for rent arrears. Mr Spruce was found to be intentionally homeless. The authority found Mrs Spruce had shared responsibility for the arrears. Mrs Spruce, however, genuinely believed arrears had been cleared; the authority had not made a correct inquiry in her case. Merely to become aware of debts, etc, when they have become so great they cannot be coped with is not to acquiesce in them. Contrast *R v London Borough of Barnet, ex p O'Connor*.[10] The facts were generally similar to *Spruce*, but Mrs O'Connor had jointly signed a massive mortgage application with her husband. She had grasped the financial situation.

6   *Lewis v North Devon District Council* [1981] 1 All ER 27, [1981] 1 WLR 328.
7   *R v Swansea City Council, ex p Thomas* (1983) 9 HLR 64.
8   *Devenport v Salford City Council* (1983) 8 HLR 54 and *R v Swansea City Council, ex p John* (1982) 9 HLR 56.
9   (1988) 20 HLR 508.
10 (1990) 22 HLR 486.

What is a deliberate act or omission?

The CoG (paras 13.5 to 13.9) pointing out applicants 'should always be given the opportunity to explain an act or omission' states certain circumstances should generally not be considered 'deliberate':

(1) acts/omissions occurring while applicants are incapable of managing their affairs because of old age, mental illness, frailty or handicap;

(2) home loss consequent on real and genuine financial hardship, eg because of loss of employment through redundancy;

(3) sale by a mortgagor, or surrender to the mortgagee, before repossession by the mortgagee where it is clear the latter has an unanswerable case to obtain possession;

(4) acts/omissions which were imprudent or lacking in foresight, but were nevertheless in good faith (see further below).

What is 'deliberate'?

Authorities must not make assumptions: the question is not 'has the applicant done this or failed to do that', but '*why* has the applicant done this, etc?'

In *R v Wandsworth London Borough Council, ex p Hawthorne*,[11] the Court of Appeal stated that where an authority has to decide whether a failure to pay rent is 'deliberate' it is bound to consider also whether that failure was caused by an inadequacy of resources to meet both rent and the needs of the applicant's children. A *conscious* decision by an applicant to devote what resources he/she has to his/her children rather than the payment of rent is not to be treated automatically as a 'deliberate' act, and inability to pay is a relevant matter in deciding whether a failure to pay is 'deliberate'.[12] Thus in a case of homelessness arising from business failure leading to mortgage default, it should be asked did the applicant know the risk he was taking when he used his home as security for his business loan?

'Deliberate' refers to the *doing* of the act, etc, not its intended or desired consequences; indeed, 'voluntary' is not an inapt synonym, for it is not necessary to show that applicants did what they did with the intention of getting themselves dispossessed.[13] To fail *deliberately* to pay off mortgage arrears so that the consequence is dispossession is intentional

---

11 [1995] 2 All ER 331, [1994] 1 WLR 1442.
12 See also *R v Southwark London Borough Council, ex p Davies* (1993) 26 HLR 677 and *R v Wandsworth London Borough Council, ex p Onwudiwe* (1993) 26 HLR 302.
13 *Devenport v Salford City Council* (1983) 8 HLR 54.

homelessness.[14] This also applies to a d*eliberate* refusal to pay rent (but note *Hawthorne* supra on the issue of what is 'deliberate'). However, failure to pay rent or mortgage repayments based on a genuine misunderstanding of material facts, such as a belief that the DSS were making the payment in the applicant's place, would be an act or omission in good faith because of lack of awareness of relevant facts, and so not 'deliberate'.[15] Authorities, it must be remembered, are required to make an inquiry into why the act/ omission occurred. Much will depend upon the inquiry process. Authorities must come to reasonable decisions based on the evidence before them;[16] the court will only intervene where a relevant matter has not been considered if it feels the authority would have reached a different conclusion had it considered the matter.[17]

Acts/ommissions which may be considered deliberate include:
(1) giving up one's home when in no risk of losing it;[18]
(2) home loss consequent upon neglect of advice from qualified persons;
(3) voluntarily relinquishing a home which it would have been reasonable for the applicant to continue to occupy;
(4) eviction following anti-social behaviour – even the anti-social behaviour of one's children;[19]
(5) voluntary resignation from a job which carries with it tied accommodation where it would have been reasonable to continue in employment;
(6) surrendering a tenancy because one can no longer pay rent because one has been imprisoned for crime.[20] See also CoG para 13.8.

What is an act or omission in good faith?

Such occurs where a person is genuinely unaware of some relevant fact, which is not the same thing as a mistake of law or bad advice, though they can be hard to distinguish in practice, see for example *R v Mole Valley District Council, ex p Burton*[1] where it was held an authority should have taken into account a woman's genuine misapprehension that, under a Trades Union agreement with local authorities, her family would be rehoused following her husband's voluntary resignation from a job carrying tied

---

14   *R v Eastleigh Borough Council, ex p Beattie (No 2)* [1984] Fam Law 115, 17 HLR 168.
15   *White v Exeter City Council* [1981] LAG Bulletin 287.
16   *R v Westminster City Council, ex p Khan* (1991) 23 HLR 230.
17   *R v Newham London Borough Council, ex p McIlroy and McIlroy* (1991) 23 HLR 570.
18   *R v Leeds City Council, ex p Adamiec* [1992] 1 FCR 401, 24 HLR 138.
19   *R v Rochester upon Medway City Council, ex p Williams* [1994] NPC 25, 26 HLR 588.
20   *R v Hounslow London Borough Council, ex p R* (1997) 29 HLR 939.
1   (1988) 20 HLR 479.

accommodation. What authorities must look for is an honest mistake, a truly genuine error or misreading of the circumstances, eg a youngster not believing her father when he said he would never take her back if she spent some time living with his estranged spouse,[2] or a couple who gave up accommodation in the UK genuinely believing there was a real business opportunity overseas.[3] Lack of awareness of a relevant fact is enough provided it is a genuine mistake made in good faith.[4] Authorities need to ask why did this person act in this way, and what was the true motivation for his/her actions bearing in mind the person's circumstances, beliefs, family background, obligations, knowledge and level of understanding.

Finally note that where a person claims to have been unaware of a relevant fact it is for the claimant to prove the facts. In this context a claim that a person from abroad believed it would be easy to find work in this country may be no more than a statement of hope on his/her part and not a 'relevant fact'.[5]

The homelessness must be a 'consequence' of the act or omission in question

The deliberate act/omission must be one in consequence of which accommodation is lost, so a continuing causal connection is needed. Nevertheless it is necessary to have *primary* regard to the position when the homelessness arose rather than at the time of the application. Thus authorities may look beyond the most immediate cause of homelessness.[6] If there is a 'chain of causation' flowing unbroken from an initial act of intentional homelessness down to the applicant's current condition, the application will be tainted by the initial act. The 'chain' *may* be broken where applicants obtain some 'settled' accommodation in which they spend a period of time between their initial state of intentional homelessness and their current condition,[7] and merely to occupy some temporary accommodation will not be enough,[8] and the cases yield few examples of where such a 'break' has been found. In the past obtaining an assured tenancy has been held to be enough, provided it is of available accommodation

2   *Wincentzen v Monklands District Council* 1988 SLT 847.
3   *R v Hammersmith and Fulham London Borough Council, ex p Lusi and Lusi* (1991) 23 HLR 260.
4   *R v Tower Hamlets London Borough Council v Rouf* (1991) 23 HLR 460.
5   *R v Ealing London Borough Council, ex p Sukhija* (1994) 26 HLR 726, CA.
6   *De Falco v Crawley Borough Council* [1980] QB 460, [1980] 1 All ER 913, and *Dyson v Kerrier District Council* [1980] 3 All ER 313, [1980] 1 WLR 1205.
7   *Din v Wandsworth London Borough Council* [1983] 1 AC 657, [1981] 3 All ER 881.
8   *R v Brent London Borough Council, ex p Awua* [1996] AC 55, [1995] 3 All ER 493, HL and see further *R v Harrow London Borough Council, ex p Fahia* [1998] 4 All ER 137, [1998] 1 WLR 1396, HL, below.

it is reasonable to occupy,[9] but not obtaining a licence of property by deception, nor occupying property as an illegal immigrant.[10] *R v Basingstoke and Deane Borough Council, ex p Bassett*[11] shows the 'chain' can be broken by some supervening independent cause of homelessness. Where an applicant seeks to rely on having obtained an intervening period of settled accommodation, what is 'settled' will be a question of fact in each case. Taking a holiday letting will not be enough,[12] nor will occupying temporary shelter found by relatives in overcrowded circumstances.[13] Accommodation in a hostel where rooms have cooking and washing facilities may be 'settled', however.[14] Whether there has been such a break is to be determined objectively, not according to the subjective intentions of the applicant. The general test is whether the applicant has legally obtained, since the act of intentional homeless, accommodation in circumstances in which it was reasonable to assume it would not be temporary.[15] In all cases the matter is one for the authority to decide as a matter of fact.[16] The length of time spent in the accommodation in question is normally a relevant consideration.

Causation

The authority must be satisfied it is reasonable to regard the applicant's acts or omissions as having caused homelessness. There must be a cessation of occupation that has taken place consequential on the applicant's conduct and in relation to premises that are 'accommodation', *and* which it would have been reasonable for the applicant to continue to occupy. Where an applicant leaves premises that do not constitute 'accommodation' no question of intentional homelessness arises.

Both the accommodation lost, and the act of causing that loss, can be outside the United Kingdom, but authorities should ensure that proper inquiries are made in such cases into the circumstances of the cesser of occupation.[17]

9   *R v Rochester upon Medway City Council, ex p Williams* (1994) 26 HLR 588, *R v Wandsworth London Borough Council, ex p Crooks* (1995) 27 HLR 660, and *R v Wandsworth London Borough Council, ex p Wingrove* (1996) 29 HLR 801, CA.

10 *R v Exter City Council, ex p Gliddon* (1984) 14 HLR 103, and *R v Croydon London Borough Council, ex p Easom* (1992) 25 HLR 262.

11 [1984] FLR 137, CA, 10 HLR 125.

12 *Lambert v Ealing London Borough Council* [1982] 2 All ER 394, [1982] 1 WLR 550.

13 *Din v Wandsworth Borough Council* (supra).

14 *R v East Hertfordshire District Council, ex p Hunt* (1985) 18 HLR 51.

15 *R v London Borough of Merton, ex p Ruffle* (1988) 21 HLR 361.

16 *R v Christchurch Borough Council, ex p Conway* (1987) 19 HLR 238, and *R v Swansea District Council, ex p Evans* (1990) 22 HLR 467.

17 *R v Reigate and Banstead Borough Council, ex p Paris* (1985) 17 HLR 103.

It must be established that the accommodation lost was available for occupation by the applicant. Under section 176 accommodation is 'available' only where it can be occupied by the applicant and by any other person who might reasonably be expected to reside with him/her. In *Re Islam*[18] it was held that a man who had lost his accommodation – a shared room – because he had brought his wife and children to live with him from overseas was not thereby intentionally homeless. Mr Islam had never actually occupied accommodation available to him *and* those persons who might reasonably be expected to reside with him, and the intentional homelessness provisions could not apply to the accommodation he had lost.[19] A useful illustrative case is *R v Peterborough City Council, ex p Carr*.[20] Ms Carr, who was pregnant, left her sister's house after her sister had refused to let the putative father of the child move in, and was found intentionally homeless. The court held the accommodation she left was not available for her occupation because it was not also reasonably available to her boyfriend, with whom she could be reasonably expected to reside.

The reasonableness of continuing occupation

Finally it must be established that it would have been reasonable for the applicant to continue to occupy the accommodation lost, ie the question is not 'was it reasonable for the applicant to leave', but, 'would it have been reasonable for the applicant to have stayed?'[1] Factors an authority may consider in coming to a decision include physical factors such as whether the accommodation is overcrowded or of poor quality, whether there is infestation by vermin and inadequacy of size.

It is arguably not normally reasonable for a person to continue to occupy accommodation where he/she has lost the right to occupy because the accommodation was tied to employment which has ended through no fault of his/hers. Though it may be reasonable to continue to occupy a damaged, but repairable, house.[2]

The courts have made it clear it is not intentional homelessness to leave property which one clearly has no right to occupy, expulsion from which one could not resist at law.[3]

---

18 [1983] 1 AC 688, [1981] 3 All ER 901, HL.
19 See also *R v Wimborne District Council, ex p Curtis* (1985) 18 HLR 79 and *R v Westminster City Council, ex p Ali* (1983) 11 HLR 83.
20 (1990) 22 HLR 206.
1 *R v Gravesham Borough Council, ex p Winchester* (1986) 18 HLR 207 and *R v Croydon London Borough Council, ex p Toth* (1987) 20 HLR 576.
2 *Miller v Wandsworth London Borough Council* (1980) Times, 19 March.
3 *R v Hammersmith and Fulham London Borough Council, ex p O'Sullivan* [1991] EGCS 110 and *R v Mole Valley District Council, ex p Minnett* (1983) 12 HLR 49.

Particular problems arise with regard to those who leave home as a result of domestic and other violent disputes and those who apply in this country after giving up homes overseas.

The CoG, para 13.7, argues a person who has fled from home in consequence of domestic violence should not be treated as intentionally homeless, even where the applicant has failed to pursue all legal remedies against the perpetrator, provided there is a well grounded fear of reprisal. It is tempting to advise such an applicant to re-obtain the home by seeking an appropriate order under the Family Law Act 1996, etc, especially where the applicant is the sole or joint tenant. In *R v Wandsworth London Borough Council, ex p Nimako-Boateng*[4] it was said there can be circumstances where the applicant should reasonably try to seek to stay and restrain the other party by court order rather than apply to the local authority as homeless. However, this would not be reasonable where the applicant stands little or no chance of gaining an appropriate order. In *Warwick v Warwick*[5] it was made clear that an order excluding the male from the dwelling would not be granted where the local authority had required such an order as a precondition of rehousing, and where it was clear the female had no intention of returning. Likewise in *Charles v Charles*[6] the court pointed out that when a woman is forced from her home by domestic violence and her partner is then excluded by a court order, to require her to return to the dwelling puts her in a place where the male knows she is and is thus enabled to further molest and abuse her.

The cases make a distinction between instances of actual domestic violence and other situations. Authorities should very seriously consider whether it is reasonable for someone to continue to occupy property where they have been subject to violence.[7] See also *R v Tynedale District Council, ex p McCabe*.[8] Here a woman fled home on account of her husband's violence. She was rehoused in Newcastle. Her husband discovered her and almost daily visited to threaten or inflict violence. She fled again to her mother's home. After a few weeks she returned to Newcastle to find her house ransacked. She applied to Tynedale District Council who found her intentionally homeless for abandoning the Newcastle tenancy. It was held the authority had failed to make proper enquiries as to the reasonableness of her continued occupation of the Newcastle dwelling.

Women are, as a result of this type of decision and insensitive housing management, particularly vulnerable to hidden homelessness owing to the lack of temporary hostels for women and by being forced to remain in violent

4   [1984] FLR 192, 11 HLR 95.
5   (1982) 1 HLR 139.
6   (1984) Legal Action (July) p 81.
7   *R v Kensington and Chelsea Royal Borough Council, ex p Hammell* [1989] QB 518, [1989] 1 All ER 1202.
8   (1991) 24 HLR 384.

relationships against their will due to the lack of alternative accommodation.

With regard to other forms of violence, much depends on the facts of each case, the nature and kind of the violence, and the level and effectiveness of police protection. In *R v Hillingdon London Borough Council, ex p H,*[9] H was an ex soldier who, with his family, left home in Northern Ireland after threats and harassment by terrorists. He applied to the authority as homeless and they held him intentionally so. The court held regard should have been had to the harassment suffered in Northern Ireland. In *R v Northampton Borough Council, ex p Clarkson,*[10] a young woman left her council house because she feared sexual harassment from her brother who was living there temporarily. The authority considered it would have been reasonable for her to stay, but it was held they had failed to have sufficient regard to the sexual harassment issue. Similarly, in *R v Westminster City Council, ex p Bishop*[11] it was held an authority should consider the issue by taking into account the needs of a dependent child, while in *R v Royal Borough of Kensington and Chelsea, ex p Kassam,*[12] it was considered the needs of the applicant's carer should be taken into account. On the other hand where threats are made to a person by criminals it may be reasonable to stay and to depend on police protection.[13]

Turning to those who apply in this country having given up accommodation abroad, authorities should take into account the customs, lifestyles and needs of an applicant's community, see *R v Tower Hamlets London Borough Council, ex p Monaf.*[14] Authorities may also consider employment conditions in the place whence the applicant came, though they need not conduct detailed inquiries into local employment conditions there.[15]

A finding of intentional homelessness bars the applicant from making further applications to the same authority based on the same facts.[16] He/she can re-apply *once there is a material change in circumstances*, or new relevant issues come to light. There is no fixed 'disqualification period' barring an applicant from re-applying, see CoG para 13.15, and also *R v Ealing London Borough Council, ex p McBain.*[17]

This issue is well illustrated by the House of Lords decision in *R v Harrow London Borough Council, ex p Fahia.*[18] In 1994 Ms Fahia was evicted from her home following a possession order. She applied to Harrow who found

9   (1988) 20 HLR 554.
10   (1992) 24 HLR 529.
11   (1993) 25 HLR 459.
12   (1993) 26 HLR 455 (determined on another issue).
13   *R v Croydon London Borough, ex p Toth* (1987) 20 HLR 576.
14   (1988) 20 HLR 520.
15   *R v Royal Borough of Kensington and Chelsea, ex p Cunha* (1988) 21 HLR 16.
16   *Delahaye v Oswestry Borough Council* (1980) Times, 29 July.
17   [1986] 1 All ER 13, [1985] 1 WLR 1351.
18   [1998] 4 All ER 137, [1998] 1 WLR 1396.

her intentionally homeless. They accordingly only owed her a time limited duty to accommodate (see now section 190 of the Housing Act 1996) and placed her in a guest house. That accommodation was due to end on 17 February 1994, but Ms Fahia did not then leave and Harrow continued to pay her rent for a further year while she stayed there. In July 1995 Harrow decided it should no longer meet the cost of her stay in the guest house, and in consequence the owner of the guest house told Ms Fahia she would have to leave. A charity asked Harrow to find her accommodation but they argued they were under no duty at all to assist her as there had been no change in her circumstances from the first finding of international homelessness. They carried out an informal investigation but concluded the stay in the guest house did not break the chain of causation from her original act of intentional homelessness because she had had no settled accommodation. It was held at first instance and in the Court of Appeal that the chain of causation can be broken otherwise than by obtaining a period of settled accommodation (see above), and Harrow *conceded* that point in the House of Lords. Harrow, however, then argued they were not bound to consider a second application from Ms Fahia unless she could show a change in circumstances which might lead to the second application being successful. The House of Lords rejected that argument. There is a *duty* to make a proper statutory inquiry once an authority have reason to believe a person may be homeless or threatened with it and may have a priority need. In the instant case Ms Fahia was clearly threatened with homelessness, and her application was not the same as her initial one – she had had an intervening year in the guest house and that changed her circumstances.

What of repeated applications to different authorities? Where a person applies to an authority and they come to a decision that he/she is unintentionally homeless, but has no local connection (see further below) with their area while having such a connection with another authority, the authority may refer the applicant to that authority who come under a duty to the applicant, notwithstanding that authority's earlier determination that he/she was intentionally homeless.[19] Each authority applied to must make its own assessment of such a repeat application without merely adopting a previous authority's determination. Where an authority use the referred provisions to refer to another authority a person previously found intentionally homeless by that authority, the 'notifying' authority must make very careful inquiries before concluding deliberations on the application, and if the authority receiving the referral is unhappy about the adequacy of the notifying authority's inquiries they should make a prompt challenge.[20] In *R v Newham London Borough Council, ex p Tower Hamlets*

19   *R v Slough Borough Council, ex p Ealing London Borough Council* [1981] QB 801, [1981] 1 All ER 601.
20   *R v Tower Hamlets London Borough Council, ex p Camden London Borough Council* (1988) 21 HLR 197.

London Borough Council,[1] it was held that where an authority refers an applicant to another authority, and that other authority has previously found the applicant intentionally homeless, that earlier finding is a relevant factor which the notifying authority should take into account.

Once an authority have completed all their inquiries and have determined the status of the applicant, they will fall under various duties which will supersede the interim duty to accommodate considered above. It may, however, be possible for an authority to transfer its obligations to another authority under the referral provisions, which may therefore be dealt with at this point.

Referral

An authority applied to *may* inquire whether there is a local connection with the district of another authority so they may refer the application to that other authority, see sections 198–200 of the 1996 Act. Before such a referral can be made it must be determined that:

(1) neither the applicant, nor any person who might reasonably be expected to reside with him/her has a local connection with the district applied to (the 'notifying authority');

(2) that the applicant etc, *does* have such a connection with another district (the 'notified authority');

(3) that the applicant etc, will *not* run the risk of domestic violence in the notified authority's district, ie a risk of violence from a person with whom, but for that risk, he/she might reasonably be expected to reside, or from a person with whom he/she formerly resided, or there is a risk of threats of violence from such a person likely to be carried out. It follows from *R v Bristol City Council, ex p Browne*,[2] that the fact an applicant suffered domestic violence in the past does not *necessarily* mean the person runs the risk of such violence in the future. Authorities are required to inquire into the issues, and the duty may be discharged simply by asking relevant questions of the applicant, though an applicant is under no duty to volunteer this information.[3] It is not sufficient simply to ask the authority to whom reference is being made whether an applicant's former home has been vacated and relet.[4]

Under section 198(4) the conditions for referral to another authority are also met if the applicant on a previous application made to that other authority was placed in accommodation in the district of the authority to

---

1 [1992] 2 All ER 767, [1991] 1 WLR 1032.
2 [1979] 3 All ER 344, [1979] 1 WLR 1437.
3 *Patterson v Greenwich London Borough Council* (1993) 26 HLR 159.
4 *R v London Borough of Islington, ex p Adigun* (1986) 20 HLR 600.

whom his/her application is now made, *and* the previous application was made within a prescribed period. This provision was specifically included to deter 'out of borough placements' by authorities. Thus if Coaltown District Council in discharge of its homelessness functions places Adam in accommodation in Coketown, that authority may refer him back to Coaltown. The prescribed period is, under SI 1996/2754, the sum of five years, *plus* the period between the date of the previous application (ie the first application to Coaltown) and the date on which the applicant was first placed in pursuance of that application in accommodation in the area of the authority the applicant has now applied to, ie Coketown.

Questions whether conditions for referral of applications are met are determined, under section 198(5) by agreement between relevant authorities, or, in default in accordance with arrangements made in directions given by the Secretary of State, see the provisions of SI 1998/1578, the Homelessness (Decisions on Referrals) Order, under which the issue of whether conditions for referral are met is to be decided by agreement between the authorities, or, in default, by a person agreed on by the authorities, or from a panel established by The Local Government Association. In *R v Hillingdon London Borough Council, ex p Slough Borough Council*[5] it was held arbitrators should consider only the issue of local connection.

'Local connection' is defined in section 199 of the 1996 Act. An applicant may have a connection with an authority's district:

(1) because he/she is, or was, normally resident there by choice (as opposed to service in the armed forces or the fact of imprisonment);
(2) because of employment in the district (which may be paid or unpaid);[6]
(3) because of family associations;
(4) because of other special circumstances (for example the medical needs of the applicant).[7]

All possible bases for finding a local connection have to be explored before a referral is made.[8]

Whether such a connection exists is a question of fact. In *Eastleigh Borough Council v Betts*[9] the House of Lords held applicants must show they have built up and established a real connection with the area of the authority applied to. They may do this by a period of residence, or employment, or because of family associations enduring in the area, or because of other special circumstances. When an application is based on residence alone it is not improper for an authority to apply the guideline in the 1979 Local Authority Agreement that to reside in an area for less than six months during the period of twelve months preceding the application

5   (1980) 130 NLJ 881.
6   *R v Ealing London Borough Council, ex p Fox* (1998) Times, 9 March
7   *R v East Devon District Council, ex p Robb* (1998) Legal Action (June) 15.
8   *R v Slough Borough Council, ex p Khan* (1995) 27 HLR 492.
9   [1983] 2 AC 613, [1983] 2 All ER 1111.

is insufficient to establish such a real connection with an area, provided the guideline is not operated as a rigid rule. Whether a referral is made in a matter of discretion, but a policy of referring *all* apparent local connection cases appears to be an abuse of discretion.[10]

Where, under section 200, an authority (the 'notifying authority') notify an applicant that they intend to notify, or have notified another authority of their opinion that the conditions for referral are met in his/her case, the notifying authority must accommodate the applicant until it is decided the conditions for referral are actually met, and once the decision is reached they must inform him/her of the decision and the reasons for it, *together with his/ her right to request a review* and the time within which that must be made. On notification that the authority applied to is *of the opinion* that the conditions for referral are met (ie they *may* be met) that authority will cease to be under any duty under section 188 (interim duty to accommodate) and cannot come under the 'main' housing duty under section 193. If the conditions for referral are then found not to be met the notifying authority must secure accommodation for the applicant *but only until they are satisfied under section 197 (see below) whether other suitable accommodation is available in their district.* If they are so satisfied then the provisions of section 197(2) supervene. Only if they are not satisfied on this point will the main housing duty become fully effective under section 193. If the conditions for referral *are* met, the *notified* authority is under a duty to secure accommodation until they have considered whether other suitable accommodation is available for the applicant in their district. If it is then again section 193(2) will apply, and, if not, then the main housing will apply. A request for a review of a decision under section 200 will not revive a duty that has otherwise come to an end – eg the main housing duty – though authorities have a *discretion* to continue accommodation pending a decision on review.

Where a notified authority make an offer of accommodation which is refused by the applicant, this will not entitle the notifying authority to claim on a *subsequent* application by the same person who has by that time acquired a local connection with them that they have discharged the duty to accommodate.[11]

It should always be remembered that the issue is whether the applicant has no local connection with the notifying authority's area while having a connection with the area of the notified authority, not whether there is a greater local connection with some other authority's area.[12]

10 *R v Harrow London Borough Council, ex p Carter* (1992) 26 HLR 32.
11 *R v Tower Hamlets London Borough Council, ex p Abbas Ali* (1992) 25 HLR 158.
12 *R v Mr Referee McCall*, noted in (1981) 8 HLR 48.

The duties owed to the homeless

As stated above a variety of duties are owed to various classed of persons.
- Where a person is found to be intentionally homeless but is otherwise eligible and has priority need the authority are, under section 190(2) to secure that accommodation is available for such a time as they consider will give him/her a reasonable opportunity of securing accommodation, and shall provide such assistance as they consider appropriate in those attempts.
- Where a person is intentionally homeless, is eligible but has no priority need, the duty under section 190(3) is to provide assistance only in that person's attempts to secure accommodation.

These duties are quite limited and appear to run from the time when the decision on the issue of intentionally homeless and the consequences thereof are communicated to the applicant.[13] Authorities should not operate inflexible policies of only giving 28-day periods of accommodation to intentionally homeless persons, but should always take the individual's circumstances into account, also any shortages of accommodation in their areas.[14] Where an authority give advice to a homeless person who thereby obtains accommodation, and who is subsequently injured by the poor quality of that accommodation it appears the authority owe no duty of care in negligence to ground a civil claim for compensation.[15]

- Where a person is homeless, eligible, is *not* intentionally homeless, but has no priority need the duty is to provide advice *and* such assistance as is considered appropriate in the person's attempts to secure accommodation.

Under section 193 where an authority are satisfied a person is homeless, eligible, in priority need and unintentionally homeless they *shall* (ie must) secure that accommodation is available to the applicant unless there is a referral to another authority (see above).

This duty continues for a 'minimum period' of two years, and thereafter the authority will have a discretion to secure accommodation, but are under no obligation to do so, see further below. However, the official argument is that this is a sufficient period, for the evidence is that the *average* length of time spent waiting for accommodation under ordinary allocation procedures is 1.2 years, thus, as the homeless will be able to register on ordinary housing lists, they should not be disadvantaged by this provision.

The 'minimum period' begins (a) where an applicant is in accommodation made available under the interim duty to accommodate (ie section 188) on the day the authority's decision that the duty is owed was notified to him/

---

13 *Dyson v Kerrier District Council* [1980] 3 All ER 313, [1980] 1 WLR 1205, CA.
14 *Eastleigh Borough Council v Betts* [1983] 2 AC 613, [1983] 2 All ER 1111, HL and *Lally v Royal Borough of Kensington and Chelsea* (1980) Times, 27 March.
15 *Ephraim v London Borough of Newham* (1992) 25 HLR 207, CA.

her, (b) where an applicant is in accommodation pending a referral but the referral does not proceed, the minimum period begins on the day the applicant is notified that the conditions for referral are not met, and (c) in any other case the day on which accommodation was first made available in pursuance of the authority's duty to accommodate.

Thus *the duty to accommodate which existed under the previous law became in many ways a duty to accommodate temporarily* with a minimum time span of two years. The authority will in any case be freed of their duty if the applicant, having been informed of the consequences of a refusal by the authority refuses accommodation the authority are satisfied is 'suitable' for him/her and the authority notifies him they regard themselves as having discharged their duty: see section 193(5). (For suitability see below.)

An authority can, however, also *cease* to be under the 'main duty' where an applicant:

(a) ceases to be 'eligible';
(b) becomes homeless intentionally from that accommodation made available for his/her occupation (eg gets thrown out of a homelessness hostel for bad behaviour);
(c) accepts an offer of ordinary housing under the general allocation procedure;
(d) otherwise voluntarily ceases to occupy as his/her only or principal home accommodation made available (see section 193(6)(a)-(d));
(e) an applicant, having been notified by the authority of the consequences of refusal as regards their homelessness duties, refuses *an* offer (one's enough) of accommodation *made under general allocation powers and* the authority are also satisfied that the accommodation was suitable, and that it was *reasonable* for him/her to accept the offer. They must also notify him/her of that outcome within 21 days of his/her refusal. For these purposes an applicant may reasonably be expected to accept an offer of accommodation under general allocation powers even though under contractual or other obligations with regard to existing accommodation, provided he/she is able to bring those obligations to an end before being required to take up the offer: see section 193(7) and (8).

Where the main housing duty is either terminated or where an authority cease to be subject to it the person to whom the duty was owed may make a fresh application: section 193(9).

Where the duty arises it cannot be deferred on the basis that the applicant owed money to the authority,[16] though an authority may bear such an issue in mind in considering what accommodation to offer.[17] Applicants should be given a reasonable time to consider the offer,[18] and

16 *R v London Borough of Tower Hamlets, ex p Khalique* (1994) 26 HLR 517.
17 *R v London Borough of Newham, ex p Miah* (1995) 28 HLR 279.
18 *R v Wandsworth London Borough Council, ex p Lindsay* (1986) 18 HLR 502.

the offer should reflect all the facts known to the authority about the applicant, including all relevant medical details, which should be taken into account before an offer is made.[19]

The limited nature of the duty to accommodate

Under section 194 where an authority have been under the duty to accommodate *until the end of the minimum period* (but not otherwise) they *may* continue to accommodate, *but only* where they have (a) carried out a review and (b) are satisfied that the person in question has a priority need, *and* (c) that there is no other suitable accommodation available for the person's occupation in their district, *and* (d) that the person wishes the authority to continue to secure accommodation for him or her.

Furthermore that discretionary continuation of accommodation can only continue for periods of two years at a time and is subject to biennial review. The review is to be carried out towards the end of each two-year period.

An authority *must*, however, cease to provide accommodation if the applicant ceases to be eligible, or becomes homeless intentionally, or is allocated a home under general powers, etc (as under section 193).

In carrying out the review authorities must undertake appropriate inquiries to satisfy themselves as to questions of priority need, etc, or whether any of the events which would end their obligation has happened. They must inform the person of their determination and what they propose to do in consequence, and the day on which they propose to cease exercising their power to accommodation.

However, the discretionary accommodation of a person may also be ended at any time, whether in consequence of a review or not under section 194(5). In such a case authorities must inform applicants of the day on which they will cease to exercise the power of their benefit and any consequential action. The person in question must be informed by notice which will have to be given at a prescribed time (28 days) before the day on which the authority will cease to accommodate.

Under section 195 the duties in respect of those who are threatened with homelessness are very similar to these in cases of actual homelessness, save that the object is to ensure that accommodation does not cease to be available for the applicant's occupation. Where accommodation other than that occupied by the applicant at the time of the application is secured, then the provisions of sections 193 and 194 apply, eg as to the period for which

---

19   *R v Wycombe District Council, ex p Hazeltine* (1993) 25 HLR 313, and *R v London Borough of Newham, ex p Laronde* (1994) 27 HLR 215.

the duty is owed and the discretionary power to continue to provide accommodation once the minimum period has elapsed.

Where a person threatened with homelessness has no priority need, or where the case is one of intentionality the only duty under section 195(5) is to provide advice and appropriate assistance. Section 196 defines becoming threatened with homelessness intentionally in terms effectively the same as those of section 191 on intentional homelessness.

The issue of 'other suitable accommodation'

Where an authority would otherwise be under a duty to secure accommodation for a person who is either homeless or threatened with homelessness *but they are satisfied* that other suitable accommodation is available for his/her occupation *in their district* (not anyone else's) their only *duty* under section 197 is to furnish him/her with such advice and appropriate assistance they consider reasonable to enable the applicant to secure that accommodation. Even this limited duty cases if the applicant fails to take reasonable steps to secure the accommodation.

Note that the word 'reasonable' occurs twice above. What is 'reasonable'? The authority must under section 197(4) consider all relevant circumstances *including* the characteristics and personal circumstances of the applicant, and the state of the local housing market and the type of accommodation available – and under section 197(5) accommodation is not to be regarded as 'available' it if is available only with assistance beyond what the authority consider reasonable in the circumstances, ie it is too expensive. Nevertheless the homelessness duties at first sight can be side-stepped if it is possible to (i) *identify some* suitable accommodation available for the applicant somewhere in the district and (ii) *by providing* advice and assistance to enable the applicant to secure the accommodation.

However, this provision is not as draconian as might be thought.

(1) The accommodation must satisfy the requirements of suitability (see section 210 below, ie the authority must consider whether it is unfit, overcrowded or in multiple occupation).

(2) The accommodation must be available for occupation by the applicant and those who might reasonably be expected to reside with him, and, pursuant to SI 1997/1741, accommodation is also not 'suitable' unless it will be available for occupation by the applicant for at least two years from the date he secures it. This innovation on the part of the incoming Labour Government did much to erode the force of section 197.

(3) Authorities in any case cannot simply rely on the existence of a generally reported healthy private rented sector in their areas, neither can they get away with giving applicants a list of landlords and houses and telling them to 'get on with it'. They are at least expected to

investigate and check and give some aid, and cannot simply say 'there is much property available at low enough rents'[20] It would appear, however that it is enough to demonstrate that there is a sufficient range of properties available without pointing to a specific house.[1] Sufficient range in this context could be properties of an appropriate size and arrangement which are also affordable by the applicant.[2]

It should, however, be particularly noted that, section 197 does *not* apply to the interim duty to accommodate under section 188, nor to the minor duty to those who are intentionally homeless (section 190), nor in the case of any person subject to referral (section 199).

Modifying the limited main housing duty

The incoming Labour Government promised to amend the main housing duty in June 1997. This they did by the Allocation of Housing (Reasonable and Additional Preference) Regulations 1997, SI 1997/1902 which came into force on 1 November 1997. Under these authorities are requested to modify their allocation schemes so that homeless persons have to be given 'reasonable' preference. Thus anyone owed the 'main housing duty' under sections 193 or 195(2), people being found accommodation after the 'minimum period' of the section 193 duty and people who have been given advice and assistance to obtain other 'suitable accommodation' under section 197 and who are still occupying it, *all* have to be given 'reasonable preference' in the allocation of ordinary council housing.

This was *not* a return to the pre-1996 law where there was the full duty to accommodate certain classes of homeless people, but it was a major modification of what would otherwise have been harsh legislation. Most authorities appear able to move homeless people quite easily into ordinary council housing within the two years of the 'main housing duty' so the change in practice from the pre-1996 position is not great. We may ask why, then, was the law changed? The answer seems to be for political reasons only, and just as 'hard cases make bad law' so does politically motivated tinkering.

Discharge of duties

Under sections 205 – 210 of the Housing Act 1996 these are known as 'housing functions'. Where an authority have such a 'housing function' under section 206 they may perform it by:

(a)   securing that *suitable* accommodation provided by them is available;

20   *R v Sefton Metropolitan Borough Council, ex p Cunningham* (1991) 23 HLR 534.
1   *R v Manchester City Council, ex p Harcup* (1993) 26 HLR 402.
2   *R v Brent London Borough Council, ex p Awua* [1996] AC 55, [1995] 3 All ER 493, HL.

(b)   securing *suitable* accommodation from some other person;
(c)   giving such advice etc as secures *suitable* accommodation from some
      other person (for 'suitability' see further below).
This enables an authority to have a degree of 'pick and choose' power over
homeless applicants. They may, subject to what is said below, accommodate
some in their own property, but the power of choice must be exercised
according to law and not unreasonably.

Authorities may under section 206(2) require the payment of reasonable
charges by those who are accommodated, either in accommodation they
provide, or in respect of sums they have to pay to providers of other
accommodation utilised to discharge a 'housing function'.

However, note that under section 207 an authority shall *not* discharge
these functions by making provision from their own housing *otherwise*
than by providing:
(a)   accommodation in a hostel falling within section 622 of the Housing
      Act 1985 (ie residences which are not separate or self contained and
      where either board or food preparation facilities are offered); or
(b)   accommodation they have leased specifically (see below);
for more than two years continuously or in aggregate in any period of three
years, and this applies irrespective of the number of applications for
accommodation or assistance made by the person in question.

Thus the duty to accommodate (which is itself temporary) is only a duty
to accommodate in specific types of accommodation (ie hostel and specifically
leased dwellings), *where* the accommodation is provided for more than two
years in any period of three years. In other words an authority's stock
cannot be permanently allocated to the homeless as such, though of course
the homeless can be allocated property according to an authority's normal
allocation scheme, but in that regard they have no special priority.

Longer term provision, for example, within the discretionary powers of
authorities can therefore, it appears, only take place in hostel or specifically
leased accommodation.

Specifically leased accommodation under section 207(2) is that leased
to an authority with vacant possession for use as temporary housing
accommodation on terms which include provision for the lessor to obtain
vacant possession from the authority on the expiry of a specified period or
when required by the lessor. That lessor must not fall within section 80(1)
of the Housing Act 1985, eg it cannot be another authority, and the authority
taking the property must not have interest in it otherwise than under the
lease or as a mortgagee.

Further provisions

Section 208 provides that so far as reasonably practicable authorities are
under a duty in discharging their housing functions to secure accommodation

for applicants within their own districts. If, however, they secure accommodation for an applicant outside their district they must give *written* notice to the council of the district in question, stating the name of the applicant, the number and description of others normally residing with him/her as members of his/her family, etc, the address of the accommodation, the date on which the accommodation was made available, and which function it was the 'finding' authority was discharging in securing the accommodation. This notice must be given within 14 days of the accommodation being made available to the applicant.

This provision is, inter alia, clearly designed to assist authorities against a person who, on moving from district to district, might seek to take advantage of the move to get round the local connection and intentional homelessness provisions.

Section 209 deals with situations where authorities make arrangements with 'private' landlords (ie landlords unable to grant secure tenancies under section 280(1) of the Housing Act 1985 as amended). Where such a landlord grants a tenancy in pursuance of an arrangement with an authority which is discharging functions under section 188, 190, 200 or 204(4), ie the various interim duties, that tenancy *cannot* be 'assured' before the end of 12 months from the date on which the applicant was notified of the authority's determination of matters, or, where there is a review of such a determination, or an appeal to the county court, the date on which the applicant is notified of the review/appeal decision, *unless* during that 12-month period the landlord informs the tenant the tenancy is to be regarded as an assured shorthold tenancy (AST) or an assured tenancy (AT). Registered social landlords will only be able to give a notice turning that tenancy (which will be only a tenancy at common law) into an AST: see section 209(2).

Where in *any other case* (eg where the tenancy is the consequence of the discharge of the 'main housing duty') a registered social landlord grants a tenancy to a person specified by the authority under its homelessness functions the tenancy *must* be an AST and the landlord cannot convert the tenancy to an AT unless it is allocated under the allocation scheme provisions of the 1996 Act: see section 209(3).

Note also that by virtue of Schedule 17 paragraph 3 of the 1996 Act a tenancy granted in pursuance of *any* function under Part VII of the Act (homelessness) is not a secure tenancy unless the authority notifies the tenant it is to be regarded as secure.

Suitability of accommodation

In the discharge of their homelessness functions, when determining whether accommodation is 'suitable' in respect of a homeless person authorities are required under section 210 to *take into account* whether the property is unfit and subject to clearance powers, whether it is overcrowded or multiply occupied; but the Secretary of State has a new power to specify circumstances in which accommodation is/is not to be regarded as suitable for a person *and* the matters to be taken into account *or* disregarded in determining whether accommodation is 'suitable for a person'. On this now see the Homelessness (Suitability of Accommodation) Order 1996, SI 1996/3204.

This indicates that in determining any issue of 'suitability' in relation to the occupation or continued occupation of property an authority shall take into account whether the accommodation was 'affordable' by that person, and in particular:

(a) the person's financial resources including:
   (i) salary, fees, remuneration
   (ii) social security benefits
   (iii) the payments due under court orders under matrimonial or children legislation
   (iv) Child Support Agency payments
   (v) pensions
   (vi) reasonably expected contributions from other members of the person's household
   (vii) financial assistance from a local authority, voluntary body etc
   (viii) insurance benefits
   (ix) savings and capital
(b) the cost of the accommodation including:
   (i) rent
   (ii) licence payments
   (iii) mortgage
   (iv) service charges
   (v) houseboat mooring fees
   (vi) caravan site fees
   (vii) council tax payable
   (viii) any deposit payable on the accommodation
   (ix) accommodation agency payments
(c) costs in respect of making payments under a court order under matrimonial or family legislation;
(d) other reasonable living expenses.

Briefly – accommodation is *not* 'suitable' it would cost too much!

(The CoG gives guidance on these duties in Chapter 15.)

Accommodation secured must comply with the above requirements and be available not only for occupation by the applicant but also by any other person who might reasonably be expected to reside with him/her. In *R v Newham London Borough Council, ex p Dada*[3] it was considered that any

3   [1996] QB 507, [1995] 2 All ER 522.

property offered to a pregnant woman should be suitable for her as a pregnant woman.

Authorities must behave reasonably in making offers. An offer must not be perverse or absurd, either as to the premises involved or the time allowed to consider it[4]. Accommodation must be habitable, and habitable by the applicant bearing in mind his medical condition[5]. With regard to time allowed to consider offers note *R v London Borough of Wandsworth, ex p Lindsay*[6] where the court said it could only intervene in relation to the amount of time allowed where the period was absurdly or perversely inadequate.

An authority may discharge its duty in stages, provided it does its best according to the resources available to 'staircase' applicants as expeditiously as possible towards satisfaction of the duty. There may be more than one move between temporary homes as the authority discharges the duty[7]. Stages on the way to the discharge of the duty, for example provision of hostel accommodation on a temporary basis, are unlikely to fulfil the duty, though this will be a question of fact and degree in each case. In *R v East Hertfordshire District Council, ex p Hunt*[8] Mann J considered that, as a matter of fact and degree, the offer of accommodation in a hostel could be of sufficiently settled accommodation to constitute a fulfilment of the duty to accommodate. This was reiterated by the House of Lords in *R v Brent London Borough Council, ex p Awua*[9]. It is not tenable to argue that a homeless person always has no 'settled residence' until there is accommodation in suitable permanent accommodation. 'Suitable' does not mean 'permanent'. Each case turns on its facts: bed and breakfast 'lodgings' are clearly temporary, a place in a hostel is likely to be temporary, but much depends on the nature of the person and the hostel. However, though the duty to accommodate can be discharged in stages, if a person is kept waiting for a long time, surely there must come a point when the failure of the authority to find permanent accommodation is an unreasonable failure to comply with the Act. Much will depend on how hard the authority in question is trying to deal with the situation if it has scant resources[10]. It may be very hard to find 'suitable' accommodation for someone with very special needs such as a wheelchair bound person, and it must be remembered the Act imposes no timetable on authorities[11]. It is different, however, where

4   *Parr v Wyre Borough Council* (1982) 2 HLR 71.
5   *R v Ryedale District Council, ex p Smith* (1983) 16 HLR 66.
6   (1986) 18 HLR 502.
7   *R v Brent London Borough Council, ex p Macwan* [1994] 2 FCR 604, 26 HLR 528.
8   (1985) 18 HLR 51.
9   [1996] AC 55, [1995] 3 All ER 493.
10   *R v London Borough of Southwark, ex p Anderson* (1999) Housing Law Monitor (March) p 9, *R v Enfield London Borough Council, ex p Akbas* (1999) Housing Law Monitor (March) p 9.
11   *R v Merton London Borough Council, ex p Sembi* (1999) Times, 9 June.

an authority has a rule that in certain circumstances, for example because of non payment of accommodation charges, an applicant's name is taken off the active rehousing list. Authorities should not penalise non payers in this way, but should proceed by way of an action for debt[12].

What then, in general, is 'suitable' accommodation? It must be suitable to the person to whom it is offered, bearing in mind all relevant medical, social, employment and emotional factors pertaining to that person as assessed by the authority[13]. Where accommodation is offered an authority is under a duty to ensure the applicant can move in and is not kept out, for example, by squatters[14], though if the authority make an offer to clear out the squatters and the applicant still refuses to even consider the property the authority's duty may be discharged[15]. Offers made should take into account whether the applicant may be subject to racial violence if offered properties in particular areas[16]. Where an offer is made and the applicant puts forward arguments that the accommodation is not suitable, the authority cannot discharge its duty unless and until it has considered the arguments[17]. Under the 1985 Act making a suitable offer of accommodation would generally, at that point of time, absolve an authority from the need to do more should the applicant unreasonably refuse the offer[18]. That did not mean the applicant was an intentionally homeless person to whom no obligation was owed unless there was an entirely fresh and unconnected incidence of unintentional homelessness. In *R v Ealing London Borough Council, ex p McBain*[19] the Court of Appeal stated that one offer of accommodation unreasonably refused satisfied an authority's obligation *pro tem*: where the applicant could thereafter show a material change in circumstances making the previous offer clearly unsuitable an authority's obligations were renewed. Most such cases will now fall within section 193(5) where the main housing duty ceases where an offer of suitable accommodation is refused, *provided* the applicant has been informed of the consequences of refusal, *and* the authority notify him they regard their duty as discharged (see also above).

Once, however, the duty to accommodate is owed it is owed indefinitely[20], irrespective of the fact that the applicant previously occupied a dwelling

12 *R v Tower Hamlets London Borough, ex p Khalique* [1994] 2 FCR 1074, 26 HLR 517.
13 *R v Brent London Borough Council, ex p Omar* (1991) 23 HLR 446 and *R v Lewisham London Borough Council, ex p D* [1993] 2 FCR 772, [1993] Fam Law 277.
14 *R v Lambeth London Borough Council, ex p Campbell* (1994) 26 HLR 618.
15 *R v Ealing London Borough Council, ex p Denny* (1995) 27 HLR 424.
16 *R v Tower Hamlets London Borough Council, ex p Subhan* (1992) 24 HLR 541.
17 *R v Wycombe District Council, ex p Hazeltine* (1993) 25 HLR 313.
18 *R v Hammersmith and Fulham London Borough Council, ex p O'Brian* (1985) 17 HLR 471.
19 [1986] 1 All ER 13, [1985] 1 WLR 1351.
20 *R v Camden London Borough Council, ex p Wait* (1986) 18 HLR 434.

under licence in a property with a destined short life which he would have had to vacate at the end of his licence period to allow substantial reconstruction of the building.

In making offers of accommodation authorities must avoid racial and sexual discrimination[1]; monitoring applications and offers is clearly important in this context and to remove such safeguards may be evidence of an arbitrary and random mode of allocating accommodation to the homeless which can be struck down on grounds of unfairness and irrationality[2]. Likewise though an authority is allowed to charge for accommodation, charges must be reasonable and not levied disproportionately on particular homeless persons[3]. Similarly accommodation provided, even temporarily, must not be cancelled 'in terrorem' to coerce an applicant[4].

Authorities may request other housing and social services authorities and registered social landlords to assist them in discharging homeless functions. Such a request, under section 213, places the requested body under a duty to provide reasonable assistance. See also Chapter 18 of the CoG. Authorities have a wide discretion whether or not to seek assistance[5], but must *not* delegate their decision-making functions[6].

It should be remembered that by virtue of Schedule 1 of the Housing Act 1985 as amended by Schedule 17 of the Housing Act 1996 a tenancy granted in pursuance of homelessness functions cannot be 'secure' unless the authority notify the tenant otherwise.

Duties of notification

Various duties of notification are imposed by section 184. When certain determinations are made they, and the reasons for them, must be given to the applicant.

These are:

(1) whether the person is eligible;
(2) if so, whether any duty – and indeed *which* duty – is owed;
(3) whether there is a 'local connection' with another housing authority.

---

1   *R v Tower Hamlets London Borough Council, ex p Commission for Racial Equality* (1991) Legal Action, (June) p 16.
2   *R v Tower Hamlets London Borough Council, ex p Ali (Mohib)* (1993) 25 HLR 218.
3   *R v Ashford Borough Council, ex p Wood* (1990) Legal Action, (December) p 16.
4   *R v Islington London Borough Council, ex p Byfield* (1991) Legal Action (March) p 14.
5   *R v Wirral Metropolitan Borough Council, ex p B* [1994] 2 FCR 1113, 27 HLR 234.
6   *R v Hertsmere Borough Council, ex p Woolgar* (1995) 27 HLR 703.

Notices must be given in writing, and if not actually received by the applicant, are treated as given only if made available at the offices of the relevant authority for a reasonable period for collection by the applicant or on his/her behalf, see Section 184(6).

In giving notice it is insufficient simply to repeat statutory wording. The applicant must be informed why and how the case has been determined in a properly articulated decision[7], and reasons must be stated in such a way that the recipient can see *why* a decision has been reached, and is thus in a position to mount a challenge if the reasoning is deficient[8]. The authority's conclusions of fact should be adequate and intelligible, though they need not be separated from other relevant considerations and judgements the authority has reached[9].

Offences

Various offences are created by section 214. Where a person, with intent to induce a belief on the part of an authority in connection with their homelessness functions as to his/her, or another's state of homelessness, threatened homelessness, priority need or unintentional homelessness, knowingly or recklessly makes statements false in material respects, or knowingly withholds information reasonably required by the authority, that person commits an offence. Applicants are required to inform authorities of material changes in circumstances arising before they receive notification of determinations. Authorities are required to explain this obligation to applicants in ordinary language.

Protecting the property of the homeless

Where an authority is under a duty to an applicant under sections 188, 190, 193, 195 or 200, and they have reason to believe there is danger of loss or damage to an applicant's personal property by reason of inability to protect it and that no other suitable arrangements have been made, they must under section 211(1) and (2) take reasonable steps to prevent or mitigate loss or damage to the property in question. A *power* exists under section 211(3) to protect property where duties under the foregoing provisions are not owed. Authorities are given wide powers by section 212 to deal with property, including powers of entry. They may under section 211(4) decline to take action save upon such conditions as they consider appropriate, for example

7   *R v Islington London Borough Council, ex p Trail* [1994] 2 FCR 1261.
8   *R v Northampton Borough Council, ex p Carpenter* (1992) 25 HLR 349.
9   *R v Islington London Borough Council, ex p Hinds* (1995) 28 HLR 302.

as to the recovery of charges for having taken action. The duty ceases when the circumstances that gave rise to it cease to apply, and authorities must notify applicants of that fact.

Challenging decisions made under the Act and enforcing the duties

Informal routes

A disappointed applicant may complain:
(1) to a senior officer of the authority who may be able to review the initial decision;
(2) to local councillors, or MPs, who may seek to have the matter reopened;
(3) to the Commission for Local Administration where there is maladministration which arises out of failure to fulfil obligations, or unreasonable delay or inefficiency, etc, causing injustice. Failure to follow the provisions of the CoG could be a prima facie instance of maladministration.

Internal Review

Despite calls for an appellate system for homelessness decisions, for many years central guidance merely *recommended* creating a system of internal review, within an initial stage dealt with by a senior officer, and possibly an appellate panel with councillors as members and an independent chair. In 1990 some 30% of authorities had such a system. The existence of an appellate system did not prevent judicial review being sought.

Statutory review

Authorities *now* have to notify applicants in writing of decisions on questions that have been the subject of their inquiries (see section 184(3) and (4)). This notice informs applicants of the right to review which exists under section 202 of the 1996 Act and of the time limits for making a review request. Such notifications therefore have to be very carefully phrased.

Applicants have the *right* under section 202(1) to request reviews of:
(a) any decision as to eligibility for assistance;
(b) any decision as to what duty (if any) is owed under sections 190-193, and 195-197;
(c) any decision to refer a case under section 198(1);
(d) any decision as to whether the conditions for referral are met under section 198(5);

(e) any decision as to any duty owed to an applicant in those cases is considered for referral or referred: see section 200(3) or (4);
(f) any decision as to issues of the suitability of accommodation offered. But under section 202(2) this is a once only matter, there is no *right* to request a review of an earlier review. Review requests have to be made according to section 202(3) within 21 days of the decision in question (it does not appear they must be in writing) or such longer period as may be allowed by the authority. No doubt legal advisers will request longer periods. There is no definition in the statute of what constitutes a request for review – is a mere expression of disappointment enough? Certainly, however, once a review request is 'duly' made a review must be carried out: see section 202(4).

The legislation itself lays down no prescribed review procedures but section 203 empowers the Secretary of State to lay down procedures in regulations, in particular requiring reviews to be carried out by persons of appropriate seniority not involved in the original decision, and the circumstances in which an oral hearing is required, and whether representation will be allowed. Where the decision is to confirm the original finding *on any issue* against the applicant's interests, or to confirm a previous decision either to refer an applicant or to inform an applicant the conditions for referral are met, the authority must notify, under section 203(4), the applicant of the reasons for such a decision. In all cases the authority must under section 203(5) inform the applicant of the right to appeal to the county court on a point of law and of the time period for making such an appeal. Regulations may provide for the time period in which reviews are to be carried out and written notice given of the decisions given.

In addition to the requirements under regulations the procedure on review must, of course, be fair and lawful. In other words the rules of natural justice must be observed, there must be consideration only of relevant issues, there must be no fettering of discretion, and the review must be carried out reasonably.

The review procedures on homelessness are now contained in the Allocation of Housing and Homelessness (Review Procedure) Regulations 1999, SI 1999/71. These give a discretion as to who is to carry out the review:
(a) where a review is to be carried out by an officer that must be someone not involved in the original decision and senior in rank to the person who took the decision;
(b) alternatively members may be involved.

Requests for reviews are to be made in general to the deciding authority, and that authority as a 'notifying' authority as to whether the conditions for a referral are met. Save in cases where the decision was made under the Homelessness (Decisions on Referrals) Order 1998, SI 1998/1578 (see above) the authority to whom a request for a review is made must notify the applicant that he/she or someone acting on his/her behalf may make representations in *writing* to the authority, and shall also, if they have not yet done so, inform the applicant of the procedure to be followed. In cases falling under SI 1998/1578 – ie cases of disputed referrals where authorities have had to go to arbitration – it is the person appointed under the 1998 order who must notify the applicant of the above matters, and, in such cases the review itself has to be carried out by a person appointed by the notified authorities, and if no such person is appointed within five days of the review request, the reviewer will be drawn from a panel established by the Local Government Association and made 'the appointed person' by the Chairman of that association. That appointed person must be given the reasons for the original decision and the information and evidence on which it was based, within five days of his/her appointment, and must in return, send to the involved authorities representations received and invite their responses. Needless to say the 'appointed person' cannot be the same person as the person who made the original decision.

In all reviews the reviewer must consider any representations made, and, if he/she considers there was a deficiency or irregularity in the initial decision, or in the way it was made, (see below for CoG guidance on this) but nevertheless is minded to make a decision against the applicant's interests on one or more matters, he/she must inform the applicant that he/she is so minded, and also that the applicant or an agent may make further representations either orally and/or in writing.

The period within which review decisions are to be notified is in general eight weeks from the day on which the review request was made, though longer periods are allowed in respect of referral reviews, and in any case the applicant and the reviewer may agree a longer period in writing. Provision is also made for reviewed referral decisions to be notified to the authorities involved.

The CoG (Chapter 19) gives considerable supplementary guidance here.

It is pointed out that there is an unlimited right to ask for a section 202 review – the applicant does not have to give grounds, while the authority's notification of the review should invite the applicant to state his/her grounds for requesting a review (if not already received) and should elicit any new information the applicant may wish to put forward. The authority's notification *may* also point out that if no representations are received they will be entitled to proceed on the basis of facts known to them, and advise the applicant that representations from representatives will be accepted and draw attention to the time period of the review. The review procedure should also be notified to the applicant if this had not already been done. It may be necessary for authorities to elicit further information during the course of the review, and they are advised to be flexible in this regard, bearing in mind, however, the need to make decisions on time, subject to obtaining the consent of the applicant to an extension of time which may be needed if significant delay is likely.

The CoG gives advice on 'irregularity in the original decision' as meaning:

- failure to take into account relevant considerations, or to ignore irrelevant matters;
- failure to base a decision on the facts;
- bad faith/dishonesty;
- mistake of law;
- decisions contrary to the policy of the 1996 Act;
- unreasonable (in the *Wednesbury* sense) decisions.

These matters may lead to an oral hearing under the regulations, of course, but authorities *may* have oral hearings otherwise if they wish, particularly where it is considered the applicant would be disadvantaged by being required to make a case in writing. But where an oral hearing is held the time limits must still be observed unless written agreement to an extension is reached. Early action to obtain such agreement is counselled wherever any significant delay is anticipated.

Good practice demands that on the review decision being made a full statement of reasons should be given, along with notification of the right to appeal to the county court. Failure to comply with good administrative practice may also lay an authority open to a maladministration investigation by the local ombudsman.

A request for a review gives an authority an opportunity to gather its thoughts on why they have taken the decision in question, and to 'tidy up' their reasoning which *may* explain why there has not been a greater amount of litigation under the right to appeal which falls to be considered next.

Section 204 provides that where a disappointed review applicant is not satisfied with the review decision, *or* is not notified of the decision on review within the prescribed time, an appeal may be made *on a point of law only* to the county court on any issue arising from the review decision *or* from the original decision. This appeal has to be made within 21 days of the review decision. There is *no* power to extend this period. 'Point of law' is not defined, and this could give rise to considerable litigation. It appears to mean the points previously taken on judicial review and questions of definition and interpretation. But it is important to remember that on appeal a decision can be rewritten, whereas on review it can only be quashed and is simply remitted to be remade.

The county court has a wide discretion on the appeal to confirm, quash or vary the decision. How will this new provision relate to judicial review? The existence of the right of appeal on a point of law to the county court will almost certainly preclude judicial review where all that is alleged is misinterpretation of the statute because the Divisional Court will refuse to exercise its discretion.[10] But it is arguable that 'JR' may be available on other

10 *R v Chief Constable of Merseyside Police, ex p Calveley* [1986] QB 424, [1986] 1 All ER 257, CA, and see *Begum (Nipa) v Tower Hamlets London Borough Council* (1999) Times, 9 November and note the right to appeal is 'once only' in respect of the original decision: see *Demetri v Westminster City Council* [1999] 45 LS Gaz R 32, CA

grounds – eg failing to take into account relevant considerations, or coming to an utterly perverse or unreasonable decision or giving an inadequate statement of reasons where this prejudices the applicant because he/she cannot appreciate the case that has been made against him/her. Additionally judicial review *might* be sought of an authority's homelessness policies, provided a person could show a 'sufficient interest' in the matter, or where there is an unreasonable refusal to extend the time for an internal review, or where one authority is seeking to challenge the legality of another's decision in connection with a referral, or where there is an unreasonable refusal to exercise the power to accommodate following the ending of the interim housing duty, or where no decision at all is made, or where a review is requested but not carried out so there is a need for an order of mandamus. In such cases there could be problems if *both* misinterpretation and, say, unreasonableness are alleged – there could be a need for both an appeal *and* a judicial review application. Furthermore pending the outcome of an appeal the county court has no express jurisdiction to grant an interim order continuing accommodation. In *Ali v Westminster City Council, Nairne v Camden LBC*[11] it was pointed out that the county court has no inherent jurisdiction to grant injunctions – unlike the High Court – and can only do so if permitted by statue. So far as homelessness is concerned the 1996 Act does not grant such a jurisdiction. Furthermore an injunction can only be granted where there is a right to be enforced.

The 'right' to accommodation comes to an end once the authority has made and notified its decision. In such circumstances the only way a decision not to continue accommodation pending an appeal can be challenged is by means of an allegation of abuse of discretion via judicial review, and that means going to the High Court.

Thus where an authority is under a duty under section 188 (interim duty in case of priority need) or section 190 (duties to the intentionally homeless), or section 200 (cases of referral or consideration for referral), section 204(4) gives them a *discretion* to continue the securing of accommodation during the period in which an appeal can be made *and* until any appeal is finally determined – including any further appeal to the Court of Appeal or House of Lords from the county court – and that discretion, prima facie, is open to judicial review. On the other hand the courts have displayed some keenness to discourage the use of judicial review. Thus in *R v Brighton and Hove Borough Council, ex p Nacion*[12] a local authority had refused to continue to provide accommodation for a person pending completion of his appeal to the county court under section 204. The Court of Appeal held that it is not normally appropriate to seek judicial review of an authority's exercise of discretion under section 204(4). Lord Woolf MR stated, however, judicial review would be an appropriate remedy where an authority had

---

11 [1999] 1 All ER 450, [1999] 1 WLR 384, CA.
12 [1999] 11 LS Gaz R 69.

failed to consider whether to exercise its discretion under section 204(4). In *R v Merton London Borough Council, ex p Sembi*[13] Jowitt J stressed that where a matter falls with section 202 applicants should pursue that route rather than seeking judicial review, and should then, if still dissatisfied pursue their remedies under section 204 where, he considered, the court could consider the same points of law as could be considered on judicial review, including *Wednesbury* unreasonableness.

This line of argument has been followed in *Warsame v Hounslow London Borough Council*[14]. Here two sisters applied as homeless persons. They accepted temporary accommodation and then refused an offer of a secure tenancy. The council had warned them that the property on offer was considered suitable and that it was reasonable for them to accept it, and that if they did not accept it the council would regard its duty as discharged, and that they would have to leave their temporary accommodation: see section 193(5). Even so the sisters continued to refuse the offer and requested a review under section 202. That resulted in confirmation of the decision that the council's duty was discharged. They appealed then to the county court under section 204 where it was held that the court had no jurisdiction to hear an appeal against a decision by an authority that it no longer has a duty to a person. In the Court of Appeal, however it was held that the right to request a section 202 review arises in relation to what duties, if any, may be owed under sections 190 to 193, and 195 to 197 of the 1996 Act. Did the authority's decision in this case fall within the notion of 'what duty, if any, did the authority owe?' If so, then did the decision on whether particular events had occurred fall within the notion of 'any decision as to what, if any, duty was owed'. The Court of Appeal considered it was clear from the statute that the answer on the first point was 'yes'. The court then went on to hold that the phrase 'any decision' in section 202(1)(b) was wide enough to cover decisions on factual matters which have to exist before any duty can be owed (eg eligibility, priority need etc), *and also* decisions as to events and facts which had occurred which had the effect of bringing any duty owed to an end. Thus the county court did have power to hear an appeal against a decision that a duty to a homeless person has been discharged.

On the other hand there have been a few cases since 1996 where the judicial review remedy has been sought with success. Thus in *R v Camden London Borough Council, ex p Mohammed*[15] an authority's decision not to continue interim accommodation pending an appeal was struck down, largely because of unfairness in the way in which the authority had failed to put its concerns about the application to the applicant, and because they

13 (1999) Times, 9 June and see the Court of Appeal in *Begum (Nipa) v Tower Hamlets London Borough Council* (1999) Times, 9 November.

14 (1999) Times, 21 July.

15 (1997) 30 HLR 315, see also *R v Hammersmith and Fulham London Borough Council, ex p Fleck* (1997) 30 HLR 679, and *R v Newham London Borough Council, ex p Idowu* (1998) Legal Action (August) p 22.

had failed to elicit an explanation of inconsistencies in her account of events. It was, however, accepted that there is no *right* to accommodation pending an appeal, that an authority is entitled to have a 'normal policy' of not providing accommodation in such circumstances; but they must consider each case on its merits and must in particular take into account new material, information and arguments raised during the section 202 review, the personal characteristics of the applicant, the consequences of a refusal to provide interim accommodation, and any other relevant considerations.

On the other hand judicial review has been held possible where it appears an authority have failed even to consider an application for interim accommodation,[16] and where an authority has tried to enforce a 'take it or leave it' policy of stating an applicant cannot both accept an offer of accommodation *and also* seek a review at the same time. It is not lawful to terminate provision of accommodation so as to force a homeless person into a property against which that person has lodged an application for review, where the result would be to expose that person to danger.[17]

Recourse to the courts will be rarely available as a remedy since they have shown they wish to leave the day-to-day administration of the Act to local authorities, and will only involve themselves on points of law. It might be thought the very large number of decisions on homelessness indicates considerable judicial intervention in homelessness practice, but this is illusory. *Judicial Review in Perspective*[18] indicated generally only 30% of judicial review applications reached a final hearing with one in six resulting in a ruling by a public body being challenged. Leave to apply for judicial review is needed and obtaining leave is something of a lottery, often depending upon which judge deals with an application, and corporate and institutional applicants are more successful in obtaining leave than are individuals. The courts will only intervene if they find an authority has erred in a point of law, ie it has clearly misinterpreted the wording of the Act, or has behaved in a procedurally improper manner, or has exceeded its powers; or has failed to obey the rules of natural justice in dealing with applications fairly; or has been random and arbitrary in the application of policies; or has behaved perversely by dealing with applicants in a gratuitously oppressive fashion; or has taken into account irrelevant factors, or failed to consider those that are relevant; or has fettered its discretion by adopting rigid rules as opposed to flexible guidelines, and certainly so where these have been developed by ad hoc groups not having formally delegated authority from

---

16 *R v Harringey London Borough Council, ex p Erdogan* (1998) Legal Action (August) p 23, and see *Ex p Nacion*, supra.

17 *R v Kensington and Chelsea Royal Borough Council, ex p Byfield* (1998) Legal Action (March) p 16.

18 Sunkin, Bridges and Mezzaros (1993).

their authority[19]. Even where error is encountered the court may decline to provide a remedy if it concludes the applicant has not suffered substantial prejudice.

It was, until quite recently, arguable that it might still be possible to rely on *Thornton v Kirklees Metropolitan Borough Council*[20] in an extreme case and bring an action for breach of statutory duty where a plaintiff could show that some right in private law had been infringed by the authority, see *Mallon v Monklands District Council*[1] where a lack of accommodation was found to have contributed to psychiatric illness, likewise *Puives v Midlothian District Council*[2] where damages of £438 were awarded following breach of an undoubted duty to accommodate. The possibility of private law rights to sue continued to be accepted in *South Holland District Council v Keyte*[3], but it was certain they could only arise after an authority had taken a decision and could not be used to force decision-taking, nor to question the validity of decisions[4]. However, it was clear that breach of the duty to make inquiries into a homelessness application is a public law matter only, and gives no right to seek damages[5]. The matter of the suitability of accommodation, irrespective of how it arises, is similarly one of public law only[6]. Despite a criticism of this line of development[7], it now appears settled that *no* right to a civil remedy arises under the 1996 Act, and earlier cases suggesting such a possibility cannot be relied on[8]. It is, however, possible for damages to be awarded in judicial review proceedings provided they are claimed along with one of the other remedies and 'arise out of any matter to which the application relates', see section 31(4)(a) of the Supreme Court Act 1981.

Under section 31 of the Supreme Court Act 1981 applications for orders of certiorari, mandamus, etc, must be made to the High Court whose leave (as already noted) must be obtained before application is made. In those cases where judicial review is still the appropriate remedy as opposed to proceeding under sections 202 and 204, a person challenging a decision will

19 *R v Tower Hamlets London Borough Council, ex p Khalique* [1994] 2 FCR 1074, 26 HLR 517.
20 [1979] QB 626, [1979] 2 All ER 349.
1 1986 SLT 347.
2 1986 SCOLAG 144.
3 (1985) 19 HLR 97.
4 *R v Lambeth London Borough Council, ex p Barnes* (1992) 25 HLR 140.
5 *R v Northavon District Council, ex p Palmer* (1995) 27 HLR 576.
6 *Ali v London Borough of Tower Hamlets* [1993] QB 407, [1992] 3 All ER 512, CA, *London Borough of Tower Hamlets v Abdi* (1992) 25 HLR 80 and *Hackney London Borough v Lambourne* (1992) 25 HLR 172.
7 Cowan, D, 'The Public/Private Dichotomy and "Suitable Accommodation" under section 69(1) of the Housing Act 1985' [1993] JSWFL 236.
8 *O'Rourke v Camden London Borough Council* [1998] AC 188, [1997] 3 All ER 23.

also need interim or 'interlocutory' relief to keep accommodation over his/her head pending resolution of the issue and a final order. Interlocutory relief by way of injunction may be sought. In *R v Cardiff City Council, ex p Barry*[9] the Court of Appeal indicated that the normal course of action where a decision is susceptible to challenge should be to grant interim relief; but only where the applicant can show there is a strong prima facie case the challenge will be successful[10].

With regard to final orders courts do not sit to substitute their decisions for those of authorities, though, in practice, a court's finding that no reasonable authority could have come to the decision actually reached may be enough to settle an issue. In those cases where judicial review is appropriate certiorari will be the principal remedy to quash a decision wrong in law, and mandamus will also be appropriately awarded to require a redetermination of issues. But in any such case specific issues of illegality must be pleaded as no order of mandamus will be granted simply to make an authority perform its homelessness obligations generally[11].

Costs may be awarded in a review application once leave is granted, and authorities who concede cases before judgment usually pay costs voluntarily, though it appears the court may award costs even on an application for leave where an authority concedes[12].

Duties under the Children Act 1989

Section 20(1) of the 1989 Act provides that social services authorities must provide accommodation for children 'in need' in their areas who appear to them to need accommodation as a result of: there being no persons having responsibility for them; their being lost or abandoned; persons who have been responsible for caring for them being prevented from providing suitable accommodation or care. Children, according to section 105(1) of the 1989 Act, are persons under the age of 18. Section 20(3) imposes a duty on social services authorities to provide accommodation for any 'child in need' within their areas who has reached the age of 16 and whose welfare they consider is likely to be seriously prejudiced if they do not provide him/her with accommodation. Section 27(1) enables a social services authority to

9   (1990) 22 HLR 261.
10 *R v Kensington and Chelsea Royal Borough Council, ex p Hammell* [1989] QB 518, [1989] 1 All ER 1120 2, and *R v Westminster City Council, ex p Augustin* [1993] 1 WLR 730.
11 *R v Beverley Borough Council, ex p McPhee* (1978) 122 Sol Jo 760.
12 *R v Secretary of State for Wales, ex p Rozhon* (1993) 91 LGR 667, *R v Kensington and Chelsea Royal Borough Council, ex p Ghebregiogis* (1994) 27 HLR 602, and *R v Kensington and Chelsea Royal Borough Council, ex p Halonen* (1995) Legal Action (December) p 20.

request the specified aid of another authority (including a housing authority) in discharging the above functions, and subsection (2) requires an authority whose help is requested to comply with that request if it is 'compatible with their own statutory or other duties and obligations and does not unduly prejudice the discharge of any of their functions'.

Under section 20 the duty is primarily to accommodate the child in question, but there is no specific exclusion of accommodating the child with the rest of his/her family. However, in *R v Tower Hamlets London Borough Council, ex p Byas*[13], the Court of Appeal considered that where an obligation is owed to a child under the 1989 Act that does not extend automatically to its parents, particularly where they are intentionally homeless. Secondly, the section 20(1) duty is owed in respect of children who are both 'in need', and who appear to need accommodation in *specified circumstances*. This definition is not the same as that of a homeless person under the 1996 Act. A child in need is defined by the 1989 Act as one who is disabled, or who is unlikely to achieve or maintain a reasonable standard of health or development without the provision of social services support, or whose health or development is likely to be significantly impaired without the provision of such support. The duty under section 20(3) in respect of general provision of accommodation to those aged between 16 and 18 is owed in respect of those who are 'in need', and whose welfare is likely to be 'seriously prejudiced' if they are not accommodated. Thus not every person aged between 16 and 18 will be able to rely on the obligation, even if 'in need', though a young person discharged from care may look for assistance to a social services authority under section 24(2) of the Act provided he/she was accommodated after reaching 16.

So far as section 27 of the 1989 Act is concerned, judicial guidance was given in *R v Northavon District Council, ex p Smith*[14] by the House of Lords. Mr and Mrs Smith, parents of five children aged under ten, had been found intentionally homeless. The Smiths then sought aid under the 1989 Act on behalf of their children from the social services authority who approached the District under section 27 and requested assistance for the Smiths in securing accommodation either by providing a full tenancy of a type commensurate with their needs, or by at least delaying their eviction from their temporary accommodation. The District refused to comply, and Mr Smith sought judicial review. In the House of Lords it was pointed out that when Mr Smith had made his homelessness application he was also entered on the Authority's housing waiting list. But there were already 2,632 names on that list and he could expect a two and a half to three year wait before rehousing: to advance Mr Smith's rehousing would have been unfair to over 2,000 other persons. As a homeless person Mr Smith's case had been

13 [1993] 2 FLR 605, 25 HLR 105.
14 [1994] 2 AC 402, [1994] 3 All ER 313.

duly considered, and he had been found entitled only to a period of temporary accommodation. He was not entitled to any priority, and the County had no power to require the District to exercise rehousing powers. When responding to a request under section 27 of the 1989 Act an authority must judge that request in accordance with the various duties it has under the 1996 Act. The appropriate response is one of co-operation. Certainly a District must consider what it can do in response to a request, and must decide what help it can give, but the duty to co-operate must not unduly prejudice the discharge of housing functions, and where a District finds it cannot lawfully co-operate with a County request any duty to accommodate children in need remains with the County. Furthermore in *R v Tower Hamlets London Borough Council, ex p Byas* (supra) the Court of Appeal held that section 27 only applies *between* authorities, *not* between departments of *unitary* authorities: an authority cannot seek aid from itself, see also section 29(9) of the 1989 Act which allows for inter-authority reimbursement of costs incurred in providing accommodation under section 27.

Even so there remains room for conflict between authorities. Further clarification is needed of what is meant by the statutory concepts 'compatible with their statutory or other duties and obligations' and undue prejudice to the discharge of functions. For example it is arguable that where an authority tenant with children has been evicted for grossly bad behaviour involving violence or racial abuse towards neighbours in breach of a tenancy condition, it would be incompatible with that authority's duties etc, if they were then required to rehouse that tenant by virtue of a section 27 request, and in such cases the duties to the children will remain with the social services authority. Outside of cases like that if a housing authority wished to resist a request for assistance it would not be enough for them merely to reiterate the statutory formulae in section 27. They would have to produce clear evidence as to the housing problems they face, and show that *in consequence* of those problems incompatibility with other duties or prejudice to their functions would be the necessary result of compliance with the social services authority's request. In fact that is what was done in the *Smith* case.

The law and homelessness: an assessment

Homelessness cannot be erradicated by passing laws. The most the law could do would be to create a framework within which resources can be justly and equitably divided. At the moment there is not even an integrated, internally coherent legal structure seeking to provide appropriate accommodation for all in need. Rather we continue to have a number of measures designed to deal ad hoc with aspects of homelessness. The 1996 Act is designed to provide assistance only to limited numbers of people who manage to satisfy certain criteria. Despite attempts to ensure consistency of practice nationwide, it is clear the application of the law of homelessness varies considerably between authorities. Initially this had a great deal to do with whether authorities had accepted voluntary responsibility for the homeless in 1974. Since then the issue has been confused by the interaction of a range of issues: attitudes of officers and councillors, local political pressures to ensure some housing stock is retained for allocation to those on the 'normal' waiting list; size and composition of the available housing stock; numbers of homelessness applications received. Certainly a cursory glance at the names of the authorities who seem to be most frequently the subject of legal action, tends to suggest that it is these districts with the most severe housing shortages where the law will most often be prayed in aid.

It has been powerfully argued (notably by Professor Ian Loveland) that the influence of the law in such circumstances is not nearly so great as lawyers might wish, with administrative practice counting for much more than might be supposed. But the law does have an undoubted part to play, and experience of working with authorities throughout the East Midlands indicates that the influence of the law varies according to levels of training received by relevant staff, the importance attached to compliance with the law by councillors and senior officers, the input into decision-taking by local authority legal departments, the nature and quality of relationships between authorities and local campaigning organisations, and the availability of legal advice to applicants either through law centres or specialist firms of solicitors.

The real problem, however, lies with the general shortage of social housing. Society has since 1945 undergone radical changes. Extended families living together have largely disappeared; the single adult unit (with or without children) is much more common. The pattern of housing demand has changed dramatically: less so the pattern of housing supply. There has also been a blithe official assurance that rising real incomes would enable more and more people to purchase their own homes; the trend throughout the century. The official mind has further been fixated since 1979 with questions of who should own social housing, and has not properly addressed the question of how much, and what sort of, social housing is needed. Not everyone wants to be, or can be, an owner occupier. It is no sin not to own one's home, nor is it a great offence to find that one needs assistance to obtain reasonable accommodation. There will always be a constituency for social housing: the homeless are the most obvious manifestation of that demand.

Further reading

Articles

Birkinshaw, P *Homelessness and the Law – the Effects and Response to Legislation* [1982] *Urban Law & Policy* 255

Bryan, M *Domestic Violence: A Question of Housing* [1984] JSWL 195

Hoath, D *Split Families and Part III of the Housing Act 1985* [1987] JSWL 15

Hoath, D *Homelessness Law After the Housing and Planning Act 1986: The Puhlhofer Amendments* [1988] JSWL 39

Loveland, I *Legal Rights and Political Realities: Governmental Responses to Homelessness in Britain* (1991) *Law & Social Inquiry* 249

Loveland, I *Square Pegs, Round Holes: The 'Right' to Council Housing in the Post War Era* (1992) 19 *Journal of Law & Society* 1

Loveland, I *Administrative Law, Administrative Process, and the Housing of Homeless Persons* [1991] JSWFL 1

Loveland, I *The Politics, Law and Practice of 'International Homelessness'* Parts I & II [1993] JSWFL 113 and 185

Robson, P and Watchman, P *The Homeless Persons' Obstacle Race* [1981] JSWL 165

Sunkin, M *Trends in the use of Judicial Review before and after Swati and Puhlhofer* (1987) 137 *New Law Journal* 731

Sunkin, M *What is happening to applications for Judicial Reviews?* (1987) *Modern Law Review* 432

Watchman, P *Heartbreak Hotel* [1988] JSWL 147

Reports

Anderson, I *Access to Housing for Low Income Single People* (1994, University of York, Centre for Housing Policy)

Anderson, I, Kemp, P and Quilgars, D *Single Homeless People* (1993, HMSO)

Garside, P *No Place Like Home* (1990, HMSO)

Greve, J *Homelessness in Britain* (1991, Joseph Rowntree Memorial Trust)

National Audit Office *Homelessness* (1990, HMSO)

Niner, P *Homelessness in Nine Local Authorities: Case Studies of Policy and Practice* (1989, HMSO)

Randall, G and Brown, S *Private Renting for Single Homeless People: An Evaluation of a Pilot Rent Deposit Fund* (1994, HMSO)

Thomas, A, and Niner, P *Living in Temporary Accommodation: A Survey of Homeless People* (1989, HMSO)

Books

Arden, A, and Hunter, C *Homelessness and Allocations: A Guide to the Housing Act 1996 Parts VI and VII*, (5th Edn, 1997, Legal Action Group)

Atkinson, R, Buck, T, Pollard, D and Smith, N, *A Regional Study of Local Authority and Court Processes in Homelessness Cases* (1999 Lord Chancellors Department Research Series, No 9/99)

Burnet, D 'Homelessness and Allocation of Housing Accommodation' (1998, Monitor Press Ltd)

Hudson, A *The Law on Homelessness* (1997, Sweet and Maxwell)

Loveland, I *Housing Homeless Persons: Administrative Law and the Administrative Powers* (1995, Clarendon Press)

CHAPTER SEVEN

Housing standards

Historical context

The issue of housing standards and the renewal of the housing stock became important issues during the nineteenth century due to the public health consequences of rapid urbanisation. Appallingly high mortality and morbidity was endemic in Victorian slum housing. As described in Chapter One the insanitary condition of urban housing was one of the principal reasons for state intervention in the housing market. As early as 1868, in The Artizans' and Labourers' Dwellings Act (the Torrens Act), local authorities with populations over 10,000 were granted considerable powers to enforce compulsory unfitness notices against landlords, and so provided for the closure and demolition of dwellings unfit for human habitation. There was, of course, at this time no financial assistance and improvement grants did not become available in urban areas until after World War Two. The Housing (Rural Workers) Act 1926 gave authorities in rural locations discretion to award grants and make loans for improvements but these powers were rarely used.

In the Artizans' and Labourers' Dwellings Improvement Act 1875 (the Cross Act) authorities were given powers to clear and redevelop *areas* of unfit housing but they had very limited possibilities to rebuild even after the Housing of the Working Classes Act 1890 and, in the absence of any significant central government funding until the conclusion of the 1914–18 war, far more slums were cleared than were rebuilt. Individual closures and the redevelopment of whole areas of housing have been enshrined in the issue of housing standards ever since.

For most of the twentieth century renovation and improvement of existing housing stock was subsumed under both the slum clearance programme and the drive for new building. It was not until the end of the 1960s that investment in the renovation of existing property became more cost effective than demolition and rebuilding due to the decline in the absolute shortage of housing stock. Renovation of existing property is, of course, one way in which new supply can be achieved – by giving existing dwellings a longer life expectancy than they would have otherwise[1]. Under the different circumstances of the 1920s the renovation and reconditioning of existing housing was promoted as an *alternative* to local authority building by the opponents of municipal housing. Bowley estimates that between 1919 and 1930 some 300,000 houses *per annum* were rehabilitated by forcing private landlords to recondition and improve their property by statutory orders against them[2]. Renovation of housing in the private rented sector thus made a considerable contribution to the inter-war drive to increase housing supply but the standard of improvement was frequently poor and many rehabilitated houses were later demolished as slums. Improvement of this stock up to the very basic standard inherited from late-Victorian housing legislation was not, therefore, an adequate response to the problem of slum housing. Accordingly a specific subsidy for slum clearance and their replacement by new houses was adopted in the Labour Government's second Housing Act 1930. This legislation was not as some commentators argue a major break in policy but, seen in the light of the reconditioning of housing in the 1920s, can be viewed as an extension of existing concern about the state of the private rented sector.

This is not the place for a detailed evaluation of the slum clearance programme and readers are referred to Chapter Two of Gibson and Langstaff's *An Introduction to Urban Renewal*[3] for a full account. The clearances were of massive dimensions and some two million dwellings have been demolished since the Housing Act 1930 (Greenwood Act) with the built environment of almost every major town and city changed as a result. Clearances were halted during the Second World War and only started again in the mid-1950s when the economy had recovered from the catastrophic consequences of the war. In the five years between 1955 and 1959 213,000 houses were demolished or closed affecting nearly 670,000 people. The clearance programme reached its post-war peak in the second half of the 1960s when between 1964 and 1969 339,000 house were demolished. The rate of clearance fell, in the mid-1970s, to about 50,000 per annum and declined sharply thereafter; by 1989 it was down to only 6,000 and has stayed below that level subsequently.

1 Needleman, L 'The comparative economics of improvement and new building' (1969) Urban Studies, Vol 6 No 2, pp 196–209.
2 Bowley, M *Housing and the State* (Allen and Unwin, 1945).
3 Hutchinson, 1982.

The current law

The rest of this chapter describes the current law and unless where expressly stated the remedies referred to apply to both public and private sector tenancies, and begins by considering the common law remedies available to tenants and others injured by the substandard condition of rented property.

Historically neither contract nor tort gave protection to tenants. The attitude of the law was encapsulated in the maxim caveat emptor, or as Erle CJ said in *Robbins v Jones*[4]: '... fraud apart, there is no law against letting a tumbledown house: and the tenant's remedy is upon his contract, if any'[5]. There was no liability in tort whether the damage arose from the landlord's mere neglect or from the careless doing of works of maintenance or installation. In *Travers v Gloucester Corpn*[6] a local authority let a house with the vent pipe of a gas geyser terminating under the eaves of the house. This dangerous installation led to a build-up of toxic exhaust fumes and as a consequence the tenant's lodger was gassed in the bathroom. The corporation was held not liable in tort.

A growing body of opinion viewed the exemption of lessors from liability in negligence with growing distaste and various attempts were made to end it. For example it was said in *Ball v LCC*[7] that landlords could be liable in *contract* to tenants for negligent installation work carried out *after* the start of the lease, though non-contracting parties could not sue under this rule. Great changes have now, however, been made in the law.

Landlords' obligations in tort

At common law

Following the decisions in *Cunard v Antifyre Ltd*[8] and *Taylor v Liverpool Corpn*[9] there is no difficulty in holding landlords liable in negligence for damage caused *by buildings retained in their occupation* to persons or to buildings let to a tenant. In *AC Billings & Sons Ltd v Riden*[10] the House of Lords stated that, irrespective of the lack of a contractual relationship,

4   (1863) 15 CBNS 221 at 239.
5   See *Gordon and Teixeira v Selico and Select Management Ltd* (1986) 18 HLR 219 for an application of this principle; see also *Southwark London Borough Council v Mills, Baxter v Camden London Borough Council* [1999] 4 All ER 449, [1999] 3 WLR 939, HL, on the point that a lack of sound insulation is no breach of covenant of quiet enjoyment.
6   [1947] KB 71, [1946] 2 All ER 506.
7   [1949] 2 KB 159, [1949] 1 All ER 1056.
8   [1933] 1 KB 551.
9   [1939] 3 All ER 329.
10 [1958] AC 240, [1957] 3 All ER 1.

persons who execute work on premises are under a general duty to use reasonable care for the safety of those whom they know, or ought reasonably to know, may be affected by or lawfully in the vicinity of the work. Thus landlords can be liable in tort for dangers created *after* the commencement of the tenancy.

In *Rimmer v Liverpool City Council*[11] , the claimant was the tenant of a flat owned, designed and built by the local authority. One internal passageway contained an unprotected thin glass panel. The tenant tripped in the passageway, put out his hand to save himself, and his hand went through the panel, as a result of which he suffered injury. The Court of Appeal repeated that *the 'bare' landlord of unfurnished premises, who has done no work on them , owes no duty of care to a tenant in respect of the state of the premises when they were let*, but held that a landlord may owe a duty of care in respect of being the *designer or builder* of premises. This duty is owed to all persons who may reasonably be expected to be affected by the design or construction of the premises, and is a duty to take reasonable care to ensure such persons do not suffer injury from design or construction defects (which *may* extend to defects in work of modernisation or conversion etc). The authority was in breach of that duty on this occasion. Liability here arose from the fact of negligent design and/or construction. Where, however, there is no evidence of negligent design or construction, the old rule survives[12] . In *Targett v Torfaen Borough Council*[13] it was held that the fact that a claimant *knows* of the landlord's bad design or construction work will not automatically negative the landlord's duty of care. The question in such cases is whether the claimant can reasonably be expected to remove or avoid the danger. It is not normally reasonable to expect a tenant to avoid a danger by giving up the property, though knowledge of a defect may point to a need for a tenant to take greater heed for personal safety, and failure to do that may result in the tenant being contributorily negligent in respect of harm suffered. See also S*harpe v Manchester Metropolitan District Council*[14] where the plaintiff took a tenancy of a flat in 1972 and found it infested with cockroaches. The authority tried to eliminate the insects for two years by using emulsified DDT, but failed in their attempts. They were found negligent in that they had failed to treat the service ducts and other spaces in the walls and floor and had used a discredited insecticide. However, this decision should not be over much relied on following *Habinteg Housing Association v James*[15] , where there was held to be *no* liability on a landlord where a flat was infested but there

11 [1985] QB 1, [1984] 1 All ER 930.
12 *McNerney v Lambeth London Borough Council* (1988) 21 HLR 188, and *Boldack v East Lindsey District Council* (1998) 31 HLR 41, CA.
13 [1992] 3 All ER 27.
14 (1977) 5 HLR 71.
15 (1994) 27 HLR 299.

was no part of the property in the landlord's possession from which an invasion of the tenant's home could be shown to have proceeded.

Under statute

Civil liability may arise under the Defective Premises Act 1972. Section 1 provides (inter alia):

'(1) A person taking on work for or in connection with the provision of a dwelling (whether the dwelling is provided by the erection or by the conversion or enlargement of a building) owes a duty:

(a) if the building is provided to the order of any person to that person; and

(b) without prejudice to paragraph (a) above to every person who acquires an interest (whether legal or equitable) in the dwelling; to see that the work which he takes on is done in a workmanlike or, as the case may be, professional manner, with proper materials and so that as regard that work the dwelling will be fit for habitation when completed ...

(4) A person who:

(a) in the course of a business which consists of or includes providing or arranging for the provision of dwellings or installation in dwellings; or

(b) in the exercise of a power of making such provision or arrangements conferred by or by virtue of any enactment; arranges for another to take on work for or in connection with the provision of a dwelling shall be treated for the purposes of this section as included among the persons who have taken on the work.'

This provision imposes liability on authorities and associations, their builders, sub-contractors and architects if they fail to build in a professional or workmanlike manner (as the case may be) with proper materials, or fail to ensure the dwelling is fit for human habitation, a phrase which may be capable of covering such matters as defective design or lay-out. It extends to necessary work not done as well as that badly done so that a dwelling lacks after the work is done some essential attribute making it unfit[16]. The duty, *which is strict*, is owed to, inter alia, those persons having legal

16 *Andrews v Schooling* [1991] 3 All ER 723, [1991] 1 WLR 783 – a house converted into flats did not have work done to prevent the progress of damp into the bottom flat from the cellar.

interests in the dwelling, for example tenants, but *not* their children or visitors. Moreover, the duty only arises in connection with *the provision*, whether by new construction, conversion or enlargement, of a *dwelling*. The provision only applies to dwellings constructed after 1 January 1974, by virtue of section 7(2) of the Act. This provision seems to have been strangely ignored by public sector tenants affected by design or construction defects.[17]

Section 3(1) of the Defective Premises Act 1972 provides:

'Where work of construction, repair, maintenance or demolition or any other work is done on or in relation to premises, any duty of care owed, because of the doing of the work, to persons who might reasonably be expected to be affected by the defects in the state of the premises created by the doing of the work shall not be abated by the subsequent disposal of the premises by the person who owed the duty'.

This statutory displacement of a landlord's immunity in negligence only applies, by virtue of section 3(2)(a), to those lettings of premises entered into after the commencement of the Act, 1 January 1974. Liability can only arise where there has been a defect created by a positive act classifiable as 'work of construction, repair, maintenance or demolition or any other work done on or in relation to premises'. It seems not *all* 'work' can give rise to liability but only that of specified kinds, or other 'work' which can be said to be 'done on or in relation to premises' such as, for example, installation of central heating. Nor does this section impose any liability for negligent omissions to do repairs.

Liability for an omission may arise under section 4 of the 1972 Act. Section 4(1) provides:

'Where premises are let under a tenancy which puts on the landlord an obligation to the tenant for the maintenance or repair of the premises, the landlord owes to all persons who might reasonably be expected to be affected by defects in the state of the premises a duty to take such care as is reasonable in all the circumstances to see that they are reasonably safe from personal injury or from damage to their property caused by a relevant defect.'

This imposes tortious liability on landlords towards tenants, their families and those other persons foreseeably likely to be in the premises, and, by section 6(3) of the Act landlords cannot exclude or restrict this duty.

17 See further *Mirza v Bhandal* (1999) Housing Law Monitor (June) 4 where a person who arranged for a house to be substantially rebuilt was found liable under section 1(4) when the house was given inadequate foundations and subsided.

This section also poses problems of interpretation. Liability can only arise in respect of a 'relevant defect'. Such is defined by sub-section (3) as

'... a defect in the state of the premises existing at or after the material time and arising from, or continuing because of, an act or omission by the landlord which constitutes or would if he had notice of the defect, have constituted a failure by him to carry out his obligation to the tenant for the maintenance or repair of the premises ...'.

Such defects must arise 'at or after the material time', which is further defined by the sub-section as being, in general terms, for tenancies commencing before the Act, the commencement date of the Act (1 January 1974), and in other cases the earliest date on which the tenancy commenced or the tenancy agreement was entered into. Liability arises out of those defects which constitute a breach of the landlord's obligations to repair and maintain. These obligations will include any express covenant to repair given by the landlord and, by virtue of sub-section (5), those implied by statute, such as section 11 of the Landlord and Tenant Act 1985. An even more extended meaning is given to 'obligation' by sub-section (4) which deems for the purposes of the section any *power* a landlord has to repair actually to be an *obligation* to repair. Such powers can arise in many situations. A landlord may have power to enter and do repairs simply because the tenant has defaulted on the tenant's repairing covenants. In such circumstances the Act provides that the landlord, while remaining liable to third parties, shall not be liable to the tenant. The effect of dicta in *Mint v Good*[18] should also be remembered. Somervell LJ said: '... in the case of a weekly tenancy, business efficacy will not be effected if the house is allowed to fall into disrepair and no one keeps it in reasonable condition; and it seems to be, therefore, necessary ... that the ... landlord should at any rate have the power to keep the place in proper repair ...'.

An implied power to enter and do repairs may arise in relation to any *weekly* tenancy of a dwelling-house and will be deemed to be an obligation to repair under sub-section (4).

In *Smith v Bradford Metropolitan Council*[19], a tenancy agreement provided the tenant should give the authority and its officers and workmen reasonable facilities for inspecting *the premises let*, their state of repair, and to carry out repairs, and the 'premises' in question were defined as the dwelling, and, where the context required, its garage, outbuildings, yards and gardens. The tenant of the dwelling was injured by the defective condition of a rear concrete patio constructed between the house and its garden by a previous tenant. The Court of Appeal found the power to enter

18 [1951] 1 KB 517 at 522, [1950] 2 All ER 1159.
19 (1982) 44 P & CR 171.

the premises fell within section 4(4) of the 1972 Act, and was a deemed obligation to repair. The context required that the patio be regarded as part of the premises in relation to which the power, and deemed obligation, to repair existed. In *McAuley v Bristol City Council*[20], however, there was merely a clause that the tenant should give the authority 'all reasonable facilities for entering upon the premises ... for any purpose which may from time to time be required by the council'. It was, nevertheless, held that this clause gave the council power to enter the premises, and that the tenancy agreement contemplated that the council would keep the premises in a reasonable and habitable condition. To give business efficacy to that understanding there had to be implied a term that the council would carry out repairs wherever there were defects in *the premises* – in this case including the garden – which would expose a tenant or visitor to a serious risk of injury. Thus because the council had the right to enter the premises they could be liable under section 4.

There are a number of subsidiary points to note about section 4. Subsection (2) provides:

'The said duty is owed if the landlord knows (whether as the result of being notified by the tenant or otherwise) or if he ought in all the circumstances to have known of the relevant defect'.

There is no need to give notice of defects provided they would be patent on reasonable inspection. Indeed there are *dicta* that a local authority landlord should carry out pre-lettings checks of houses to detect defects.[1]

In *Clarke v Taff Ely Borough Council*[2], Mrs Clarke visited her sister's council house and was injured when the rotten floorboards gave way beneath a table on which she was standing. The house was one of a number of pre-war council houses known to have a potentially dangerous floor construction. The authority's chief housing surveyor agreed that in view of the age of the house, its type and the presence of damp it was foreseeable that rot would occur. Damages of £5,100 were awarded.

A very extended meaning is given to 'tenancy' by section 6 of the 1972 Act. The term includes leases and underleases, tenancies at will and sufferance and statutory tenancies, and rights of occupation given by contract, see also section 4(6).

Even so, to rely on section 4 the claimant must show that there has been harm caused as a result of a relevant defect, so that tripping over a slab leaning against a wall of a house is not enough where the landlord's

20 [1992] QB 134, [1992] 1 All ER 749, CA.
1   *Morley v Knowsley Borough Council* (1998) Legal Action (May) 22.
2   (1980) 10 HLR 44.

obligation is 'to repair' as the situation is not one where a lack of repair can be shown.[3]

Liability under the Occupiers' Liability Act 1957

The common law imposes liability on landlords for defects on their premises, eg the common parts of blocks of flats, which cause injury to their tenants. The Occupiers' Liability Act 1957, section 2, also imposes liability in such circumstances, and the 1957 Act adds to the landlord's obligation by stating in section 3(1):

> 'Where an occupier of premises is bound by contract to permit persons who are strangers to the contract to enter or use the premises, the duty of care which he owes to them as his visitors cannot be restricted or excluded by that contract, but (subject to any provision of the contract to the contrary) shall include the duty to perform his obligations under the contract, whether undertaken for their protection or not, in so far as those obligations go beyond the obligations otherwise involved in that duty.'

The effect is that landlords cannot by virtue of their contracts with tenants reduce obligations to tenants' visitors below the standard required by the Act, the 'common duty of care'. Furthermore tenants' visitors are enabled to claim the benefit of any more onerous obligations inserted in the lease, unless the lease itself specifically excludes this.

LANDLORDS' OBLIGATIONS IN CONTRACT

At common law

Contractual remedies only apply as between contracting parties. Any third party injured by the defective state of a dwelling-house must find a remedy in tort. That said, landlords may be liable to tenants for a breach of express covenants to repair and maintain a dwelling-house. In such a case the extent of the liability will depend upon the wording of the covenant. Such express covenants are rare, particularly as many leases of ordinary dwelling-houses in the past have been created orally on a weekly basis under section 54(2) of the Law of Property Act 1925. Where authorities and registered social landlords use express terms in their tenancy agreement these frequently do no more than replicate the statutorily implied terms considered below.

---

3   *Boldack v East Lindsey District Council* (1998) 31 HLR 41, CA.

However, such terms may go further and relate not just to the dwelling-house but to the whole of the premises let. They may also impose specific burdens such as promises that particular items of repair will be carried out within particular periods of time. Express covenants are construed taking into account the state of the dwelling at the time it was let, its age and locality[4], thus a simple covenant to repair is not to be interpreted to require a landlord to renew a decayed hovel by turning it into an up-to-date home. However, a covenant to keep a building in 'good and tenantable' condition may require a landlord to put it into that state even where it has not previously attained it, *Crédit Suisse v Beegas Nominees Ltd*[5].

The common law has also been unwilling to imply terms into leases. In *Smith v Marrable*[6], Parke B implied a term into a letting of *furnished* premises that, at the start of the lease, they would be in a habitable condition. According to *Sarson v Roberts*[7], the obligation will not arise if the premises become uninhabitable during the course of the lease. What is likely to make a house unfit for habitation in this context are matters likely to affect the health of incoming tenants such as infestation by bugs, or defects in drains, or recent occupation by a person suffering from an easily communicable disease. The meaning given by the common law to 'unfit for human habitation' is therefore different from the meaning the phrase has under the unfitness provisions of the Housing Act 1985. If furnished premises are 'unfit' at common law the tenant is entitled to quit them by repudiating the tenancy, and may also sue for any loss suffered, see *Wilson v Finch Hatton*[8], and *Charsley v Jones*[9]. This implied condition is limited to lettings of furnished dwellings. In *Sleafer v Lambeth Borough Council*[10] it was said that where a landlord lets unfurnished dwellings there will generally be no implied term that they are free of defects.

However, in *Liverpool City Council v Irwin*[11] the House of Lords implied a term into a letting of a flat in a high rise block. The authority owned a tower block of flats, access to which was provided by a common staircase and electrically operated lifts. The tenants also had the use of internal chutes into which to discharge rubbish. The condition of the block deteriorated, partly as a result of vandalism, and defects included: failed lifts; a lack of lighting on the staircases, and blocked rubbish chutes. The tenants refused to pay rent and the landlord applied for possession orders

---

4   *Anstruther-Gough-Calthorpe v McOscar* [1924] 1 KB 716.
5   [1994] 4 All ER 803; see also *Smedley v Chumley & Hawkes Ltd* (1981) 44 P & CR 50.
6   (1843) 11 M & W 5.
7   [1895] 2 QB 395.
8   (1877) 2 Ex D 336.
9   (1889) 53 JP 280.
10 [1960] 1 QB 43, [1959] 3 All ER 378.
11 [1977] AC 239, [1976] 2 All ER 39.

on the flats, to which the tenants replied with a counter-claim that (inter alia) the landlord was in breach of covenant of quiet enjoyment. The House of Lords said this was a contract in which the parties had not themselves fully expressed the terms and the court could imply certain terms solely to prevent the contract of letting from becoming inefficacious and absurdly futile. The House of Lords then went on to state:

(1) the tenants had in their leases an implied right or easement to use the stairs, lifts and rubbish chutes as these were necessarily incidental to their occupation of high-rise flats;

(2) the landlord was therefore under an implied obligation to take reasonable care to maintain those common areas and facilities;

(3) such an obligation is not, however, absolute because tenants of high-rise blocks must themselves resist vandalism and co-operate in maintaining the common areas in reasonable condition, and

(4) the courts have no power to imply such terms in tenancy agreements as they think 'reasonable'. They may only supply such terms as are truly necessary for the functioning of the contract.

Thus in *King v South Northamptonshire District Council*[12] where a wheelchair bound tenant was forced to use a rear access path, over which she had only a right of way, as the way into her home, and it was clear the dwelling could not be enjoyed without that access way, an obligation on the part of the landlord was upheld to keep the path in repair.

There are dicta supporting an argument that where a landlord has let out flats on long leases in a block (for example by virtue of the Right to Buy) the landlord is under an implied obligation to take reasonable care to see that those parts of the block that the landlord retains do not damage the flats that have been let[13].

Under statute

Parliament has on a number of occasions attempted to remedy the omission of the common law, but, sadly, the courts have adopted a somewhat restrictive interpretation of the legislation, while Parliament itself has been remiss in not keeping some of the remedies up-to-date. This is particularly true of the provision which began life as section 12 of the Housing of the Working Classes Act 1885, and which is now section 8 of the Landlord and Tenant Act 1985. This states that in a letting to which it applies there is an

12 (1991) 24 HLR 284.

13 *Gordon and Teixeira v Selico Ltd and Select Managements Ltd* (1986) 18 HLR 219, though the unwillingness of the courts generally to imply obligations to repair the structure of blocks of flats was reitterated in *Adami v Lincoln Grange Management Ltd* [1998] 1 EGLR 58; but see also *Loria v Hammer* [1989] 2 EGLR 249.

implied term of fitness for human habitation at the commencement of the tenancy and that the landlord will keep it so fit throughout its currency.

The problem is that section 8(3) limits its applicability to contracts of letting where the rent was not originally, on or after 1 April 1965, more than £80 in relation to Inner London Boroughs or £52 elsewhere in the country, and thus hardly any properties are now covered. The courts have 'discovered' other difficulties in the wording of the provision, and these have hardened into rules of interpretation which apply not only to section 8 but also to section 11 of the Landlord and Tenant Act 1985. Thus *Middleton v Hall*[14] and *Ryall v Kidwell & Son*[15] state that only the tenant can sue. While these decisions have been effectively overruled in tort by section 4 of the Defective Premises Act 1972 (see above) the technical rule remains that privity of contract limits the possibility of suing on the implied covenant only to the contracting parties. Next it should be noted that landlords cannot be liable under the implied covenant unless tenants have previously given notice of the defect. This was decided, in the case of patent defects, by *McCarrick v Liverpool Corpn*[16], and was applied to latent defects by *O'Brien v Robinson*[17]: again remember the tortious remedy under section 4 of the Defective Premises Act 1972 is not made so dependent upon the giving of actual notice. In the case of authority dwellings, it was held in *Sheldon v West Bromwich Corpn*[18] that where an appropriately qualified authority employee knows that premises are defective that knowledge will be treated as giving the authority notice, and notice does not have to be given personally by the tenant.

In *McGreal v Wake*[19] though it was stressed that tenants should inform landlords of works necessary to meet breaches of repairing obligations, it can be enough to 'trigger' a landlord's responsibilities if the tenant complains to the local authority and they then serve notice requiring works under their Housing Act 1985 powers. Similarly in *Dinefwr Borough Council v Jones*[20] a district valuer's 'right to buy' report to an authority which specified defects was held to constitute notice, even though it was not submitted as a disrepair complaint.

A solicitor's letter complaining about a lack of repair can be sufficient to put a landlord 'on notice' and need not specify the exact nature or degree of the disrepair, provided it makes clear to the landlord that the tenant is giving notice the work should be done[1].

---

14 (1913) 108 LT 804.
15 [1914] 3 KB 135.
16 [1947] AC 219, [1946] 2 All ER 646.
17 [1973] AC 912, [1973] 1 All ER 583.
18 (1973) 25 P & CR 360; see also *Griffin v Pillet* [1926] 1 KB 17.
19 (1984) 269 Estates Gazette 1254.
20 (1987) 19 HLR 445, see also *Hall v Howard* (1988) 20 HLR 566.
1 *Al Hassani v Merrigan* (1987) 20 HLR 238.

The most serious limitation on section 8 was imposed by the Court of Appeal in *Buswell v Goodwin*[2]. Here a cottage was statutorily unfit and, as the local authority had made a closing order on it, the landlord had commenced possession proceedings against the tenant. He argued the house was only unfit because the landlord was in breach of implied contractual obligations under section 8. The Court of Appeal, however, restricted the ambit of operation of the implied covenant to cases where houses are capable of being made fit at reasonable expense. The obligation is not absolute. Where a house has fallen into an extreme state of disrepair the tenant can no longer rely on the implied covenant. The paradox thus emerges of tenants of the worst housing receiving the lowest level of legal protection. Furthermore where statutorily unfit houses are retained by authorities under their Housing Act 1985 powers, section 8 will not apply to letting such houses, see section 302(c) of the Housing Act 1985.

Section 11 of the Landlord and Tenant Act 1985

A similar process of judicial reasoning has emptied much of the meaning from the other statutorily implied covenant: section 11 of the Landlord and Tenant Act 1985. This applies, under section 13 of the Act, to leases of dwelling-houses granted on or after 24 October 1961 for terms of less than seven years, so a lease for a term of seven years is not caught[3]. The obligation is to keep in repair the structure and exterior of the dwelling, including its drains, gutters and external pipes, *and* to keep in repair *and* proper working order the mains services installations, including basins, sinks, baths and sanitary conveniences, but excluding appliances etc, for making use of a mains service, eg a refrigerator, *and* to keep in repair and working order space and water heating installations. The standard of repair required is determined by having regard to the age, character, prospective life and locality of the dwelling. It is not possible to contract out of this obligation, see section 12 of the Act, save with the consent of the county court.

The provision now requires, with regard to tenancies granted on or after 15 January 1989, that a landlord is to keep in repair the structure and exterior of *any* part of a building he/she owns of which the tenant's dwelling forms part, see section 11(1A) of the 1985 Act. A similar extension of the original section 11 covers mains services installations which serve a dwelling-house directly or indirectly *and* which either form part of any part of the building in which the landlord has an interest or are owned by the landlord

2　[1971] 1 All ER 418, [1971] 1 WLR 92.
3　*Brikom Investments Ltd v Seaford* [1981] 2 All ER 783, [1981] 1 WLR 863 and *Demetriou v Poolaction Ltd* [1991] 1 EGLR 100, CA.

or are under the landlord's control. However, the landlord's obligations can only be relied on where the disrepair, etc, is such as to affect the tenant's enjoyment of the dwelling or of the common parts of the property in which it is, see section 11(1B). Nevertheless this provision may be relied upon by, for example, tenants of flats adversely affected by disrepair of stairways and access paths. It appears liability in respect of defects in retained common parts is absolute, and that a landlord here can be liable, even in the absence of knowledge: see *Passley v Wandsworth London Borough Council*[4] where water pipes in a block of flats burst in freezing weather and flooded a tenant's flat. The obligation 'to repair' implied an obligation to 'keep in good order'.

The policy of Parliament in creating the implied covenant was to prevent unscrupulous landlords from imposing unreasonable repairing obligations on tenants. It cannot be said, however, that the law has been successful in *preventing* disrepair and bad housing conditions. Tenants are generally ignorant of their rights, and often do not complain about disrepair until it becomes exceptional and intolerable. Alongside this there exists the same restrictive judicial attitude already seen in relation to the section 8 covenant.

This can be seen in decisions as to which matters fall within the scope of the implied covenant. In *Brown v Liverpool Corpn*[5], paving flagstones and shallow steps leading to a house were held to be part of its 'exterior'. They were necessary for the purpose of gaining access to the house and fell within the scope of the implied covenant. In *Hopwood v Cannock Chase District Council*[6] slabs in a back yard were held not to fall within the scope of the covenant as the back yard was not the essential means of access to the house. In *Irvine v Moran*[7] it was considered ' structure' is that which gives a property its 'essential stability and shape', not the ways and means in which a house is fitted out, eg garages, gates, wall plaster, door locks, internal decoration, though external doors, windows, window glass and painting are part of the 'exterior'. So far as flats are concerned, dicta in *Campden Hill Towers Ltd v Gardner*[8] are most important. Where the structure is concerned the landlord's obligation extends to anything which can ordinarily be regarded as part of the structure or exterior of the dwelling in question. Thus section 11(1)(a) applies, irrespective of the words of the lease, to the outside walls of a flat (even though they may have been excluded from the lease), the outer sides of horizontal divisions between flats, the outside of the inner party walls of the flat and the structural

4   (1996) 30 HLR 165; see also *Stockley v Knowsley Metropolitan Borough Council* [1986] 2 EGLR 141 a case where the tenant had warned the landlord of a problem of frozen pipes in an adjacent flat.
5   [1969] 3 All ER 1345.
6   [1975] 1 All ER 796, [1975] 1 WLR 373.
7   [1991] 1 EGLR 261.
8   [1977] QB 823, [1977] 1 All ER 739.

framework and beams directly supporting the floors, ceilings and walls of a flat. The test to be used in determining the scope of the implied covenant is whether the particular item of disrepair affects the stability or usability of the particular flat in question.

In *Douglas-Scott v Scorgie*[9] the Court of Appeal held that the roof of a building above a top floor flat may be part of the structure and exterior of that flat, irrespective of whether or not it forms part of the demised premises. The content of the obligations of public and private sector landlords are the same under this implied covenant[10].

The covenant is one to repair, so what is the meaning of the word 'repair'? In *Ravenseft Properties Ltd v Davstone (Holdings) Ltd*[11] a distinction was made between the process of repair and a completely different process which is replacement. Replacement is a process of reconstruction so drastic that at the end of the lease the landlord receives back a wholly different property from that which he/she demised. 'Repair' on the other hand, according to the decision in *Greg v Planque*[12], simply means making good defects, including renewal where necessary. In other words, simply keeping the property in a condition suitable for the purpose for which it was let. The distinction between these two processes is the scale and degree of the work involved. The fact that work, because of modern statutory requirements or building practices, has to be done to a higher standard than that of the original does not necessarily mean that it cannot be classed as 'repair'. Work will not be classifiable as 'repair' if it results in a reconstruction of the whole, or substantially the whole, of a building.

In *McDougall v Easington District Council*[13] Mustill LJ put forward three tests which may be applied 'separately or concurrently' to decide whether a matter is one of repair or renewal/replacement:
(1)   do any alterations go to the whole, or substantially the whole of the structure;
(2)   is the effect of the work to produce a building of a wholly different character from that which was let;
(3)   what is the cost of works in relation to the building's previous value, and what is their effect on its value and life expectancy?

Thus if the landlord can show that the work required on any given house is so drastic that it would amount to his/her getting back, at the end of the term, a substantially different house from that which was let, then that work is outside the obligation to repair. In *Pembery v Lamdin*[14] a landlord let certain old premises not constructed with a damp-course or with

9   [1984] 1 All ER 1086, [1984] 1 WLR 716.
10   *Wainwright v Leeds City Council* (1984) 270 Estates Gazette 1289.
11   [1980] QB 12, [1979] 1 All ER 929.
12   [1936] 1 KB 669.
13   (1989) 21 HLR 310.
14   [1940] 2 All ER 434.

waterproofing for the external walls, and covenanted to keep the external part of the let premises in good repair and condition. The tenant claimed this put the landlord under an obligation to waterproof the outside walls and render the premises dry. It was held the obligation was only to keep the premises in repair in the condition in which they were let. In this case the landlord would be required only to point the external brickwork. However, contrast *Elmcroft Developments Ltd v Tankersley-Sawyer*[15]. The court found that replacing an incorrectly laid *and existing* damp proof course in a block of flats was an act of 'repair'. Similarly, contrast *Mullaney v Maybourne Grange (Croydon) Management Co Ltd*[16] and *Reston Ltd v Hudson*[17]. In the former the replacement of wooden framed windows with double glazed ones was considered an improvement, in the latter the comprehensive replacement of all windows at one time when only some were rotted was considered a 'repair'.

The burden of proving a particular repair is needed is, moreover, on the person alleging its need and as a landlord may normally repair on a piecemeal 'make good as we go' basis,[18] should the tenant wish to argue for a major replacement evidence will have to be adduced showing why a piece meal job is no longer enough[19].

It is also necessary to show disrepair as opposed to a lack of amenity or inefficiency, see *Quick v Taff-Ely Borough Council*[20]. Here a council house built in the early 1970s was thermally inefficient with uninsulated concrete window lintels giving rise to condensation that produced intolerable living conditions. The Court of Appeal accepted that the eradication of a design defect, such as affected the dwelling, may fall within the ambit of the implied covenant, provided the work required does not amount to substantial reconstruction or improvement, *and* provided the work is necessary to remedy disrepair. To repair is to make good some damage: eradicating a design defect that simply makes a dwelling inefficient or ineffective as a habitation is not automatically therefore repair. In *Quick* the court found the condensation simply made the house function badly or inefficiently, there was no damage or deterioration as such to any components of the structure of the dwelling. The obligation to repair only arises where there is damage or deterioration, though where this can be shown to exist, discharging the obligation may require eradicating a design defect giving rise to the damage so that to some extent the dwelling is 'improved'. Note also *Stent v Monmouth District Council*[1] where there was actual deterioration damage

15 [1984] 1 EGLR 47, CA.
16 [1986] 1 EGLR 70.
17 [1990] 2 EGLR 51.
18 *Dame Margaret Hungerford Charity Trustees v Beazeley* (1993) 26 HLR 269.
19 *Murray v Birmingham City Council* (1987) 20 HLR 39.
20 [1986] QB 809, [1985] 3 All ER 321.
1   (1987) 19 HLR 269.

of a badly designed and installed entrance door which could be characterised as 'disrepair'.

The content of the obligation to repair has also been the subject of judicial attention. In *Newham London Borough v Patel*[2] the Court of Appeal considered the forerunners of section 11(3) of the Landlord and Tenant Act 1985. This states that the standard of repair is to be determined by having regard to the 'age, character and prospective life of the dwelling-house and the locality in which it is situated'. Mr Patel's house was a poor, old dwelling in bad condition shortly destined for redevelopment. The court concluded the prospective life of the dwelling affected the content of the section 11 duty. The authority could not be required to carry out repairs which the court categorised as 'wholly useless'.

On the other hand a landlord cannot always justify a poor standard of repair simply on the basis of a low rent being charged for an old house, see *McClean v Liverpool City Council*[3] and *Sturolson & Co v Mauroux*[4]. To succeed on this basis a landlord would need to show that the rent is truly 'nominal' or very low, while any repairs needed would be wholly useless, or that the dwelling has no prospective life.

Once the landlord has notice of disrepair the work should be carried out within a reasonable time – this will depend upon the nature of the work needed, any problems associated with obtaining the necessary materials, the landlord's work load, etc – and the burden of proving unreasonable delay in doing work lies on the tenant[5].

Even where a landlord is in breach of an express or implied repairing covenant, liability will only extend to those matters which are foreseeable consequences of the breach.[6]

Tenants are not, however, entitled to treat their homes in a cavalier fashion. It was made clear in *Warren v Keen*[7] that tenants are always under some sort of obligation to look after their homes. In the case of a long lease, say 99 years, the tenant is usually made subject to full repairing covenants.

On the other hand weekly tenants are usually bound to use the premises in a tenant-like manner. This means taking proper care of the premises, for example cleaning chimneys and windows, replacing electric light bulbs, mending fuses, and unstopping blocked sinks. In *Wycombe Health Authority v Barnett*[8] it was stated that in very cold climatic conditions a tenant *may*

2   [1979] JPL 303.
3   [1987] 2 EGLR 56, CA.
4   (1988) 20 HLR 332.
5   *Morris v Liverpool City Council* [1988] 1 EGLR 47, CA.
6   Stumbling on stairs which the tenant has to use because lifts are out of action (in breach of covenant) is not foreseeable, while being burgled via a front door which is clearly in a state of disrepair is; contrast *Berryman v Hounslow London Borough Council* (1996) 30 HLR 567 with *Marshall v Rubypoint Ltd* (1997) 29 HLR 850.
7   [1954] 1 QB 15, [1953] 2 All ER 1118.
8   [1982] 2 EGLR 35, CA.

have to lag water pipes, or use additional heat, or turn off the water supply according to the circumstances, such as the severity of the cold, the duration of contemplated absence from home and the internal condition of the house, in order to behave in a tenant-like manner. See also *Mickel v M'Coard*[9] where a tenant left a house for a month, without telling the landlord, in very cold weather and was held liable for burst pipes.

Remedies for breaches of covenant

Specific performance

Though there appear to be few reported cases on the issue, section 17 of the Landlord and Tenant Act 1985 permits orders of specific performance to be made in cases where tenants' alleged breach of landlords' repairing covenants occur. The remedy is available whether or not the breach relates to a part of the premises let to the tenant, and notwithstanding any equitable rule which would otherwise restrict the scope of the remedy, eg that the tenant does not have 'clean hands' because of arrears of rent. Specific performance is, however, a discretionary remedy and the court will not order a landlord to do unnecessary or extravagant work. Though the remedy is available as a final[10] or an interim order[11] it is arguable an interim order would only be made before a decision on liability for repairs where the situation was extreme and some immediate danger needs to be removed.

Landlords may give undertakings to do works or consent to mandatory orders made in repairs proceedings: neglect to honour these may result in contempt proceedings[12].

Appointing a receiver

Where a landlord is neglectful, and in breach which is likely to continue, of repairing obligations, so that serious deterioration of the dwelling(s) in question is likely, and it can be shown that the landlord is taking no real interest in the property, either to collect rent or to perform obligations, it may be possible to apply for the appointment of a receiver by the High Court if it appears just and convenient. The receiver will then manage the property

---

9   1913 SC 896.
10 *Francis v Cowcliffe* (1976) 33 P & CR 368; see also *Rainbow Estates Ltd v Tokenhold Ltd* [1999] Ch 64, [1998] 2 All ER 860.
11 *Kotecha v Manchester City Council* (4 October 1982, unreported, County Court).
12 *Mullen v Hackney London Borough Council* [1997] 2 All ER 906, [1997] 1 WLR 1103 and *R v Wandsworth County Court, ex p Munn* (1994) 26 HLR 697.

in accordance with the lease until further order, see *Hart v Emelkirk Ltd*[13] . However, this remedy may not be sought by *local authority* tenants, see *Parker v Camden London Borough Council*[14] . Though even against a local authority landlord a mandatory order commanding performance of repairing obligations may be made if there is a clear breach of a covenant which gives rise to major discomfort and annoyance *and* a real risk of damage to health consequent on the breach.

Where the premises consist of two or more flats in a block, section 21 of the Landlord and Tenant Act 1987 permits a tenant to apply for the appointment of a manager of the premises, though a preliminary warning notice has to be given to the landlord under section 22 specifying the grounds on which the court will be asked to appoint a manager. A manager may be appointed where the landlord is in breach of obligation, where that breach is likely to continue and where it is just and convenient to make the appointment. See section 24 of the 1987 Act as amended in 1996. This power, does *not*, however, apply to any premises where the landlord is 'exempt' (eg a district or London borough council, an urban development corporation, a housing action trust, the Housing Corporation, a housing trust or a registered housing association) or where the premises are on the functional land of any charity. The power to appoint a manager has been vested in Leasehold Valuation Tribunals under section 86 of the Housing Act 1996.

Self help

In *Lee-Parker v Izzet*[15] it was held that, irrespective of the common law rules as to set off, occupiers of property had a right to recoup themselves out of *future* rent for the cost of repairs to the property, in so far as the repairs fell within the landlord's express or implied covenants, provided the landlord was in fact in breach, and only after due notice had been given. Tenants have no rights to *withhold* payment of rent to compel landlords to carry out repairs, and if they do they will be in breach of their own obligations under the lease. The rule only authorises the deducting of the *proper* costs of repairs from future rent: a tenant is not entitled to expend vast sums and then present the landlord with the bill. The following steps should be taken before reliance is placed on the rule:

(1) the tenant *must* notify the landlord of the disrepair which itself must arise from a breach of the landlord's covenants;

(2) the tenant should obtain at least two builders' estimates as to the likely costs of the repairs and send them to the landlord, warning that if repairs

13 [1983] 3 All ER 15, [1983] 1 WLR 1289, and see *Daiches v Bluelake Investments Ltd* (1985) 17 HLR 543.
14 [1986] Ch 162, [1985] 2 All ER 141.
15 [1971] 3 All ER 1099, [1971] 1 WLR 1688.

are not affected the tenant will carry out the work and will deduct the cost from future rent;
(3) to be absolutely safe, a county court declaration should be obtained authorising this course of action, and
(4) having given his landlord time to execute the repairs, the tenant may then proceed to do them.

Some authorities phrase their tenancy agreements in such a way as to attempt to exclude the operation of the *Lee-Parker* principle. Such a clause, provided it specifically denies the right to 'set-off' and is not merely a clause denying a right to make deductions from rent may be sufficient to exclude the *Lee-Parker* principle[16].

In *Asco Developments Ltd v Lowes*[17] a landlord sought summary judgment for arrears of rent under RSC Ord 14 alleging that there was no defence to the action. The tenants sought to defend on the grounds that the landlord was in breach of repairing obligations. Megarry V-C held that in certain special circumstances the *Lee-Parker* principle could be applied to monies accrued in rent arrears, and the tenants could defend the action. However, the court stated that nothing in the decision should be taken to encourage rent strikes as a means of forcing action on the part of a landlord. It was made clear in *Camden Nominees v Forcey*[18] that it is no answer to a claim for rent by a landlord for the tenant to say that the landlord has failed to perform his obligations. If tenants are to use the *Lee-Parker* principle in respect of rent arrears, they must specify to the court the sums and costs in question, and must particularise the issues. A judge faced with such issues should act with considerable discretion before allowing the tenant to defend the claim for rent.

In *British Anzani (Felixstowe) Ltd v International Marine Management (UK) Ltd*[19], Forbes J indicated that *in equity*, as a set-off raised by way of defence, unliquidated damages, for example claims for inconvenience and loss of enjoyment, might be recoverable against rent under a tenancy agreement. The tenant must be able to show it would be inequitable in view of the condition of the dwelling to allow the landlord to recover the whole amount of rent claimed. The tenant's contention should be raised as a defence to the landlord's action, and the tenant should make a counter-claim which particularises the nature of the landlord's breach of obligation and the consequent damage. Though it is not *absolutely* necessary that a claim and counter-claim should arise from the same contract, both must stem from very closely connected transactions so that equity can recognise that the tenant's counter-claim goes to the very root of the landlord's claim.

16 *Electricity Supply Nominees Ltd v IAF Group plc* [1993] 3 All ER 372, [1993] 1 WLR 1059.
17 (1978) 248 Estates Gazette 683.
18 [1940] Ch 352, [1940] 2 All ER 1.
19 [1980] QB 137, [1979] 2 All ER 1063.

A set-off of unliquidated damages is a defence to as much of the plaintiff's claim as is represented by the eventual amount of the award made. If defendants limit damages to a sum less than that claimed from them then they must pay the balance over and above the counter-claim. But where the defendants' damages are claimed at large, finally to be decided by the court, and where it is bona fide claimed they top the claimant's claim, even though they are not yet quantified, then the defendant's set-off amounts to a complete defence to the whole of the claimant's claim.

However, this equitable relief is discretionary, and as 'he who comes to equity must come with clean hands', it is unlikely to be available to a tenant who has been guilty of wrongdoing in relation to the transaction in question.

Damages

What damages can be recovered for breach of a covenant to repair? The law was exensively reviewed in *Calabar Properties Ltd v Stitcher*[20]. The object of damages is to restore the tenant to the position he/she would have been in had there been no breach. In relation to periodic lettings the measure of damages will, in general, be as stated in *Hewitt v Rowlands*[1], ie the difference in value to the tenant of the premises, from the date of notice of want of repair down to the time of the assessment of damages, between the house in the condition in which it currently is and the condition in which it would be had the landlord, on receipt of notice, fulfilled the obligation; in other words the difference in value to the tenant of the premises in their current condition and the condition in which they should be, bearing in mind age, character and locality. This sum is likely to be what the tenant would have to spend in performing the landlord's obligations for him, though it may be a sum computed by reference to a proportion of the periodic rent, plus a sum in respect of inconvenience and discomfort.

Where the dwelling is occupied under a 'long' lease the appropriate measure of damages will be *either*, where the tenant wishes to sell the dwelling, the difference in the price he/she received for the dwelling as damaged and the price it would have fetched on the open market had it been repaired, or, where the tenant wishes to remain in the dwelling, the cost of taking reasonable alternative accommodation, the cost of redecorating plus some compensation for inconvenience in addition to the cost of repairs.[2]

It is not enough simply to claim 'damages', the issues must be particularised. 'Special damage' ie the precise amount of pecuniary loss

20   [1983] 3 All ER 759, [1984] 1 WLR 287.
1   (1924) 93 LJKB 1080.
2   *Bradley v Chorley Borough Council* (1985) 17 HLR 305.

suffered by the tenant flowing from the facts must be specifically pleaded. This means that claims for, inter alia, damaged personal property, money spent discharging a landlord's obligations, or remedying damage consequent on a landlord's failure to act, costs of redecorating, the cost of taking alternative accommodation, should this be reasonable, have to be specified. Some general damage, compensation for which will be computed by the court according to the nature of the tenant's interest in the property, must also be generally pleaded, and this includes matters such as inconvenience and discomfort, as mentioned above.[3]

Awards of damages historically varied, but the trend is for awards to be increasing following *Calabar Properties*. It will be of no avail to a landlord to plead a low rent has been paid where a tenant has had to endure extremely poor living conditions for a long period of time, and where a tenant is clearly a victim of a landlord's default a substantial award of damages is acceptable, see *Chiodi's Personal Representatives v De Marney*[4], and *Davies v Peterson*[5].

It should be remembered that the onus of proof in relation to these matters is on the tenant, see *Foster v Day*[6], and tenants should act in good time and ensure relevant defects are brought to their landlord's attention, otherwise general damages may be reduced[7].

The existence of a 'tariff of damages' for discomfort and inconvenience, has been judicially noted with a range of £1,000 to £2,750 per annum. Such damages are payable in appropriate cases, and it is irrelevant that the tenant is otherwise on state benefits which go towards paying the rent: tenants are not to be doubly penalised for poverty and poor living conditions.[8]

The right to repair

Section 96 of the Housing Act 1985 and SI 1985/1493 established a 'right to repair' under which *secure* tenants were entitled to carry out certain repairs for which their landlords were responsible and to recover the costs from their landlords. In practice this right was little used.

---

3 See *Ezekiel v McDade* [1995] 2 EGLR 107 where a sum of £4,000 was awarded for the inconvenience of living in a substandard home, and *Lubren v Lambeth London Borough Council* (1987) 20 HLR 165 where the offer of alternative accommodation made to the tenant was held *not* to affect the question of damages.
4 [1988] 2 EGLR 64, CA.
5 (1988) 21 HLR 63; see also *Brent London Borough Council v Carmel (Sued as Murphy)* (1995) 28 HLR 203 where the £50,000 was awarded on a counterclaim for lack of repair raised as a defence to a possession action for non-payment of rent – the disrepair was characterised as 'appalling and intolerable'.
6 (1968) 208 Estates Gazette 495.
7 *Minchburn Ltd v Peck* [1988] 1 EGLR 53, CA.
8 *Wallace v Manchester City Council* [1998] 3 EGLR 38, CA.

A new section 96 was substituted by section 121 of the Leasehold Reform, Housing and Urban Development Act 1993. This empowers the Secretary of State to make regulations to allow local authority secure (and introductory) tenants to have certain repairs carried out at their landlord's expense. (Housing association tenants were excluded from the scope of the statutory scheme, but a scheme appropriate to associations was drawn up by the Housing Corporation: see Housing Corporation Circular 33/94.) The basic notion of the scheme is that landlords should inform tenants of the existence of the right to repair and should maintain lists of approved contractors (which may include the landlord's own workforce) prepared to carry out qualifying repairs.

The matters as specified in SI 1994/133 (Schedule) (as amended by SI 1994/844, and SI 1997/73) *include*: electrical power/lighting faults; faults in or loss of gas supply; faults in or loss of water supply; loss of heating (November to April); burst pipes, blocked or leaking foul drains and WCs, leaking central heating pipes and cisterns; water penetration of roofs; non-flushing WC; loss of heating (May-October); loose handrails; weeping pipes; seized stopcocks; defective WCs and unusable or insanitary sanitary ware; blocked flues; solid fuel heating defects; entryphone defects; non-securable doors and windows; rotten timber flooring; failed extractor fans. Most such defects should be repaired in one working day, though some may take three and others up to seven. For a repair to qualify, a financial limit of £250 is also imposed, while a landlord must also have at least 100 houses let on secure tenancies to fall within the scheme.

Tenants may apply for qualifying repairs to be carried out. Landlords must then inspect, if this is felt necessary, and if satisfied the disrepair in question in 'qualifying' must issue a notice specifying the nature of the repair, the listed contractor by whom it is to be carried out and the target time by which any work is to be done. Where such a notice is issued the tenant must be provided with a copy. If the initially specified contractor fails to carry out the work in the prescribed time, the landlord must (if the tenant states he/she requires another contractor to do the work) issue a further notice specifying a new target time for the work. The landlord may be liable to pay some compensation to reflect the inconvenience of delay to the tenant determined in accordance with the regulations if a repair remains incomplete after the second target time has passed.

The right to information

Section 104 of the Housing Act 1985 (as amended) requires landlords who grant secure tenancies to publish within two years of the commencement of the Act (and thereafter to revise and republish) information, in simple terms, about their secure tenancies. This information must explain, inter alia, the effect of the implied covenant to repair under section 11 et seq of the Landlord and Tenant Act 1985. All secure tenants must be supplied at least yearly with a copy of this information.

PUBLIC LAW REMEDIES FOR DEALING WITH SUB-STANDARD HOUSING

Grudging Parliamentary interference with the contractual relations of landlords and tenants has never been enough by itself to deal with bad housing conditions. In many – maybe most – cases tenants have lacked the financial and other resources to enable them to vindicate their rights via breach of covenant actions, while, historically, some dwellings have been in such poor conditions as to be beyond the help of 'repair' within the meaning outlined above. The existence of *areas* of substandard housing also made it unrealistic to expect action to depend solely on individual initiative. The Artizans' and Labourers' Dwellings (or Torrens) Act 1868 first made provision for clearance, while the subsequent Artizans' and Labourers' Dwellings Improvement (or Cross) Act 1875 coupled clearance with area redevelopment procedures. However, little use was made of this or subsequent legislation until after the First World War when the Acquisition of Land (Assessment of Compensation) Act 1919 – coupled with Exchequer subsidies for new council house building – helped to lay an effective legal basis for authorities to acquire sub-standard dwellings and rehouse their occupants. Even so many of the acquisition procedures remained cumbersome until the Housing Act 1930 was passed which streamlined the process and led to a demolition rate of some 90,000 houses per annum by 1939.

Area action was then interrupted by the Second World War and it was not until 1955 that area clearance of poor housing recommenced and continued into the 1970s. Housing *improvement* was not a new policy in the 1970s. The Moyne (1933), Ridley (1945) and Hobhouse (1947) Reports had all drawn attention to the need to prevent housing decline and to take action on improveable property. Some limited powers in this connection were given by the Housing Act 1935, but it was the Housing Act 1949 which introduced grant aid for housing improvement.

Powers to bring about *area* improvement were introduced by the Housing Act 1964, and an area based rehabilitation policy to deal with sub-standard housing was promoted by the Housing Acts of 1969 and 1974. This policy remains the basis of dealing with poor quality housing conditions although it has been of limited success in reaching the poorest households in the very worst housing. Legislative changes introduced in the Local Government and Housing Act 1989 were an attempt to deal with this and put into formal order policy changes heralded in 1983 by the Green Paper

Home Improvements: A New Approach, Cmnd 9153 which promised the introduction of means testing for grant aid to target grants at those in most financial hardship while at the same time reducing public expenditure. Further massive changes were wrought by the housing legislation of 1996 to which attention will be paid below.

The 1989 legislation also provided an opportunity for revision of the definition of unfit housing which had by then become hopelessly outmoded, the version on the statute book being traceable back to 1909.

The 1989 fitness requirements

Section 605 of the Housing Act 1985, inserted in 1989, imposes a *yearly* obligation on district and London borough councils to inspect their areas to consider action in relation to:
(1) repair notices;
(2) slum clearance;
(3) houses in multiple occupation;
(4) housing renewal areas;
(5) grant aid for housing.

DoE Circular 6/90 indicates this means there should be a yearly planning exercise to:
(a) identify types and numbers of unfit housing, and the best ways of dealing with problems;
(b) monitor action in progress;
(c) initiate regular physical surveys;
(d) develop comprehensive renewal strategies to direct funding more effectively;
(e) consider data available from other sources.

These powers apply to dwellings generally, ie houses, houses in multiple occupation, flats, 'bedsitters' and indeed any property used as a dwelling[9].

Sub-standard housing may also be brought to the attention of authorities by individuals. Authorities must take account of reports of unfit housing made by their 'proper officers' while local magistrates and parish and community councils may also complain in writing to such an officer that a dwelling is 'unfit', and that imposes a duty on the officer to inspect and report on the dwelling, see section 606 of the 1985 Act. The consideration of information received activates the specific duties to take action.

Authorities must in the discharge of functions pay attention to the new unfitness standard of section 604 of the 1985 Act (as substituted). This is

9   *Ashbridge Investments Ltd v Minister of Housing and Local Government* [1965] 3 All ER 371, [1965] 1 WLR 1320.

stricter and more up to date than previous law, and lists criteria which must be positively met if a dwelling is to be classed as 'fit'.

The criteria for houses (including HMOs) are is the house:

(1) structurally stable;
(2) free from serious disrepair[10];
(3) free from dampness prejudicial to health of occupants;
(4) adequately provided with lighting, heating, and ventilation;
(5) adequately provided with wholesome water;
(6) adequately provided with facilities for cooking/preparing food, including a sink with hot and cold water;
(7) provided with a suitably located water closet for occupants' exclusive use[11];
(8) provided with a suitably located bath/shower and basin with hot and cold water for occupants' exclusive use;
(9) provided with a system for water drainage?

Thus:

(a) a house is unfit if, in the opinion of the authority taking into account the effect of the defect on the dwelling as a whole, it fails to meet one or more of the above criteria, *and*
(b) by reason of that failure it is not reasonably suitable for occupation.[12]

The criteria for *flats* are as for houses, but a flat may also be unfit if the building of which it is part is affected by structural instability/disrepair/dampness/inadequate ventilation/an ineffective drainage system, and by reason of that the flat is not reasonably suitable for occupation.

Though there is considerable room for subjective evaluation in a decision as to whether a property is/is not 'fit', the 1989 standard encourages a 'check list' approach to decision making which prevents authorities considering the effect of an accumulation of minor defects, which was the position under the previous law, and some authorities now consider a property which might previously have been considered unfit because of its cumulative defects may now evade control: it does not fail to meet any one of the stated criteria, see further DoE, *Monitoring the New Housing Fitness Standard*, HMSO, 1993, pp 45–47. See also further below on the relationship between sections 189 and 190.

Further guidance on the new fitness standard is to be found in Annex A of DoE Circular 17/96: *Private Sector Renewal: A Strategic Approach.* This stresses that the various matters listed in the statute are to be considered separately to determine whether there is a complete failure under any of them. Where '*serious disrepair*' is concerned, however, it may be

---

10 A fall of ceiling place can be such a disrepair: – *Porter v Jones* [1942] 2 All ER 570, 112 LJKB 173.
11 Defective lavatories and guttering can make dwellings 'unfit': *Horrex v Pidwell* [1958] CLY 1461.
12 *Hall v Manchester Corpn* (1915) 84 LJ Ch 732.

the result of a single item or a combination of a number each of which in itself would not be 'serious', provided the cumulative effect is. In *Dover District Council v Sherred and Tarling*[13] the Court of Appeal stated that, inter alia, the absence of imminent danger to the occupants in relation to an item of disrepair is a factor to consider in relation to whether disrepair is 'serious', for the test remains as posited in *Morgan v Liverpool Corpn*[14] – whether or not the state of repair is such that by ordinary use damage may naturally be caused to the occupants. The Court of Appeal further added that while local authorities must apply the unfitness test in an objective fashion the experience and wishes of the occupants can be taken into account as not irrelevant in determining the standard of 'ordinary use', and this could extend to the standards accepted by neighbours living in identical housing. It is, however, for the judge to determine whether any given set of premises are/are not 'fit', though clearly the judge must take account of expert evidence on technical matters which are not within the everyday competence of the court; such evidence is relevant to identifying the existence and degrees of risk.

General guidance on the fitness standard

Further guidance on the criteria is given in DoE 6/90 Annex A. 'Unfitness' is primarily to be determined in terms of health and safety, having regard to the severity, location, persistence, duration and extent of any defects in the property, though discomfort, inconvenience and inefficiency may also be considered. The standard should be applied by considering the dwelling rather than its occupants, though a house should be suitable for all types of occupants who might reasonably be expected to occupy it, including, as appropriate, the elderly and children. Each of the statutory criteria must be considered, individually and in relation to each other, and thorough internal and external inspection of each relevant dwelling is counselled. Authorities must not only consider failure to meet the criteria, but whether by virtue of that failure the dwelling is not reasonably suitable for occupation. A mere minor failure to meet a criterion does not doom a property otherwise perfectly sound. However, if a defect is persistent it may lead to action being necessary. Decorative condition is generally not to be considered, though its exterior lack may have led to an independent problem of disrepair. Dwellings should be assessed on their 'as now' condition.

DoE Circular 6/90 makes the following points about the various statutory criteria. The structural stablility criterion is concerned with the overall integrity of a building, while 'serious disrepair' arises usually from

13 (1997) 29 HLR 864.
14 [1927] 2 KB 131.

deterioration. Disrepair can arise from a single item or a combination of individual smaller items. Disrepair should be considered against a background of whether it prejudices safety, or prevents a property from being normally used, or prevents surfaces from being cleaned, or gives rise to risk of fire/ explosion, toxic fumes or electrocution, or to a risk of water penetration or other structural risks. The criterion is concerned with seeing that houses function as intended, and are wind and weather tight, and do not give rise to long term deterioration so as to prejudice the integrity of the dwelling. However, it must be remembered the courts have held that the test of 'serious disrepair' is whether by ordinary use of the property personal injury or injury to health by damage may naturally be caused to the occupier[15], irrespective of whether an individual item of disrepair is one that can be quickly and easily repaired. In coming to a decision on such matters authorities must act in a judicial spirit[16].

Dampness *which is prejudicial to health* may either be rising or penetrating damp or persistent condensation damp arising primarily from design/construction defects. The ventilation, lighting and heating criterion allows authorities to consider, inter alia, whether a dwelling's main living room has fixed heating provision which can maintain a room temperature of 18°C(+) when the external temperature is –1°C. Wholesome water supplies are those which are adequate and continuous with piping that does not contaminate the water and adequate taps at sinks, while the food preparation criteria enable authorities to consider matters such as the adequacy of work surfaces, cookers and the size and layout of kitchens, the porosity of kitchen surfaces and their ability to be cleaned. Foul water systems must also be considered with regard to any propensity to be blocked, their ability to cope with rainfall and their siting so as to prevent flooding or the spread of ice.

Certain matters are not listed as criteria for fitness, for example infestation by bugs or vermin, a lack of gas or electricity or modern wiring or insulation, though such matters may be considered, *provided* a dwelling also falls in some way to satisfy the statutory criteria, and, of course, they may be evidence of serious disrepair, see *Steele v Minister of Housing and Local Government*[17].

Once an unfit dwelling is discovered a duty to take action arises, and under the 1989 amendments action is primarily to take place according to an integrated area based policy. Section 604A of the 1985 Act provides that authorities must consider with regard to sub-standard housing the most satisfactory course of action, whether it be repair, closing, demolition, etc.

15 *Morgan v Liverpool Corpn*, supra, and *Summers v Salford Corpn* [1943] AC 283, [1943] 1 All ER 68.
16 *Hall v Manchester Corpn* (1915) 84 LJ Ch 732.
17 (1956) 168 Estates Gazette 37; see also *Stanton v Southwick* [1920] 2 KB 642 (infestation by rats) and *Thompson v Arkell* (1949) 99 LJ 597 (infestation by fleas).

This is to ensure a flexible area based response to the eradication of bad housing, which allows for an approach that is appropriate to the problems and needs of the area ranging from renovation to demolition and rebuilding, *in conjunction with the private sector* according to central policy.

But what is the most satisfactory course of action? Using powers under section 604A the Secretary of State issued a code of guidance which formed Annex F to DoE Circular 6/90. The current guidance is now also to be found in Annex B of DoC Circular 17/96.

The Code

This is a 'factor to be taken into account' (compare the Code under Part VII of the 1996 Act), but it is so detailed that it will be hard for authorities to adopt alternative modes of proceeding. It lays down the following principles.

First, identify the need for action either by means of survey, or complaints from tenants or applications for grant aid. Where a survey is required, the *recommended* means is the Neighbourhood Renewal Assessment (NRA) which has the following components: (a) stated purposes, (b) defined aims and objectives, (c) a defined area, (d) a physical survey, (e) a survey of residents' socio-economic characteristics, and their views and preferences, (f) a survey of the non-residential characteristics of the area, (g) a socio-environmental assessment, (h) consideration of scope for private investment, (i) creation of a broad range of options for dwelling(s) in the area and (j) development of options into workable categories for option appraisal on economic and socio-environmental bases, and (k) reporting the *reasoned* preferred option for the dwelling(s).

Socio-environmental factors should have equal weight with economic issues, though costs are also to be considered over a period of years using a formula which is to include *all* action costs, including administrative costs, not just those attributable to publicly aided/required works. This enables authorities to consider the overall economics of various forms of action over a 30 year period. It may be necessary to work the formula more than once in relation to any given property to consider both its individual fate and that of a group of dwellings in which it is situated. While the formula is expressed in the circular in algebraic form, there is considerable room for subjectivity in its application. Though the NRA formula was developed as a means of determining whether or not to take action by way of declaring a renewal area (see further below), DoE Circular 6/90 Annex F para 8 points out it can be adopted as a basis for other forms of housing action, while Annex G argues its applicability to individual premises. In all circumstances the object is effectively to allow authorities to take decisions following a series of sequential steps designed to enable the costs and socio-environmental implications of decisions to be explored, with a systematic appraisal of alternative courses of action, so as to identify the option likely to produce the greatest community benefit on a long term basis.

Second, consider most satisfactory course of action by taking into account a wide range of issues such as: (a) costs, (b) social implications of any action taken, (c) alternative courses and their implications, (d) impact of the various forms of action on other nearby dwellings, (e) area strategy factors, (f) the local character and life of the community, (g) the views of those affected by the work/action, (h) the effect of any action in relation to the total needs of an area, and (i) the size of the area against which the effect of the work is measured.

The 1996 Guidance in addition stresses the need for authorities to deal with unfit housing as part of the strategy for an entire area, and thus the effect of any action which could be taken – eg a repair notice under section 189 of the 1985 Act – must be considered according to the context of the property within its area. This, of course, means that authorities have to determine what the appropriate area for this contextual determination is, and that depends on the geographical location and type of the dwelling. The object of the NRA in such circumstance, it is reiterated, is to ensure that economic, social and environmental issues are considered when determining the most appropriate course of action, together with the long-term consequences of the action, and the effect of the action on any neighbouring properties. Following completion of the NRA an authority should consider:

- each option within the context of the overall private sector renewal strategy and the resources available for its implementation;
- the practicability of any given option, bearing in mind the physical condition of the premises and others on which they abut;
- the potential life of the property if repaired;
- the relationship of the premises with neighbouring properties and their condition;
- proposals for the future of the area as a whole – eg, whether it is to be a conservation area;
- the nature and circumstances of the owner/occupier of the dwelling and their wishes and proposals for the future of the property;
- the management record of the landlord (if any);
- the effect of each option on the local community;
- the way in which an option will affect the local environment and its appearance.

The courts have been unwilling to interfere overmuch in this exercise which, it is recognised, must inevitably be somewhat subjective and imprecise. Thus it is not appropriate for a court to attempt to review the balance between socio-environmental and economic factors struck by an authority, and a decision should only be upset if it can be shown to be clearly wrong in law, or *Wednesbury* unreasonable[18].

---

18 *R v London Borough of Southwark, ex p Cordwell* (1994) 27 HLR 594.

A similar judicial line was taken in *Taggart v Leeds City Council*[19] where it was alleged no socio-environmental assessment of the kind envisaged by the Code had been carried out, and that the socio-environmental issues should have been placed before the relevant committee of the local authority instead of being merely considered by council officers. It was further alleged that the economic issues had been incorrectly considered so that the recommendation of the officers was weighted against renovation of the property in question and in favour of its closure. The court pointed out that the provisions of the Code are not mandatory, nevertheless there should have been more socio-environmental material in the report to the committee, so that these could be weighed against the economic issues, for the ultimate responsibility lay with the committee not the officers. However, even if all the issues had been presented to the committee, there was no possibility that their decision would have been different, as it was clear the socio-environmental factors themselves weighed in favour of closure. Neither could it be said that the methodology adopted by the officers was irrational.

Thus while socio-environmental and economic factors are to be given equal weight in the generation of options for the future of a property, and while the decision taking bodies need to have before them the material needed to enable them to reach a decision, the courts are unwilling to interfere with the exercise of 'housing' judgement in this area – which may be contrasted with their increasing willingness to intervene with regard to selection and allocation issues examined above in Chapter Three. The courts are only likely to interfere where an obviously important issue is completely ignored, or where weight is given to a clearly irrelevant one.

The courses of action available

After the evaluation process described above authorities should be in a position to make a choice as to which course of action to take in relation to the area/property in question. (However, see further below on the possibility of 'deferred action'.)

Individual houses (including flats)

A number of choices are available, the 'most satisfactory' should be chosen from: serving notice under section 189(1) or 189(1A) of the 1985 Act (repairs procedure), or under section 264 (1) or 264(2) (closure of whole premises or parts), or under section 265 (1) or 265(2) (demolition). (For action under

19   (1998) 31 HLR 693.

section 289 clearance procedure for areas, or group repair action, see further below.) Section 604A(2) provides that the Secretary of State may issue guidance in relation to the choice of action. That guidance is contained in Annex F of DoE Circular 6/90. This provides that general considerations in relation to *all* choices include: considering premises in their setting, and the effect of action on neighbouring dwellings and on the area; the size and nature of the area in question; the costs of action and their long term social implications; the views of those likely to be affected by any decision.

With particular regard to action under section 189 authorities should consider the physical condition of the dwelling; its life expectancy as repaired; comparison of repair costs as against other courses of action; other proposals for the area; condition of neighbouring properties; group repair proposals (see below); the need (long and short term) locally for the type of accommodation provided by the dwelling; owners'/occupants' wishes and ability to carry them out; local environment.

With regard to section 264 the following are relevant: comparison of cost of closure versus other options; whether the building is listed or in a conservation area; position of dwelling with regard to neighbouring buildings; the need locally for accommodation as provided by the dwelling; wishes of owners/occupants, and alternative uses for the building; effect of closure on the cohesion etc of area; availability of accommodation for displaced residents.

With regard to section 265 the following are relevant: relationship of the dwelling to neighbouring buildings; comparison of costs of alternative action; the need for the type of accommodation provided; future proposals for area – eg conservation area status; availability of accommodation for the displaced; wishes of owners/ocupants etc; prospective use of the cleared site; the local area, its future residentially, and the impact of the cleared site on it.

Where the building in question contains flats some of which are unfit the authority should additionally consider the condition of the common parts, and the proportion of fit to unfit flats – a 75% level of unfit flats points to demolition of the building, as also where defects threaten stability.

The object of these provisions as modified is to ensure flexibility of action in respect of unfit dwellings. It appears judicial review of an authority's decision is available should irrelevant factors be taken into account, for example a general desire to protect the environment when it was alleged a cottage was unfit because it discharged sewage directly into a stream, see *R v Forest of Dean District Council, ex p Trigg*[20], and this remedy is available to tenants as well as landlords.

20 (1989) 22 HLR 167.

The legal procedures

Action under section 189 etc (repair notices)

Where an authority is satisfied this is the most satisfactory course of action in respect of a dwelling house or house in multiple occupation (HMO) they *must* serve a repair notice on the person having control, or, in the case of a HMO, on its manager. With regard to unfit flats, whether or not in multiple occupation, where the cause of unfitness is the condition of another part of the overall building notice is served on the person having control of the relevant part. 'The person having control' is defined by section 207 of the 1985 Act as the person who receives the rack rent of the premises, ie a rent of not less than two thirds of their full net annual (or 'rateable') value, or who would receive it if the premises were let. Thus the 'person having control' is that person who is in a position to let the premises out, *and* to receive, a rack rent of them.[1] Where only part of a building is made subject to a notice the person to be served is the fee simple owner in relation to that part of the building and who in the opinion of the serving authority ought to have executed the works.[2]

A repair notice requires the execution of specified works of *repair or improvement* which are to be begun by a reasonable date, not earlier than 28 days after the notice is served, and are to be completed within a specified reasonable time. The notice must state that in the authority's opinion the works will make the property fit for human habitation. Copies of the notice must also be served on the freeholder, mortgagee or lessee of the property. The notice becomes operative if there is no appeal at the expiry of 21 days from its date of service, and is then a local land charge. The notice must specify works, though over much technical precision is not required, and it may be enough simply to require a roof to be overhauled.[3]

An authority is not, however, under a duty to serve a repair notice if, though satisfied the property in question is unfit, they determine that the premises form part of a building which would be a 'qualifying building' in a group repair scheme, and that they expect to prepare such a scheme for the building within a period of 12 months, see section 190A of the 1985 Act. See further below on group repair schemes.

---

1   *Truman, Hanbury, Buxton & Co Ltd v Kerslake* [1894] 2 QB 774.
2   Section 207 of the 1985 Act as amended – this covers flats, and common parts in blocks of flats.
3   *Church of Our Lady of Hal v Camden London Borough Council* (1980) 255 Estates Gazette 991.

Action under section 190

A repair notice *may* also be served under section 190 where an authority is satisfied a dwelling house or HMO is in such a state of disrepair that though it is *not* unfit either *substantial repairs* are necessary to bring it to a reasonable standard considering its age, character and locality, *or* though not unfit that the state of disrepair is such as to interfere materially with the personal comfort of the occupying tenant, or persons occupying the HMO as the case may be. These powers extend to buildings containing a flat under section 190(1A), whether singly or multiply occupied, where though the flat is not fit, *either* substantial repairs are required to parts of the building outside the flat to bring it to a reasonable standard in view of its age, character and locality, *or* where the condition of part of the building is such as to interfere with the personal comfort of occupying tenants. But under section 190(1B) such a notice may *not* be served, unless there is an occupying tenant of the dwelling house or flat in question, *or* the property is within a renewal area within Part VII of the Local Government and Housing Act 1989 (see further below). An 'occupying tenant' is a person *other than* an owner occupier, who occupies the dwelling as a lessee, while an 'owner occupier' is a freeholder or 'long' leaseholder, ie one for more than 21 years. The person served with the notice will normally be the 'person having control', ie generally the landlord or owner of the premises, see section 207 of the 1985 Act as amended, but in the case of a HMO notice may be served on the manager, see section 190 (1C). Copies must also be served on any other person having an interest in the property as freeholder, mortgagee or tenant, see section 190(3).

The notice may *not* require the doing of works of internal decorative repair, section 190(2), and must be clear on its face as to what works are required, see *Our Lady of Hal Church v Camden London Borough Council*[4]. Once a repair notice has become operative it is a local land charge, see section 190(5), and a deliberate failure to comply with a notice is a criminal offence under section 198A.

Section 190 contemplates action against two kinds of property, houses in need of substantial repair and fit houses in disrepair where conditions interfere with the personal comfort of occupying tenants, and though there is evidence to suggest authorities make less use of these powers than they could, the powers have been recognised as permitting action to prevent properties becoming unfit, and as allowing the consideration of wider policy issues in the taking of decisions on houses falling into disrepair[5]. However, what is this provision's relationship with section 189? Section 189 deals

---

4 (1980) 255 Estates Gazette 991.
5 *Kenny v Kingston upon Thames Royal London Borough Council* (1985) 17 HLR 344.

with properties that are *unfit*, section 190 with those that are *fit*. Yet a property may be unfit and *also* affected by other defects which fall only within section 190. It appears *practice* is to serve notices under both sections each requiring specific works to commence on the same date, yet it would be preferable if section 189 was amended to allow the requiring of works to make a dwelling fit *and* to bring it up to a reasonable standard considering its age, character and locality.[6]

Appeals and challenges

A person aggrieved (a phrase undefined by the statutes, though here it may extend to include tenants) by the service of a repair notice may, under section 191, within 21 days of service appeal to the county court. There are particular grounds of appeal, without prejudice to the general right to appeal, allowing the appellant to argue that some other person who is an owner of the property ought to execute required works or pay their cost in whole or full, see section 190(1A), and, *in the case of a notice under section 189*, that some other action, such as closure or demolition would have been the most satisfactory course of action, see section 190(1B). On an appeal the court has discretion to confirm, quash or vary the repair notice, and all relevant factors can be taken into account such as the expense of the works required, the value of the property, the financial position of the owner[7], though where an appeal is brought under section 190(1B), see above, the court *must* have regard to the guidance issued under section 604A. Where an appeal against a section 189 notice is allowed and the reason is that making a closing or demolition order would be the most satisfactory answer the judge shall, if requested by the appellant or the authority, include a finding to that effect in his judgment. A notice incorrectly served, for example where the person does not have control, may be ignored as invalid,[8] while it appears a notice illegally served could also be challenged by way of judicial review.[9]

Enforcement of repair notices

Authorities have power under section 191A to execute required works by agreement with the person having control of the property, at that person's

6   *Monitoring the New Housing Fitness Standard*, p 78.
7   *Hillbank Properties Ltd v Hackney London Borough Council* [1978] QB 998, [1978] 3 All ER 343.
8   *Graddage v London Borough of Haringey* [1975] 1 All ER 224, [1975] 1 WLR 241.
9   *R v London Borough of Southwark, ex p Lewis Levy Ltd* (1983) 8 HLR 1.

expense. Otherwise, if a repair notice is not complied with authorities have power under section 193 to do required work, and may recover their costs under Schedule 10 of the 1985 Act. 'Compliance' in this context means that the works specified in the notice must be begun and completed within the due time allowed, see section 193(2), while section 193(2A) also allows authorities to do required works where it appears that reasonable progress is not being made towards compliance before the end of the appropriate period for doing the works. Written notice of intention to exercise the section 193 powers *must* be given to the person having control of the property, and may be given to any owner of them, see section 194, while section 195, inter alia, empowers a magistrates' court to order a person who has received notice of intended action (and who prevents the officers, servants or agents of an authority from carrying into effect any of the relevant statutory provisions) to permit all things requisite to be done, on pain of committing an offence. Powers of entry for survey and examination purposes before or after a repair notice has been served are given by section 197 which enables authorities to authorise their officers in writing to enter premises for a specified purpose(s), and thereafter such an officer may enter the premises by giving seven days' notice to the occupier and owner, and it is an offence under section 198 to obstruct such an authorised officer. It is a further offence under section 198A for a person having control of premises subject to a repair notice to fail intentionally to comply with that notice *either* by not starting the works by their due commencement date *or* by not completing works on time, and the obligation to complete required works continues notwithstanding that the period for their completion has expired.

It should be noted that under section 203(3) no action taken under, inter alia, section 189 and 190 etc, prejudices or affects any remedy available at common law or under statute to the tenant of any premises against the landlord.

Action under section 264 etc (closure/demolition)

Section 264 (as substituted in 1989) provides that where an authority is satisfied, having considered the Secretary of State's guidance, that a dwelling house or HMO or one or more of the flats in a building is unfit and that the most satisfactory course of action is closure of the relevant premises it shall make a closing order. This is an order under section 267(2) which prohibits the use of the premises in question for any purpose not approved by the authority, though such approval is not to be unreasonably withheld, and a person aggrieved by its withholding may appeal to the county court.

Section 265(1) (as substituted in 1989) provides that where an authority is satisfied that a dwelling house (but not a flat) or an HMO (but not a flat multiply occupied) is unfit and that demolition is the most satisfactory course of action it must make a demolition order. Where a building contains one or more flats and some or all are unfit and the authority considers demolition is the most satisfactory course of action it must make a demolition order under section 265(2). Such an order requires premises to be vacated within a specified period (of at least 28 days) from the time it becomes operative and to be demolished within six weeks after the end of that period, or if not vacated before the end of that period to be demolished within six weeks of when it is vacated, though the authority may specify such longer period as they consider reasonable, see section 267(1). The provision that the premises are to be required to be vacated is mandatory, even where they are vacant when the order is made[10]. It should further be noted that where a closing order has been made the authority may at any time revoke it – save where the building in question is listed, or the dwelling is a flat – and substitute a demolition order, see section 279.

Where a demolition or closing order is made copies must, under section 268, be served on any person who is an owner of the premises and on any reasonably ascertainable mortgagee. Where the premises in question is a building containing flats notice must in addition be served on those who are the owners of the flats, see section 268(1A). An order against which no appeal is brought becomes operative at the end of 21 days from its date of service, see section 268(2). A person aggrieved by such an order thus has 21 days under section 269 to appeal to the county court, though this right does not extend to any person who is in occupation under a lease with an unexpired term of three years or less, however, such a person may be able to challenge by way of judicial review where there is clear illegality[11].

The grounds of appeal include, under section 269 (2A) that another course of action, eg a repair notice, was the most satisfactory course of action rather than demolition/closure as the case may be, and in such cases the court must consider the Secretary of State's guidance in coming to a decision. Otherwise the court has considerable discretion in deciding appeals.

Once a demolition order has become operative in respect of any premises the authority must serve on any occupier of them, or any part of them, a notice which states the order's effect, the date by which the premises are to be vacated and requiring the surrender of possession before the vacation date. Possession may thereafter be obtained by order in the county court,

10 *Pocklington v Melksham UDC* [1964] 2 QB 673, [1964] 2 All ER 862 and *R v Epsom and Ewell Corpn, ex p RB Property Investments (Eastern) Ltd* [1964] 2 All ER 832, [1964] 1 WLR 1060.
11 *R v Woking Borough Council, ex p Adams* (1995) 28 HLR 513.

irrespective of any security of tenure existing under the Rent Act 1977 or the Housing Act 1988, see section 270. But a property owner may not recover damages for loss as a result of an authority's failure to serve a section 270 notice on a sitting tenant[12] . It is an offence under section 270(5) to enter into occupation of premises, or to permit someone to enter into occupation, after the date by which an order requires it to be vacated, provided it is known that the order has become operative and applies to the premises. Similar provisions apply in respect of closing orders under sections 276 and 277.

Section 271 and 272 grant powers to authorities to demolish relevant premises in default of action by their owners and to recover their expenses. They may also secure, under section 273, the cleansing of premises subject to demolition orders of vermin.

Once a demolition order has become operative the owner of the premises, or any other person in a position in the opinion of the authority to put his/ her proposals into effect, may propose the reconstruction of the premises, including their enlargement or improvement. If satisfied this work will lead to the creation of one or more fit dwelling houses or houses in multiple occupation, as the case may be, they may afford the person an opportunity to do the work by extending the period within which demolition is required, and further extensions of this time may be granted provided satisfactory progress with no unreasonable delays is being made on the work. If this is then completed to the authority's satisfaction they may revoke the demolition order, see section 274. (A similar power to determine a closing order on relevant premises being rendered fit exists under section 278.) Section 275 permits the substitution by an authority of a closing order for a demolition order where proposals are submitted by the owner of relevant premises, or by any other person interested in them, for their use other than as housing accommodation.

Where either a closing or a demolition order is made under sections 264 or 265, compensation must be paid to affected owners under section 584A. The basis of compensation is the diminution in the compulsory purchase value of the property determined in accordance with the Land Compensation Act 1961. But where such an order is brought to an end, any compensation received must be repaid, see section 584B.

A building which is 'obstructive', ie dangerous or injurious to health simply because of its contact with or proximity to other buildings, may be made subject to an obstructive building notice which gives the owner notice of a time and place when the building's demolition will be considered by the local authority, see sections 283 and 284 of the 1985 Act. After giving the owner a hearing on this matter the authority may determine, by an obstructive buildings order, to demolish the building or part of it, and to require its vacation. If no appeal is then made the order will then become operative on the expiration of 21 days from the date of service of the order on the building's owner(s). A person aggrieved by such an order may, however, within that time appeal to the county court under section 285, though this right does not extend to occupiers who hold the building under leases or agreements whose unexpired term is three years or less. The court has wide discretion to confirm, quash or vary the order on an appeal, the making of which suspends the order until the final determination of the appeal. Once such an order has become effective the authority may serve notice on the occupier stating the effect of the order and requiring vacation of the premises; thereafter possession may be obtained by court order, irrespective of any security of tenure under the Rent Act 1977 or the Housing Act 1988, see section 286. The prime responsibility for executing an order lies on the relevant building owner(s), under section 287(2) but such owners may, before the end of the period within which an obstructive building is required to be vacated, sell their interests to the authority for the compulsory purchase value of the premises, and the authority is then under a duty to carry out demolition, see section 287(1). Where there is a failure by owners to carry out demolition the authority is under a duty under section 287(3) to do the necessary work and they may recover their expenses from owners under section 288.

Note that buildings other than houses can be dealt with under these provisions[13], while they are specifically excluded from applying to buildings owned by local authorities, and statutory undertakers unless in this case they are used as dwellings, showrooms or offices, see section 283(2).

Where an authority would otherwise be required under sections 264 or 265 to make a demolition or closing order in respect of a dwelling house, HMO or the whole of a building, they may, under section 300, where it appears to them that the premises can be made to provide accommodation of a standard 'adequate for the time being' purchase the property instead. Notice of determination to purchase the property must be served on those persons who would otherwise have been served with copies of a demolition/ closing order. Thereafter the property may be acquired by agreement or compulsorily. This provision only allows authorities to acquire property on a temporary basis, it may not be used to add to an authority's permanent housing stock[14].

---

13 *Jackson v Knutsford Urban Council* [1914] 2 Ch 686.
14 *Victoria Square Property Co Ltd v London Borough of Southwark* [1978] 2 All ER 281, [1978] 1 WLR 463 – 'temporary' use may, however, continue for quite a while; 24 years in *R v City of Birmingham Corpn, ex p Sale* (1983) 9 HLR 33.

Deferred action

Important changes in the law on unfitness were made by the Housing Grants, Construction and Regeneration Act 1996 to give authorities a little more leeway with regard to taking action.

Under section 81 of this Act where an authority are satisfied a dwelling house or HMO is unfit but are also satisfied that serving a *deferred action notice* (DAN) is the most satisfactory course of action they are to serve such a notice. A DAN states:

(i)   that the premises are 'unfit',
(ii) the works required in the authority's opinion to make them 'fit',
(iii) the other courses of action available to the authority if the premises remain unfit.

Such a DAN becomes operative, where no appeal is brought, on the expiry of 21 days from its date of service and thereafter is final, and while it remains operative it is a local land charge. However, the existence of a DAN does not prevent the authority from taking other action with regard to the premises.

DANs are to be served under section 82 of the 1996 Act on the person 'having control' of a dwelling house or HMO as the case may be (see sections 207 and 398 of the Housing Act 1985). Such a notice may also be served in respect of a flat or flat in multiple occupation, but in the case of an HMO the notice may be served on the manager rather than the person having control. Other appropriate freeholders, mortgages and lessees of the property are also to be served.

A person aggrieved by the service of a DAN under section 83 may appeal to the county court, and may *in particular* argue that a more satisfactory course of action would be to require repairs, closure or demolition. In such a case the court is required to take account of the guidance issued by the Secretary of State: see further above. The court has a wide discretion on appeal but where it allows an appeal and the reasons include that another course of action would have been more satisfactory the court must, if the appellant requests, include a finding as to *the* satisfactory course of action. Bringing an appeal defers the operation of the DAN.

Authorities may at any time under section 84 of the 1996 Act review any DAN and *must* do so at two yearly intervals having carried out an inspection for this purpose. The DAN must be renewed if the authority conclude this is the most satisfactory course of action, but again an appeal against such a finding is possible on the same terms as outlined above. In deciding on the most satisfactory course of action authorities must, of course have regard to guidance issued by the Secretary of State: see section 85 of the 1996 Act.

The ability to serve a DAN will, inter alia, enable authorities to hold back from taking action in relation to technically unfit properties (bearing in mind that the number and range of these were increased where the criteria for unfitness were revised in 1989) where, eg, the conditions are not too bad and where the occupant is, say, an elderly person who would be seriously upset or affected by requirements for extensive works. On the occupant's death or removal to more suitable premises the authority may then take other action to bring the property up to standard.

Power to 'improve' enforcement procedures

Under section 86 of the 1996 Act the Secretary of State may, by order, require authorities to act in a specified way before taking any of the following types of action:
(i)   serving or renewing a DAN;
(ii)   serving a repair notice;
(iii) serving repair notice on house not yet unfit;
(iv)   making a closing order;
(v)   making a demolition order.
   Such an order may provide that authorities must, as soon as practicable, give the person against whom action is intended an 'appropriate notice' and must not take any further action before the end of a specified period. Such a notice is one which:
(i)   states the nature of remedial action the authority thinks should be taken;
(ii)   explains the grounds on which it appears to the authority a statutory notice of any of the specified varieties might be served;
(iii) states the nature of the action which might be taken and whether there is either a right to make representations before, or a right of appeal against, taking such action.
   The order may further provide that before an authority takes *any* action against a person they must give that person a written notice stating they are considering taking the action and the reasons why, and that that person may make written representations or oral representations before some other person to be determined according to the Secretary of State's order. Any representations made must be considered. This is known as the 'minded to' procedure. It was introduced under the Conservative's deregulation policy, the object being to avoid unnecessary formal action.
   The section goes on to provide, however, that nothing is to preclude an authority from taking immediate action against a person, or requiring immediate remedial action where such appears 'necessary'. This is clearly designed to deal with emergency cases where it is imperative that immediate action is taken. Notices are thus not to be served 'out of the blue' on 'persons having control'. Indeed provision is made for a preparatory

process – an initial notice stating the authority is considering taking action, and why, and allowing for representations to be made and considered and/ or stating that there is a right of appeal. The object is to ensure that some premises will be dealt with informally without the need to resort to the full legal procedure.

'Meat' was placed on the bones of the statue by the Housing (Fitness Enforcement Procedures) Order 1996, SI 1996/2885. This provides that before an authority takes enforcement action of the types specified above, save in cases of emergency, they must

(a) give to the proposed subject of their action a written notice stating:
    (i) that they are considering taking the specified action and the reasons therefor – that is the 'minded to' notice;
    (ii) that the recipient may, within a specified period (not less than 14 days) make *either* written representations to the authority, or (where the recipient so requests) oral representations to the authority in the presence of an officer appointed by them – a request to make oral representations must be made not later than seven days beginning with the day the 'minded to' notice is given;
(b) consider any representations duty made and not withdrawn.

Failure to comply with this procedure will be an additional ground of appeal against any enforcement action taken in addition to those already existing under the statute: see Regulation 3.

Charging for enforcement action

Under section 87 of the 1996 Act authorities are given power to make *reasonable* charges to recover their administrative costs and certain other specified costs where:

(i) they have served/renewed a DAN;
(ii) they have served a notice under section 189 (1985 Act);
(iii) they have served a notice under section 190 (1985 Act);
(iv) they have made a closing order under section 264 (1985 Act);
(v) they have made a demolition order under section 265 (1985 Act).

Specified costs include expenses incurred in deciding whether to service a notice, identifying works to be specified (where appropriate) therein and actually serving the notice. However, a ceiling may be set on such costs by an order made by the Secretary of State, and if the court allows an appeal against a notice it may further order a reduction or cancellation of any charge made. Charges may be recovered, under section 88 of the 1996 Act from persons on whom notices are served, and are recovered by serving a 'demand for payment' on the person from whom recovery is sought, whereafter the demand becomes effective on the expiry of 21 days unless an appeal is brought. The sum recoverable will then be a charge on the property which the authority may recover by selling or leasing the property or by appointing a receiver as if the authority were a mortgagee acting under the Law of Property Act 1925.

The maximum charge is fixed by the Housing (Maximum Charge for Enforcement Action) Order 1996, SI 1996/2886. Regulation 2 fixed the maximum charge at £300.

Clearance area procedure under section 289 et seq

Clearance area procedure remains available where, after survey procedures (see above) an authority is satisfied this is the most satisfactory way of dealing with the condition in the area. Authorities must therefore consider alternative options, the views of residents, rehousing provision, after use of the area, and the ability to attract private sector investment. They must then be satisfied that the residential buildings in the area (ie houses, HMOs or buildings containing flats) are unfit, or are by reason of their poor arrangement, or by virtue of the narrowness and poor arrangement of streets, dangerous or injurious to the health of inhabitants, and that other buildings in the area are similarly dangerous or injurious to health, see section 289(2)(a) and (b). 'Houses' has been interpreted as covering a wide range of premises eg shops and garages with living rooms over them, see *Re Bainbridge, South Shields (D'Arcy Street) Compulsory Purchase Order 1937*[15], and *Re Butler, Camberwell (Wingfield Mews) No 2 Clearance Order 1936*[16], and also tenement houses, *Quiltotex Co Ltd v Minister of Housing and Local Government*[17].

Clearance area procedure was modified in 1989 so that section 289 (2B)-(2F) of the 1985 Act now provide that consultation with those persons directly affected (ie freeholders, lessees and mortgagees of affected buildings) must be undertaken before a clearance area is declared, with notice served on every person having an interest in any building in the area, while other occupants of residential property should be informed of the authority's proposals. Local press advertisement must take place and representations invited and considered. As a matter of good practice consideration should be given to ensuring the provision of the above information in languages other than English where appropriate. At least 28 days shall be allowed for the making of representations. The consideration of representations procedure necessitates that those who are asked for their views should be given full information as to the proposals so that they may make a properly

15   [1939] 1 KB 500.
16   [1939] 1 KB 570.
17   [1966] 1 QB 704, [1965] 2 All ER 913.

informed response; there is, however, no obligation to consult *before* the initial resolution to proceed by way of clearance area procedure[18]. Before deciding to declare a clearance area an authority should also consider the relative proportions of fit and unfit dwellings in the proposed area.

As a result of considering representations the authority may decide to declare/not declare a clearance area, or declare it subject to the exemption of certain unfit residential buildings, see section 289 (2F)(a), (b) and (c). Where they decide to declare a clearance area, the authority must pass a resolution to that effect and have the area defined by a map, but *excluding* any residential building which is not unfit, or dangerous or injurious to health, any residential buildings which though unfit have been exempted, and any other buildings which are not dangerous or injurious to health. A clearance area should, generally, be a contiguous area of land, with no outlying separated parcels of land, see section 289(5B), though the authority may also include land in a clearance area which belongs to them, provided they could have included it had it not belonged to them, see section 293(1). Furthermore before the resolution is passed the authority must be satisfied that, in so far as suitable accommodation does not exist for those who will be displaced by clearance, they will be able to secure such accommodation as it becomes necessary and that they have the necessary resources to carry their resolution into effect, section 289(4). 'Suitable accommodation' in this context means suitable *dwelling* accommodation[19], while the need for an authority to be satisfied as to its resources does not require the placing before the authority of specific figures[20]. Upon making the resolution the authority must 'forthwith' send a copy to the Secretary of State together with a statement of the number of occupants of buildings in the clearance area on a specified day.

Where a residential building which is unfit is *not* included in a clearance area, for example because of exemption under section 289(2F)(b), the authority is under a duty to take action in respect of it under whichever of sections 189, 264 or 265 it considers the most appropriate course of action.

In addition *before* declaring a clearance area the authority must also consider whether they have the resources to pay relocation grants under sections 131 to 140 of the Housing Grants, Construction and Regeneration Act 1996. Such grants allow owner occupiers (freehold or leasehold where their term is for more than a year) to relocate to designated areas on the acquisition of their homes within the clearance area. Grants are discretionary, including their amount, which is also means tested and subject to a limit: see section 134 of the 1996 Act. Grants made are conditional on the grantee

18 *Fredman v Minister of Health* (1935) 154 LT 240.
19 *Re Gateshead County Borough (Barn Close) Clearance Order 1931* [1933] 1 KB 429.
20 *Goddard v Minister of Housing and Local Government* [1958] 3 All ER 482, [1958] 1 WLR 1151.

remaining an owner-occupier of the dwelling purchased, and are repayable if the grant conditions are broken: see sections 135, 136 and 138.

As soon as the authority have declared land to be a clearance area they must, under section 290, proceed to secure its clearance by purchasing the land and undertaking clearance themselves, or by otherwise securing demolition of buildings. The power to acquire the land (which may be exercised by agreement, or under compulsory powers if authorised by the Secretary of State) extends to land surrounded by the clearance area acquisition of which is reasonably necessary for securing a cleared area of convenient shape and dimensions, and adjoining land whose acquisition is reasonably necessary for the satisfactory development or use of the cleared area. Such adjoining land must be shown by the authority, should they wish to acquire it compulsorily, to be reasonably necessary as a question of fact. The land must be partly contiguous with land in the clearance area.[1]

Detailed treatment of compulsory purchase procedure is beyond the scope of this work, but it should be noted that since 1 April 1990 under sections 578 and 578A of the 1985 Act, the appropriate procedure is generally that under the Acquisition of Land Act 1981, Part II, under which the authority makes a compulsory purchase order on the land in prescribed form, which is then given publicity in local newspapers, while notice of the effect of the order is also served on all owners, lessees and occupiers of relevant land, except tenants for a month or less. The order is then submitted for ministerial confirmation which may not be given until after any objections to the order have been heard and considered. Once the order is confirmed the acquiring authority must publicise that fact locally, and serve notice of that fact on the affected landholders. Compensation for compulsorily acquired unfit property is paid on the same basis as acquisitions of fit property assessed under the Land Compensation Acts 1961 and 1973, which is, effectively, market valuation. Where a person is displaced from a dwelling in consequence, inter alia, of its compulsory acquisition, and he/she occupied that dwelling as an only or main residence for a period of one year ending with the displacement, by virtue of an interest in it or as a statutory tenant under the Rent Act 1977, etc; a *home loss payment* may be claimed under section 29 of the Land Compensation Act 1973, and the position is similar where a *tenant* is displaced by the acquisition of the *landlord's* interest in a property *by agreement* by an authority possessing compulsory purchase powers, see section 29(6). Where the conditions relating to entitlement to claim a home loss payment are *not* met a discretionary payment may still be made to a displaced occupier, see section 29(2) of the 1973 Act as amended. Note that a person is not 'displaced' if he/she gives

1   *Coleen Properties Ltd v Minister of Housing and Local Government* [1971] 1 All ER 1049, [1971] 1 WLR 433 and *Gosling v Secretary of State for the Environment* [1975] JPL 406 and see *Bass Charrington (North) Ltd v Minster of Housing and Local Government* (1970) 22 P & CR 31.

up occupation before the date on which the acquiring authority was authorised to acquire under section 29(3). Claims must be made in writing, with particulars as required by the authority, within six years of displacement, section 32. The amount of a home loss payment for a periodic tenant is fixed at £1,500 by section 30 of the 1973 Act. Similar payments may be payable to local authority tenants who are required to move because their homes are being redeveloped. In such cases it appears alleged rent arrears due from the tenant can be deducted by way of set-off by the landlord from the statutory sum.[2]

A *disturbance payment* may additionally be payable to a tenant displaced by compulsory acquisition under section 32 of the 1973 Act and this will cover, inter alia, reasonable removal expenses, see section 38. To qualify for a disturbance payment a person must be in lawful possession of the land in question, and must have no entitlement to compensation under another statute.

It is clear policy that clearance and compulsory purchase procedure should only be used where there is a compelling case for their use on grounds of public interest, with the burden of justification falling on the acquiring authority. An authority must be satisfied that clearance is the most satisfactory way of dealing with the area, and must have considered alternative uses for the area, the views of residents, arrangements for rehousing and after use of the land. More than one survey may be needed to satisfy an authority on these issues. Compulsory purchase orders will be confirmed where the Secretary of State is satisfied that the economic and other interests of an area are best served by clearance. Authorities must argue their case for being granted compulsory purchase powers in a written document. This will include statements of the reasons for concluding relevant buildings are unfit, the proposals for rehousing residents and relocating any commercial or industrial uses, evidence as to the proposed after use of the site, evidence that the economic aspect of clearance has been considered, see DoE Circular 6/90 para 68. Circular 5/93 adds to this, para 11, that compulsory purchase is *generally* justified as a 'last resort' where a clear housing gain can be achieved and where other means of bringing about housing improvement have failed, and normally the Secretary of State does not expect an owner occupied house to be included in a compulsory purchase order unless it has defects adversely affecting other housing. Paragraph 63 of Circular 6/90 concludes by stating that 'Where authorities acquire any property or land they will wish to consider disposing of it to the private sector,' a clear indication that it is policy that slum clearance powers should be used to facilitate action by the private sector rather than to build up public sector land banks.

2   *Khan v Islington London Borough Council* [1999] EGCS 87, CA.

Once an authority has acquired land under section 290, section 291 requires them to ensure that buildings on the land are vacated and are then demolished, though they may, under section 301 postpone the demolition of residential buildings on land they acquire if they consider those buildings are capable of providing accommodation of a standard 'adequate for the time being'. Such property will almost certainly be of a standard lower than that of 'fitness', but it must not be of such a poor quality that it is prejudicial to health or a nuisance, otherwise its occupants will be in a position to take statutory nuisance proceedings against the authority, see further below *Nottingham Corpn v Newton*[3] and *Salford City Council v McNally*[4]. The period of postponement of demolition can be quite long – 24 years was considered not unreasonable on the facts in *R v Birmingham City Council, ex p Sale*[5]. However, in that case Forbes J argued that exercise of the power to postpone requires more than that the housing is 'capable of providing accommodation adequate for the time being'. There must be some exceptional reason why demolition is postponed over and above 'need' for houses and the fact that the houses in question can be maintained to the standard of adequacy. The scheme of the Act is that once demolition is decided on, demolition should proceed unless proper and exceptional reasons justify postponement of demolition. Section 583 of the 1985 Act further permits authorities to permit continuation of tenancies of houses compulsorily acquired and to continue in use as housing accommodation. In such cases they may serve notice on the occupants authorising continued occupation on specified terms.

Those who are displaced from residential accommodation as a result of compulsory purchase action, and who have no suitable alternative accommodation available to them on reasonable terms, are entitled to look to the acquiring authority for housing, see further below on section 39 of the Land Compensation Act 1973.

An assessment of the use of unfitness powers

In 1993 the Department of the Environment published research undertaken by the Legal Research Institute of the University of Warwick, *Monitoring the New Housing Fitness Standard,* following local authority concern at possible variation in interpreting the 1989 fitness standard.

With regard to the ways in which unfit dwellings may come to authorities' attention, it was found that 65% of inspections arose following grant

3   [1974] 2 All ER 760, [1974] 1 WLR 923.
4   [1976] AC 379, [1975] 2 All ER 860, HL.
5   (1983) 9 HLR 33.

inquiries, 19% were responses to occupiers' complaints, while there was generally wide variation between authorities in the reasons for undertaking an inspection. Fewer than half the authorities surveyed had conducted a house condition survey representative of all dwellings in their areas within the previous five years while some authorities had insufficient staff and financial resources to respond to unfitness, and most authorities considered their resources before inspection. Of the 1,369 dwellings which fell within the survey, 68% were held to fail the fitness test, but once again there was a wide variation between authorities in the proportion of dwellings which failed, while dwellings inspected after a grant inquiry were more likely to be found unfit than those inspected following complaint by an occupier. The pattern of fitness was in any case found to be affected by local conditions such as underlying geology, mining subsidence and construction technique. Local officials were found to determine more dwellings to be unfit than a central group of re-surveyors of the properties, but in only 16% of instances was there complete disagreement between members of the two groups. Local officials reported that most failures of the fitness standard were due to disrepair and dampness, while a dwelling failing on one requirement of the standard was also likely to fail on more. However, when attention was concentrated on HMOs the most common reasons for officers determining property to be *unfit for multiple occupation* were in connection with failures under section 352 of the 1985 Act in respect of means of escape from fire and other fire precautions, see further Chapter Eight below.

It was found that the phrase 'not reasonably suitable for occupation' allowed divergent findings as to fitness because of the element of subjective evaluation, and officials indicated they would welcome clarification on a number of issues, for example the requirements as to stability, heating, cooking facilities and locations of water closets. Similarly there is often local confusion as to what is meant by a 'building' for the purposes of the legislation. When it comes to taking action in respect of properties found to be unfit, in 54% of instances local officials were likely to recommend action by way of grant aid (see further below) with repair notices being served in 23% of instances, and clearance, demolition or closure is an option in 3% of cases. Some authorities, however, have an informal 'do-nothing' option where an occupier is unwilling to undergo disruption consequent on works needed to make a dwelling fit.

The research concluded that overall the new fitness standard can be uniformly applied by authorities and their officers, but clarification of particular issues was recommended ie structural stability, dampness, lighting, heating and ventilation, water supply, food preparation facilities, water closets and drainage. It was also suggested that certain other indicators of fitness should be included in an amended section 604, ie internal arrangements and dangerous design features, thermal and sound insulation, hazards outside a dwelling, eg problems of gaining safe access, fire precautions and precautions to guard against radon penetration., It was further concluded there is still too much room for subjective variation in the application of the section 604 standard and that the phrase 'and, by reason of that failure, is not reasonably suitable for occupation' should be repealed.

The research also pointed to the plethora of guidance available on the fitness standard. What is needed is guidance advising on *attainment standards* ie the standard a dwelling should reach on the completion of any works, while any guidance should clearly state the purpose for which it has been issued. Guidance on model approaches to housing surveys, specifications to make houses fit and on setting pricing guidelines for common repair items would also be welcome.

Authorities would also like wider powers simply to close parts of dwellings unsuitable for habitation, and to require the doing of certain works only so as to avoid the disruption to certain occupiers consequent on the determination than an extensive package of works is needed to make a dwelling fit. See now, however, the DAN procedure outlined above.

One particular issue relating to modernising the fitness standard, however, can be dealt with at this point – energy efficiency. Cm 2453 *Energy Efficiency in Buildings*, the response of the government to a report from the House of Commons Select Committee on the Environment in 1994 indicated official unwillingness to make energy efficiency a criterion for assessing the fitness of dwellings. It was accepted that creating such a criterion would increase the number of dwellings classified as unfit and the cost of making dwellings fit. There remains also doubt about the numbers of sub-standard dwellings. The 1994 report *Papering Over the Cracks* (National Housing Forum) argued for an immediate £7 billion programme to bring privately owned housing up to fitness standards, and stated more than one owner occupied dwelling in 20 does not meet the fitness standard, while one home in every 13 overall is unfit.

Unfitness: the future?

The Internet summary of the English House Condition Survey 1996, issued by DETR in 1999, indicates that:
- the number of dwellings lacking basic amenities, for example a bathroom, is approaching an irreducible minimum of some 200,000, approximately half of which are vacant;
- on the basis that a 'modern' dwelling is one with kitchen and bathroom facilities installed post 1964, modern electrical wiring and central heating less than 30 years old, 78% of the housing stock qualifies, most of these being in the owner occupied and registered social landlord

sectors, but modern kitchens and bathrooms are less likely to be found in the privately rented and local authority stock;
* while 80% of dwellings have some fabric faults, the majority of these are minor;
* higher levels of disrepair are still found concentrated in the private rented sector and such dwellings of all ages (save those provided after 1964) are in noticeably worse states of repair than dwellings of similar ages in other sectors;
* of the local authority stock it is the post 1964 dwelling which tend to have the highest disrepair problems, largely due to the presence of numbers of purpose built high rise flats;
* the highest levels of disrepair are in the London boroughs, large urban districts, and older resort and university towns;
* there remain 1,522,000 unfit dwellings, some 7.5% of the housing stock, a similar proportion to that found in 1991, but some half million of the then unfit dwellings have since been made fit, while an equal number have since become unfit;
* the most common reasons for unfitness are unsatisfactory facilities in which to prepare and cook food, disrepair and dampness;
* the number of dwellings unfit on more than item was more in 1996 than in 1991, with the greatest rates of unfitness found in pre 1919 houses and converted flats, and the incidence by sector is 6.0% owner occupied, 19.3% privately rented, 7.3% local authority rented and 5.2% rented from registered social landlords;
* though private tenants suffer the greatest proportional incidence of unfitness, more than half all unfit homes are owner occupied, largely because of the size of this sector, and this proportion has increased since 1991;
* 'poor housing' ie that which is unfit, or needs substantial repair or essential modernisation afflicts 14.2% of the population, and is particularly prevalent amongst ethnic minority households, the young, the unemployed, the part-time employed, the elderly and lone parent households;
* 'poor living conditions', ie concentrations of poor housing and/or environmental problems afflict 6.6% of the population, again with ethnic minority and unemployed households suffering most.

The picture that emerges is of a housing stock that is overall in good condition, but with stubborn 'pockets of problems'.

Most people, even those in 'poor housing' are satisfied with their homes or their state of repair. It is those groups suffering the highest degree of what is now often called 'social exclusion' who are most dissatisfied, ie the young, the unemployed, lone parents, private tenants, ethnic minorities and households with infants. The search for a more appropriate standard of fitness for the start of the next century has therefore to be set against the background of continuing relative deprivation in society, and should be considered not just as a 'bricks and mortar' issue but as a contribution to bringing about a more inclusive society.

In February 1998 the DETR issued a consultation paper on the housing fitness standard. This raised a number of important issues for the future of the law.

(1)   A statutory housing fitness standard should be retained, but of what sort?

(a)   Is it preferable to keep the present standard with expanded requirements embracing health and safety issues; or

(b)   to adopt a new standard?

To adopt (a) would more than double the number of unfit properties as it would bring in properties with poor energy efficiency ratings, those subject to radon gas, those with poor internal arrangements and those with poor fire safety – the unfit total would rise to 3,245,000 dwellings. To adopt (b) would mean a new approach whereby scarce resources are budgeted to deal with dwellings with the greatest health and safety risks, whereby houses would be rated according to a range of characteristics rather than 'passing/failing' – as under the current law. A specific minimum level would be set below which a property would be deemed unfit, and the new system would allow better targeting of enforcement action and grant aid. The new rating system would also allow the characteristics of the occupants to be taken into account – eg particular vulnerabilities.

The features of the new system would be:

(i)   a physical survey covering all the current issues *plus* thermal efficiency, radon and health and safety issues;

(ii)   concentration on the effect of the defect, not the defect itself.

(iii)   concentration on the severity of the problem posed by the condition of the dwelling.

Matters to be considered would include risk of falls, fire safety, exposure to extremes of cold and heat, radon, burning and scalding hazards, electrical hazards, mould and damp, presence of pollutants, exposure to lead, presence of asbestos, injuries caused by falling objects and explosions, problems caused by doors and windows, sanitation and drainage and hygiene problems, food safety and other infection problems, noise exposure, crime and fear of crime problems, space and privacy issues, lighting difficulties.

The system would depend on an assessment of the probability of any given defect causing a hazardous event measured against the likely health outcome of the event. The overall 'rating' of a house would be the sum total of the scores given in respect of each given defect's likely effect – thus a single high probability of severe injury would result in a 'higher' rating than a multiplicity of minor defects. The scores would be placed in 'rating bands' as a guide to determining outcomes.

(2)   Should the law be based on powers rather than duties, as currently? The questions posed were as follows.
(a) Is a power to take action more consonant with a discretionary grant system (see further below on grant aid)?
(b) Would use of powers rather than duties lead to an inconsistency of approach between authorities and also lead to more legal challenges?
(c) Should the present ability of authorities to serve deferred action notices be abolished?
(d) Should there be a differential approach according to the nature of the tenure involved – eg a duty to enforce in the private rented sector, a power only in the owner occupied sector? It is desirable to have inequality of treatment?
(e) If the fitness standard approach outlined above were to be adopted should there be a duty to enforce in respect of houses below the deemed minimum standard and a power in respect of houses above it?

(3)   Should there be a harmonisation of the various enforcement powers to bring together the criteria applicable to section 190 of the Housing Act 1985 (fit but in disrepair), section 352 (unfit for number of occupants) and section 80 of the Environmental Protection Act 1990 (statutory nuisance)?

At the moment there are discrepancies between these provisions, relating to:
(a) periods for commencing work – in some cases immediate action can be required, in others 21 or 28 days' notice has to be given;
(b) mental elements – 'intentional failure' to comply as opposed to failure to comply 'without reasonable excuse';
(c) variety of levels of fines – ranging between £2,500 and £5,000 upper limits.

(4)   Should the 'minded to' provision of section 86 of the Housing Grants, Construction and Regulation Act 1996 (see above) be repealed and replaced by a voluntary concordat on good practice with regard to taking enforcement action?

(5)   Should the power to charge in respect of enforcement action introduced in 1996 be retained?

(6)   Should the current guidance on interpreting the current fitness requirements (ie Annex A of DoE 17/96) be retained on an interim basis until the new fitness rating approach is adopted?

(7)　Should the fitness standard be made applicable to areas within dwellings applicable to each household or 'unit of accommodation' enabling authorities simply to close down parts of a dwelling while leaving the rest in use?

(8)　Should the fitness standard be made enforceable against local authority dwellings and, if so, by who? Possible enforcers include the Health and Safety Executive, the Environment Agency or the Housing Corporation; alternatively a new independent body could be created, or a 'proper officer' of the authority could be instituted to enable an authority to enforce against itself.

Action is still awaited on these proposals.

HOUSING RENEWAL AND IMPROVEMENT

Renewal areas

Improvement of poor housing conditions on an area basis has been a policy option available to authorities for many years. The Housing Act 1969 introduced the notion of the General Improvement Area (GIA). Housing Action Areas (HAA) were introduced under the Housing Act 1974 to deal with more run-down areas. These types of action continued to be available under the Housing Act 1985, but the law was subject to criticism in that it did not provide one single, comprehensive mode of dealing with poor housing and also because it tended to separate consideration of housing conditions from other important issues such as employment, education facilities etc. Though changes have been made to the law it is by no means certain that these have come about as a result of desires to answer the foregoing criticisms as opposed to wishes to foster individual effort to target resources and to reduce overall public expenditure. Under the changes made by the Local Goverment and Housing Act 1989, HAAs and GIAs can no longer be declared, see section 98 of the 1989 Act.

In place of GIAs and HAAs the 1989 Act introduced the concept of the Renewal Area (RA) and Annex C of DoE Circular 6/90 made it clear that land within a GIA or HAA could be instead designated as, or as part of, a RA.

The new law is part of the overall 'flexible approach' to a renewal and improvement strategy introduced by the 1989 Act. Renewal action is to be undertaken after careful appraisal of the options available for an area. Where declared, RAs will be larger than GIAs and HAAs were, and will normally last for ten years, during which time comprehensive action is to be undertaken to renew housing and tackle social and environmental problems. The basis is akin to partnership between the authority, residents, associations, and the private sector, including financial institutions for the object of using local authority powers is to give others 'market confidence' in the area, so helping to reverse processes of decline and to encourage spin offs for the local economy in the form of employment and training opportunities. Authorities are required by section 605 of the Housing Act 1985 to consider declaring RAs. This will involve selecting appropriate areas for action. DoE 6/90 made it clear the worst will not necessarily be the first; in some cases preventive action in respect of areas in danger of decline may be more appropriate. RAs will be declared against a policy background of choosing the 'most satisfactory course of action' which runs as a skein throughout repair and renewal legislation. Within a RA there may also be a need for pockets of clearance and/or group repair schemes etc (see further below). Further guidance is to be found in DoE Circular 17/96.

The statutory basis for declaring a RA is a report prepared under section 89 of the 1989 Act which must include particulars of the living conditions in the area in question, the ways in which they could be improved, powers available to the authority, the authority's detailed proposals for using those powers, costs of the proposals and the financial resources actually, or likely to be, available for implementing proposals. The report must also contain a reasoned recommendation as to whether a RA should be declared. In considering whether to make a declaration an authority must have regard to guidance issued by the Secretary of State, and must comply with any directions given as to publicising their proposals and receiving representations. DoE Circular 6/90 Annex E required authorities to publicise proposals in local newspapers, and also to post site notices indicating their intentions. The details are now to be found in ministerial directions forming part of Annex C1 of DoE Circular 17/96. The publicity must identify the area and name a place where a map defining it may be inspected, and the place to which representations should be sent. Similar information must be posted to each address in the area along with a summary of the section 89 report. Any representations received must be considered before declaration takes place. Authorities must also be satisfied that the living conditions in the area, which must consist *primarily* of 'housing accommodation', are unsatisfactory and that this problem can be most effectively dealt with by declaring an RA. Housing accommodation, see section 100, means dwellings (buildings occupied or intended to be occupied as separate dwellings), HMOs and hostels.

The report referred to above should, on the basis of DoE Circular 6/90 para 26, be based on use of NRA principles, see earlier notes, and should also draw on a wide range of relevant expertise, eg in planning, valuation, accountancy, environmental health, highway planning and the social services, together with the views of private sector agencies.

Certain conditions also have to be met before a RA can be declared, see section 90 of the 1989 Act. The actual conditions are laid down in DoE

Circular 17/96, Annex C1, para 3. Thus an RA *must* have at least 300 dwellings in it. 75% of the dwellings in the area must be privately owned; RAs are not designed to deal with the needs of run down public sector estates, these are the subject of other programmes administered by the DETR as funding for authorities.

Action on run down authority estates is possible, but takes place largely within an administrative structure. Elsewhere it is the law which lays down the parameters within which action takes place, as the following paragraphs make clear with regard to RAs.

The physical condition of dwellings in a RA must be such that 75% are 'unfit' or would qualify for works under sections 112, 113 or 115 of the 1989 Act (see further below), and the financial circumstances of those living in the area must be such that at least 30% of them appear dependent to a significant extent upon certain state benefits, eg housing benefit, income support, etc.

If the above conditions are met an authority may proceed to declare a RA, and section 91 requires them to publicise this fact, and take steps to inform those who reside, or who own property, in the area, particularly as to the name and address of the person to whom inquiries and representations concerning action to be taken should be addressed. Information and advice should also be provided for those wishing to carry out works on housing accommodation. Certain specified information also has to be sent to the Secretary of State, see DoE Circular 17/96, Annex C1, para 4. The duty to publish information on action taken or to be taken, and assistance available in respect of carrying out works in a RA is a continuing one once the area is declared, see section 92, and once again the Secretary of State may issue directions as to fulfilling this duty, see DoE Circular 17/96 Annex C1, para 5.

Under section 93 of the 1989 Act extensive powers are conferred on authorities to implement RA strategy. They may, under section 93(2), acquire land by agreement or compulsorily, and provide housing thereon. Such activity must serve one or more of the following objectives, ie the improvement or repair of relevant premises, the proper and effective management of housing accommodation, or the well being of residents. Land may also be similarly acquired for the purposes of effecting or assisting the improvement of the amenities of the area, section 93(4). Authorities may carry out works on land they own and may assist in respect of works on other land by making grants, loans and providing guarantees and materials, etc.

The compulsory purchase procedure to be used is that under Part XVIII of the 1985 Act and the Acquisition of Land Act 1981. Land may be acquired to secure the improvement or repair of housing either by the authority or another body to whom they wish to transfer the land, eg a registered social landlord, *or* bring about the proper and effective use of housing in the area, *or* to secure the well being of the residents of the area.

Section 96 of the 1989 Act empowers the Secretary of State to grant subsidies to authorities in respect of RAs, though this is effectively entirely at the discretion of central government. Circular 17/96, Annex C1, para 8, details the expenditure towards which contributions will be paid, these *include* street works, traffic management schemes, landscaping, improving the exteriors of buildings, converting buildings to provide community facilities and other environmental works, but *exclude*, inter alia, works on the interior of houses, works on commercial or industrial premises, works to improve or provide facilities which are intended primarily to produce revenue for the authority, and works of routine maintenance. The rate of contribution is 50% of costs per annum up to a limit of 'aggregate eligible expenditure' of £1,000 multiplied by the number of dwellings in the area. See also DoE Circular 17/96 Annex C1, para 10.

Though the general expectation is that RAs will last for ten years, they should be kept under constant review, though re-surveys may be needed not more than once or twice. Section 95 gives power by resolution, however, to exclude land from a RA or bring designation to an end. Before doing this there must be compliance with the Secretary of State's requirements under DoE Circular 17/96 Annex C1, para 6 which requires local publicity for the proposal, delivery of statements about the proposal to each address in the area, consideration of any representations received, delivery to the Secretary of State of specified information. Thereafter the resolution may be made and its making and effect must be publicised.

Grant aid

Improvement of dwellings, either by their owners or tenants, and on either an individual or group basis, under the aegis of Grant Aid given by authorities has been a feature of housing improvement for many years, and there have been many forms of grant aiding scheme, see inter alia the House Purchase and Housing Act 1959 and the Housing Act 1974. Between 1989 and 1996 the relevant law was to be found in Part VIII of the Local Government and Housing Act. This has now been repealed and replaced by the Housing Grants, Construction and Regeneration Act 1996, the chief object of which was to reduce the amount of central funding for housing improvement by moving away from a mixed pattern of mandatory and discretionary grants to one in which nearly all grants are discretionary. [References to Section numbers following are to the Housing Grants, Construction and Regeneration Act (HGCRA) 1996 unless otherwise specified]. (see also DETR Circular 06/99 on Part 1 of the 1996 Act.)

The types of grant available

Section 1 of the 1996 Act lists grants as:

- Renovation grants – those for the improvement or repair of dwellings or their provision by conversion of houses or other buildings;
- Common parts grants – those for the improvement or repair of the common parts of a building;
- Disabled facilities grants – those to provide facilities for a disabled person in a building;
- HMO grants – those for improving or repairing HMOs, or to provide an HMO by conversion.

Grant applications must be made in due form under section 2 of the Act, and must in particular give details of the works in respect of which a grant is sought, and, normally, must be accompanied by at least two contractors' estimates of the costs of carrying out those works.

Applicants must be 'eligible' under section 3 ie they must be aged 18 or more, and public bodies such as authorities are specifically excluded from eligibility, while the Secretary of State has further powers to prescribe further classes of ineligible persons. Furthermore under section 4 a grant application may not be *entertained* in respect of premises provided by construction or conversion less than ten years before the date of the application, save where the application is for a disabled facilities grant, or for an HMO grant in respect of an HMO provided by conversion. In addition no grant is *payable* in respect of works excluded from grant aid under regulations made by the Secretary of State: see section 5.

Renovation grants (RG)

Under section 7 an authority may not entertain an application for RG unless satisfied that the applicant has or proposes to acquire an 'owners interest' in the property, ie the freehold or a leasehold term of at least five years: see section 101, *or* in the case of an application *other than one for conversion* that the applicant is a qualifying tenant and does not have an owner's interest. A qualifying tenant is one whose tenancy requires him/her to carry out relevant works on the dwelling and whose tenancy is not an 'excluded' one under regulations, *or* whose tenancy is of a class specified by the Secretary of State. Specified licensees may also apply.

Where an owner's application is made it cannot, under section 8, be entertained unless accompanied by an owner-occupation certificate, or a certificate of intended letting of the dwelling. The former states the applicant has, or proposes to acquire, an owner's interest and intends to reside (or that a family member shall reside) in the dwelling. The latter makes a similar statement in respect of the letting of a dwelling on a residential basis. Section 9 then provides that a tenant's application cannot be entertained unless there is an accompanying certificate that the applicant is a 'qualifying tenant' and that the tenant (or member of the tenant's family) intends to live in the dwelling as his/her only or main residence. An authority may also require a certificate of intended letting from the tenant's landlord.

Section 10 generally imposes a prior qualifying period requirement on applicants before their applications can be entertained, though this does *not* apply to a landlord's application, nor to a conversion application, nor one in respect of a dwelling in a renewal area, nor one in respect of works to provide means of escape from fire or other fire precautions. The qualifying requirement is that an ownership or tenancy condition has been met throughout a qualifying period, *and*, where the application is accompanied by an owner-occupation certificate or tenant's certificate, that the applicant lived in the dwelling as his/her only or main residence throughout that period. The qualifying period is one of three years, and the ownership or tenancy condition is, as specified in section 11, that the applicant has had a qualifying owner's interest in the property or was a qualifying tenant. Thus the owner, or tenant as the case may be, must have had the appropriate qualifying interest for the appropriate period. The object here is to ensure grant aid goes to those who are bona fide long term residents in an area and who are not seeking to 'carpet bag' grant aid, but there are exceptions as outlined above to this rule.

RG *may* be approved under section 12 for the following purposes:

- Complying with notices under section 189 or 190 of the Housing Act 1985;
- providing adequate thermal insulation or adequate facilities for space heating;
- providing satisfactory internal arrangements;
- providing means of escape in case of fire or other fire precautions;
- to ensure the dwelling complies with specifications issued by the Secretary of State;
- to ensure compliance with requirements as to the provision of services or amenities within the dwelling;
- where the application is for conversion, in order to provide for the provision of one or more dwelling.

Authorities have power to vary an application where they conclude it is for works more or less extensive than are necessary to achieve the purpose in hand.

Section 13 then provides that an authority may *not* approve an RG application unless satisfied than the works proposed are *necessary* for one of the foregoing purposes, nor may they approve an application from someone who proposes to acquire an owner's interest until satisfied he/she has done so.

Before approving an RG application under section 13(4) the authority must consider whether the premises are 'fit', and if the premises are not, they may not approve unless satisfied that on completion of relevant work (and any others proposed) they will be 'fit', *and* that the carrying out of the works is the 'most satisfactory course of action'. They must also consider the expected life of the building.

Common parts grants (CPG)

Under section 17 the purposes for which a CPG application may be approved are broadly similar to those applying to RG applications, save that added to them is one that an application may be approved to comply with a notice under section 352 of the Housing Act 1985 – notices requiring works to render a HMO fit for the number of occupants, etc. Once again approval is discretionary as with RG, but under section 18 approval may not be given unless the authority is satisfied that the works are necessary for one or more of the purposes specified in section 17. Furthermore the authority must consider whether the building in question satisfies fitness requirements, and if it does not they may not approve the application unless satisfied that on completion of the works the building will be fit etc, just as with an RG application. Section 57 defines further 'Common Parts' – see further below.

Disabled facilities grants (DFG)

Section 19 lies down initial application requirements very similar to those for RG applications, ie that the applicant has or proposes to acquire an owner's interest in the relevant property *or* that the applicant is a tenant of the relevant dwelling, though note in this case the tenant applicant does not have to be under any tenancy obligation to carry out the works. Furthermore 'tenant' in this context *includes* secure and introductory tenants amongst those who may apply. The applicant need not be the 'disabled occupant' for whose benefit the work is intended, but such a person there must be: see generally section 20. As with RG applications, where an owner's application is received there must be a certificate of intended residence by the disabled occupant in the dwelling (see section 21) and a similar certificate is required in respect of a tenant's application under section 22, while, once again, the authority must also require an owner's certificate from the tenant's landlord unless they consider it unreasonable in the circumstances to do so.

DFG are *mandatory* – an exception to the generally discretionary nature of grant aid – and the purposes for which an application *must* be approved are:

• facilitating access to the dwelling or the building in which it is situated;

* making the dwelling/building safe for the disabled occupant and others residing with him/her;
* facilitating access by the disabled occupant to the principal family room;
* facilitating access by the disabled occupant to, or providing for that person, a sleeping room;
* facilitating access by the disabled occupant to, or providing for that person, a lavatory;
* facilitating access etc to a bath or shower room;
* facilitating access etc to a room with a wash hand basin;
* facilitating the preparation and cooking of food by the disabled occupant;
* improving the heating system to meet the disabled occupant's needs, or providing a suitable system;
* facilitating use by the disabled occupant of sources of power, light and heat – eg by repositioning switches;
* facilitating access around the dwelling by the disabled occupant in order for him/her to care for someone else normally resident there;
* other purposes as specified by the Secretary of State.

There is an additional *discretionary* ground of approval where DFG is sought to make a dwelling/building suitable for the accommodation, welfare or employment of the disabled occupant in any other respect. See also section 24 on the mandatory nature of DFG, but note that an application even for such a grant may not be approved unless the authority are satisfied that:

* where the application is from an intending owner of the property that he/she has acquired an owner's interest;
* the relevant works are necessary and appropriate to meet the needs of the disabled occupant and that it is reasonable and practicable to carry them out having regard to the age and condition of the property (and in relation to this issue the opinion of the Social Services Authority must be sought). Authorities must also consider whether the dwelling in question is fit, and must take that into account in determining whether it is reasonable and practicable to carry out relevant works. On DFG generally see DoE Circular 17/96 Annex 1.

It should be noted generally that in relation to determining DFG issues an authority are not entitled to have regard to their resources, and that taking such an issue into account is taking account of an irrelevant consideration open to judicial review[6].

---

6   *R v Birmingham City Council, ex p Mohammed* [1998] 3 All ER 788, [1999] 1 WLR 33.

HMO Grants (HMOG)

Once again, under section 24, an authority may not entertain a HMOG application unless the applicant has or proposes to acquire an owner's interest in the property on which relevant works are to be carried out. It will thus be noted that the tenants in an HMO cannot apply for HMOG in respect of it. Under section 25 the applicant must accompany the application with a statement that he/she has or proposes to acquire an qualifying owner's interest in the property, and that he/she intends that the property will be residentially occupied under tenancies or licences (excluding holiday lettings) by persons not connected with the owner. This is known as a 'certificate of future occupation'.

Section 27 provides that HMOG may be payable in respect of the same range of purposes as apply to RG, plus, once again, securing compliance with notices under section 352 of the 1985 Act. Section 28 further provides that approval is discretionary, subject to requirements that the authority must be satisfied the works proposed are necessary for section 27 purposes, and the usual range of requirements as to the acquisition of an owner's interest and compliance with fitness requirements.

General restrictions on grant aid

Where works subject to a grant application are *commenced* before approval under section 29 the general rule is that the authority *may* still approve the application (and that applies to otherwise mandatory grants) provided they are satisfied there were good reasons for commencing work without approval. This discretion is *not* available in respect of *completed* works. Nothing in section 29, however, applies to an application in respect of works necessary to render a dwelling fit, or to comply with a notice under sections 189 or 190 of the Housing Act 1985 (repair notices) or to meet the requirements of section 352 (1A) of the 1985 Act (fitness for number of occupants).

Means testing

Not only are grants now generally given only on a discretionary basis, they are also under section 3 means tested in the case of applications from owner occupiers, tenants or those seeking DFG. The means testing formula is contained in regulations made under section 30(5) but proceeds on the well tried basis of comparing the applicant's financial resources (income, assets, needs and outgoings – including those of spouses, persons living with the applicant and dependants) against the 'applicable amount', ie an amount fixed by regulations in relation to grants, so that where 'resources' exceed 'applicable amount' the amount of any grant otherwise payable is proportionally reduced. For the detailed rules see the Housing Renewal Grants Regulations 1996, SI 1996/2890, as amended by SI 1996/3119, SI 1997/977, SI 1998/808 and SI 1999/1523.

In the case of landlord's applications the amount of grant to be paid is broadly at the discretion of the authority under section 31. Authorities must, however, have regard to:

- the extent to which a landlord will be able to charge an increased rent because of the grant aided works and
- such other matters as may be directed by the Secretary of State.

In addition authorities may seek and act upon the advice of rent officers in relation to any matter: see further the Rent Officers (Housing Renewal Grant Functions) Order 1997, SI 1997/778.

Where tenants make an application for CPG and it is approved, the authority must initially decide how much of the cost of the relevant works is attributable to the applicants – the 'attributable cost'. That is an amount equal to the following proportion of the cost of relevant works:

- where it *is* ascertainable, the attributable cost is the proportion that the aggregate of the respective liabilities of each of the applicants to carry out, or to contribute to the carrying out of, the relevant works bears to the aggregate of all such liabilities on the part of all persons;
- where it is *not* ascertainable, the attributable cost is the proportion that the number of applicants bears to the total number of people liable to carry out, or contribute, to the carrying out of works to the building.

So, for example, under the first limb of the formula if a block of flats has six flats with contribution costs such as service charges evenly divided, and three flat holders make the application the 'attributable costs' are 50% of the cost of relevant works. If for some reason the second limb is applied the approach to adopt is a numerical one; so where there are ten flats and only two applicants the attributable cost would be 20%.

Once the attributable cost is determined it has then to be portioned out amongst all applicants using a similar formula to determine individual entitlements.

The Secretary of State has power under section 33 of the 1996 Act to fix a maximum level of grant, though authorities have a limited discretion to exceed this on the case of DFG: see, inter alia, the Disabled Facilities Grants and Home Repair Assistance (Maximum Amounts) Order 1996, SI 1996/2888.

Decisions, notification and payment

Section 34 requires authorities to notify applicants as soon as reasonably practicable, and in any case not later than six months from the date of application, of the outcome. Authorities approving an application must also inter alia determine those relevant works which are eligible for assistance according to the formulae for the various grants, the amount of the expenses which in their opinion are properly to be incurred in carrying out eligible works, and the amount of grant they have decided to pay. They must inform the applicant of approved eligible works and the amounts they have determined. Where a grant is refused reasons must be given.

An approved grant may be redetermined under section 34(5) if circumstances beyond the applicant's control lead to increases in costs. Section 35 requires an authority to pay *approved* grants either in whole after the completion of eligible works or by instalments as the works progress with the balance paid on completion. While the grant determining function is essentially a matter of public law only open to challenge by way of judicial review so that, for example, a refusal to approve a grant application would give rise to no cause of action for damages, where an application *has been approved*, and payment is withheld because of disputes over fulfilment of grant conditions, it appears an ordinary action may be brought to enforce payment of the grant[7]. However, conditions may only be imposed on approved grants if allowed for under the Housing Grants, Construction and Renovation Act 1996, or consented by the Secretary of State: see section 34(6) of the 1996 Act.

Payment of mandatory DFG may be delayed under section 36 but only up to a period of 12 months from the date specified in the notification of the decision on the application.

Grant payment conditions

Under section 37 there is an implied condition in *all* grants that, as a general rule, eligible works are carried out within 12 months of the approval date. Authorities *may* also require that works are carried out according to their specification. Payment is in any case, however, conditional upon works being carried out to the authority's satisfaction, and their being provided with appropriate invoices and receipts for the work – ie proof of expenditure.

Section 38 imposes a condition that, in general, the works may only be carried out by a contractor whose estimate accompanied the application, while under section 39 grants may be paid in whole or part to the contractor, provided the work has been done to the applicant's satisfaction, and provided the applicant was told before approval that this method of payment might be adopted.

Section 40 of the 1996 Act applies a general principle that where an application is approved and the applicant ceases to be a person entitled to the type of grant in question before the 'certified date' ie the date certified

---

7 *Dennis Rye Pension Fund Trustees v Sheffield City Council* [1997] 4 All ER 747, 30 HLR 645, CA.

by the authority as the date on which the execution of eligible works was completed according to their satisfaction (see section 44(3)(b)) no grant is to be paid, or no further instalment, as the case may be. This would apply, for example, where an owner ceased to have an 'owner's interest, or where a tenant ceased to qualify. Where a change of circumstance, however, affects a disabled occupant between the date of approval of a DFG application and the 'certified date', as, for example where the works are no longer appropriate for that person's needs, or where that person ceases to occupy the dwelling in question, section 41 enables the authority to take such action as they consider appropriate, including determining that no grant should be paid, taking into account all the circumstances of the case.

Authorities may under section 42 recalculate, withhold or demand repayment of grants in a number of circumstances including cases where they discover that the amount of a grant was decided on the basis of inaccurate or incomplete information so that it exceeds the applicant's entitlements, or where eligible works were begun before approval or were not completed within the due time, or were carried out by the incorrect contractor. Where after approval it appears that an applicant was not entitled to a grant of the type approved, under section 43 no grant, or further instalment as the case, may be, is normally to be paid – though there is a little discretion in the case of CPG approved following a landlord's application – and the authority may demand repayment with interest. This is a provision designed to inhibit fraudulent grant applications, which may themselves be the subject of separate criminal investigation and prosecution.[8]

General grant conditions

Section 44 et seq provide for a number of general grant conditions, in particular section 44(3)(a) provides that the 'grant condition period' – a phrase encountered in a number of places in Part I of the 1996 Act, shall be five years from the certified date which, has already been said, is the date the authority certify as that on which the execution of eligible works is completed to their satisfaction.

There then follow conditions relating to repayment on disposal of RG (section 45), CPG (section 46) and HMOG (section 47). These follow a generally similar pattern: where the owner of the premises (landlord in the case of CPG) makes a 'relevant disposal' other than an 'exempt disposal' (see below) of the whole or part of the premises after any instalment of grant has been paid and before the certified date, *or* makes such a disposal on or after the certified date and before the end of the grant condition period, the amount of grant paid becomes repayable at the demand of the authority,

8   *R v Parker* (1993) 26 HLR 508.

though authorities in general have a discretion not to demand repayment or to seek less than the full amount. In addition so far as RG is concerned there is similar latitude where the owner is elderly or infirm and is making the disposal in order to move into some form of sheltered or supported housing (such as a hospice), or to move elsewhere into care, *or* is making the disposal so that he/she may go and live with and care for an elderly or infirm member. Note that there is no scale whereby liability to repay is reduced over the grant condition period, also that the condition in each case is a local land charge, binding on other persons (though not on a local authority or registered social landlord in the case of HMOG).

'Relevant' and 'Exempt' disposals are defined by section 53 and 54. The former *includes* a freehold transfer or assignment of a lease, or the grant of a lease for a term of more than 21 years other than at a rack rent. The latter, inter alia, is a disposal to a 'qualifying person' by way of freehold conveyance or leasehold assignment, or under a will or an intestacy, or following compulsory purchase, or where the conveyance/assignment is made by a person at least 70 years old and is done to raise annuity income for that person who will remain entitled to live in the dwelling, or where the disposal is made under a matrimonial order under section 24 or 24A of the Matrimonial Causes Act 1973, section 2 of the Inheritance (Provision for Family and Dependants) Act 1975, section 17 of the Matrimonial and Family Proceedings Act 1984 or Schedule 1, paragraph 1 of the Children Act 1989. A person is 'qualifying' if he/she is the person or one of them by whom the disposal is made or is the spouse or former spouse of that person (or one of them) or is a member of the family of that person (as defined be section 113 of the Housing Act 1985).

Section 48, 49 and 50 impose various occupancy conditions. Where RG is given on an owner occupier's application it is a condition under section 48 that throughout the grant condition period the dwelling is to be occupied as stated in the owner-occupation certificate, and a similar condition applies under section 49, mutatis mutandis, in the case of a dwelling renovated for the purpose of letting. A similar condition applies under section 50 where HMOG has been given. In all these cases the grant aiding authority can demand evidence of compliance, and breach of condition leads to liability to repay the grant (save that that does not generally apply under section 48 where there is an exempt disposal). Authorities, however, have discretion not to demand repayment, or may demand a lesser sum than the full amount. The conditions in all cases are local land charges.

Section 51 empowers authorities, subject to the consent of the Secretary of State, to impose a condition requiring the applicant to take reasonable steps to pursue 'any relevant claim' and then to repay the grant out of the proceeds. Relevant claims include insurance claims and those for damages in respect of the property. As before non-compliance with the condition entails a liability to repay the grant. Other conditions may be imposed with the consent of the Secretary of State under section 52, while under section 55 grant conditions cease to have effect on the voluntary repayment of a grant.

Supplementary provision

Section 57 empowers authorities to make agreements with the owners of dwellings (occupying tenants in the case of CPG) to enable an authority to carry out at the owner's expense, any grant aided or grant aidable works, and any additional works, and any additional works the authority consider necessary or desirable. Note also section 58 under which, inter alia, 'common parts' for CPG purposes include the structure and exterior of the building, and any common facilities provided in the building or elsewhere for the occupiers.

Group repair schemes (GRS)

Authorities are empowered by section 60 to undertake group repair schemes to put 'buildings' into a reasonable state of exterior repair, and/or to render them structurally stable. This is the latest version of the notion of 'enveloping' whereby public funding is devoted to exterior works while the occupants remain liable for the internal condition. A 'building' includes the whole or part of a terrace of houses or other dwelling units. However, under section 61 the 'buildings' in question must also be 'qualifying', and a GRS must relate to at least one qualifying building, while each of the other qualifying buildings in the scheme must satisfy the requirements of being an 'additional' building. A building qualifies if at the time the GRS is prepared it satisfies the conditions laid down for qualification in relation to a GRS. The basic notion is that each GRS will contain a *primary* building and *additional* buildings. The primary building may be all or part of a terrace or houses or some other dwelling units such as a converted warehouse of factory. Furthermore some part of the exterior of that building must not be in reasonable repair, or all or part of its structure must be unstable. Under the Group Repair (Qualifying Buildings) Regulations 1996, SI 1996/2883, the primary building must contain at least two dwellings, while an 'additional' building must contain at least one dwelling. As a further precondition the carrying out of the work on the primary and additional buildings at the same time must also be the most effective way of ensuring the repair or stability of each of them: see further DoE Circular 17/96.

'Scheme works' under section 62 of the 1996 Act are to be directed towards securing the 'reasonable repair' of the exterior of the buildings, ie any part of the building which is exposed to wind or rain or otherwise faces into open air, while 'reasonable repair' under section 96 is to be determined by having regard to the age, character and locality of the dwelling, and by *disregarding* its state of internal decorative repair; though in addition under section 62(6) there is a requirement that to meet a 'reasonable' standard of repair the building after the works are done must be substantially free from rising or penetrating damp. Alternatively works may be directed towards making buildings structurally stable, which includes work to the structure or to the foundations of the building.

A GRS requires the approval of the Secretary of State under section 63, but this has been given generally to schemes meeting criteria laid down in Annex D2 of DoE Circular 17/96.

Just as with grant aid, only certain persons are eligible to participate in a GRS under section 64 – 'eligible participants' – and these are those who have an 'owner's interest' (ie freehold or leasehold with five years unexpired: see section 101) in *a* dwelling or other premises in a relevant building, who can give possession of any part of the building subject to proposed scheme works *or* who have the consent of the occupier of the relevant part to the carrying out of the works. Eligible participants *may* also be 'assisted participants', where they can certify they are owner occupiers and intend to live in the dwelling, or where they give a certificate of intended letting of the dwelling, or, where the property in question is a HMO, they give a certificate that they own the property and will continue to make it available for residential occupation by others. The certification given must relate to residential occupation for a period of five years beginning with the completion of the works – this is known as 'the protected period': see section 69. Public bodies such as authorities and registered social landlords are excluded from being 'assisted participants' who are able to seek grant aid towards the cost of the GRS.

The general principle under section 65 is that eligible participants must signify their consent – 'scheme consent' – to the scheduled scheme, otherwise no work may be done on part of a building in respect of which no eligible participant has signified consent, and must then, under section 67 make their duly apportioned contribution to the cost of the scheme. The eligible participants may apportion the contributions by agreement, otherwise equal division of costs is the rule. As assisted participant whose interest as an owner is in premises other than a dwelling or HMO only has to make a proportionate contribution to costs according to the formula: 25% for buildings in renewal areas, 50% elsewhere. For other assisted participants, eg those who are owner occupiers or landlords of houses, the amount payable is to be determined by the relevant authority, though it may *not* exceed 25% or 50% as the case may be.

A scheme once completed is to be certified by the authority to the assisted participants as having passed its 'completion date' under section 66, but schemes may be varied at any time before completion – eg to allow more people to participate. Such variation is subject to consultation with existing participants, and the consent of the Secretary of the Secretary of State – though this has been generally given: see Annex D2, DoE Circular 17/96.

Section 69 imposes conditions on those who are assisted participants for a period of five years following completion, and these are similar to the conditions on grants already encountered. Thus under section 70 there can be liability to pay on demand to the authority a sum of money – known as the 'balance of the cost' – should an assisted participant make a 'relevant disposal' which is not an 'exempt disposal' of relevant premises (see above for the meaning of these terms). Similarly under section 71 there are occupation requirements which, if breached may lead to a demand for payment of the balance of cost.

Home repair assistance (HRA)

Section 76 of the 1996 Act empowers authorities to give financial assistance in cases *other* than grant aided works or where a GRS does *not* apply. There are otherwise generally very strict limits on the HRA. Thus an applicant, under section 77, must be aged 18 or more, must live in the dwelling in question as his/her only or main residence, must be either the owner or tenant of the dwelling (*including* a secure tenant), must have a duty or power to carry out the work in question, and must be in receipt of some form of state benefit, such as income support. There are some limited exceptions to these restrictions, for example the state benefits restriction does not apply to applicants who are elderly, disabled or infirm, as defined under section 100. The amount of HRA is also subject to limits imposed centrally by regulation, currently £2,000 per annum or £4,000 in any three-year period: see SI 1996/2888.

It should finally be noted that the Secretary of State has power to give financial assistance to authorities in respect of their grant aiding functions – and to recover contributions where grants have to be repaid: see sections 92 and 93 and Annex C1 of DoE Circular 17/96.

Further central guidance on Grants etc, can be found in DETR Circular 1999/6.

REMEDIES UNDER THE ENVIRONMENTAL PROTECTION ACT 1990

So far as housing is concerned the general object of this Act is the protection of public health, the measures being derived from the Public Health Act 1936 which in turn followed on from the 'great' Public Health Act 1875. The law is therefore here not so much designed to lay down housing standards as to protect the health of individuals. The existence of separate housing and public health 'codes' of legislation has undoubtedly caused confusion over the years, though the ability of, for example, a tenant to initiate criminal sanctions against a neglectful landlord under public health law has undoubtedly enabled individuals to bring about improvements in their housing conditions. One thing is clear: compliance by a landlord with standards under housing legislation will not automatically mean there is compliance with public health standards under the 1990 Act, see *Salford City Council v McNally*[9]. Likewise the fact that a tenant is seeking a parallel civil remedy in respect of a housing defect is no reason for refusing a remedy under the 1990 Act[10].

It is the duty, under section 79 of the 1990 Act, of district councils and London boroughs, and in Wales county and county borough councils to inspect their areas from time to time, and also to investigate complaints from the inhabitants of their areas, in respect of 'statutory nuisances'. These include: premises; accumulations or deposits; animals; noise emitted from premises, or from vehicles, machinery or equipment in a street, though *not* from general traffic noise[11]; any other matter declared by statute to be a statutory nuisance, provided in each case the matter is prejudicial to health, ie actually injurious, or likely to cause injury, to health, or a nuisance, see section 79(7). Health seems to mean physical as opposed to mental health, see *Coventry City Council v Cartwright*[12]. This case arose out of an alleged nuisance caused by dumping of rubbish, the Divisional Court gave some consideration to whether mental health could be within the protection of the law but reached no concluded opinion on this point. It can be argued that a breakdown in mental health can be caused as a result of a person having to live in a sub-standard house. However, judicial opinion seems to disagree, and to hold that conditions that are 'prejudicial to health' are those which are likely to cause physical illness or disease or to result in an infestation by vermin.

If premises are to be shown to be a statutory nuisance their condition *as a whole* must be so serious that in consequence they are a real risk to health or are a nuisance; a mere lack of internal decorative repair is not enough: see *Springett v Harold*[13]. Nor is any matter which merely affects the *comfort* of the occupants, even if it amounts to an act of harrassment. However, it is unnecessary to prove that a dwelling is *both* prejudicial to health, *and* a nuisance. It may be enough for conditions to be 'prejudicial

9   [1976] AC 379, [1975] 2 All ER 860.
10 *R v Highbury Corner Magistrates' Court, ex p Edwards* (1994) 26 HLR 682.
11 *Haringey London Borough Council v Jowell* [1999] EGCS 64, and section 79(1)(ga) and (6A) of the 1990 Act.
12 [1975] 2 All ER 99, [1975] 1 WLR 845.
13 [1954] 1 All ER 568, [1954] 1 WLR 521.

to health' if they are such as to cause a person who is already ill to become worse: see Kelly CB in *Malton Board of Health v Malton Manure Co*[14].
In *Bennett v Preston District Council*[15] it was held that defective wiring in a dwelling may be prejudicial to health. This may now be open to question following the decision in *R v Bristol City Council, ex p Everett*[16] that poor internal arrangements in a house leading to a risk of physical *injury* – in this case a steep staircase – are not capable of being statutory nuisances. In *Southwark London Borough Council v Ince and Williams*[17] it was held that noise penetrating a dwelling made it prejudicial to health. This case may be limited to its own particular facts as it concerned both road *and* rail noise, and was decided before amendments made to the 1990 Act excluding street traffic noise from the definition of statutory nuisances, see footnote 11 supra.

Furthermore condensation may amount to a statutory nuisance, even where the structure is unaffected, see *Dover District Council v Farrar*[18] and *Greater London Council v Tower Hamlets London Borough Council*[19], especially where it gives rise to extensive growths of mould and dampness, and results from a condition arising from the failure of the responsible person (in this case the landlord) to take remedial or preventative action, such as the installation of ventilation, insulation and heating systems[20]. The cases appear to support the propositions that a landlord may be liable for a statutory nuisance arising from condensation caused by an unsuitable or defective heating system, lack of a reasonable system of heating and ventilation, design and construction defects and disrepair. Once, however, a proper system of heating, insulation and ventilation is provided it is for the tenant to use that system sensibly so as to avoid condensation. It remains a moot point as to whether questions of the expense of running a heating system can be considered in determining whether the system is reasonable and proper. In *Scotland* it appears that where an adequate heating system is provided the failure of the occupier to use it properly can negate liability on the part of the landlord of premises[1]. Certainly a refusal by a tenant to allow a landlord to instal a heating system will act as a defence in statutory nuisance proceedings.[2]

14 (1879) 4 Ex D 302 at 305.
15 (1983) Environmental Health (April).
16 [1998] 3 All ER 603, [1999] 1 WLR 92; affd [1999] 2 All ER 193, [1999] 1 WLR 1170, CA.
17 (1989) 21 HLR 504. This case is unlikely to be followed in the light of comments in the House of Lords in *Southwark London Borough Council v Mills* [1999] 4 All ER 449, [1999] 3 WLR 939, HL, that a lack of sound insulation gives a tenant no civil claim for breach of covenant for quiet enjoyment.
18 (1980) 2 HLR 32.
19 (1983) 15 HLR 54.
20 See further *Birmingham District Council v Kelly* (1985) 17 HLR 572.
1 *Anderson v Dundee City Council* [1999] 11 ELM 24 and *Robb v Dundee City Council* [1999] 11 ELM 84.
2 *Carr v Hackney London Borough Council* (1995) 28 HLR 749.

Premises may also come within the statutory definition if they are 'a nuisance'. Does this mean that any common law nuisance is also *ipso facto* a statutory nuisance? The answer is partly 'yes'. For a person to prove an allegation based on the 'or a nuisance' limb of the definition he/she must show that the act or default complained of is either a public or private nuisance, ie something causing deleterious affectation to a class of Her Majesty's subjects, *or* a substantial interference with land (or the use and enjoyment thereof) arising outside that land and then proceeding to affect it. So much is clear from *National Coal Board v Neath Borough Council*[3]. However, there is a judicial tradition stretching back to *Malton Board of Health v Malton Manure Co*[4], *Great Western Rly Co v Bishop*[5], and *Bishop Auckland Local Board v Bishop Auckland Iron and Steel Co*[6], that situations contemplated as falling within the 'or a nuisance' limb of the definition must have some relation to health.

Furthermore whether something is either prejudiced to health, or a nuisance has to be objectively determined, and not according to the subjective news of the occupant of premises[7]. However, the layout of a house may be 'prejudicial to health' if it requires a person to traverse a kitchen in order to wash hands following use of a lavatory because then there is a objective risk of infection[8].

Thus where it is alleged that premises are 'prejudicial to health' it will not matter that only the occupier is affected by the acts, defaults or state of affairs complained of. Where on the other hand it is alleged that the premises are 'a nuisance' the act or default, etc, *must affect persons other than the occupier of the premises*. Furthermore in this latter situation the person must, it appears, be able to prove that the nuisance is one that in some way affects, or has relevance, to health. It must also be remembered that *R v Newham Justices, ex p Hunt* and *R v Oxted Justices, ex p Franklin*[9] established that proceedings brought in respect of a statutory nuisance are criminal in nature and thus the burden of proof on any informant will be correspondingly high. In *Patel v Mehtab*[10] the court pointed out that the question whether premises are prejudicial to health will turn upon expert evidence, and that the magistrates must pay due heed to the expert testimonies given by one or both sides, and not advance their own lay

---

3   [1976] 2 All ER 478, [1976] 1 WLR 543.
4   (1879) 4 Ex D 302.
5   (1872) LR 7 QB 550.
6   (1882) 10 QBD 138.
7   *Cunningham v Birmingham City Council* (1997) 30 HLR 158.
8   *Oakley v Birmingham City Council* (1999) Times, 8 January.
9   [1976] 1 All ER 839, [1976] 1 WLR 420; see also *Botross v Hammersmith and Fulham London Borough Council* (1995) 27 HLR 179 and *R v Inner London Crown Court, ex p Bentham* [1989] 1 WLR 408.
10 (1980) 5 HLR 78.

assessments of the facts over those of expert witnesses. Similarly magistrates are not entitled to ignore expert evidence from Environmental Health Officers that premises are 'prejudicial to health' and to demand medical proof[11] .

The procedure for taking action in respect of a statutory nuisance

Local authorities and private citizens may take action in respect of statutory nuisances: it is convenient to consider authorities first.

Section 80 of the 1990 Act provides that where an authority is satisfied a statutory nuisance exists, *or* is likely to occur or recur, they *must* (see further, however, below) serve an abatement notice which will require the nuisance's abatement or prohibit or restrict its occurrence *or recurrence*, and may require the execution of works or taking of steps for such purposes, specifying the time within which compliance is required[12] . Where works are required they must be specified for notices must be clear and certain both as to the works and the time within which they are to be done, for the recipient must be able to know what is required[13] . It is not necessary for the notice to specify whether the nuisance is 'prejudicial to health' or 'a nuisance'[14] . This notice is to be served on the person responsible for the nuisance, save in cases of nuisances arising from structural defects, or where the person responsible cannot be found, in which case the owner is to be served. This is apparently so in relation to structural defects even where the tenant is responsible[15] . The 'owner' is the person who receives the rack rent, ie the economic rent, of the property, or who would receive it if it was let, whether in his/her own right, or as an agent[16] . Failure to comply with a notice without reasonable excuse is an offence. However, it should be noted that authorities are not statutorily bound to prosecute offences (see further below) even though they may have taken default action themselves under section 81(3), which enables them, under section 81(4) to recover their expenses. Section 81(5) further empowers authorities to commence High Court proceedings

11 *R v Knowsley Metropolitan Borough Council, ex p O'Toole* [1999] 22 LS Gaz R 36.

12 See also *Bristol Corpn v Sinnott* [1918] 1 Ch 62.

13 *R v Wheatley, ex p Cowburn* (1885) 16 QBD 34; *R v Fenny Stafford Justices, ex p Watney Mann (Midlands) Ltd* [1976] 2 All ER 888, [1976] 1 WLR 1101; *Kirklees MBC v Field* (1997) 30 HLR 869; and *Network Housing Association v Westminster City Council* (1994) 27 HLR 189.

14 *Lowe v South Somerset District Council* (1997) 96 LGR 487.

15 *Warner v Lambeth London Borough Council* (1984) 15 HLR 42.

16 *Pollway Nominees Ltd v Havering London Borough Council* (1989) 21 HLR 462 and *Camden London Borough Council v Gunby* [1999] 4 All ER 602.

where they are of the opinion that statutory nuisance proceedings before the justices would provide an inadequate remedy. Authorities undertaking works under section 81(3) may recover their reasonable expenses under section 81(4), and these may be recovered as a charge on the premises under section 81A, even though payment may be made by instalments under section 81B.

A person served with an abatement notice may, under section 80(3) of the 1990 Act, appeal to the justices within a period of 21 days beginning with the date of service of the notice. Schedule 3 to the Act enables regulations to be made concerning such appeals. The Statutory Nuisance (Appeals) Regulations SI 1995/2644, provide in reg 2 as grounds of appeal that: the abatement notice was not justified; there has been an informality, defect or error in, or in connection with the notice; the authority has unreasonably refused compliance with alternative requirements, or the notice's requirements are otherwise unreasonable in character or extent or unnecessary; a reasonable amount of time has not been specified for compliance; that specific statutory defences are applicable under section 80(7) or (9), but these are not relevant to premises cases; the notice should have been served on some other person (eg the owner where a nuisance arises from a defect of a structural character) or it might lawfully have been served on someone else, or on someone else in addition to the appellant. On hearing proceedings on appeal the magistrates have a wide discretion to dismiss the appeal, quash the abatement notice or vary it. However, they must consider whether the notice was justified as at the date of service, not the date of the hearing[17]. Making an appeal leads to the abatement notice being suspended, but an authority may prevent this by making a non-suspension statement in the notice.

Certain general requirements from decisions on the previous law relating to statutory nuisances would also seem to apply under the 1990 Act. Thus the legislation lays down a procedure which an authority has to follow in the abatement of statutory nuisances, and it would seem from *Cocker v Cardwell*[18] that this procedure is mandatory once an authority decide to act. Where an authority are satisfied of the existence of a statutory nuisance the Act says they 'shall serve' an abatement notice on the person responsible requiring the abatement of the nuisance. However, it was said in *Nottingham Corpn v Newton*[19], the first case where an authority was successfully prosecuted in respect of unfit property also constituting a statutory nuisance, by Lord Widgery CJ that 'shall' is not mandatory. Where *an authority has a choice of remedies* between the 1985 and 1990 Acts the courts may not order them to use the latter in preference to the former. The

---

17 *Surrey Free Inns v Gosport Borough Council* (1998) 96 LGR 369.
18 (1869) LR 5 QB 15.
19 [1974] 2 All ER 760, [1974] 1 WLR 923.

Encyclopaedia of Housing Law and Practice, however, argues the 'requirement to serve an abatement notice is mandatory ... the local authority have no discretion'. The point is not therefore entirely clear or decided.

It is a defence to a prosecution under section 79 to show that there was a 'reasonable excuse', see section 79(4). If evidence of such an excuse is put forward by the defence, it is for the prosecution to disprove it according to the criminal burden of proof[20].

Taking action in respect of statutory nuisances by private citizens

The majority of statutory nuisances are dealt with by authorities but an individual wishing to proceed may rely on section 82 of the 1990 Act. This provides that the magistrates may act on a complaint made by a 'person aggrieved', and where they are convinced the alleged nuisance exists, or although abated is likely to recur, they must make an order to require the defendant to abate the nuisance, and execute any necessary works, and/ or may prohibit a recurrence of the nuisance. Where a recurrence is forbidden there is no need to state a specific compliance date[1]. The magistrates may also fine the defendant. In addition the magistrates have powers to direct the local authority to take abatement measures in respect of a nuisance where neither the person responsible or the owner/occupier of the premises can be found, and to prohibit the use of premises for human habitation where a nuisance renders them unfit for that purpose, see section 82(1) and (3). As with local authority proceedings it is the person responsible for the nuisance who is generally to be proceeded against, though where the nuisance is of a structural character, or where the 'person responsible' cannot be found, it is the owner of the premises who will be liable. Before complaining to the magistrates, however, the person aggrieved must give the potential defendant written notice of intention to commence proceedings, specifying the matter complained of. In the case of alleged noise nuisances three days' notice must be given, in all other cases not less than 21 days' notice is required, see section 82(6) and (7).

A notice served under section 82(6) is *not*, however, the equivalent of an abatement notice, and therefore does not have to specify works needed, nor to identify the capacity in which the defendant is to be proceeded against ie as 'owner' or 'person responsible'. There is no prescribed form for a section 82(6) notice, all that is needed is a specification of the matters complained of, so that the recipient has a chance to remedy the situation.

20 *Polychronakis v Richards and Jerrom Ltd* [1998] Env LR 346.
1 *R v Tunbridge Wells Justices, ex p Tunbridge Wells Borough Council* (1995) 160 JP 574.

While it is desirable that the notice should give as much information as is reasonably possible, the courts accept that section 82 exists to give remedy to citizens and are unwilling to see it bogged down in unnecessary technicalities.[2] Similarly attempts by landlords to require formalities by stipulating that notices may only be served at their principal offices have been judicially disapproved.[3]

Who is a 'person aggrieved'?

It was held in *R v Epping (Waltham Abbey) Justices, ex p Burlinson*[4] that a private citizen can proceed against a defaulting local authority under this provision, and in *Salford City Council v McNally* (supra) it was further held that the fact that the nuisance arose as a result of an authority's exercise of Housing Act powers was no defence to an action taken by one of their tenants deleteriously affected in consequence. In order to use the provision an individual must be a 'person aggrieved'. In the present context this includes anyone whose health has actually been injured by the nuisance, or any occupant of the premises or indeed anyone with a legal interest in a house which is permanently affected by the nuisance. In *Gould v Times Square Estates Ltd*[5] , even a squatter in an empty former shop and dwelling accommodation was held able to use this procedure, but the applicability of this provision to trespassers was expressly left undecided in *Coventry City Council v Cartwright* (supra). Where, however, a person is a tenant in a block of flats and only some of the flats are in sub-standard order, it is not possible for that person to be 'aggrieved' in relation to the whole block[6] .

The consequences of action taken

Once the court is satisfied under section 82(2) that a statutory nuisance exists, or though abated is likely to recur on the same premises, they *must* make an order as outlined above[7] . Similarly, evidence of the existence of a statutory nuisance will normally require the court to issue the necessary summons against the defendant[8] .

---

2   *East Staffordshire Borough Council v Fairless* (1998) 31 HLR 677, and *Pearshouse v Birmingham City Council* (1998) 31 HLR 756.
3   *Hall v Kingston-Upon-Hull City Council* [1999] 2 All ER 609; overruling *Leeds v Islington London Borough Council* (1998) 31 HLR 545.
4   [1948] 1 KB 79, [1947] 2 All ER 537.
5   [1975] LAG Bulletin 147, Camberwell Magistrates Court.
6   *Birmingham District Council v McMahon* (1987) 19 HLR 452.
7   *Coventry City Council v Doyle* [1981] 2 All ER 184, [1981] 1 WLR 1325.
8   *R v Highbury Corner Magistrates' Court, ex p Edwards* (1994) 26 HLR 682.

In this context the *Newton* case states clearly that the justices *must* issue a nuisance order if the existence or future recurrence of the nuisance is proved. But they have a very considerable discretion as to the *terms* of the order. When deciding the terms of the order justices should consider all the circumstances of the case including the possible gravity of the danger to the health of the occupants and the imminence of demolition. They may properly require work to be done in phases, allowing for absolutely necessary jobs to be done first, while other tasks can be left till later, perhaps to be rendered unnecessary by demolition, thus saving expense.

A decision illustrates the ambit of the justices' discretion. In *Lambeth London Borough Council v Stubbs*[9], an authority owned an old house the tenants of which were Mr and Mrs Stubbs. The condition of the house constituted a statutory nuisance, which was admitted by the council before the justices in proceedings commenced by the tenants. The justices refused to adjourn the hearing so that the authority could obtain vacant possession, and instead made a nuisance order requiring the remedying of the most serious defects within 21 days of the vacation of the premises and of the others in 42 days. Shortly thereafter Mr and Mrs Stubbs were rehoused and the house was simply left vacant until it was demolished. The question for the court was whether the action of the council in securing vacant possession was sufficient abatement to comply with the nuisance order. It was held that it was not. Where a house is prejudicial to health simply to move the present occupiers out does not cure the problem, for if other occupiers should move in at a future date their health will then be imperilled. Where justices make a nuisance order requiring the doing of remedial work, that work must be done; moving the sitting tenant is not enough. See also *Coventry City Council v Doyle* (supra), where it was, however, pointed out that different considerations might apply in a case where the premises have been effectively rendered incapable of occupation. Of course where the authority intend to demolish the property within a very short time the court should take that into account when drawing up the order. In such circumstances the authority should ask the justices to exercise their discretion to order that the house shall not be used for human habitation. Such an order will remove the need for great expenditure. Any order made, however, must be clear and certain.

Where on the hearing of proceedings in respect of an alleged nuisance it is shown that the nuisance did exist when the initial complaint was made, then, irrespective of whether it still exists or is likely to recur at the date of the hearing, the court is to order the defendant to compensate the complainant for expenses incurred in bringing the proceedings: see section 82(12). The court may also direct the relevant local authority to perform any requirements of an order to abate a nuisance where the defendant is in default, see section

82(11). Section 82(12) is mandatory and requires the justices to award costs once they are satisfied that the nuisance existed at the time the complaint was made. They may not refuse to award costs where they believe proceedings should not have been brought, for their only discretion is in relation to deciding the sum believed 'reasonably sufficient' to compensate the complainant for any expenses properly incurred in taking action[10]. Properly incurred costs may be awarded even where a claim for a compensation order (see further below) fails,[11] and indeed magistrates have a very wide discretion on how to assess costs, there being no formal assessment procedures[12]. It has, however, been argued that, as a matter of course, a complainant should give advance notice of cost claims, so that the respondent may indicate whether the claim is accepted or challenged. Furthermore the magistrates should take proper steps to investigate how a claim for a substantial amount has been arrived at, and on what basis it is challenged[13].

Where a tenant commences and then withdraws proceedings the award of costs against him/her is limited by sections 16 to 19 of the Prosecution of Offences Act 1985, which limits costs in cases where there has been no unnecessary or improper conduct by the tenant[14].

Compensation orders

As proceedings under section 82 are criminal in nature, compensation may be awarded to the complainant under section 35 of the Powers of Criminal Courts Act 1973[15]. This power exists to ensure compensation is paid in cases where a civil remedy might not otherwise be available. It is inappropriate to use it to award substantial sums for what may generally be classified as personal injuries. Furthermore the absence of a civil remedy does not mean that a compensation order should be made[16], and the fact that a complainant might not succeed in a civil claim should be taken into account by the magistrates. Furthermore a compensation order can only be made in respect of the period of the offence as alleged in the information. Thus compensation may be awarded only for that injury, loss or damage as is proved to have been caused by the continuation of the nuisance after the expiry of the period stated in the notice under section 82(6) until the date of the hearing.

10   *Hollis v Dudley Borough Council* [1998] 1 All ER 759, [1999] 1 WLR 642.
11   *Davenport v Walsall Metropolitan Borough Council* (1995) 28 HLR 754.
12   *R v Southend Stipendiary Magistrate, ex p Rochford DC* [1994] Env LR D15.
13   *Taylor v Walsall and District Property and Investment Co* (1998) 30 HLR 1062.
14   *R v Enfield Justices, ex p Whittle* (1993) Legal Action (June) p 15.
15   *Herbert v Lambeth London Borough Council* (1991) 24 HLR 299 and *R v Inner London Crown Court, ex p Bentham* [1989] 1 WLR 408.
16   *Davenport v Walsall Metropolitan Borough Council (supra).*

Section 35 does not give to magistrates' courts a power to take account of the whole period for which a nuisance is alleged to exist. For while such courts may be able to award sums up to £5,000, they should be wary of involving themselves in what are effectively civil claims, though a compensation order if sufficiently large to be punitive may be imposed instead of as well as in addition to a fine[17].

The relationship between the Housing and Environmental Protection Acts

It cannot be sufficiently stressed that the requirements of the two 'codes' are separate and equal. Remedial action taken under one will not necessarily satisfy the requirements of the other. Of course action taken to eliminate unfitness in a house will nearly always ensure that it will not be prejudicial to health because in general the standards required by the 1985 Act are higher than those under the 1990 Act. This can be illustrated by a simple example: if a house is unfit through dampness caused by the lack of a damp-proof course then the 1985 Act would require the insertion of such a course to make the house fit and free from damp; if the same house is prejudicial to health because of damp, then the 1990 Act will only require it to be made reasonably free from damp on a periodic basis which may be achieved by lining the walls with damp-proof paper.

There are times when the two codes do appear to be in conflict: thus in the *Newton* case the court said local authorities have a discretion as to how best to deal with sub-standard housing; in *R v Kerrier District Council, ex p Guppy's (Bridport) Ltd*[18] the unfitness provisions were said to be mandatory, while in the *Salford* case action taken under the Housing Act was said to be no defence to subsequent prosecution under the public health legislation. In fact there is no real conflict between the codes and the cases can be reconciled. The question always to bear in mind in these situations is: w*ho* is seeking to do *what to whom* by *which* procedures? This question can receive different answers in different circumstances as the following instances will show.

The individual sub-standard house in private or housing association ownership

This situation can be illustrated by the facts of the *Kerrier* case. The landlords owned two unfit dwelling-houses, both tenanted. The owners were prepared to make one good house of the two but could not do so

---

17 *R v Liverpool Crown Court, ex p Cooke* [1996] 4 All ER 589, [1997] 1 WLR 700, and *R v Knightsbridge Crown Court, ex p Hobin Abdillahi* (1998) Legal Action (May) p 24.
18 (1975) 30 P & CR 194.

without obtaining vacant possession, and had no accommodation for the displaced tenants. The local authority said it had no accommodation either and decided to commence proceedings against the landlords under the Public Health Act 1936 (predecessor of the 1990 Act) to require remedial action on the roofs of the houses. The landlords countered by alleging the houses were statutorily unfit and that the authority were in breach of mandatory duties under the unfitness provisions if they failed to proceed under them. The court accepted the landlords' contention. Thus where a *local authority* commence proceedings under the 1990 Act in respect of any house which is a statutory nuisance, the *owner* of the house may allege that they are in dereliction of duties under the Act of 1985 and may apply for mandamus to compel the performance of relevant duties. Even here it must be remembered that mandamus is a discretionary remedy and so landlords are not guaranteed success if they adopt the counter argument developed in the *Kerrier* case. Where the proceedings are between the *tenant* and the *landlord* the authority's duties have no relevance save insofar as the landlord, having begun separate proceedings against an authority to compel performances of their duties, might argue that the justices should consider the possible outcome of those proceedings when deciding the content of any order issued under section 82 of the 1990 Act.

The sub-standard house in local authority ownership

The unfitness provisions do not apply to a local authority's own houses *within its own area*, save in the cases where another person also has a relevant interest in the property, for an authority cannot serve a housing order on themselves, see *R v Cardiff City Council, ex p Cross*[19]. However, in such circumstances provided the existence of a statutory nuisance can be proved, the 1990 Act can be used and any prior action taken under the 1985 Act will be no defence to the local authority.

This was the situation in the *Salford* case. In 1967 Salford Corporation declared certain areas to be clearance areas, and at the same time made compulsory purchase orders on the houses within the areas. However, the Corporation realising it could not rehouse all the residents quickly, deferred demolition of the houses for a *minimum* period of *seven* years. By 1974 Mrs McNally's house suffered from an accumulation of refuse, dampness, defective sanitary fittings, unsealed drains, rats, defective windows and/or doors, a leaking roof, defective drainage, and defective plaster work. She commenced proceedings in respect of the statutory nuisance comprised by her house and succeeded. The House of Lords held that the resolution to defer demolition was no defence to statutory nuisance proceedings. It must

19   (1982) 6 HLR 1.

be remembered, however, that where an old sub-standard house is made the subject of a nuisance order the justice's discretion should be so used as to prevent expenditure of unnecessary sums. The best that can be hoped for is a 'make and mend' operation designed to make the house reasonably bearable as a dwelling, though following *Saddleworth UDC v Aggregate and Sand Ltd*[20], a lack of finance does not seem to be a reasonable excuse for not complying with a nuisance order. Landlords cannot plead poverty in the hope of entirely escaping from the requirements of nuisance orders!

The sub-standard modern council-built house

Evidence is not lacking that bad construction, poor design, unproved building techniques and misguided planning policies have led to the erection of many council houses and flats whose inhabitants frequently have to endure extremely unpleasant living conditions. In some modern council properties there are severe problems of damp and condensation which can lead to ruined furniture and clothes and illness in the occupants.

The decision in *R v Cardiff City Council, ex p Cross* (supra) of course applies to council built as well as council acquired housing. But statutory nuisance proceedings can bring some relief to tenants. In *Birmingham District Council v Kelly*[1] the proceedings concerned council built dwellings comprising low rise flats. The dwellings had defective windows, and were also extensively affected by mould which was found to be prejudicial to health. The mould was found to be the result of the act, default or sufferance of the local authority because of, inter alia, the poor thermal quality of the flats, the absence of heating provision in the hallways, a gap under the front door of one flat, the poor quality of ventilation in bathrooms and kitchens. In some, but not all cases, mould could be attributable, in part to disrepair, though the court found that there was no breach of any obligation laid on the authority as a landlord qua landlord. But that was not enough to prevent inquiry into whether there was liability for the existence of a statutory nuisance. The court pointed out that three questions arise: is there a statutory nuisance, is it due to the act, default or sufferance of the local authority, and what steps are necessary to abate it? The court concluded that the answer to the first two questions was 'yes': the mould was a consequence of condensation attributable to design defects in the flats. But the court pointed out that magistrates should use discretion as to the terms of a nuisance order, and that statutory nuisance proceedings should not be used as a means of obtaining for tenants benefits which they were aware did not exist when they took their tenancies, and which would over

20　(1970) 69 LGR 103.
1　(1985) 17 HLR 572.

generously favour them in relation to other tenants of the authority. An authority may be required to do works of improvement, but the need for such works must be justified by the evidence and the circumstances. Magistrates should behave reasonably in imposing orders on local authorities, bearing in mind the heavy duties already laid upon them. Even so it appears that use of the statutory nuisance provisions, while enabling individuals to secure improvements of their conditions, can also have the effect of disrupting planned maintenance and improvement programmes devised by authorities as they are forced to switch resources from the programme into reactive responses to individual problem premises whose existence and needs have been made inescapable following actual or threatened statutory nuisance proceedings.

Statutory nuisances – an uncertain future?

Statutory nuisance proceedings are particularly unpopular with some local authority landlords who allege their misuse by lawyers and community workers, pointing out that where an individual tenant secures an individual remedy under the 1990 Act, this does not necessarily lead to an upgrading of the circumstances of neighbours who may be suffering equally bad conditions, while resources to comply with a court order may have to be diverted from elsewhere disrupting planned maintenance and improvement programmes. Following DoE sponsored research in 1996 it was recommended that section 82 of the 1990 Act should be amended to:
• 	define clearly the initial offence;
• 	allow for a 'reasonable response' to be made to the person aggrieved's notice, *either* that the landlord is doing or what is needed to abate the nuisance, *or* to enable service of a counter notice which specifies works to be done and gives a timetable for doing them;
• 	allow for action other than works to be ordered as a means of abatement;
• 	allow enhanced discretion to the courts over questions of costs.
Action to translate these proposals into law is still to be taken.

A restriction on the ability of solicitors to undertake statutory nuisance claims on behalf of clients could have arisen under the terms of the Access to Justice Bill 1999. This provided in clause 27, that no criminal proceedings could be the subject of a conditional fee agreement, ie where the client pays the lawyer if the latter is successful and costs are gained. Statutory nuisance proceedings are, of course, criminal in nature.

As summary criminal proceedings statutory nuisance cases are ineligible for legal aid. However, an agreement between a complainant and his/her solicitors that costs will not be paid out of the complainant's resources had been apparently lawful provided the solicitors have sought no more than ordinary profit costs and disbursements in the event of a successful outcome to the case.[2]

Despite arguments that the Bill's provisions might breach the European Convention on Human Rights because they could amount to a denial of the means of obtaining a fair hearing of grievances via an effective right of access to the courts (see Article 6(1)) the government's response was that it believed law centres would be prepared to take on statutory nuisance actions, and to resist amendments to the Bill which would extend legal aid to cases brought in magistrates courts under section 82 of the 1990 Act. However, the Access to Justice Act 1999 as enacted on 2 July now provides in section 27 (amending section 58 of the Courts and Legal Services Act 1990, and also adding section 58A to that Act) that the proceedings which cannot be the subject of an enforceable *conditional fee* agreement are (a) criminal proceedings and (b) family proceedings, *apart from proceedings under section 82 of the Environmental Protection Act 1990.*[3]

Rehousing displaced residents

Section 39 of the Land Compensation Act 1973, as amended, provides:

'(1) Where a person is displaced from residential accommodation on any land in consequence of
  (a) the acquisition of the land by an authority possessing compulsory purchase powers;
  (b) the making ... or acceptance of a housing order ... or undertaking in respect of a house or building on the land;
  (c) where the land has been previously acquired by an authority possessing compulsory purchase powers or appropriated by a local authority and is for the time being held by the authority for the purposes for which it was acquired or appropriated, the carrying out of any improvement to a house or building on the land or of redevelopment on the land; ...
and suitable alternative accommodation is not otherwise available to that person, then, subject to the provisions of this section, it shall be the duty of the relevant authority to secure that he will be provided with such other accommodation'.

---

2 *Thai Trading Co (a firm) v Taylor* [1998] QB 781, [1998] 3 All ER 65, CA.
3 This does not legalise *contingency fee* arrangments, ie one that *costs* are payable only if a prosecution is successful: see *Wells v Barnsley Metroplitan Borough Council* (1999) Times, 12 November.

Within the context of action on unfit properties, this means that authorities have an obligation to rehouse persons displaced as a result of the making of demolition, closing or clearance orders or the accepting of undertakings under section 264 of the Housing Act 1985. Some authorities adopt a wider obligation as a matter of administrative practice, and the strictly limited nature of the section 39 obligation should be noted. It does not apply to squatters, nor to persons permitted to reside in a house pending its demolition or improvement. The duty only applies, in general terms, to persons resident in the dwelling on the date when the order, or undertaking, etc, was made or accepted or when notice of its making was published, as the case may be. Moreover, in the case of displacements arising out of the doing of works of improvement, the obligation is only owed to persons who are *permanently* displaced.

The greatest restriction on the obligation is that it confers no right on persons displaced to have priority over other persons on the housing waiting list. In *R v Bristol Corpn, ex p Hendy*[4] the applicant lived in a basement flat where he enjoyed Rent Act security of tenure but which was also statutorily unfit. Mr Hendy had a history of rent arrears with another local authority and Bristol Corporation offered him only temporary accommodation, pending an offer of suitable residential accommodation, on the terms usually offered to prospective municipal tenants. He applied for an order of mandamus to compel the authority to fulfil their rehousing duty, contending this was to provide him with permanent accommodation on terms that gave him a security of tenure equivalent to that which he had enjoyed under his former tenancy. The Court of Appeal refused the order. They concluded that the duty is only to act reasonably and to do the best practicable job in providing a displaced person with other accommodation.

NB Where a dwelling is closed for human habitation by order of the justices under section 82(3) of the Environmental Protection Act 1990, there is no obligation to rehouse on the local authority under section 39 of the 1973 Act.

4   [1974] 1 All ER 1047, [1974] 1 WLR 498; see also *R v East Hertfordshire District Council, ex p Smith* (1990) 23 HLR 26.

Further reading

Burridge, R, Ormandy, D, Battersby, S *Monitoring the New Housing Fitness Standard* (DoE/HMSO 1993)

DoE *The Use of Section 82 of the Environmental Protection Act 1990 against Local Authorities and Housing Associations* (HMSO, 1996)

Hadden, T B *Compulsory Repair and Improvement* (Centre for Socio Legal Studies, Wolfson College, Oxford, 1978)

Hadden, T B 'Public Health and Housing Legislation' (1976) 27 NILQ 245

Hawke, J N and Taylor, G A 'The Compulsory Repair of Individual Physically Substandard Housing: The Law in Practice' [1984] JSWL 129

Hughes, D 'Public Health Legislation and the Improvement of Housing Conditions' (1976) 27 NILQ 1

Hughes, D 'What is a Nuisance? The Public Health Act Revisited' (1976) 27 NILQ 131

Hughes, D 'Housing and Public Health – A Continuing Saga' (1977) 28 NILQ 233

Hughes, D 'Housing Repairs: A Suitable Case for Reform' [1984] JSWL 137

Luba, J *Repairs: Tenants' Rights* (Legal Action Group, 3rd Edition, 1999)

Reynolds, J I 'Statutory Covenants of Fitness and Repair' (1974) 37 MLR 377

Watkinson, D 'Legal Remedies for Condensation Damp in the Home' Legal Action November 1985, p 153 and April 1986, p 49

CHAPTER EIGHT

Multi-occupancy and overcrowding

Introduction

Multi-occupation and overcrowding may occur together to convey an impression that they are always associated evils. In fact the problem of overcrowding is not restricted to multi-occupied dwellings, nor even primarily associated with them. Nor should it be assumed that conditions in all multi-occupied houses are bad.

Multi-occupation and overcrowding arise for totally different reasons in areas of varying housing types. In the past a typically overcrowded house was 'two-up-and-two-down', situated in industrial towns and cities. They were overcrowded either because of the sexual composition of the families occupying them, or because they were simply too small to be able to accommodate large families. The law relating to overcrowding developed to deal with situations of the above kind.

In our day the problem is different. Anyone familiar with British urban geography will be aware that one great unanswered problem of housing policy is the use and management of larger older houses in inner suburban areas. Obviously ripe for conversion into multi-occupation, where that is sympathetically done the result is the provision of much useful accommodation. However, unthinking or unscrupulous owners indulge in unsatisfactory divisions, failing to provide proper cooking and sanitary facilities, and frequently resorting to overcrowding individual units of accommodation to extract the maximum financial return. The result is danger, particularly from a fire safety point of view, and squalor. In properties such as these multi-occupation and overcrowding occur together.

A further issue consequent on the expansion of the universities is the rapid increase in the number of houses of a variety of sorts occupied by students. It is frequently hard to determine whether these are in single or multiple occupation.

The current problem and the policy response to multiple occupation

The size of the problem

The 1985 Physical and Social Survey of Houses in Multiple Occupation in England and Wales (Thomas & Hedges) published in 1986 concluded there were at least 290,000 Houses in Multiple Occupation (HMOs) in England and Wales, providing accommodation for 2.6 million people. Four fifths of HMOs then surveyed were unsatisfactory in relation to management, occupancy or provision of amenities. Half needed repairs costing more than £10,000, and only one-quarter were assessed as of a 'good' standard. In most houses occupants had only a single small room each. Damp and condensation were frequently encountered physical problems, while four fifths of HMOs had defective, inadequate or non-existent means of escape from fire, a problem particularly associated with smaller HMOs and those owned by private landlords. The occupants of HMOs tended to be young, single and hard up; they rarely occupied such accommodation out of choice.

These findings were largely reinforced by the English House Condition Survey of 1996. This discovered in England in 1996 some 800,000 private rented HMOs containing 860,000 households, some 1.5m people. Most residents are aged under 30, and it is rare to find households with children. By 1996 those in full time education were over represented in HMOs, a sector of housing continuing to be characterised by a transient population of tenants tending overall to be on low incomes, either because they are students or are economically inactive or are working in low paid jobs. Repair and safety problems continue to affect the HMO sector of housing, though the worst problems appear to affect what the DETR now categorises as 'traditional HMOs', ie pre 1919 houses of three or more storeys with five or more habitable rooms, commonly encountered in or near city centres. These properties are likely to have both internal and external faults, a higher level of outlay needed to remedy their defects, a slightly higher rate of unfitness for human habitation than other rented property, and a very high rate of being unfit for multiple occupation by virtue of inadequate fire safety. Almost two-thirds of all 'traditional' HMOs are 'unfit' under either sections 604 or 352 of the Housing Act 1985.

The policy response

Following the Thomas & Hedges survey certain changes were made in the law in 1989 and in 1996 following further consultative exercises in 1994 and 1995, but before these are detailed current central policy on HMOs must be examined. The principal documents here are currently the HMO Management Guide (The Guide) issued by the DoE in 1992, and DoE Circular 12/93.[1]

These point to wide variation in local authority policy with regard to HMOs, and encourage adoption of best practice to harmonise standards throughout the country. The Guide is also both a strategic and a detailed advice document.

Section 395A of the Housing Act 1985 inserted in 1996 provides for Codes of Practice to be approved by the Secretary of State which would replace the current guidance. As yet no code has been approved, though one went out for consultation in 1997. This issue will be referred to below when considering the future of the law.

Policy: The first steps

Authorities are encouraged to produce formal policy documents on HMOs, providing for *aims* – eg to stimulate a thriving market in acceptable quality accommodation in HMOs, *objectives* – ie steps on the way to achieving *aims* – *targets*, ie administrative action to facilitate achieving aims and objectives, such as serving all requisite notices within pre-set time periods – *performance indicators*, and *provision for review of aims, objectives, etc.* A realistic budget in respect of the foregoing is recommended.

A strategy is needed to meet the requirements of section 605 of the Housing Act 1985 to provide for a regular review of HMOs in an area, and also to ensure that authorities do not proceed in a fragmented and inefficient way in dealing with HMOs. Policy should bring together and harmonise the practices of planners, environmental health and housing officers who otherwise might apply different criteria and policies with regard to HMOs. The policy should also be debated *at corporate level* so that the entire authority is committed to it.

Drawing up the policy

Both The Guide and Circular 12/93 counsel authorities to gather accurate information on numbers, types and conditions of HMOs, which may require

1   See also DoE Circular 12/92.

specially commissioned research. The local housing market should then be considered to determine what level of demand there is for housing at particular prices and the relative advantages/disadvantages of HMOs as opposed to non-HMO provision. Authorities should also consider information about residents' attitudes to existing HMOs, demographic and environmental issues and the spread and location of HMOs throughout their areas. Policy should address three key issues:

(1) maximising HMO contribution to safe, quality accommodation;
(2) minimising risks from unsafe accommodation;
(3) using planning controls to ensure that HMOs do not have an unacceptable environmental impact.

Central guidance urges authorities not to accord too low a priority to HMO work in the allocation of resources. However, the policy an authority develops should reflect its needs and problems – eg whether it has a real scarcity of accommodation.

Implementing policy

Guidance stresses the need for a multidisciplinary approach to the HMO issue: either the creation of a specific inter departmental team (costly in terms of resources); or setting up project teams of key staff from relevant departments who have regular meetings to inform colleagues of their work. The latter approach is recommended for small authorities with fewer HMO problems.

Both The Guide and Circular point to raising standards as a central element in any authority's HMO strategy, and suggest this can be done via formal enforcement action or, eg by contractual requirements when an authority itself is a major customer of HMO landlords for bed and breakfast accommodation for the homeless. Authorities are encouraged to use whatever means are most conducive to achieving policies, and to link tactics in a concerted attempt to improve conditions.

Where, however, a sanctioning approach is adopted authorities are advised to ensure that what they require is formulated in the light of local housing conditions, bearing in mind the risks and discomforts of occupants relevant to the size and type of property in question, *enforceable, defensible* and *justifiable* in court. Neither should a sanctioning approach be inflexibly applied.

Where a sanctioning approach is adopted authorities should delegate legal authority to officers to ensure that powers are effectively and expeditiously used. Effective communication is needed so that relevant officers receive all necessary information and advice. In any case staff must receive proper written guidance in the form of a manual to ensure standardisation of approach and operational consistency in relation to all HMO powers and duties. Standards should be regularly reviewed and amended where necessary in the light of experience. In connection with prosecutions authorities were particularly counselled by The Guide to consider the implications of prosecution, eg will it have a deterrent effect, or secure the doing of necessary works; what are the financial implications for the authority of either doing the works themselves or relying on a prosecution? Authorities were also advised to consider how well landlords have been made aware of legal obligations: moral and economic issues play a part in prosecution policy. It is the culpable rather than the deficient landlord who is likely to be prosecuted.

Supervision of multi-occupation by planning control

Under planning law 'development' may not generally be carried out without planning permission from the local planning authority. Can authorities use planning powers to prevent the inception of undesirable multi-occupation developments?

Section 55(1) of the Town and Country Planning Act 1990 defines development as:

'the carrying out of building, engineering, mining or other operations in, on, over or under land, or the making of any material change in the use of any buildings or other land'.

Section 55(2)(a) excludes from this definition:

'the carrying out for the maintenance, improvement or other alteration of any building of works which (i) affect only the interior of the building or (ii) do not materially affect the external appearance of the building...'

But Section 55(3)(a) goes on to provide:

'For the avoidance of doubt it is hereby declared for the purposes of this section – the use as two or more separate dwelling-houses of any building previously used as a single dwelling-house involves a material change in the use of the building and of each part thereof which is so used'.

Unfortunately doubt has not been avoided. It is uncertain whether any change from single residential to multi-occupied use inevitably constitutes an act of development by falling within section 55(3)(a) above, and so requiring planning permission. In *Ealing Corpn v Ryan*[2] a planning authority alleged unauthorised development had taken place in that the use of a house had changed from being a single dwelling to use as two or more separate dwellings. The house contained several families who all shared a common kitchen, and presumably the lavatory and bathroom also. It was held the house had not been divided into *separate* dwellings. A house may be occupied by two or more persons living separately under one roof, without their occupying 'separate dwellings', provided they are sharing certain common living accommodation, which, following *Goodrich v Paisner*,[3] includes kitchens. Multiple occupation by itself *may* be insufficient to bring section 55(3)(a) of the Town and Country Planning Act 1990 into operation. That is designed to deal with situations where new dwellings can be regarded as truly separate, self-contained and independent; here the existence of physical reconstruction will be a factor of great importance.

But multi-occupation may still constitute development where conversion amounts to a material change of use under section 55(1) of the 1990 Act. In *Birmingham Corpn v Minister of Housing and Local Government and Habib Ullah*[4] three former singly-occupied houses were let in parts to a number of occupants each paying a weekly rent. The Divisional Court pointed out there had been a change of use. The houses, which had previously been used as single family accommodation, were being used for gain by their owner letting them out as rooms. The material change of use is constituted by alteration from family/residential to commercial/residential use.

It has been argued, following *Duffy v Pilling*[5] that where a single person owns or rents a house and lives there with lodgers, generally providing meals for them but sometimes allowing them to provide for themselves, there is no change of use unless there is some physical division between the parts each person occupies. This decision is most unsatisfactory. The better view of the law is that a material change of use occurs as soon as a predominantly single family use alters into a predominantly non-family use. Once the lodgers predominate then a change of use has taken place. In *Lipson v Secretary of State for the Environment*[6] a change of use of premises from self-contained flats to individual bed-sitters was found to be a material change of use. The test is to ask a simple question of fact in each case: 'who has control over the property?' If control is in the hands of one person who has a small number of others living with him/her there is no material change of use, but if effective control has been 'parcelled out' amongst individuals,

2   [1965] 2 QB 486, [1965] 1 All ER 137.
3   [1957] AC 65, [1956] 2 All ER 176.
4   [1964] 1 QB 178, [1963] 3 All ER 668.
5   (1977) 33 P & CR 85.
6   (1976) 33 P & CR 95.

the best evidence of which is physical partitioning of the premises, then multi-occupancy will have arisen and a material change of use. See also *Panayi v Secretary of State for the Environment*[7], where use of four self-contained flats as a hostel to house homeless families was held to constitute a material change of use.

Central guidance points out that housing and planning policies on HMOs should complement each other. But there can be conflicts between housing and planning functions in an authority – particularly where one department wishes to improve a property which another wishes to eradicate. Use of corporate strategy should help to minimise conflict, while placing policies on HMOs in development plans is another way of ensuring harmonious relationships.

It is questionable how far an authority may go in using planning powers to prevent the spread of undesirable multi-occupation. An outright policy of refusing any application for planning permission to convert premises to multi-occupation would be an illegal fetter on discretion. Nor would it appear generally proper for an authority to take into account the character of the person applying for planning permission. Past housing misdeeds are matters relevant to other areas of law and do not raise planning issues as such. Neither could an authority impose restrictive conditions designed to regulate future behaviour on a grant of permission; the whole thrust of the cases is that planning conditions must always relate fairly to physical development, and not subsequent use by developers of powers of letting and management.

On the basis of ministerial decisions on planning appeals the proper factors to be taken into account by a planning authority in deciding applications to convert houses to multiple use include: density of housing; possibility of overcrowding; amenities of the neighbourhood; any locally prevailing shortage of accommodation; suitability of premises for conversion; architectural considerations and, occasionally, problems that might arise from an increase in numbers of cars that incoming residents might wish to park. All these are proper land use considerations.

The Guide and Circular 12/93 remind authorities that, under section 171B of the Town and Country Planning Act 1990, any unauthorised change of use to multiple occupation acquires immunity from planning enforcement action, and becomes a lawful use of land, once ten years have elapsed from the time the change was made. They also point out that enforcement action does not have to be taken, and where *planning considerations* indicate that no action would be appropriate then an unauthorised change of use may be allowed to continue, though permission may be retrospectively granted and subjected to conditions. Where, however, it is desired to take enforcement action a number of considerations should be borne in mind before it is taken, eg effects on residents and on any housing action that has been, or may be, taken to improve the state of the property.

One issue worthy of special mention is whether taking housing action may undermine subsequent planning action. The Guide made it clear that safeguarding the occupants of HMOs is the first and most important consideration. Where dangerous housing conditions exist they should not be left unremedied simply because planning enforcement action is pending. Where the situation is not one of danger it should be remembered the Housing and Planning Acts are separate codes. Use of one does not preclude use of the other provided what is required is reasonable, and provided one is not used as a covert way of achieving the objects of the other. In practical terms this means where an unauthorised HMO is discovered and planning enforcement is a possibility, housing action should be limited to requiring what is reasonable in the circumstances, bearing in mind the overriding duty to protect health and safety, and the need to minimise wasteful expenditure.

The supervision of multi-occupation under the Housing Acts

Section 345 of the Housing Act 1985, Part XI is the principal legislation, as amended in 1989.

The definition of multi-occupation

Section 345 of the Housing Act 1985 as amended, provides that multi-occupancy arises when a house 'is occupied by persons who do not form a single household'. 'House' is not defined by the legislation, though it *includes* any part of a building which would not, apart from the requirements of the statutory provision, be regarded as a house, and which was *originally constructed* or *subsequently adapted* for occupation by a single household. Similarly a unit of accommodation which is a flat can be in multiple occupation. DoE Circular 5/90 explains this change was introduced to ensure that Part XI powers could be used in relation to individual flats, such as large flats in mansion blocks, a circumstance not entirely clear before amendment.

A great deal of artful device has been employed by devious landlords trying to ensure their premises are not 'houses', so as to escape regulation. Property has been described as 'hostels' or 'hotels', and has been deconstructed and reconstructed. The judges have responded by giving an extended meaning to the word 'house'. Whether or not any given property is a 'house' is a question of mixed fact and law – 'fact' in that the first question is to determine all relevant facts about a building, and 'law' in that the application of the word 'house' is a matter for judicial interpretation of relevant statutory provisions. Essentially a house is a building used for ordinary dwelling purposes, see *Reed v Hastings Corpn*[8], or one constructed or adapted for use as a dwelling. A shop with living accommodation attached may be a house, as may premises consisting of a workshop with dwelling rooms over it. A building used partly for residential and non-residential purposes may be a house, even an unfinished house may be a house. Hostels and lodging houses may be houses, and properties subdivided into flats may remain houses – indeed a good 'rule of thumb' which has a degree of judicial approbation is 'once built as a house, always a house', see *Pollway Nominees v Croydon London Borough Council*[9]. A large holiday home may be a house, and only a totally drastic process of rebuilding would take a property built as a house outside that classification, see *R v Kerrier District Council, ex p Guppys (Bridport) Ltd*[10]. The basic principle is that 'house' covers any place fitted and used and adapted for human habitation[11]. This approach was most recently confirmed in *Living Waters Christian Centres Ltd v Conwy BC and Fetherstonhaugh*[12] where the court held 'house' must be broadly interpreted, and emphasis must be placed on the purpose for which a property was originally built. In this case two old houses used for religious retreats were held to be HMOs: they provided sleeping accommodation and communal dining facilities.

On the question of whether premises are a HMO or a house in which individuals merely board (in which case they will fall within *fire* controls under the Fire Precautions Act 1971 and SI 1972/238), see *R v Mabbott*[13]. There the Court of Appeal held the distinction is a matter of fact and degree; where persons are transient occupiers that is a factor to take into account. However, the court also considered it would be wrong to conclude that in *all* cases premises that are boarding houses cannot be HMOs. Premises can be both, and satisfying the requirements of the 1971 Act will not necessarily absolve those responsible for a property from compliance with the 1985 Act and vice versa. The important point is that the 'label' placed on a property by its owner is not conclusive of its status, see also *Thrasyvoulou v Hackney London Borough*[14].

'Household' is also undefined. In *Wolkind v Ali*[15] Mr Ali occupied certain premises which he used as a lodging house. The local authority

8   (1964) 62 LGR 588.
9   [1987] AC 79, [1986] 2 All ER 849.
10 (1985) 17 HLR 426.
11 *R v Southwark London Borough, ex p Lewis Levy Ltd* (1983) 8 HLR 1 and *R v Hackney London Borough, ex p Evenbray Ltd* (1987) 19 HLR 557.
12 (1998) 77 P & CR 54, CA.
13 [1988] RVR 131.
14 (1986) 18 HLR 370.
15 [1975] 1 All ER 193, [1975] 1 WLR 170.

served on him notice prescribing the number of persons who could lawfully sleep in certain rooms. These restrictions were observed by Mr Ali until he was joined by his large family from abroad. Thereafter the premises were occupied solely by the family. The Divisional Court held multi-occupancy powers did not apply to this house as it was being used only by a single household.

In *Okereke v Brent London Borough Council*[16] it was held that once a property is divided between separate households it makes no difference whether multiple occupation arises from physical division of the building or not. Here a house built originally for occupation by one family had been converted into separate self-contained dwellings. The basement and ground floor were each occupied by one family and the first floor by two or more families, who shared a bathroom, water closet and kitchen. The second floor was unoccupied and unfit for occupation. It was held the house as a whole was multi-occupied.

Where there is a clear division of control over a house between two or more households the multi-occupancy powers apply. Likewise where a person lives in or occupies a house, and shares control with others living there, as a commercial enterprise, a multiple occupation arises. 'Occupied' in this context generally means 'lived in', even where that occupation is of a transitory nature.[17]

But what about the situation where persons live together freely and communally in a house? In *Simmons v Pizzey*[18] Mrs Pizzey occupied a property in a London suburb as a refuge for 'battered women'. The local authority fixed a maximum number of persons who might lawfully occupy the house. Mrs Pizzey was subsequently charged with a failure to comply with this. Her defence was that the house was not multi-occupied as all residents lived there communally as one household. The House of Lords rejected this and laid down tests to be applied in deciding whether a group of persons do/do not form a single household.

(1) The number of persons occupying the property, and the place of its location must be considered. 30 or more persons occupying a suburban house can hardly be regarded as forming a single household.

(2) The length of time for which each person occupies the property must be considered. A fluctuating and constantly altering population is a clear indication that the property is multi-occupied.

(3) The intention of the owner of the property has to be taken into account.

This approach was applied in *Silbers v Southwark London Borough Council*[19]. Here a common lodging house was used for accommodating

---

16 [1967] 1 QB 42, [1966] 1 All ER 150.
17 *Living Waters Christian Centres Ltd v Conwy BC and Fetherstonhaugh* supra.
18 [1979] AC 37, [1977] 2 All ER 432.
19 (1977) 76 LGR 421, CA.

some 70 women; some were alcoholics, others were mentally disturbed. They stayed for varying periods or indefinitely. It was held such a fluctuating group could not be regarded as forming a single household. It is not necessary for persons to have exclusive possession of different parts of the property for them to form individual households. Indeed it seems from dicta in *Milford Properties v London Borough of Hammersmith*[20] that a multi-occupancy can arise even where some occupiers are in the premises unlawfully, for example as unlawful sub-tenants. In *Hackney London Borough v Ezedinma*[1] the court stressed what constitutes a household is a question of fact and degree. Students each of whom has a separate tenancy of a room in a house may nevertheless group together to form a 'household'. On the other hand, homeless families may be so accommodated in a house as to occupy it not as a single household, see *Thrasyvoulou v Hackney London Borough*[2] . Many so called 'hotels' are occupied on this basis. Circular 12/93 also counsels authorities to consider the way in which cooking and washing facilities are used, whether occupants eat and clean communally, whether each has a separate contract, and whether the landlord or the occupants fill any vacancy casually arising. In *Barnes v Sheffield City Council*[3] it was indicated the sort of issues to be considered include:

- did the occupants originally come to the house as a group or were they individually recruited;
- what facilities are shared;
- are the occupants responsible for the whole house or merely individual parts;
- are occupants able to lock other occupants out of their rooms;
- if an occupant leaves, whose responsibility is to replace him/her;
- who allocates rooms to occupants;
- what size is the property;
- how stable a group are the occupants?

The official guidance further stresses the need to consider whether there are separate cooking and washing facilities, whether there is communal dining, whether cleaning is a communal task, and the nature of each occupant's contract with the landlord.

On the basis of the foregoing the following types of premises *may* constitute HMOs:

- those occupied as flatlets or 'bedsits', ie rooms with full self catering and a degree of self containment;

---

20   [1978] JPL 766.
1   [1981] 3 All ER 438.
2   (1986) 18 HLR 370.
3   (1995) 27 HLR 719, see also *R v Kensington and Chelsea RBC, ex p Westwoods Ltd* (1995) 28 HLR 219.

- houses where though accommodation is not self-contained, there is self-catering;
- houses where in addition to the householder there are numbers of lodgers living independently;
- properties labelled 'hostels', 'guest houses', 'boarding houses' and 'bed and breakfast';
- registered residential homes;
- houses divided into self-contained flats with common parts;
- premises occupied by two or more households;
- premises occupied by persons whose relationships are so tenuous that they cannot be regarded as a household;
- premises with one main and other separate subsidiary households.

In all cases, however, the question whether there is a HMO will be a matter of fact and degree, and cannot be decided in advance by the application of predetermined local policies or professional guidelines: *this in itself is a problem.*

The problem is the clash between legal and administrative ways of thinking. The lawyer's approach to the HMO problem is to consider the definition given by the law and then to determine on a case by case basis whether any given property is a HMO. Housing Management and Environmental Health officials on the other hand need clear cut categorisations to assist them in their work – and they may further wish to include within their concept of HMO properties which do not fit into the parameters allowed by section 345. The Chartered Institute of Environmental Health (CIEH) definition, for example, classifies HMOs into six groups.

- A – houses occupied as individual rooms where each occupant has some exclusive and some shared accommodation and lives independently of all others (compare DETR group (i) below);
- B – houses where the occupants 'share' the dwelling in the sense of having exclusive bedrooms but communal living spaces – eg student houses – many of these would *not* be classified as HMOs under section 345;
- C – houses occupied by persons whose occupation is ancillary to their education or employment, eg a hall of residence;
- D – hostels, guest houses, bed and breakfast hotels, providing accommodation for people with no other permanent dwellings;
- E – registered homes for persons in need by virtue of age, disability, mental disorder, drug or alcohol dependence;
- F – other houses/buildings which by erection or conversion comprise self-contained dwellings – eg a large old house converted into self-contained flats.

The DETR classifies properties as follows:

- Group (i) – converted houses providing flatlets, bedsits and rooms each occupied by a single household with sharing of facilities and common circulating areas as stairs – 'traditional' HMOs;

- Group (ii) – shared houses – eg student houses;
- Group (iii) – houses with lodgers who share the house with the occupier/occupying family – these will hardly ever fall within section 345 as it stands;
- Group (iv) – purpose-built HMOs, eg sheltered accommodation with private rooms and some shared facilities;
- Group (v) – hostels, guest-houses, boarding houses, 'bed and breakfast' (compare CIEH Category D);
- Group (vi) – self-contained flats converted from a single house.

For the purposes of the law shared houses and houses with lodgers (CIEH Category B – DETR Group (iii)) are not likely to be classified as HMOs – which can lead to problems for over zealous environmental health officers. It must be open to question whether a legal definition so much at variance with administrative and managerial practice is desirable or defensible.

Some harmonisation of thinking and action may result following the Court of Appeal decision in *Rogers v Islington Borough Council*.[4] Mr Rogers had a three-storey, ten-bedroomed house let out to up to nine single, young, professional adults on individual verbal agreements. Each had the right to a room and the right to share communal facilities, and each lived there for about two years. Mr Rogers lived in France but kept a room for himself, and he called the premises a private residential club because though new occupants were recruited via newspaper advertisements current occupants decided whether or not a person should be admitted. Was this house a HMO?

Nourse LJ, referring to *Barnes* and the unhappiness of some authorities with that case concluded a good working test of multiple occupation was needed, and found a way forward by clarifying what constitutes a 'household'. A 'household' exists where a number of people live together in some form of relationship, and that can include a house where an occupier has a few paying guests living with the family. Students can form such relationships – where a group of students club together to rent a property they are to be recognised normally as forming a household, even though they were unknown to each other before coming to university, and pay rent individually. They have a reason to live together and form a community, be it comradeship, or as a means of reducing the cost of living. In such case, as in *Barnes*, where four of five people come together and take a house as a preformed group for a predetermined length of time, they will form a 'household'. In the instant case there was no such relationship, and the label placed on the house by Mr Rogers did not change its status; it was a HMO.

4   [1999] 37 EG 178, CA.

Local authority housing and fire precaution powers

Registration

Section 346 of the 1985 Act (as inserted in 1996) empowers authorities to make various registration schemes for HMOs for the whole or part of their area, these need not apply to all types of HMO.

Registration schemes may contain 'control' or 'special' conditions, for which see further below. Under section 346A, inserted in 1996, once a scheme is in force it is the *duty* of those persons specified in it, for example the owners and managers of relevant properties, to register their HMOs. In general registration is for a period of five years and is renewable; 'reasonable' registration fees are payable on registration, and half fees on renewal, subject to limits to be set by the Secretary of State: see SI 1997/229 as amended by SI 1998/1813. Schemes specify the details to be registered, and it is the duty of persons subject to the scheme to notify the details and any changes in them.

Section 346B enables the Secretary of State to prepare model schemes and any local scheme confirming to a model requires no central confirmation – unlike schemes under the previous law all of which required individual confirmation. Schemes not conforming to a model still require central confirmation and the Secretary of State may modify such a scheme before confirmation. Two model schemes exist and are contained in DoE Circular 3/97. Scheme CI is a simple scheme which merely requires the notification of HMOs, while Scheme C2 is more elaborate and contains control provisions. Such provisions exist under section 347, as substituted in 1996, enabling limits to be set on the number of persons occupying a HMO, and preventing multiple occupation of a house unless it is registered. Under section 348G it is a criminal offence to break or otherwise fail to comply with the requirements of a registration scheme once it is in force.

Section 348, as substituted, enables local authorities on an application for the first registration of a house, or on the renewal or variation of a registration, to:
- refuse the application on the basis that the property is unsuitable for multiple occupation and is incapable of being made suitable;
- refuse the application on the basis that the person having control – ie the person who receives the rent of the property on his/her own account or as an agent (see section 398) – is not a 'fit and proper person';
- require the carrying out of works on the property;
- impose conditions as to the management of the property.

Written reasons must be given where an application to register is refused or where works are required or conditions concerning management are imposed, and in such cases the applicant has 21 days in which to appeal the matter to the county court – and also where the authority fail to determine an application within five weeks of receiving it. The county court has a wide discretion on appeal to confirm, vary or reverse the authority's decision.

Section 348A further enables authorities who have control schemes at any time during a period of registration to alter the number of persons or households permitted in the house, or to revoke registration altogether, on the basis the house is unsuitable for such occupation as is permitted by the registration and is incapable of being made suitable, or to alter the number of permitted persons or households until specified works are executed within a set time to make the house 'suitable'. registration may also be revoked where the authority conclude the person having control of the house, or the person managing the HMO (ie the person who owns the premises and who receives the rents from them either directly or via an agent, *or* who would receive those rents but for the existence of an arrangement with a third party: see section 398) *is* not fit and proper, (which appears to cover situations where ownership has changed hands) or where there has been a breach of the conditions of management relating to the HMO. Again written reasons must be given for such an action and there is a 21-day right of appeal to the county court.

A critique of registration schemes

The new provisions are an advance on that previously existing, and contain power to take action against a person who is not 'fit and proper', which at one point it was thought would not be incorporated in the law during the passage of the Bill leading to the 1996 Housing Act. However, that expression is not defined in the Act – does it, for example, extend to a person who has a history of convictions for the harassment of tenants generally or only in respect of specific offences relating to HMOs? Furthermore it is arguable that the DoE model schemes which may be adopted without further ministerial confirmation, are too lax in that they exempt from control far too many types of HMOs – eg those occupied by persons forming only two households, or those with no more than four persons who form no more than two households, or only by three persons in addition to the controller/manager of the property. Also excluded are childrens' homes, registered homes, and self-contained flat conversions passed under the Building Regulations as well as health service properties and those belonging to registered social landlords, and universities. This exemption removes most student occupied HMOs from control. Furthermore it is not clear where the section 348A powers may be used. Arguably they could be used in situations where culinary or sanitary facilities have so deteriorated that the number of occupants must be reduced, or remedial measures instituted, but this does not allow an authority to improve conditions beyond the standard applying at the beginning of the period of registration: see section 348A (2) which prevents authorities from imposing more stringent requirements part way through the registration period. It will be noted that under the current law there is no compulsory registration of all HMOs, nor compulsory licensing of their owners and managers: this may, however, change: see further below.

Special control provisions

Sections 348(B) to 348(F) insert special controls in respect of hotels/hostels which, it is alleged, are sometimes the scene of drug abuse and other forms of anti-social behaviour. Under these powers authorities may insert additional control conditions in a registration scheme, and also to control occupancy levels (in both cases an appeal is possible). Once an authority has determined to have a registration scheme with *control* provisions, additional *specific controls* can be included to prevent a HMO or the behaviour of its residents from *'adversely affecting the amenity or character of the area'*. Authorisation may be given for registration to be refused, the number of occupants reduced, and for conditions to be imposed on registration. In particular authorisation may be given for the revocation of registration where a house is occupied by more households than are permitted or where a breach of conditions has occurred and this is due to a 'relevant management failure'. Such a failure is 'relevant' (under section 348F) where the person having control of or managing the HMO has failed to take reasonable steps to prevent the HMO or the behaviour of residents from adversely affecting the amenity or character of the area in which it is situated, or to reduce such an effect. Note, however, that a special control provision cannot be used to authorise the refusal of an application for the first registration of a HMO which was operated as such before the introduction of the registration scheme with special control provisions, nor of any application for renewal of registration of a HMO previously registered under such a scheme, save where there has been a relevant management failure. In a case where special control provisions apply when considering an application for registration of a HMO authorities may also take account of existing HMOs in the vicinity of the proposed HMO.

Special control provisions are draconian in effect, and the debates leading up to the passing of the Housing Act 1996 indicated that they are to be targeted at situations where, inter alia, large numbers of people on state benefits are drawn to particular areas by the availability of cheap accommodation – eg where large seaside hotels otherwise vacant are proposed for turnover to multiple occupation. Even so it appears no consent to the incorporation of special control provisions will be given unless an authority can show their area is already adversely affected by the existence of one or more HMOs, or that such a problem is likely to arise from deteriorating conditions in existing HMOs or the creation of new ones, see DoE Circular 3/97 Annex A, paragraph 9. It is important to remember that no 'model' scheme of special control provisions exists, and thus any such scheme would have to be specifically drawn up and submitted for central authorisation.

Where special control provisions are included in a scheme provision must also be made under section 348C for notification of decisions and for appeals. Where an application is refused or the conditions or registration are varied or there is a revocation the authority must give written reasoned notice of its decision. Then there is a 21-day right of appeal to the county court. The court has power to vary or reverse the authority's decision if some *material* informality, defect or error is found, or where the authority behaved unreasonably in acting as they did. The court may direct the authority to grant applications either as made or as varied. Conditions imposed may also be varied.

Under section 348D special control provisions in a scheme may allow an authority to direct that where registration should be revoked, they may also direct that the level of occupation is to be reduced to such a level where the registration scheme no longer applies. The making of such an 'occupancy direction' is dependent on the authority concluding there has been a relevant management failure, and in doing this must balance the interests of occupants against those of other local residents and business.

Where such an occupancy direction is given those who have control of or who manage the HMO must take all reasonably practicable steps to comply with it, and security of tenure for assured tenants and assured shorthold tenants in the property is effectively removed for this purpose. Again written reasoned notice must be given and there is a right of appeal to the county court: see section 348E.

Under section 349 authorities proposing to make registration schemes conforming with the central model must publish notice of their intention one month before the scheme is made, and must give local notice of the actual making. Similar requirements apply to local schemes needing the Secretary of State's confirmation. The publicity must explain what steps will have to be taken before a HMO can be registered. The scheme must be available for public inspection, and the local press must also be utilised to give publicity to schemes. Section 350 grants further powers to authorities to obtain information in connection with registration schemes.

Registration remains, however, a voluntary activity, and many authorities have been reluctant to introduce this form of control. They are wary in particular of putting forward proposals that may not match the concept of what should be a 'model scheme'. It appears, however, that following the return to power of the Labour party in May 1997 that the attitude of the DETR to registration schemes not conforming to the central models may have softened, and that there is an informal 'invitation' for authorities to put forward their own schemes in a draft form for discussion prior to submission in order to facilitate the subsequent granting of approval.

Management regulations

By virtue of section 369 of the Housing Act 1985 (as amended) the Secretary of State has power to make a code to ensure proper standards of management in HMOs, see the Housing (Management of Houses in Multiple Occupation) Regulations 1990 SI 1990/830. By virtue of Schedule 9 of the Local Government and Housing Act 1989 the code automatically applies to HMOs, and its breach may lead to immediate prosecution under section 369(5), and service of a notice under section 372 of the principal Act requiring rectification of specified relevant defects of management. Under section 369(5) it is an offence either *knowingly* to contravene management regulations, *or* to fail without reasonable excuse to comply with the regulations (an offence of *strict* liability, though it is for the prosecution to prove the absence of a 'reasonable excuse')[5]. Central guidance, however, counsels authorities to publicise their powers well before resorting to prosecution and always to ask how far any given landlord could have been reasonably expected to comply with the code.

The regulations generally require managers of HMOs to ensure that:
(1) all means of water supply and drainage are maintained in repair, clean condition, good and proper working order, with water fittings (which includes baths and WCs) being protected against frost damage;
(2) supplies of water, gas and electricity to any resident are not unreasonably interrupted;
(3) common parts are maintained in repair, clean condition and good order, reasonably free from obstruction, with handrails and bannisters replaced, maintained and provided where necessary on grounds of safety;
(4) specified installations in common use, or serving parts of premises in common use, are maintained in repair, clean condition and good working order, including installations for supplying gas and electricity for lighting and heat, sanitary provision, sinks, installations for cooking/ storing food;
(5) internal structures of any part of a house occupied as living accommodation are in clean condition at the start of a period of residence, and are maintained in repair, with mains installations being kept in repair and working order, though managers are absolved from

5   See *City of Westminster v Mavroghenis* (1983) 11 HLR 56 and *London Borough of Wandsworth v Sparling* (1987) 20 HLR 169.

carrying out repairs needed in consequence of failures by residents to use accommodation in a tenant-like manner;

(6) windows and means of ventilation are to be maintained in repair and proper working order;

(7) means of escape from fire and associated fire precautions and apparatus are in good order and repair and are unobstructed, with suitably displayed signs indicating all means of escape from fire;

(8) outbuildings, yards, areas, forecourts, gardens in common use are to be kept in repair, clean condition and good order, with boundary walls, fences and railings so maintained as not to be dangers to residents;

(9) refuse and litter are not to accumulate (this appears to extend to enable action to be taken against old cars and rubbish kept in the front garden of a HMO by the landlord)[6];

(10) reasonably requisite precautions are taken to ensure residents are protected against injury having regard to the design and structural conditions of any given HMO, including where needed, preventing access to any unsafe roof/balcony;

(11) the name, address and telephone number of the manager is to be visibly and suitably displayed;

(12) information is given to the authority as to numbers of individuals and households accommodated in response to specific written requests by that authority.

Residents are required to assist managers in the effective discharge of the above duties. A 'manager' in the present context it should be remembered is (a) that person who as owner or lessee of premises receives directly, or via an agent or trustee, rent or other payments from residents, (b) an agent or trustee who receives rent etc on behalf of the owner/lessee, see section 398(6).

Powers to require the doing of further works

If in the opinion of a local authority a HMO is defective because of neglect in complying with the management regulations they may serve notice under section 372 of the 1985 Act on the manager specifying and requiring execution of works necessary to make good the defects. It is not enough merely to specify the effect of required works, they must themselves be specified.[7] The notice must allow at least 21 days for doing the works, though this may be extended from time to time with the written permission of the authority. Information of service of the notice must also be served on all other persons known to the authority to be owners, lessees or

---

6   See (1999) Housing Law Monitor, June, p 7.
7   *Canterbury City Council v Bern* [1981] JPL 749.

mortgagees of the house. Following service the person served has, under section 373, a period of 21 days (or such longer period as the authority may allow) to appeal to the county court. The grounds on which an appeal may be made are that:

(1) the condition of the house did not justify the authority in requiring execution of the specified works;

(2) there has been some material error, defect or informality in, or in connection with, the notice;

(3) the authority have refused unreasonably to approve execution of alternative works, or that works required are otherwise unreasonable in character or extent, or are unnecessary;

(4) the time allowed for doing the works is not reasonably sufficient, or the date specified for doing the works is unreasonable, or

(5) some person other than the appellant is wholly or partly responsible for the state of affairs, or will benefit from the doing of the works, and therefore ought to bear the whole or part of their costs.

The appeal powers can be productive of delay in implementing remedial action; delays of between 15 and 18 months have not been unknown.

Power to require execution of works to render premises fit for number of occupants

Section 352 of the 1985 Act, as amended in 1989 and 1996, empowers authorities to require execution of works to render premises fit for the number of their inhabitants. An authority may, subject to section 365 which relates to means of escape from fire, serve a notice, on the person 'having control' ie the person receiving the rent, or on the person managing the house, where (a) it considers a HMO fails to meet one or more of a number of stated criteria, and (b), having regard to the number of individuals or households (or both) accommodated in the premises, by reason of that failure the premises are not reasonably suitable for occupation by the individuals or households in question. The listed criteria are, under section 352(1A):

(1) are there satisfactory facilities for storage, preparation and cooking of food including adequate numbers of sinks with hot and cold water;

(2) is there an adequate number of suitably located WCs for exclusive use by occupants;

(3) similarly are there fixed baths/showers and wash hand basins with hot and cold water for occupants;

(4) subject to section 365 are there adequate means of escape from fire, and

(5) are there other adequate fire precautions.

Note that there is no power to fix an occupation level for a HMO under this section: that falls to be done under section 354, see below.

This special standard of fitness for HMOs is in *addition* to the general fitness standard for houses existing under section 604 of the 1985 Act. Under section 189 notice may thus be served to ensure a HMO is provided with adequate lighting, ventilation and heating, while action may be taken under section 190 to deal with disrepair, see further Chapter Seven.

Worthy of special note are the provisions relating to means of escape from fire and other fire precautions. It was argued by DoE Circular 5/90 that the power relating to 'other adequate fire precautions' enables authorities to take steps to require fire detection and warning systems along with fire fighting equipment in addition to 'means of escape from fire' an expression in the past regarded by fire law experts as not extending to matters such as smoke detection systems – a distinction being made between a means of escape from fire and a means of warning people to make use of that means of escape.

Authorities have a general discretion under section 352(2) to serve notice requiring works to be done to make a property fit for the number of occupants for the time being accommodated or for a smaller number the house would reasonably accommodate if the works were carried out. Notices may *not* specify works to premises outside the house, and must specify *works*[8], while subsection (2A) provides that where an authority have exercised or propose to exercise powers under section 368 to secure closure of part of a house, they may in their section 352 notice specify such work as is necessary to make the house fit bearing in mind that a part has been closed. Where a section 352 notice is served the authority is under a duty, under subsection (3), as amended, to inform the occupiers of the property, as well as the person having control and the house's manager, while notices once served become local land charges, thus warning future potential purchasers of the property, see section 352(5A). Notices served must be noted in a public register open to public inspection, free of charge at reasonable hours.

Where notice is served section 352(4) provides that the person served must begin required works not later than a specified reasonable date – which must not be earlier than 21 days after the date of service of the notice, and must further complete them within a specified reasonable period. This enables authorities to think about and fix a definite period within which work must be done. Where notice is served in respect of section 352 requirements and the specified works are carried out a further notice may not be served within a period of five years, unless the authority consider there has been a change of circumstances, eg in relation to the correlation of the premises; see section 352(7) and (8). However, a notice may not be served merely because an authority have adopted enhanced standards.

8   *Canterbury City Council v Bern* [1981] JPL 749.

Further guidance on implementing the fitness standard required under section 352 is contained in DoE Circular 12/92. This continued a trend in DoE housing standards guidance in being extremely detailed, thus tends to restrict local discretion, despite encouragement to use discretion in Circular 12/93 para 4.2.1. The more detailed the guidance the harder it is to depart from it, despite the somewhat platitudinous statement in Annex A para 1.3 'The Guidance is advisory. Authorities are reminded they must be flexible in forming their own opinions.' More restrictive is the warning against adoption of over strict standards a little later where: 'Authorities are reminded that excessively high standards of accommodation may deter landlords from making accommodation available at all'. Authorities are also effectively barred by Annex A para 1.5 from applying fitness requirements higher than those generally applying to new buildings 'and buildings may be expected to fall considerably short of current regulation standards and codes before they fail to meet the requirements of section 352'. General guidance touches upon matters such as the nature of premises, arguing, for example, it would be inappropriate to insist on provision of separate catering facilities for all residents in a HMO where the property is a hotel or hostel where meals are centrally provided. Similarly the nature of occupancy is always to be considered. The Circular argues it may be appropriate to set different standards for HMOs let for only a few days at a time or on an unfurnished basis as opposed to those occupied furnished and long term. General consideration should also be given to the Institution of Environmental Health Officers' guidance setting differing standards for different size categories of HMOs, though these, legally, may not be applied as rigid rules.

Turning to specific requirements under section 352 what does the 1992 Circular recommend? So far as satisfactory food preparation facilities are concerned it points to avoiding food having to be carried between floors, and the desirability of providing sufficient cooking facilities, which should be well laid out, and adequately screened. Reference is made to other standards which may be used as guidance, eg BS 5482 on domestic butane and propane gas burners. To come to a decision under this part of section 352 authorities are recommended to have regard to the type of provision and location of facilities, the scale of provision, the suitability of sinks, H & C supplies, cookers, work surfaces, food storage facilities, layout and lighting and ventilation issues. The aim is to provide *generally* adequate kitchen facilities in each unit of accommodation, or access for each unit to shared facilities on the same floor.

So far as WCs are concerned the Circular makes specific reference to using the Building Regulations BS 6465 and DoE Design Bulletin 24 as yardsticks for assessing the fitness of a HMO, though once again it adds: 'failure to meet these would not in itself, necessarily constitute grounds for unfitness'. The basic factors to consider are type, provision, scale, location, suitability, and layout of WCs and like facilities, their compartmentation, lighting and ventilation; the *ideal* is separate facilities for each unit of accommodation.

With regard to fire safety the Circular draws upon, and replaces, the earlier 'blue' guide on means of escape from fire and related issues jointly published by the Home and Welsh Offices with the DoE.

Only a brief overview can be given of the guidance which relates to hostels and houses divided into two or more units of accommodation, including 'bedsitters' and properties divided into flats. Authorities should seek *adequate* means of escape from fire and other fire precautions, with *basic provision* of means of escape always being necessary, the principal aim being to ensure all occupants of a HMO should be able to leave safely in the event of fire. This is to be achieved by combining measures to *prevent* the spread of fire with those to provide escape routes and means of warning of fire, bearing in mind: protection and fire resistance of escape routes against products of combustion; distances to be travelled to make a final exit from premises; nature of means of escape and their suitability to occupants, eg width of corridors, steepness of stairs; need for precautionary and warning systems. The Circular reminds authorities that HMO management must be conducive to maintenance of fire safety standards, with regular maintenance of alarms and extinguishers, etc. The adequacy of management to meet such standards must be considered: inadequacy could lead to service of closing orders, see further below. Authorities are urged to counsel managers to hold fire drills and advise residents of good fire safety practice, and are also recommended to distribute checklists of fire safety reminders to residents of non-hostel HMOs. With regard to hostels it is recommended that staff should be instructed in fire safety and drills.

Supplemental provisions

Section 352A (inserted in 1996) enables authorities to levy reasonable charges in respect of their administrative expenses on persons served with section 352 notices. Theses are limited to expenses incurred in determining whether a notice should be served, identifying the works and actually serving the notice – and there is a statutory limit of £300 per notice: see SI 1997/228. Furthermore under section 377A, again inserted in 1996, before a notice under section 352 can be served a preliminary or 'minded to' notice must be served on the potential recipient of the full notice informing that person of the authority's intentions and the requirements they intend to specify. This gives the recipient an opportunity to make representations (oral or in writing) to the authority to which they must have regard before proceeding. This provision does not, however, preclude an authority from taking immediate action to serve a section 352 notice where they deem this to be 'necessary': see section 377A(7), SI 1997/227 and DoE Circular 3/97.

Section 377A also applies to notices requiring the execution of works under section 372: see further below.

Appeals against section 352 notices are available under section 353. It is a ground of appeal that, inter alia, the condition of the premises in respect of means of escape from fire and fire precautions did not justify requiring the specified works, and further that the date specified for beginning these works, is not reasonable. It may alternatively be argued that an authority has no power to serve the notice because the property is not an HMO. This may be done by way of appeal to the county court rather than by judicial review[9].

Further supplemental provisions to section 352

The power of authorities under section 354 to limit the number of occupants of a house so as to prevent the occurrence of, or to remedy, a state of affairs otherwise calling for service of notice under section 352 was modified in 1989, and further amended in 1996. They may limit by direction the number of occupants allowed for a HMO based on consideration, inter alia, of whether the property has adequate means of escape from fire and other adequate fire precautions in addition to consideration of whether it has adequate cooking and sanitary facilities. This power also extends to parts of houses, see section 354(2). At least seven days before making a direction the authority must serve on the owner and every known lessee, notice of their intention, and also post a copy of this notice in the house in some place accessible to the occupants. A right to make representations is given to those on whom notice is served. The direction once given makes it the duty under section 355, of 'the occupier', which includes any person entitled or authorised to permit individuals to take up residence in the house, to keep the number of persons within the permitted number. In *Hackney London Borough v Ezedinma*[10] a managing estate agent was held to fall within this definition: he had been authorised to let out rooms. Copies of the direction must be served, within seven days of its making, on the owner and known lessees of the house, and also posted within the house in some place where the occupants can have access to it. It is an offence under section 355(2) knowingly to fail to comply with a direction while a direction under the section is a local land charge under section 354(8). Once the notice is in force it appears that the limit placed on occupation is to be achieved by 'natural decline' in the number of occupants, ie persons will leave and are not to be replaced.

A section 354 direction can only be issued when the house to which it applies is multi-occupied, and further multiple occupation of the premises

9   *Nolan v Leeds City Council* (1990) 23 HLR 135.
10   [1981] 3 All ER 438.

at the time of an alleged offence is an essential requirement for liability. However, it seems from *Simmons v Pizzey*[11] that once a direction is validly given temporary cessation of multiple occupation does not end the direction but merely suspends its operation; it will revive and be applicable as soon as the house is again multi-occupied. There is no right to appeal against a section 354 direction as such. However, authorities have power under section 357 to revoke or vary directions, following changes of circumstances affecting the house, or the execution of works there, on the application of anyone having an estate or interest in the house. An unreasonable refusal to exercise this power can form the subject of an appeal to the county court. A section 354 notice may be served in addition to, or instead of, one under section 352. The latter is designed to ensure that facilities in a HMO are adequate for the number of occupants, while the former is used to specify a maximum number who may occupy the house with existing facilities. If served together they may specify the maximum number of occupants for a HMO after works have been carried out.

Special provisions with regard to fire

Section 365 of the 1985 Act (as amended in 1989 and further in 1996) gives authorities wide power of choice in cases where a HMO presents fire risks. Where an authority considers a HMO fails to meet the requirements of section 352, and one reason, or the reason, why they are of this opinion is because there are *no* adequate means of escape from fire *or* no other adequate fire precautions, they may, as an alternative to requiring works, accept an undertaking *or* make a closing order under section 368.

Section 365(2) (as amended) provides that where the foregoing powers are available, the authority's discretion is total; it is up to them to make whichever order seems appropriate. However, they are under a duty to make some appropriate order where the house is of such a description, or is occupied in such a way, as may be specified by the Secretary of State in an order, though the Secretary of State is also given power by section 365(2A) to specify houses of a particular description or occupied in a particular way in respect of which the range of powers is not to be exercised. Properties subject to the *duty* to take action are those specified in the Housing (Fire Safety in Houses in Multiple Occupation) Order 1997 SI 1997/230. These are those which comprise at least three storeys – excluding any storey lying wholly or mainly below the floor level of the principal entrance to the house – and which are not otherwise excluded. The *excluded* properties are:
- houses used as children's homes;
- houses registered under the Registered Homes Act 1984;

11 [1979] AC 37, [1977] 2 All ER 432.

- houses occupied by health service bodies;
- houses for which the responsible person is a university or further education body;
- houses approved centrally for the purposes of the probation service;
- houses in which the local housing authority has a freehold or leasehold interest;
- houses subject to control orders (see further below);
- houses occupied by persons forming only two households;
- houses occupied by no more than four persons, or by three persons in addition to a responsible person and any other member to that person's household;
- houses consisting of self-contained flats where at least one-third are *either* let on leases of more than 21 years to their occupiers, *or* are wholly occupied by any freeholder of the house, *or* when the flats were created they complied with building regulation requirements;
- houses in respect of which the responsible person is a registered social landlord

The 'responsible person' is the person having control or the person managing the property, see further above.

The *duty* is to come into force on a phased basis between 30 September 1998 and 29 February 2000 in order to allow authorities whose areas contain large numbers of HMOs to have time to take action, and to concentrate their resources first of all on those properties of *four* or more storeys. Apart from those cases specified by the Secretary of State, the 'fire powers' are discretionary: there is no general duty to take action in respect of HMOs save that under section 605 of the 1985 Act (as amended) whereunder authorities must at least once every year, consider housing conditions of their district to decide what action to take in pursuance of, inter alia, their HMO powers, though they are subject to direction by the Secretary of State in relation to this. Furthermore the fitness provision, the substituted section 604, though specifically declared in section 604(3) to apply to HMOs, contains no specific reference to means of escape from fire or adequate fire precautions as criteria for determining whether a house is fit.

It is accepted that there is an overlap between sections 352 and 604. Circular 12/93 counselled authorities to pursue the most satisfactory course of action on a house by house basis, bearing in mind the need to minimise risks on an interim basis. There is no common law duty of care arising in respect of these fire safety powers[12].

However, before action can be taken under section 352 in respect of remedying want of adequate means of escape from fire, the housing authority must under section 365(3) consult the relevant fire authority.

---

12 *Emphrain v London Borough of Newham* (1992) 25 HLR 207.

Circular 12/92 indicated HMOs constitute a significant fire hazard. Between 1978 and 1981 550 people died in HMO fires, while in 1986 alone in Bayswater there were 50 HMO fires. The risk of death or injury from fire in a HMO is ten times that in other houses. Local housing authorities *must consult* with the fire authority where:

- they are under a duty to exercise section 365 powers (see above);
- they have a discretion to exercise such powers and the house is one falling within a description specified by the Secretary of State, ie children's homes, registered homes, houses occupied by health service bodies (eg nurse's homes) houses for which the responsible person is a university of further education body, houses approved for probation service purposes: see SI 1997/230.

Where an authority is considering taking enforcement action against a HMO and the 'minded to' procedure described above would apply, DoE Circular 3/97 points out it is prudent to consult with the fire authority before any preliminary notice is served in respect of the property.

The consultative requirements are designed to ensure that where a property is capable of being dealt with under both the 1985 Act and the Fire Precautions Act 1971 – eg it is also a 'hotel' or 'guest house', that differing burdens are not imposed by different authorities, and also that such properties do not 'fall between the two stools' of the legislative regimes. Furthermore Circular 7/97 points out that where a valid fire certificate under section 1 of the 1971 Act is in force enforcement activity should normally be left to the fire authority.

Where (subject to section 365) it appears that means of escape from fire would be adequate if part of a house ceased to be used for human habitation, the authority may under section 368 secure that. They may also secure closure of part of a house while serving notice under section 365 specifying works necessary to supply the rest with adequate fire escapes. In the execution of these powers they may after consultation with owners or mortgagees accept undertakings from such persons that part or parts of houses will not be used for human habitation without the consent of the authority. An undertaking need not take the form of a formal contract with an offer and acceptance, but can arise by clear conduct and correspondence.[13]

It is an offence to use, or to permit use of, any part of a house subject to a closing undertaking. Where such an undertaking is not accepted, or if one accepted is found to be broken, the authority may make a closing order on the relevant part of the house. The provisions of Part IX of the 1985 Act apply to closing orders made under section 368 including rights of appeal under section 269, see Chapter Seven. Use of section 368, is, however, subject to section 365, and it appears authorities should use this in preference to more drastic closure powers.

13 *Desmond v London Borough of Bromley* (1995) 28 HLR 518.

The term 'means of escape from fire' was given a wide meaning in *Horgan v Birmingham Corpn*[14] to include not just fire escapes as such but also ancillary matters such as screens operating to keep escape routes clear of smoke. In deciding what 'means' to require authorities should consider the personal circumstances of the occupants of any given HMO, eg their ages and whether they are supervised, see *Kingston-upon-Hull District Council v University of Hull*[15].

If a notice under section 352 or 372 is not complied with, or if persons on whom they are served inform the authority in writing that they are unable to do the works, section 375 of the 1985 Act allows the authority to do the work. They may recover reasonable expenses under Schedule 10 of the Act from the person on whom notice was served, or where an agent or trustee was served, in whole or part from the person on whose behalf the agent or trustee was acting. Recovery may be by action in the county court or the authority may sequestrate rents from the property. Authorities may even recover costs where the works have been belatedly done after they have started the work in default.

A *wilful failure* to comply with notices issued under sections 352 or 372 of the 1985 Act is, by virtue of section 376(1), an offence punishable by a fine. Under section 376(2), where a person initially convicted of the offence created by section 376(1) commits a further new offence if he/she then wilfully leaves the work undone for the obligation is continuous.[16] This meaning of 'wilful failure' to do works was stated in *Honig v Islington London Borough Council*[17] to include voluntary omissions to act, irrespective of motive. It appears the only allowable reasons for not acting are force majeure, accident or impossibility.

Section 377 of the 1985 Act applies where any person, being an occupier, or owner of premises, and having received notice of intended action under sections 352 or 372 of the Act prevents the carrying into effect of proposals. A magistrates' court may order that person to allow doing what is necessary. The magistrates may not question whether the works are required, though they may refuse an order if, for example, a person in a part of a building to which access is sought is too ill for such access to be allowed[18]. Failure to comply with a court order is an offence.

14 (1964) 63 LGR 33, CA.
15 [1979] LAG Bulletin 191.
16 *Camden London Borough Council v Marshall* [1996] 1 WLR 1345.
17 [1972] Crim LR 126.
18 *Wandsworth London Borough Council v Bowes* (1989) 23 HLR 22.

Further powers to prevent overcrowding in multi-occupied houses

Section 358 of the Housing Act 1985 applies where it appears to an authority that an excessive number of persons, having regard to the number of rooms available, is being, or is likely to be, accommodated in a HMO. They may serve on the occupier, or on the person exercising management of the house, or on both, an 'overcrowding notice'. This must state, under section 359, in relation to every room what the authority consider to be the maximum number of persons who can suitably sleep therein, if any. Special maxima may be included where some or all of the persons occupying the room are below a specified age. An authority may require a number of courses of action from persons on whom such notice is served. The first, under section 360, is to refrain from:

(1) knowingly permitting any room to be occupied as sleeping accommodation otherwise than in accordance with the notice, or

(2) knowingly permitting persons to occupy the premises as sleeping accommodation in such numbers that it is not possible to avoid persons of opposite sexes, not living together as husband and wife, and over the age of 12, sleeping in the same room, it being assumed that persons who occupy the premises as sleeping accommodation sleep only in rooms for which the notice sets a maximum, and that the maximum for each room is not exceeded.

The alternative course of action, under section 361, is that the person on whom notice is served must refrain from:

(1) knowingly permitting any *new* resident (ie a person not living in the premises immediately before the notice was served) to occupy a room as sleeping accommodation otherwise than in accordance with the notice, or

(2) knowingly permitting a new resident to occupy part of the premises for sleeping if that is not possible without persons of opposite sexes, and not living as man and wife, sleeping in the same room.

Not less than seven days before serving notice, under section 358(2), the authority must:

(1) inform the occupier of the premises, and any person appearing to exercise management, in writing of their intention to serve the notice, and

(2) ensure, so far as reasonably possible, that every other person living in the house is informed of their intention.

Those informed must be given an opportunity of making representations regarding this proposal. A person aggrieved by such an 'overcrowding notice' may, under section 362, appeal to the county court within 21 days of service. The court may confirm, quash or vary the order. Once an order is in force it is an offence to contravene it.

A notice may, under section 363, be revoked or varied at any time by the authority on the application of any person having an estate or interest in the house. If they refuse, or fail to notify the applicant of their decision, the applicant may appeal to the county court.

During the currency of overcrowding notices, under section 364, authorities may give notice requiring occupiers to furnish them with written particulars as to:
(1) numbers of individuals on specified dates using the premises as sleeping accommodation;
(2) numbers of families or households to whom the individuals belong;
(3) their names, and the names of heads of families and households;
(4) rooms used by those individuals and families or households respectively.

It is an offence to fail to supply such particulars or to file a false return. Even so it appears hard to amass evidence to bring a successful prosecution for 'Part XI overcrowding'. Furthermore the provisions grant only powers, and there is an element of subjectivity in their application.

General supplementary powers

Authorities have a number of supplementary powers to assist in the exercise of multi-occupation functions. Under the Housing Act 1985, section 395(1) an authorised officer may enter any house, after giving 24 hours' notice in writing of his intention to both occupier and owner, if the latter is known, in order to determine whether multi-occupation powers should be exercised. By virtue of section 356 at any time after a section 354 direction is in force an authority may serve further notice on the occupier of the house requiring a written statement of:
(1) numbers of individuals living in the house (or part of it) on a specified date;
(2) numbers of families or households to which those individuals belong;
(3) names of individuals, and of heads of families or households, and
(4) rooms used by those individuals and families or households respectively.
Failure to reply, or making a false reply, is an offence.

The Housing Act 1985, section 395(2) empowers authorities to enter houses to ascertain whether there has been contravention of any regulation or direction made under sections 348G (registration schemes), 355 (direction limiting number of occupants), 358 (overcrowding notices), 368 (contravening undertakings), 369 (contravention of management code), 376 (failure to comply with notices by not executing works) of the Act, and in such a case notice need not be given in advance.

Control orders

To deal with HMOs in the worst condition authorities may make 'control orders' allowing them to take over management for up to five years and act as if they were the owners. It is a proper use of this power to make an order to ensure continuance in use and operation of a house, see *R v Southwark London Borough Council, ex p Lewis Levy Ltd*[19]. An order allows an authority to take the necessary steps (other than sale) to bring a property up to a satisfactory standard.

Under section 379 of the 1985 Act an order can be made if:
(1) a notice has been served under sections 352 or 372 (execution of works) or if a direction has been given under section 354 (limits on numbers of occupants); *or*
(2) it appears to the authority that the state or condition of the house is such as to call for taking any such action, *and*
(3) it also appears that the state of the house is such that it is necessary to make a control order to protect the safety, welfare or health of persons living therein.

Control orders are designed to deal with the most squalid and dangerous conditions and while there is no lengthy legal procedure as to their making much staff time and effort may be consumed. An order comes into force when made (section 379(2)) and as soon as practicable thereafter the authority must enter the premises and take such immediate steps as are necessary to protect residents' health, welfare and safety. A copy of the order has to be posted in the house where it is accessible to residents. Copies must also be served on every person who, before the order, was the manager of the house, or had control of it, or was an owner, lessee or mortgagee. These copies must be accompanied by a notice setting out rights of appeal under section 384 of the 1985 Act (see below).

The effect of a control order

A control order transfers full possession and control of the house to the authority (see generally section 381) and cancels orders, notices or directions already made under the management provisions, but without prejudice to criminal liabilities incurred. It is possible to exclude from control, under section 380 of the Act, any part of the house occupied by an owner or tenant of the whole house. Such a part will be subject under section 387(3) to the authority's right of entry for purposes of survey etc. The authority may grant, under section 381(2), weekly or monthly tenancies within the property, but rights and obligations of existing residents are protected by section 382.

Section 385 then lays a double duty on the authority:
(1) to maintain proper standards of management and take any action necessary under the management provision of the Act, and
(2) to keep the house insured against fire.

19   (1983) 267 Estates Gazette 1041.

Thereafter section 386 requires them to prepare a scheme and to serve a copy on the dispossessed proprietor and on all other owners, lessees and mortgagees, not later than eight weeks from the making of the control order. The object of such an order is to ensure the property is in a proper condition to accommodate its occupants, not to ensure an increase in the amount or quality of the accommodation.[20]

The scheme must, under Schedule 13 Part I, provide for execution of, and payment for, works involving capital expenditure needed to satisfy statutory requirements. The scheme must state what the authority consider to be the highest number of individuals who should be allowed from time to time to reside in the house, and also an estimate of the balance of the moneys that will accrue to the authority in the form of rents, etc, from residents, after they have paid the dispossessed proprietor compensation (see below), and disbursed all other payments, other than those in respect of management powers under the Act, ie capital expenditure. Throughout the life of the control order the authority must also keep half yearly accounts under Schedule 13, para 4. They must balance capital expenditure against surplus balances (revenue) arising from the rents, etc, referred to above. The cost of expenditure constitutes a charge on the premises.

During the currency of a control order section 389 of the 1985 Act requires the authority to pay the dispossessed proprietor (ie the person otherwise entitled to rents from the property) compensation at an annual rate of one half of the rental value of the house, ie the amount the house might reasonably be expected to fetch if let, see Schedule 13 of the 1985 Act as amended.

Appeals and compulsory purchase of HMOs

Any person having an estate or interest in the house, or otherwise prejudiced by a control order, may appeal to the county court under section 384. A similar right exists under Schedule 13 against the authority's scheme. The period for appeal runs out six weeks after a copy of the scheme has been served.

Control orders expire after five years, unless they are revoked earlier by the authority; Housing Act 1985, section 392. A person may apply, with reasons, for early revocation. If this application is rejected, or ignored for six weeks, he/she may appeal to the county court for revocation of the order. An unsuccessful appeal generally precludes further applications for a period of six months: see section 393.

---

20 *Orakpo v London Borough of Wandsworth and Secretary of State for the Environment* (1990) 24 HLR 370.

An authority has power under section 17 and Schedule 13 Part IV of the 1985 Act to make a compulsory purchase (CPO) on a property subject to a control order. Where they make the CPO within 28 days of making the control order they need not prepare or serve a management scheme until after the decision of the Secretary of State to reject or confirm the CPO. Provision is made for satisfaction of the financial obligations of both authority and owner: the latter is to receive any surplus revenue balance in the hands of the authority; they may recover their capital expenditure on necessary works from revenue balances derived from rents received from the house or from the compulsory purchase compensation. A CPO is a last resort measure, generally only authorised where an authority proposes to transfer the property on or after improvement to an acceptable manager such as an association, see also DoE Circulars 6/85, 3/89 and 12/93. A CPO may not be used merely to punish a landlord, but is to be used where it is clearly improbable a landlord will be able to do required works, see *Bell v Secretary of State for the Environment*[1] and *Riddle v Secretary of State for the Environment*[2]. A CPO may be made even after a lapse of time from obtaining a control order provided the authority can show that despite the landlord being given repeated opportunities to do remedial works these have been ignored, see *Orakpo v Wandsworth London Borough Council*[3].

Further general guidance on the use of control orders is given by both DoE Circular 12/93 and the 1992 Management Guide. Where possible preliminary studies should be undertaken to assess the effects of making an order, but where action is needed in a hurry, however, streamlined procedures and detailed coordination of steps within authorities are essential. Once an order is in place there must be an appropriate management structure for the house, and a properly thought through and costed strategy for its improvement in which the authority may wish to involve a local housing association as a manager. The need for procedural correctness was stressed by the Court of Appeal in *Webb v Ipswich Borough Council*[4] where, despite shortcomings, a landlord was able to upset a control order on appeal by showing that officers had not followed their authority's procedure before serving the order.

HMOs: The future?

Section 73 of the Housing Act 1996 introduced a new provision into those on Multiple Occupation in the 1985 Act.

1   [1989] 1 EGLR 27.
2   [1988] 2 EGLR 17, CA.
3   (1990) 24 HLR 370, CA.
4   (1989) 21 HLR 325, CA.

Section 353A would create a new duty imposed on the persons having control of HMOs and their managers to keep premises fit for the number of their occupants so that action under section 352 is not needed, and if this duty is broken any tenant in the HMO or any other person who suffers loss, damage or personal injury would be able to sue the person in breach. It would also be an offence to fail to comply with the duty: see section 353A(2), (3). An example of such a situation might be a badly maintained flight of stairs in a HMO whose condition would entitle the local authority to serve a section 352 notice, so that an injured person could regain damages and a prosecution could also be mounted. But how easy would it be to adduce evidence to support such action – how often would inspection of HMOs take place to ensure repair, etc, duties are being complied with? It has always been uncertain when this section would be commenced, and at the time of writing this work it appears this provision will not be brought into effect. This is largely attributable to problems in connection with section 395A, also introduced in 1996.

Section 395A would allow the Secretary of State to approve codes of practice with regard to the regulation of HMOs. Breach of such a code would give rise to no civil/criminal liability, but would be admissible in evidence in civil or criminal proceedings. Work on a code of practice on HMO standards was in hand for some time, and approval of the code would have enabled the Secretary of State to commence the new 'duty' provisions laid on landlords.

The provisions relating to the code were due to be in place by mid 1998, according to the DETR's late 1997 plans. A draft was out for consultation in late 1997 with a view to its finalisation by the middle of 1998. The duty on landlords under section 353A was then to be commenced in 1999/2000. It then transpired, however, that the DETR considered the scheme 'unworkable'; so where did we go from there?

There is arguably some political controversy here between the DETR and the Home Office. The main problem with HMOs remains the fire safety issue. There are those in the Fire Service and the Home Office who argue regulation of HMOs should be taken out of local housing control altogether and become a matter of fire safety and risk assessment under a new Fire Precautions Act (FPA). The logical corollary of this is that *all* residential premises irrespective of occupancy status should be subject to such controls (domestic properties are currently outside FPA regulation). However, all new homes have to have smoke detectors under the Building Regulations so that pass is already partly sold.

Would the DETR give up its powers over HMOs? One way forward would be to modify the existing consultative duties of local housing authorities with regard to HMOs, so that not only do they have to consult with fire authorities, they would also have to *comply* with fire authority wishes. This would be in line with Scotland where Local Environmental Health Authorities are the 'lead' bodies re HMOs, but all HMO inspections are carried out by fire authorities who are then in a position to secure compliance with their wishes. However, would fire authorities take proper account of housing needs?

The long term

The DETR proposed to consult in 1997/98 on a compulsory licensing scheme of HMOs and their landlords and managers with new legislation before Parliament in 1998/99, and the whole scheme in place by 2001/2002. This timetable cannot now be met, but the DETR did launch a consultation scheme in March 1999 on the licensing of HMOs with the promise of a further exercise on risk-based HMO standards to follow.

The essence of the 1999 consultation proposals was as follows.

• There should be a duty on persons managing or controlling a HMO to ensure that it is licensed, *and* that there is a nominated person resident in the UK responsible for ensuring compliance with licence conditions; these persons should ensure the licensee has sufficient resources to carry out his/her duties.

• There should be a power in the licensing authority to refuse a licence if the licensee or the person managing, or the person having control are not considered 'fit and proper'.

• HMOs should be broadly defined as houses occupied by members of more than two *families* (ie related persons – this would catch student houses), but there should be exemptions – eg those subject to alternative regulatory regimes; houses converted into self-contained flats let on long leases; those occupied by the freeholder/long leaseholder who has his/her only or principal home there, and which are occupied only by not more than two persons in addition to the owner-occupier's family; those occupied or managed by local housing authorities.

• Licences should specify a maximum number of occupants for a house to reflect its condition and the standard of management, with an alternative power to refuse a licence unless particular parts of a house are not used – eg attic bedrooms with no fire escapes.

• The term 'fit and proper person' could be defined instead of being left as at present to local authority discretion, but it is not yet clear whether this would be done by legislation or by guidance, or what the criteria for 'fitness' would be. Certain criminal offences involving fraud or violence or breaches of housing or health and safety law would disqualify a person.

• Authorities should have 'special control' powers to refuse or revoke licences on the basis that an HMO has or would have a detrimental affect on an area, but, as under the current law, this would be subject to ministerial consent.

- It might be possible to allow applicants for licences to provide a certain amount of information about their premises on a self-certification basis so that an initial assessment could be carried out, thus removing the need for inspection of all premises before a licence is granted.
- Where premises have been registered under a control scheme and meet its standards, they should be deemed to be licensed for the rest of the registration period.
- Failure to meet licence standards should result in revocation of the licence, with the local authority being empowered to ensure acceptable standards in the house while the number of the residents are reduced. Where it is necessary to close a HMO immediately following its unlicensing the local authority should have a duty to rehouse residents, or to acquire and manage the house as with current control order powers, or a reputable registered social landlord could be given control of the property.
- It is open to argument that a person who loses a licence on the basis of not being fit or proper should be open to blanket disqualification by a court either for a specified period or indefinitely.
- A hefty level of fine is needed to ensure persons do not own unlicensed HMOs.
- Failure to comply with licence conditions could be an offence in its own right, as could making false statements in support of a licence application.
- An appeal system against refusal/revocation of licences is needed; this could be the existing county court appeal, or a newer cheaper system depending on a specialist tribunal. In general a licence should continue in force pending an appeal, but subject to immediate revocation where there is a risk to health and safety.
- Licences should be make periodically renewable, and could also be made issuable for varying periods of time.
- Provision needs to be made for specific types of property where the local authority should be the fire authority, and clear and unambiguous demarcation of responsibility is needed.
- As a condition of getting a licence written evidence of gas safety checks of all relevant appliances would be needed – evidence might also be required of continuing safety checks as a condition of a licence.
- Fees for licensing could be charged.

New primary legislation would be needed to bring in such a scheme, and no undertaking was given in 1999 as to when a Bill could be introduced. Further legislation is envisaged with regard to detailed standards on fire safety, health and safety and the provision of amenities and facilities in HMOs. The current legislation reflects conditions and aspirations prevalent many years ago when it was drafted – it must be remembered that the 1985 Act only consolidates material dating from many years before then – and, long term, the government wish to repeal *and* replace all the current Part XI of the 1985 Act. There would then be a new general duty on HMO landlords to ensure the health and safety of their tenants.

Interim reform

As an interim measure the DETR sent a *letter* to local housing authorities on 9 June 1999 which gave supplementary guidance on HMO standards.

- Health and Safety standards should be goal based and related to risk, and thus an element of flexibility is desirable to allow alternative solutions to problems to be put forward, provided these achieve the goal set.
- DoE Circular 12/92 should not be treated as a set of prescriptive rules, rather authorities should take account of all relevant factors concerning the health, safety and welfare of HMO residents when exercising their powers, and should examine all available options to eliminate or reduce risk considering the cost and practicability of those options. Benefits to be gained by way of risk reduction or improvements in living conditions should be balanced against their cost to landlords.
- Requirements for HMOs should be set on the basis of reasonably foreseeable occupancy factors – eg higher standards are appropriate in premises to be used as a hostel for vulnerable persons.
- Authorities should consider lenient timescales for requiring the carrying out of less pressing improvements and should require immediate action in relation to those matters where health and safety are at risk.
- The removal of certain types of furniture – eg that which is foam filled – can reduce fire risks, but such a removal does not fall within the concept of 'works' for the purposes of section 352 of the 1985 Act. Removal may, however, be required under the terms of a registration scheme, and the DETR model scheme makes provision for this.
- Fire safety requirements should be based on risk assessments, which take account of the building and its condition, its layout, the number and type of occupants, and standard of management, with mains powered smoke alarms being required as a minimum.
- Where a HMO is found on inspection to be in breach of gas safety legislation, this should be immediately reported to the Health and Safety Executive. Furthermore registration schemes can contain powers for authorities to insist on seeing current gas safety certificates before a house can be registered.

Multi-occupation and the powers of fire authorities

Section 10(1) of the Fire Precautions Act 1971 (as substituted) applies, inter alia, to any premises which are being, or are proposed to be, put to use to provide sleeping accommodation other than single private dwellings. With regard to such premises where the fire authority consider use of the premises involves, or will involve, a risk to persons so serious that their use ought to be restricted or prohibited, they may serve on the occupier a prohibition notice stating and specifying the issues, and giving directions as to the use of the premises until remedial measures are taken. In the case of imminent risk of serious personal injury a prohibition may take immediate effect. It is an offence under section 10B of the 1971 Act to contravene a prohibition notice, though section 10A allows an appeal to the magistrates' court within 21 days of service of the notice. The court may cancel, affirm or modify the notice. This statutory mode of appeal, it appears, is a preclusive mode of challenge, even where it is alleged the premises do not fall within the fire authority's jurisdiction, see *R v Chesterfield Justices, ex p Kovacs*[5].

The powers of fire authorities with regard to multi-occupied premises are extensive. It should be a matter of good practice for housing and fire authorities to work together in an integrated and co-ordinated way to ensure premises are not made subject to conflicting sets of requirements. Over zealous use of fire control powers may result in premises being closed with their occupants, only some of whom may qualify as 'homeless', displaced to the streets. On the other hand protection of human life demands vigilance from fire authorities for it appears it is not negligent for a housing authority not to have a system of pre-inspection of multi-occupied properties to which *non-priority* homeless persons may be referred, see *Ephraim v London Borough of Newham*[6]. Much depends upon the attitude of individual fire prevention officers and the nature and quality of relationships between authorities and their officers. (Cross reference should also be made to the grant aiding powers of authorities concerning HMOs in Chapter Seven. Concern has been expressed that reductions in grant aid may especially prejudice implementation of fire precaution measures in HMOs.) For landlords' duties in respect of gas appliances see the Gas Safety (Installation and Use) Regulations 1994, SI 1994/1886, as amended by SI 1996/550 and SI 1996/2541. Note also that a landlord who fails to maintain gas appliances as a result of his gross negligence may additionally run the risk of a conviction for manslaughter should a tenant die of certain monoxide poisoning.[7]

5   [1992] 2 All ER 325.
6   (1992) 25 HLR 207, HL.
7   *R v Singh (Gurphal)* [1999] Crim LR 582, CA.

Overcrowding

Local authority powers with regard to overcrowding are found in Part X of the 1985 Act. This is derived from older legislation, and standards are open to criticism as out of date. Under sections 324 and 343 of the Act overcrowding powers apply in relation to 'dwellings' ie premises used or suitable for use as a separate dwelling. This would seem apt to include caravans, see *DPP v Carrick District Council*[8].

Overcrowding appears now to be largely a problem of the past. The preliminary results of the 1997/98 Survey of English Housing released by the DETR early in 1999 argued that taking as the 'best measure' the 'bedroom standard', ie the difference between the number of *bedrooms* needed to avoid undesirable sharing and the number of bedrooms a household actually has, only 2% of households are now overcrowded. Overcrowding is, moreover, largely concentrated in the council sector with 5% of households being overcrowded.

The legal definition of overcrowding

A dwelling is overcrowded when the number of persons sleeping in it contravenes *either* section 325 (room standard) or section 326 (space standard). Under the former, contravention occurs when the number of persons sleeping in a dwelling and the number of rooms available for sleeping is such that two persons of opposite sexes, not living together as man and wife, must sleep in the same room. Children under ten are left out of account in the calculation, and rooms are available for sleeping if they are locally used *either* as bedrooms or living rooms, see section 326(2)(b). Under the latter standard contravention occurs when numbers sleeping in a dwelling exceed the permitted number having regard to numbers and floor areas of rooms in the dwelling available for sleeping. The permitted number for a dwelling is whichever is the *lesser* of *either* the number specified in Table I below, or the aggregate for all rooms available for sleeping in the dwelling of numbers of persons specified in Table II in relation to each room of the floor area specified in that table.

Table I

Number of rooms	Number of persons
1	2.0
2	3.0
3	5.0
4	7.5
5 or more	2 for each room

8   January 1985, unreported, Truro Magistrates Court, 'Housing Aid'.

Table II

Floor area of room	Number of persons
110 square feet or more	2.0
90 – 100 square feet	1.5
79 – 90 square feet	1.0
50 – 70 square feet	0.5
Under 50 square feet	NIL

A child under one and a half years is not reckoned in these calculations, and a child between one and a half and ten counts as half a unit.

All persons who use the house as their home should be counted when deciding whether there is overcrowding, not just those sleeping there at any given time, otherwise the law could be ignored by persons sleeping on a shift basis. In *Zaitzeff v Olmi*[9] a daughter at a boarding school was held to be living at home for the purposes of the permitted number standard.

Section 330 of the Act permits authorities to license occupiers to exceed the permitted number standard, but only up to numbers specified and only for periods of up to 12 months. Within that period the licence may be revoked by the authority giving the occupier one month's notice. Licences may be granted to take account of seasonal increases of population in a district, for example to allow for the accommodation of migratory agricultural workers, or in other 'exceptional circumstances' – an otherwise undefined phrase.

Offences

These are principally defined by sections 327 and 331 of the 1985 Act and can be committed by the occupier of a dwelling-house and by the landlord where the property is let. The occupier who causes or permits overcrowding commits a summary offence save where acting under licence granted under section 330 (see above), or where the case falls within either section 328 or 329. Under the former where a dwelling becomes overcrowded solely by virtue of a child attaining the age of ten, then the occupier commits no offence *provided* he/she applies, or has so applied before the relevant birthday, to the housing authority for suitable alternative accommodation, *and provided that all persons* sleeping in the dwelling are those who were living there when the child reached the relevant age and who live there continuously afterwards, or are children of those persons. The exemption ceases to apply if either suitable alternative accommodation is offered to the occupier and he/she fails to accept it or otherwise fails to take reasonable steps to secure the removal of persons not members of the family from the house. A mere visit by a member of the occupier's family who normally lives

9   (1952) 160 Estates Gazette 154 (county court).

elsewhere which causes temporary overcrowding is not an offence, see section 329.

Section 342 of the Act defines 'suitable alternative accommodation' as a dwelling-house where the following conditions are satisfied:
(1) the house must be one where the occupier (and family) can live without causing it to be overcrowded;
(2) the authority must certify the house to be suitable to the needs of the occupier (and family) as respects security of tenure, proximity to place of work and otherwise, and in relation to the occupier's means; and
(3) where the dwelling is a local authority house, it is certified as suitable to the needs of the occupier and his family, with a two bedroom dwelling providing accommodation for four people, three bedrooms accommodating five people and four bedrooms seven people.

Landlords commit offences under section 331 and are deemed to have caused or permitted overcrowding if:
(1) after receiving notice from the local authority that a house is overcrowded they fail to take reasonable steps to abate the overcrowding, or
(2) the house was let with the landlord having reasonable cause to believe that it would become overcrowded.

To aid landlords section 101 of the Rent Act 1977 takes away security of tenure in a house which is so overcrowded that the occupier is guilty of an offence, while authorities themselves may take possession proceedings under section 338 of the 1985 Act. Note there is no equivalent provision to section 101 in respect of assured tenancies under the Housing Act 1988.

Landlords are under a duty, see section 333 of the Housing Act 1985, to inform authorities within seven days of overcrowding within any of their houses that has come to their knowledge.

In order to inform occupiers of their rights, section 332 of the 1985 Act requires that a summary of Part X of the Act shall be contained in any rent book or similar document given to the tenant, together with a statement of the permitted number of persons in relation to the house. Authorities are under an obligation to inform either occupiers or landlords if any apply, of permitted numbers of persons in relation to relevant houses.

Enforcement and remedial powers and duties of local authorities

The Housing Act 1985, section 339 makes it the duty of authorities to enforce the overcrowding provisions, and only they may prosecute. Where an authority is responsible for overcrowding they can be prosecuted only with the consent of the Attorney-General. An authority may serve notice on an occupier requiring, within 14 days, a written statement of the number, ages and sexes of the persons sleeping in the house. Failing to comply with this request or deliberately making a false return is an offence, see section 335 of the 1985 Act.

Authorities are also under a general duty under section 334 of the 1985 Act to investigate overcrowding of which they become aware, to make a report to the Secretary of State of findings, and the number of new houses needed to relieve overcrowding. The Secretary of State may direct an authority to make such an investigation and report.

Further reading

Blake, J 'Safe as Houses?' *Roof* January/February 1995, pp 34–35

Department of the Environment *The HMO Management Guide* DoE (1992)

Grosskurth, A 'Lives on the line' *Roof* November/December 1984, pp 11–14

Kirby, K, and Sopp, L *Houses in Multiple Occupation in England and Wales* (HMSO, 1986)

National Consumer Council *Deathtrap Housing* (NCC, 1991)

Randall, G, Brown, S and Piper, J *Houses in Multiple Occupation, Policy and Practice in the 1990s* The Campaign for Bed Sit Rights, 1993

Thomas, A D and Hedges, A *The 1985 Physical and Social Survey of Houses in Multiple Occupation in England and Wales* (HMSO, 1986)

Department of the Environment, Transport and the Regions *Fire Risk in Houses in Multiple Occupation: Research Report* (HMSO, 1998)

Department of the Environment, Transport and the Regions *English House Condition Survey 1996: Houses in Multiple Occupation in the Private Rented Sector* (HMSO, 1999)

Index

Anti-social behaviour order
application for, 247
housing authority obtaining, 157,
158
Arbitration
landlord-tenant disputes, of, 190
Assignment
secure tenants, by, 158, 159
Assured shorthold tenancy
Codes of Practice, 175, 176
meaning, 175
new association tenants, regime for,
186
new investment, failure to induce,
46, 47
new tenancies automatically being,
175
rent provisions, 232
security of tenure, 184, 185
Assured tenancy
break-up of marriage, transfer on,
248-252
Codes of Practice, 175, 176
excepted classes, 174, 175
fixed term, termination of, 176,
177
meaning, 174
new association tenants, regime for,
185-187
new investment, failure to induce,
46, 47

Assured tenancy—*contd*
periodic, termination of, 176
property, as, 266
rent provisions, 229-232
residence requirement, 174
right to acquire, 68, 69
security of tenure, 176
separate dwelling, of, 174
succession to, 273
Asylum seekers
accommodation, provision of, 292-
294

Back-to-backs
meaning, 9
Betterment levy
abolition, 28
Business Expansion Scheme
housing, tax relief for, 47

City of London Common Council
housing functions, 57
Clearance area
compulsory purchase in, 382, 383
declaration of, 381
demolition of buildings in, 384
disturbance payments, 383
home loss payments, 382
procedure-
availability of, 380
modification, 380

Clearance area—*contd*
procedure—*contd*
representations, 380, 381
use of, 383
purchase and clearance of land, 382
relocation grants, 381
unfit building not included in, 381
Closing order
acquisition of building otherwise
subject to, 376
appeal against, 374
charges, 379
compensation, payment of, 375
power to make, 373
service of, 374
Compulsory competitive tendering
defined activities, 164
end of, 164
extension of, 49
housing management, 164, 165
introduction of, 164
Compulsory purchase
displaced residents, rehousing, 419,
420
house in multiple occupation, 454
renewal areas, in, 392
statutory provisions, 60
Council housing
abolition of subsidies, 24
allocation-
additional preference, 122-3, 316
appeals from decisions, 124
disability discrimination, 112,
113
duties of authorities, 114
general duties, 114
housing register, 118-121
judicial review of decisions, 106
new principles of, 108
obligations of authorities, 114,
115
persons already tenants, to, 124
political, 107
priorities, 114, 124
qualifying persons, 115-118
racial and sexual discrimination,
109-112
reasonable preference, 122-3, 316
reasonable, to be, 107
reform, 108
scheme. *See* allocation scheme,
below
statutory provisions, 106

Council housing—*contd*
allocation—*contd*
statutory rules, 113-121
waiting list, through, 108
allocation scheme-
additional preference, persons
having, 122, 123, 316
administration of, 124
combined, 123
consultation, 124
date order, 123
points, 123, 124
publication, 121
reasonable preference, persons
having, 122, 123, 316
requirement to have, 121
types of, 123, 124
authority to build, 2
building, 12, 13
building after 1964 election, 33
building standards, 33
capital receipts, release of, 52
capital spend, cutting, 44, 45
Conservative pledges, 28
decline in building, 28
demunicipalisation, 45
Design Manual, 20
economic crisis, effect of, 33
failure of private housing, filling gap
left by, 10
first Labour Government, under, 20-
22
high-rise flats, 29, 30, 34, 35
housing association properties,
proportion in relation to, 3
inter-war period, in, 19, 20
Labour Government of 1945, under,
27, 28
Labour manifesto, 1964, 32
Labour view of, 37
mass, beginning of, 18
National Housing Plan, 33
necessity, acceptance from, 19
new crisis in, 31
occupants of, 2
origins of-
Addison Act, 6
public health, 6-10
payment for, 18
peak of, 5
poor, for, 22, 23
poorest households, occupation by,
44

Council housing—*contd*
post World War 1, 16-20
post World War 2, 26
private builders, subordinate role to,
    20
provision, social purpose of, 54
qualifying persons-
    examples, 117
    exclusion policies, 117, 118
    habitual residence, 116
    homeless, 116
    housing register, 118-121
    immigration control, exclusion
        of people subject to, 115
    initial exclusion, 115-117
    meaning, 115
    regulations, 115
    restrictions, imposition of, 117
quantity of, 14
re-lets, 2, 44
reduction in, 2
sale of, 42, 67-70. *See also* RIGHT TO
    BUY
statutory provisions, 2
stock of, 2
stock transfer, 50
Thatcher years, in, 41-45
Wheatley's view of, 20, 21
County council
housing functions, 57

Defective premises
inspection and repair, facilities for,
    344, 345
liability for, 342-346
notice of defects, 345
obligation to repair, 344
omission, liability for, 343
relevant defect, meaning, 344
tenancy, meaning, 345
Demolition order
acquisition of building otherwise
    subject to, 376
appeal against, 374
charges, 379
compensation, payment of, 375
possession of premises, obtaining,
    374, 375
power to make, 374
reconstruction of premises, 375
service of, 374
sitting tenant, failure to serve
    notice on, 375

Demolition order—*contd*
vermin, cleansing premises of, 375
Development
multi-occupation, 426-429
Disability discrimination
housing allocation, in, 112, 113
District councils
housing functions, 57
Domestic violence
associated persons, rights and
    remedies of, 246
Family Law Act 1996, provisions
    of, 245, 246
ground for possession, as, 259, 260
homelessness, as factor in, 284,
    285, 306
jurisdiction, 247
meaning, 244
non-molestation orders, 26, 247
refuges, 244
regulation, authorities taking pro-
    active role, 263
statutory provisions, 245
tangle of remedies, 247, 248
transfer of tenancies, 246
unmarried persons, remedies for,
    245

Eviction
summary, 16

Flats
definition, 70
equivalent of house, where treated
    as, 57
fitness requirements, 363
high-rise, 29, 30, 34, 35
long lease, right to buy, 70. *See also*
    RIGHT TO BUY
reconstruction of premises as, 56
unfit, action relating to, 368, 369

General Improvement Area
abolition, 390
introduction of, 35, 390
Germany
private sector housing, 15
trade unions, 15

Harassment
protection from, 247
Homeless persons. *See also*
    HOMELESSNESS

Homeless persons—*contd*
accommodation-
    adults under disability,
        application by, 289
    application for, 286, 288, 289
    child, application by, 289
    children in need, for, 332-334
    domestic violence, risk of, 284,
        285
    location and quality, factors of,
        284
    none, determining, 285, 286
    offer of, 320, 322
    other suitable, availability of,
        315
    permanence, lack of, 320
    reasonableness of, 283, 284
    refusal of, 293
    right to, ending, 328
    room, offer of, 285
    suitability, 318-322
    treatment as having, 283
classes of, 285
council accommodation, route into,
    281
council housing, qualification for,
    116, 123
decisions, challenging-
    breach of statutory duty, 331
    courts, recourse to, 330
    informal, 324
    internal review, 324
    judicial review, 328-332
    statutory review, 324-332
dependent children, with, 296-298
deserving, duty to house, 38
disintegration of relationship, effect
    of, 263, 264
duties owed to, 298
    cessation of, 313, 314
    discharge of, 316, 317
    duration of, 312
    limited nature of, 312, 314
    modification, 316
    nature of, 312
    other suitable accommodation,
        availability of, 315
    stages, discharge in, 320
    temporary accommodation, 313
    threatened homelessness, on,
        314, 315
eligibility for assistance-
    asylum seekers, position of,
        292-294

Homeless persons—*contd*
eligibility for assistance—*contd*
    classes of, 290-292
    definition, 290
    immigration control, persons
        subject to, 290, 294
historical context, 276-278
increase in, 32, 38
law, in, 283-286
local authority-
    accommodation outside district,
        securing, 317, 318
    discharge of duties, 316, 317
    duties of. *See* duties owed to,
        above
    housing functions, 316, 317
    initial contact with, 286-288
    inquiries by, 286-288
    interim duty to accommodate,
        294, 295
    notice of decision, 288
    notification, duties of, 322, 323
    obligation to provide
        accommodation, 293
    officers of, 286
    post-initial application inquiries,
        289
    private landlords, arrangements
        with, 318
location of, 279
offences, 323
official statistics, 279-281
overlapping jurisdictions, 278
pregnant, 296
priority need, 295-298
property of, protection, 323
registered social landlord, tenancy
    granted by, 318
responsibility for, 277
security of tenure, lacking, 285
statutory provisions, 278
statutory review of decisions-
    grounds, 326
    irregularity in initial decision,
        meaning, 326, 327
    notifications, 324, 325
    point of law, appeal on, 327-
        329
    procedures, 325
    representations, 326
    request for, 325, 326
    statement of reasons, 327
temporary accommodation,
    provision of, 277

Homeless persons—*contd*
varying policy stance on, 279
vulnerable, 297
Homelessness. *See also* HOMELESS
   PERSONS
acceptances-
  declining number of, 280
  number of, 279
actual or threatened, 283
advice and assistance, availability
  of, 282
assessment of law, 334, 335
Code of Guidance, 281, 282
court decisions on, 330
criteria for determining
  reasonableness of
  accommodation, 283, 284
current position, 280
housing problem, recognition as,
  276
intentional-
  accommodation abroad, giving
    up, 307
  act or omission, acquiescence in,
    300
  causation, 304, 305
  consequence of act or omission
    in question, as, 303, 304
  continuing occupation,
    reasonableness of, 305-9
  deemed, 299, 300
  definition, 298
  deliberate act or omission, 301,
    302
  domestic violence, fleeing from,
    306
  effect on duty to accommodate,
    298
  failure to pay rent, on, 301
  finding, effect of, 307, 308
  good faith, act or omission in,
    302, 303
  inquiries as to, 299
  Northern Ireland, fleeing from,
    307
  relevant matters, 299
  repeated applications, 308
  sexual harassment, fleeing from,
    307
law on, 281-283
legal concept, as, 283
legal nature of, 279
local connection, referral to area
  having, 309-311

Homelessness—*contd*
preventive measures, 282
rise in, 280
shortage of housing, problem of,
  335
threat of, duties on, 314, 315
Hostel
definition, 60
multiple occupation. *See* HOUSE IN
  MULTIPLE OCCUPATION
occupation, nature of, 102
House
premises being, determining, 56
House in multiple occupation
administrative expenses, charges
  for, 444
authorities having control of, 455
authorities, powers of, 451
compulsory licensing scheme,
  proposed, 456-458
compulsory purchase order, 454
control orders-
  appeals, 453, 454
  compulsory purchase order on
    property subject to, 454
  effect of, 452, 453
  expiry, 453
  power to make, 451, 452
  property, bringing up to
    standard, 452
  purpose of, 452
definition, 429-434
fire authorities, powers of, 458, 459
fire controls, 430
fire precautions, 442, 444, 446-449
fire risk, house presenting, 446-449
fire safety, 455
fitness of premises, standard of,
  442, 443
food preparation facilities, 443
grants, 398
groups of premises, 433, 434
house, meaning, 429, 430
household, meaning, 430-432, 434
housing legislation, 429
interim reform, 458
legal and administrative views of,
  433
management regulations, 439, 440
number of occupants, power to
  limit, 445, 446
occupants, safeguarding, 429
overcrowding, prevention of, 450,
  451

House in multiple occupation—*contd*
persons in control, duties of, 455
planning control, supervision by,
    426-429
policy-
    documents, 424
    drawing up, 424, 425
    first steps, 424
    housing and planning, 428
    implementing, 425, 426
    issues, 425
registration-
    refusal of application, 435
    revocation, 436, 438
    voluntary nature of, 438
registration schemes-
    control conditions, 435, 437,
        438
    critique, 436
    model, 435
    notice of intention to make,
        438
    special conditions, 435, 437,
        438
regulation, codes of practice, 455
sanitary facilities, 443, 444
surveys, 423
two or more households, division
    between, 431
types of premises, 432, 433
works-
    power to require, 440, 441
    required to render premises fit
        for number of occupants,
        441-444
Housing Action Areas
abolition, 390
introduction of, 35, 390
Housing Action Trusts
consultations, 96
creation of, 97
designation of areas, 96
disposal powers, 98
establishment of, 46, 47
introductory tenancy, power to
    grant, 127
objectives, 97
planning authority, as, 97
practice, in, 99
proposals, drawing up, 97
purpose of, 96
statutory provisions, 96
tenants, rights of, 98, 99

Housing Action Trusts—*contd*
transfer of housing and land to, 97
Housing Association Grant
calculation, 220
capital programme, 220
capital regime, 1988, 221-223
introduction of, 40, 41
pre-1989 system, 220
replacement of, 48
**Housing Association Tenants
    Ombudsman Service**
determination of investigations,
    196-198
proposals for, 195
Housing associations
assured tenancy regime, 185-187
auditing and performance
    monitoring, 41
charitable status, 61, 62
council properties, sale of to, 3
definition, 61
fully mutual, 62
funding, allocation of, 48
funding regime, 3
independent rented sector, in, 220
judicial review, not subject to, 61
loans for, 32
market forces, exposure to, 48
mergers and transfers, 3
National Federation, 59
number of, 48
number of properties, 3
private renting, as alternative to, 37
provision of housing by, 59
registered social landlords,
    becoming, 1
rise of, 40, 41
rules, 62
status, 61
succession to tenancies of, 273, 274
tenure of dwellings, 173
Housing Corporation
acquisition of land by, 60
disposal of land by, 60
dwellings or hostels, provision and
    improvement of, 60
function of, 32
general regulatory powers, 65-67
grants by, 223, 224
housing management, issue of
    guidance on, 65, 66
information, disclosure of, 65
lending, power of, 59, 60

Housing Corporation—*contd*
objects of, 189
operating procedures, revision of, 188
powers and resources, 40
registered bodies, grading, 188
registered social landlords-
accounts, audit, 188, 189
mismanagement or misconduct, transfer on, 189
regulation of. *See* REGISTERED SOCIAL LANDLORDS
regulatory powers, 187-190
restructuring, 220
social housing grants, power to give, 64, 65
statutory provisions, 59
Housing finance
change in, 204
current expenditure-
HRA subsidy, 211
main items, 210
new regime, 209, 211
notional HRA, 209, 210
sources of income, 210
system in 1980s, 209-211
house building, capital controls over, 208, 209
legislation, 39
local authority capital spending-
allocation, 205
capital receipts, use of, 205, 206
existing housing, renovation and rehabilitation of, 204
financing, 206
housing improvement, for, 205
meaning, 204
new regime, 207, 208
proportion of, 206
top-slicing, 205
problem of, 12, 35
review of, 35
Thatcherite policy, 39
Housing for Wales
setting up, 220
transfer of functions, 59, 61
Housing management
best value consultation, 170
Best Value Performance Plans, 165, 166
compulsory competitive tendering, 164, 165
delegation of functions, 167

Housing management—*contd*
estate management committees, 163
inspection powers, 165, 166
meaning, 162
participation by secure tenants, 162-164
proactive tenant management, 167-170
registered social landlords, agreements with, 170
tenant participation compacts, 170-173
transfer arrangements, 167
Housing policy
change in direction, 34
Major Government, under, 48-51
national, 12
New Labour, under, 51-54
origins of-
issue of, 5
public health problems, dealing with, 7
regeneration, 48-51
rehabilitation, 34-36
Review Green Paper, 35, 36
right to buy, 43
Thatcherite, 39, 41-45
urban renewal, 50
Housing renewal. *See* RENEWAL AREAS
Housing Revenue Account
debits to, 212, 213
future changes, 214
government control over, 211
HORAS, determining, 213
housing stock, sums debited and credited for, 212
notional, 209, 210
rents and charges credited to, 212
requirement to maintain, 207
rules for keeping, 212
special cases, credits in, 213
subsidy, 211, 213
Housing rights
break-up of marriage, adjustment on, 248, 249
disintegration of relationship, on-
departmental boundaries, 262
disability, effect of, 266
diversity of practice on, 263, 264
domestic violence, on, 244-248
homelessness provisions, use of, 263, 264

Housing rights—*contd*
  disintegration of relationship, on—
      contd
    housing consequences, 261-266
    joint tenancy, issue of, 252-258
    legal action, requirement as pre-
        condition of obtaining
        tenancy, 263
    long term rights, 248-260
    one parent families, guidelines
        for, 261
    policies, need for, 265, 266
    rehousing following, 261
    statutory provisions, 243, 244
    transfer of tenancies, 246
    transfer orders, 249-252
    welfare and employment
        benefits, use of, 265
    women, position of, 262
  future of, 274
  joint tenancy, under, 235
  non domestic situations, in, 242,
      243
  relationships, within-
    English law, recognised by, 235
    general, 234
    legal framework, 234
    social developments, 234
  subsistence of relationship, during-
    cohabitant status, 237
    joint tenancy, 235
    matrimonial home rights, 236
    non-tenant spouses, of, 236
    occupation orders, 237-242. *See
        also* OCCUPATION ORDERS
    recognised relationships, 235
  succession. *See* SUCCESSION RIGHTS
Housing standards
  area improvement, 361
  contract, landlord's obligations in-
    common law, at, 346-348
    covenants, 346, 347
    disrepair, complaints of, 351
    fitness for human habitation,
        implied term of, 349, 350
    implied covenants, 351
    implied terms, 347, 348
    notice of defects, 349
    repairing covenants. *See*
        REPAIRING COVENANTS
    statute, under, 348-355
    structure and exterior of
        dwelling, keeping in
        repair, 350-355

Housing standards—*contd*
  contract, landlord's obligations in—
      contd
    tenants, obligations of, 354
    third party, position of, 346
  current law, 340
  enforcement powers,
      harmonisation, 389
  existing property, renovation of, 339
  fitness standard-
    check list, 363
    consultation paper, 388
    criteria, 363, 364
    dampness, 365
    energy efficiency, 386
    enforceability, 390
    future of, 386-390
    guidance on, 363-366
    infestation, effect of, 365
    interpretation of requirements,
        389
    part of building, for, 390
    rating system, 388, 389
    reports on, 362
    serious disrepair, 363-365
    unfitness, determining, 364
    use of powers, assessment,
        yearly review, 362
  historical context, 338-340
  Housing and Environmental
      Protection Acts, relationship
      between, 415
  improvement. *See* IMPROVEMENT
  liability for, 340
  public health codes, and, 406
  public health issues, 338
  renewal. *See* RENEWAL AREAS
  repairing covenants. *See* REPAIRING
      COVENANTS
  slum clearance. *See* SLUM CLEARANCE
  statutory nuisance. *See* STATUTORY
      NUISANCE
  sub-standard, public law remedies-
    area improvement, 361
    Code, 366-368
    courses of action, 365, 366
    economic factors, 366-368
    fitness requirements, 362-364
    individual houses, 368, 369
    issues, 367
    legal procedures, 370-390. *See
        also* UNFIT DWELLINGS
    Neighbourhood Renewal
        Assessment, 366, 367

Housing standards—*contd*
sub-standard, public law remedies—
contd
reports, 361
socio-environmental factors,
366-368
statutory provisions, 361
tenants' right to repair, 359, 360
tort, landlord's obligations in-
common law, at, 340-342
defective premises, for, 342-346
designer or builder of premises,
as, 341
negligence, in, 340-342
occupier's liability, 346
statute, under, 342-346
unfit dwellings. *See* UNFIT DWELLINGS

Housing subsidies
basis of calculation, changes to, 45
Conservatives, under, 38-40
debt burden, reduction of, 38
growth in, 40
post-World War I, 17
renewal areas, in, 393
return to private landlords,
encouraging, 17
size and standard, variation in, 22
sources of payment, amalgamation,
46
Thatcher years, in, 41-45
Thatcherite policy, 39
Wheatley, 20-23
withdrawal of, 18

Improvement
grant aid-
amount of, 399
carrying out of works, 403
common parts grants, 396
decisions on, 399, 400
disabled facilities grants, 396,
397
general conditions, 401-403
general restrictions on, 398
HMO grants, 398
means testing, 398, 399
occupancy conditions, 402
payment conditions, 400, 401
relevant and exempt disposals,
402
renovation grants, 394-396
repayment on disposal, 401, 402
statutory provisions, 393
types of, 394

Improvement—*contd*
group repair schemes, 403-405
home repair assistance, 405
powers, 361
secure tenants, by, 159-161

Injunction
acts or conduct, relating to, 154
area, for benefit of, 154
bad behaviour, restraining, 154
breach of tenancy conditions,
against, 152, 153
ignoring, contempt of court, 157
limitations on use of, 155
possession proceedings, combined
with, 153
power of arrest, 154-156
tenancy status, relevance of, 155,
156

Insanitary dwellings. *See also* UNFIT
DWELLINGS
power to close and demolish, 7, 8
unfitness, test of, 8

Introductory tenancy
adoption of, 130, 131
authorities having power to grant,
127
conditions for, 128
information, publication of, 130
legislation, 127
possession order, grant of, 129
security of tenure, 128, 129
succession to, 129, 130, 272
tenancy ceasing to be, 128
termination of, 127
value of, 131

Joint tenancy
break clauses, 254
deed of release, 259
disintegration of relationship, on,
252-258
long-term commitment, grant on,
271
notice to quit-
injunction against service of, 255
new sole tenancy granted on,
257
order against one tenant, effect
of, 255
property adjustment order
sought, effect of, 256
proposed intention to serve,
restraint of, 256
requirements, 254

Joint tenancy—*contd*
  notice to quit—*contd*
    suitable accommodation,
        availability of, 257
    unilateral, 252-254
  one joint tenant leaving, effect of,
      254
  refusal to surrender, effect of, 257,
      258
  right to buy, 71
  rights under, 235
  surrender, 254

Landlord
  housing standards, obligations. *See*
      HOUSING STANDARDS
  private sector-
    First World War, in, 17
    influence, lack of, 14
Licence
  examples of, 102, 103
  secure, 106
  short term accommodation,
      provision of, 103, 104
  tenancy distinguished, 101
Local authority
  byelaws, 8, 9
  capital expenditure, controls on, 35
  council housing. see COUNCIL HOUSING
  enablers, as, 45, 46
  house building, capital controls
      over, 208, 209
  housing. *See* LOCAL HOUSING AUTHORITY
  housing finance. *See* HOUSING FINANCE
  housing management, criticism of,
      45
  housing management system,
      market testing, 49
  housing provided by, 1
  Housing Revenue Accounts. *See*
      HOUSING REVENUE ACCOUNT 207
  public health powers, 7
  role as developers of public housing,
      ending of, 45
Local government
  Local Ombudsman. *See* LOCAL
      OMBUDSMAN
  New Labour reform, 53
  reform, 11
  urban services, administration of, 12
Local housing authority
  accommodation, provision of, 58
  acquisition of land by, 59

Local government—*contd*
  allocation of council housing. *See*
      COUNCIL HOUSING
  anti social behaviour orders,
      obtaining, 157, 158
  bodies being, 57
  byelaws, 58
  complaints mechanism, 199
  duty to provide housing, 57-59
  housing conditions, consideration
      of, 57
  housing register-
    de-registration, 119
    establishment and maintenance
        of, 118
    persons put on, 118, 119
    prescribed information, 118
    review of decisions, 119, 120
    rights of information, 121
    time limit for decisions, 120
  housing stock, holding, 58
  injunction against tenants,
      obtaining, 154
  introductory tenancy, power to
      grant, 127
  needs of district, consideration of,
      57
  recreation grounds etc, provision of,
      58
  reports to tenants, 200
  roads and streets, laying out, 58, 59
  voluntary stock transfers-
    central powers over, 93, 94
    consent to, 91
    consultation provisions, 92
    continuation of, 94
    guidelines, 92, 93
    number of, 91
    right to buy, effect on, 95, 96
    tenant, position of, 91, 92
    terms of, 93
Local housing company
  participation in, 223
  structure, 62, 63
  transfers to, 50
Local Ombudsman
  complaints to-
    maladministration, investigation
        of, 190, 191
    procedure, 191, 192
  exclusions from remit, 192
  good practice, promotion of, 199
  investigation of decisions by, 190

Local Ombudsman—*contd*
  local government, supervision of,
    190
  public awareness, 194
  recommendations of, no obligation
    to implement, 193
  remedy, effectiveness in providing,
    192-194
Lodger
  occupation, nature of, 102
  secure tenants, of, 158
Lodging house
  definition, 11
London
  housing accommodation, provision
    of commercial premises with,
    58
  housing authorities, 57

Matrimonial home rights
  spouses, conferred on, 236
Metropolitan District Councils
  housing functions, 57
Model dwelling companies
  management of dwellings, 8
  private companies, as, 13
  re-housing by, 8
  social housing, as source of, 12
Mortgages
  First World War, control in, 16
  option, 37
  tax relief, 37
Multi-occupation. *See also* HOUSE IN
    MULTIPLE OCCUPATION
  overcrowding, and, 422
  problem, size of, 423
  reasons for, 422

National Housing Agencies
  proposal for, 189
Nuisance
  premises being, 408
  statutory. *See* STATUTORY NUISANCE

Obstructive building notice
  demolition of building, 375, 376
  service of, 375
Occupation orders
  applicant in occupation, as to, 240
  associated persons, 238, 239
  cohabitant status, 237
  cohabitants or former cohabitants,
    provisions applying to, 241

Occupation orders—*contd*
  discretionary exercise of powers,,
    239
  disposition of dwelling by tenant,
    effect of, 255
  effect of, 237, 240
  former spouse, provisions applying
    to, 240
  issues taken into account, 240, 241
  landlords, significance for, 242
  mandatory requirements, 241
  neither party having entitlement to
    occupy, where, 242
  relatives, definition, 238
  risk of significant harm to applicant
    or child, where, 239, 240
  statutory provisions, 237
Occupier's liability
  landlord's obligations, 346
Overcrowding
  enforcement powers, 462
  investigation of, 462
  legal definition, 460, 461
  local authority powers, 460
  multi-occupation, in case of, 422
    prevention in, 450, 451
  offences, 461, 462
  problems of, 8
  reasons for, 422
  remedial powers, 462
  suitable alternative accommodation,
    offer of, 461, 462
Owner-occupation
  boom in, 28
  encouragement of, 19
  expansion, Conservative
    Government favouring, 28
  fiscal advantages of, 37
  increase in 1980s, 43
  Labour attitude to, 36-38

Poor relief
  abolition, 6
**Possession (assured shorthold
    tenancy)**
  grounds for, 184
  order, 184, 185
Possession (assured tenancy)
  grounds for-
    demolition or reconstruction,
      intended, 180
    deterioration in condition of
      dwelling, 182
    discretionary, 181-184

Possession (assured tenancy)—*contd*
  grounds for—*contd*
    domestic violence, 260
    employment, dwelling let by
      virtue of, 183
    furniture, ill treatment of, 183
    holiday purposes, dwelling
      required for, 179
    landlord, dwelling required for,
      178
    minister of religion, occupation
      by, 179
    mortgagee, exercise of power of
      sale by, 179
    nuisance, 182, 183
    periodic tenancy, devolution on
      death of previous tenant,
      180
    persistent delay in paying rent,
      182
    rent arrears, 181, 182
    student accommodation, 179
    tenancy obligation, breach of,
      182
  notice of intended proceedings, 177,
    178
  order, 183, 184
  procedure for obtaining, 177, 178
  suitable alternative accommodation,
    provision of, 181
Possession (secure tenancy)
  alternative remedies, 152
  date of, 136
  decision, review of, 142, 143
  grounds for-
    arrestable offence, conviction
      of, 139, 140
    assignment by exchange,
      premium having been
      paid, 144
    bad behaviour, 140-143
    breach of covenant, 137, 138
    charity, occupation conflicting
      with objects of, 146
    demolition or reconstruction,
      landlord intending, 145
    deterioration in condition of
      dwelling, 144
    disabled person, dwelling suitable
      for not occupied by, 146
    discretionary, general
      considerations affecting,
      147-149

Possession (secure tenancy)—*contd*
    domestic violence, 259, 260
    drug taking, 142
    employment, dwelling let by
      virtue of, 144, 146
    false statement, obtaining
      tenancy by, 144
    furniture, ill treatment of, 144
    harassment, 138
    immoral or illegal purposes, use
      of premises for, 138, 139
    locality, issue of, 139, 140
    menacing and abusive behaviour,
      140, 141
    nuisance, 135, 138-143
    original dwelling, completion of
      works in, 145
    overcrowding, 145
    preconditions, 137
    redevelopment scheme, dwelling
      in area subject to, 145
    rent arrears, 137, 138, 149-152
    special needs, dwelling required
      for person with, 146, 147
    unsuitably large accommodation,
      tenant by succession
      occupying, 147
  judicial review of decision, 148
  notice of proceedings, 135, 136
  order for-
    appeals, 148, 149
    conditions, 147
    execution of, 149
    homelessness consequences of,
      148
    limitations, 136
    stay, suspension or
      postponement, 147, 148
  suitable alternative accommodation,
    nature of premises, 137
Private sector housing
  Bevan, opposition by, 27
  building, slump in, 40
  failure of system, 17
  fair rents, 38
  Germany, in, 15
  home ownership, promotion of, 32
  inter-war period, building in, 24,2 5
  Labour Government of 1945,
    controls, 27
  landlords-
    First World War, in, 17
    influence, lack of, 14

Private sector housing—*contd*
 new investment, failure to induce,
  46, 47
 other European countries, in, 5
 poor economic return, 31
 pressure on, 14
 profitability, reduction in, 10
 provision in 19th century, 6
 Rachmanism, 31
 renewal, 32
 repair and maintenance, power to
  compel, 31
 revival, 30, 46
 security of tenure, 38
 structural collapse, 14
 subsidies, 13-15, 38
 taxation, 14, 15
Property rights
 break-up of marriage, adjustment
  on, 248, 249
Public health
 environmental protection, 405, 406
 housing policy, as origin of, 6-10
 housing standards, issue of, 338
 insanitary dwellings, powers over, 7,
  8
 insanitary housing, power to clear
  areas of, 7
 local authorities, powers of, 7
Public sector housing
 administration and governance,
  complexity of, 4
 agencies providing, 5
 byelaw, 9, 10
 changes in, 54
 continuation as major supplier of
  housing, 36
 council housing. *See* COUNCIL HOUSING
 elderly, for, 30
 financial regime, 45
 First World War, effect of, 15-20
 function of, 28
 law-
  meaning, 1
  purpose of, 1
 residual role, 29
 state expenditure, withdrawal of, 35
 statutory framework, evolution
  of, 5
 structure and purpose, change
  in, 2
 suburban, growth of, 9
 turning point, 1960s, 35

Public transport
 growth of suburban housing, cause
  of, 9
Public Works Loan Commissioners
 registered social landlords, loans to,
  65, 224

Racial discrimination
 housing allocation, in, 109-112
Registered social landlords
 accountability, 187-201
 accounting requirements, 64
 accounts, audit, 188, 189
 actions against, 66
 adjudicatory systems, 190
 allocation policies, 125, 126
 approved schemes for dealing with
  complaints, 195, 196
 assured tenancy regime, 185-187
 borrowing by, 59, 60
 capital regime, 1988, 221-223
 complaints mechanism, 200
 creation of, 3
 deregistration, 63, 64
 determination of investigations,
  196-198
 financial arrangements, 219-224
 financial regulation, 1996 system,
  223, 224
 financial risk, 222
 general regulatory powers, 65-67
 generic term, as, 63
 grading, 188
 guidance on accountability, 198
 homeless person, grant of tenancy
  to, 318
 housing associations. *See* HOUSING
  ASSOCIATIONS
 Housing Corporation, regulatory
  powers, 187-190
 housing management agreements,
  170
 housing ombudsman, jurisdiction of,
  195
 housing provided by, 1
 insolvency, 66, 67
 lettings policies, 125, 126
 local housing companies, 62, 63
 mismanagement or misconduct, 189
 number of, 48
 ombudsman service, intention to
  create, 194-196
 provision of housing by, 59

Registered social landlords—*contd*
Public Works Loan Commissioners,
loans from, 65, 224
register, maintenance of, 63
registration, 61
application for, 63
criteria for, 64
eligibility for, 63, 64
regulation of, 64
rents-
assured shorthold tenancies, 232
assured tenancies, 229-232
de-regulation, 228, 229
determining, 226, 227
fair, registration of, 225, 228
secure tenancies granted before
1989, 225-228
sinking fund, 221
social housing grants, 64, 65
succession to tenancies of, 273, 274
tenure of dwellings, 173
types of tenants and housing, 222
voluntary disposals by, 69
Renewal areas
action in, 390
compulsory purchase procedure,
392
declaration of-
conditions, 391, 392
publicity for, 392
requirement to consider, 391
statutory basis for, 391
duration, 393
implementation of strategy, 392
introduction of, 390
physical condition of dwellings in,
392
subsidies, 393
Rent
arrears-
authority handling, 218
breach of repairing obligations,
where, 356-358
possession on ground of
secure tenancy, 149-152
assured tenancy, 181, 182
reasons for, 217
recommendations, 218, 219
serious, 217, 218
assured tenancies, 229-232
challenging, 217
comparisons, 216
council house, pegging to local
house prices, 39

Rent—*contd*
de-regulation, 228, 229
fair rents system, 38, 39
fixing, discretion in, 215, 216
increasing, 216, 217
court challenges to, 4
local capital value, relating to,
46
market levels, increase to, 29
percentage of income paid in, 11
persistent delay in paying, 182
private and public sectors, disparity
between, 38
reasonable-
current legal framework, 215,
216
notion of, 214
requirement of, 23
rebate schemes, 23, 24, 29
registered social landlords, under-
assured shorthold tenancies, 232
assured tenancies, 229-232
de-regulation, 228, 229
determining, 226, 227
fair, registration of, 225, 228
secure tenancies granted before
1989, 225-228
strikes, 34
Rent controls
decontrol, 31
First World War, in, 16
introduction of, 17
patchwork of, 31
Rent to mortgage scheme
application of, 82
exclusion of, 82
exercise, notice of, 83
freehold, transfer of, 83, 84
interest of landlord, transfer of, 83
introduction of, 82
landlord's share-
calculation, 83
redemption, 84
lease, grant of, 84
minimum initial payment, 82
notice relating to, 79
statutory provisions, 50, 79
terms and consequences of
acquisition, 83
withdrawal of claim, 83
Repair notice
appeals, 372
enforcement, 372, 373
execution of works, requiring, 370

Repair notice—*contd*
substantial repairs required, where,
371
unfit dwelling, service on, 370
Repairing covenants
breach-
damages for, 358, 359
information, right to, 360
notice of defects, 349
payment of rent, withholding,
356-358
receiver, appointment of, 355,
356
right to repair, 359, 360
self-help, 356-358
specific performance, 355
express-
breach of, 346
construction of, 347
repair, meaning, 352
structure and exterior of dwelling,
keeping in repair-
disrepair, showing, 353
obligation to repair, where
arising, 353
renewal or replacement,
meaning, 352, 353
repair, meaning, 352
standard of, 354
statutory provisions, 350-355
tenants, obligations of, 354
time for, 354
Right to buy
assured tenants, of, 68, 69
change of landlord, effect of, 80
completion-
effect of, 81
notice requiring, 80
discount, 74-76
dwelling-house, definition, 70
exceptions, 72, 73
exercising, 76-80
flats-
improvement contributions,
notice of, 78, 79
loan, right to, 78
long lease of, 70
service charges, notice of, 77,
78
freehold and leasehold sales, terms
common to, 87
Housing Act 1985, under, 70-81
initial notice of delay, 81
introduction of, 68

Right to buy—*contd*
joint tenants, of, 71
landlord's notice, service of, 76, 77
leasehold terms, 84-87
liability to repay discount, 76
loss of status, effect of, 74
meaning, 42
members of family, of, 71, 72
mortgage, right to, 81, 82
new secure tenant, position of, 80
number of houses sold, 43
preserved, 95, 96
price, 42, 74-76
purchasers, profile of, 43, 44
reference period, 77
rent to mortgage scheme, *See* RENT
TO MORTGAGE SCHEME
replacement of properties,
prevention of, 44
resale, restrictions on, 87-89
sale in contravention of exception,
73
Secretary of State, powers of, 89,
90
secure tenants, of, 70
service charges, 86
tenant's notice, service of, 76
two years, arising after public sector
tenancy for, 70, 71
ultimate tenant's right, as, 4
valuation, procedure for, 79
vesting order, 89
voluntary stock transfers, effect of,
95, 96

Scotland
landlord and tenant, contract
between, 16
Scottish Homes
role of, 61
setting up, 220
Secure tenancy
assignment, 267, 268
break-up of marriage, transfer on,
248-252
conditions, 131-135
divorce, assignment on, 267
excepted classes, 132-134
information, right to, 360
introduction of, 4
loss of status, 134
possession. *See* POSSESSION (SECURE
TENANCY)
property, as, 266

Secure tenancy—*contd*
  rent, increasing, 216
  right to repair, 359, 360
  rights of tenants, 131
  security of tenure, 135, 136
  succession. *See* SUCCESSION RIGHTS
Secure tenants
  collective rights-
    development of, 201
    housing management,
      participation in, 162-164
    information, publication of,
      161, 162
    proactive tenant management,
      167-170
    tenant participation compacts,
      170-173
    transfer arrangements, 167
    variation of terms, as to, 161,
      162
  improvements by, 159-161
  subletting and assignment by, 158,
    159
Security of tenure
  assured shorthold tenancy, 184, 185
  assured tenancy, 176
  basic rule, 135
  introductory tenancy, 128, 129
  possession. *See* POSSESSION (SECURE
    TENANCY)
  secure tenancies, 135, 136
Sexual discrimination
  housing allocation, in, 109-112
Shared ownership lease
  right to, 82
Slum clearance
  effect of, 8
  evaluation, 339
  problem, tackling of, 23
  programme, 29
  resistance to, 34
  subsidies, 24
Social Exclusion Unit
  establishment of, 51
  report, 52
Social housing
  disposal of-
    council houses, 67-70
    general powers, 90
    Housing Action Trusts. *See*
      HOUSING ACTION TRUSTS
    Large Scale Voluntary Transfer,
      68

Social housing—*contd*
  disposal of—*contd*
    registered social landlords, by, 69
    restrictions, 91
    right to buy. *See* RIGHT TO BUY
    Secretary of State, powers of,
      89, 90
    vesting order, 89
  financing, change in, 204
  grants, 64, 65
  meaning, 56
  ownership and control of, 201, 202
  route of entry into, 113
  shortage of, 335
  voluntary stock transfers-
    central powers over, 93, 94
    consent to, 91
    consultation provisions, 92
    continuation of, 94
    guidelines, 92, 93
    number of, 91
    right to buy, effect on, 95, 96
    tenant, position of, 91, 92
    terms of, 93
Statutory nuisance
  action in respect of-
    abatement notice, service of,
      409. 411
    appeals, 410
    authorities, by, 409-411
    compensation orders, 414
    consequences of, 412-414
    expenses of, 413, 414
    persons aggrieved, meaning, 412
    private citizens, by, 411
    reasonable excuse, evidence of,
      411
  common law nuisance, and, 408
  condensation, 407
  condition of premises as a whole,
    consideration of, 406
  conditions prejudicial to health,
    406-408
  criminal proceedings, 408
  duties of authorities, 406
  nuisance order, issue of, 413
  rubbish, dumping, 406
  types of, 406
  uncertain future of, 418, 419
Subletting
  secure tenants, by, 158, 159
Succession rights
  assured tenancy, to, 273

Succession rights—*contd*
introductory tenancy, to, 272
registered social landlords, tenants
of, 273, 274
secure tenancy, to-
assignment, 267
fixed term tenancy, 269
homosexual partners, position
of, 270
member of family, definition,
269-271
minor, by, 270
one only permitted, 271, 272
qualified persons, 269
registered social landlords,
tenants of, 273, 274
residence requirement, 270
successor, determining, 268, 269

Tenancy
assignment, possibility of, 258
assured. *See* ASSURED TENANCY
assured shorthold. *See* ASSURED
SHORTHOLD TENANCY
breach of conditions, injunction
against, 152-154
commencement, requirements for,
126, 127
conduct and agreement of parties
creating, 104
exclusion from secure status,
termination of, 135
exclusive possession and
occupation, 104
finding of, 102
introductory. *See* INTRODUCTORY
TENANCY
legal estate binding third parties, not
creating, 105
licence distinguished, 101
meaning, 101, 104, 105
nature of agreement, 105
repairing obligations, existence of,
106
secure. *See* SECURE TENANCY
transfer orders, 249-252
Tenants
collective rights-
development of, 4
evolution of, 53, 54
Housing Action Trust areas, in, 98,
99
legal rights, strengthening of, 4

Tenants—*contd*
right to buy. *See* RIGHT TO BUY
secure. *See* SECURE TENANTS
treatment, fairness of, 53
Trade unions
building industry, in, 21
Labour Party representing, 15

Unfit dwellings
action regarding, 365
appropriate notice in relation to,
378
attention of authorities, coming to,
384, 385
building, meaning, 385
clearance areas. *See* CLEARANCE AREA
clearance of, 338, 380-384
closure, 373-376
deferred action notice-
appeals, 377
charges, 379
effect of, 377, 378
review, 377
service of, 377
demolition, 373-376
displaced residents, rehousing, 419,
420
energy efficiency, 386
enforcement action, charges for,
379
enforcement procedure, 379
fitness standard-
application of, 385, 386
future of, 386-390
modernisation, 386
Housing and Environmental
Protection Acts, relationship
between, 415
housing association ownership, in,
415, 416
individual, courses of action for,
368, 369
local authority ownership, in, 416,
416
modern council-built houses, 417,
418
Neighbourhood Renewal
Assessment, 366, 367
not reasonably suitable for
occupation, meaning,
385
private ownership, in, 415, 416
repair notices. *See* REPAIR NOTICE

Unfit dwellings—*contd*
  statutory nuisance. *See* STATUTORY
    NUISANCE
  strategy for area, dealt with under,
    367
  use of powers, assessment, 384-386

Unitary authorities
  housing functions, 57

Wales
  housing authorities, 57